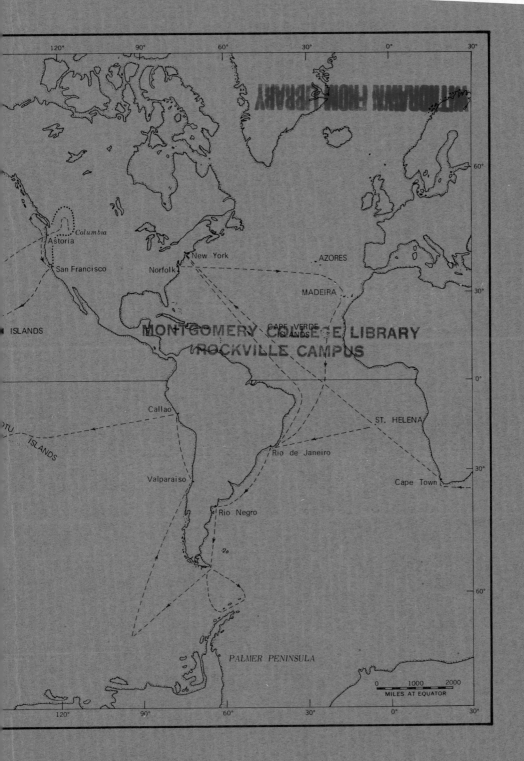

120°   90°   60°   30°   0°   30°

60°

Columbia
Astoria
San Francisco

New York   AZORES

Norfolk

MADEIRA

ISLANDS

CAPE VERDE
ISLANDS

0°

Callao

ST. HELENA

OTU ISLANDS

Rio de Janeiro

30°

Valparaiso

Cape Town

Rio Negro

60°

PALMER PENINSULA

0   1000   2000
MILES AT EQUATOR

120°   90°   60°   30°   0°   30°

The Great United States
Exploring Expedition of 1838-1842

University of California Press

BERKELEY   LOS ANGELES   LONDON

The Great
United States
Exploring Expedition
of 1838-1842

Many shall run to and fro . . .

by WILLIAM STANTON

UNIVERSITY OF CALIFORNIA PRESS
BERKELEY AND LOS ANGELES, CALIFORNIA

UNIVERSITY OF CALIFORNIA PRESS, LTD.
LONDON, ENGLAND

ISBN 0-520-02557-1

Library of Congress Catalog Card Number: 73-84390

Printed in the United States of America

Dit voor Jos

Contents

Preface

A book should stand on its own feet. But as the elements of this one are diverse and perhaps not altogether what one expects on opening a book about exploration, a few words by way of introduction may be justified.

To the exasperated question, "Why be a historian?" I once heard a wise historian reply with two words and a hyphen: "Self-indulgence." This book results from the steady application of that selfish principle. Its subject first piqued my curiosity fifteen or more years ago when, reading through the letters of various American scientists of the early nineteenth century, I many times came upon the query, "What of the Ex. Ex.?" When the other side of the correspondence was available, I found the answer to be that, some ass or other having been given a place in a good man's stead, the Exploring Expedition was in dire straits and the cause of science in America hopeless, or that the collections of sea shells returned were enormous and represented the dawn of a new age for American science. Here was an invitation to indulge.

Yet for a hedonist, the historian bears a remarkable burden. No less than the anthropologist, he must ever be aware that he is addressing himself to an exotic culture. He must purge himself of the preconceptions of his own to become one with it, yet cleave to skepticism all the while in the dismaying knowledge that his very touch is transforming, that success can only be the lesser failure.

In the story that follows I have let the characters speak for themselves, most particularly those who sailed the ships, for theirs was a culture within a culture and they tried, with the means peculiar to their own, to make some sense of other cultures utterly foreign. The American past holds few extended adventures which have produced so many first-hand accounts, for, aware that theirs was a historic venture, the explorers sought to record it all. The result is an exercise in the picaresque. Like Huck on the river, they tell as much about themselves as about what they saw, and so we know them by what they see.

The self-indulgent naturally accumulate debts. Mine are many—to librarians, curators, foundations, and to friends who, listening, yet remained clear of eye. Among librarians I am most particularly indebted to Herbert B. Anstaett, then of Franklin and Marshall College, who, before I was aware of its existence, put before me William Reynolds' magnificent journal, then granted me every indulgence in its use; to Archibald Hanna of the Western Americana

Collection at Yale, who so obligingly displayed the riches over which he presides; to Ralph W. Thomas, Curator of the New Haven Colony Historical Society; Mrs. Lazella Schwarten, Librarian of the Arnold Aboretum at Harvard; David C. Mearns, then Chief of the Manuscripts Division of the Library of Congress, and his staff; Whitfield Bell, Mrs. Gertrude Hess, and Murphy D. Smith of the American Philosophical Society; Howard C. Rice and Alfred L. Bush, Princeton University Library; Gerald E. Holsinger of the Library of the American Museum of Natural History; Stephen T. Riley, Director of the Massachusetts Historical Society; Samuel T. Suratt, then Archivist of the Smithsonian Institution; Herman R. Friis, Senior Specialist in Cartographic Archives, National Archives; to the many librarians I never met who provided photographic copies; and finally to the long-suffering staff of the Hillman Library, University of Pittsburgh.

At critical periods of my research I received financial assistance from a Ford Foundation Public Affairs Research grant from Williams College, from the American Philosophical Society, the Division of the Social Sciences and the Faculty Grants Committee of the University of Pittsburgh, the Solomon R. Guggenheim Memorial Foundation, and the Richard Prentice Ettinger Fellowship. To all I am grateful.

In the making of this book I have greatly benefited from conversations with Nathan Reingold of the Smithsonian Institution, whose knowledge of the manuscript sources of American science is simply unparalleled, and Samuel T. Suratt. At one stage the manuscript was read by four one-time colleagues at the University of California at Berkeley, Kenneth M. Stampp, Winthrop D. Jordan, Roger Hahn, and John Heilbron, and by my three respected friends, Donald Fleming, who has now for the second·time performed this act of friendship, Irving Bartlett, and Thomas Philbrick. That the manuscript is no longer at that stage testifies to the esteem in which I hold their advice.

Alto dos Castelos
Praia do Carvoeiro

1 Republican Longitude

Tocqueville: How are roads made and repaired in
America?
Poinsett: It's a great constitutional question. . . .

George Wilson Pierson, *Tocqueville and Beaumont in
America*

Captain William Smith of the *Williams*, a merchantman out of
Blyth, England, discovered the South Shetland Islands in February 1819. They
were the southernmost known land, and the discovery was dealt with in the
efficient English way perfected in the course of a long history of geographical
discovery: Smith reported to the Admiralty, the Admiralty hired a surveyor,
and in due course the three-hundred-mile-long chain appeared on the
charts—English charts.

In January 1820, while the surveys were in progress at Clarence Island on
the eastern end, two sealers arrived—the Argentinian *Espírito Santo*, whose
captain perhaps was acting on information from Smith himself, stealthily
followed by the Stonington, Connecticut, brig *Hersilia*, Captain James
Sheffield. Sheffield could take only nine thousand skins, owing to a shortage of
curing salt, but he saw three hundred thousand more.

First on the scene for the next season (1820–1821), Smith was astonished at
the traffic that ensued. "To your Memorialist's surprize," he reported to the
Admiralty, "There arrived from 15 to 20 British Ships together with about 30
sail of Americans"—Americans from Stonington, Nantucket, New Bedford,
Salem, Boston, New Haven, and New York. Of the 300,000 seals of the
previous season, the herds on Livingston Island, the largest of the chain, were
all slaughtered by the end of January—the species was extinct in the islands
within a decade—and Captain John Davis of the New Haven ship *Huron* set

1

off in search of new beaches. On February 7, according to his log, he made "a Large Body of Land" and sent a boat ashore in what is now known as Hughes Bay. On its return he closed the day's entry—and the earliest known documentary evidence of a landing on Antarctica—with the words, "I think this Southern Land to be a Continent." Very interesting. Unfortunately, the men had found no seals.

In the season of 1822–1823, Benjamin Morrell of Stonington, searching for rookeries south of the South Sandwich Islands, which lie to the east of the South Shetlands, set his *Wasp* on a southerly course that by March 15 carried him, he said, to 70° 14' S., where there lay before him still an open sea that would have borne the *Wasp*, he was sure, to eighty-five degrees.* But, low on water, without fuel, without the instruments necessary for effective exploration and, he lamented, "without the aid of such scientific gentlemen as discovery ships should always be supplied with," he was compelled to put his ship's head to the north. Morrell comforted himself with the hope that the government might be persuaded to launch an expedition, for the glory of attaining the Pole should go to "the only free nation on earth." [1]

The experience of these three Antarctic seasons suggested that if ever the United States developed an interest in overseas exploration it had better look elsewhere than among seal hunters for its Balboas and Cooks. For what was required was single-minded pursuit of geographical knowledge, and the sealers sought only the seal.

But even had they selflessly sought to increase geographical knowledge, they would have found it difficult to do so. The other frontiersmen of the sea are a case in point. By the turn of the century they had followed the whale round the Horn and launched the China trade, and soon the island world of the Pacific was beckoning irresistibly those quick spirits who sometimes craved adventure no less than dollars. Its largely uncharted expanses held forth the alluring prospect of new discoveries, and little niches in immortality awaited those who came upon unknown islands. Threading the *Hope* through the Marquesas in the spring of 1791, Captain Joseph Ingraham became the first discoverer of no less than five islands. In the twenties, because discovery of the great whaling ground off the coast of Japan attracted many vessels to the far Pacific, new islands were sighted with such frequency that on numerous occasions one would be "discovered" and named two or more times before it appeared on a chart. Soon the Pacific was dotted with the names of

* Morrell was in the Weddell Sea, which, less than a month before, the English sealer James Weddell had penetrated to 74° 15' S.

Nantucketers, their ships, presidents, wives, daughters, and miscellaneous relations.

For that the discoverers owed thanks to the British Admiralty and to the East India Company's hydrographer. Their own government provided no charts. Sailing with her husband, Abby Jane Morrell was "mortified" to discover that they could leave New York harbor only by an English chart and ingenuously confessed that she was "not wise enough to understand" why it was that though Americans plowed all the seas of the world and made discoveries big with promise for mankind, the government could not act for the "general interest" by printing charts and sailing directions. "It were well . . . that we should do something for the world whose commerce we enjoy." Besides, she added, "we have now a name to support, and what have we done to raise its glory?" In regard to the science of the sea, nothing much.[2]

Though respected for their seamanship, American shipmasters had no great reputation as navigators. It was no wonder. They relied almost exclusively on dead reckoning—finding their way by compass, taffrail log, and soundings. To be sure, they did develop this elementary system into an art that served well enough in coasting voyages and Atlantic crossings, but on Pacific voyages and circumnavigations it left a good deal to be desired. Celestial navigation was far more accurate but was possible only by the use of lunar tables or the chronometer (available ever since the Englishman John Harrison had developed an accurate instrument in the middle of the eighteenth century), both of which provided the means of determining longitude. The prosperous and influential Boston firm of Bryant & Sturgis expressed the attitude typical among shipping merchants when in 1823 they reprimanded one of their East-India masters for having spent two hundred and fifty dollars for a chronometer. It must come out of his own pocket, not theirs: had they known he would be governed by such extravagant whims, "we would have sett fire to the Ship rather than have sent her to sea." Almost certainly they were bluffing, unless the conflagration promised a profit. When commerce was booming, delays or even shipwreck occasioned by faulty navigation constituted little more than negligible expense. When it was not, making equipment available for the improvement of navigation was considered an unheard-of extravagance. The War of 1812 showed that a great many ships and men could be lost without noticeably discouraging the intrepid merchant.

Virtually in self-defense, then, the shipmasters of Boston, Salem, and Newburyport established marine societies, of which Salem's East India Marine Society (1799) came to be the best known. By restricting membership to master mariners and supercargoes who had "actually navigated the Seas near the Cape of Good Hope or Cape Horn," and providing each with a blank sea journal to be deposited on completion in its library, the Society became a clearinghouse for navigational knowledge.

One of its members alone took up a great share of the obligation the merchant shunned. While on a Pacific voyage in his youth, Nathaniel Bowditch (1773–1838) was struck by the paucity of information available to the navigator. Lacking chronometers, he turned to lunar observations and taught the technique to the ship's officers, and in 1801 brought out his *New American Practical Navigator*. Cheaper by far than the chronometer, "Bowditch" soon became and has since remained the standard treatise. Abby Jane Morrell found that his book was on "every officer's table" and, for a wonder, "highly esteemed by navigators of other countries."

The only other American contribution to navigation was made by Bowditch's benefactor and publisher, Edmund Blunt (1770–1862) of Newburyport, who in his *American Coast Pilot* (1792) provided sailing directions in the form of courses, distances, and descriptions—crucial because there were yet no buoys and lights—for the coast of the United States. The book quickly came into general use, and for good reason. Merely by correctly locating South Shoal off Nantucket, Blunt reduced the passage to European and Southern ports by twenty-four hours. In the preface to the last edition he compiled, Blunt observed in truth that he had taken up a duty which "belonged rather to the Government than to an individual." [3]

Americans of Blunt's and Morrell's persuasion found their spokesman in John Quincy Adams. Believing that the great object of government is "the improvement of the condition of those who are parties to the social compact" and that knowledge is the chief means of that improvement, President Adams urged Congress in 1825 to establish universities and other public institutions, including astronomical observatories—"light-houses of the skies" was his elegant phrase—to reform the patent laws, set up uniform standards of weights and measures, and launch an exploring expedition. Vigorous action on these lines would elevate not only the condition of the American people, but America herself in the eyes of a world forced to acknowledge that at last this nation had assumed her obligation "to contribute her share of mind, of labor, and of expense to the improvement of those parts of knowledge which lie beyond the reach of individual acquisition, and particularly to geographical and astronomical science." That the engagement had not been honored in the half century since independence was not for want of example. French, British, and Russian voyages had made glorious contributions to "the improvement of human knowledge." "We have been partakers of that improvement," Adams admonished in measured tones, "and owe for it a sacred debt." To fail to return "light for light" would be to doom the Republic to "perpetual inferiority."

Virtually all that Adams proposed had been urged during the Constitutional Convention almost four decades earlier and there disputed by enlightened men of good will toward science. Yet because many of them bore toward government the fear and hatred that for America was to be the crippling legacy of the colonial experience, the constitution they wrote left scant room for government encouragement of science. And the reception accorded Adams' program suggested that Americans in 1825 were little inclined to use the room that was there. The editor of the Richmond *Enquirer* spoke for many when he asked indignantly, "If we are in *debt* to Europe for her scientific discoveries, how much does she *owe* us for the *splendid* example we have furnished of a *free government*; the blood that has been shed, the treasure that has been expended to keep up 'this light-house' of the earth?"

Though disheartening, the situation was by no means hopeless, for the very poverty of the scientific climate made those cultural patriots who were dedicated both to republican institutions and the pursuit of knowledge determined that the new nation should cease to be an intellectual colony of the Old World. There had been some successes over the years. President Jefferson had managed, if by a devious course, to persuade Congress to put up an initial twenty-five hundred dollars for sending out the Lewis and Clark Expedition, which proved a popular success and made some important contributions to knowledge. But its success as a scientific enterprise was limited for reasons of government inadequacy. "An expedition's usefulness to science itself," one historian has pointed out, "depends on classifying the collections and reporting the results. The library, museum, and herbarium were as much a part of scientific exploring as were keelboats and trinkets for the Indians." Congress had been persuaded to part with keelboats and trinkets but was in no mood to establish libraries, not to mention museums and herbariums. The expedition's papers and some of its collections found their way to Philadelphia, and the botanical collection, which proved to be outstanding, was finally described not by an American but by a German living in England. The journals were not published in their entirety until the twentieth century and not then at public expense. Later and lesser ventures were accorded similar treatment.

The attempt to survey the nation's coastline best illustrates the awkwardness of relations between science and government. The Coast Survey, authorized in 1807, came into existence when a few enlightened minds both in and out of government were able to dazzle Congress with visions of the practical benefits that would accrue. A skilled geodesist, Ferdinand Hassler, arrived from Switzerland with instruments of appealing accuracy in his baggage and at Philadelphia fell in with members of the American Philosophical Society, who brought him and his apparatus to the attention of two fellow-members, Thomas Jefferson, who happened to be President of the United States, and the Secretary of Treasury, Albert Gallatin. Swayed by the prospect of commercial benefit, the prospect of having American charts of the American coast, and probably by military considerations as well (during the War of 1812 inhabitants of the coastal areas would be astonished at seeing British ships "sailing boldly" into inlets where Americans in light coasting craft never dared venture), Congress appropriated fifty thousand dollars and placed the Coast Survey under Hassler's superintendence. It owed its existence to "an intellectual oligarchy," Hassler's biographer rightly notes, "that knew better what is good for the people than the people themselves knew."

Unfortunately, progress was not immediately forthcoming: charts were slow in coming from the press, some native Americans wondered why a foreigner should hold so lucrative a post, the cantankerous Hassler showed no grasp of the democratic obeisances, the Navy showed jealousy, and the enterprise proved to be dismayingly expensive. In 1818 Congress dismissed Hassler and excluded from the Survey all but military and naval officers. Senator Mahlon Dickerson of New Jersey, who opposed Hassler's removal, told him frankly that the members were unwilling to pay "what is absolutely required for the accomplishment of so great a work, by men of competent science to complete it." But the critical reason for Congress' action went beyond jealousy and parsimony. Hassler wanted a survey that would be of practical benefit to be sure, but also one that would be a credit to American science. Congressmen, by contrast, looked upon the enterprise as in no way different from the surveys of Ohio: surveyors, "using compass and chain, produced maps on short notice, Hassler had not done so, hence should be dismissed." The premium was on utility, economy, dispatch. When afterwards the instruments fell into disuse and, worse, misuse, European observers drew the obvious conclusion. "In Russia your talents would have been better appreciated," Admiral A. D. von Kruzenstern wrote Hassler from St. Petersburg.

Science was expensive in time and money, and controversy as well. As Congressmen generally preferred the comfortable groove of strict construction, the only force likely to divert them was public opinion, and the prospect of its decreeing government sponsorship of science was dim. What did excite popular feeling in these years was national pride, a particularly volatile element in the decades after 1815. The unlikeliest issues aroused it. In 1819 the subject of a prime meridian was before a committee of Congress. Some patriots took a firm stand for an American prime meridian on the ground that the Meridian of Greenwich was a monarchical one and wholly unsuitable for the United States. "Are we *truly* independent, or do we appear so," one asked, when on leaving his own country every American is "under the necessity of casting his 'mind's eye' across the Atlantic, and asking of England his relative position"? It was calculated "to wean the affections. . . . What American seaman has not experienced this moral effect?" [4]

Probably few Americans were inclined to carry banners through the streets over the issue of a national prime meridian. But the sentiment was typical enough of the many who insisted that the Republic must take its rightful rank among the nations, and it was a force that, applied to some object of rather more popular appeal, might shake a niggardly and doctrinaire Congress from its parochial course.

What was required for the launching of Morrell's and Adams' exploring expedition, then, was a popular cause and a leader. As matters developed, the cause was fully as unlikely as that of the native meridian. So was the leader.

2 Symmes' Hole

All men dream, but not equally. . . .

T. E. Lawrence

The first American ancestor of John Cleves Symmes, Jr., came to Massachusetts Bay in 1634 in the same ship with Mistress Anne Hutchinson. Perhaps something of her independent quality of mind was quietly absorbed into the family strain to rise to the surface in the sixth generation.

Born in New Jersey in 1780, the nephew of the Revolutionary patriot and Ohio impresario of the same name, Symmes received only a common school education before entering the army in 1802 in order, as he later recalled from his hillock of renown, "to merit and obtain distinction, and accumulate knowledge, which I had seldom tasted but in borrowed books." In the War of 1812 he obtained distinction at Lundy's Lane and Fort Erie and by 1818, retired from the army, he felt he had accumulated sufficient knowledge to issue his "Circular Number 1," sending copies to "each notable foreign government, reigning prince, legislature, city, college, and philosophical society, quite around the earth," as he later explained. Dated "St. Louis (Missouri Territory), North America, April 10, 1818," and addressed "To All The World," it was the first public proclamation of a system that had been ripening in Symmes' mind for some years. "I declare that the earth is hollow and habitable within; containing a number of solid concentric spheres, one within the other, and that it is open at the poles twelve or sixteen degrees. I pledge my life in support of this truth, and am ready to explore the hollow, if the world will support and aid me in the undertaking." To show that he was no mere theorizer—the Republic accorded no very high repute to mere theorizers—he briefly outlined a plan of action: "I ask one hundred brave companions, well equipped, to start from Siberia, in the fall season, with

8

reindeer and sleighs, on the ice of the frozen sea; I engage we find a warm and rich land, stocked with thrifty vegetables and animals, if not men, on reaching one degree northward of latitude 82; we will return in the succeeding spring." He sensibly appended a certificate of his sanity.

The years 1819 and 1820 were wonderfully green years, when merely leafing through a book of voyages, or musing on a rainbow or a bird seen through the study window, would often lead into promising avenues of investigation. In the late summer of 1820 Symmes fell to reflecting on the habits of martins, a species of bird, he noted, "that migrate in a peculiar manner. It appears to be unknown from whence they come, and whither they go." In nearby Cincinnati they built nests about the houses and seemed to "delight in the society of man," and one might reasonably infer that they did so elsewhere, too. But where? The proper mode of proceeding, it occurred to him, was to attach to their legs small bands bearing the date and perhaps "a rough drawing of a ship, with the national flag, and drawings of some of the animals of the climate, as a sort of universal language; also, a request for the reader to attach a similar label about the time of the return of the birds in the spring, and to publish the circumstance in a newspaper of the country." Then "if we do not by such means learn, soon or late, where the martins go, it will be inferrible that they go to some unlettered people or unknown country"—in all likelihood of course "Symmes' Hole," as it soon came to be called in the West—and "the more reasons we find for presuming there are unknown countries, the more we will be disposed to exert ourselves in research." [1]

Many who were so disposed stepped forward, for Symmes' theory was commonsensical; it well accorded with popular presupposition, religious as well as scientific, by disclosing the "most sublime economy of nature, in her arrangement of those majestic forms of matter, in the best possible way 'to save stuff,'" as one eager follower put it; it could be tested by "brave companions"; and, not least, it appealed to local and national pride. One of their own, the Captain was a standing refutation to the notion that Americans who went West reverted to "savagism." The "*silence* of all *scientific* men on the matter" merely indicated that they, at least, believed that Symmes would be proved correct, for it was "mortifying to the pride of science that more discoveries have been made by *untaught geniuses* than by regular *savans*." Finally, Symmes was a man of appealing presence. Of medium height, with a straight nose, generous but firm mouth, hair slightly wavy but lying close to the head, forehead high and heavily lined, he was a little wrinkled about the eyes, which looked out from massive brows. The expressive countenance suggested intelligence and probity, and if the New Theory, as it was called, suggested

The Newton of the West: John Cleves Symmes, Jr. and
his hollow earth, "Drawn by John J. Audubon Aug.
1820, for the Western Museum." (Courtesy The
New-York Historical Society.)

massive ego, yet the man possessed an attractive humility and when asked how he was able to make "further discoveries than others," freely confessed to standing on the shoulders of giants who had provided "all the numberless prior discoveries, ready formed and stated, as a base whereon to found new ones."

The modest disclaimer brought to mind the unassuming Newton. There were other parallels. Symmes suffered the *odium theologicum* for neglecting to identify the origin of the earth's rotation ("This implies that matter generated it; and this denies it creation," charged one clerical crank); and he suffered imputations on his originality (having lifted the theory, it was variously asserted, from Scots, Germans, Swiss, Englishmen, and Mohawk Indians). His very tribulations made converts. Still, common sense and Western boosterism, religious complacency and contempt for learning, even Symmes' sweet nature, would have counted for little had the New Theory fallen elsewhere than on the seedbed richly manured with equalitarianism and—an element closely allied in its ideological chemistry—cultural patriotism. The equalitarian contempt for learning, coupled with the persistent call for an American Newton who would establish the equality of Americans with other peoples, were already distinguishing the United States as pre-eminently the country of the queer fellow. And in the second quarter of the century, when equalitarian sentiment was flourishing as never before, so was many another heady new theory: a leading educator of women overthrew Harvey with her discovery that it was the lungs that provided the motive power in the circulation of the blood; millenarians leaped from steeples at the appointed hour; and a new religion, impeccably American, rose upon a fundament of golden tablets dug out of the otherwise barren soil of Vermont. In such company the cold eye of reason might seem to flicker in approval at the sight of Symmes' Hole.

One indication of the prevalence of cultural patriotism and the awareness of America's backwardness in science is that even Symmes' opponents regarded him as an effective, if wrong-headed, proponent of national support for science. The Cincinnati mathematician Thomas Johnston Matthews, who dismissed Symmes as one in whom "observation becomes the mere pioneer of fancy, collecting a heap of learned rubbish," nevertheless urged that the federal government dispatch Symmes on his proposed expedition, for even "if the region he goes in search of, should prove a fairy land, still his enterprising spirit would be likely to render us better acquainted with the arctic zone" and just might find a northwest passage. Matthews promised to devote the proceeds from the sale of his own printed attack on Symmes' theory to promoting the "contemplated polar expedition." [2]

Memorials began to reach Congress in 1822. The first suggested that

"I declare that the earth is hollow": John Cleves
Symmes' wooden model of his inspiration. (Courtesy
The Academy of Natural Sciences of Philadelphia.)

Congress outfit two vessels for northern polar exploration. Though a motion was offered to refer it to the Committee on Foreign Relations, it was tabled instead. The following January a similar one was presented to the House, asking that Symmes be entrusted with the conduct of an expedition for exploring the unknown polar region, not only in order to test the "new theory of the earth" but also to open new avenues of commerce. Whatever may be said of the new theory, it concluded, "there appear to be many extraordinary circumstances, or phenomena, pervading the Arctic and Antarctic regions, which strongly indicate something beyond the Polar circles worthy of our attention and research." So it went. Holes in the poles or no, there was probably something there worth investigating. Again the memorial failed, but the following month seven more appeared, five from Ohio, one from Pennsylvania, and one, marvelously, from Charleston, South Carolina. However briefly, Symmes had gained the attention of the lawmakers and with it that of the country, because for Americans Congress was Parliament, Hyde Park, Covent Garden, and Ascot rolled into one. More important, Symmes made a convert of a man who understood the uses of publicity much better than he, and one who was to become in turn his disciple, chief publicist, bitterest enemy, and successor.[3]

Jeremiah N. Reynolds was born in Cumberland County, Pennsylvania, in 1799, and moved with his family to Clinton County, Ohio, at the age of ten. There, he had gained but two years of schooling, followed by three years at Ohio University at Athens. By 1824 he was settled in Wilmington, Ohio, as editor of the *Wilmington Spectator*. It was the prospect of national glory that attracted Reynolds, who had some reservations about the finer points of Symmes' theory. Yet he was an almost ideal acquisition as proselytizer. Undistinguished in appearance, of medium but solid stature, with a short nose and broad face, he possessed both a lively sense of humor and the good sense to keep it well in hand when lecturing on the hollow earth. These qualities, together with his unrelenting energy, effectively complemented Symmes' gentle, though indomitable, equanimity.[4]

True to the form of converts, Reynolds was soon expressing dismay at the master's lack of fervor and laying plans that to Symmes had been only dreams. To bring the theory to the People, Reynolds proposed a nationwide lecture tour. Although Symmes had little wish to leave home, for the prospect of addressing the sophisticated audiences of the great eastern cities found him unenthusiastic, Reynolds' impatient eloquence prevailed and they set off in September 1825.

The disciple had found his proper element on the boards, and his tour was a remarkable performance. Like the skeptical editor of the local newspaper, many in Reynolds' audience in Chambersburg, Pennsylvania, where he was lecturing in January 1826, had thought of Symmes' speculations as the "wild effusions of a disordered imagination" and attended the first of Reynolds' lectures out of "mere notions of curiosity," promising themselves "much amusement." But, addressing the well-filled house in a "clear, forcible and candid manner," he had scarcely begun before they were "completely enchained" and, the editor reported, "a breathless silence prevailed." For he swayed them with "facts, the existence of which will not admit of a doubt, and the conclusions drawn from them are so natural, so consistent with reason, and apparently in such strict accordance with the known laws of nature, that they almost irresistibly enforce conviction on the mind." Many in the delighted audience joined the editor in the hope that the government would encourage the enterprise, for the "cost of an experiment would be trifling, and discoveries of importance would most probably be made, tho' Symmes' theory should be found erroneous." The response of Chambersburg was one with that of the western towns where this "young pioneer in philosophy" had been heard: "*give them an out-fit.*" At Harrisburg, where the young pioneer addressed the legislature, fifty of the lawmakers responded with an enthusiastic letter that urged the government to equip an expedition, for the promise it held out was "quite as reasonable as that of the great Columbus" and "better supported by facts."

Even the knowing audiences of Philadelphia, "the Athens of America," succumbed. However, a shift in emphasis was becoming evident. Reynolds had launched his long campaign to put a polar expedition to sea. Soon Symmes would be forgotten and, after a little longer, the Theory itself. Even now Reynolds was suggesting that the notion of a habitable interior was perhaps overly elaborate and that while it would require an expedition to determine the matter, the Theory just might prove erroneous. Reynolds had the soul of the entrepreneur and, sailing now upon different seas, he trimmed his sails accordingly. He understood how much enthusiasm for Symmes' Theory in Ohio and elsewhere in the West had stemmed from pride in the Western Newton, and putting the West behind him, he effectively supplanted that attraction by emphasizing two aspects of the Theory that proved to have universal appeal—a simple concept of the universe, simply expressed, and national pride at the prospect of launching an exploring expedition. In short, he made an urbane hypothesis of a backwoods doctrine of the cosmos and became for a time a popular evangelist of science. Symmes came on to Philadelphia, too, but his health was precarious, and Reynolds agreed to

SYMMES' HOLE

assume most of the burden of lecturing. But only at a price. Weary of Symmes' exasperating vagaries, the young man laid down his terms. Symmes must recognize that the great object of their efforts was to procure assistance in "testing the truth of the Theory," that Reynolds was to enjoy complete freedom in carrying this message to the public, and even be permitted his own interpretation. The Pennsylvania legislators had commended the courage of one who disdained to stand "in awe of the world's dread laugh," but the laugh did grow a bit tiresome. "To spend the prime of life, in an adventure of this kind, is a matter of some moment," Reynolds reflected plaintively. But Symmes refused any terms and the two parted ways. The master moved on to address audiences in upstate New York, New England, and Quebec and to display a hollow globe, demonstrating with magnet, iron filings, and a bowl of sand to the students at Harvard and Union how all tends to the centrifugal and concentric. Bad health put an end to his tour in the winter of 1827, though it left his imagination unimpaired, for he issued a communiqué from his sick bed, declaring that "animal heat originates from food, and *is produced to active heat in the heart, and not in the lungs* as physiologists have contended." Exhausted from his labors, Symmes went home to die—in May 1829, at the age of forty-nine. He was buried at Hamilton, Ohio, with a hollow sphere to mark his grave.[5]

Once free of Symmes and his quirks and quiddities, Reynolds set about disassociating himself still further from the more extravagant reaches of the Theory. To this end he sought to attract to his banner the many advocates of the open polar sea, a concept as old as the known existence of America. Stemming originally from the assumption that the continents of the Old and New Worlds must be accessible to one another, if not conveniently by land, then at least by water, it received stimulus early in the nineteenth century from the researches of Alexander Humboldt, which showed that the equator was not the parallel of maximum heat, and those of David Brewster, which indicated that the poles were not the points of maximum cold. In Reynolds' day and after, the notion was thriving in the most respectable scientific circles. He combed the *Transactions* of the Royal Society and collections of voyages for mariners who had found open water in all directions in extremely high latitudes. Then, having melted the ice caps with the weight of authority, he emphasized how extensive was the field for "enterprise and discovery," and suggested, with a flourish of the flag, how such an expedition as he proposed would reflect the national glory.[6]

But Reynolds was no burner of bridges. Aware that Congress might not act, he managed to keep before the public the alternative of a private expedition, "a plain practical common sense undertaking," as he described it, that would have government sanction and possibly material assistance. When Reynolds began addressing his appeal to shipowners he sounded new notes. Predicting a happy union for science and commerce, he pointed out that the exploring scientists just might discover the winter retreats of seals. Also, he now put the northern Verge behind him along with other ideological jetsam and urged an expedition to the South Polar regions as more promising. That was where the seals were. But he had other and better reasons for fixing his sights on the Antarctic seas. Recognizing that the southern hemisphere contained a smaller land mass than the northern, and believing with many another that ice formed only in the presence of land, he reasoned that there would be less obstacle to exploration at the south. The English sealer James Weddell had found an open sea there and reached 74° 15', a record that was to stand till almost mid-century. And, by comparison with the northern polar regions, the Antarctic was virtually unknown. For nearly 340 degrees of longitude, the Antarctic Circle had never been approached.

When early in 1828 the House Committee on Naval Affairs, softened up by heavy bombardment of memorials during the previous months, requested a statement of Reynolds' views, his reply showed how much he had learned about the art of lobbying. He now said less of how Antarctic exploration would further scientific knowledge, and nothing whatever of holes in the poles. Swinging into the prevailing wind, he had consulted merchants and captains engaged in the Pacific trade, ships' logs and journals kept between 1805 and 1820, and reports from commanders to the Navy Department, and he now offered the Committee a sweeping survey of American economic activity in the Pacific and South Sea, together with a plea for government to "look after the merchant there" by sponsoring scientific exploration. Since the whaling fleets of Nantucket and New Bedford alone were producing over four million barrels of oil annually, the industry would decline unless new sources were found. The sealing industry was already slipping—in good measure from Americans having taken an estimated seven million skins since first venturing into the Pacific. The sandalwood trade with the Sandwich Islands, which two Boston captains had launched twenty-four years earlier and which now yielded about three hundred thousand dollars annually, was in danger. (Within a few years sandalwood was extinct in those islands.) Only exploration could find the whale, the seal, the sandalwood, launch a feather trade, and summon up a fishing industry.

Many found his plea persuasive, and one Democrat from North Carolina eloquently defended such a voyage as long "due as our contribution to the general stock of geographical and nautical science." But it was a pity no one called attention to the preparations Britain was currently making to contribute again to that stock, for while the House was debating, H.M.S. *Chanticleer* put to sea under the command of the noted navigator Henry Foster (1796–1831) and at the suggestion of the Royal Society, to make observations on magnetism, meteorology, and oceanography, and to determine by pendulum observations the specific ellipticity of the earth. But that comfortable and fruitful relationship between government and science was a part of the baggage Americans had left behind when they fought their way out of the Empire in search of liberty, and to retrieve it now, some believed, might well return them to the grip of another powerful government, no less oppressive for being their own. Fearing that in the face of such qualms a bill might not command the necessary support, friends in the House pushed through a resolution on May 21, 1828, requesting the President to dispatch one of the smaller public ships to the Pacific to examine "coasts, islands, harbors, shoals, and reefs," if that might be done without special appropriation.[7]

Timid and stingy as it was, President Adams confided to Reynolds, whom he had first met at a sideboard supper that February, that nothing during the past session had given him more pleasure than that resolution. Adams was soon fretting over the details and pressing his Secretary of the Navy (and Reynolds' friend), Samuel Southard, to ready a ship for sea, for he faced an election in November and was under no illusion about the probable outcome.

Reynolds was appointed special agent of the Navy Department to obtain information about islands and reefs, about the extent of American enterprise in the Pacific and South Seas, and other data useful in drawing up sailing instructions for the expedition. He took up the assignment with characteristic enthusiasm. Going directly to the men who had won the United States commercial dominance in areas little known to the world at large, he consulted the sealing and whaling captains of New England, some "more than 70 years of age—doubled Cape Horn 20 times, taken 30 thousand barrels of oil, and traversed more than one million miles by sea." At Nantucket he drew out every whaling captain he could find ashore and pored over their logs, journals, and charts. These men, adept beyond the ordinary in the art of navigation, he found eager to share their knowledge and not the least concerned over the threat to states' rights that in other quarters the expedition was said to represent.

The sealing captains were a good deal less informative. The "skinning trade," as the men of Stonington called it, led them far beyond the common whaling routes on voyages of "the most daring kind," and some had actually taken seal within the Antarctic Circle. They would talk freely enough about how best to bring a vessel through the ice, how far south they had been and what the weather was like, but "would rather give you money than the position of their sealing islands" and regularly destroyed all log books on their return. But it was worth knowing that some had sailed beyond seventy degrees south to find moderate weather and a clear sea and that all agreed that ice first formed only where sea and land met and that more ice was to be seen between sixty-two and sixty-eight degrees than farther south.[8]

Reynolds found that his every previous estimate of opportunities for discovery had fallen far short. Of the long list of islands, rocks, and reefs sighted at one time or another by American mariners but still incorrectly charted, most lay in the Pacific. Assembled from the fragments of individual experience by the commonsense device of consulting those who had sailed in unknown seas, his report was the first extensive survey of the American whaling and sealing industries and, because "those seas are truly our field of fame," he was fully justified in claiming that it constituted a fund of information that the admiralty of no other nation possessed.

But his heart was clearly in the high southern latitudes frequented only by the secretive seal hunters—that "mighty space of which the world is yet ignorant and will long remain so, if the enterprise of our Government does not explore it." It was exposure to Edmund Fanning (1769–1841) that most whetted Reynolds' appetite for Antarctic adventure. With little exaggeration he described Fanning as "the Father of all Sealers." Born into a remarkable family of Stonington seafarers, Fanning shipped at fourteen as cabin boy. A voyage in command of the ninety-three-ton *Betsey* in 1797–1798 made his fortune and in a measure the sealing industry itself. Sailing from New York with a cargo of trinkets for the island trade, he rounded Cape Horn, took a load of sealskins near Juan Fernandez, rescued a missionary in the Marquesas, where he narrowly escaped shipwreck and massacre by natives "shouting, or blowing their war conks" (for which escape he thanked "Kind Providence," good discipline, and the small vessel's maneuverability), discovered and named four islands in the South Pacific, took aboard the survivors of an East India Company supply ship wrecked on Tinian, disposed of his cargo at Canton and obtained another of "teas, silks, nankeens, China ware, &c.," then returned to New York to sell the cargo for $120,000, despite some of the tea's having become waterlogged. Fanning's appetite for profitable voyages was equaled only by his enthusiasm for the sea, the islands, and all their fruits. He knew the ways of polar ice and the habits of the sea's elephants, leopards, and lions; he knew where to find the best stands of sandalwood, how to choose "eatable

SYMMES' HOLE

bird's nests," and the ways of curing "Beache la mer." He knew that coral moss, so highly prized in China, was very "like a vessel's bilge water" in both smell and taste. Intensely curious about the Antarctic, he was a strong believer in the open polar sea, and Weddell's accomplishment hung before him like a vision.* Somewhere in that sea, he was sure, lay a continent.[9]

In the course of his tour Reynolds also seized every opportunity to draw out support for the expedition and interview scientists and navy officers who sought to accompany it. Dr. James Ellsworth De Kay (1791–1851), the New York physician-naturalist and mainstay of the New York Lyceum of Natural History, was eager to join up as naturalist. Supporting De Kay, the Lyceum urged in the interest of national honor that due attention be given the natural sciences and, pressing home their point, assigned nine of their number to prepare reports for the guidance of the scientific corps. In reply, Southard promised to make the expedition "as extensively serviceable to commerce and to Science" as the means would permit. Though both De Kay, who tactfully applied for the post of navy surgeon, and Southard were well aware that the practice of employing civilians had been a tender issue in the aristocratic navies of Europe ever since exploration had become a scientific endeavor in the middle of the eighteenth century, they also knew that service to science required it. Men of science in the Navy could virtually be counted by the ears on one's head, and for good reason. Such men did not seek careers in the Navy and, aside from the often ludicrous attempts to teach them mathematics while at sea, officers rarely acquired any science.

That employment of civilians could be an issue in a republican navy, too, was not immediately evident, though from the vantage of hindsight that lack of perception would appear inexcusable. In casting about for a suitable astronomer, Reynolds first brushed against young Charles Wilkes, lately promoted lieutenant and exceedingly anxious to join the expedition. Quite unaccountably in a navy officer, Wilkes had been subjecting himself of late to a rigorous course of training in some of the sciences—under the tutelage of Nathaniel Bowditch in mathematics and Ferdinand Hassler in the triangulation methods used by the Coast Survey. His brother-in-law James Renwick (1792–1863), professor of natural philosophy at Columbia College and probably the nation's most widely respected engineer, was providing instruction in the practical aspects of geomagnetism. Though Wilkes' acquirements

---

* In 1812 Fanning had obtained a commission from President Monroe for a privately financed "voyage of discovery and in pursuit of physical science, particularly in natural history," to be made in Fanning's *Volunteer* and *Hope*, but with the outbreak of the War of 1812 the enterprise came to nothing.

would have failed to attract passing notice in the scientific community at large, they stood out in bold relief in the Navy. At twenty-seven, two years Reynolds' junior, Wilkes was a member of an influential New York family, and what caught Reynolds' attention was less the lieutenant's abilities than the "movements making" to get him on the expedition as astronomer. Reynolds summed him up as "enterprising and ambitious," though "exceedingly vain and conceited." There was a "spirit of dictation about Wilks and Renwick," he reported to Southard, "that I dont like." And he learned that some prominent members of the Lyceum, who were friends, or friends of friends of the Wilkes-Renwick-Brevoort-Colden clan, were suggesting, "with that kind of look and emphasis, which indicate authority," that the Department might not see fit to send Reynolds himself on the expedition. Though puzzled, he decided to attach "no importance to this *ebulition* of envious feeling" and after Wilkes called on him several times during the first week of November 1828 to discuss the expedition, Reynolds finally assented that he should have an appointment, though not as astronomer. That must go to a scientist of established reputation. Accordingly, Southard delegated Wilkes to collect the astronomical instruments needed.[10]

There was little reason to put it down as a fateful choice. Prospects seemed bright for an early sailing. The sloop-of-war *Peacock*, entirely rebuilt at the New York Navy Yard under Reynolds' watchful eye, was launched at the end of September 1828 in a colorful ceremony. Crowds cheered and cannon thundered as the first vessel ever built by the American government for overseas exploration slid down her ways. Perhaps many reflected on this occasion, with the editor of the *New-York Mirror*, that the ship bespoke the liberal "spirit of the age" and foretold "a long career of glory and usefulness" for the Republic. For him the great moral of the launching was that these blessings were to be secured as much by "cultivating the arts and sciences in times of peace" as by "energy and valor in time of war." Or, as Reynolds once coolly explained to Southard, "Nations as well as children must have play things, and the expedition will do for our country as well as any thing else"—and a good deal better than some of the usual playthings of nations, he might have added.

To judge from the numbers in the Navy and out who wished to sail with the expedition, the enthusiasm was widespread. Many of the most promising midshipmen and lieutenants applied for positions, experienced sealing captains coveted the posts of pilot and navigator, others offered their ships, artists sought appointment as draughtsman, medical doctors begged to be taken along as surgeons. Scientists of every description asked to go, some, including the distinguished entomologist Thomas Say, pleading merely for any place at all in the scientific department. A few, bearing no particular gifts, applied for the post of "journalist," or captain's clerk, or begged to go before the mast, even without pay.

To most Southard could only reply that the date of sailing remained uncertain and that the applicant's record was on file in the Department. But in September he appointed De Kay "principal naturalist" and as his assistants the exploring naturalist-painter Titian R. Peale and the Albany geologist James Eights. Lieutenant Wilkes would assist the principal astronomer, Robert Treat Paine of Boston. Southard also named the expedition's commander, the able veteran Thomas ap Catesby Jones. As Jones was "a flaming Jacksonian," the dismayed Reynolds predicted that future charts would be littered with "Jackson Islands, Hamilton Capes, McDuffie Promontorys, Benton Inlets, Van Buren Harbors." But Southard understood the expediency of placating the political opposition and Reynolds soon found he could get on famously with Jones.[11]

Southard chose Jones against the advice of Lieutenant Wilkes, as well. He had asked Wilkes, a lieutenant of only two years' standing but the only one in the Navy who advertised his calling as essentially scientific, for his views on whether his fellow officers were capable of conducting an exploring expedition. It appeared that Wilkes had very decided opinions. In an astonishing performance, the twenty-seven-year-old officer proceeded down the Navy List, parading his superiors for inspection. The commander of an exploring expedition, he cautioned, must possess "energy, intrepidity, perseverance, skill as a seaman," and knowledge of science, "not only in his profession, but in a great degree out of it," that he might direct the researches of the scientific corps and be able to point out to them "the easy method of execution." He must display "amiability that he may attach those . . . under his command" and "talents, and education, to narrate what occurs to the expedition in a clear, simple, and unaffected language." And with all this, he must have "a happy fertile genius to be able to meet the arduous situations he may find himself placed in." It was a large order. Wilkes could vouch for the amiability and energy, even literary talents, of several in the Navy List but, in all conscience, not for their science and in the end was sorry to have to confess that the Navy had no one to offer. Admittedly, he was not well enough acquainted with Jones to pass judgment, but he doubted that Jones would be "anything remarkable."

Turning to officers of his own rank, Wilkes advised that lieutenants ought to be selected from the bottom of the Navy List, for the simple reason that they had recently passed their examinations and not yet forgotten what too many officers had "entirely forgot; I mean the Science that enabled them to pass." He was thus able to reduce the matter of selection to a formula: officers were qualified "in the ratio of the times from their examinations." Science aside, younger officers were less likely to "lounge & seek amusement in public places" and contract "dissipated habits," and more susceptible to proper discipline, a point of which Wilkes made much, for word was getting round that rank was to signify little on this expedition. This was an unfortunate rumor that he felt obliged to bring to the Department's attention, for the *Peacock* ought to be "in conformity to a man of war."

Wilkes delicately refrained from offering opinions on the scientific corps beyond observing that he was fully confident of performing the duties of astronomer to the full satisfaction of the Department, providing he met with no obstructions from the commander. Yes, and one other stipulation: "my pride would not allow me to act subordinately to any one not belonging to the Naval Service." The proper way of proceeding, therefore, was to give him command of the second vessel and name him second in command of the expedition, thereby freeing him, and science, from the regulations of the commander's ship.

What respect Southard accorded these views is not known. He appointed Jones anyway, but he might well have resolved to keep an eye on the young lieutenant who offered them.

In his Annual Report, sent to Congress with the President's Message in December, Southard noted that the *Peacock*'s outfit was now nearly complete and expressed the hope that Congress would again consider the bill reported but not acted on before the close of the previous session. Reynolds did what he could to help and later confessed to having persuaded twenty persons that "the right time to go south, is, when the sun is in his northern declination." He improved other opportunities. When Congressman George Wolf urged the name of a fellow Pennsylvanian as surgeon to the expedition, Reynolds went to work on him. Decision rested with the Secretary, of course, but considering the great interest the Congressman had always taken in "our enterprise" and the "lively recollections the Department had of his past valuable services," Reynolds was sure the Secretary would give his nomination the "most favourable construction." The "countenance of the Hon. Geo." brightened, he reported, "and just as he was . . . trying to recollect, what he had done to give the Department so favourable an impression of him,—I observed, that if only two vessels went on the Expedition, there was no possible hope for his friend, but if Congress authorized three immediately, he would then be taken into consideration." Wolf agreed to help. "Give me latitude," Reynolds proclaimed, "and I will strike bold for immortality."

In December the House beat down by eighty-four to seventy-one a substitute bill that would instead have sent out an expedition to explore the territory west of the Rockies and, attaching an appropriation of fifty thousand dollars, passed the bill by a handsome margin. The northern seaboard states overwhelmingly supported it, the inland southern states overwhelmingly opposed it. The West divided. Congressman George Wolf voted yea.[12]

Reynolds was delighted, not least with his own appointment as historiographer, which involved writing the journal of the expedition and completing his survey of American commercial enterprise in the Pacific and South Seas. All now seemed well with "the first American Expedition of discovery—the first to go to the south Pole, and the first from any Republican Government; three grand points that can never happen again."

Then, just when prospects appeared brightest, things began to go wrong. The Navy Board of Examiners, no doubt resenting the attempt to induct civilians, denied De Kay a surgeon's commission and shortly afterward that of the doctor who sought appointment as assistant surgeon so that he might go as assistant botanist. On top of this, the surgeon of the regular Navy who was scheduled to serve announced that he would not go without De Kay. The Adams administration was waning and its authority even over navy officers waned with it.

Then there developed a flurry of jealous bickering among the officers in New York who wanted to join the expedition. Such conduct was not unusual among American navy officers, perpetually cacophonous in their endless debate over the pecking order, but Reynolds spied the hand of the ambitious Wilkes, who seemed to think that his "transcendent powers and unmatched attainments" had been overlooked by the Department. In the Navy it was always possible to cloak professional jealousy in the generous folds of esprit de corps, and, unfortunately, De Kay reported, the commandant of the navy yard, Isaac Chauncy, was not the man to control the situation, for he looked upon the expedition as "a queer matter, right in itself because England does the same thing," but "out of his line." De Kay had a suspicion that Wilkes, "expecting nothing from the present Administration & hoping much from the next," would throw in the way whatever obstacles presented themselves and urged all dispatch in getting the enterprise to sea before the new administration could lay hands on it. And indeed Wilkes was collecting the scientific instruments—the pendulum apparatus, astronomical clock, theodolite, transits—with something rather less than the haste that was necessary if the ships were to sail before March 4. (Privately determined that they should not, Wilkes happily confided to Jones that the delay would allow the officers time enough to prepare themselves for all the scientific duties, and so render it unnecessary to employ civilians. After all, the assistants in the astronomical department need not be Newtons but only men of steady habits. True, something more would be required of the chief astronomer, whose duties would consist largely of experiments with the pendulum, in the technique of which only two Americans were thoroughly competent—"a Professor of Columbia College" and the navy lieutenant he had trained. Better then to appoint a navy man, so that duties might be performed with "much more harmony.") Reynolds was disgusted with the officers and announced firmly, "All the collision with these boys must be done on shore." [13]

But it was the boys in the Senate who delivered the coup de grace. Getting wind of the controversy, Senator Robert Y. Hayne of South Carolina, Chairman of the Committee on Naval Affairs, objected to the expedition on the ground that the civilian scientists, who ought to be the "mere agents and instruments" of the officers, would reap the "glory of the enterprise, if any glory was to be acquired in it." Secretary Southard coolly replied that it was no reproach to the officers that they could not "furnish the lights which would do most credit." In their own profession they had no superior, but if too much was sought for them all would be lost to them. It was a sensible enough view of matters, but some officers were sure the Navy had been slandered—and slandered, by God, by its own chief—and turned to Hayne as their champion. Wilkes expressed "great regret that the Secy should possess so little espirit du corps," and as the date of the inauguration approached and his assurance grew, he wrote Jones that he would have nothing more to do with the present Secretary and requested that in the event Southard should choose to dispense with the indispensable and succeed in putting the ships to sea with another as astronomer, Jones would please return all the plans he had drawn up for the scientific apparatus, as he was unwilling that they should be made use of by those who sought to deprive the Navy of the opportunities it was "justly entitled to." He begged Jones not to think this view "ungenerous," as it only proceeded from a "strong feeling of spirit de corps."

Three days after passing the House, the bill was sent to the Senate, where it fell into the clutches of Robert Y. Hayne. As he was to make abundantly clear in his classic debate with Webster the next year, Hayne was one of those federal officers who considered it his duty to forestall government's every action beyond the minimum necessary to protect property, personal and chattel. Party lines formed, and on February 5, 1829, Hayne launched his attack. Any geographical discoveries an expedition might make, he argued, would be "fraught with the most serious evils"—defense expenditures, a spirit of adventure, "visionary hopes," emigration—and mark "abandonment of the fundamental principles" which had hitherto restrained the Republic from forming "unnecessary connections abroad." Anyway, it would be "altogether superfluous to attempt the discovery of unknown lands" while there remained unexplored regions at home. In short, explorers should see America first, though even that effort might prove too expensive to be practicable. Sound Southern doctrine provided the political moral: commerce and science, like agriculture, might be "safely left to the enterprise of individuals, which, with an instinctive sagacity, that puts to shame, the assumed wisdom of governments, is invariably directed to the pursuits most profitable to themselves, and most to the welfare and honor of the country."

When it was all over, Democrats and professional Southerners (only one Whig voted against consideration) were heard to rejoice that the "South sea bubble" had burst. As the friends of exploration saw it, all was left to the "limping gait of State legislature and private adventure," and the American Union, as a moral person in the family of nations," was to "live from hand to mouth." [14]

Reynolds was disappointed, of course. So was Lieutenant Wilkes. Wilkes had seen a vision, rather late in the day but the more vividly for the odds being, as he understood, "now so much in favor of the Navy having all the duty to themselves." But he was not without resources. In a long, anonymous letter-to-the-editor on the whole subject, he confessed that although he had had his "fits of enthusiasm" for Reynolds' scheme, he had never entertained the absurd notion of employing public vessels to convey Symmes' "proselyte" as a "diplomatic agent to Symmesonia," or to plant the flag on the southern axis, or even to reach beyond the *ne plus ultra* of Cook. No such grand design: "all our ideas were common-place ones" of a modest enterprise to discover whether reported but uncharted islands really did exist. (He did not for a moment believe they were to be found to the "incredible" number of two hundred that the "poor fellow" Reynolds had listed.) Now that Southard (whose support of exploration had merely betrayed his political desperation) was out of office, the time had come to get rid of "that Mountebank Reynolds" and place the whole enterprise in the hands of the very men the late Secretary and his learned but impractical master had slandered by declaring to the world their inability to fill any of the literary or scientific situations and by appointing civilians of "little attainment" in their stead—the officers of the Navy.

If Reynolds' disappointment was the greater, his resourcefulness was no less. With Edmund Fanning and the other sealers he had met in the course of his lecturing and research he organized a "South Sea Fur Company and Exploring Expedition" to test the "instinctive sagacity" that Senator Hayne professed to find in private enterprise. He signed up the young Philadelphia artist John Frampton Watson, and of the scientists who had sought to join the enterprise that grounded in the Senate chose James Eights (1798–1882) of Albany, whom Amos Eaton had recommended as "one of the most competent geologists in North America." Though some of the members were skeptical of mixing scientific curiosity with the profit motive, the New York Lyceum of Natural History subscribed five hundred dollars toward Eights' expenses.[15]

In the sailing in October 1829 of the brigs *Seraph* and *Annawan* and the schooner *Penguin* the editor of the *New-York Mirror* saw a proper rebuke to the "narrow policy and contemptible economy of our national rulers" and a glorious tribute to the "indefatigable originator of the scheme" and the "active and enlightened merchants" and scientists who had come to his aid.* The little expedition might well make discoveries that would attract private enterprise, "promote the cause of science, and add to the reputation of the country."

Unfortunately the only discovery was how little enthusiasm the crews, suffering from cold and damp and the onset of scurvy, manifested for science and the national reputation. They had signed on for their lays or shares of the catch, and finding the catch negligible, they fled this queer voyage at various points on the coast of Chile. When at Talcahuano the *Seraph*'s remaining crew confronted their captain with "a stern determination to desert," it was decided to turn homeward while men enough remained to work the vessels. They sailed without Reynolds who, finding it a hard task "to inspire these men, with the feeling, that there is something worth living for, besides money," went ashore with Watson at Santa Maria, to spend the next two years tramping through Chile.

In all charity it was difficult to ascribe much scientific importance to the enterprise. It did return some fifteen chests of specimens to the collections of learned societies (Reynolds' own collection of some four hundred bird skins, plants, shells, minerals, and the like he gave to the Boston Society of Natural History, where it made the first large addition to their cabinet), and the sweeps

---

* The vessels were commanded by three of Stonington's Antarctic sealers: the *Seraph* by Benjamin Pendleton, the *Annawan* by Nathaniel B. Palmer, and the *Penguin* by his brother Alexander Palmer. Nathaniel Palmer was long credited in the United States with having discovered the Antarctic Continent in 1820, while with a fleet under Pendleton's command.

of the *Annawan* and *Penguin* in their search for land were of value in establishing its absence. James Eights' work admittedly was of a high order. Attached to the *Seraph*, he collected flora and fauna on the east coast of Patagonia and Staten Island (Argentina) and the islands of southern Chile, and conducted oceanographic and zoological investigations in the South Shetlands. Of the species he described, one of trilobites was not redescribed until seventy years later, and another, an unheard-of ten-legged pycnogonid, was not again described until 1905. As the vessels cruised westward from the Palmer Peninsula, he made regular observations of the icebergs and concluded from the rocks they bore—like none seen in the islands visited—that land was near. He noticed algae drifting in the sea which grew only in the vicinity of rocky shores, and penguins and terns whose habit, he had observed, was not to leave the land any great distance behind. Furthermore, in the South Shetlands, whose predominant formations were sandstone and basalt, he found granite boulders lying about and could only conclude that they had been carried there by icebergs from "their parent hills on some far more southern land." * That a southern continent existed he would not venture to state on the basis of this evidence alone, but that there were "extensive groups, or chains of islands yet unknown," he did not doubt.

But like Reynolds, who carved only a few literary pieces out of his journals—though one of these, an old tar's tale of "Mocha Dick, the White Whale of the Pacific," that appeared in the country's leading literary monthly, *The Knickerbocker*, must have caught the eye of Eights' fellow-townsman Herman Melville—Eights published few of his observations and these only sporadically in a variety of journals over the next two decades. His labors constituted a purely personal triumph in a region that would become significant only for the opportunities it offered science, which he had been the first to seize.

Scientists complained with America's most distinguished botanist, John Torrey, that "it turned out just as several of us suspected, that the Expedition was destined, not for discovery, & for scientific purposes—but to catch seals!"

---

* On seeing a reference to Eights' incongruous boulders in the published instructions of l'Institute de France to Captain Dumont d'Urville's Antarctic expedition of 1837, Charles Darwin connected them with the large boulder that Captain John Balleny of the *Eliza Scott* and *Sabrina*, returning in 1839, had reported on an iceberg floating fourteen hundred miles from the nearest known land (Enderby Land); he concluded that all of them might well be the antipodean counterparts of what puzzled geologists of the northern hemisphere were calling "erratic boulders," clusters of stones that bore no generic relationship to the local formation, and what leaped to his mind was the possibility that all had been deposited by moving ice. It was a theory that British and European geologists, most notably William Buckland and Louis Agassiz, were just then substantiating.

Even less pleased were the investors in the enterprise, who grumbled that they were out of pocket for having attempted to give aid to science.

Everyone involved understood the reason for its failure. Fanning coupled his plea for compensation with a petition for a national expedition, arguing that the failure of this private enterprise, though well planned and outfitted, demonstrated that only a national expedition could succeed. With feelings "mortified to their utmost," the *Seraph*'s captain concurred fully: "I am now convinced . . . that an exploring expedition, by any private means can never produce great or important national benefits; it must be clothed with authority from government, and the officers and men on regular pay." [16]

When Reynolds returned to the United States in the spring of 1834 he found a different nation from the one he had left. At the top the statesman of broad culture and solid accomplishment had been supplanted by the new style American democrat, or rather, the current embodiment of the chaotic aspirations of the American people in a new age, for it was all but impossible then as now to discern Andrew Jackson beneath the ideological nosegays flung upon him. The nosegays are important. In that new topsy-turvy world Jackson possessed a great political advantage in not having been exposed to any formal education worth the name. Rather, he had been educated in "nature's school" and was therefore the "natural" man. If Jackson possessed intellectual interests, he also possessed the political astuteness to conceal them. Whatever his policies, the unlettered leader stood out to good advantage in this heyday of romantic primitivism against the learned, intellectual, "artificial" and "aristocratic" Adams.

After the defeat of 1828 a lesser man than Adams might well have sought seclusion from the mob. Instead, he chose to battle the monumental cupidity from a seat in the House of Representatives and could be counted upon to lend his assistance when Reynolds again took up his campaign. And so could Samuel Southard, whom the New Jersey legislature returned to the Senate in 1833. To their presence add the absence of Robert Y. Hayne, who had departed in disgust with national politics (making his way back down the political ladder—his kind of politics told him the direction was up—he became successively Governor of South Carolina, Mayor of Charleston, and president of the Louisville, Cincinnati & Charleston Railroad) and grounds for optimism emerged. Though the ranks of the Navy still seethed, its present head, Mahlon Dickerson, was an amateur scientist and so might be counted on. Even the Jacksonian program as announced in the Inaugural Address, a copy of which Reynolds read in Chile, held out promise. The new president had struck a nice balance by announcing his intention to respect the powers of the states and to practice "a strict and faithful economy," and then affirming nevertheless that "internal improvement and the diffusion of knowledge, so far as they can be promoted by the constitutional acts of the Federal Government, are of high importance." Though no respecter of hayseed or, in any particular way, of successful generals, Reynolds thought parts of the address "pretty good." [17]

There were other developments in the course of Jacksonian rule of which he was to approve. Though Jackson's administration was the first one frankly to embody the anti-intellectual aspirations inherent in the American concept of equality, it was by that very token in a position to institute some of the distinctly intellectual aspirations of its predecessor. The sullen element was largely for domestic consumption in election years and not for export. And even at home it was tempered by another element in the American variety of equalitarianism, one common enough to new nations and shared by the Jacksonians with the Adams administration—confidence that the Republic was at least a match for other nations in the realm of intellect.

Ironically, then, it was the Jacksonians, with their impeccable equalitarian credentials, who in 1830 gave Ferdinand Hassler, whom Jackson himself rather admired, charge of regulating standards of weights and measures, then two years later reinstituted the Coast Survey with Hassler as its chief—though taking care to specify that this was no authority for establishing an astronomical observatory. But even Adams' lighthouse of the skies, which the Jacksonians had laughed out of the democratic court, was to evolve in the heyday of their power, when, seemingly in subversion of the popular will, Charles Wilkes mounted a three-and-a-half-foot portable telescope in the small depot of charts and instruments the Navy had set up in 1830. By 1836 Secretary Dickerson was suggesting to Congress than an astronomical observatory might be considered "remotely," at least, "necessary to the defence of our country." Less remotely, it was necessary to "our navy, our commerce, and scientific pursuits." Already an "officer of science," as he put it, had to be employed to care for maps and charts and philosophical apparatus. Why not set up an inexpensive observatory and assign all these duties to its superintendent? Before they surrendered power to the cool manipulators of log cabins and hard cider, the Jacksonians were to take his advice.

Then too, it was Jackson's own administration that first responded to the call for support of the shipping and trading interests in the Pacific by dispatching two ships—one of them the *Peacock*—and appointing a special agent to make treaties in the Far East. The Jacksonians are to be known for their deeds as well as their sounding brass. If the country could have a lighthouse of the skies, and a diplomat sent to procure respect for a flag that flew in those faraway lands mainly in the interest of the mercantile enterprise of the New England states, why not, it might reasonably be asked, an exploring expedition? The obstacle was the same: Jacksonian equalitarianism and commitment to the negative principle that the world is governed too much.

Reynolds believed with Adams that government big enough to prevent America from becoming the intellectual pariah of the Western world might well be tolerated without fear of destroying equality at home, and within a few months of his return, memorials were once more arriving at the House of Representatives. The most eloquent of the lot was from the East India Marine Society of Salem, whose members had been the pioneers of American commerce in the East. They called attention to their experience with a single island group and let it serve as an index to the rest. "The Feejee or Beetee islands—what is known of them?" Although thought to consist of at least sixty islands they remained uncharted, and the consequences for the Salem ships that collected "beach le mar" and shell for the China trade were these:

Ship Clay, brig Quill, have returned; brig Faun lost at the island; ship Glide, Niagara, also lost; and barque Peru, greatly damaged, and, in consequence, condemned at Manilla; brig Spy damaged, but repaired again; brig Charles Daggett, barque Pallas, brig Edwin, ship Eliza, ship Emerald, Ship Augustus, and brig Consul.

The Charles Daggett has recently returned, in consequence of having a portion of her crew massacred by the natives. The ship Oeno, of Nantucket, was lost on one of these islands, and her officers and crew, consisting of 24 in number, were all massacred in like manner, save one.*

* The bare list of disasters, far from complete, concealed a multitude of cruel detail. The Nantucket whaleship *Oeno*, having completed a highly successful voyage (during which she had discovered Oeno Island northeast of Pitcairn) had sailed again the same year. In the Fijis the vessel struck a reef and quickly broke up. Escaping in the boats, the crew made Turtle Island (Vatoa), where only the cooper, William S. Cary, survived massacre. Adopted by one of the chiefs, he remained in the Fijis a year before meeting a fellow Nantucketer, David Whippey, who had settled in the islands by choice some years before and now sat very near the throne on the nearby island of Ovalau. Two and a half years after the wreck of the *Oeno*, Cary was picked up by the *Clay* of Salem, Captain Benjamin Vanderford. From the *Clay* he shipped aboard the *Quill*, then took a berth in the *Glide*. The *Glide*, too, struck a reef but the crew repaired her and were trading with the natives when suddenly attacked. Two were killed. In March 1831, while the vessel was riding at anchor, a squall drove her on another reef. While the men were held captive the captain and a few of the crew set out in one of the boats for an island two hundred miles distant, where it was rumored a vessel had arrived. It had indeed: the *Niagara* had been driven on a reef and broken up in the same storm that destroyed the *Glide*. By the summer of 1831 most had been picked up by the *Peru* of Salem, Captain John H. Eagleston, shortly afterward herself to be lost, as the memorial noted. Cary came home to Nantucket in 1833.

The scientific was not far behind the maritime community in urging exploration. Taking heart from the forthright action of the shipmasters of Salem and spurred at sight of the "extensive & highly interesting" collection of objects of natural history that Reynolds had gathered, the Boston Society of Natural History drafted a memorial to point out that scientific as well as commercial advantages might be expected and urged Congress—it would mean "but little additional expense"—to attach a corps of scientific men to the proposed expedition, that the United States might join England and France in the great task of completing "the chain of created nature."

The call to arms that foretold victory was an address that Reynolds delivered in the Hall of Representatives on the evening of April 3, 1836. With the candor and good humor that were his hallmarks, he spoke for the "spirit of the age" as he sought to reason on behalf of science with the disciples of the "sylvan nursery philosophy," who preached the imported creed that it would be best for Americans to remain on the farm "and suffer other nations to come and take the productions of our soil in exchange for their own manufactures," and the latter-day "utopian enthusiasts," who declaimed upon "the purity of a primitive people, and the contaminating effects of commerce." When masts and spars are required, he informed them, "neither Fauns nor Dryads can protect the grove," and the vision of the Founding Fathers, who had often lamented that they could not live to see "the fruit of the garden they had planted," was coming to pass. This generation of Americans had every reason to rejoice that "Providence has cast our lines in such pleasant places, in such auspicious times."

But it was not to commerce that he now declared allegiance. His appeal was for a scientific enterprise. To those who would ask if tangible benefits might be expected from exploration, he replied with truly remarkable insight into the nature of scientific activity, an insight that was seldom publicly voiced and rarely comprehended outside the community of science. "Scientific research," he bluntly informed his audience, "ought not to be thus weighed," for by an "immutable law of nature" that applied to "all matters of science" as well as geographical discovery, "utility cannot be computed in advance." As it happened, the benefits of past exploration had been great beyond all expectation. Britain's attempt to find a northwest passage had revealed the extent of the continent and opened up the riches of the Hudson's Bay fur trade, the cod fishery of Newfoundland, and the whale fishery of Davis's Strait. "Yet not one of these rewards of enterprise was anticipated, or formed an element in the calculation, when her Cabot, her Davis, her Hudson and Baffin, were dispatched on their perilous voyages."

On his recent voyage to the Pacific, Reynolds had seen, of all things, a Prussian discovery ship, when that nation had "scarcely an hundred tons of shipping" in the entire ocean. It was quite simply a matter of "national dignity and honour." Now, "while the treasury, like the Nile in fruitful seasons, is overflowing its banks," was the time to send forth an enterprise "worthy of the nation," that was to say, "nothing on a scale that has been attempted by any other country." Here for the first time he fully described the vision that had beckoned since first he heard Captain Symmes lecture. Designed "to throw back on Europe, with interest and gratitude, the rays of light we have received from her" and thereby "wipe off, at one glorious effort, the taunting imputation so long cast upon the American character," the expedition was not simply to correct the errors of former navigators, but "to collect, preserve, and arrange every thing valuable in the whole range of natural history, from the minute madrapore to the huge spermaceti, and accurately to describe that which cannot be preserved; to secure whatever may be hoped for in natural philosophy; to examine vegetation, from the hundred mosses of the rocks, throughout all the classes of shrub, flower, and tree, up to the monarch of the forest; to study man in his physical and mental powers, in his manners, habits, and disposition, and social and political relations; and above all, in the philosophy of his language, to examine the phenomena of winds and tides, of heat and cold, of light and darkness . . . in fine, there should be science enough to bear upon every thing that may present itself for investigation."

Science enough indeed. To those of his open-mouthed hearers who were asking themselves how all this might be effected, Reynolds calmly offered his prescription: "By an enlightened body of naval officers, joining harmoniously with a corps of scientific men, imbued with the love of science." Carefully chosen, the officers and the "lights of science" would, "like stars in the milky-way, shed a lustre on each other, and all on their country!"

At some point in the course of his campaign Reynolds had devoted a great deal of thought and observation to the role of scientists in the Republic, and he now emerged as their champion. In its employment of these men he urged government to recognize that scholars qualified for such station "do not hang loosely upon society" and to reverse the unhappy tendency that had made this country "a by-word" among nations for "pitiful remuneration of intellectual labours." A nation with no "stars and ribands, no hereditary titles" to award its men of genius could only show its appreciation by monetary reward. Therefore let us "stamp the value we set on science . . . by the price we are willing to pay."

It was an eloquent performance, and its effectiveness lost nothing in its careful timing. For two weeks earlier, Senator Southard had reported an expedition bill for his Committee on Naval Affairs and recommended a naval expedition accompanied by civilian scientists to sail in two small surveying vessels, a tender, storeship, and a sloop-of-war. The Senate approved and, at Southard's urging, recommended an appropriation of a hundred and fifty thousand dollars. In the House the bill occasioned extensive debate, touched off by the Jacksonian Democrat Albert Gallatin Hawes of Kentucky. Though Hawes came of a distinguished family of Virginia politicians, he affected the popular Davy Crockett stance. He was not willing, he announced, to see money "wrested from the hands of the American people" expended on a "chimerical and hairbrained notion" that would "take the vessels and seamen of the United States, and send them to the South Seas, exposing them to all the diseases, hurricanes, and mishaps of that climate." But Hawes' snarl from the backwoods was ignored and efforts to strike out the expedition were put down by the instant opposition of two members from Ohio, Bellamy Storer, who as a young Cincinnati lawyer twelve years before had introduced John Cleves Symmes to a local audience as the Newton of the West, and Thomas L. Hamer, who thought Hawes' provinciality understandable enough in one "never out of sight of land in his life" but pointed out that it must not be allowed to prevail over "Enlightened public opinion," the "great moral lever which, in a good degree, now governs the civilized world." The House voted for exploration on May 9. It only remained for the new Secretary of the Navy to see to the administrative details.[18]

Mahlon Dickerson (1770–1853) seemed, on the face of it, an ideal Secretary of the Navy to handle such an assignment. An amateur botanist and member of the American Philosophical Society, he was a man of both education, holding a degree from Princeton College, and considerable social position, having inherited New Jersey's Succasunna Iron Works. As a political opponent of Southard, he had served New Jersey both as Governor and Senator. To the Jackson administration he now brought protective coloration. As an advocate of the tariff—he had been one of the founders of the policy—he gave the lie to charges that the administration was doctrinaire on the issue of free trade, which he denounced as "a system as visionary and impracticable as the ever-lasting and universal pacification of the world." And as one who had gone as a trooper to put down the Whiskey Rebellion forty years before, his presence suggested that the administration did not mean to subvert property rights, as some persons of property charged. Further, he was as sound as the pigs of his own foundry on the issue of centralized government. Believing that the federal government possessed but few legitimate functions, he himself

Mahlon Dickerson: "Cautious not to attempt too much business." (Courtesy The New-York Historical Society.)

performed no more than was necessary to keep the Navy Department alive. Even so, his years in the cabinet were a great bother and none more so than those in which the exploring expedition made demands on his energies, as his diary of 1836 attests. March 15: "Cold & chilly—my face swelled—declined dining with Mr. Maxy [sic]—forgot the Cabinet Meet^g—had two hands in my garden." July 7: "Hot weather—very busy at my office—plagued with the Exploring expedition." July 11: "Plagued with J. N. Reynolds." October 1: "plagued with the correspondence of Capt. Jones & J. N. Reynolds." December 31: "end of the most perplexing & busy year of my life." Forever plagued and perplexed, this aging bachelor found delight only in botanizing expeditions, dinner table gossip with cronies, and a flourishing flower garden. Popular in society, at his post he was essentially a courthouse politician, complacent and inflexible, yet capable of remarkable heights of petulance when crossed. Having been saddled by his Whig enemy in New Jersey politics with the organization of an enterprise with which he had no sympathy whatever, Dickerson was bitter. One of his first acts was to try to kill the expedition in cabinet meeting by pointing out to Jackson that it was a resurrection of a favorite project of Southard's, whom Jackson also heartily disliked. But Jackson responded that Southard then had at least one good idea to his credit and that steps must now be taken to put it into effect.[19]

Dickerson's chief colleague in the preparations was Thomas ap Catesby Jones, the same Jones who has been chosen to command the aborted expedition of '28. Now forty-six and a commodore, Jones had had a varied career. Member of a Virginia family of Welsh origin, he had entered the Navy in 1805 at the age of fifteen and had been a comrade-in-arms of General Jackson at New Orleans, where he had been severely wounded in the crucial battle on Lake Borgne. A stern, soft-spoken little man hunched protectively over the musket ball lodged in his shoulder, Jones was popular with those who served under him and both Southard and Reynolds thought highly of his abilities. By 1836 he had commanded the Pacific Squadron and was regarded as one of the Navy's best. Jackson ordered Dickerson to let Jones have his choice for flagship, the *Macedonian*, the Navy's smallest frigate, so new it was still in the stocks at Norfolk. Though there were objections to using so large a vessel for exploration, this famous ship, like her commander, was thought to be a fitting symbol of America's declaration of cultural independence. For she was originally a British warship captured by Stephen Decatur in the *United States* in 1812, and though now entirely rebuilt, she still mounted the original British guns. With a length of 164 feet and a beam of 41, the frigate offered safe and comfortable accommodations for a corps of scientists and adequate stowage for both their instruments and the survey boats. For the rest, Jones suggested two brigs of about two hundred tons, two schooners of one hundred, and a storeship of three. When Dickerson resisted, Jones called again on the General, who simply announced that the request, less one schooner, was to be complied with and the expedition to sail in October. Still resisting, Dickerson carried over to the White House the seven volumes of the recently published *Voyage de la Corvette L'Astrolabe* to show how much of scientific value J. S. C. Dumont d'Urville's small expedition of 1826–1829 had yielded. But Jackson merely concluded that if that much could be accomplished by a small force, so much the more might be done by a large one. Left with no choice but to acquiesce, Dickerson issued orders to the Board of Navy Commissioners for fitting out the *Macedonian*, completing the storeship *Relief*, then building at Philadelphia, and constructing the brigs and schooner, the latter, at Jones' suggestion, to be specially strengthened in timbers, knees, and planks.[20]

But neither the Board, the commandants of the navy yards, nor the navy agents, who handled the financial affairs of the Department, knew quite what to make of the expedition. By the end of August, Jones was complaining to the Secretary that preparations were far behind schedule. Dickerson so reported to the Commissioners. And the Commissioners, bewildered by the whole extraordinary enterprise, signed more orders and drafts and asked the Secretary's advice when at a loss. To what appropriation was construction to be charged? When was the sailing date, that ship's bread might be baked? What proof must the whiskey be?

All felt much put upon, but the greatest burden fell on Jones. He was to outfit and command not only the first American overseas scientific expedition, but the largest to sail under any flag. His task would have been difficult even with the enthusiastic cooperation of everyone concerned, and as matters stood cooperation was a rare commodity indeed. Early in June 1836, on the eve of retiring to Tennessee for a rest, Jackson informed Dickerson that he felt a "lively interest" in the expedition and was "anxious that nothing should be wanting on our part to secure its success, and, if unsuccessful, that no blame should rest upon us." Jones, he announced, was to be given overall responsibility for superintending the outfit, and the Secretary, after consultation with the Commodore, was to appoint commanders for the ships, who would assist him in the preparations. It was a sensible enough arrangement, yet contention quickly developed between Jones and Dickerson over the appointments. Jones was firm on the issue of seniority, which was the very backbone of the Navy's organization. When, having pored over the Navy List and weighed ability and seniority, Jones announced his selection of those (all personally unknown to him) best fitted to command the smaller vessels of the squadron, Dickerson refused to appoint them. For without consulting Jones he had promised commands to two favorites. He had already sent Charles Wilkes, brother-in-law of his friend Professor Renwick, to Europe to purchase the instruments that Wilkes reported unobtainable in the United States, and he had promised him command of one of the smaller vessels as well as superintendence of the surveying party. Hoping to supplant Reynolds, he had also promised both a command and the position of historiographer to Lieutenant Alexander Slidell, whose books of travels were enjoying some popularity. Dickerson justified these choices to Jackson on the ground that since "the officers were to bear much of the responsibility, labor, and danger of the expedition," they should have the honors as well.

Surprised and hurt, Jones announced that his objections were insuperable, and a lengthy correspondence ensued. Though Jones was willing to accept Wilkes as the logical person to take charge of the surveying party and the instruments, Slidell, about whom he felt some deep misgiving, he would prefer not to have in any situation. Not least, he roundly objected to Slidell's being clothed with authority "to give his own version of my acts and doings!" and suggested that if "belles-lettres attainments" were to be the chief qualifications for commanders, then Washington Irving, James Fenimore Cooper, James Kirke Paulding, and Charles S. Stewart should be given careful consideration —especially the Reverend Stewart, who as a Navy chaplain had more sea service to his credit than did Slidell, and in addition had resided some years among the South Sea islanders.

Dickerson's insistence that Slidell be appointed, that the scientific corps be exclusively naval, as well as his well-publicized search for suitable candidates in the ranks and his vigorous objection to exploration in the polar region, all flowed from his animus for the author of his miseries, J. N. Reynolds. Reynolds' popularity with both the public and the scientific community galled the Secretary, whose distaste for the man had been formed at least as early as 1835, when the exploration bill was before Congress, and had been sharpened when during the session of 1836 Reynolds had invaded Dickerson's home territory and elicited a memorial from the New Jersey legislature, a maneuver that had forced Dickerson to allow the category "exploration" to appear in the bill of appropriations for the year. Thereafter it had been one defeat after another—as he worked with friends in the House to have the appropriation stricken out and as he attempted reduction in ships and men. Even when it was clear that he would have to accept the expedition if he was to remain in the cabinet, he did not budge from the position he had taken when Reynolds had called at his office on the eve of the bill's passage: short of another act of Congress, he would "not allow a civilian to have any control in the enterprise." [21]

Understandably, therefore, Dickerson was dismayed to receive a memorandum from Jackson stating that Reynolds was to be appointed to the expedition, then a second hasty prodding note on the same July day: "It will be proper that Mr. Reynolds go with the expedition. This the public expect." Still he balked. Taking advantage of a verbal error of Jackson's, whose correspondence abounded in them, he sought to thwart Reynolds by offering him the post of secretary to Jones, who in any event had already chosen his secretary. As the President had stated and the administration newspaper announced that he was to be "corresponding secretary and commercial agent," Reynolds declined to accept a "clerkship." Moreover, he had hopes of being chosen to write the official account of the cruise, hopes justified by a letter, signed by forty-three supporters of the expedition in Congress, calling the Secretary's attention to Reynolds' "unremitting zeal" in "the cause of his Country and of science."

With the Secretary of the Navy struggling to wrest from its commander the control of an expedition he privately hoped would never put to sea and simultaneously caught up in a rancorous quarrel with its originator; and with many officers of the Navy jealous enough of civilian participation to support the designs of a Secretary they secretly contemned, it made for a poisonous atmosphere in which to organize the "great national expedition," and it was no wonder that despite Jones' almost frantic activities over a period of nineteen months after passage of the authorizing act, preparations languished. Unable to secure appointments for the commanders he had chosen and therefore, so the system of seniority decreed, without officers even for his own ship (though as first officer of the *Macedonian* he did have the assistance now of the red-faced, brandy-swilling but able James Armstrong, master-commandant who became the Captain Claret of Melville's *White Jacket*), Jones was forced to carry virtually the entire burden of many tasks. He had to see to alterations to the *Macedonian* (including erection of a poop cabin for the commander, displaced from his customary accommodations on the gun deck by the corps of scientists); he had to supervise construction of the brigs and schooners (Jones still insisted on the need for two) to novel specifications so that they might bear up under the stress of Antarctic ice yet be buoyant and swift despite the added weight in timbers and planks; and he had to arrange for a multitude of other details—ships' boats that would be sturdy yet light and of shallow draft for use in surf, special foul-weather gear (he hoped to use the new india-rubber cloth), special heating arrangements for sailing in high latitudes, trinkets for the islanders, whiskey for the crews, cutlasses and muskets, cannon and hammocks.[22]

(Keeping a sharp eye on the preparations, lest the "pompous Yankee enterprise" become the "laugh and ridicule" of all Europe, Edmund Fanning expressed concern about the brigs being built at Boston, and after their launching he voiced his dismay. Pointing out that only a man who had wintered in "the icy regions, observed the making, forming, and breaking up, of those ice islands, bergs, floats, &c., and navigated amongst them in trying positions" could be considered competent to direct their building, he offered his services, only to collide with the Department's determination to make this a Navy enterprise from start to finish. In August, he offered to build them himself, for those in the stocks would be "dismasted by the Woollies." But he was promised only "due consideration.")

The storeship *Relief* was launched in the middle of September at Philadelphia. She was unique in several respects. The only storeship the Navy possessed worthy the name, she was also the first Navy vessel to be equipped with spencer masts (which carried a fore-and-aft sail) at both fore and main, making it possible to sail her much closer to the wind than could be done with squaresails alone. She even had a commander—Lieutenant James Glynn. Then, over Fanning's alarmed protest that no "talent or ability ever can do or obtain, with such vessels, what our citizens or the world will expect from the American character, nation, and its gallant navy, by and from this national enterprise," the two brigs were launched at Boston late in October. One newspaperman reported them to be "as strong as wood and iron could make them, but very like an old-fashioned demi-john in their model." On November 2 the *Macedonian*, a deep-water ship drawing over seventeen feet and bearing as her figurehead the likeness of Alexander the Great, was launched at the Norfolk yard and a week later the brigs, re-rigged as barks, were awarded the names *Pioneer* and *Consort*. The little schooner launched at New York was christened *Pilot*.[23]

When, through Jackson's intercession, commanders were finally chosen for the *Pioneer* and *Consort*, Jones made a tour of the navy yards to inspect the vessels before they sailed to Norfolk, which, persuaded that "hard winter" would arrive before preparations were completed, he had chosen as the rendezvous in place of New York. In the course of the stormy passage from Boston in January 1837 it was found that the two barks leaked annoyingly and that the new anthracite galley stoves (the invention of Commodore James Barron, they were assumed to be a great advance over the usual wood burners as less stowage was required for fuel) were a great bother from the difficulty of getting up the fire, which once got up threatened to fire the ship.

As a further test the *Pioneer* sailed for Vera Cruz at the end of January with the unpopular Mexican Napoleon, General Santa Anna, on board. The General's return in good health by the United States Navy occasioned widespread criticism, but more important to the expedition was the captain's appraisal of his vessel after eighty days at sea. A mere rip "that would not jeopard the safety of a boat" would set her to pitching heavily, and having "pitched away three jibbooms, a foretopgallant-mast, and mizen-top mast" and stove in the stern boat, he was convinced that the *Pioneer* was "totally unsuited" for a cruise "on which our business is to *seek* and not to *avoid* dangers." One of the hands wrote home that her movements were "sufficient to frighten the monsters of the deep."

As the *Consort* and *Pilot* were built on similar lines, the the rumor quickly spread through the maritime community that the exploring ships were unfit. Blaming the rig and the extra armament installed for the Mexican cruise, Jones made the necessary alterations and at the conclusion of an eight-day cruise pronounced them "fair-sailing vessels" that could carry more sail in a heavy sea than could the merchant vessels they had hailed. But to improve them further he sent them into drydock at Norfolk. Once these alterations had been made, little more remained to be done in Jones' area of responsibility. Though there was still a shortage of officers, nearly five hundred men had been recruited and most of the stores gathered.

Preparations in the scientific department were in no such state of forwardness, as Jones had pointed out to Dickerson a number of times. As commander, he required information on a variety of matters centering about the scientific corps. Where was the expedition to go, precisely? How long would it be at sea? How many "scientific gentlemen" would there be, and how were they to be governed? Who, if anyone, was to write a history of the voyage?[24]

3 A Glorious Prospect

Exult O shores, and ring O bells!

Whitman

Newspapers most solicitous of the "national character" consoled themselves with the reflection that "the proper arrangement of an expedition, whose results are to be judged by the whole scientific world" could not be "too carefully defined."

Reynolds himself well knew how much depended on the quality of the scientific corps. On his first voyage Captain Cook had inaugurated the era of scientific exploration by assigning purely scientific duties to two botanists. Since then, every exploring expedition of importance had been accompanied by scientists. Yet, largely because all duties had been assigned to one or two persons, these had been less than genuinely scientific affairs. For example, the Russian voyage of 1815–1818, commanded by Otto von Kotzebue, had carried a well-known "investigator of nature in all her departments," Adalbert von Chamisso. In botany and zoology Chamisso's work turned out to be valuable, but in geography and linguistics it could with charity be described only as "rather unfortunate." Science had made such strides since Cook's day—and Kotzebue's, too, for that matter—that it was no longer possible for a man to acquire a competent knowledge in many of its departments before age unfitted him for exploration. What Reynolds therefore planned, as the *North American Review* discerned, was the first expedition, with the possible exception of Napoleon's into Egypt, with a "Scientific Faculty, complete in all the departments." This was radical innovation, and Reynolds understood that its uniqueness placed all the greater burden on the expedition's conductors, for if they failed, they could not expect successors to complete the design. Indeed they could not expect government again to look with enthusiasm on sponsoring scientific expeditions.[1]

Predictably, Dickerson had shown no great haste in choosing scientists for the corps. But by August, when the President again nudged him into action, the Secretary had reached the dismaying conclusion that they were not to be found in the ranks of the Navy. Dispatching Wilkes to Europe to purchase the instruments the latter thought necessary, he wrote to the leading scientific societies of the country for their advice on the selection of "scientific gentlemen of suitable age"—among cronies he called them "oyster and clam catchers"—who were "well acquainted with geology and mineralogy, with botany, with zoology in all its numerous branches, with meteorology, magnetism, electricity, and other subjects connected with natural history." He also required a philologist and an artist to paint the portraits of the natives along the route, together with a list of scientific subjects deserving special investigation.

It was little enough information on which to recommend a man—no mention of the duration of the voyage, of pay, of the place of the scientists in the chain of command, no mention of instruments, equipment, books, accommodations. Nevertheless, individual applicants appeared in considerable number, stressing friendship with this or that politician, dropping a few academic names, proclaiming devotion to the Democratic Party and detestation of the Bank of the United States, or simply pleading poverty. But by that time Reynolds had considerably lightened the Secretary's task. Spending the year in New York, he discussed the make-up of the corps with his friend of '28, James De Kay, who himself declined to go, because he had just accepted a job with the Natural History Survey of New York. But De Kay introduced Reynolds to the young botanist Asa Gray, then twenty-five and in New York as librarian and curator of the Lyceum of Natural History. The previous spring Gray had published his first book, *Elements of Botany*, which by introducing the "natural system" of classification in place of the "artificial" Linnean system would influence the course botanical studies in America would take, and even then was making something of a stir. Reynolds urged him to apply for the position of botanist and probably sought his advice on the other appointments, for in August, Reynolds went up to New Haven to consult with Benjamin Silliman (professor of most scientific subjects at Yale and founding editor of the only national scientific publication, the *American Journal of Science*, usually referred to simply as *Silliman's*), and to call on Gray's friend and junior by two years, James Dwight Dana. Dana had trained in geology and chemistry under Silliman and after graduation in 1833 had spent a year in the Mediterranean teaching mathematics to midshipmen aboard the *Delaware*

James Dwight Dana in 1843, age 30. (Geology Library,
Yale University.)

and the *United States* before returning to New Haven to become Silliman's
assistant and to complete his own first book, *A System of Mineralogy*.[2]

On Gray's urging, Dana accepted the post of geologist that Reynolds
offered. And it was probably Gray also who suggested a third contemporary,
Charles Pickering, aged thirty and oldest of the group. Pickering was the
grandson of Colonel Timothy Pickering, the Revolutionary soldier and
statesman of Salem, Massachusetts, in whose home he was brought up, and
nephew of the distinguished philologist John Pickering, with whom Reynolds
also consulted on expedition affairs that summer. Charles Pickering had taken
a medical degree at Harvard in 1826 and becoming interested in botany had
moved to Philadelphia, where in 1836 he was librarian of the Academy of
Natural Sciences and member of the American Philosophical Society as well.

Though he had published little and was remarkably retiring, he had a reputation among naturalists of his generation as a zoologist of great erudition and subtlety.[3]

Reynolds was understandably attracted to these young men of his own generation who shared his concern for the role of science in America and America's role in the world—it had been Gray's conscious attempt in his recently published book to help close the gap between European and American science—and, ably supported by De Kay and the New York Lyceum, he urged them to apply for positions in the corps. Still, his choice of these three argues a remarkable discernment, for Gray and Dana—Pickering's independent nature effectively precluded any such role for him—were to be the leaders of what may be termed the first generation of professional scientists in the United States.

They responded in kind, and for reasons quite apart from the man's geniality and infectious enthusiasm, for he offered them the Pacific. Ever since the first voyage of the incomparable Cook, this last great area of the earth to be opened to Europeans had been regarded as the most fruitful field for both geographical and scientific exploration, a fact which the British Admiralty, the British Museum, and the Royal Society had recognized to their immense benefit. Already, scientific discovery there had raised a most tantalizing problem by putting the first real strain on an ancient theory generally accepted as comprehending the whole world of living nature—the concept of the Great Chain of Being. In 1817 the first President of the Linnean Society of London had noted that in working among the natural productions of Australia the botanist "finds himself as it were in a new world. He can scarcely meet with any fixed points. . . . The whole tribes of plants, which at first sight seem familiar to his acquaintance, as occupying links in Nature's chain, on which he is accustomed to depend, prove, on a nearer examination, total strangers, with other configurations, other economy, and other qualities; not only the species themselves are new, but most of the genera, and even natural orders." In the end, of course, the problems the Pacific posed were resolved only when viewed within the wholly novel frame of thought provided by Charles Darwin and sustained by Joseph Dalton Hooker and Thomas Henry Huxley, three who spent the formative years of their careers on scientific voyages in the greatest of the oceans.[4]

That frame of thought still lay in the future, and when Reynolds first approached the young Americans natural history was still governed by the influence of Linnaeus, and the accepted approach to it was the empirical path laid down by him and blessed by Francis Bacon—the collection and

A GLORIOUS PROSPECT

classification of specimens from as many areas as possible. Reynolds now held out the opportunity to explore the unknown aboard a floating laboratory with every needed book and instrument at hand. Small wonder they took J. N. Reynolds to their heart.

They had yet another reason. In striving to raise science in America from the status of an avocation, subsisting on the kind of Sunday botanizing that Mahlon Dickerson so much enjoyed, to a profession nourished by seven-day specialization in one or more of the great number of branches that were emerging, they were almost painfully conscious of the uniqueness of their role in American life. A nation devoted to getting ahead tended to look askance at young men who insisted on devoting themselves to pastimes and who, like that odd Swiss import Ferdinand Hassler, looked for recognition not to society at large, but to their professional peers. Public acclaim they neither sought nor desired, but the opportunity to practice their profession they absolutely required. In a nation so remarkably prosperous the opportunities to do so were remarkably few. Economic hardship had driven Gray from practicing medicine to teaching and finally to writing his *Elements of Botany.* His tiny salary at the New York Lyceum had come as a godsend. Dana had sailed as schoolmaster as much out of the desire to have an income as to see the world, and on his return he had written an anxious father that he almost wished he had entered the family store, "where it appears to me that I should not have had to have lived a life of so much doubt and uncertainty as appears now to be my prospect." He was saved for science by Silliman's invitation to become his assistant in the chemical laboratory at Yale. Except for Hassler's Coast Survey and the natural resources surveys conducted by the states, opportunities for scientific employment were confined to the scarce and subordinate posts that fell vacant from time to time—most often in the new backwoods colleges— and the very few librarianships and curatorships offered by the scattered scientific societies.

The situation was well described by a member of the Boston Society of Natural History who had urged the expedition upon Congress. After taking due note of the commercial advantages that might be expected—the scientist's sop to the national ethic of useful work—he set about linking the welfare of the American scientist with the national honor: "The peculiar circumstances connected with the settlement & subjugation to the purposes of life on a new soil have hitherto been the reason that little attention has been given to the Nat. Sciences & few men have had either the opportunity or the means of making much advance in them. But the time has come when great numbers of learned men are turning their attention to these subjects." Though "of vast importance to the community at large," these subjects unfortunately yielded no recompense but personal gratification and so could be extensively pursued only with government patronage. This the "honor of the nation" now demanded, for with the patronage enjoyed by their counterparts in Britain and France, American scientists "might hope to boast of a Buffon, a Latreille, a Cuvier."

What Reynolds and the Lyceum's committee thus saw in Dickerson's innocent if grudging request was the opportunity to gain for these scientists and for the nation itself the recognition they so desperately craved. De Kay put it bluntly to the Secretary. It would be "injudicious economy" to jeopardize "the great object of the expedition" by employing second-raters willing to work on the cheap. He suggested that the principals be offered a salary of thirty-five hundred dollars with rations.

But Dickerson, whose natural element was black ink, thought two thousand sufficient. While it would not "command the services of those who have lucrative businesses at home," it was unlikely, he suggested comfortably, that such persons would wish to accompany the expedition whatever the pay, and a larger amount would only antagonize the officers. He was doubtless correct about the explorer's salary not attracting the businessman-scientist, and for once and all unwitting, the man's mania for economy performed a useful service by excluding from the expedition the older generation of leisure-time naturalists and beckoning the rising and struggling generation of professionals. For the latter, even the salary that Dickerson proffered was, as Gray put it, "no small inducement." Though with the pride of the outcast some were chary at first, "not quite ready for Treasury pap," as Charles Pickering remarked, they were attracted to the man who first offered government as a patron to science and freely gave him their loyalty. They were correspondingly repelled by him who strove to destroy the expedition.[5]

However reluctant Dickerson was to follow the hated guide, he now had little choice if, as he had proclaimed in an unguarded moment, he wanted men of talent, for Reynolds had rounded up the best that American science had to offer.

In the end the Secretary professed himself satisfied with the qualifications of Pickering, Gray, Dana, and also with the protégé of the American Philosophical Society, the artist-naturalist Titian Ramsey Peale, already experienced in exploration and now manager of the Philadelphia Museum founded by his father, the Federal artist Charles Willson Peale. However, the year 1836 was drawing to a close—it was the year the *Beagle* returned to England with Charles Darwin ("a zealous and unpaid tributary to the cause of science" who had "labored unremittingly" during the voyage, the *Army and Navy Chronicle* reported)—and still Dickerson made no appointments. This delayed the purchase of equipment and books and the organization of the corps.

Dana thought it "astonishingly singular" that "they make no appointments for an expedition that is to sail so soon." Eager to put to sea but, he wrote Gray, having "no friends at Washington," he feared the worst for himself. Dana's fear of political appointments was shared by many in the scientific community. Richard Harlan (1796–1843), one of the founders of vertebrate paleontology in America but then more widely known as an able zoologist with an exceedingly acid tongue, remarked with some insight to John Torrey that "Polytical influence" was "about to mar the whole concern," and that men "of real merit, must wait to see if the President may not have some friends to serve!" He understood that other appointments were coming of which they might not wholeheartedly approve—another botanist, whom "no one knows as a botanist," and three more zoologists, one of them the Philadelphia physician Reynell Coates (1802–1886), who by his own admission was largely unfamiliar with the subject but had influential political friends. This in spite of the fact that four qualified zoologists did "not exist in this Country." If this criterion was adhered to, Harlan suggested, the time might soon come when the "real *horses* of the expedition may decline working in the same team with the asses."

The political botanist turned out to be one William Rich of Washington, probably a botanizing buddy of the Secretary. When the country's premier botanist, John Torrey, wrote Dickerson in alarm to ask, who was Rich? and to urge that the man's duties be clearly defined that they might not infringe on Gray's, Dickerson replied vaguely that Rich was "not a distinguished botanist," to be sure, but had made himself "very useful in discoveries of plants, and their properties and uses." Finding himself "fatigued," Dickerson offered no further explanation for the appointment of a man whom none had recommended and few even heard of. Fearing that the enterprise would be further "marred by improper appointments," Gray gave thought to remaining behind.[6]

But having met defeat in his attempt to appoint Slidell and Wilkes, Dickerson did not relish humiliation at the hands of the scientific community and when, after further nudging from the President, the appointments were finally published in January 1837, they proved to be not nearly so bad as had been feared, and, with the exceptions of Rich and Coates, horses all. Besides these two, and Pickering and Gray, he named as zoologist Titian Peale, and as specialist in organic remains, James Eights; as conchologist, James Pitty Couthouy (1808–1864), a young Boston merchant and ship captain who had acquired some reputation in working with the sea shells of New England and, eager to join, had pleaded his case before Jackson himself; and as entomologist, young John Witt Randall, recently graduated from Harvard. Walter R. Johnson (1794–1852) resigned his professorship at Philadelphia's Franklin Institute to take direction of the physical sciences. At the recommendation of Yale professor Josiah Gibbs, Horatio Hale, still a student at Harvard, was named philologist.

The choice of artists and draughtsmen was a delicate matter, for the success of the natural history research depended in considerable measure upon their work. (In Torrey's opinion the country had none qualified to make the best botanical drawings; he himself relied on Paris.) In the end, the choice for botanical draughtsman fell on Alfred Agate, a painter of miniatures only just returned from two years in France and Italy and one of New York's most promising young painters. Gray thought that with some training he might be made to do. Joseph Drayton of Philadelphia, a draughtsman of recognized competence, would draw other specimens. The landscape painter chosen was Raphael Hoyle of Newburgh, New York, whose work was much esteemed by his fellow artists Henry Inman, Thomas Cole, and Samuel F. B. Morse.[7]

Only the position of astronomer remained to be filled. Wilkes was unreceptive, there being little about this expedition of which he approved. The frigate was too large to be of use, Jones' adherence to the rule of seniority denied experience to younger officers, and the very existence of a civilian corps was an insult to the Navy. It would anyway be impossible for him "to serve with Captain Jones advantageously in any situation."

When, regretfully, Dickerson sought a civilian astronomer, he was astonished to discover that none was to be had. Professor James Dean of the University of Vermont, who had been eager to join the expedition of eight years earlier, was now over sixty and felt himself too old to embark on so arduous an enterprise. And Nathaniel Bowditch was both too old and too busy with the affairs of his insurance company even to recommend anyone. Denison Olmsted of Yale announced that he was much too occupied with college affairs to draw up instructions for the astronomer.

When Dickerson, puzzled, asked Robert Treat Paine, who had also sought to join the earlier expedition but no longer evinced any enthusiasm, to consult Bowditch personally, it was only to learn that neither Bowditch nor Paine knew anyone in New England—and the rest of the country was a total loss—"sufficiently qualified" who would be willing to accept the position.

Paine coolly suggested the reason for this remarkable state of affairs. "The astronomers of this country," he wrote, "have always deeply regretted the disinclination of Congress to do any thing for the advancement of their favorite science. With them, the establishment of a national observatory at Washington has ever been a favorite project; they therefore did not view the proposed expedition with much favor, not only because the expense of it will exceed more than ten times the cost of an observatory, but because, should the result of this gigantic equipment be inadequate or unsatisfactory, they greatly feared that Congress for many years would be indisposed to do any thing more." Whether Dickerson found the explanation enlightening is to be doubted, but then it was an uncommon kind of revolt. It was suggested that the distinguished astronomer-geologist Joseph Nicholas Nicollet (1786–1843), who was an experienced explorer, be offered the post, but nothing came of it, probably because of the determination (novel in the history of exploration and muted, but everywhere understood) to employ none but native citizens in the corps. There, so far as the department of astronomy was concerned, matters rested.[8]

In the meantime, Wilkes, dispatched in mid-1836 to buy books and instruments in Europe, was overdue. Pickering had provided the Navy Department with a list of requirements in the autumn, but between a temporary indisposition ("must be cautious not to attempt too much business") and a miserliness that was becoming legendary among the scientists, Dickerson took his good time in forwarding the order to Wilkes. Why learned gentlemen charged with collecting facts should require so many books was beyond the Secretary's grasp. Suspecting a "disposition to fill the ship with books," he cautioned the corps to confine their purchases to "such only as are indispensable." When Wilkes did return in the latter part of January 1837, he brought what was then not only the largest collection of scientific apparatus ever purchased by this government, but the largest provided by any government for its explorers, and the lieutenant announced proudly that it comprised "all that can, in any way, be useful."

Unfortunately, the scientists found his acquisitions sadly lacking. Somehow he had neglected to buy microscopes. They charitably put it down to ignorance and Gray remarked crisply, "As that gentleman is not a naturalist, and appears not to have consulted any naturalist abroad, he was, of course, not aware of the omission." And though Wilkes had assembled some zoological works, Pickering remarked with unwonted acerbity that "if we are reduced to the gauge of taking 'only such as are indispensable,' I should say most of them might be left behind." That some member of the scientific corps should visit

Europe was now considered essential. "Foreign governments," he pointed out, "have not scrupled to send agents to examine our institutions whenever they have thought any thing was to be learned by it; and it seems . . . but wisdom on our part to take advantage in return of the labors of other nations."

But to lay in the necessary books and instruments, whether ordered at home or abroad, required free consultation among the scientists and allocation of their duties. Otherwise all would be duplication and confusion. On this matter, as on others when the need arose, the corps took a surprisingly firm stand. Pointing out these facts to the Secretary during a visit to Washington early in March, Pickering, Gray, and Coates announced it as their joint decision that they would not submit lists of books and instruments until they had been placed on duty. For another reason, too, they insisted on this point. Some, assuming at the time of their appointments that the ships would soon sail, had given up jobs to devote their energies to the preparations and were now in want of income. (Couthouy cooperated only on his lawyer's assurance that compliance would legally obligate the Secretary to pay his salary.)

Again surprised that so little progress had been made and, like Adams before him, anxious that the expedition be a credit to his administration, President Jackson issued his commands to the Secretary: "The exploring squadron must now soon sail: and it is now proper that the scientific corps should be called forthwith into service, to receive each their orders, that each may prepare and be ready to embark the moment Commodore Jones gives the orders. This done, no blame can attach to the Executive department on the score of supineness or neglect. Please attend to this." But the Secretary nevertheless managed to stall through this last month of Jackson's administration, which drew to a close with the expedition little nearer the polar regions and the islands of the Pacific than it had been eight years earlier.[9]

By this time it was clear that, as Gray put it in a letter to his father, there was a "strong attempt to break" the expedition. Spearheaded by Dickerson and "the naval influence," there was a movement in the Senate to eliminate the frigate, and Reynolds pleaded with Southard to arrest it, for if the frigate and the accommodations it afforded were lost, the expedition would cease to be a scientific enterprise.

While Commodore Jones was still seeking information about the scientific corps, news arrived from Paris that the French, who already had three small expeditions afloat, were to send yet another of two vessels under Captain J. S. C. Dumont d'Urville, with instructions to explore the Antarctic regions and the islands of the western Pacific. That this was France's response to the zeal of the American government in promoting science seemed confirmed by further news received in July. Louis Philippe had promised a reward to the sailors if they should reach 75° South. Beyond that, the reward would increase with latitude, and if they should reach the pole, the King proclaimed, "then every thing will be granted to the sailors that they may demand." France had set her heart on a new *ne plus ultra*.

Unimpressed by the challenge, Dickerson on June 3 reported to now President Van Buren that there was a "general want of confidence" in three of the exploring ships and indeed in the enterprise itself "under its present organization." Urging reduction in ships and men on the ground that to rob the Navy of so large a force would leave the nation's commerce exposed, he charged a board of commodores to inquire into the fitness of the vessels for exploration that, he took care to emphasize, would venture "in the high southern latitudes" as near the pole as possible.[10]

Reynolds and Jones promptly recognized this tactic for what it was. By encouraging the belief that an expedition led by an armed frigate and equipped with botanists and zoologists was being sent to attempt the pole, Dickerson held it up to ridicule and, since it was authorized under the commerce clause, to the charge of unconstitutionality as well. Reynolds was a patient man, but as patience is no match for true phlegm, he now burst into the newspapers with a series of angry letters. Writing under the pseudonym "Citizen," he enumerated the Secretary's depredations on the expedition, and delicately suggested that both Dickerson and the squadron be sent speedily on their way. For his part, the disgusted Jones frankly told the commodores that he would much prefer not offering "a single remark to a Board called into being" for such a purpose, but in obedience to the Secretary's order wrote out a narrative of his dreary adventure and an able brief for the expedition as organized. The present impasse, he suggested magnanimously, was owing to failure of perception: that in the magnitude of its purpose this expedition had no precedent, for the legendary explorers of the Pacific were but *"pioneers, who made vast discoveries,"* to be sure, but for want of *"time, means, and the necessary equipments* for extensive and accurate surveys, were *compelled* to leave *an infinite* amount of work to be executed by some humble follower." The Navy was indeed in a sad state, he concluded pointedly, if it could not spare its smallest frigate for such a service without endangering the nation's commerce.

The commodores reported in the middle of July that the ships were "sound, strong, and well built" and that while they did not combine to perfection the qualities of sailing and working well, great strength and capacity, probably no ship could. With a few alterations, soon completed, they would prove satisfactory for the purpose. They advised against anything more than slight reduction in officers and men, for great expense had already been incurred and further delay raised the spectre of defeat of the whole enterprise.

While alterations began anew on the *Pioneer* and *Consort* at the great granite drydock at Norfolk, Jones set off in company with Reynolds to find a replacement for the *Pilot*, which it had been decided might better be left at her mooring. The scientists were left in a limbo of "floating reports & predictions," but Dana heard that the President was pleased with the board's findings and determined that the expedition *"shall go."*

That the President was so determined became clear when—at the end of June 1837, six months after Congress had made appropriation for their pay—Dickerson placed the scientists on duty and on the payroll as of July 4, truly a day of independence for those who had devoted months to the service and suffered hardship for their pains. But making an exception to the Navy's usual practice, he refused to permit advances on their pay, badly needed by some for the purchase of personal gear, until the very eve of sailing. Eights was in poverty as usual. Couthouy had laid out so much of his own time and money in preparing dredges and other apparatus and gathering books for the department of conchology that he was in danger of arrest from creditors. While Dickerson assumed a businesslike stance and refused to employ a debtor, Couthouy finally extricated himself by pledging his shell collection. And the corps were startled to learn that their salaries were to be paid only from July instead of the date of appointment the previous January. Rejecting the cynical permission to resign, "if so disposed" which Dickerson granted the protesting scientists, young Hale announced that he hardly knew "any inconvenience short of absolute starvation which would induce me to renounce the opportunity." [11]

While the French Antarctic expedition was making its final preparations (such was the enthusiasm it elicited in France, Reynolds reminded Dickerson, "that some of the most promising youth in the kingdom have volunteered their services even before the mast; while *you* hold up a similar enterprise as degrading to the officers of our navy!") the Secretary journeyed up to Philadelphia on Department business and while there managed to spend a part of an evening with some of the corps at the home of the Philosophical Society ("meeting with the Scientific corps at the Philosophical Hall—on the invitation of my old friend John Vaughn—who treated with wine strawberries confectionary &c.—delightful," was his complete account of the event in his diary) before proceeding to New York to call on his friend Professor Renwick. He professed surprise that many books and instruments were still wanting but

A GLORIOUS PROSPECT

assumed a liberal stance for the occasion and promised an abundance of every necessary article and even, he added warmly, "a little more." He now thought the squadron might sail within seventy days.

Hopes rose again. Dana found the little corps "an agreeable company." Everywhere they enjoyed the hospitality of the seat of American science, whose libraries, both public and private, were thrown open to them. At least one evening was spent at one of the popular "scientific Soirées" frequently given by the distinguished geologist and craniologist, Dr. Samuel George Morton, who had shown a "lively interest" in the preparations. In August they finally met their commander. As Jones seemed "desirous of consulting the comfort & wishes of the corps in every respect," Dana thought him "just the man for such an expedition."

As alterations to the *Pioneer* and *Consort* neared completion in September, so that they were no longer the "clump, misshapen things" that had ridden the same waters a few months earlier, Jones urged the Secretary to have the books, charts, and instruments taken out of storage in Washington and sent down to Norfolk. In the meantime he would bring the ships round to New York for installation of their heating apparatus. The Commodore was sufficiently emboldened by the prospects on the eve of sailing to read to officers and crews his "General Order No. 1." He could promise that all, even the unpopular marines, would be well cared for. In the regions of "extremist cold," there would be extra warm clothing issued at the Navy's expense, "ample supplies of good and wholesome provisions," and a "liberal allowance of Hospital stores" and antiscorbutics, all of which, as every man who had served a hitch well knew, was without precedent. For this was no ordinary service: "Towards the United States Surveying and Exploring Expedition are turned the eyes of all Europe; and your successful labours . . . will . . . enlarge the bounds of knowledge, and diffuse the blessings of civilization and Christianity among nations now unknown." England, France, and Russia now had expeditions afloat, "and that nation which wins the prize by pushing her discoveries farthest . . . besides reaping the rich harvests of present and contingent commercial advantages, will acquire the proud distinction of Benefactor of the Human Race."

There was one difficulty. Many had already served one-third of their enlistment. Getting them home in the midst of the voyage would be awkward, so to those who would sign new articles on the first of November he would pay three months' bounty on their arrival in New York.

Anchoring in the North River, the squadron made "a fine appearance" and attracted much attention. Senator Southard and other dignitaries paid a visit and professed to be "much gratified" with the state of things. No doubt enthralled by visions of the national destiny and the present and contingent commercial advantages, the men signed over and received their bounties. Then, to the consternation of all, one hundred and fifty-five of these benefactors of the human race deserted.

While officers took up the chase, outfitting continued. A heating contraption was installed in the *Macedonian*, a large furnace in the fore-peak that was entwined within and without by a coiled pipe that conducted hot water through the vessel. Supplies were stowed aboard—india-rubber floats, crates of instruments, and "only men of science knew what else," as one of the bemused young officers recalled. Everyone remarked on the comfortable accommodations afforded by this vessel "built according to the most approved lights of modern science."

The officers found themselves "the Lions of the day" ashore. On their arrival at the theater the actors let the performance slide to give " 'Three Cheers'! from the Sovereign People." One lieutenant confessed to feeling "a little foolish" at receiving such acclaim "before we had performed any thing" but was gratified to find so much enthusiasm for the expedition, "even yet." And the scientists, confident now, turned a deaf ear to the few pessimists among them who were sourly predicting that "we shall eat our Christmas dinner in this country" and organized their private mess to supplement the dreary navy ration. By omitting liquor and wine, they were able to reduce individual assessments to a remarkably low one hundred and twenty dollars and were unprepared for the resulting praise. As "a *strictly temperance body*," oneeditor intoned, they imparted "a *moral* as well as an intellectual dignity" to the "great national enterprise." [12]

Outfitting was continuing at a satisfactory pace when, suddenly, on November 9 sailing instructions arrived from Washington, describing the general area of operations, apportioning the duties of the corps, and including the reports of the advisory committees of the Philosophical Society, the East India Marine Society, the Naval Lyceum, and a memorandum on the Pacific and South Seas by Admiral Kruzenstern. All of which on the face of it was very helpful indeed, but actually, as Dickerson very well knew, these were non-sailing instructions issued to facilitate another of the non-departures he had been announcing for twelve months past. He had not sent the scientific instruments from Washington as Jones had requested, he knew they were not going to arrive in the near future, and he issued an appointment which rendered it unlikely that the expedition ever would sail under Jones' command.

A GLORIOUS PROSPECT

The problem of the instruments was handled with an inefficiency remarkable even for this enterprise. Soon after the arrival of the twenty thousand dollars' worth of equipment and books Wilkes had purchased, Walter Johnson expressed the wish to familiarize himself with them, only to be informed that the scientific corps would soon be assembled in Washington and the instruments placed in their charge. When no such steps were taken, he wrote again in April, but to no effect. Finally, in July, Dickerson granted him permission to examine the instruments stored at the New York yard. Happy at last to be able to do "something effectual" but pointing out that the whole time since receipt of his appointment should have been devoted to observation and adjustment of the instruments, Johnson was surprised to find on arrival that all the chronometers, necessary to verify the accuracy of other instruments, had been shipped to Washington a month before, that many of the books had been lent to Wilkes and others, and instruments to Professor Renwick, and that a shockingly large number of instruments and parts of instruments were inexplicably missing. He packed up the remainder and shipped them to Philadelphia, where, with the permission of the city authorities he set up a small observatory in Rittenhouse Square for testing them—assisted by several young officers who, somewhat to their surprise, discovered that "the lamp of Science held more charms" than the "many fair Cyprians" who infested the city.

Renwick discovered a few of the missing instruments in his apparatus room but knew nothing about the others. Dickerson acknowledged having lent some of the instruments to Wilkes, and coolly asked that others be lent him for a survey to be made of Georges Bank. When the disgusted Johnson observed that as Wilkes and Renwick had been permitted use of the chronometers, it did seem that "at least equal facilities and advantages should be accorded to those who are intending to go," Wilkes professed himself startled at the man's want of delicacy. "Mortified," he wished to be absolved of all responsibility. Some of the missing apparatus was on board his command, the *Porpoise*, including six sextants brought aboard by mistake, and some at his house in Washington. As for the rest, he could only suggest that Johnson, "through ignorance," did not know how to assemble them properly.

Working in Philadelphia with borrowed timepieces, Johnson grew increasingly restless as the summer wore on and in exasperation pointed out to Dickerson that philosophical instruments, after all, were not like "muskets or cutlasses, which, after undergoing a rough and hasty proof, may be put into the hands of any soldier or marine, sure of fulfilling their purpose." Jones backed him up, suggesting that the Secretary appoint officers to "hunt up" the missing pieces as soon as possible, for the *Macedonian* was alongside the wharf and all was at a standstill until it should be determined "who and *what* is to be embarked, and *all persons and things*" ordered aboard.

But no one knew which were the forty-seven chronometers chosen for the expedition, or what their rates and errors were. When finally ordered to deliver them up, Wilkes became suspicious that his honor had been impugned and wrote to the Department to demand copies of relevant correspondence. Then it was discovered that many surveying instruments were also missing. When forthrightly ordered to delay sailing in the *Porpoise* until he had delivered up all the instruments in his possession the Lieutenant discovered that he had some of these, too, others had been lent to officers in Boston and Philadelphia, some were in storage at one of the navy yards, and about the others again he had no knowledge. Then it was found that even without the missing instruments so much scientific equipment had been gathered that it was necessary to remove more of the frigate's guns and install instrument rooms on the berth deck.

Utter chaos. But Jones was past caring. At last exasperated beyond endurance, he resigned command in the middle of November. Though he somewhat belatedly offered reasons of health—and indeed he was bedridden and hemorrhaging at the lungs—what finally prompted his departure was the appointment, revealed to him only in the sailing instructions and made with the view of precluding any role for Reynolds, of a Navy chaplain as historiographer. There was an end to the matter as far as he was concerned. During the entire seventeen months of his command he had faced the most "uncompromising opposition" and "procrastination the most extraordinary." The squadron was now to be found in New York in the midst of the only season in which it was possible to operate in Antarctic waters, with provisions a year old and officers and men "harassed and wearied out by delay—opposition, derision, and uncertainty." He hoped another commander would be found promptly that the expedition might sail within a month.

Two days after the resignation news arrived from France—where it was assumed that the delayed departure of the Americans was owing to careful planning for every contingency—that the *Astrolabe* and *Zélée* had sailed from Toulon in August, with "wine for two years" and instructions to advance as near the South Pole as possible and thereafter to visit "all the islands of the South Seas." [13]

Edmund Fanning saw in these events a godsent opportunity for government to take his advice on the construction of exploring vessels, but most others ascribed them to a more mundane source. At the Boston Yard

A GLORIOUS PROSPECT

Lieutenant John ("Mad Jack") Percival, who himself had reason to be grateful to Dickerson for once having rescued him from the "persecution of the Missionaries" in Hawaii, wrote the Secretary frankly that in Boston, the city most closely identified with the Pacific trade and now suffering like the rest of the country from the financial panic, Dickerson's policy toward the expedition had aroused "a feeling of unrelenting unkindness" toward him. It aroused similar feeling in Congress, where resolutions were introduced calling for explanations and a futile attempt made to disband the expedition on the ground of "the present organization of the Navy Department, to say nothing of the incompetence at the head of it."

Dickerson's appointment in December 1837 of a new board of survey occasioned no surprise in Boston or elsewhere. The board recommended that the *Macedonian* be replaced by a lightly armed sloop-of-war and that in place of the schooner the expedition take along materials for building a decked-over boat that might be assembled when needed. As it had already been discovered that the supplies and equipment gathered at the New York yard were too much by several hundred barrels to be stowed in the ships, the recommendation meant that there must be a corresponding reduction in personnel. The scientists rightly suspected that they would have to bear the brunt of it.

When news of the new survey reached Reynolds, he immediately stepped forward to enlighten the public on the virtues of the original plan. Would it not be "honourable to our national character," he asked, "if, when any doubt was raised concerning the position, natural history, or language of any island, an appeal to the records of the South Sea exploring expedition should be sufficient to set the question at rest?" The means were at hand, for assembled and ready to sail was no body of mere collectors, but a national task force of scientists each of whom had "his favourite division; while possessing, at the same time, more or less knowledge of the branches consigned to his companions." Only give the signal to weigh anchor, then observe the efficient way they bring their talents to bear: The frigate, home and laboratory and transport, has come to anchor at, say, one of the Fiji Islands. While magnetic and pendulum observations are made from a station on shore, the specialists proceed under escort into the interior, where the "productions of the whole, the valleys, and the mountains," the language and the culture come under their practiced eye—and all without delaying the expedition beyond the time required for the hydrographical survey, because the unique "division of labours" makes possible "a perfect system of reciprocity. The botanist, while plucking a flower would not overlook the insect feeding upon it; because the entomologist would repay the courtesy by gathering for him a plant; and each would be able to give to the other all requisite information of their respective localities." [14]

It was a preview of the coming organization of science. But for the scientific community as a whole, still informed by the tradition of the naturalist, its appeal was less than persuasive. In Philadelphia, which Constantine Rafinesque had hated because science there was in the hands of a few "aristocrats" but could not avoid because it was still the capital of American science, Pickering had watched the traditional sentiment gather and crystallize among the influential dilettantes of the Philosophical Society and the previous autumn had occasioned some stir in their ranks by submitting his resignation. He had been very frank: "Having long seen with regret that the objects of your Institution were not appreciated among yourselves as a body, I have . . . looked upon your position in the Public eye as unfortunate, and a regard for the Infant cause of Science in our Country . . . induces me to decline the association hereafter."

Chief among his antagonists were the armchair naturalist George Ord (1781–1866), the testy and perennial critic of Audubon; John K. Kane (1795–1858), a Philadelphia lawyer whose accomplishment in science was confined to writing obituaries of the Society's members; and Clement C. Biddle (1784–1855), a self-educated Philadelphia banker said to be very agreeable in personal intercourse and faithful in attending meetings of the Society. As a director of the Philadelphia Museum (formerly the renowned Peale's Museum) Kane fixed a covetous eye on the prospective natural history collections of the expedition and had been cultivating Dickerson's favor by reporting gloomily on the activities of Reynolds, Gray, Dana, and others he lumped together as the "New York Clique." Except for his friend Peale and a few others, Ord, a ship chandler and ropemaker become a "wealthy gentleman of leisure," thought the corps "the most intriguing, presumptuous, cross-grained animals that ever were herded together" in such an enterprise and no *"gentlemen"*: two of them had been expelled from a New York hotel for "inebriation." To a friend abroad, he reported that the expedition itself was a farce got up by a "self-taught genius" and "disciple of the renowed Captain John Cleves Symes" and, thinking with many others in the spring of 1838 that the enterprise had collapsed, found "not much cause to regret."

All three were naturalists of the old school, who preferred a little banking in the morning and botanizing in the afternoon, and they bitterly opposed all that the expedition represented. What it represented in part was the democratization of science, for the coming of the specialist, however much it

A GLORIOUS PROSPECT

was to be deplored on a variety of grounds, meant at least in America, where the tradition of self-help prevailed and the government supported vicarage did not exist, that for the first time the investigator need not possess wealth in order to practice his profession. The passing of the naturalist was to make possible the pursuit of science as a profession. But the rays of a new dawn are rarely relished by the old order and, pulling up the covers of tradition, these three sturdy dabblers of the Philosophical Society muttered angrily against the new day. In the eyes of the aristocratic naturalist, there clung to the specialist in science something of the grubbiness of the mechanic: he could never be quite respectable. As the aristocrat is nowhere so jealous of his privileges as in a democracy, where, if few, they are nonetheless of his own making, Reynolds with his popular following was the embodiment of all they deplored, and by using their influence in Washington they tried to close the ranks of science against him. Mistaking Reynolds' vision for naïveté, they argued that the size of the corps bore no relation, unless an inverse one, to the expedition's success. Their prescription was to reduce the corps to "manageable form" by assigning astronomy and hydrography to navy officers commanding two of the vessels, turning meteorology and the natural history of man over to navy surgeons, and restricting the rest to their particular favorites, Peale and the draughtsman Joseph Drayton, a botanist and a machinist. "Above all else," Ord remarked bitterly, "I would urge the necessity of excluding from any share, directly or indirectly in this enterprise, that incendiary fellow——: a man that I should avoid with as much caution as I would the approach of a mad dog or a rattlesnake." It was a snarl from a generation of scientists that was nearing extinction, to survive into the future as the superficial and essentially harmless philosophers of nature in the popular press and the Boy Scout movement. But the recommendation of these worthies helped to shape the course the expedition was to take, which so far as the organization of science was concerned was a journey not into the future but into the past.[15]

Warily optimistic, Dana predicted that "Strange things may take place first, but there is no doubt that we shall be off at last." He was correct on both counts. The immediate problem was to find a commander, and an awkward one it proved to be. In December 1837 and the following January, Dickerson offered the command to three veteran captains. The first declined because, it was said, he thought the *Macedonian* unsuited for such an expedition. The second, who announced that he would not "lend his aid to pluck a single plume" from the squadron as its sailing was now "a matter of *honor*," took command with a burst of energy (thinking that canvas was filling at last, Dana sent to New Haven for his guitar), but then the *Macedonian* was plucked and he resigned. The third, Matthew Calbraith Perry, refused the command for unspecified "reasons of an imperative character."

Blaming the Secretary, one perceptive member of the House suggested that he be placed where "his imbecilities could bring no dishonour upon the country hereafter," and Van Buren himself, though ever careful to avoid offending, gave evidence of agreement when he requested Secretary of War Joel Poinsett, who had a reputation both as an amateur scientist and an able administrator, "to aid the Secretary," as Poinsett was to put it delicately to a puzzled correspondent, "with my counsel whenever he may think proper to request it."

To put an end to what was developing into a national scandal and an international joke, Poinsett on January 30 simply ordered Lieutenant Francis H. Gregory to the command. As squadrons were customarily commanded by captains, the Senate cooperated by confirming Gregory's promotion next day, but both Poinsett and Congress reckoned without Mrs. Gregory. An emotional warrior, the Captain was soon pleading for release on the ground that his absence would bring "ruin and desolation" upon his family. Though disappointed, for the "character of the navy" was in jeopardy, Poinsett relented in a letter so full of the "spirit of patriotism" that it caused Mrs. Gregory to drop "one tear at the sacrifice of her feelings" and give her consent. The Captain would be off for New York on the morrow. But on the morrow he observed that though Mrs. Gregory said nothing it was so apparent that a "sacrifice has been made, to my interest and fame, that cannot fail to entail upon me endless regrets," that he must again beg off. Poinsett again consented—less fervently this time.

Giving up his flirtation with firmness, he offered the command to Captain Joseph Smith. Smith accepted on condition that Charles Wilkes and two other lieutenants experienced in survey work could be induced to command the vessels. (Wilkes had served under Smith early in his career and the older man had remarked on his "promptness & attention to duty—rather inclined to your own way in most matters," was the way Smith put it, "but always efficient.") But at a secret session in the Hall of the Navy Department, Wilkes declined going on the expedition in any capacity. When Smith, thinking he might still accept command if only the two other lieutenants would come along, asked Wilkes to set up the pendulum and show him how to use it, Wilkes pettishly refused. Smith was offended. Having offered commands to three junior lieutenants, he could not now offer them to their seniors on the

Navy List without giving offense and so had no choice but to hand in his resignation.[16]

Poinsett was less chagrined at the latest resignation than he might have been, for on consulting Professor Renwick about Wilkes' availability for command of one of the vessels he found Renwick's recommendation of his brother-in-law's talents enthusiastic enough to suggest that the lieutenant might play a larger role than Smith had cast him in. Renwick was not at all certain that Wilkes would consent to have anything to do with the expedition, for he had been much offended by the appointment of Walter Johnson. But he assured Poinsett that Wilkes would be the making of it. His surveys of Narragansett Bay and Georges Bank attested to his talents in hydrography and geodesy. In magnetism Renwick had once been his mentor but Wilkes was now beyond him. With such acquirements he probably had nothing to gain "in reputation or standing" by participating, but quite inexplicably he might on certain terms be persuaded. These would include control of all the departments of physical science and some increase in pay, though nothing like as much as a civilian scientist would require—a great saving there. Also, the Department might have to agree to publish the results of his pendulum experiments in London and New York, as also his determination of the longitude of Columbia College, an accomplishment "of the utmost scientific importance."

On April 19 Poinsett secretly recommended the appointment of Wilkes to the command, not of a single vessel, but of the entire squadron and suggested that Dickerson order him to New York to make selections from among the instruments, stores, and crews. Appointment of so junior an officer (of forty lieutenants on the Navy List thirty-eight had more sea service) to such a command was unprecedented in the service, and as secrecy is the fountainhead of rumor, the rumors that now spread through the ranks and into the public domain clung to Wilkes' reputation like bloodsuckers for many years afterward. In view of his standing on the Navy List the opprobrium was probably inevitable, but his having refused command of one of the vessels while Smith was commanding the expedition lent credence to the suspicion that he had maneuvered himself into high place. From Washington, Jane Renwick Wilkes wrote her husband in New York that "the town is in a blaze," and one lieutenant reported the officers in Norfolk "all up in arms." Captains and lieutenants, bitter that a junior of no particular "professional attainments" —a category that did not include attainments in science—had been selected over seniors of proven ability, carried their complaints all the way to the

President and there was suddenly an abundance of volunteers for the command.[17]

Wilkes' friend John Percival passed appropriate judgment on all such by remarking that if qualified post captains and senior lieutenants would not accept command of a service unpopular in the Navy "they had no right to complain" now. Poinsett replied to the protests by announcing that this was a special service of non-military character to which navy tradition did not specifically apply. Which was as good a response as any to protests based on the antiquated system of seniority. But the appointment nonetheless did violence to a system cherished by old veterans who had influential friends and left a heritage of hatred for the expedition in the ranks of the Navy and pockets of distaste in the country at large. When Southern senators, protesting that it would be "fatal to chivalry," were reminded that both James Cook and Edward Parry had been promoted lieutenants that they might command exploring expeditions, which was precedent enough for giving this one to a lieutenant who far surpassed them in scientific talent, Henry A. Wise suggested that perhaps the singular scientific talent that had won Wilkes command was his pledge to dismiss not only members of the scientific corps who were "obnoxious to the Department," but also "Mr. Reynolds, who has done so much in getting up this expedition." But even those who had never seen any point in sending grown men "to catch birds and flies, toads and fishes" were still not willing that "the honor of the country should be tarnished" by abandoning the enterprise. The fact of the matter was, the expedition had become an acute embarrassment. There was no longer any hope of reaping popular acclaim for an expedition once very popular indeed, and Whig and Democrat found themselves in agreement when old John Quincy Adams called at the War Department and left word that all he "wanted to hear about the exploring expedition was, that it had sailed."

Poinsett therefore worked closely with Wilkes but at the same time granted him a degree of autonomy never accorded Jones. Wilkes accepted it as no more than his due, and when in May he was briefly treated to a display of the Dickerson dilatoriness he took the Secretary briskly to task. It quickly developed that Wilkes' notions of the proper organization coincided to a remarkable degree with Poinsett's. When in the midst of public speculation, he announced his choice of ships, the sloops-of-war *Vincennes* and *Peacock*, the *Relief*, and the brig-of-war *Porpoise*, which Wilkes had been commanding in his survey work for some months past, the choice was as much Poinsett's as his. So it was, too, when in the summer two schooners were added, thereby bringing the total tonnage above that of the original squadron. "A singular kind of reduction," Dana remarked, aware by now that science had lost its battle with the Navy.

The corps was to be overhauled almost as completely. "All the duties appertaining to Astronomy, Surveying, Hydrography, Geognosy, Geodesy, Magnetism, Meteorology, and Physics generally to be exclusively confined to the Navy Officers," Wilkes wrote in a memorandum to Poinsett, confident that no others were "so well qualified to perform them." And the lesser departments of science that he allowed a place—zoology, geology and mineralogy, botany, conchology—he proposed to "fill up as far as can be done from among the Medical corps" attached to the expedition. Only if medical officers of sufficient learning could not be found were civilians to be appointed, and they were to be placed "entirely under the control and direction of the Commander of the Expedition." [18]

It was not only the haunting spectre of further delay that impelled Poinsett to accept Wilkes' terms, for such they evidently were, but his own predilections as a scientist. Poinsett, who wrote papers on unusually large cypress trees and the antiquities of Mexico, was a naturalist like Dickerson—whom Reynolds had lately been chiding as having developed some small reputation as a botanist "before botany became a science"—and to him it was simply foolish to send out a battery of specialists whose minds, though sharp of perception, ranged only narrowly. Dismissing the entire lot would be "injudicious," as it would produce "much clamour," but Poinsett agreed that the number should be brought as "low as possible" and was probably correct in the opinion that the "philosophical Societies" of the country would agree to "the propriety & even necessity" of doing so.[19]

Like Dickerson before him, Wilkes was disappointed in his search for learned officers in or out of the medical corps. He could not turn up even a respectable naturalist. One navy surgeon told him frankly that none existed in the service. Having then no choice but to fall back on the best "civilian" talent the country could offer, he took up the matter of reduction with the one full-fledged naturalist in the corps. Late in April he journeyed down to Norfolk, whence it was again decided the expedition should depart, and on the last day of the month had "a long conversation and a very satisfactory one," he wrote Poinsett, "with Mr. T. Peale." As an experienced explorer (he had accompanied the Long Expedition as painter in 1819, had collected birds in Florida for Charles Lucien Bonaparte in 1825 and a variety of natural history specimens in Colombia in 1832), Peale considered himself well qualified to advise. The corps should be sharply reduced, he agreed, for it prescribed a "division of labours" that was "too nice," as he put it, "to have

Titian Ramsay Peale, self-portrait, ca. 1825–1835.
(Courtesy The American Museum of Natural History.)

terminated in harmony, for by it the gentleman who might have discovered a new animal was not entitled to describe its anatomical structure or the parasites found in or about it, or the geologist to have figured among fossils &c &c." Moreover, it made for too much separation between the scientists and the officers, who ought to be "as closely amalgamated as possible . . . their interests in the success of the enterprise being the same." He and Wilkes concluded that with the assistance of some navy officers Peale and Pickering, with Dana, Gray, and Couthouy, whom they thought the best qualified members of the original corps, would constitute a sufficient number. Of the others, Randall was "not agreeable," Coates was "out of his senses," Eights' "habits" were "not of the best," and Johnson and Hale, the taxidermist and three painters could be "dispensed with" on grounds of economy.

Though he approved of "leaving home all the block-heads and taking the best fellows," Asa Gray was not otherwise enthusiastic for the new organiza-

A GLORIOUS PROSPECT

tion. He kept his own counsel and waited. Dana was discouraged for once and gave thought to resigning but, persuaded that Gray would remain, resolved his doubts and kept his place. In Washington, where with some others of the corps he had been scheming to get the whole enterprise removed from the jurisdiction of the Navy Department, Pickering spent an evening with "our new Commodore" and, he confessed to Gray in surprise, found himself going "over to the enemy." He thought some of Wilkes' ideas "not bad," the man was invested with "unlimited power," and he understood the administration had promised "an honourable station . . . to our friend Reynolds."

Pickering was surely unaware of Wilkes' proposal for dealing with the superfluous members of the "ridiculously over-grown corps": only "suffer their pay to continue until the sailing of the Expedition, which will keep them quite quiet, as that has undoubtedly been the motive which has induced many of them to get employment in the expedition." Superfluous now himself, Dickerson received the news gratefully and, to forestall congressional investigation of his administration, resigned at the end of June to retire to his estate, explaining that he did so after four years of "the most arduous duties" because within the last two "the difficulties and perplexities arising from the exploring expedition" had rendered his labors "intolerable." Still, he professed great pride in his major accomplishment: "The exploring expedition has been reduced nearly fifty per cent," though it was still "upon too large a scale" and would never make "an adequate return for the enormous expense." [20]

As scientific values were said to be rated by the new administrators, philology was patently the most "useless" of the departments of the original corps, and the probability of Hale's being eliminated caused a stir. From Yale Josiah Gibbs protested in alarm. From Salem John Pickering sought to disabuse his friend Poinsett of Wilkes' strange notion that "any man in the Expedition can pick up languages well enough to make vocabularies." Hale's mother, the indomitable literary widow Sarah Josepha Hale, whose place in history would be secure even had she not written "Mary Had a Little Lamb," heard the rumors and took time from editing the *Lady's Magazine* and books on cooking and housekeeping, plays, romances, and annuals, to plead the cause of Horatio, who had "always sustained the reputation of extraordinary talents in all his literary pursuits," whose "character and habits" were "of the purest order," and whose feelings were "warmly enlisted in the cause of his country and Democratic institutions." Mrs. Hale refused to believe "that President Van Buren will permit such a course to be pursued." Hale had made a name for himself in the scientific community while a seventeen-year-old sophomore at Harvard by publishing a vocabulary of a hitherto unrecorded

Algonquin dialect, which he compiled by mingling with a visiting tribe from Maine that was camped near the College grounds. But when Poinsett notified Hale on July 30 that he was among the chosen his decision to overrule Wilkes turned less upon the young man's promise—for how greatly that promise would be fulfilled no one could know—than upon his conviction that the learned of America and Europe expected philology to be represented on an expedition that was labeled scientific.[21]

Other mothers' sons, left to their own devices, fared less well. One of the artists who had left his regular employment two years before "for the honor of being connected with such an expedition" appealed to Poinsett: "It is not the money I speak of—I am willing to go any how—do any thing rather than be left behind." One by one their letters of inquiry arrived at the Department, for the most part tentative queries at first, then expressions of astonishment and, finally, outrage. The earliest query, the greatest astonishment and outrage, were Walter Johnson's, whose inquiries over the months had elicited nothing resembling a direct reply. He had devoted his full time to expedition affairs since early the previous year. Jones had called upon him to conduct all manner of investigations—from the best method of heating ships in polar regions to the qualities of india rubber cloth. Late in July he learned that Wilkes had been "permitted to do pretty much as he pleased in regard to the Scientific corps," that, sharply reduced, the expedition would sail about August 10, and that those left behind would receive formal notice of their superfluity only after the ships had sailed. What astonished Johnson more than anything else was "that a young officer of the Navy," without reputation in science, had been made arbiter of the scientific qualifications of members of the corps. Well, Walter Johnson was one, he assured the Department, who would not offer his qualifications "to such an arbitration."

A few days later, "feeling considerable anxiety on the subject," Eights wrote from Albany to ask if he were still considered a member of the corps. As the other letters arrived Poinsett blandly sent them over to the new Secretary of the Navy, James Kirke Paulding. Reynolds did what he could. When Southard was preparing an exposé of the Navy's mismanagement Reynolds pressed him not to waste words on Dickerson—it would be "kicking a dead ass"—but rather to defend the "retiring and unobtrusive class of citizens" engaged in science, showing how much their "ill-requited labors" elevate the national character and how government therefore should always be "paternal and just" toward them that their services might be commanded in the few instances in which government has the power to encourage "liberal pursuits." Reynolds then went to Paulding with a plea for the castaways. Dickerson had stopped their pay six months since on various grounds—once, incredibly, in a letter to Johnson, on the ground that the corps had been "extravagant" in their purchases—and having borrowed or pledged their half-pay tickets to meet the expense of their own now useless outfits, most were very hard up. Every man of "liberal and just feelings" would surely agree that they should receive at least the advance customarily paid officers on the eve of sailing. But Paulding was helpless and though Poinsett recommended payment, those left behind were still trying to collect some form of compensation long after the ships had sailed.

In the future American scientists might think twice before turning to government for patronage. Asa Gray took second thought during the summer

The gardener: William Dunlop Brackenridge.
(Courtesy Smithsonian Institution Libraries.)

and in the middle of July brusquely informed Paulding that he would "decidedly prefer not to accompany" an expedition "so essentially different from the original." Gray's resignation was an incalculable loss for his was the finest talent of all. Though he generously promised to aid the amateur Rich both before its departure and after its return, his separation meant that the expedition would sail with a second-rate, Sunday botanist. For Gray himself, it meant, in the words of his biographer, that he would be known forever after "as a 'closet botanist,' a man who studies nature second-hand in the garden and herbarium. The faint aura of pedantry—unjust though it is—which still clings to his name would never have formed about a shellback of the United States Exploring Expedition." And his promise to help Rich would cost him dearly when years later he would struggle with the stale and brittle collections that lay in chaos about him. But for the present it was assumed that William Dunlop Brackenridge, a twenty-eight-year-old Scot, would help to take up the slack. At nineteen he had been head gardener at the Edinburgh Botanical Gardens and had since headed a department at the British Gardens. He had come to Philadelphia only the previous year, as foreman to the nurseryman Robert Buist (1805–1880), who had popularized the spectacular plant that Poinsett had introduced from Mexico in 1833, and who recommended Brackenridge for the post. While the Scot's chief duty would be to care for the live plants collected, he seemed knowledgeable enough and might be depended on to collect specimens, too.[22]

The shabbiest affair in a shabby business was the treatment of Reynolds, whose suspicion that he also would probably be jettisoned had never lessened his efforts on behalf of the expedition. In the face of heavy congressional disapproval, on August 13 Reynolds was formally notified that his services were no longer required. Some said a bargain had been struck between Poinsett, who sought to uphold the honor of the administration by covering up for the incompetent Dickerson, and Wilkes, who had schemed to get the command and now was willing to reject and deceive most of the scientific corps and to refuse a place to Reynolds.

Unmoved, so far as anyone knew—for he was not one to confide—by the broken hopes and careers strewn in his wake, the seemingly imperturbable Wilkes continued busily with his preparations. Taking time from his work with the instruments in New York, he journeyed down to Norfolk to survey the ships and inquire who among the officers wished to accompany the expedition under his command, for unlike Jones, he was allowed to choose his own officers. Many did. One midshipman who had been with it "upwards of sixteen months—the disagreeable part of it," offered his services anew. Another, still aboard the rejected *Consort,* had volunteered in 1828, then again in 1836, and now, still seeking "to embark on such a duty," volunteered once more. Wilkes signed them on, together with two pilots—John Percival's brother Isaac, an experienced sealer fallen on hard times from a fondness for the bottle but now pledged to "abstain from all Simulating lickers" during the cruise, and the experienced Pacific captain from Salem, Benjamin Vanderford, who was now to see the Pacific for the last time.[23]

True to the principle of selection he had outlined to Southard a decade earlier, Wilkes chose most of the midshipmen, or "young gentlemen" as they were called, from among those who had most recently passed their examinations.* (It was the principle Reynolds had observed in choosing scientists.) He then turned to the crews, half of whom had deserted, "having got discouraged by the dilatory movements of this humdrum affair," as one who chose to remain explained in a letter home. When they learned in March that the expedition had a new commander, "All the Ships Company" of the *Macedonian,* comprising "first-rate materials," it was said, signed a memorial to the Secretary of the Navy pointing out that they had signed over the previous November with assurance from Jones that they would sail "with him as our Commodore." Some had been shipped for seventeen months now, and "had we ever dreamed . . . that any other than him could or would have been appointed to take the command we do solemnly assure you sir we would not have re entered." Wilkes solved the problem by bringing the ships round to Norfolk and giving liberty. Lieutenant Thomas T. Craven, in command of the *Macedonian,* which served as receiving station while the other vessels were readied, reported with surprise that the first liberty group "came off punctual to the hour." Though one night in August two of the *Vincennes'* crew took direct action and jumped overboard into Norfolk harbor, the problem was much reduced once it seemed that the expedition would sail after all.[24]

---

* One American who sailed before the mast in the thirties addressed himself with some relish to the question, What are midshipmen? "Midshipmen are usually the progeny of naval captains and members of naval bureaus—of United States senators—of members and ex-members of congress—and of other great men. . . . The consequence of this is, that midshipmen commonly look upon themselves as being somebody. . . . Hence their very messes become seasoned with a strong smell of aristocracy. . . . Their duty is to muster the watches, to run errands, to carry orders and messages, to command the boats when absent on duty, and to keep a general watch and supervision over the movements of the men. They are at sea something near what constables are on land—the summoners, reporters and informers, while their superiors may be styled the executioners of the law. Though in general they are looked upon with contempt by the men, yet the laws protect them from insult." After serving five years, three of them on active duty at sea, and successfully passing an examination, these unfortunates became passed midshipmen. Of the fourteen passed midshipmen who sailed with the expedition, nine attained the rank at the examinations held by the Board of Captains between May 28 and June 22, 1838. All but one stood among the first seventeen.

Given a free hand by Poinsett, who alerted every naval facility to his needs, Wilkes organized matters with remarkable dispatch. Setting August 15 as the date of departure, he had some of the instruments (all readily located for once) sent directly to Washington for testing and packing, while he tested the remainder at New York and arranged for simultaneous astronomical observations to be made during the cruise at Boston by William Cranch Bond (1789–1859) and at Washington by Lieutenant James Melville Gilliss (1810–1865), a promising young officer of scientific bent who was then in charge of the Depot of Charts and Instruments. These basic matters arranged to his satisfaction—the outfitting of the ships he left to their commanders and to Commodore Lewis Warrington of the Norfolk yard—he consulted those experienced in Pacific and polar navigation on what islands and reefs of uncertain position had been reported, the best points for rendezvous and repairs, what were the prevailing winds in the Sea of Celebes, the healthy months in the China seas, and the best means of conducting trade in Soo Loo Land.

While Poinsett made arrangements for depositing the expedition's scientific collections in J. K. Kane's Philadelphia Museum, on the tenth of July Wilkes reported the squadron nearly in readiness. He had taken the *Vincennes* and *Peacock* from the hands of Commodore Warrington a few days before. The *Relief*, afloat so long that her bottom was foul, was being overhauled. The *Porpoise* would be ready by the twenty-fifth. With matters in such good train, he wrote Paulding to ask that the passed midshipmen be given temporary appointments as acting lieutenants. Paulding acceded without a murmur. The Governor of Virginia paid a visit to the squadron and was received with a salute of nineteen guns and manned yards. Later in the month Wilkes came down, and the *Vincennes* and *Peacock*, now equipped with spar decks and staterooms constructed on the gun decks so that they resembled small frigates, moved from the Navy Yard out to the naval anchorage, where the *Relief* soon joined them. With the storeship lying off Town Point, next the *Peacock*, then the *Macedonian* and *Vincennes*, and s?mewhat lower down, "in all the solemn grandeur of a ship of the line," the venerable *Constitution*, they presented "a martial spectacle." The reporter from the Norfolk *Beacon* could not recall such a display since "the days when the British fleet burdened the waters of the Chesapeake." (Though no one remarked, the people of Norfolk were witnessing the first of the curtain calls of the long age of sail: on the twenty-third of the previous April the *Sirius* and *Great Western* both arrived off Sandy Hook to inaugurate regular Atlantic steamship service.) On the twenty-fifth President Van Buren, accompanied by Poinsett, Paulding, and Commodore Warrington, came to give his blessing. Cannon at the navy yard and on the ships fired salutes, and the *Macedonian* and *Vincennes* were gorgeously decorated with flags. Reynolds was not present to hear the cannon boom. Satisfied that the reality was unworthy of their dream, he and Asa Gray went up to Saratoga Springs to think on other things for the first time in many years. Meanwhile Peale's aristocratic friends in Philadelphia staged "a little festive gathering" in honor of his—and their— success. They invited Lieutenant Wilkes.[25]

Early in August txe *Porpoise* arrived from New York and the two schooners, *Sea Gull* and *Flying Fish*, took their places in the squadron. Small and bandy-legged Chaplain Jared Leigh Elliott stumped aboard with a sizeable cargo of "the important means of grace"—Bibles for each mess, a testament for each man, a fine selection of the publications of the American Sunday School Union, a complete set of the bound volumes of the Tract Society, and thirty thousand additional pages of assorted tracts—and voiced a fervent prayer "that every ship shall become a Bethel." By the fifteenth all was in readiness and the squadron, riding "gallantly abreast of Fort Monroe," waited to sail with the first fair wind. All aboard were said to be "in fine spirits, elate with anticipations of the peaceful triumphs, not less worthy of the wreath of fame than those of 'grim visaged war,' which await the successful results of scientific research." Up the coast at New Haven, a South Sea whaler docked with news of the *Astrolabe* and *Zélée*. On March 12 her captain had called at Port Famine in the Straits of Magellan to collect letters from the barrel set up on its barren shore for the convenience of mariners. He found that Dumont d'Urville had replaced it with a secure and sprightly box and left his dispatches within. These told that his ships had arrived safely the previous December and would proceed south toward the end of the month, weather permitting.

On the afternoon of the eighteenth of August, a Saturday, the wind rose slightly just when the tide began its ebb. On the *Vincennes* the signal "prepare to weigh" was run aloft, orders were shouted, boatswains' shrill whistles split the languorous air, and the crews took their stations at windlasses and yards. On the quarterdecks the first lieutenants shouted into their trumpets, the sails dropped, filled, and the vessels of the United States Exploring Expedition stood to sea under full sail. There were rumors at the last minute of a show of mutiny aboard the *Peacock*, but one rumor more could not harm the enterprise, and the incident proved to be only a matter of a single sailor using "improper language." He was duly punished and the six vessels sailed with the best wishes of those who still cared. "Admitting the truth of the old adage, that 'A bad beginning will have a good ending,' " one reporter who was barely able to believe his eyes remarked with apt irony, "they have a glorious prospect of success." [26]

4 Behold! Now, a Nation

It is a great doctor for sore hearts and sore heads, too,
your ship's routine, which I have seen soothe—at least for a
time—the most turbulent of spirits.

Conrad, *The Mirror of the Sea*

The wind slackened during the night but freshened again. And
at seven thirty in the morning they sailed past the lightship off Willoughby's
point, discharged the pilot (who had not been heard to use "a vulgar or
profane expression" during all his time aboard, the chaplain noted with
satisfaction), and at signal from the *Vincennes* formed a "line ahead
order"—the *Vincennes* in the lead, followed by the *Relief, Porpoise, Peacock,*
and the two schooners, *Flying Fish* and *Sea Gull.*

It was a unique squadron, the last of the overseas exploring expeditions to
rely solely on sail and the first in a good many years to be dispatched on polar
exploration with ships unadapted for the peculiar hazards of such service. But
as the *Peacock*'s captain noted, the first consideration of all hands had been to
put the squadron to sea, even if needs be in ill-adapted and hazardous vessels.*

At the bulwarks with the rest to enjoy a last lingering gaze, Lieutenant
George Foster Emmons of New Haven, who had joined the *Peacock* at her
launching ten years before, remarked to himself with as much surprise as
gratification, "So here I am at last aboard the first man of war that I was ever
launched in, & the first Vessel that was ever built by our government for
Exploring Service." Officers took a lively satisfaction in the knowledge that the
very act of weighing anchor had "silenced all the croaking of such incredulous
individuals as were in the constant habit of affirming that the Expedition

* A thing of wood and canvas through most of the century, the Navy possessed only one steam
vessel, built in 1837.

73

never could leave the waters of the United States." They were embarked at last on an enterprise "which may prove perilous, must be interesting and which we trust will prove by its results, that the confidence of the Government was not misplaced."

The *Vincennes*. (Photograph of model in The Smithsonian Institution.)

The *Vincennes*, a sloop-of-war of the second class, was a favorite in the service. Built in New York in 1826, she was a vessel of 780 tons and a length of 127 feet and by far the largest of the squadron. In 1828–1830 she had been the first ship of the Navy to circumnavigate the globe and had spent a good part of her life with the Pacific Squadron. For a fat ship—she was thirty-five feet in the beam—the *Vincennes* was surprisingly fast, by many considered the fastest of her class in the service, and her beaminess discouraged pitching in heavy weather. Like most of the navy vessels built during the twenties, she was plain, the ornate carvings and figureheads having largely disappeared, and painted

BEHOLD! NOW, A NATION

the customary navy black. For her present complement of 190, a light deck had been added to the original single deck, so that her accommodations, if not commodious, were less cramped than those of the other vessels.

Second in line as the capes faded into the distance was the *Relief* with a complement of 75. Completed only two years before and the only ship of Commodore Jones' squadron to be retained, she was built expressly as a vessel of burden for the regular cruising squadrons. Though the expense of constructing this vessel of 468 tons and 109 feet had been thought scandalous, she was particularly handsome and in the many months before departure was a great favorite with visitors, who found her "fitted out in the most complete manner" and her accommodations "exceedingly snug." But she was a slow sailer. Having already, like the lubberly visitors, developed a warm affection for her, her captain and officers blamed overloading, but after several days spent lying-to, Wilkes suddenly had enough and late in August ordered her to make her own speed for the Cape Verde Islands, where the squadron would rendezvous, or failing that, Rio.

The gun-brig *Porpoise* followed, a vessel of 224 tons built at the Boston yard two years before. Two-masted and rigged as a brigantine, with a length of 88 feet and a beam of twenty-five, she was a particularly good sailer and responsive to the helm. Wilkes, who had commanded her in his survey on the coast of Georgia the previous spring, thought well of her and most conceded that she was the fastest ship in the squadron. For the present service a poop-cabin and a forecastle had been set upon her deck. She carried 65 men.

The *Peacock* had been built at the New York yard in 1828 supposedly on a few pieces of her namesake, a practice the Navy resorted to when Congress refused to appropriate funds for new construction. A sloop-of-war of 680 tons and 118 feet between perpendiculars and smaller than the *Vincennes* (though both were pierced for eighteen guns), she was a full-rigged ship. After the collapse of the expedition planned for 1828 she had cruised with the West India Squadron off the coast of Brazil, then in the East Indies, where she delivered Edmund Roberts with his treaty for the Sultan of Muscat. That had come near being her last cruise, for she had lain on a coral reef at the mouth of the Persian Gulf for sixty hours, and it was only by throwing over extra spars, shot, guns, and even provisions, that she was saved, to return home round the world in time to join the Expedition. Though sharp and with uncommonly hollow ends, the *Peacock* had not shown herself particularly fast. But with armament sharply reduced, she was now to show the speed she promised. Strongly constructed of liveoak, she had the round stern fashionable of late, which offered much greater strength than the old transom, and the quarter galleries with their tall casements added a touch of elegance. The *Peacock* was a ship to inspire confidence. She carried 130 men.

Bringing up the rear were the two schooners purchased at New York at the last minute and converted from pilot boats—the *Flying Fish* of 96 tons, and the *Sea Gull* of 110. Between their purchase on August 3 and their joining the squadron at Norfolk nine days later, their rigging had been reduced and outfits completed with remarkable dispatch. Carrying fifteen men each, they were both good sailers, though on the third day out the *Flying Fish* split her jib and mainsail in trying to keep the pace.[1]

All except the greenhorns regarded the voyage to Rio as uneventful. Wilkes kept his own counsel and his officers were a little surprised to find that they were making for Madeira and the Cape Verde Islands instead of directly for Brazil. But these ports lay in the path of the prevailing winds and close enough to the points at which Wilkes was instructed to search for shoals that past navigators had reported to lie in the eastern Atlantic. As they were regular ports of call for American naval vessels, many of the old tars among officers and crews had seen them before and were not to be impressed by another visit.

There was brisk weather during the first week and "irritable stomachs and lugubrious countenances" appeared on every hand, one of the *Peacock*'s surgeons noted. Largely unaccustomed to shipboard life, the scientists suffered most from this near ultimate in human misery, but the "green ones" soon recovered their spirits and once more, as a midshipman put it in a letter home, everyone had "a smiling face & a good appetite."

Aside from a few floggings which all hands were called to witness—one of the *Vincennes*' lookouts fell asleep and two men got drunk and had to be punished, as the chaplain noted with professional regret but military approval, for the safety of all—the only events worthy of note were the discovery from the masthead of what was thought to be a wreck but which on inspection from the boat turned out to be a huge cottonwood tree with a long limb extending upward for all the world like the stump of a mast (aware that he was on a scientific expedition, one of the lieutenants determined that it was 120 feet long and 14 around) and a few days later a real wreck, the deserted hulk of a lumber brig that had been washing about the seas for years perhaps. Specimens of the barnacles were carefully removed for examination by the "Scientific Gentlemen," while the crew of the *Relief* caught enough fish from the school surrounding the wreck to make a mess for the ship's company.

Taxidermist John W. W. Dyes described the other occurrence as "a merecul." One day when the order was given on the *Vincennes* to loose the main topgallant sail, Seaman George Porter somehow got himself caught by the neck in the buntlines and was flung from the yard. He was discovered perhaps a minute later, a human pendulum swinging with the roll of the ship eighty or ninety feet above the deck. On reaching the top with his kit, the astonished doctor found him still alive, though badly bruised. (A temperance enthusiast, Dyes was disgusted when at the afternoon roll to grog Porter grumbled at the doctor's orders, finding it "dambt hard that he must not have his Grogg, because he came near Braking his Neck." And when the purser came in a few minutes later to inquire how Porter felt, Dyes was "surprised to here this wicked man Remark that he knew Dambt well what that Damd shark wanted to know if there was any likely Hood of his dying it was not Him that he Cared a Dam for but it was the 50 Dollars that he was in Debt.")

Three weeks out of Norfolk the surgeon of the *Peacock*, pleased with his lot, was "inclined to believe that the inconveniences so much complained of at sea, are some what exaggerated," but three weeks is a small part of four years. The officers spent their time experimenting with the sextant, a novel exercise for many, and calculating the ship's position, and generally seeing to the endless details that served to keep the vessels in spanking navy condition. The scientists put their instruments in order and rearranged their gear in hopes of gaining a little more living space in their cramped quarters. Peale, who had done as much as any man with the exception of Wilkes to reduce the expedition, was somewhat surprised, as he wrote his young daughters in Philadelphia, to discover that his stateroom on the *Peacock* was "just about as large as your mother's bedstead; in it I have a little bed over and under which is packed clothes, furs, guns, Books and boxes without number, all of which have to be tied fast to keep them from rolling and tumbling about, and kept off the floor as it is sometimes covered with water." When time hung heavy they fished for sharks and dolphins and bonito, occasionally netted a hovering bird, and were sometimes reduced, as the amused commander of the *Relief* noted, to "overhauling pieces of Kelp." They busily took notes on everything, writing down "many hard names," as Passed Midshipman William Reynolds observed, while the artists made sketches. Peale, to pass the time, painted a giant eagle on the back board of the *Peacock*'s dinghy, which he had decided would make a fine boat for his hunting expeditions into creeks and bays.

Sometimes the appearance of a strange sail would serve to break the monotony, and they would seize the opportunity to ask the news and send letters home, a time honored custom at sea, but an amenity that American merchantmen were often loath to observe. On one occasion when the vessel refused to heave to, the *Peacock* gave chase. This met with no response and Captain Hudson ordered a musket fired. As the vessel continued on her way, he fired one of the *Peacock*'s thirty-two pounders. It was then amusing, Lieutenant Emmons noted, "to see the difference a little louder noise makes—for no sooner had this last gun been fired when this personification of republicanism backed his main & mizen topsails & allowed us to speak him." Lieutenant Oliver Hazard Perry boarded her and was given newspapers dated seventeen days after the squadron's departure.

During calms the men were allowed to swim in the basin of a sail spread in the water to protect them from sharks. A musical band might have helped to pass the leisure hours, but Wilkes had left it behind as an expensive frivolity, and the only substitute that could be found was a poor bugler on the *Vincennes*. When his cracked notes rasped out across the sea, Peale on the *Peacock* declared that he much preferred to hear "one of the crew tinkling on a mandolin."

Some found diversion in the divine services conducted each Sunday. On the *Vincennes*, Wilkes and his uniformed officers seated themselves along the starboard side, while the men, in neat duck frocks and trousers, blue jackets and tarpaulin hats, stood on the port and Elliott preached from a grating laid across two shot boxes, using the flag-draped capstan for a pulpit. With "the blue arch of heaven as the ceiling of our temple," as he put it, Elliott weekly assured all that His eye was on the sparrow and urged them to shun profanity. But as the weeks wore on, many came to consider the rite something of a trial. On the *Peacock*, Peale complained that the sermons Hudson read were for "comfortably seated" shore congregations and not for those who "stand and balance ourselves to the motions of the ship which becomes rather tiresome."

In fair weather, the officers would break out the boats and visit, exchanging messes or simply gathering for talk around a bottle and drinking to "Wives and Sweethearts"—"May they never meet," added the cynical. Some were invited to dine with their commander, who sought in this fashion to ascertain, as he put it to himself, "the capacities I was obliged to use" and at the same time express "in as it were a social way many things I wished to inculcate." Many had known one another for years in the service, for good friends sailed in this squadron. Others now met for the first time on a voyage that was to link their lives for four long and arduous years and carry them thus joined in memory for many more to come.

The officers were an uncommonly youthful lot. Most had entered the service within the past decade and five within the year. Passed Midshipman William Reynolds wrote his sister how strange it was "to look around & find none but youthful faces among the officers—a Young Captain, with boys for his subordinates—no gray hairs, no veterans among us, none of those 'hard a weather' characters. . . . We are all in the spring time of life." "May we," he added, "live to reach its winter." Senior in age as well as length of service was Lieutenant William Leverreth Hudson, the amiable captain of the *Peacock* and second in command of the Expedition, then forty-four years of age. A New Yorker, he had entered the Navy as midshipman in 1816, two years before Wilkes. Only Poinsett's persuasiveness and Secretary Paulding's proclamation divesting the expedition of all military character had overcome Hudson's scruples against serving under a junior, and even so there was reason to suspect that his capitulation was being charged against his reputation. Wilkes had known him for some years and held a high opinion of his capabilities. And Commodore Ridgely, aside from Wilkes the only one of his brother officers who urged him to accept the subordinate command, had also pressed Hudson because of his known superiority as a seaman.

Commanding the *Relief* was Andrew K. Long, who had entered the service the same day as Wilkes, January 1, 1818, though his commission as lieutenant had been conferred a year after his commander's. Long was (at most) Wilkes' second choice for the post.

Lieutenant Cadwallader Ringgold, only slightly their junior in the service, commanded the *Porpoise*. He had entered the Navy in 1819, had seen service with Commodore Porter's "Mosquito Fleet" in suppressing piracy in the West Indies, and his commission as lieutenant was now ten years old. At thirty-six, this member of a distinguished family of Maryland's Eastern Shore (General John Cadwallader of the Revolution was his grandfather) was highly regarded in the service. He had accepted the command at Wilkes' particular invitation.

Command of the schooners (everyone long continued to call them pilot boats) was given to passed midshipmen—a departure from navy practice that occasioned some grumbling among lieutenants serving in subordinate capacities aboard the larger vessels, but one which expressed Wilkes' determination to give the younger officers as much responsibility as possible. The *Sea Gull* was presently commanded by James W. E. Reid, son of Governor Robert E. Reid of Florida, who had seen only seven years' service, and the *Flying Fish* by Samuel R. Knox, small and balding, who appeared older than his twenty-nine years. Knox adapted easily to the command: both his father and grandfather had been Boston pilots. In the service for ten years now, he had managed to see something of the world both afloat and ashore, for after serving with the Mediterranean and Pacific Squadrons he had spent three and a half years in overland exploration of the Northwest before taking up navy duty again.

"The best sailor in the Squadron and one of the best in
the Service." Captain William L. Hudson. (Narrative,
2: frontispiece. Western Americana Collection, Yale
University Library.)

When he did so it had been in command of the schooner *Hadassah* surveying
the Savannah and May Rivers and Georges Bank with Wilkes. He had been a
passed midshipman for a year.

The subordinate officers were the cream of the Navy, and there were among
them a good number of future captains and admirals. Many came from
distinguished families—the Gansevoorts of New York, the Lees of Virginia,
the Aldens of Massachusetts, the Pinkneys of Maryland, the Blairs of
Jacksonian Washington, and the Perrys and Dales of Navy fame. One,

William May, was the son of President Washington's personal physician, and among the "young gentlemen" were Hudson's son and Wilkes' nephew.

Assistant Surgeon Silas Holmes of the *Peacock*, who had been a classmate of Dana at Yale, surveyed the lot. He anticipated times of peril and "scenes of strange adventure" but concluded that "in whatever situations of doubt or danger we may be destined to be placed, I am certain that the firm & gallant spirit which should be characteristic of American officers will support us bravely." * Considering that the commander kept the squadron's instructions secret and that only he was to know what the next port of call would be, this was a remarkable expression of confidence.

Soon after leaving Hampton Roads, Wilkes ordered all officers to keep a journal in which they would daily record navigational and meteorological data (ship's position, day's run, course, current, wind, temperature on deck and at the masthead, strange sails discovered, and the like) and, a point he emphasized, "all occurrences or objects of interest, which may, at the time, be considered even of the least importance." Upon their return these, like the scientific collections, would be surrendered to the government, to be used in writing the history of the expedition. But during the cruise they were to be regularly submitted to the commander, who thereby became monitor of minds as well as shaper of destinies. With some grumbling and many modest disclaimers, the officers and scientists became journalists.

One young officer had already begun a journal, and though aware that its retention might be construed as a direct violation of the order, he could not bear to let it go "before any one's Eyes" and resolved to keep two in future. There was no more enthusiastic explorer in the squadron than this dedicated journalist, Passed Midshipman William Reynolds of Lancaster, Pennsylvania, twenty-two years old when he set sail in the *Vincennes*, having already spent seven years in the service. He confided freely to his private journal, which he filled with visions of Glory and Duty and rhapsodies on sea and sky. He was in love with his profession ("which certainly calls forth the noblest & most daring traits of mans nature") infatuated with his ship, and excited at the "goodly prospect of strange lands, & wild adventure." With such youthful innocence he was, but for his intelligence, a Billy Budd. Standing at night under a full spread of canvas, well braced against the wind and the roll of the ship, had lost none of its fascination for William Reynolds, who returned to his journal to describe an experience he must have known hundreds of times before and

---

* Four years older and disproportionately wiser, Holmes pasted over this passage with the comment, "I look upon it to be sheer nonsense."

The secret chronicler, William Reynolds. (Reproduced
from David B. Tyler, *The Wilkes Expedition*, American
Philosophical Society Memoirs, vol. 73, p. 43, from
photograph in possession of Mr. and Mrs. John H. K.
Shannahan.)

write of "the towering pyramids of canvas, & the multitude of ropes, like bars
of ebony, reaching from spar to spar, with all the accuracy of a picture—all
human voices are hushed; the eternal moaning of the masts & the murmuring
of the water, are the only sounds that break the stillness of the night, unless it
be the warning cries of the lookouts, at half hourly intervals, & the solemn
tones of the bell—these coming from the lofty heights, and different portions
of the ship, have almost an unnatural effect."

Reynolds' enthusiasm for the present enterprise, which he continued to call
"the first, great, national Exploring Expedition," was boundless. He got on
well with the scientists from the first. Peering into the microscope at the
animalculae brought up in their nets, he marveled to "see how Nature has

provided for them, and how many beauties are disclosed that were not perceptible to the naked Eye," and was soon making it "part of my days amusement to look over the labours of the Scientifics," preferably in their own quarters, where they lived among "dead & living lizards, & fish floating in alcohol, and sharks jaws, & stuffed Turtles, and vertebraes and Animalculae frisking in jars of salt water, and old shells, and many other equally interesting pieces of furniture hanging about their beds, & around their state rooms." And he watched in fascination as the learned landsmen, at first "greatly mystified at the multifarious, and apparently complicated, and confused operations on ship board," adjusted themselves to the new environment.[2]

To be sure, Reynolds' view was not universally shared and some of the officers looked upon the lubberly "scientifics" with at best amused contempt. On the *Peacock*, Dana found to his dismay that, though ordered by Wilkes to assist with the observations, only a few did so with any care. Dana's other shipmates among the scientists were the soft-mannered, amiable linguist, Horatio Hale, and the naturalist Peale, prickly and, owing to the role he had played in reducing the corps, no great favorite with his colleagues. The *Vincennes* bore three of the scientifics, Charles Pickering, the exuberant conchologist Joseph P. Couthouy, and the Philadelphia artist and engraver Joseph Drayton, in his forties the old man of the corps. Drayton had brought along his violin and often entertained the men with concerts on the forecastle. Botanist William Rich and artist Alfred Agate berthed in the *Relief*.

The scientific corps was not the only novelty to be found in this adventure. Reading of the hardships of earlier voyagers during the passage to Madeira, several of the officers remarked the contrast to their own well-found vessels and modern methods of navigation. But the greatest novelty of the present enterprise was its nationality. "Behold! now, a nation," wrote William Reynolds, "which but a short time ago, was a discovery itself . . . is taking its place among the enlightened of the world, and endeavoring to contribute its mite, in the cause of knowledge." The long struggle to launch the expedition had been "most fortunate" insofar as it had brought to the command a leader of "great talent, perhaps genius," who had worked his way up from cabin boy and distinguished himself in science the while. "Long life to him!" When early in the cruise Wilkes gave Lieutenant Craven a vigorous dressing down for bullyragging Reynolds, the latter discovered that the commander was a gentleman, too, and one of "high souled sentiments" who knew what was "due to one Gentleman from another."

There was in fact every reason for intelligent and ambitious young officers to take heart at the organization of this expedition. Those who now for the first time berthed in staterooms in place of the squalid quarters in steerage traditionally assigned to midshipmen delighted in having quarters of their own with couches, curtains over the ports, plated candlesticks, and a brussels carpet. They even found themselves exercising the duties of officer of the deck, trumpet in hand, directing the management of the ship—an honor that on other service most would not have been accorded for some years yet. "I cannot explain to you the feeling," Reynolds wrote his sister, "for though we only take advantage of, or oppose, the wind & waves it seems as if we directed them . . . oh! the excitement is good & glorious. . . . My profession, above any other in the world—hurrah! for the Exploring Expedition!"

On the first leg of the cruise the explorers sought to take measure of their commander, whose long pocked face with its long nose and firm mouth they saw at every turn and whose influence they everywhere felt. Each morning he would hail the schooners and, calling them up to each quarter, order their tiny crews paraded for his inspection. While the men strove to toe a seam of the slippery and tossing decks and their passed-midshipmen commanders stood by, Wilkes would coolly survey them through an eyeglass, then shout into the trumpet,

"That third man, Mr. Bacon, his legs are dirty Sir! The next man's head has not been combed! Look at that lubbers neckerchief! Stand up, you rascals!"

Those who had served with him on Georges Bank spoke of him with an enthusiasm that communicated itself to others "ready to believe that the object of such generous praise must be the very *beau ideal* of a Captain for the hazardous Enterprise in which they had embarked," as one of the officers later recalled.

(There were exceptions. Had Wilkes glanced upward through the cabin skylight on the night of August 29 he would have seen Charlie Erskine, who stood looking down with an iron belaying pin dangling delicately from his fingers. On the Georges Bank survey this young seaman had fetched the mail for the *Porpoise* and once when the letters got soaked Wilkes had him stretched over a gun and flogged with the knotted rope sailors called a colt. Sore in body and spirit, Erskine had determined to avoid the volatile lieutenant in the future and shipped with the Mediterranean Squadron, but in spite of everything he had found himself on board the *Vincennes*. As he now stood over the skylight he felt again the colt's sting and waited for the ship's weather roll that would make his aim more certain. But then, as with so many other near murderers of the century, the "upturned face" of his mother appeared before him, and he replaced the belaying pin, though it was some moments before his hand could release it.)

"The very *beau ideal* of a Captain for the hazardous
Enterprise." Charles Wilkes, by Thomas Sully.
(*Narrative*, 1: frontispiece. Western Americana
Collection, Yale University Library.)

Unfortunately, the *Peacock* was not all that fresh paint and polished brass
suggested. Early in the cruise Captain Hudson found one of the pumps so
rusted that it crumbled in use, and the gear furnished for others did not fit the
bore. These were matters serious enough in themselves, but they were made
worse when it was discovered that the vessel badly needed caulking. The berth

deck and dispensary were flooding from a leak in the fore apron, and Hudson found his cabin "half leg deep in water, carpet floated up, and myself almost floated out."

Wilkes saw to it that hydrographical and meteorological observations were made regularly and accurately. They determined the current by a simple but time-consuming device. Two kegs linked by a five-fathom line were put over from a boat, one sufficiently weighted to sink its air-tight companion to just below the surface. With the log line fastened to the connecting line it was possible to get a reading uninfluenced by wind and wave. And by frequently taking the temperature of the sea they were able to trace the course of the warm Gulf Stream. On the three legs of their voyage to Rio they searched for the reported shoals laid down on the charts or in the sailing directions of the English hydrographer John Purdy, but though backing and filling and sounding for days and nights together with the vessels deployed over some twelve miles, they found no shoal water whatever in the locations given— which they could determine with a combined total of thirty chronometers, as Captain Hudson observed wonderingly—and no sign of the submarine volcano that Admiral Kruzenstern thought he had sighted in the eastern Atlantic. In this way they laid to rest many ghosts that had long haunted mariners.

The ten days at Madeira, where they arrived September 16, were a welcome relief. The ships no sooner anchored than the scientists were off to "scour the Country," as Lieutenant Robert Johnson observed with amusement, with their "trunks and all the paraphernalia pertaining to their professions," though Peale, to his disgust, was detained with the officers to pay the customary visit to the governor. These excursions were short and hurried, for Wilkes required that all return aboard by ten o'clock each evening. No one knew why. When it was discovered that an American brig lying in the harbor was shortly to sail for the States, Wilkes seized the occasion to box up the broken and rusted pieces of one of the *Peacock*'s pumps and send them along with Hudson's report on the state of his ship directly to the Secretary of the Navy, as evidence of the kind of workmanship practiced at Commodore Warrington's Norfolk yard. Wilkes was privately of the opinion that Warrington should be dismissed from the service for thus endangering the great national enterprise, though to be sure he was merely the tool of the "machinations of its secret foes," in particular the embittered Navy Commissioners, who had ordered him to obstruct the outfitting in every way possible. (In Washington the package created something of a stir, and the president of the Board of Navy

Commissioners pronounced it "a great piece of impertinence on the part of so young an officer.")

With the ships newly painted, watered, and provisioned with Madeira's famed fruits and vegetables, and with deserters recaptured, the squadron stood down Funchal Roads early in the afternoon of September 26 with a smacking breeze from the east and next day was well into the trades. Fair weather and favorable winds made the passage to the Cape Verde Islands a pleasant one for all, except the commander, who was annoyed by the failure of the schooners to keep station. On October 6 they anchored in the harbor of Porto Praia. Horatio Hale was able to get ashore long enough before they sailed next day to converse with the slaves and compile a Mandingo vocabulary. Peale shot some quail for the *Peacock*'s mess and some birds of brilliant plumage for the collections. The officers who went ashore were not impressed. Surgeon Silas Holmes was happy to return to the ship's boat, followed all the way, he complained, "by hogs, dogs, monkeys & jackasses." Not a man deserted.

The westward crossing to Rio was effected rather more promptly than the eastward had been. The search for shoals continued, but the reported locations were fewer, and some of the officers now took the opportunity to improve their knowledge. George Foster Emmons, twenty-nine-year-old third officer on the *Peacock*, addressed himself to meteorology, not only to improve himself in a science which had "every thing to recomend it to the Nautical profession," but also because, as he saw it, this expedition was uniquely prepared to "prosecute a regular series of simultaneous observations in various parts of the globe." It was true that few were trained observers, but this might be considered rather an advantage than a handicap, as meteorology was still in its infancy as a science. Various theories had sprung up within the past few years—most notably those of Redfield and Espy. William C. Redfield (1789–1857), the versatile Connecticut saddler, concluded after the great gale of September 1821 that storms were progressive whirlwinds and elaborated his theory in a long series of scientific papers; James P. Espy (1785–1860) of Pennsylvania, who came to be known as the "Storm King," attributed storms to the rising and expansion of heated air and the consequent rush of heavier air to fill the vacuum. Espy, as a member of the Philosophical Society's committee on instructions for the Expedition, had drawn up those relating to meteorology. The two theories were at swords' points at the time, and Emmons thought that the squadron's unskilled observers might provide a way out of the impasse, since they were not "prejudiced in the favor of . . . preconceived opinions." His friend Dana did have some training in the science and moreover was devoted to Redfield and his theory. But as the corps was organized these matters lay outside Dana's "department" and his efforts in meteorology were to bring him, all unwitting, into collision with Wilkes.

Shortly after first sighting the Southern Cross and the Magellanic Clouds, Emmons and Dana secured the assistance of Hale and Passed Midshipman Henry Eld, Emmons' New Haven neighbor, and on some nights the commander's young nephew, Wilkes Henry, and dividing the night and the sky between them, systematically observed the heavens in preparation for the anniversary of the great shower of shooting stars that (in association with Tuttle's Comet) had burst over New England in 1833.

The *Peacock* was first to sail into Rio's grand harbor, anchoring in the early morning of November 21. Daylight disclosed the frigate *Independence*, Commodore John Nicholson, swinging at anchor nearby, and at sight of the explorer her band struck up "Hail Columbia" in the early morning air. "The heart of every American on board responded," Emmons noted. That was the only response the *Peacock* was prepared to make, her own band consisting of only "a drummer & an indifferent fifer." On the twenty-fourth the *Vincennes* appeared and the brig and schooners, and three days later the *Relief*. The *Relief* had been bedeviled by calms and light airs, and lumbering along for days and nights together at no more than three knots, had made the passage in one hundred days, which everyone, including her rueful but loyal officers, believed to be a record for slowness. The feat destroyed what little confidence Wilkes had in Captain Long, whom he blamed for failing to find the trades. (Not one to lightly forgive, Wilkes went to the trouble some years later of compiling a list of passages from the United States to Rio and had the satisfaction of finding that indeed the *Relief* did hold the record.)

The stay at Rio meant further delay before the squadron could take up its appointed rounds. But the condition of the ships, particularly the *Peacock*, made repairs imperative before rounding the Horn and, it was hoped, venturing into the Antarctic. But if delay was inevitable, Rio was the best of all places to enjoy it. Although some of the less traveled were taken aback at first sight of ladies riding astride rather than sidesaddle, and Chaplain Elliott, alarmed at the prevalence of "French works of the most obscene and pernicious character," predicted "scenes of Infidel Havoc" for the city, all such were silently rebuked by one of the petty officers who had seen rather more of the world and pointed out that "local custom is the only true standard of virtue and delicacy."

The ships were painted, repaired, and provisioned and futile efforts made to smoke out the cockroaches from the *Vincennes*. "Battened down the Hatches and kindled a Brimstone and Charcoal fire," Lieutenant Hartstene recorded; "in the Morning took off the Hatches and found them unscathed." Purser Waldron saw to replacing the one hundred and twenty-five gallons of whiskey that it was discovered amid widespread lamentations had leaked from one of the *Vincennes'* casks. And the scientists took up their hunt for specimens. Couthouy scoured the harbor for shellfish, Pickering and Brackenridge made a botanical excursion into the mountains, Peale went shooting for birds, and Drayton and Agate busily sketched the specimens brought in. Since here also were Negroes "fresh from the African Coast" representing tribes from all middle and southern Africa, Hale resumed his task of compiling vocabularies. But in most respects Rio had been well worked over by previous scientists and the Expedition's stay was no more than an interlude in their adventure. Officers and scientists alike were unhappy with the delay, for if they were to attempt the Antarctic this season no time was to be lost.

Wilkes' own enthusiasm for observation kept him fully as busy. When informed that the hot and rainy season had arrived—discouraging news, for this would play havoc with the pendulum and astronomical observations—he consulted meteorological tables provided by a resident American, found that the inhabitants were quite incorrect about the intervals of their seasons, and proceeded with his observations. As it happened, clear weather held until the squadron's departure. He arranged for the exclusive use of deserted Enxados Island at the harbor's mouth and detailed officers to take readings from the instruments—apparatus for variation and dip, barometers, thermometers, and tide staff, among others—every hour round the clock. A marine guard was stationed to protect the instruments and as the boats were hauled up for repair and refitting the island became a navy yard as well as an observatory.

In the scientific work, Wilkes held every officer rigorously to his duty. Just how rigorously Lieutenant Emmons learned when he and Lieutenant Joseph A. Underwood, third officer of the *Relief* and a friend of previous voyages, set out one morning to scale the monumental Sugar Loaf mountain overlooking the harbor. By pushing and pulling one another over the precipitous parts they reached the rocky summit thoroughly winded, only to find a message in a bottle informing them that they had been preceded the previous May by a group of Her Britannic Majesty's officers. But as they were anyway the "*first Americans* that ever reached the top of this pinnacle," they added their names to the Englishmen's, emptied their flask of wine to the success of the United States Exploring Expedition and, gathering plants on the way, scrambled down the mountainside to return on board just after dark, exhausted but certain their accomplishment would earn at least "the silent approbation of the Commander of the Expedition—but in this," Emmons remarked in rueful wonder, "it appears we were mistaken," for on the following morning Captain Hudson handed them a note from Wilkes: "Sir, I learn with surprise & regret that an officer of your ship made an excursion to an important height in this vicinity without obtaining the necessary instruments for its correct admeasurement; as it results only in the idle & boastful saying that its summit has been reached, instead of an excursion which might have been useful to the expedition." Undaunted, Underwood and the conscientious but independent Emmons collected the requisite instruments, retraced their steps, and determined the "admeasurement."

So the commander expected every man to do his duty. That he was also interested in his officers' professional welfare was confirmed when Lieutenant Charles H. Davis, of the *Independence*, a nascent astronomer (whose reputation as a scientist would one day surpass Wilkes') sought to join the Expedition, for though Wilkes readily accepted two midshipmen, he steadfastly refused to have Davis, explaining to the junior officers that he did not wish to see one more lieutenant standing in the path of their promotion. Davis was offended.

Soon his commander was, too, though for other reasons. A roly-poly bachelor of easy grace, John B. Nicholson, Commodore of the Brazil Squadron, was popular throughout the service. He obligingly complied with Wilkes' request that he exchange volunteers from the *Independence* for the squadron's invalids and also with Wilkes' "requisition" of additional volunteers. But on discovering that, contrary to Wilkes' representations, the invalids were wholly unfit for duty (one deranged, another epileptic, others consumptive), Nicholson refused to have them and pointed out that it was Wilkes' duty to provide their passage home. But despite this provocation and the fact that the *Independence* was already short-handed, the Commodore dispatched thirty-one volunteers. There matters rested—Nicholson a little taken aback at the pre-emptory tone of this lieutenant, Wilkes disgruntled at having to return the invalids and affronted because the volunteers were less prompt in stepping forth than he thought respectful—until it was discovered that the squadron's bread was infested with worms and weevils. Wilkes suggested that it would be "a great saving to the Government" if Nicholson would purchase the bread for his crew. Still unruffled, Nicholson replied that serving condemned foodstuffs would violate regulations and proposed that Wilkes sell the bread at auction. When Wilkes professed "great astonishment" at the Commodore's unconcern for economy and pronounced his advice "too ridiculous to merit attention," Nicholson replied that this was "language which even a senior officer would not intentionally address to a junior without he was a child or an idiot." Properly incensed, Wilkes accused him of lack of respect for the "great national enterprise" and upbraided him for neglecting to address him as "Captain Wilkes," a title which he felt the extent of his command conferred.

Flabbergasted, Nicholson wished Wilkes success in attaining the rank he claimed and, rather than delay the Expedition by bringing charges against its commander, bundled the correspondence off to Washington to give the Secretary an opportunity to make of it what he would.*

Wilkes' having sent the *Relief* ahead to Orange Harbor at the tip of Tierra del Fuego, the squadron got up their anchors on Sunday, January 6, 1839. On clearing the harbor both the *Vincennes* and the *Peacock* ran afoul of an English brig and, though no damage resulted, the officers, never before having witnessed such a mishap involving a vessel of the United States Navy, were "much mortified, because the thing *looked lubberly*—and right in the very face of every body, among them all the men of war." Then the breeze failed just outside. Chaplain Elliott, who wanted to call a halt to the Expedition every Sunday, found a moral in these untoward events: "Any attempt to gain time by unnecessary work on the Sabbath is frequently defeated by some detention or accident." The breeze lifting again in the evening, they again weighed anchor (from which conchologist Couthouy carefully removed the Tubularia) and stood down the coast.[3]

* Wilkes never forgave Nicholson for reporting him to Washington. In writing his autobiography many years later, he gave a different and incorrect account of their disagreement, which he closed with this clinical observation: "In the last years of his life he became dissipated, and finally lost his mind, and died uncared for—such was his end, he was a native of Virginia."

5   First Blood

An anchor is a forged piece of iron, admirably adapted to
its end. . . .

Conrad, *The Mirror of the Sea*

The weather grew colder on the passage down the coast, and the special "exploring clothing" was issued with the understanding that if the crews "conducted themselves like men" they would not have to pay for it. This consisted of blankets, large peajackets, and immense boots, and it quickly became apparent that once again, as so many times in the past, some supplier had practiced his enterprise freely upon the Navy. For the jackets were of poor stuff and the boots, Surgeon Holmes noted, had only "this good quality, that if water gets into them it will very soon run out, they seeming to be constructed on the sieve principle." Only the blankets were what they pretended to be. As cold and dampness, generally thought to be the causes of scurvy, increased, lime juice and pickles were issued to each mess.

After a passage in light and variable winds, on January 25 the squadron arrived off the low sand hills surrounding the mouth of the Río Negro, where they were to investigate the area's potentialities as a port. They found little to detain them, learning only now that the *Beagle* had spent two months surveying here, though the results were not yet published. But the schooners, which ran upon the shifting sand bar across the river's mouth, came near being detained permanently, especially the *Sea Gull*, which rode out a severe pounding that lasted four hours. Opinion differed as to the damage suffered. Wilkes professed himself satisfied that there was none, but Peale, who was aboard at the time, felt that her masts would pitch overboard any second, and Lieutenant Micajah G. L. Claiborne thought she "came near going to pieces."

Here began the internal troubles of the Expedition. There had been flickerings of animosity from time to time. They were inherent in any enterprise carried out by the United States Navy and compounded in this one by the presence of the scientists. Wilkes had anticipated difficulties. Indeed his anticipations nourished them. He was suspicious about the good faith of the officers he had inherited from Commodore Jones, and he set out determined to play the martinet. One afternoon while the survey was in progress and Wilkes was prostrated by one of the violent headaches that periodically attacked him, he noted that the boats were clustered about the *Porpoise.* Investigation revealed that the officers had "overlooked their duty, and joined in a merry making." Since the commander of the brig, Lieutenant Ringgold, was away on special duty at the time, Wilkes fixed responsibility on Lieutenant Craven, who was in charge of the *Vincennes'* boats, and immediately suspended him from duty for permitting and, indeed, "joining in the jollification." It was an instance of "failure to preserve the discipline" that was "too outrageous" to be borne, and Wilkes promptly elevated his trusted lieutenant of former surveys, the diminutive Overton Carr, to Craven's place and consoled himself that things now "went on as usual." To all appearances they did, but appearances were deceptive, and the "usual" was soon to describe a new state of affairs.

The scientists were well aware that theirs was an awkward role in an expedition that Wilkes had sought to convert from a scientific to a predominantly naval enterprise. So was Wilkes, who, enjoining cooperation, had assured them that they might feel free to call upon the assistance of the officers, and urged the officers to take full advantage of the unparalleled opportunity to improve their own knowledge of the sciences. That some of the officers resented the presence of the scientifics was understandable. The civilians were men of education and knowledge, in the face of which the officers could not take refuge even in their own familiarity with the applied science of navigation, of which few had a firm grasp. Several of the scientists—Dana and Couthouy, certainly—were as expert at it as anyone in the squadron. Moreover, the officers were aware that while their own roles were to be their customarily anonymous ones, the civilians stood to win fame through publication of their findings. Thus it would have required an unparalleled degree of selflessness for the officers to be unfailingly helpful to the scientists, and often, when called upon for aid, some were pleased to be able to explain (with regret) that at present professional duties forbade.

At the Río Negro, professional duties forbade Ringgold's sending a boat to collect Peale and Surgeons Fox and Holmes, who had gone exploring on the pampa, where Peale, a fine hunter, had killed a buck for the *Peacock's* mess.

By the time they reached the landing they had carried the carcass several miles through the hot sand and were thirsty. While Peale skinned it, Fox signaled the boats. One of the *Sea Gull's* arrived, but only to inform them that Ringgold had ordered that no communication be held with the shore. Peale, who was rather hot tempered anyway, thought this very "uncivil treatment" and left the venison to spoil on the beach while he quenched his thirst with brackish water and returned to the hunt. While most of the bird skins they had collected also spoiled, they spent the night fighting fleas in the bush. All next day their signals were ignored until they walked down to the river's mouth and attracted the attention of Captain Hudson, who sent a boat for them. Much offended, Peale reported Ringgold's conduct to Wilkes.

He misread his commander. Wilkes had grown suspicious that some of the officers were "combining to produce difficulties" and, persuaded that some of the scientists were inclined to side with them, he encouraged Peale to make a formal complaint. With this in hand he sought to mark "the line between the officers & the scientific corps" by informing Peale, and through him the other scientists, that they had no right to call for assistance from the officers: "their only true course was to appeal to me." The pronouncement probably healed the breach between Peale and Ringgold but it opened one between Peale and Wilkes that would never close. The pattern was set. Friction that developed anywhere in the squadron was invariably noted by the suspicious commander, evidently through informers on the various ships. Just as invariably, Wilkes then took action, and the animosity was turned against him.

Having assured themselves that the Río Negro would never become a significant port, the squadron got underway after divine service on February 3 and stood to the south before a brisk wind. The wind increased until they found themselves plowing through heavy seas that, to Peale's dismay, deposited a "cheerless swash of water" on his cabin floor. As the schooners had difficulty in keeping the pace on the downwind course, Wilkes ordered them to make the best of their way to Orange Harbor on Hoste Island, some eighty-five miles northwest of Cape Horn. The temperature fell steadily, and the gales continued until the thirteenth, when they made the high and broken coast of Cape San Diego and entered the Straits of Le Maire, through which the squadron "glided along with all its canvas spread to the breeze, scarcely making a ripple under the bows," as Wilkes described it with satisfaction, and in three hours completed the passage. On the seventeenth they rounded iron-bound Cape Horn and, six months after leaving Norfolk, encountered the long smooth swell of the Pacific. Early in the night of February 19 they came into Orange Harbor to see the small fires of the Indians blazing on the

"A safe & beautiful anchorage, secure from all storms."
The squadron in Orange Harbor, Tierra del Fuego, by
Alfred T. Agate. (*Narrative*, 1: p. 124. Western
Americana Collection, Yale University Library.)

surrounding hills and a large one on Burnt Island at the harbor's mouth that
the men of the *Relief* had set as a beacon. Moving into the inner harbor in the
morning, they found themselves in "a safe & beautiful anchorage, secure from
all storms," where the supply ship and schooners rode gently at anchor, and
seals and penguins flapped and waddled on the beaches. Since their own
arrival on January 30 the *Relief*'s crew had cut a large supply of firewood for
the squadron, taken soundings of the harbor, and hunted geese and ducks to
their hearts' content—carefully preserving the skins, as one of them noted, "to
adorn some Museum and enlighten the publick." On February 15 and 16 the
Flying Fish and *Sea Gull* had arrived, the cynosure of every officer's eye. "Who
would not sooner command one of these fine Schooners on such an important
cruise as this," Sailing Master George T. Sinclair of the *Relief* asked himself as
the handsome little vessels came in past the island, "than be first Lieutenant of
any Frigate in the Navy?" Events were shortly to show that many would.

Immediately upon arrival Wilkes commenced preparations for a cruise to the south. The season was probably too far advanced for any spectacular achievements, but Wilkes was hopeful of approaching Captain Cook's farthest south, 71° 10′ (longitude 106° 54′ W.). At the least, they would gain some experience in sailing among the ice that would be useful in their major effort the following season.

Accordingly, Wilkes disposed of officers and ships in the manner he conceived likely to obtain the best results and supplied the vessels with a year's provisions—a margin of safety against their being frozen in. He announced that he would go aboard the *Porpoise* with Ringgold. Lieutenant Robert E. Johnson (who had already served aboard the three larger vessels) would command the *Sea Gull* and Lieutenant William M. Walker (from the *Peacock*) the *Flying Fish*. Hudson would bring the *Peacock*. His decision to replace Passed Midshipman Knox on the *Flying Fish* was made the easier when he discovered one night that a "drinking bout" was in progress aboard her. He had a considerable respect for the abilities of both Knox and Passed Midshipman Reid and had maintained them in their commands over the muted but continuous protests of several of the lieutenants, but that kind of frivolity was to be discouraged. Besides, if they remained in command, the senior officers he wished to take along would be serving under them—an impossible situation. Wilkes mollified the men of the *Vincennes* by promising them their fill of Antarctic cruising the following year. To mollify certain of the officers was rather more difficult, indeed impossible, and he was afterwards to term the stay at Orange Harbor "the turning point of the discipline of the cruise."

In the months since leaving Norfolk the officers had become attached to their ships, to their own quarters, their own messes and shipmates. Wilkes, however, viewed them as a mobile labor force that might be shunted from ship to ship as he judged best, and because of his annoying policy of secrecy regarding the movements and arrangements of the squadron, his announcement now took everyone by surprise. As the infirm members of the crews were transferred to the *Vincennes* and the pick of her own men sent on board the other vessels, even William Reynolds—unknown to Wilkes, probably his warmest admirer in the squadron—was inclined to complain somewhat. The "whole domestic arrangement of the Squadron was to be overturned."

But beyond the inconvenience was the issue of seniority. Wilkes had offended against tradition by giving command of the schooners to passed midshipmen when lieutenants were serving in subordinate capacities aboard the larger vessels. And the stroke of Poinsett's pen that divested the Expedition of military character had in no wise cooled ambition or undermined allegiance to the principle of seniority. While Knox, and probably Reid, too, protested their removal, lieutenants senior to Johnson and Walker claimed the commands for themselves. Lieutenant Claiborne claimed the *Sea Gull* and, in the event of his "rights being disregarded," requested that he be detached and returned to the States. He found the contingent request granted with alacrity, for he was immediately ordered from the *Porpoise* to the *Relief* and assured that as soon as his services could be spared he would receive orders to report to the Secretary of Navy in Washington. The response of the first lieutenant of the *Peacock* was rather more vigorous. In staking his claim to command of the *Sea Gull*, Lieutenant Samuel Phillips Lee of the Virginia Lees wrote Wilkes a letter "disrespectful in its tenour." He was immediately dispatched in Claiborne's wake.

Lieutenant Johnson was surprised to find himself in a command and not altogether gratified. He was unhappy to replace Reid and dismayed at being the cause of discontent among his seniors, especially since his good friend Lieutenant Walker complained at the injustice of Johnson's having the larger schooner—by fourteen tons. Lieutenant Robert F. Pinkney, who took Lee's place in the *Peacock*, protested that he was entitled to the command assigned Johnson but saw the inadvisability of attaching an ultimatum. Johnson was a cool observer of the internal troubles of the Expedition but was devoted to it and "sorry to see a bad feeling in the Squadron." With others of like mind, he tended to blame "the devilish Schooners" and Wilkes' excuse that they were not proper commands for lieutenants. So many requests to be detached reached Wilkes that he issued a statement in the hope of clarifying matters: the two schooners were to be considered equal commands, and seniority of rank, when vacancies occurred elsewhere in the squadron, would "at all times be regarded."

Lee's dismissal involved transfers and reassignments for eleven officers but, cutting through the fog of jealousy and discontent, Wilkes issued these in an hour's time and congratulated himself that his decisiveness had rid the squadron of Lee, whom he suspected of endeavoring "to poison the minds of those well affected" toward the Expedition, and broken the back of a "mutinous cabal." His suspicions worked strongly upon his imagination. In view of the history of the expedition before its sailing, that he should entertain suspicions was no wonder, and his imaginary mutinous cabal was staffed almost solely with officers Commodore Jones had appointed. But the fact pointed less to their culpability than to the accuracy of Jones' insight: the Navy could not bear a temporary disruption of its hidebound custom even for the glory of overseas discovery. Shunting the disaffected into the *Relief* did little to restore good feeling. The quarreling continued, with the vectors of animosity converging more and more upon the commander, until Wilkes came to see himself in a world peopled with isolated friends and cabals of enemies. And indeed it was difficult for any man in the squadron to remain indifferent or dispassionate toward this seemingly omnipresent commander, who knew of events in every ship almost as soon as they happened and who regularly examined the thoughts they chose to record in their journals. But the fund of good humor was not exhausted. Chaplain Elliott, whose choice of topics for his sermons was often uncannily inept, helped immeasurably when the following Sunday he chose to address these men so near the end of the earth on the subject of Belshazzar's Feast and the "sin and danger of intemperate revelry."

Most of the scientists, with their equipment and collections, were also bundled into the *Relief*, which was to conduct surveys in the Straits of Magellan, and could look forward to fruitful work along its shores before their return to Orange Harbor. Peale asked to remain aboard the *Peacock* for the southern cruise, and Couthouy, hoping to make a more careful examination of Orange Harbor, to stay with the *Vincennes*. Wilkes granted both requests.

Their equipment completed, the *Peacock*, *Porpoise*, and the schooners weighed anchor and stood down the harbor early in the morning of February 25, while the crews of the other vessels gave three hearty cheers. The *Relief* stood to sea the following day, leaving the *Vincennes* at anchor on the smooth waters of the nearly landlocked harbor. Lieutenant Craven was in charge of the *Vincennes*, having been restored to duty after addressing a last minute apology to Wilkes—and suffering the further humiliation of having it rejected in first draft as too submissive for "a high toned officer and gentleman." Lieutenant Carr set up the observatory on shore, while Lieutenant James Alden took charge of a survey party with instructions to chart the area of Nassau Bay and the Hermite Islands at the tip of Tierra del Fuego.[1]

This survey party—consisting of Alden, Reynolds, and ten of the men—set out "in the most stormy month, of the most stormy part of the world" with a small and, as it happened, unreliable chart (the most recent to be had, Reynolds noted; older ones "would answer just as well for any other place") and the full knowledge that their thirty-five-foot launch would be unable to weather a gale, and that if caught out in a "S.W. blow, and driven off the Land, we would be *lost!*"

On the twelfth of March, while they were in the passage between Wollaston and Hermite, a squall sent them flying under the lee of the latter. When other squalls followed in quick succession and it became clear that their

FIRST BLOOD

visit would be prolonged, they set up a kitchen among the rocks and dined on limpet soup and the ducks and geese that flew over in clouds—fine fare that they washed down with champagne and the "Burden's choice Madeira" they had had the foresight to bring along. They passed the time between feasts in listening to the men spin yarns. "And such yarns," Reynolds recalled, "I thought *I* knew some little thing about a roving life."

It was March 25 before they dared venture out again. The frequency and violence of the gales (which they later learned had caused the *Vincennes* to drag her anchor in Orange Harbor) persuaded them that to attempt the survey of the islands in the open sea would be foolhardy, and they hugged the coast instead. On the twenty-seventh they sighted the *Sea Gull* and fired their small brass cannon to attract her attention. She had returned from the southern cruise and was conducting a second search for them. When the survey party was safely aboard the *Sea Gull,* another gale swept down, wrecking the empty launch and testing even the *Sea Gull's* mettle. But they found her perfect in model and balance and freely predicted that she could outlive "the heaviest gale that might blow." She brought them the eighty miles into Orange Harbor in seven hours. The twenty-five-day cruise of the launch had been little more than a gastronomical occasion.

On the eleventh the *Flying Fish* arrived with adventures of a different magnitude to report. Wilkes had divided the force in the attempt to make the most of the small chance of significant discovery. With the *Sea Gull* he would explore the southeast coast of Palmer's land (what is now called the Antarctic Peninsula) and if possible press beyond, while the *Peacock* and *Flying Fish* would take a westerly course to Cook's *ne plus ultra.* From the first day out of Orange Harbor the squalls were nearly continuous. On March 1 the *Porpoise* and *Sea Gull* made Ridley's Island off the northern tip of the South Shetlands and on sighting Cape Melville filled away for Palmer's land, raising it two days later.

They found it ringed with ice, which to Johnson seemed "utterly impassable." But Wilkes stood on with the schooner in his wake until the ice was so thick that the latter's helm was "put to starboard and port every instant" to avoid collision. They had been sailing in a mist, but now snow began to fall, or rather to blow, "in such piercing flakes as to prevent looking out to windward" as they cruised among icebergs of fantastic size and shape and color—opal, green, even black—in which Johnson found that it required only a little imagination to "recognize the ruins of some ancient city, where Palaces, & Cathedrals, with every manner of edifice, statues of men, birds & beasts were conmingled." But it was no place to be caught in by the gales that

The *Sea Gull* and the *Porpoise* at 63° 10′ S., from
sketch by Charles Wilkes. (*Narrative*, 1: p. 142.
Western Americana Collection, Yale University
Library.)

seemed to be in fashion in these latitudes, and they changed course to coast
the land to the northeast, heaving-to at night and proceeding under reefed
sails during the day. By March 5 they were certain that no open water lay
between ice and shore. The boisterous weather made soundings and determination of the current impossible, the decks were sheets of ice, and the rigging
of the *Sea Gull* so iced up that it was nearly impossible to make sail. Wilkes
hailed the schooner and ordered her back to Orange Harbor, giving the
latitude as he had determined it—a somewhat less difficult feat aboard the
steadier brig—as 63° 10′ S.

Freely confessing, as Johnson put it, that "constant wet decks, and the
certainty that the crew could not stand many nights of such hardship . . . are
rather dampers to *penetrating* enthusiasm," they beat the ice from the rigging,
and shaped a return course to the west through Bransfield's Strait. On March

10 they put into the drowned crater that forms the harbor of Deception Island in the South Shetlands to spend a week in fruitless search for the self-registering thermometer placed in a cairn by Captain Henry Foster of H.B.M. *Chanticleer* ten years before, making their mess on the penguins that covered the hillsides. With over half the crew too sick for duty and all suffering from the unremitting cold and damp, on the seventeenth they stood to the north, pausing en route to Orange Harbor only long enough to survey Wollaston Island.

On parting from the schooner, Wilkes also shaped his course to the north, making Elephant Island in the eastern South Shetlands, where the sea was too high to permit a landing, on the seventh. On March 16 they were again off the Straits of Le Maire, when the storm that held the launch under the lee of Hermite sent them running for Good Success Bay, some seventy-five miles to the northeast. Here, where two of Joseph Banks' servants had perished from the cold while botanizing for their master in 1769, Lieutenant Dale landed with a party to explore the country, but was unable to get off again through the rising surf. A boat sent to their rescue capsized, its men saved by their india rubber life preservers, and it was five days before the gale fled howling. At Orange Harbor again Dale found himself suspended from duty for having failed to bring his boat back through the surf.

The *Flying Fish* was more successful. Separated from the *Peacock* on the second day out of Orange Harbor, she proceeded to the southwest through gales that twice split her jib and mainsail and heavy seas that smashed both boats and washed the port binnacle overboard, injuring the helmsman (the schooner was steered by tiller in the open cockpit) and lookout and half filling the cabin. Once, as though to join in the sport at her expense, a whale came up from the deep and "rubbed his vast sides" against the vessel. Every rope became an icicle and the men swathed their feet in blankets. They made two more rendezvous, hoping for medical aid from the *Peacock*, for three of the crew of ten were disabled, one with a fractured rib. His shipmates knew their cordage and mended his bones with a woolder.

Walker shaped his course for Cook's farthest south, heaving-to during the nights to avoid the ice islands. They were among schools of whales as well, and once a right whale, larger than the schooner itself, lay so obstinately in their path that the men had to fend it off with boathooks. On March 19 they awoke to find the fog lifted and before them a wall of ice fifteen to twenty feet high, extending east to west as far as the eye could see. They fancied that their vessel must have looked like "a mere skiff in the moat of a giant's castle," and noted here one of the many weird tricks of the polar atmosphere. "The voice had no

"A mere skiff in the moat of a giant's castle." From
sketch of the *Flying Fish*, by Alfred T. Agate. (J. C.
Palmer, *Thulia: A Tale of the Antarctic*, New York,
1843, p. 33.)

resonance: words fell from the lips, and seemed to freeze before they reached
the ear," and while the icebergs ponderously rose and fell their caverns sent
forth "a fitful roar, like moans from some deep dungeon."

By alternately luffing and bearing away they managed to avoid contact with
the barrier as they coasted it to the west. On the twenty-first they made
latitude 68° 41′ S., longitude 103° 34′ W. and stood due south at eight knots,
confident from the state of sea and weather that before noon next day they
would "get beyond Cook." In place of their smashed thermometers they hung

FIRST BLOOD

up a tin pot of water and resolved to press on until it froze. They were learning a thing or two about navigation in these seas, finding it wise to keep in the lee of the bergs in a stiff breeze, when the larger mass was blown ahead of the many fragments that trailed in its wake, and to windward in light weather, when the smaller pieces drifted more rapidly with the current. But the fog closed in suddenly and "our hopes," Walker lamented, "were blasted in the bud: it soon became so thick we could not see at all." From fear of the floating ice they hove-to for the night, but the weather only grew thicker and on the morrow they found themselves surrounded by ice "stretching in all directions as far as the eye could reach, and beyond, icebergs, packed and floating ice." Walker managed to escape from their isolated pond only by gathering six knots way and smashing through the "sutures" that ran at intervals through the ice—this in the face of the alarmed protests of the carpenter, who hurried aft to warn that the vessel could not bear the strain. Dodging the ice islands against which the sea broke "with the roar of thunder, and to the height of eighty to one hundred feet," the *Flying Fish* drove westward. On the twenty-fourth they were forced to repeat the performance of cutting through the sutures, a more difficult, yet more imperative task now, for as the breeze "died away into a murmur, a low crepitation, like the clicking of a death-watch, announced that the sea was freezing," and all suddenly realized that the wind's breath was the breath of life to them. It came, and crowding on all sail, they smashed away for four hours to gain the open sea.

With the sun now tending the northern hemisphere daylight lasted only a few hours, and fearful that the vessel's copper might be cut through, they decided to return north, comforting themselves with the reflection that on March 22 they had reached "about" 70° S., 101° 11′ W. (cloudy weather had prevented good sights) and on the nineteenth had seen ice discolored with a "deep earthy stain," which gave the appearance of being "but lately detached from land," and on the twenty-third, "appearances of land"—just what appearances Walker did not specify. They had reached a point some one hundred miles north of what is now known as Thurston Peninsula, where the Walker Mountains and Cape Flying Fish commemorate their feat.[2]

When the schooner spoke the *Peacock* a month after losing her in the gale, the crews cheered ship, but Walker's report dampened the remaining hopes of the *Peacock*'s officers, who of course had contended with the same weather. The captain of her maintop dead from injuries suffered in falling from the yard, her decks and rigging frozen over, and her bows bearing a great mound of ice (and finally watertight, Hudson noted, from the work of the "Antarctic Caulker"), the *Peacock* had reached 68° 08′ S., 97° 58′ W. Now, on receiving

Walker's report that to the south all was ice, Hudson called a council of his officers, who decided, "sorely against our will," Peale recorded, "but by the dictates of common prudence," that in a further attempt in so unfavorable a season there was nothing to gain and everything to lose. The kindly Hudson, who as a courtesy on the first day out of Orange Harbor had revealed his instructions to the officers and who as the weather grew colder ordered hot coffee served to the watches—two innovations everyone remarked on—assembled the crew on the maindeck to inform them of the decision and commend their conduct during the cruise. They afterwards dispersed in silence, but Lieutenant Emmons observed that only a few betrayed disappointment, perhaps at not "having obtained a piece of the South Pole, or discovered a new continent," goals, for all anyone knew, equally unlikely of attainment. Promising one another success next season they put up the helm and stood to the north.

By the light of a young moon and the roar of a large horn on the *Peacock* that blew almost constantly, the two vessels ran through the ice in company. There was a bad scare aboard the larger ship on the night of March 29, when she filled with smoke and the drums beat to quarters. Waking from a sound sleep to the news that his ship was on fire, Hudson rushed forward in his underwear. But it was only a bag of coffee in the hold that had taken fire from roasting in the galley during the day. On April 1 the vessels parted company, in accordance with instructions, the *Peacock* bound for Valparaiso, the *Flying Fish*·once more for Orange Harbor.

As the rest of the squadron returned to anchor beside the *Vincennes*, her men listened eagerly to the tales of the polar explorers. Their own adventures had been of a milder cast. On calm nights the placid waters of the harbor resounded with the breathings of whales, "loud & shrill as the whistling of a tempest," and in the clear moonlight, Reynolds recorded, "we could see their huge black forms, heaving out of the water, & the jets of spray that they flung aloft!"

Exploring the countryside that from the sea appeared so green and lush, they found it everywhere moss and spongy turf, with here and there a gnarled tree. Only the tops of the hills were firm underfoot, and they were frozen. And if the southern explorers had learned something about sailing in the ice, for their part the Orange Harbor party had stories to tell of the local inhabitants. Often met singly searching for mussels in the coves, the Fuegians were the first savages most had ever seen. For a generation well-steeped in the laws of nature that underpinned the institutions of their society and with an idea or two about "natural" man, undefiled by the artificial influences of civilization, the encounter with the barrel-chested but otherwise spindly and bowlegged Fuegians was a shock. One morning early in March three canoes appeared, keeping well off the ship, each with a family seated around a small fire flaring fitfully on a mound of sand and stones at the center. In one a man stood up and delivered what Couthouy described as "a sort of recitative chant," ending by "suddenly changing his key to a minor & falling several notes." Putting away the brass spyglasses, which seemed to give alarm, the officers enticed them alongside with strips of red flannel and bright buttons. A few of the men were induced to come aboard, though the women would not even rise for the presents offered, thereby "showing a degree of modesty hardly to have been expected," Couthouy noted primly, considering "the fact of both themselves & the men being entirely naked." They kept up a cry of "Yah me scone, Yah me scone," that no one could make anything of.

They readily traded their handsome fish spears, which, ten feet long, tipped with whale tooth and perfectly hexagonal, everyone marveled at, for trinkets, but remained exceedingly timid. Hoping to break down their reserve, Couthouy took one by the hands and, singing, waltzed him around the deck. The native followed both steps and notes exactly. Arm-in-arm they "figured away," to the amusement, Couthouy noted, of some of the officers and men who found the exhibition "excessively ridiculous." Perhaps it did seem a ludicrous caper, he reflected, but it was serious enough in purpose. "I view the matter very differently. Thrown as we are likely to be among many savage tribes during this expedition, we must, to win confidence with the timid, as well as propitiate the warlike, unbend a little . . . & consent for a time to be all things to all men." Artist Drayton got out his violin and struck a few notes, which the natives imitated, as they did, too, the notes of a flute played by one of the crew. Drayton suddenly had an idea. Pointing to the sky and joining his hands in the attitude of prayer, he found that the natives did likewise, which led him to conclude happily that they had "some knowledge of a supreme being." But further acquaintance with their amazing talent dispelled the notion. "They were the greatest mimics I ever saw," remarked a petty officer, for "altho' they could not understand they could repeat every word spoken to them as plain as he that spoke it." Though amusing, their mimicry made it impossible to form a vocabulary of the tongue, for one of the explorers would point to his eye and solemnly pronounce the word, "eye," only to find to his exasperation that the native did the same.

One fellow they called "Jim Orange" paid a longer visit. The men gave him a scrubbing, trimmed his hair and beard, "clothed him decently," and made him a member of the mess. Though he remained "a great glutton and eat to

"Pity then the Poor Naked Savages." Fuegians and
canoe, by Joseph Drayton. (*Narrative*, 1: p. 127.
Western Americana Collection, Yale University
Library.)

repletion of all the dishes that pleased his taste," he learned to do so "with
perfect propriety." They grew fond of him but, Reynolds noted in surprise,
"he left one day, without any show of ceremony or affection & never showed
himself again."

The explorers responded variously to their first exposure to man in a state
of nature. Remarking their "perfect state of nudity" and filth, most found in
the Fuegians "a field for the Philanthropist." "Pity then the Poor Naked
Savages now shivering by your side," mused Long, "Poor creatures: You do not
seem to be so well provided for as the beast of the forest." Passed Midshipman
Joseph Perry Sanford scrutinized their bark canoes, kept "on the stretch" by
many small hoops athwart the bottom ("You can hardly ascribe a particular
shape to them"), in the construction of which, he confessed, "some ingenuity
is visible," and their low, oval huts, formed of twigs and roofed with woven
swatches of grass. Dismayed that "Something, having the shape of 'Gods
noblest work' " was to be found here at the world's end "living in a state of the
most abject misery and wretchedness," he unhesitatingly blamed the environment. "A more chilling, desolate or dreary country" could not be imagined,

FIRST BLOOD

and "civilization could not have a being where all the ingenuity man usually brings into play for his subsistence would be of no avail."

Perhaps others were brought to similar reflections. William Reynolds put his own thoughts in order without any trouble at all: "If *they* be the children of Nature, I am thankful that I am a member of a more artificial community, & will waive forever the belief, that those barbarous ones who have the fewest wants, lead a more enviable existence, than the great civilized mass, who are always wanting."

On April 13, two months after entering Orange Harbor, the *Vincennes* and *Porpoise* set sail, with only the commander knowing what was to be their next port of call. The *Flying Fish* and *Sea Gull* were to wait ten days more for the laggard storeship, then open sealed instructions that directed them to join the other vessels at Valparaiso. Wilkes pressed his ship with sail in a way that was "startling, even to the oldest hands," Reynolds noted, rather taken aback but admiring the man's nerve. One day with studding sails set, "at a tremendous risk to spars & canvas," they logged over two hundred and seventy miles, "a wondrous speed." (It is the last expression of admiration for Wilkes to appear in Reynolds' long journal.) On May 10 they made the island of Mocha and on the fifteenth, Valparaiso, where the *Peacock* had been at anchor nearly three weeks.

They learned that the *Relief* had appeared on April 15 then proceeded up the coast to Callao. That was welcome news, for her failure to return to Orange Harbor had occasioned some fears. As it happened, these were not misplaced, for the storm that caused the *Vincennes* to drag her anchor in the protected waters and sent Alden's launch scurrying under Hermite had come near closing the career of the storeship. Long's orders were to proceed northwestward along the treacherous coast, entering the Straits from the west through Cockburn Channel, and rejoin the squadron at Orange Harbor by completing a circuit of that part of Tierra del Fuego separated from the mainland by the Straits of Magellan. For several days out they experienced heavy weather, with contrary winds that prevented their making way to the west, and Long determined to follow a southern tack. Then the wind failed, they drifted with the strong current, and for some days the weather signs were favorable—a point Long noted with apprehension.

On March 18 "a gentle air from the S & E paid us a visit, seeming to say, put yourselves under my auspices, and I will conduct you to a haven of rest," recalled Lieutenant Claiborne of the enticing moment. "Parties began to be talked of, some to go in search of Specimens in the Animal, Vegetable & mineral kingdom, others to ascend lofty mountains . . . vain dream—delusive hope!" About halfway to the point at which they were to enter the Straits, a gale descended suddenly and furiously. Hurriedly shortening sail, they ran on in thick mist between rocky shores. Just as night was coming on, the air cleared for a moment and they made out a few miles distant what they took to be Noir Island. It was a heartening sight, especially as King's sailing directions described it as an "excellent roadstead." In any event, the fury of the storm convinced Long that anchoring under its lee was the only way to save the vessel. Finding that the two anchors held, they felt comparatively safe. But during the night the gale increased and the sea smashed the port waist boat. Next day they put down two more anchors. Sailing Master Sinclair took a look about and returned to his quarters to write out his own sailing directions. "This part of the Coast only requires to be known to be the more avoided, so say I, but here we are at the very worst season of the year & in an Equinoxical gale. All that we can do now is to do our best & trust the rest to a bountiful providence." Wind and sea increased again next day, wrenching away the port sheet anchor. Then the port bow chain went suddenly slack. The cable had broken. The night of the nineteenth was to live vividly in the memories of all—dark and dismal it was, the wind screaming through the rigging, a sea as high as the mastheads, men and officers all on deck, straining to hear the fateful rumble of the cables that would signal the dragging over the stony bottom of the last remaining anchors. They heard it in the early morning. For a few hours the anchors caught on a reef, but just before noon the ship gave a heavy lurch, the cables parted, and, Long recorded, "we found ourselves at God's mercy." Perhaps it stood them in good stead, for the wind both shifted and abated, and daylight broke. They cleared the reef astern by half the length of the ship and, putting on a heavy press of canvas, departed the "excellent roadstead" with all dispatch. "I hope I shall never be unmindful," wrote Long thankfully as they gained the Pacific's wide waters, "that 'A sweet little cherub sits up aloft / Who keeps a look out for poor Jack.' "

Without anchors, Long concluded that it would be madness to enter the Straits and no less to attempt returning to Orange Harbor and therefore opened his sealed orders. Learning that the squadron was to rendezvous at Valparaiso, he shaped a course to the north, submitting now, as Lieutenant Claiborne freely confessed, "with the utmost complacency to whatever kind of wind & weather, God in his wisdom, thought proper to send us."

It had been the fiercest storm anyone on board had ever met with, and in reflecting on their experience they marveled at their own calm in the face of almost certain disaster, and especially at Captain Long's. Full of praise for the way he had taken the trumpet and worked his ship "with great coolness," they agreed that there was no one to whom they would more willingly trust their lives in the future. And they commented, too, on the sangfroid of quiet little Pickering, who at the height of the storm retired to his cabin, wrapped himself in his cloak, stretched out on the deck and went to sleep. Even Wilkes, who was not disposed to a favorable view of this particular passage of the *Relief*, praised this "philosophic act."

At Valparaiso they had to borrow an anchor from H.M.S. *Fly* before entering the harbor.

The *Flying Fish* arrived on May 19—alone. Her commander, Passed Midshipman Knox, reinstated after the southern cruise, reported that the schooners had left Orange Harbor in company on April 28 in heavy weather. They had last sighted the *Sea Gull*, under Passed Midshipmen Reid and Bacon, at midnight, lying-to with her head to the south under False Cape Horn. Shortly afterward a furious squall struck and Knox fled back to Orange Harbor to wait it out.

Hopes rose on June 6 when the telegraph on the hill reported a schooner standing along the coast. For a while everybody was sure it was their "lost companion," but it proved to be only a passing vessel. While they waited, Carr set up the observatory once more and the scientists scattered along the seashore and into the mountains on two separate excursions, once venturing a hundred miles inland to an altitude of fifteen thousand feet, both times neglecting, to Wilkes' great annoyance, to take along instruments for the proper determination of altitude.

Wilkes professed no alarm at the *Sea Gull*'s delay. Rather he seized the occasion to detach Lieutenant Craven from the squadron, to take command of the schooner on her arrival, he said. That did nothing to mollify the officers who felt that he should send the *Flying Fish* in search, and it did not deceive Craven, who, Wilkes noted in surprise, was "very sore upon the subject."

The *Porpoise* was dispatched to Callao for needed repairs, clearing the harbor on a Sunday without mishap. And on June 6, the *Vincennes*, *Peacock*, and *Flying Fish* followed, the *Vincennes* disgracing herself in the harbor by twice fouling the *Peacock*. Their decks in an uproar, the two ships appeared to Reynolds to be "engaging each other in bitter strife," like "Gladiators of the Sea." Then on clearing the harbor the *Vincennes* fouled a Danish ship. "Crazy with shame and vexation," Reynolds put it all down to Wilkes' "mismanagement & obstinacy." On the eighteenth and twentieth they came to anchor at the sand island of San Lorenzo off Callao harbor, where final preparations were to be made for the Pacific cruise.

Aside from repairing the ships and taking on the provisions just arrived from the States, preparations included putting into effect plans for the better discipline of the squadron that Wilkes had been laying privately for some time past. Initially these involved only disposition of the *Relief* and her commander, but as they took effect events unfolded that involved other and more far-reaching decisions. Wilkes read Long's report on the *Relief*'s late cruise with "much surprise and mortification" and demanded an apology for his impertinence in having sent a copy to the Department in Washington. He blamed Long ("one of Jones' officers") for all the storeship's tribulations since clearing Norfolk and even for the absence of the *Sea Gull*. Had Long returned to Orange Harbor or even sent word through the Straits, the schooner would be with them now. Those unacquainted with the unremitting burden of command might find the reasoning unimpressive, even devious, but Wilkes had long since learned the importance of assigning responsibility—and affixing blame.

Wilkes' reprimand was so harsh that Long requested a hearing before a court martial, but to the commander's mind another and happier course presented itself. The storeship was slow, her commander incompetent, and he soon persuaded himself that it was obligatory "to forego her services and that of her Commander especially." It would save government money. He laid his plans quietly, as was his wont. Then when the *Vincennes* sailed into Callao harbor she brought news of changes that, as Emmons noted with deceptive mildness, "created considerable excitement." Informing Long that there was no time to be spared for a court martial, he bundled the request off to the Secretary, together with his own report on the affair. Long was inclined to keep his opinions to himself, but one of the officers noted that "much difficulty & diplomacy there was in quieting Captain Long."

The decision to detach the *Relief* meant that officers and men must be reassigned. Wilkes had earlier rid himself of unwanted scientists by merely sailing away from them. He could do the same with navy officers and laid his plans accordingly. The decision came too late to provide transportation for Lieutenant Lee, who had already departed in the *Henry Lee*, a ship named for his uncle.

Every day during the third week of May a gun was fired aboard the *Peacock* and the jack flew from her mizzen to signal that a court of inquiry was convened to investigate the conduct of Lieutenant Dale, who at Good Success Bay had failed to return his shore party to the *Porpoise* before the rising surf had rendered return impossible. The court exonerated him. But when Wilkes' order restoring him to duty was read to the assembled ships' companies, Dale—one of the "Old Explorers" who had "sailed in Rittenhouse Square" with the "Great Unbegun Undertaking" under Commodore Jones—found himself sternly forgiven for incompetence. His many friends among the lieutenants were incensed and when their reasonable request that they be shown the decision of the court met with rebuff, Dale addressed a letter of complaint directly to the Secretary—and immediately found himself assigned to the *Relief*. Wilkes saw to it that his friends accompanied him.

Already promised early passage home for his conduct at Orange Harbor, Lieutenant Claiborne now joined the *Relief*, and Lieutenant Hartstene, who had once served as Jones' first lieutenant aboard the *Consort* but had passed some heated words with Ringgold at Valparaiso and reported him to Wilkes, had to carry his kit aboard, too. With them went pilot Isaac Percival of the good but failed intentions and Passed Midshipman Hunn Gansevoort, suffering from "the Venereal," who nonetheless had been with the Expedition long enough to be able to inform his cousin Herman Melville about it.[3]

Thus when the light of dawn fell upon Callao Harbor on June 21 the *Relief* had on board very nearly the same officers as had sailed in her from Norfolk. But "ere the clock had told ten," her sailing master noted in dismay, only her commander was scheduled to remain. Her crew had been drafted for the *Vincennes* and their place taken by "the Lame Blind & disaffected. We are an ignorant people," he lamented, "& know not today what is to turn up tomorrow. Yesterday we had a three years cruise in contemplation—today we are newly officered & . . . half manned & bound home." There were yet others whom Wilkes would have preferred to add to its cargo of castoffs. Indeed, could he have but seen a little way into the future, the storeship could never have accommodated the numbers. He had taken a strong dislike to two of the medical officers. Doctor Charles Guillou was "much wanting in common sense" and "a novice in medicine" and Doctor Edward Gilchrist had not the proper "feeling towards the Expedition" and was "greatly overrated in his profession." But as the *Peacock*'s surgeon had to be invalided home Wilkes had no choice but to retain the two offenders. One had perforce to accept disappointments as they came, and to his mind much had been accomplished toward remolding the expedition into a better disciplined force, a task that nagging scientists and importunate politicians had not allowed him to carry out at home. Prospects for the next three years appeared considerably brighter.

And indeed nearly three weeks were to pass before the next eruption of feeling. Hope for the *Sea Gull* waned and foreboding became "deep & general." Some speculated that she had sustained hidden damage while aground at the Río Negro, but there was no knowing and the explorers turned to the tasks at hand. In an effort to destroy the voracious packs of rats that had taken their tithe of the stores and even gnawed a hole in the cutter, they burned three barrels of charcoal in the storeship's holds, transferred her library and scientifics to the *Vincennes*, and stowed the bird skins, minerals, dried plants, samples of the sea bottom, and shells for the long voyage home. With them went fresh stores to be deposited for the squadron at Honolulu and Sydney, including a quantity of whiskey. Loading whiskey was a critical performance, and as was the custom a guard of marines was stationed aboard to keep a sharp eye on the crew. But now marines and sailors fell upon the whiskey together. All got hilariously drunk, spent the night in irons, and sobered up under twenty-four of the cats next day, which, again observing that time did not permit a court martial, Wilkes simply ordered out of hand.

Full of drunken and unemployed American soldiers of fortune who had come to fight in the war between Peru and Chile, Callao was "the dirtiest of all places" and really uninhabitable, where in a half hour's time a man would find himself "black with fleas and spotted nearly all over with blood," and all who could seize the time chose instead to see the sights of Lima, including women that Reynolds found "lovely beyond belief," dressed in the saya, close-fitting and, for a wonder, "short enough to display the ancle." But the licentiousness of Lima made Silas Holmes, who had left Valparaiso "not without regret," very much the New Englander again. He was particularly oppressed by the popular dances, one of which, he complained, "is danced by a male & female, & is an exact & most disgusting imitation of the generative act! As might be supposed," he added tartly, "the foundling hospital is well supported & is under very good management." The crews were less prudish, and Lieutenant Emmons, who was something of a disciplinarian, thought their conduct ashore vacated whatever claim they might have had to liberty, but then reflected with philosophic resignation that always and everywhere "*Grog & women* . . . play the duce with the better resolves of a sailor."

On the Fourth of July the *Vincennes* dressed ship to celebrate the Republic's sixty-third birthday. Salutes were fired from ship and shore and the crews received an extra ration of grog—all except the men of the *Peacock*, who had managed to get theirs earlier in the day with the aid of a thoughtful shipmate in the boats who filled hollowed-out pumpkins with liquor and set the little fleet adrift on the current ahead of the ship. It was a bit of artistry that led George Emmons to reflect admiringly on the ingenuity of the American seaman.

Restive with the repeated delays, the explorers were impatient to be off, for their hearts were "in the Islands," as Reynolds put it, and thus far many had not been out of the "old & beaten track." Particularly annoying was the air of mystery that concealed their next destination; it was especially annoying for the scientists, whose explorations carried them some distance inland, even the mild-mannered Pickering wondering why the length of stay in port must always be "a state secret of the Commander's." But, certain that these matters were none of their concern, Wilkes left rumor to fill the void, and with a new story flying through the squadron every day, not surprisingly many came to the same conclusion Henry Eld reached. "I positively do not believe the Commander of the Expedition knows from day to day what he is going to do," he wrote home. "So great a nation are we." And bundling disaffected officers into the storeship, though it encouraged circumspection, did not perceptibly increase the fund of good will. Many of the discarded lieutenants had good friends among those remaining and even among the midshipmen, though it must be said that the remonstrations of the latter had been less than clamorous at the time of the dismissals. Wilkes had early won the loyalty of the midshipmen by assigning them duties hitherto reserved to lieutenants, thus opening the way to earlier promotion. Their regret at the dismissals was real, but so was their ambition and so, ultimately, was their loyalty to Wilkes.

They soon learned that their loyalty counted for curiously little with Wilkes, who had ambitions of his own. At Valparaiso they had anchored near the *Falmouth*, whose commander, Captain Isaac McKeever, had been most helpful, sending replacements from his own ship for the squadron's lost boats and otherwise displaying an enthusiastic interest in the enterprise. Surprised to come upon a captain of the United States Navy who wished the Expedition well, Wilkes was much gratified. His officers also remarked the novelty. Still solicitous, McKeever put in at Callao with three deserters from the *Vincennes* (who in violation of regulations were awarded three dozen lashes each when Wilkes again decided that time did not permit a court martial) and, "almost kissing the foot of Capt Wilkes," as one of the officers put it, showed himself eager to oblige with any further service. As sailing master, McKeever had aboard his twenty-year-old nephew, Lieutenant Edwin J. De Haven, who wanted very much to join the Expedition. Lieutenant Johnson hoped that McKeever had no "sinister designs" but noted that the sailing masters of the squadron were wary.

With bitterness, Reynolds described succinctly the event that gave the lie to Johnson's hope: "McKeever gave us his launch, his cutter and his nephew, which latter, was heartily wished at the d---l by us all." Two passed midshipmen, Hunn Gansevoort and Henry A. Clemson went to the *Falmouth* in exchange. (Poor Gansevoort found himself on a tour of the harbor, ordered from the *Peacock* to the *Flying Fish* to the *Relief* and finally to the

Falmouth.) De Haven, who had been an officer since the age of ten, was later to make a name for himself in Arctic exploration, but when, showing "anything but a proper feeling," he joined the *Vincennes* as sailing master, he closed off prospects for a dozen or more midshipmen, some of whom had been with the Expedition for two years now, and who felt that Wilkes had reneged on a promise. So far as experience in the squadron was concerned, the midshipmen were as dedicated to the principle of seniority as were their erstwhile superiors among the lieutenants, and now "to have the sweet cup dashed . . . by a stranger," as Reynolds rather floridly put it, was too much for their faith in Wilkes' justice.

A more sensitive man might have redeemed himself in their esteem. Not Wilkes, who gave little thought to the matter at the time and was by nature incapable of accepting responsibility for the mistrust and bitterness with which the squadron was launched upon Pacific exploration.

Officers took up the by now customary search for deserters and with ships repaired and provisioned and good will destroyed the squadron set sail on July 12, broken now, the "saucy little beauty" *Sea Gull* given up for lost by all but Wilkes, and the *Relief*, stripped of all her original officers except Long and his boatswain, cast aside. The storeship lay still at anchor off San Lorenzo with instructions to sail for Honolulu on the sixteenth. None aboard her knew any more of the squadron's destination than did the officers of the other ships—some said the Sandwich Islands, some the Marquesas, some thought the commander himself uncertain—and if the men of the *Relief* cheered ship when the other vessels departed, no one cared to note it in his journal.[4]

6 A Fathom of Tapa

Point Venus is the most lovely spot I ever saw without
exception.

Assistant Surgeon J. S. Whittle

"Apparently very happy," observed Lieutenant Emmons of the
crew as favorable winds bore them westward in pleasant weather. On Hudson's
Peacock, the happiest ship in the squadron, they gathered on the forecastle
every fair evening to sing and dance.

Only two events proved worthy of note. One of the seamen shipped at
Callao came down with smallpox. The surgeons hastily banished him to a cot
on the spar deck and waited in dread. But no other cases appeared and the
man recovered in a few weeks.

Lieutenant Johnson noted precisely the time of the other occurrence. At
10:20 on the morning of July 18, the blue broad pennant was seen to fly from
the *Vincennes* in place of the customary coach whip of a lieutenant
commanding. The officers of the *Porpoise* got out a spyglass and saw their
commander upon the quarterdeck bearing an epaulet on each shoulder. He
was a captain now. Almost immediately the same little drama was staged on
the *Peacock*. Unknown to the observers, the four pieces of braid were
intended to smuggle back into the squadron the military aspect of which the
Secretary had divested it, for, still smarting at not having the temporary
appointment of captain which he thought the responsibility warranted, and
was required to maintain proper discipline among the "heterogeneous mass"
(as he had described his command in an irate last-minute letter to the
President), Wilkes had persuaded Hudson to join him in the deception.

Thirty days passed, a good many of them devoted to tiresome and fruitless
searches for islands earlier reported, before on August 13 the explorers made

the low green island of Clermont Tonnerre (Reao), easternmost of the Tuamotu Group, or Low Islands, the cloud of some eighty atolls that stretches fifteen hundred miles across the Pacific, and to everyone's delight found themselves at last among "the tempting Edens of the South Pacific," as the excited Reynolds put it. Though Clermont was well known to the chartmakers, the French explorer Louis I. Duperrey having discovered and surveyed it in 1823, some doubt concerning its precise position had since developed. Wilkes intended to settle the question. Also, since it was known to be inhabited, he thought it a good starting point from which to trace the island cultures from one end of Polynesia to the other.

No more than a lagoon ringed with coral and fringed with trees, Clermont was typical of these low coral islands, hardly any of which rises to more than thirty feet above the sea, a circumstance that with their hidden reefs had led Bougainville to name them the Dangerous Archipelago. But it was big with meaning for the explorers. Captivated at first sight of it, William Reynolds scurried up for a better view and clung to the royal yard for an hour, "entranced with the singular & picturesque loveliness of that gem of the ocean." Here was the vision that had drawn volunteers to the Expedition and comforted those dragooned. "No debts, no duns—no house rent, no coach hire—no Lawyers, no Doctors, no butchers bills, no nothing, but to pluck the golden fruits & pull the willing fish to the Shore."

To the astonishment of the scientists, the three vessels began a running survey without making any motions toward landing them. Peale was incensed and put it down as "a sorry business" that the commander should leave them on board to peer through spyglasses while he took up his own work. On the next afternoon, however, two boats put out from the *Vincennes* bearing Couthouy and Pickering and several officers, including Wilkes. When the surf proved too high for landing, the irrepressible Couthouy and Passed Midshipman Simon Blunt simply dove overboard and swam to the beach, where they immediately gave "three cheers for the expedition." They were probably the first white men ever to set foot there, since neither Duperrey nor Captain Frederick W. Beechey, who called in 1826, appears to have made a landing. The others soon managed to land and for two hours they rushed about collecting plants, working inland as far as the lagoon and returning on board without having seen a single inhabitant. When they returned the following afternoon, however, a crowd of seventeen natives, dressed in the Polynesian fiber *maro* that hung from the waist, appeared on the beach brandishing long spears with angry menace.

Shortly after clearing Callao, Wilkes had issued a general order forbidding the use of force except in self-defense and proclaiming that in the islands the squadron must display "peace, good-will, and proper decorum to every class," that future American visitors might be accorded a friendly reception. This was a situation, then, seemingly made to order for John Sac. Sac was a New Zealander, a ferociously tattooed fellow whom an American captain had brought to the States for exhibition some years before and who was now returning home as the squadron's interpreter. Shouting in the Tahitian dialect, he tried to make it clear that this was a friendly visit, with no other object than to distribute presents. The response proving less than hospitable, Wilkes stood tall in his boat and called out to Sac, "Tell them," he shouted, "tell them that I am the *big chief.*" Watching closely, Couthouy could describe their response only as "very unfriendly." Wilkes then ordered a number of blank cartridges fired, but that made no impression, either. Two of the midshipmen leaped out and swam to the beach but beat a hasty retreat when the natives began thrusting their spears in the air with an irregular staccato motion.

Couthouy was disgusted. Grabbing up a handful of medals and mirrors, the conchologist swam in and, holding out the presents, advanced toward one he took to be the chief. The man continued to back away until Couthouy was within a yard, then, suddenly joined by another, he stopped and raised his spear with a shout and "a distortion of feature," Couthouy observed, "that was anything but encouraging." Taking no notice of the looking glass dropped at his feet, he made a pass with his spear. When others took up stones, Couthouy, as though to complete this curious dance, began backing toward the beach. The chief made another thrust, but the recoil of the surf carried the conchologist out of reach and he gained the boat under a hail of stones. Then a club came hurtling at the boats, thrown "so truly and with such force" that it would have knocked one of the officers overboard had not the majestic John Sac, standing naked in the bow, coolly warded it off with a boat hook that he brandished aloft "with as much dexterity," Couthouy noted admiringly, "as any savage among them." It was difficult to recognize "one of the most orderly peaceable men of our ship's company in the fierce looking savage warrior before us."

His patience exhausted, Wilkes discharged his fowling piece loaded with mustard shot and ordered others to do the same. It became a bloody business, for the natives took the tiny shot in "breasts, faces, arms, & legs." Still, they calmly washed off the blood before moving into the trees with "deliberate dignity," carrying their chief, who had refused to flinch before the fire. Some of the officers were a little disconcerted by the "unconcern and contempt" they showed.

When, busy at collecting, Pickering and Couthouy were a little slow in observing the evening recall signal, Wilkes blustered them and threatened to keep all the corps aboard in the future if they did not pay closer attention to orders.

Coming from the commander of a scientific expedition the threat was ludicrous, surely made in a moment of distemper. But unpredictable as this commander was, one could not be certain, especially as, so Peale put it, he seemed not to think "the resources of a land of equal importance with its hydrographic position."

After taking a final set of measurements next day, the squadron stood to the northwest, not wishing, remarked yeoman Ezra Green in reflecting on these tetchy people, further to "interfere with their prejudices." The officers reflected, too, on this first contact with the islanders. Lieutenant Johnson thought he detected some contradiction of the compassionate order issued on their departure from Callao, and Surgeon Holmes mused over "how much might have been added to knowledge" and to "the credit of our squadron, by a 7 hours ramble of our scientific corps," for he was aware that the "reputation of the expedition will depend upon the verdict of scientific men." The reception that would be tendered the next white men to appear at Clermont occupied the thoughts of some, and Peale remarked sarcastically that its "geographic position is highly interesting."

While still in sight of Clermont, the squadron made another island very like it and also of uncertain position, Serle's (Pukarua), and again commenced a survey. "Scientific Corps as before all idle," Peale grumbled. Finding their collections valuable and hoping for more from Serle's, the scientists were the more eager when Lieutenant Alden reported that the natives were swimming out to the boats to trade ornaments, maros, and tortoise-shell tools. They tried to steal everything in sight—ring-bolts and oarlocks, the copper from the oar blades—but without any injury intended or sense of wrong, for one who was swimming away with a notebook returned it immediately on observing the owner's anxiety. The scientists were cheered when Wilkes announced that they might go ashore early next morning.

But their hopes were blasted during the night when they woke to the "crash of breaking spars." The *Vincennes* had put her helm up without giving signal and the *Porpoise* collided with her, carrying away the latter's starboard quarter boat and her own jibboom. When the ruined boat, which Wilkes insisted on searching for, was recovered eight hours later, Serle's was out of sight and Wilkes gave the order to stand away. The scientists put it down as another lost opportunity and one for which small excuse could be found.

They made Honden (Pukapuka) in the northeastern Tuamotus on the first anniversary of casting off their pilot at the Virginia capes. It was an occasion for reflection. Fully aware that when they had finally got to sea after all the ridiculous delays they had proceeded to waste a year in places already well known to the world's naturalists, Couthouy spoke for all the corps as, all but frantic, he wrote in his journal, "Our cruise may be considered as just now beginning. . . . I am continually dissatisfied with myself because I cannot do enough."

At four o'clock next afternoon Wilkes allowed them to go ashore—for two hours. The brief excursion provided a tantalizing taste of riches in natural history, for though discovered over two centuries earlier by Jacob Le Maire, president of the Dutch ship *Eendracht*, the island remained in its "primitive freshness," the multitude of frigate birds so tame that Peale climbed the trees and plucked them like fruit from the branches, and Couthouy was certain that a thorough examination here would yield "a richer addition to our collections than a month passed at places which have been ransacked twenty times over." The island's potential for natural history was the greater, for isolated as it was from the main group, there could be no doubt that its productions varied "materially" from those of the more central islands, and as it was uninhabited, no danger attached to its thorough exploration. The anniversary scrutiny of Honden was afterward to stand in the minds of the corps as the supreme example of their commander's contempt for science. The conduct of the Expedition had assumed a disagreeable pattern. They were allowed ashore only late in the day with orders to remain within sight of the boats so as not to miss the signal for return. If they did miss it, they were not thereafter to go ashore at all. Couthouy thought it "a mere burlesque" under these circum- stances to call the present enterprise anything more than a surveying expedition.

On August 23 they made the cluster of little islands discovered by John Byron in the *Dolphin* in 1764, which, unable to land because of the surf, he had named the Disappointment Islands (Napuka and Tepoto). Perched aloft, William Reynolds found that "to sweep along the shores, with a Glass, presented a series of the most lovely pictures that can be conceived of— Oh! but they were beautiful." The blue lagoon set in the green island looked "as if it could have been created for no impurer use than to yield up the Pearls that abound in its depths." On the beach the natives stood waving white flags, and next day long outrigger canoes came off, paddled by "fine robust looking men," avid for anything the explorers chose to toss them, "leaping overboard for the merest trifle," singing, laughing, and waving all the while the white cloth that the explorers were to learn was the native tapa, the common coin of Polynesia. While the scientists fretted aboard and the islanders watched in curiosity from the beach, the vessels took their stations for the inevitable survey. This survey was the first to fix the position of the Disappointments with accuracy. The next day was Sunday, and after beating back to the island—the vessels stood off and on overnight, there being no anchorage—divine service was dutifully observed ("style bombastick & reasoning Shallow," Brackenridge observed of the sermon), and at four in the afternoon boats went off bearing the scientists.

When Couthouy swam in laden with trinkets, the natives helped him to his feet, rubbed noses and traded tapa for buttons, but would not allow him to advance beyond the beach, leading him repeatedly "with a gentle force down to the water making a satisfied sort of grunt as I left, & still carefully helping me up as oft as I returned." With force less gentle Peale and some of the officers pushed back and tramped on to the village.

Back aboard at sunset they received a written reprimand from Wilkes for having collected specimens in so dangerous a situation, which Peale thought "quite a literary curiosity as coming from a commander of a Scientific expedition," and at nearby Tepoto next day the *Peacock*'s scientifics were not allowed ashore. Those who were met a similar reception—eager trading (the Scots gardener observed that "they took particular good care that the pieces of cloth which they threw us was such as was pretty well wore out."), much rubbing of noses accompanied by a "soothing noise" that Couthouy thought very like "that by which men try to propitiate the feelings of some beast of whom they are suspicious," and the gentle pushing. A poor swimmer but good marksman, Brackenridge stood for a time in the stern sheets "ready with a brace of Pistols to shoot down the first Savage that might offer violence to any of our party," but soon found it difficult to keep a straight face, for "It was real laughable to see some of our people who endeavoured by dint of Stratagem to pass the Natives—how they were packed by two or three stout Indians & led like lambs back to the Surf." They had finally to give it up, but not before having "to rub the greasy noses of the whole tribe," Couthouy observed with amused distaste.

Standing to the southwest from the Disappointments, the scientists reflected bitterly on the irony of their situation. They had sent home fifty thousand specimens from Rio, but though five unexplored islands had just been "*surveyed*," the collections from them would not fill "a cigar-box," Couthouy estimated. "The people of the United States expect much from us after our long delays & vexations," Peale sourly explained to his journal: "to them we owe a long apology."

At sunrise on August 29 they raised a small round island which, not laid down on the chart, Wilkes named King's after the man at the masthead who first sighted it. This was Taiaro, which Captain Fitzroy had discovered but not visited in the *Beagle* in 1835. The surveys commenced immediately and at the seemingly magical hour of four in the afternoon the scientists of the *Vincennes* were allowed ashore to make what collections they could before sunset. Dana, Peale, and Hale were kept aboard the *Peacock* all day, close in to the island, which, Peale remarked before finally exploding, they could see "abounded in Scientific riches, & boats were swinging idly to the davits, men were looking as to a paradise, but no, a survey is made, nothing more is requisite, and time flies. *What was a Scientific Corps sent for?*"

They made Raraka next day, twenty miles to the southwest, and the scientists fared better, getting ashore soon after the survey began. The natives, gorgeously tattooed about the buttocks, were friendly and some of the younger women "very good looking," Couthouy noted in surprise. With more freedom than they had grown accustomed to since Callao, the scientists once more began to muse on the possibilities of this expedition. Hurrying along its beach, Couthouy found Raraka particularly rich in coral specimens. There was no man in the squadron more ambitious for the expedition or industrious in swelling its collections than Boston's learned mariner, the swarthy conchologist, but he had no sooner recovered his enthusiasm than he ran up against another facet of the commander's omnipresent authority. As he stepped out on deck after breakfast next morning it was to hear Wilkes call out that he "would not have the whole ship lumbered up with coral," which gave off a disagreeable smell and "endangered the health of the crew by producing malaria." When Couthouy protested that he took no more than was necessary for determination of specific characters and that previous expeditions had experienced no difficulty in preserving large and numerous specimens, Wilkes replied testily that he "did not care a damn for what had been done in previous expeditions, or consider himself in any way to be governed by it." He himself would decide all matters relating to the collections and decide them according to his own views. Couthouy, who had seen illustrations of the magnificent coral formations in European collections, thought this an absurd position to take up but held himself in check, remarking in his journal, "of course there is no reply to this."

As they proceeded along the archipelago to the northwest another problem arose in the scientific department. After a day of collecting on Manihi, Couthouy found himself confronted with what he called "the old vexed question of collections." Wilkes had ordered the officers to assist in gathering specimens, which he announced were to be considered public property. But as some of the officers were themselves proud owners of small cabinets, particularly of shells, and others, seeing that they were, willy-nilly, to collect, sought to set up cabinets of their own, they had intimated to Couthouy at Orange Harbor that if they were not allowed to retain specimens their future contributions would be few. Some told him candidly that there were "ways and means of evading such an order & they would not scruple to do it," and that he and the rest of the scientifics had "no right whatever" to call upon the officers "to aid them in earning their pay." Further remarks had been more personal.

Persuaded that this was no bluff, he saw that government must choose between having the major part of large collections or the whole of small ones and was in favor of allowing the officers to retain surplus specimens as an inducement to their participation. When in April Wilkes had issued a definite order that all collections were to be surrendered the threats came into the open again, and as the man in charge of the one branch of science for which there was a general taste, Couthouy bore the brunt of the officers' displeasure.

When the matter boiled over again in the Tuamotus he found Wilkes in no mood to retreat. Already in a pet because Peale had been forty minutes late in returning from shore and because one of the *Peacock*'s men had chosen not to return at all, Wilkes flatly declared that the officers must "disregard all personal interest in the collections." Nothing was really settled and the question remained vexed.

To hasten their arrival at Tahiti, their next port of refreshment, Wilkes divided the squadron at Kauehi (which he named "Vincennes Island," though again Fitzroy had discovered it four years earlier) for survey duty in the northwestern Tuamotus. Responding promptly to this "agreeable surprize," on September 1 the *Porpoise* set off on a sweep that carried her to Raraka, Katiu, Makemo, Carlshoff (Aratika, with nearby Taenga sometimes called Buyers Group), and Kruzenstern's (Tikahau). The *Flying Fish* was left to survey King George's Group (Takapoto and Tararoa) while the *Vincennes* and *Peacock* proceeded northwest to Rurik (Arutua) and Waterlandt (Manihi, which Byron had called Prince of Wales, and which on some charts appeared as Dean's), then southwest to Makatea and Tetiaroa. All were to rendezvous at fabled Tahiti.

Shortly after daylight on September 10 the men of the *Vincennes* had a foretaste of Tahiti when they landed on Aurora (Tetiaroa), where, though annoyed by the flies they were charmed by the inhabitants, who lived in houses of woven mats slung from frames of breadfruit logs, slept on pillows filled with sweet basil, and who understood "acts & Epistles" yet wore flowers in their hair. They brought to Couthouy's mind a verse of Byron's *Don Juan*: "A group that's quite antique / Half naked, loving, natural, and Greek." Surgeon Holmes was utterly nonplussed when the wife of one of the native missionaries was "very forward in her advances."

Next afternoon they sailed into Matavai Bay and anchored at sunset a mile to the west of Point Venus, next to the *Porpoise*. Every man in the squadron had waited long for this moment. In this respect they differed little from other men in the Western world, for the South Seas had come to occupy a significant place in Western thought in the past seventy-five years, and Tahiti was their heart. The island's discoverer, Captain Samuel Wallis, had arrived in H.M.S. *Dolphin* in 1767 in hopes of finding the great land mass that many believed must lie thereabouts to give the earth stability. The revolution in thought that this disappointingly small island produced could hardly have been greater had the predictions of the learned been confirmed. Voyagers' accounts—Bougainville arrived in 1768 and Captain Cook in 1769 and 1773—found a receptive audience in generations nurtured on the natural rights philosophy. It had always been difficult to find historical confirmation of the notion of a state of nature, which to John Locke had been little more than a logical necessity, but with the discovery of Tahiti the noble savage became believable. The historians of Eden had somewhere gone astray: here where bread and milk grew on trees were the true children of a benevolent nature, living in peace and freedom by the exercise of the natural reason with which every man was endowed.

Efforts had been made to keep Wallis' discovery secret but the memories of his ship's company were too vivid to be concealed, and all the world soon knew what delights a nail or two would buy there. Perhaps some had learned by word of mouth that his men were obliged to sleep on the deck from having bartered away their hammock nails and were pulling nails from the ship's timbers before their depredations were discovered.

Unfortunately, the good news from the Pacific had coincided with a new manifestation of the Anglo-Saxon folkway, the evangelical revival. English Baptists and Methodists read the published voyages of the explorers and were not amused. In 1787, bearing commissions from the London Missionary Society, they had brought the apple to Tahiti, mastering as best they could a language that "abounds with vowels," as one complained, and a moral code, another noted, that abounded with "painful conflicts for spiritual self-denying missionaries." They were very nearly the first observers of a society untouched by civilization. They made themselves the last.[1]

Of late years a lively controversy had developed over the extent of their success. Glowing reports had been published, most notably the English missionary William Ellis' *Polynesian Researches* (1829) and the New York minister, Pacific missionary, and Navy chaplain Charles S. Stewart's volumes of travels of 1828 and 1831. Neither the Russian explorer Otto von Kotzebue nor the English captain Frederick William Beechey had been impressed and had sharply disputed their claims. "To pray and to obey," Kotzebue had remarked, "are the only commands laid upon an oppressed people who submissively bow to the yoke, and even suffer themselves to be driven to prayers by the cudgel!" The criticism had occasioned some fulminations on both sides of the Atlantic, for the missionary saga itself had widespread romantic appeal. "The Missionaries!" sighed William Reynolds in a letter home, "the Christians leaving their homes, to wean the Savage from his Idol Gods & from his human sacrifice & feasts." Aware that this was "a subject of earnest inquiry," the explorers were determined "to contemplate without prejudice." [2]

The landscape of Matavai Bay, with the groves of breadfruit and coconut and orange trees stretching out along the shore in either direction and the high irregular volcanic peaks rising to crown the island, captivated everyone except Wilkes, who thought it lacking in tidiness. "After looking at so many of those low treacherous coral reefs," Couthouy found the appearance of "high solid looking land . . . truly refreshing." Canoes came out in swarms with offerings of fruit and eggs, and as soon as the anchor was down, several of the principal chiefs came aboard to extend a formal welcome and collect the officers' linen for their wives to wash. Yeoman Ezra Green took one look at the handsome Tahitians and went below to write in his journal that here were "desidedly the most interesting people on the globe." In the evening, lights gleamed here and there among the trees and a gentle land breeze wafted the island's own welcome to the explorers—the perfume of the orange groves.

Wilkes briskly took matters in hand, astonishing and antagonizing the officers by ordering all to be aboard "their respective ships," a favorite phrase of his, by sunset. He likewise required all to attend the missionary church on Saturday, the missionary Sabbath,* and officers and men, as Ezra Green described it, formed "in Collum upon the beach, surrounded by hundreds of

---

* Saturday was the Pacific Sabbath because the original missionary contingent, out of neglect or more probably ignorance, had not adjusted their timepieces to antipodal time.

Natives," and marched to the bamboo church to hear a sermon preached by old Charles Wilson, the converted baker's apprentice who had come out in the *Duff*. A hospital was set up on Point Venus, where Cook had made his observations of the transit of Venus, in one of the huts erected for Captain William Bligh of the *Bounty* in 1768. Another nearby was taken over for the observatory.

A crowd quickly gathered about the little station, swelling daily as the curious came from distant parts of the island to sell pigs and fruit—for money now, not baubles, the explorers noted. A happier people they had never seen. Lieutenant Henry Eld was astonished "to see that the whole time we were there . . . although these people were Eating drinking and sleeping together never such a thing was seen or heard as a quarrel among them, although they were all sorts mixed together of Every . . . rank & disposition still Every thing was harmony & playfullness & good humour. What an example these people set to us who pretend to call ourselves civilised." Purser Speiden of the *Peacock*, worthy and pious like his captain, taught the girls hymns not yet learned from the missionaries, and the crews the work songs that sailors sang. They could be heard along the beach until two or three in the morning, when some would swim out to the ships and beg to be taken aboard. They were invariably refused, the accounts say.

The missionaries had banned native songs and dances, but the girls' "love for their own" was irresistible, Eld found, and one night on the beach in the moonlight about twenty of them performed a peculiar and most indecent dance. In rhythm to what Eld described as "a kind of grunt set to music," they threw their arms in all directions with fingers extended, "all the while keeping perfect time & Making the same Noise simultaneously." Gradually the sound swelled until they seemed "perfectly frantic & Excited. . . . Every blood vessel appears to be ready to burst & you can see the red in their faces showing thro the Copper." Suddenly, one springs into the center of the ring "& commences dancing & Making all the grimaces that can be conceived accompanied with the most lascivious Motions of the body, the Music still increasing & perhaps two or three of them get up in this way, it now appears to be at its highest pitch & gradually begins to grow less & less for some time when they suddenly kick up their heels above their heads & fall heavily to the ground which is the signal that they have finished." * This time they danced till daylight, then

* When word had reached Wallis' ship that every man on board might have one of the "Young Girls" with the blessings of the chiefs, "Even the sick which had been on the Doctors list for some weeks before," observed the sailing master, "now declard they would be happy if they were permitted to go ashore, at same time said a Young Girl would make an Exelent Nurse, and they

crawled into the bushes to sleep. Even so, they were collected around the tents again at eight o'clock.

Best qualified to balance the old culture against the new were the scientists who joined the party that George Emmons led across the top of the island. Carrying a back-breaking load of equipment, they were to ascend and determine the height of Orofena, the "prodigious high mountain," as Cook had called it, lying near the island's center, pausing along the way to sketch atmospheric phenomena, determine the temperature of springs and the air at various heights in both sun and shade, to take meridian altitudes for longitude, and half-hourly readings from the sympiesometer, the sensitive barometer for determining altitude. From Paparno on the northeast coast they proceeded along the Papenoo River, followed by a troop of boys and young women with white blossoms in their hair. Where the river was too deep to ford, the girls simply stripped off their missionary garments and struck out as boldly as the men, "laughing and shouting to each other in high glee," Couthouy recorded in delight, "their garlanded heads and wild mirth" recalling pictures "by some of the old masters, of water nymphs or troops of joyous baccinale. It all seemed perfectly natural too." Their ancient guide took them over the site where twenty-four years before he and the other Christian converts had slaughtered the "idolators," driving many over a high precipice and crushing the heads of the rest, and his "expression of furious satisfaction" as he relived the battle gave Couthouy the distinct impression that he thought the old days, "when they could cut one another's throats or beat out their brains, and get drunk as often as they pleased—as far preferable to their present peaceable life."

Emerging on the southeast coast on the fifth day, they breakfasted on a baked pig with "a splendid scarlet hibiscus stuck in each ear and surrounded by a double rampart of Taro and bread fruit," then joined the crowds headed for the midweek lecture. Neatly turned out in calico frocks and large bonnets and making up three-quarters of the congregation, the women sang with fervor and "considerable taste in a minor key," Couthouy noted. Struck by their "most exemplary" deportment, he was reflecting on how much the worthy missionaries had accomplished in their brief tenure when on gaining the out of doors these same women flocked about to evince by age-old gestures their availability, and "One most respectable woman," he noted in astonishment, "actually offered her two daughters as an inducement for us to visit her house."

---

were Certain of recovering faster under a Young Girls care nor all the Doctor would do for them." Bligh laid the mutiny on the *Bounty* in part to the attractions of these "Young Girls."

A FATHOM OF TAPA

Accompanied by "a joyous laughing troop" of girls and boys, they sauntered toward Papeete and "as the train appeared and disappeared at intervals, through the dense foliage of Guyavas & orange trees that overlooked the road," Couthouy felt that "the whole scene had an arcadian aspect that would have filled the soul of a painter or poet with delight." It was a pleasant jaunt along the bowered "Broom Road" that Herman Melville was to make famous, the surf booming against the reef, the explorers helping themselves to coconuts along the way. Nearing Papeete, they found the people "less civil, though more civilized," demanding a price "for the least little service or thing," and often dressed in cast-off seamen's clothes.

In the town a few days later Couthouy met several of the royal family (though not Queen Pomare, who, far gone with child, was decently in confinement) the missionaries had foisted upon Tahiti in place of the traditional chiefs. The heir to the throne, a barefoot princess of seventeen, begged him to play the jewsharp and in turn sang God Save the Queen in Tahitian while he hummed a bass. He also met the two leaders of the missionary contingent, Charles Wilson and John Muggridge Orsmond (1784–1856), with whom he and Pickering had some unexpectedly frank conversations. They found both men, and particularly Orsmond, who had been at pains to inform himself on Tahitian ethnology, pessimistic, freely confessing that their success had been much exaggerated. Thus primed, Couthouy wrote into his journal a little essay on the one-sided struggle between "natural" man and the Spirit of the Age.

The missionaries had totally stamped out human sacrifice and idol worship and inculcated a regard for private property (the squadron lost nothing by theft here), and these were "great points." They also made much of having eliminated that strange religious institution the *arioi*. Touring the coastal villages by canoe, the greatly respected members of this society had provided Tahitians with theater and church, satire and worship. But their practice of killing the infants born of their exhibitions had horrified the missionaries as much as the exhibitions' licentiousness, though it had made sense of a kind to Thomas Malthus. Couthouy shared the missionaries' horror of infanticide, but he thought that its elimination brought them little credit in view of the "unbridled licentiousness" still everywhere to be observed and the substitution of abortion. Husbands hospitably offered their wives to strangers and women offered themselves, and, Couthouy observed, "there is no one to 'cast the first stone.'" To his "certain knowledge," the royal family itself was no exception, and the throng of soliciting women about the station on Point Venus—within sight of the Reverend Wilson's windows—left none of the explorers with any

"An arcadian aspect." The Broom Road, Tahiti, by
Alfred T. Agate. (*Narrative*, 2: facing p. 32. Western
Americana Collection, Yale University Library.)

A FATHOM OF TAPA

doubts on his head. The most seasoned among them had never seen anything like it. "And still you hear the Missionaries preaching up the great change they have wrought in their morals?" asked the *Vincennes'* armourer sarcastically. "If there is any change it certainly must be for the worse."

Couthouy detailed the change: Sabbath observance for the native religious holidays, obscenity ("carried to an extent in word & gesture, of which those who have never witnessed it can form no conception") for profanity, clothes (calico bags and flapping straw bonnets that gave the women "exactly the air of Irish washerwomen") for nakedness. Silas Holmes, as might be expected, sought to apply the devil's workshop rule, but without much success, for how, he asked himself, could a people blessed with such natural abundance be expected to keep themselves busy? and he suspected that the licentiousness had something to do with the rigorousness of the imported morality which, by prohibiting dancing and all songs except hymns and God Save the Queen, caused the natives to regard the missionaries with about "as much affection as a prisoner may feel for the turnkey." Having read his Ellis and Stewart, William Reynolds expected to find these people "well advanced in civiliza-tion—to see the mechanical arts flourishing . . . to look upon a busy population tilling the earth, & having the regularity & system of an enlightened community . . . & conducting themselves like a sober, decent & religious people." Mechanical Arts, Diligence, Morality: the Trinity of Jacksonian America. Reynolds was staggered by the reality. Nothing was to be seen of mechanical arts, natural abundance decreed indolence, and as for morality, "here," he concluded primly, "I must draw the veil." Confronted thus, he very nearly broke free. "Who can judge one nation by another?" he asked.

Though even Wilkes thought the missionaries' practice of maintaining segregated schools and services of worship for their own offspring a self-defeat-ing measure that smacked of hypocrisy, it would not have occurred to him to venture upon such treacherous waters as those, and at least two in the squadron would have recoiled in outrage. Sanctimonious John W. W. Dyes, observing that liquor was to be had in plenty at a dollar a bottle, hastily rounded up the *Vincennes'* few temperance men for a renewal of vows. And James Dwight Dana, who had undergone a strenuous and emotionally debilitating bout of religious conversion shortly before the squadron sailed, and who had written Asa Gray in horror that "No people on the globe stand more in need of the renovating principles of the Bible" than the Fuegians, was left speechless by the Tahitians. Like the missionaries whose fortitude he greatly admired, he blamed the seamen, or more precisely the "immoral influence" of the foreign seamen. "I might tell you many things," he wrote his brother in Utica, "which would lead you in tears to prayer to God for them," but could not bring himself to do so. Devout in a less frantic way, Captain Hudson thought the missionaries were doing a wonderful job.

On September 20, anxious to make Sydney in time for the Antarctic summer, Wilkes ordered the *Porpoise* back to the Tuamotus to complete the survey of Kruzenstern's Island. From there she was to rendezvous with the rest of the squadron at Rose Island in the Navigator Group. The time had come to round up deserters. It was almost a ritual now. When two of the *Peacock*'s men had deserted at Tetiaroa, Emmons had found himself unable "to credit common sense or forethought to men that would leave a comfortable ship where little duty is required of them & every indulgence that could be reasonably asked granted them, in exchange for a residence of any duration upon one of these Islands." At Tahiti the problem assumed an entirely different magnitude. To insure prompt delivery, Wilkes offered an unheard-of one hundred and fifty dollars for the capture of men who, desperate at the prospect of leaving this happy land, made off in the ship's dinghy. A party of natives tracked one group all night and brought them to bay atop a high ridge in full view of the ship. The mode of their return might have been thought punishment enough, for they were carried like so many pigs, dangling by hands and feet from long poles, but Wilkes required each man to place thirty dollars in the hands of his captor before (no time for court martial) the cats fell thirty-six times upon his back. To prevent similar annoyances in the future, Wilkes addressed a letter of advice to Queen Pomare, urging "the absolute necessity" of providing police and a lock-up. As this was soon done—and in time for the "Calabooza Beretanee," a mile out of town on the Broom Road, to receive its most famous prisoner, Herman Melville—the Expedition had the honor, for what it was worth, of helping civilize Tahiti.

After presenting a "Musical box" to the two delighted young princesses, outrageously got up in western finery for the occasion, Wilkes took the *Vincennes* over to nearby Eimeo (Moorea) on the morning of the twenty-fifth. There, as though to assure that memories of these islands should never wither nor their image tarnish in the years for reminiscence that lay ahead, two girls came down to the beach and began the low provocative humming that was the invariable prelude to one of their dances. Leaning over the bulwarks, Couthouy watched in fascination.

When repairs to the schooner's mainmast and keelson were completed, many a seaman, adjusting his buttons or wiping illicit gin from his lips, returned on board with a blessing for this isle and, it may be, a curse for the

United States Exploring Expedition. When the *Peacock* and *Flying Fish* stood to sea at early daylight on October 10, it was with the discovery that two more men had deserted during the night. Hundreds of canoes followed for a time in the ships' wake. Eld was sure there was not a "single soul" in the squadron who did not leave "this simple & kind hearted people" with regret. For in spite of faults that would not be tolerated in Rhode Island, Surgeon Holmes observed that they "were always good natured, cheerful, gay, & happy, . . . & our visits always seemed to please." [3]

7 Samoa

Here comes a candle to light you to bed,
Here comes a chopper to chop off your head.

Tommy Thumb's Pretty Song Book

The *Vincennes*, laden with fruits and pigs sent by Queen Pomare as a present to the ship's company, stood to the west before a steady breeze. It was Cook's course of 1769, past Sir Charles Saunders' Island (Tupa-a-manu), Huahine, Tahaa, Borabora, Maupiti, and Motu-iti. On the last day of September 1839, she made Bellingshausen, an uninhabited atoll at the western extremity of the Society Group, where Couthouy and Pickering got ashore in the first boats for about four hours, while Wilkes conducted his magnetic experiments and collected birds, which seemed as tame as those on Honden.

A week later they made Rose, easternmost of the Navigator Islands, now coming to be known by the native name, Samoa, where the *Porpoise* was standing off and on, having arrived the day before from Kruzenstern's and Lazaroff (Suvarov), southernmost of the Northern Cook Group, where Surgeon Guillou loosed a pullet and cock and planted beans for the benefit of future voyagers.

In company once more, next day they made the high Manua Islands a few miles to the northwest, which Jacob Roggeveen had discovered in 1722 on the same voyage on which he discovered Easter, Rose, and other of the major Samoan Islands. Natives came out now in large canoes, gunwales ornamented with white shells (of the *ovula oviformis*, Couthouy promptly noted) that glistened in the brilliant sunshine. A flying survey of the two islands was begun immediately and the next day Couthouy, Pickering, Drayton, and Brackenridge, the last just recovered from the bout of sickness that had laid him low in

Tahiti, went ashore on the larger island, Tau. They were promptly surrounded by islanders who set up a clamor for "Baca" and were happy to accept one fishhook for a fowl, a half dozen coconuts or a bunch of bananas. But the women were less pretty than the Tahitians, and seemingly less licentious. Mistrusting first impressions, some of the officers tested this one with tempting presents, pointing out that no missionaries were within sight or hearing. One of the girls, "pointing upward," Holmes noted approvingly, "replied with great solemnity, 'Mittinay there.' " The story, and perhaps it was no more than that, spread rapidly through the squadron, the journalizers professing strong approbation of this expression of simple wisdom. Wilkes, noting primly that these temptations were "unauthorized," found the girl's response "a just and severe rebuke."

When on the tenth both vessels raised the rugged green island of Tutuila, William Reynolds was so captivated he chose to sleep on a "soft plank" on the spar deck that he might wake to the sight of it. While the *Vincennes* anchored in the deep and narrow harbor of Pago Pago, the *Porpoise* stood on to Savai'i, westernmost and largest of the group, for, to speed their examination of these islands, Wilkes divided the squadron, reserving Tutuila for the *Vincennes* and assigning Upolu to the *Peacock* and *Flying Fish*.

They remained in the islands a month, sounding, surveying, collecting, refreshing, exploring in every direction. While the brig surveyed Savai'i, Pickering examined its natural productions. Brackenridge suffered a relapse, probably brought on from attempting to keep pace with the seemingly inexhaustible Couthouy, who went striding about Tutuila as he had about Tahiti—to climb the highest peak and later, with Dana and Surgeon Whittle, to cross Upolu in both directions, stopping on the way to sound from atop a couple of floating logs a lake said to be inhabited by eels the size of coconut trees. From an English resident of Upolu, Couthouy learned that the *Astrolabe* of Captain Dumont d'Urville's expedition had called here about a year before, and Couthouy reported in his journal, doubtless with ulterior motives, that the French had made "immense collections in the way of natural history and curiosities" and "actually sent off several boat loads of shells & corals from the reefs, and nearly as many plants, and that the ship's berth deck was a complete museum."

Apart from a rumor at Rio, this was the squadron's first news of the three other national expeditions that were abroad in these years. In addition to the French voyage of the *Astrolabe* and *Zélée*, England in 1836 had sent Commander Edward Belcher (1799–1877) to the Pacific in the *Sulphur* to conduct hydrographic and magnetic and, in a small way, botanical surveys on the western coasts of North and South America and the islands, and would soon dispatch another, under Captain James C. Ross (1800–1877) in the *Erebus* and *Terror* to the Antarctic.

When the *Peacock* and *Flying Fish* arrived on October 18 Peale promptly disappeared into the interior, where he set a pace that soon collapsed the fragile Rich. On one of these excursions he learned from a missionary that the natives practiced circumcision, which he took to be "a pretty strong proof of Asiatic origin." On another he traversed the island from north to south, climbing an extinct volcano, measuring waterfalls and banyan trees, and collecting birds.

One of the more sweeping excursions was made by William Reynolds and Lieutenant Underwood, who surveyed the shoreline of Tutuila in two of the ship's boats. Reynolds cut quite a figure in his own eyes—barefoot, with a large floppy white hat, "Sailor's trowsers," an old shirt, and a knife belted at the waist. "I adopted my habits to the climate & the people," he explained, "& I was a great favorite wherever we went!" Putting in for the night round the island's south point, he strolled along holding the hands of two pretty girls of no more than fifteen, one the chief's daughter and "Extremely handsome," and could not but notice that as they proceeded through the settlement "my two sweethearts were the Envy of the Village." Such conditions were perhaps not the most conducive to the cool objectivity expected of scientific explorers, but Reynolds kept his eyes open.

Not far from Massacre Bay, where several of La Pérouse's men had been slaughtered in 1787, they reached one of the "big houses," kept clean by the villagers and provided with sleeping mats for travelers and the single people of the village. Reynolds awoke in the early light to find the house full of sleepers and his own nearest neighbors "two or three young girls, who were dozing away, in all the confidence of simple innocence," and lay back to reflect on "the wide difference between them & my own race." On rising, he found some momentary awkwardness about making his toilet "in the midst of bright Eyes & pretty faces," but summoned "sufficient brass to proceed; & Why not?" Then came the questions. Why "*two* shirts, *two* trowsers, a waistcoat, stockings & shoes, & *a hat*"? a procession of curious villagers wanted to know. Why "a Kerchief for the throat & one for the pocket, and a toothpick & penknife, and a *toothbrush* and towels"? Why knives and forks, salt and pepper, butter and mustard? People were "very foolish to have so much trouble" at meal time. All wanted to peer through the spyglass at the neighboring village and hear the ticking of the watches. They were astonished that the visitors did not open their meals with prayer and could not understand, either, Reynolds noted, why "We laughed, danced & sang; the Missionaries were grave at all times" and he and Underwood left them, as he thought, "Wavering in their Minds."

At a big house in a "heathen" district farther along the coast, the villagers staged a dance for their benefit. It lasted all night in the glare of torchlight and was "highly immodest & indecent," Reynolds recorded, "it might safely be called wanton & lascivious." But at the end of six days of as pleasant survey duty as he was ever likely to have, he found his view of the world fast broadening. On the Samoan institution of the "Big House" he could now reflect, "No one need make any provision for his journey" in clothing, food, or money. "Such is the custom of a people who never had the rule inculcated by *their* religious creed. . . . Yet such Charity . . . is extended to the meanest being, by those whom *we* call *Savages!*"

It is not recorded that Wilkes held a maiden's hand, or was subjected to the ribald ridicule the Tahitians directed at Cook for not taking a mistress—no doubt the natives were now more accustomed to such idiosyncrasy in their guests. He sought rather to impress upon these people that a presence was among them, as he set about reordering island affairs in this particular or that, moving with easy gravity from the scientific to the judicial to the diplomatic. At times, though, the Samoans could be terribly obtuse and then exasperation showed a little. The capture by a party of officers of a native accused of murdering a New Bedford sailor a year before, early occupied his attention; relinquishing observatory affairs to Carr, with Hudson's assistance he assembled the principal chiefs as a court of justice in Apia's big house—officers and missionaries on chairs, chiefs and spectators crosslegged on mats, a missionary interpreting. Even though "the customs of civilized people were explained to them, the Mosaic law . . . expounded," prosecutor Hudson's demand that the chiefs put the man to death gave rise to "much argument," Reynolds noted with unconscious irony. The chiefs pleaded on behalf of the prisoner (who, standing in the center of the circle, freely confessed to having killed the man for his clothes) that he was a "heathen" and "in darkness," and that they themselves, who had just emerged from darkness, "should not be subjected to the operation of laws destined for a much more elevated state of society." They urged Hudson "to remember that the gospel which they had just embraced, taught them & him alike, to be merciful." Of course, now that they had been made aware of "what was right they were willing to establish such a law in such cases & bind themselves to adhere to it hereafter." Holmes thought their plea displayed "much ingenuity." Siding with the chiefs, Wilkes handed down the decision: the prisoner would be exiled to an uninhabited island. He was accordingly returned to the *Peacock,* with a crowd of weeping natives in train, and his wife loud in lamentation.

The scientists returned with their bag of words and worms and flowers. On November 10 the *Porpoise* and *Flying Fish* came in from Pago Pago, deserters were rounded up and flogged, and early in the afternoon the squadron got under weigh, having surveyed all the larger islands of the group and gathered large collections.

This second prolonged exposure to island life brought further reflections on the contact of cultures. It is impossible to say to what extent the ranks of the doubters were increased, but certainly the romantic Reynolds could be reckoned among them. On crossing Upolu to the south, he and Emmons had met many natives in the mountains who were on their way to see the ships at Apia, and "I could not help thinking," he recalled, "how much better it would be to let them go on their own old way: but No, No! We must have all the world like us, if we can!" Admittedly the white man oftentimes came with the best intentions, but even with "pity & commiseration for the benighted savage," he brought "a black train of consequences." Still, increasing contact was inevitable, and with it would come "difficulties & evils of all kinds: discord, war, domestic strife," until "the original nature of the people will have left them forever."

As for that most pervasive medium of change, the missionary, the doubt planted at Tahiti came to flower in Samoa. One of the missionaries who preached on board the *Vincennes* was the celebrated John Williams, the English ironmonger's apprentice who had been born again in adolescence. Residing now at Apia, where construction of another of his train of luxurious island residences was bringing large numbers under his influence, for many years he had been stamping out idleness and lesser sins from Tahiti to Samoa, teaching the natives to be happy, for the Lord's sake, in the work he made for them, fighting Catholic and Polynesian heathenism with an ardor born of faith in God and Trade, distributing Mother Hubbards and coal-scuttle bonnets, torturing natives who tatooed themselves, and of late awing them with magic lanterns, electrical shock devices, and other gadgets of civilization. Reynolds was astounded by the great man's sermon: "such a gross, absurd tissue of Nonsense, ignorance & fanaticism . . . I never listened to." The islands seemed not to render the ignorant wiser or less fanatical but to work a less desirable change, for even those who came with the best intentions, he observed, "a little While, & they sink the Missionary, in the Merchant, the preacher in the Magistrate." These were novel thoughts, and he was rather apologetic about entertaining them. But it is clear that his disillusionment went beyond the conduct of these simple bigots to embrace the wisdom of contact with island cultures in any form.

But if the Samoan culture was doomed, the explorers nevertheless had enjoyed the magnificent opportunity of observing it before the ravages were complete. In the heathen districts the custom of tatooing the buttocks persisted, and the colorful public ceremonies of rupturing the hymen of intended brides just previous to marriage, and dances too lascivious to describe. Not a hand in the squadron but was gratified at the refreshments the islands offered—the fresh meat and water, fruits and girls—and fond memories of the good things of Samoa were to warm them through many an Antarctic night.

Unfortunately, the visit had done nothing to improve domestic relations in the squadron. Wilkes had conceived a violent dislike for the industrious Couthouy, and the stay at Apia brought their relationship to a boil. Perhaps the matter of the stinking corals continued to rankle with the commander, or perhaps he resented the presence in the squadron of another ship captain. It was only while in Samoa that Wilkes found time to read the journals that most of the officers and scientists had kept more or less regularly since leaving Norfolk, and he proved to be remarkably sensitive to the relatively mild criticisms they dared record in them. His wrath fell officially upon the conchologist, whose remarks on the awkward situation regarding collections he found particularly offensive. In the great cabin of the *Vincennes* and in the presence of Hudson, Dana, Carr, and Surgeon Gilchrist, Wilkes accused him of fomenting discord. Couthouy coolly stood his ground, reiterating his criticisms of the conduct of the scientific affairs of the Expedition. Incensed, Wilkes hotly asserted that he had afforded every facility to the scientists consistent, as he revealingly expressed it, with his "other and paramount duties in the Expedition," and threatened to detach the conchologist if he persisted in his mistaken course.

And Dana, even before the frustrating and humiliating experience in the Tuamotus of having to cool his heels aboard ship while the officers set about their appointed tasks, had written Asa Gray from Valparaiso to congratulate him on his decision to remain at home and to convey Couthouy's congratulations to the scientists left behind on their "narrow escape from Naval servitude." Though hard pressed with his work in geology and the crustacea, Dana did what he could in meteorology, too, on the assumption that free exchange of information and ideas was to be the rule for this expedition. Perceiving that the data gathered by each of the ships on the storm that held them under Noir Island during those never-to-be-forgotten days and nights and struck the *Vincennes* at Nassau Bay and the brig at Good Success, provided a unique opportunity to trace a storm's path, at Callao he had gone over to collect the data from the *Vincennes'* log, informing Wilkes that he wished to compare the facts with Redfield's theory. Instead of encouraging this effort to further the expedition's scientific achievement, Wilkes refused permission, adding that he had the subject in mind himself and that it was anyway not an appropriate one for civilians. After that rebuff the astonished Dana resolved in the future "not to excite his jealousies . . . by *interfering* in what he considered his department."

The scientists also continued to chafe under the secrecy that kept them in the dark regarding sailing dates and destinations and prevented their communicating their discoveries to colleagues at home. But they got on well with one another, rather better in fact since Peale, whose conduct in the organization of the corps had occasioned some resentment, had seemingly lost all influence with Wilkes. The mutual dislike that developed at the Río Negro had since been exacerbated when Wilkes, discovering that Peale possessed a copy of the published congressional document containing the sailing instructions issued to Commodore Jones, borrowed it, then refused to return it on the ground that Peale's possession violated the rule of secrecy.

But the distaste in which the scientists had come to hold their commander was as nothing compared to the officers' feelings. Whatever jealousies and bickerings had existed among them, or, what the projectors of this enterprise had most dreaded, between them and the scientific corps, rapidly dissolved on the Pacific cruise. Wilkes' conduct in one incident after another created a bond of unity that could hardly have existed under a more popular commander. At some point on the cruise he conceived an especial dislike for Lieutenant Robert F. Pinkney, now commanding the *Flying Fish*, and in addressing him habitually placed sarcastic emphasis on "*Mister* Pinkney." While under way one night in August, Wilkes hailed him with orders to heave-to. Unable to hear in the wind, Pinkney brought the schooner alongside. Wilkes repeated the order and Pinkney, knowing that to heave-to in this position would result in collision, waited for the opportunity to comply. Wilkes shouted a third time, "Why dont you heave to Sir, heave to immediately." Pinkney did so and the schooner shot up into the wind across the *Vincennes'* bows, just clearing the latter's flying jib boom, and clearing it, not through the prompt action of Wilkes, who did not act at all, it was noted, but of Lieutenant Underwood in stopping the way of the *Vincennes.* Bustling forward and stamping the deck, Wilkes sang out through the trumpet,

"What do you mean, what do you mean by such conduct as this. I never saw the like of it in my life."

"I hove to in obedience to your orders," replied Pinkney.

"God damn it Sir," the commander shouted, fairly dancing in his fury, "I never ordered you to heave to under my bows." Midshipman Clark heard this much on coming out of the schooner's hatchway before Wilkes caught sight of him and ordered him back below for being out of uniform.[1]

One incident at Samoa had particularly offended the officers. At Wilkes' orders, Pickering and Passed Midshipman William L. Maury were landed on Savai'i, where for a period of ten days Pickering was to survey the natural history of the island and Maury, unassisted, was to take hourly readings around the clock from the tide staves placed a half mile off shore. Inevitably, some of the nighttime hours on his chart were left blank. Foreseeing the result, Pickering, who was a physician, furnished him with a letter testifying that the duty was physically impossible of performance in full. But to no avail. Wilkes saw that orders had not been obeyed, and Maury received a written censure accusing him of gross neglect of duty and "consulting his own ease."

Wilkes consulted no one's ease, least of all his own. Even those who admired him least readily testified to his astonishing industry. He was everywhere, and everywhere busy. When the man rested was a mystery. Surgeon Fox, who kept an eye on all matters affecting health, concluded that Wilkes set aside no more than five hours for sleep and at times "the number of hours spent without sleep was extraordinary." Fox could not know how many were spent pondering the "cabals" and musing on "mutiny" as one officer after another turned against him. In view of the Expedition's turbulent past, a certain wariness was indicated, was indeed to be commended, but Wilkes' suspiciousness surpassed any justifications to be found there. Trifles assumed significance as they confirmed one or another in the maelstrom of suspicions, and then came the headaches that drove him to his berth. Anger, anxiety, and decisions, decisions.

Underwood (a particular target), Reynolds, Blunt, Alden, Sinclair, North, May, the surgeons—though all these and more felt the lash of his tongue and remembered it, Wilkes might yet have elicited their respect had he displayed those abilities most esteemed in the profession. But in these as in leadership he was no James Cook. (Though perhaps he permitted himself the comparison: the great navigator was Wilkes' present age at the time of his first voyage; both were lieutenants, and the elaborateness of the present enterprise might compensate for whatever edge, if any, Cook might have held in genius.) As a seaman he left a great deal to be desired, and his officers were prompt to observe the lack. Moreover, in time of crisis he repeatedly showed himself indecisive, asking the opinions of all and sundry while disaster brushed near. On the August night when the *Porpoise* collided with the *Vincennes* the officers again observed this strange behavior. Flurried and almost incoherent, Wilkes appeared hurriedly on deck and began exclaiming excitedly, "My God! What is the matter? How is this? What shall we do?" and gave the irrelevant order to call all hands. In the midst of the performance one of the officers recited the necessary commands and the vessels separated.

The *Peacock* and *Vincennes* in the harbor of
Pago-Pago, Samoa, from sketch by Charles Wilkes.
(*Narrative*, 2: p. 75, Western Americana Collection,
Yale University Library.)

If there were recriminations on that occasion, they have been lost. More typical was the time when in attempting to beat out of Pago Pago's narrow harbor the *Vincennes* twice missed stays and was drifting perilously near the surf that was breaking on the bold and rocky shore. Learning that they had got sternway, Wilkes withdrew to the weather gangway, while the officers, their fate in the hands of the pilot now, narrowly eyed the rocks below. After an agonizing time the ship began to claw off, and they turned to see Wilkes leaning on the booms with his face in his hands. It was the closest of escapes and, once clear, Wilkes refused to heave-to to discharge the pilot, despite his protests, until well at sea. When the pilot finally did gain his boat, he turned and called up with cool insolence, "You may fill away now, Sir! fill away, as soon as you like."

"Captain W could have eaten him," Reynolds observed. And Captain W did suggest to commander Ringgold that he "flog the Pilot Foxhall, with a dozen of the Cats, if he should ever come aboard the Porpoise."

One sees him then, standing in the wind as the *Vincennes* rides the long Pacific swells, angrily goddamming Mister Pinkney, or Mister Sinclair, or in the great cabin passing derogatory judgment on James Cook, or King, or Duperrey, or disputing with Surgeon Gilchrist the nature of the disease that carried off a corporal of marines, or again, wandering uninvited and unwelcome into the wardroom, the commons of the lieutenants, to track down and mash under thumb the spiders that inhabited the pantry. One has the impression of a man at bay, a man of acquirements but little beyond the ordinary who yet bears an extraordinary responsibility in commanding, as he never tired of explaining, the First Great National Exploring Expedition. He had gained some reputation as a scientist in a Navy that knew nothing of science beyond the dread of it and now found himself in command of a scientific corps of distinction. In the midst of one of his tirades William Reynolds watched Hudson turning to go below and later wrote home that "the Nature of the man has become changed—he is as one possessed by a demon." And so he was.

Thus the ships sailed west, every man aboard save the informing "fo'c'sle rats" roundly cursing a captain aspiring to be the republican Cook but more and more displaying the less endearing qualities of Bligh. They passed Manono, Apolima, Savai'i, westward until Wallis Island came in sight on November 12. Here they paused for a survey. In the midst of these operations their Samoan prisoner was brought up to the gangway. Respectably dressed in a suit of clothes now, he shook hands cordially with his guards and was put into a canoe alongside to become a slave to the chief of Wallis, a "*not uninhabited* Island," Emmons rather insolently noted. For another week they ran in company and out as pleasant weather gave way to a gale that damaged the *Peacock*'s rigging. Beyond the two high Horne Islands they swung onto a southwesterly course for Matthew's Rock, an isolated volcano, sometimes active, that towered almost twelve hundred feet above the sea, which the *Vincennes* sent a boat to examine.

On November 29 high land was discovered from the masthead of the *Peacock*. By eight in the evening they made out a glow which they took to be the Port Jackson light. The entrance to the harbor was difficult, as some of the officers well knew. To a vessel approaching from the east only a high palisade was visible. Closer in a niche appeared and the perpendicular face divided. Those well acquainted with the channel ran straight into the niche about two shiplengths, then turned on the heel to port, and in two or three lengths more the great harbor opened up. The wind here could be tricky, and if you failed to turn quickly enough you were on the rocks. The explorers were running in darkness, yet the *Vincennes* stood boldly in as the wind came in puffs out of the ravines on either hand. There was consternation aboard the *Peacock* as she followed the *Vincennes'* blue lights, for none knew that Wilkes had as quartermaster a one-time Sydney trader.* At ten-thirty they were anchored among the shipping abreast of Sydney, New South Wales.[2]

* In later describing this bold maneuver in his narrative of the Expedition, Wilkes neglected to mention the presence of the quartermaster, an oversight William Reynolds promptly detected.

8 Sydney

On the whole it would appear to be for the best that the
great majority of human beings should go on living in the
place in which they were born. . . .

T. S. Eliot, "Notes Towards the Definition of Culture"

Even the lookouts in the semaphore station at the harbor's
mouth had failed to detect their passage, and the explorers delighted in the
surprise and chagrin of official Sydney next morning at sight of the Yankee flag
flying from two naval vessels riding quietly at anchor. The newspapers were
full of jokes at the expense of the authorities, which the Americans found
"highly flattering" to the "Nautical Skill & daring" of the squadron. But no
one took offense, not even at Wilkes' not very humble apology to the
governor. The *Porpoise* and *Flying Fish* anchored later in the morning and in
the afternoon the *Camden*, John Williams' missionary brig which they had
earlier towed out of Apia harbor.

The *Camden* brought tragic news. At Erromanga in the New Hebrides,
where she called to deposit native teachers, the islanders attacked without
warning, killing Williams and another and dragging their bodies into the
bush—for a feast, it was said. The explorers heard the story from one of the
survivors who preached on board the *Vincennes*, and Lieutenant Emmons
found in it only "another proof to thousands already recorded of the
treacherousness of these barbarians." They were forewarned.

Arrangements were promptly made for the use of Fort Macquarie
overlooking the harbor as an observatory station, and overhauling of the
vessels began next day. Replacements were ordered for the sprung masts of the
schooner, and all the vessels were caulked and painted. Provisions were loaded
from the stores deposited by the *Relief*, which had sailed for home some ten

143

days earlier after an uneventful cruise, her officers apprehensive at the prospect of rounding the Horn with her crew of invalids. As a matter of fact, the *Relief* made the passage from Sydney to Cape Horn in the very good time of forty-one days.

Weary of the steady island diet of fresh pork, their heads full of "Visions of Beef Steaks" and well filled decanters, the explorers were pleasantly surprised at the amenities the little city afforded (including for Dana a flourishing Missionary Society) and delighted by the stream of invitations to dinners and dances and "Pic-nics." Instead of a "den of abominations, tenanted exclusively by . . . the offscouring of the earth," as the fastidious Surgeon Holmes put it, they discovered a "well built and very flourishing colony" with a "refinement and elegance" scarcely to be expected in a settlement only five decades old.

But outside the military and the upper crust they soon learned to exercise tact in the subtle and intricate social relations that prevailed. It was dangerous, Reynolds observed, "to whisper *transportation* in the Street . . . families pass you in splendid equipages, Convicts once! rich rascals now." And for rascality, Peale reported, Australian immigrants would "shame Texas." Some visited a convict ship recently arrived and were surprised to find it specially built for the service—filled with bunks, each accommodating five persons, with iron-spiked barricades and plenty of light and fresh air. The usual shipboard punishment, they learned, was to place the offender in an upright box on deck, so narrow that he was compelled to stand erect for the duration of his sentence. Wilkes thought it all most efficiently ordered. Some visited the women's prison at Paramatta, quaintly but aptly styled a "factory," where the inmates loomed cloth, plaited straw, and picked oakum but showed little of the good will they had come to expect in Sydney, and the commander was a little discomposed by the "malignity and hatred" to be read on their "disgusting leering faces."

The only other exception to the welter of Anglo-Saxon good feeling appeared within the squadron itself. The stay at Sydney was peppered with occasions for distaste. Assistant Surgeon Guillou, whose "insubordinate disposition" Wilkes put down to his "French extraction," was reprimanded by both Wilkes and Ringgold and charges were preferred against him over an affair that grew out of the doctor's requisitioning of a pestle and mortar. The same day Lieutenant Maury, sore from being reprimanded for his conduct of the tidal observations at Savai'i, was suspended from duty for having written a "disrespectful letter" to the commander. On the eleventh Surgeon Gilchrist was suspended for the same reason and his request to be detached and sent home refused. Lieutenant Johnson was in trouble with both Ringgold and Wilkes over another letter. The captain of the *Flying Fish*, Lieutenant

Pinkney, fed up with Wilkes' persecution at Samoa, had asked to be detached and been refused. And Wilkes was keeping a sharp eye on others in whom he thought he detected signs of disrespect, a "cabal," he called it. In short, relations were much as usual when the squadron was together.

Less affected by these contretemps than the officers, the crews found Sydney much to their liking. These people spoke a sensible language and lived in houses very like those to be found in Boston; their George Street was New York's Broadway; and Sydney Cove, full of "old Fagins and old Fagin's pupils," where nations gathered in a miniature world to pass their time in "eating, drinking, singing, dancing, gambling, quarreling, and fighting," Sydney Cove was Boston's Ann Street, Philadelphia's South Street, Norfolk's River of Styx, Cincinnati's Sausage Row, New York's Five Points or Hook. At the Jolly Sailors' Inn there were separate tables for the English, who drank their 'alf and 'alf out of pewter mugs and sang "Rule Britannia," the French, who took their claret in thin glasses and roared the "Marseillaise," the Russians, who with the Americans drank "something harder" and sang something incomprehensible, and of course the Americans, who treated all to an occasional round of "Yankee Doodle." It was a sailor's port. But not even in Boston or New York had they seen such depravity—"half-dressed, dirty soldiers" and "dirty and drunken women, staggering along the public streets, brawling and fighting," and English women married to black men. The explorers found themselves in pretty firm agreement with the appraisal of an earlier governor of the colony, that there were but "two classes of people in New South Wales, those who had been convicted and those who ought to be." [1]

The scientifics enjoyed Sydney, too, but in a different way. Dana fell in with the Reverend William B. Clarke, the first trained geologist to reach this continent—he had studied under Adam Sedgwick at Cambridge—and their work in the field together marked the beginning of a lifelong friendship. The others busied themselves preparing the Pacific collections for shipment home by a bark bound for Boston, visited the extensive Botanical Gardens just outside the city, and made short excursions into the rolling, unpicturesque bushlands about. They found the seeming desolation of the country deceptive, and on one three-mile jaunt early in December Brackenridge alone collected some one hundred and fifty species of plants. On another they met several parties of the aborigines, remnants of a dying culture. One of the seamen who went along found their features uglier than the Fuegians' though their forms "more manly." A queer lot they seemed, who acknowledged no masters or chiefs, but there was something to admire in a people who considered one man "as good as another, as long as he behaves himself," and who, by hurling a spear or flinging a bent stick, could live off the country. The explorers were fortunate in witnessing one of their weird dances, held at night before the fire in a little clearing. Some twenty men came out of the bush in quick succession, the skeletons of their dark bodies outlined in front with white pipe clay. A "hideous, frightful, and ugly" group. They stood motionless for a long time, "staring wildly at us, then all of a sudden they jumped up and yelled like so many hyenas" and "kept on jumping up and down, throwing their whole arms and legs about as if they had no ankle or knee joints or elbows." Then one after another they would vanish, merely by turning around becoming invisible. The men found the affair "strangely suggestive of Hades," which was an apt enough characterization of the aborigines' own predicament. In the towns they were beggars and in the country were hunted down like wolves for killing the white men's cattle. Wilkes predicted that a few years more would see their total extinction. It was a situation familiar enough to Americans.

"Strangely suggestive of Hades." Aborigine dance, by Alfred T. Agate. (*Narrative*, 2: facing p. 198, Western Americana Collection, Yale University Library.)

Just how the scientists would occupy themselves on the coming Antarctic cruise was clear to no one, and when Wilkes proposed that they spend the next three months as they saw fit, though in diligent application, to be sure, and rejoin the squadron at Bay of Islands in New Zealand the following March or April, all decided to remain behind. Two were laid up, anyway, Brackenridge from a fall at the gangway and Couthouy from overwork and exposure. Couthouy had taken a cold in Samoa that settled in the lungs and rendered him totally inactive for once. The surgeons recommended rest in a milder climate, and Wilkes accordingly ordered him to meet the squadron at the Sandwich Islands, where it was expected to arrive the following May or June.

Much of the talk overheard in the barracks and grogshops or at the elite Australian Club, frequented by the officers, rather put the explorers on their mettle. Many of the visitors to their ships knew that the English and Russian vessels that cruised near the Circle were specially constructed and reinforced for battle with the ice, and perhaps some had read of the elaborate preparations being made this year for Captain James Clark Ross' expedition to the Antarctic. The American ships were too frail, it was said. They carried no great ice saws, they had no watertight compartments for buoyancy, their heating systems were rudimentary. As they could stow no more than a seven months' supply of fuel even after installation of additional coal lockers at Sydney, or provisions for a twelvemonth even on short rations, they were doomed if frozen in and forced to winter.

Of all who watched these "young Americans, foolhardy and reckless," outfitting their rather old-fashioned expedition—some shaking their heads in resignation as "they supposed that we would go on," Charlie Erskine recalled—one would most like to have the opinion of John Biscoe. Now in Sydney, the onetime master in the Royal Navy had commanded the brig *Tula* and cutter *Lively* on a combined sealing and exploring voyage for the Enderby Brothers in 1830–1831. Sailing eastward from the South Sandwich Group more or less along the Antarctic Circle, he made land on February 28, 1831 at 66° 25′ E. and named it Enderby Land. In some quarters it was hailed as the discovery of a continent—and was indeed the first known landfall on the main body of Antarctica. Returning north to Hobart, Tasmania, where he met the famous James Weddell, still active in sealing, he refitted and recruited and in January 1832 continued his cruise to the east. On February 14 he discovered Adelaide Island off the western coast of the Palmer Peninsula and a few days later the group slightly to the north now known as the Biscoe Islands. Unaware of Bellingshausen's discovery of Peter I and Alexander I Islands, he assumed that he had found the southernmost known land, for both his discoveries were south of the northern point of the Palmer Peninsula, which, "a high continuous land" beyond, he named Graham Land. Though he probably did not know of the latest events south—John Balleny's discovery of the five Balleny Islands on the Antarctic Circle at 164° 29′ E. earlier in this year 1839—Biscoe knew what land looked like in the Antarctic and where to seek it. The old-fashioned private explorer of polar seas·might have conveyed much useful information to the commander of a squadron engaged in a scientific enterprise supported by the resources of government. As like as not he did. Wilkes was to make no mention of a meeting, but he was to make none of the Port Jackson quartermaster, either.

The squadron's situation was actually even more perilous than its critics knew. Not only were all but the *Peacock* unadapted to such service, but that ship was in the worst condition of all. After giving the vessel a thorough inspection Carpenter Jonas Dibble reported that her sheer strake was pretty well rotted, together with the waterways of the gun and berth decks and that the stanchions supporting the bulwarks of the spar deck were in such a state of decay that they could not be relied upon to support the rail and the boats attached to it "under anything more than ordinary circumstances." As the circumstances of this cruise were expected to be something more than ordinary, Hudson reported the condition of his ship to Wilkes, and pointing out that to repair its defects now would preclude its joining in the southern cruise, added that it was his duty to contend with the defects. Wilkes agreed that "the credit of the Expedition and the country" required the *Peacock*'s participation: otherwise, "improper imputations and motives would be ascribed to us." Sensitive as always to improper imputations and with another curse for the Norfolk Navy Yard and the disruptive cabal at home, he gave orders to hasten the preparations that they might sail well before the end of December.

There were more deserters this time and, though the Sydney police were uncommonly prompt in rounding them up and English captains leaving the harbor most obliging in permitting search, enough were successful that additional men had to be shipped. On December 15, when her decks were still lumbered with provisions and with the new masts and rigging, five of the *Flying Fish*'s crew of seven made off in one of the boats and, though a reward of a hundred and fifty dollars was offered, they were not to be found. Wilkes blamed the Sydney "crimps," who made a profitable business of kidnapping seamen and selling their services to other captains at five dollars a head, but it was clear enough that it was the usual combination of attraction and repulsion that bore them out of the squadron. The schooner's crew was filled out with difficulty and on December 25, while officers of the other ships were enjoying a final round of entertainment ashore, Pinkney and Sinclair were hard at work readying the little vessel. Somewhat downcast and perhaps giving thought to the missing *Sea Gull*, Sinclair put down his entry for Christmas Day, 1839: "I do not suppose that a vessel ever Sailed under the U.S. Pendant with so Miserable a crew as we have now. We have no cook and only 7 men, four of them are not in my opinion worth their salt, but they are all we can get. It will be a great wonder if we return from the South."

The *Vincennes* gathered up and stowed the observatory equipment (the scientists had carted off their gear the day before) and the vessels dropped a little way down the bay to anchor off Pinchgut Island. Early on the morning of the twenty-sixth, they weighed and stood to sea, bound, all hoped, for a land where man had never trod. "In their passage outwards," the *Sydney Herald* announced, "they were not merely beautiful, but grand." Aesthetics, anyway, was well served.[2]

9 Ruffled Feathers

Ease the sheet, and keep away;
Glory guides us south today.

J. C. Palmer, "Antarctic Mariner's Song," 1843

At the very outset the *Vincennes* missed stays in attempting to clear the bay and had to anchor. It was mid-afternoon before she could be got under weigh and for the next eight days the ships were continually heaving-to to communicate by boat, compare chronometers, or wait for the schooner to catch up. Wilkes insisted that the squadron keep in company and in the event that proved impossible he laid down two rendezvous: Macquarie Island, some eight degrees south of Sydney and a little to the east, where each vessel was to stand off and on for forty-eight hours, and, farther south, Emerald Isle, of whose position or even existence no one was certain. From there they were to proceed to the south "as far as the ice will permit," thence pursuing a westerly course to 105° east longitude until March 1.

From all reports this was to be a particularly favorable season in the latitudes they were to explore. Loose ice was reported farther to the north than usual, promising less of it in the southern sea. On New Year's Day aboard that happiest of ships the *Peacock*, Captain Hudson left his cabin and the midshipmen their quarters in steerage to dine in the wardroom and drink "a happy New Year to our absent friends" and "success to the Expedition." But they also reduced sail to allow the schooner to keep up. Though the *Vincennes'* carpenter seized these opportunities to construct double doors over the hatches in order to keep the temperature below decks near the optimum fifty degrees that by Wilkes' reckoning would have the wholesome effect of "inducing the men to take exercise for the purpose of exciting their animal heat," the rest chafed at the exasperating delays. This was to be their last chance to strike for national glory, and if many were too young to remember the vision of Captain Symmes that had launched their expedition in the public imagination twenty years before, all knew the occasion was a historic one. They were the first sent expressly to determine whether land existed at the South Pole. "May it please the Almighty to grant us success" was the prayer of George Emmons and the fervent hope of all. Beyond that, every man wanted the glory of discovery for his own ship.

The delays made little sense. The feeling was widespread that sailing in company had been a mistake in the Pacific, where by making one track instead of four, they had sharply reduced the chance of discovery, and in the fog and ice of the unknown polar sea it seemed dangerous as well. To William Reynolds, aware how many voyages there had failed for want of time, this "dilly dallying was Maddening" and aroused his suspicions that Wilkes was either timid or was purposely delaying the other ships that the *Vincennes* might claim the honor, if honor there was to be.

Only the officers of the *Flying Fish* failed to complain of the policy. Short of crew and stores, they sailed with a marked lack of enthusiasm. Then one of the three competents of the crew fell sick and the three officers had to pitch in and work ship with the rest. If this was their condition in mild weather with only one man sick, "what will it be when we get South, among the Ice," asked sailing master George Sinclair in the only journal now extant for this voyage of the schooner. He recorded his answer with ready rhetoric: "if the ghosts of the departed are ever allowed to visit this Earth, I shall certainly pay a visit to a certain individual, as I suppose Ghosts are allowed to say what they think." On the last day of the year the *Vincennes* sent over a code of signals to be used in fog. That was thoughtful but, Sinclair remarked sourly, "as we have neither Balls, Gong, or Horn they had as well been left out."

New Year's was stormy. They took in the mainsail, but early in the afternoon the topsail split, leaving them to scud under foresail and jib. Then the foresail jibed several times and finally broke the jaws of the gaff. They proceeded under jib alone while they repaired the gaff. Then the jib sheet parted and the schooner was helpless. At just this moment the *Vincennes*, though near enough to observe their plight, signaled to make all sail. They could hardly believe their eyes when she bore away "and deliberately left us to whatever fate the gods of the Winds might have in store." "A few deep toned curses," Sinclair noted with some satisfaction, "accompanied her." By night they had completed the repairs and reset the foresail, but before midnight the gale forced them to heave to with a sea breaking violently over the deck. The schooner's officers were every bit as suspicious of the commander's motives in deserting them as was William Reynolds at the commander's insistence on sailing in company, and the motive ascribed was the same. "There is but one opinion on board this Schooner on the subject and were I to live to be as old as the Patriarchs of the Bible, I could never forgive the act."

Out of range of the epithets, those aboard the other ships rejoiced at the successive departures from station that, it was said, gale and sea and fog made inevitable. For a while they kept company by firing the big guns, but by January 4 the *Vincennes* was out of sound as well as sight and Reynolds, happily banished to Hudson's ship for having appeared on deck without taking respectful notice of Captain Wilkes, jotted succinctly in his journal, "Captain & all hands, happy to be clear of her."

As the temperature dropped into the forties Hudson had stoves set up on the *Peacock*'s half deck and served out the exploring clothing again—to each man a pea jacket, a "Macanaw Blanket," as Emmons put it, a jersey frock, a dozen pairs of drawers in hopes one might remain dry, and a pair of trousers, but nothing to keep the feet dry, for the Sydney boots were no more suitable than the shoddy stuff designed for exploration by the entrepreneurs at home.

The *Peacock* made the high land of Macquarie on the morning of January 10, hove to off the southeast end and sent a boat ashore under Passed Midshipman Henry Eld. In roughly the same latitude as Cape Horn, the island had first been discovered by the crew of an unknown ship whose wreckage was found upon its shores in 1810 by a Sydney captain. It remained uninhabited, and after one good look about Henry Eld determined to inhabit it no longer than necessary. While the quartermaster planted the flagstaff with a message announcing their arrival to the other ships, Eld collected specimens of the "natural productions," nudging aside the penguins that strutted in his path. The stench of their rookeries was fearsome and their gabble "Enough to deafen one," but from the summit this "Army of lilliput soldiers" presented a "Novel & beautiful sight." Then, having dutifully kept her appointed rendezvous, the *Peacock* gathered up her explorers and with almost unseemly haste filled away to the south.

Beating up for the island, the officers of the *Flying Fish* had watched her for fifteen minutes before the fog closed in. Unable to signal as their sole gun was stowed below, they stood off and on hoping to speak her on the morrow, for the rope purchased at Sydney was poor stuff and they had lost a jib stay on January 14. Thereafter they had sailed through heavy seas and thick fog, accompanied by jackass penguins that hurtled through the water like porpoises and sometimes rose close under the bows to "stare wildly at us & then plunge under again, uttering a most doleful cry."

To their dismay the *Peacock* was nowhere to be seen next morning, but as soon as the fog lifted a little they obediently kicked a path through the penguins to plant their own signal, together with a bottle stuffed with letters which, Sinclair remarked, still smouldering, "if they should Ever be found & we not heard from more, will tell the sad tale of our doleful condition, & inform our friends to what cause to attribute our loss." With all but four of the crew incapacitated they stood on next day for the second rendezvous.

Assistance would have been prompt enough had the *Peacock* sighted the schooner, for memories of her sister's fate remained fresh. But instead they hurried onward for they now guessed that Wilkes had ignored the rendezvous. The *Vincennes* and *Porpoise*, after a half-hearted attempt to beat up to Macquarie, wasted no time at all on the second rendezvous. The *Peacock* herself passed a full degree eastward of the reported position of Emerald Isle and Hudson decided not to lose time in beating up to it. Only the despised schooner took the trouble and on January 15 sailed over the position without sighting land.

As such voyages went, these Americans in high latitudes for the second consecutive season were Old Antarctic Hands, and they drew comparisons and contrasts with phenomena observed their previous cruise on the other side of the Pole. For one thing, the icebergs, the first of which they met along the sixty-first parallel, were generally tabular instead of the fantastic shapes seen before. On all the ships they noticed how much the binnacle compasses were affected by local attraction—by the stoves in wardroom and cabin, or a belaying pin at a distance of four feet. Even a small iron button held four inches east or west of the pivot would draw the south point across twenty degrees. They were near the magnetic pole and Emmons hoped that on the return they might be able to determine its exact position. At the same latitude they dispensed with the binnacle lights. Stepping out on deck one night to take the mid-watch, William Reynolds found the men reading *Pickwick*. As the temperature fell into the thirties the pint of hot coffee served to each man standing watch was held in higher esteem than grog, which was thought to be just as well. What struck them most was the relative mildness of the weather, for on crossing the sixtieth parallel they left the squalls behind. Though frequently cloudy and punctuated with snow flurries, there were days of brilliant sunshine and, as Reynolds noted gleefully, "None of the tempestuous Violence of Cape Horn." It was not so cold, either. The temperature rarely fell below freezing and the ships were a good deal more comfortable than the previous season.

The *Peacock* sighted her first berg in 61° 36′ on the afternoon of January

13, one of the fantastic variety that attracted the enthusiasm for the picturesque. "We all came on deck," Reynolds recalled, "and we all gazed, till our very vision ached, on the dazzling Ice, that we were passing slowly by: and that which we were looking on, was neither Earth nor Sea!" There were more bergs that day and the next, but still no sign of the barrier, and many concluded from the unexpected mildness of the weather that there could be none short of a very high latitude, perhaps the seventy-fifth parallel. Even the steady Emmons began to believe that they would not bring up short of the seventieth. A fine breeze was holding and the few bergs, coupled with continued daylight, made it unnecessary to heave to at night to avoid collision. When at noon on January 15 and in latitude 65° 25′ no ice could be seen from the masthead, it dawned on all of them that next day they would be farther south than the ship had reached the previous season. A little more, Reynolds speculated, and "We would pass 70°—Eclipse Cook, & distance the pretender Weddell . . . we were all in a perfect fever of excitement!" On the *Porpoise* the skeptical first lieutenant was writing a letter when the first iceberg was sighted. He thought they might get far enough south "to equal the expectations of the world at home" and declared that all were "willing to undergo much suffering from cold and exposure to effect something which will give the Expedition a name, for we shall not find those who appreciate such sufferings unless accompanied with success."

With everything seemingly in their favor, a yet more enticing prospect appeared: they might fall in with land in these high latitudes instead of ice. After all, "Palmer's Land" extended several degrees north of the latitude they were now in. Reynolds thought they might find "a Continent, the Existence of which has been so much disputed; if we do . . . the Nation May reap the fame of having at last Contributed Something to the general Knowledge of the World!" It was a heady vision of national glory. But visions are but airy things.

An halation dispelled this one. During the afternoon they fell in with floe and brash ice, then an ice island towering some eighty feet, perfectly flat on top, and a half mile long. At four they sighted the long white streak on the horizon called an ice blink, "our old Offender," as Eld put it ruefully, "the Never failing forerunner of the Ice field's all our hopes all our fancies glory & the southern Continent Evaporated." Dismay was general. "Our dreams were at once destroyed!" Reynolds recorded.

There had been some fog during the day and when it lifted a little they sighted the barrier extending (everyone took care to note) "as far as the eye could reach." * It was a hard moment. The still hopeful reminded themselves

* Properly speaking, barrier ice is shelf ice attached to the land. This breaks off to form ice islands that are often many miles long. From the sea itself, sometimes frozen to a depth of eight

with Henry Eld that "it is supposed where there is Ice the land Must be Near."
They coasted the barrier to the westward, running through floe and brash but
keeping well off to avoid the larger drift ice. Whales were sporting all about
and there were many kinds of birds to be seen, among which Emmons
recognized the rare sheathbill, only two stuffed specimens of which were said
to exist. Reynolds at sight of it all was moved to put down a stanza of *The
Ancient Mariner*:

> The fair breeze blew, the white foam flew,
> The furrow followed free—
> We were the first, that ever burst
> Into that silent sea.

They were the first by the narrowest of margins, for within an hour after
sighting the barrier they discovered a sail to leeward. It was the *Porpoise*.
Rounding to under their stern Ringgold reported that he had made the barrier
on the evening of the eleventh at 63° 28′ 45″ S., 161° 08′ 30″ E., had parted
from the *Vincennes* in a fog the next day despite all efforts to keep her in
sight, and had since been coasting the barrier, searching for an entrance in the
bays that on occasion opened up. (Ringgold really had attempted to keep
station, making the seas resound with horns, bells, and guns, all to the dismay
of Bob Johnson, for whom separation "greatly multiplied" the squadron's
chances "for the acquiring fame as polar explorers." On learning next morning
that the din had been in vain, he recorded with some temerity, "Three
cheers!!!")* These bays made for pleasant sailing, and Surgeon Holmes found
the sea within them as smooth as "the Narragansett on a calm Sunday
Morning in Midsummer," but they led little farther south. All the *Porpoise*
had to show for the work of the past four days were the carcasses of two sea
elephants that Johnson had taken from an iceberg and now sent to the
Peacock for preservation.

Filling away to the west, the two vessels beat along the barrier in company.
There was a bad moment next day, January 16, when a sail was made hull
down on the lee beam, for everyone supposed it to be the *Vincennes*, but
passing behind an iceberg, which reduced it to a plaything, it disappeared from
view. Later the brig, too, disappeared in the fog. But two aboard the *Peacock*

---

feet, comes another species of ice, sea ice broken up by the winds and separated from the barrier
by a lane of open water. Bunched by winds, this becomes pack ice. When the explorers refer to the
"icy barrier," it is clear that they include much pack ice in the description. Confusing the two is
not at all difficult.

* The *Flying Fish* gained the barrier at 159° 36′ E., the *Porpoise* and *Vincennes* at between
161° E. and 165° E., all between the sixty-third and sixty-fifth parallels.

Henry Eld, the big New Englander who, with William
Reynolds, first sighted the Antarctic Continent.
(Western Americana Collection, Yale University
Library.)

found that there was more to be seen from her masthead that day than their
sister ships. The morning was unusually fine, with intervals of bright sunshine
and a dimpled sea. "Never experienced such delightful weather before S. of
50°," Emmons remarked. The leadsman ran out 850 fathoms of line without
finding bottom but just before ten o'clock, when the ship was within a mile
and a half of the barrier, two frequenters of the rigging, William Reynolds and
Henry Eld, "from a Motive of Curiosity," as the former put it matter-of-factly,
"went to the Masthead: we wanted to obtain a good view of the field of Ice,
that Spread away beneath us." The sight was "grand & singularly imposing"
and rendered them speechless, for "to look over such a vast expanse of the
frozen Sea, upon Which human Eye nor foot had Ever rested, & which . . .
presented an impassable boundary to the Mysterious region beyond, filled us
With feelings, Which we were powerless to utter." Eld's account of what they
saw conveys with immediacy their elation: After contemplating this "*Barrier of
Ice* so Called" for some time, he wrote, "Mr Reynolds & myself almost at one
accord Exclaimed this is land, but not trusting the Naked Eye went on deck

RUFFLED FEATHERS

for a Spy Glass, which only Confirmed what we had before felt sure of, so unlike the usual appearance of the barrier was it that it burst upon [us] with the utmost Vividness & we unhesitatingly pronounced it the Southern Continent. The Mountains could be distinctly seen towering over the field Ice & Berg's in the back ground stretching to the S & W as far as we could discern any thing. Two peaks in particular were very distinct running up to an immense height in a conical form & others the lower parts quite as distinct but their summits lost in a light fleecy cloud tho few of which were to be seen in that quarter for the weather was remarkably clear & the sun shining brightly ridge after ridge with their sides partially bare connecting the Eminences that I have just spoken of which Must be from one to two thousand feet in height & alone is Enough to Establish its identity, for no berg or Ice Island Ever seen was one quarter its Altitude." *

After gazing for half an hour they returned to the deck, from which the peaks remained visible, to make their report, a "duty too important to be neglected." While Reynolds pointed out the distant land to Lieutenant Thomas A. Budd, officer of the deck, Eld went to break the glorious news in the cabin. To his astonishment, Hudson merely nodded in assent. He had no doubt of it. Probably most of the large bergs and ice islands ahead were aground. But the wind was light and the ship close in with the barrier. "At all events," Hudson added, "we shall see more of it in two or three days."

Hudson did not bother to come on deck. Budd did not record the report in the logbook. No lookout was sent aloft to confirm. No orders were issued the leadsman. And presently the ship went onto the opposite tack and crawled off through the fog that had closed in, leaving the excited pair to cool their heels in "Disappointment and mortification." These were the greater because of their certainty that what they had seen was "nothing else but terra firma." It was far too high to be an ice island. Moreover they had observed from previous experience that all ice islands attached to the barrier were "table topped in large Square masses," and did not become the rugged, picturesque variety until weathered. And what they had seen was not a cloudbank, either, for it was a beautiful day before the fog closed in in the evening, with only scattered patches of light cumulus that floated well above the horizon. They thought Hudson's response "a singular way to receive a report of *Land!*" in these latitudes.

The next day was cloudy with a moderate breeze from the south and

* The *Peacock*'s noon position was 65° 18′ S., 157° 36′ 38″ E. The two peaks here on the George V Coast bear the names Wilkes later gave them, Eld's and Reynolds' peaks.

occasional spits of snow. The *Vincennes*, discovered to windward, reported fruitless forays into ice bays then stood off, once more "allowing us (agreeable to the wish I believe of all on board)," Emmons solemnly remarked, "to explore by ourselves." During the next two days the icebergs were numerous and only intermittently did the weather permit a glimpse of the barrier, the *Vincennes*, and the *Porpoise*.

What they saw on the nineteenth stopped the mouths of most of the skeptics. The day began with fog and snow but when it cleared a little toward noon the *Peacock* was found to be in the mouth of a bay of ice some twenty miles deep, just within the Antarctic Circle. Its south side was lined with bergs and field ice that Reynolds thought resembled "the ruins of an ancient City, With its towers & buildings tumbling from decay" and the penguins strutting about "with Solemn aspect, might have been taken for the Melancholy remnant of the inhabitants." Its north side was drift ice. The barrier proper lay ahead to the west. Within, the sea was like a mirror, with a murkiness in its depths that Emmons attributed to an unusual abundance of "animalculae &c." A number of iceblinks gave the horizon a beautiful luminescence. Hoping to find a further opening, a bay within a bay, they made all sail and stood in through the innumerable pieces of broken ice that were drifting slowly out to sea. At 1:40 P.M. they lost sight of the *Vincennes* as she continued along the barrier to the westward. At 3 P.M., from the masthead ice was made out at the head of the bay and indeed in all directions except their wake. "However," recorded Emmons, "stood on—everyone delighted with our River sailing & eagerly spying at every thing appearing at all unusual"—until the wind gradually hauled ahead and drove the ship into the drift ice to the side of the bay, where they were forced to go about.

Shortly before four the attention of some of the men was caught by a sea elephant that swam alongside, looked up and gaped, and there was some scurrying about for a gun before he disappeared. But the attention of others was caught by something in the distance "peering over the compact Ice at the head of the bay—very much resembling high craggy land covered with snow." Suddenly, Emmons noted, "*Discovery stock* ran high—Spy glasses were in great requisition." That captain of the crosstrees, William Reynolds, had been aloft again, with one of the "young gentlemen," Midshipman George W. Clark, perched just below him. Reynolds had no sooner settled himself, hitched up his spectacles and glanced around than he saw land "as plain as possible" and, pointing toward the head of the bay, sang out to his companion, "Do you see that?" Swinging round, Clark agreed, "It must be land." What they saw was of "great height," of "rounded uneven Summit, &

broken sides." They scrutinized it for some time before descending to the deck, where Reynolds reported to the officer of the deck, George Emmons. Agreeing that it looked promising, Emmons summoned Hudson. Captain and all hands were soon aloft and to Reynolds' joy nearly all were convinced. "Well," he recorded with satisfaction, "it was Land!"

Through the afternoon and evening the *Peacock* sloshed through the ice on short tacks in the hope of finding a passage, the officers all on deck or in the rigging. Someone made a sketch of the "vast amphitheater" they were in, with the peaks in the background. Aloft for some three hours, Henry Eld was "merely Confirmed" in his belief that they had seen land three days before. There was a great deal of excitement and, he noted, "The first land Ever discovered in the Antarctic was the talk, & consequences & surmises arising there from, Castles built in the air & fame anticipated."

They reached the head of the bay about eleven o'clock and, no further passage appearing, lay there until it grew lighter. At this point they estimated that the formation was some fifteen miles distant. But Emmons remained skeptical and the cautious Hudson began to doubt. He turned to the officer of the deck, Passed Midshipman Alonzo B. Davis, and remarked, "Our land has turned out to be an Iceberg." Davis, who himself had no doubts whatever, accordingly changed his entry in the logbook to state that the supposed land was merely ice. Reynolds was disgusted when he returned on deck shortly after midnight to be told that the formation had proved to be only another ice island, "for it was *all white*." The reasoning left him unimpressed. "I really did not expect to see *Much bare earth* in *this region*," he observed sarcastically.*

In any event there was no hope of getting nearer, or getting a boat safely through the floating pieces. Nothing was to be gained by further gazing, and if the wind should shift they might find themselves in a most awkward situation. A blow from the north would shut them in and the resulting sea would grind the vessel to pieces. So Hudson gave orders to wear round, the *Peacock* worked free and stood down the bay through rafts of broken ice and whales that were spouting all around with a noise that reminded Emmons of "our own high pressure Steam Boats on the Ohio." Though she was sailing nearly before the wind, gaining the mouth of the bay required skillful maneuvering. Going aloft early in the morning, Eld found a shortcut, and by eight they were at its outer mouth standing for a passage between two large and beautiful bergs. Suddenly it occurred to the officer of the deck that the two just might

* Wilkes named this projection of land Cape Hudson. In 1959, the Australian National Antarctic Research Expedition identified it as the tip of Mawson Peninsula.

be joined beneath and he mentioned the thought to Eld. Of course. They had seen just such formations before. Eld hastened aloft once more even though it was now too late to change course and found to his immense relief that there was no such danger. There was a moral here that "I shall remember all my life," he recorded, "give an iceberg a good birth for ⅝ of these Mountains are under water." This perilous passage set them free upon the accustomed heavy swell and they resumed beating to the westward.

The weather turned thick, with snow in the afternoon that fell in large dry flakes, a double reefed topsail breeze that blew in squalls and a considerable head sea—"such weather," Emmons remarked, "as makes one think he has done his country a service after keeping a four hour's Watch on deck." On the twenty-first it improved somewhat though cluttery still, and during the morning watch they discovered the *Porpoise*, which remained in sight for twenty-four hours. But there were many bergs and the *Peacock* kept away from the barrier. The wind moderated on the twenty-second and they had pleasant weather again, with a beautiful Italian sky at the rising and setting of the sun that everyone remarked on, as they did, too, the sun's setting in the east. But then, remarked Emmons, "we witness more curious things in this region that our friends but little appreciate at home." In the afternoon they witnessed a gory battle between a whale and a killer clamped to its spout hole, the whale leaping in open-mouthed agony and dyeing the sea crimson for some distance around. The spectacle brought every man on deck. The behavior of the compasses was also curious. Once the ship's head lay due south by one of them while the other told due north. Only a vigorous shaking would make them function properly.

Sailors had an expression to signify the imminence of doom: "It is all day with them." And in these latitudes, where it was perfectly light for twenty-two hours and never dark, the men made frequent play on the words. One of the old quartermasters came up to Eld on January 22 and remarked gravely, "It is a Curious Country we are in—this, Sir, it is all day with us now, the ship works in 4 points & the sun sets in the East." But it was only a pun. The *Peacock*'s men remained in good health and, as usual on Hudson's ship, in good spirits as well, busying themselves in devising new ways to keep warm, playing games and, Eld noted, "stamping about the decks the whole day in the Most Merry mood & . . . dancing & singing most of the time."

But they had not come to frolic, and as the *Peacock* continued beating westward the propitiousness of their circumstances—mild weather, everlasting daylight, no more than light frost—only heightened their exasperation with the seemingly interminable barrier. It was as though fate had singled them out for sport and Eld took it almost personally. "It appears hard & most unfortunate," he grumbled, "that we cannot find an Entrance into the Ice while Every thing is favorable."

January 23 was another surprisingly clear day, with light breezes from the southwest, and began most auspiciously. They made the barrier once more, extending by compass NNE and SSW, and ranged some three miles off its projecting fingers, where it appeared as a kind of open-air ice museum, displaying all possible varieties of the substance against a background of ice islands varying from fifty to eight hundred feet in height. In the afternoon they entered a bay in the ice at 151° 43′ E. from which they spied the *Porpoise* emerging.* Hudson stood in a little way then hove to, to make observations for magnetic dip and intensity and determine the feasibility of taking ice from a berg to replenish the supply of fresh water.

Lieutenant Walker found that the ice made potable enough water. On another berg Eld and Hudson's clerk, Fred Stuart, completed their observations, though with some difficulty as the berg's movement necessitated constant readjustments, and returned with a penguin they had stunned with a boat hook. It set up "a Most inordinate Noise" in the boat, attacking everyone within reach "with such vigor as to Make it a Caution," until they put a lashing on its beak. No sooner was the bird quieted than they heard a great hullaballoo from the ship and looking up to see the men in the rigging in the act of giving three cheers naturally assumed that the applause was directed at them, "we being the first," remarked Emmons, who had gone along with a rifle in hopes of bagging a sea elephant, "that had landed upon Ice within the Antarctic regions." They gave an answering cheer only to find on getting aboard that the applause was not for them at all.

The *Peacock* had got soundings at 320 fathoms, the line coming up coated with blue mud and bearing in one of its bends a rock fragment an inch and a half long.† Here was certain indication of the proximity of land. "The old Ice

---

* Presumably this was Deakin Bay, which Wilkes was to name "Peacock Bay."

† In blue water, sounding was a tricky operation. The ever-increasing friction on the descending line and the freaks of submarine currents tended to neutralize the momentum of the lead, making it all but impossible to determine the moment of touch bottom beyond a depth of eight hundred or a thousand fathoms, the more so as the line, its weight greatly increased by absorption of water, would continue to run out long after the plummet had buried itself in the ocean bed. In consequence, remarkable depths of eight and ten miles had been reported in unlikely places. Often, too, with the life stretched out of it, the line would break in hauling in, so that the work of hours might yield no reliable result. To obviate these difficulties in some part, the Expedition used copper wire, the joints carefully twisted and soldered, and these were among the first ships of any nation to sound with wire. But much of it was lost in hauling in and the practice was abandoned before the squadron returned.

rang" with cheers. There was a general spirit of holiday, and "all was hustle about the decks." Below, men played shuffleboard and rolled ten pins on the gundeck—so smooth was the sea within this bay. At the leadline men coiled to the music of a fiddle, occasionally bursting into songs and hurrahs, until all hands were called to splice the main brace. "We were a happy ship," Reynolds recalled, "little did any one think of the change that few short hours would bring about!"

For yet a little while their star rose on. The captured penguin provided a great deal of amusement, for its pompous gait was droll. Eld watched in admiration as it stood for its portrait—forty-five inches from bill to tip of tail, and rotund with a girth of thirty-three, black and gray on the body, black head and yellow throat, "& take it all in all . . . a Most beautiful Creation." But then Science intervened, for it was a particularly fine specimen of the king penguin and its skin, Emmons hoped, would be preserved for "our National Museum—should we come to be blessed with one."

But the poor beast bore a significance beyond that, for its craw yielded five pebbles, and on dressing it later the entrepreneurial cook found twenty-seven more, which he flogged to the men at fancy prices as "South Pole stones." Thus, remarked Eld, "our Australian Continent was vended about in so small portions as a single pebble about the size of the End of the little finger . . . in so high Estimation was it held."

Reynolds saw his favorite captain come on deck grinning broadly: "poor Man! he was nearly beside himself with joy!!" None of your Cape Flyaways, here was evidence a seaman could grasp. Hudson was heard to voice the firm opinion that the field of ice which, studded with bergs, formed the shores of this bay was "hard & fast aground" and that the high eminences beyond were land. Even George Emmons was convinced, and none were happier than those who now believed more firmly than ever that they had seen land on January 19, fifty miles from here. "The question then was," remarked Eld, "how were we to get hold of it?" Crossing the vast field of ice was really a small problem compared to that of reaching the field itself through the drifting pieces that lined the shores to create a deadly moat where a man could neither walk nor float.

After sounding again at 340 fathoms they made sail along the western shore of the bay to have a closer look at what appeared to be high land to the south and southeast. The sun set at ten, and most of the officers and men, excited at the prospect, stayed up to see it rise at two, when its reflection upon the ice produced "a Splendid Effect, glorious to the Eye, dazzling & confounding to the imagination," as the scene was described by Reynolds, who had the watch.

In the northwest black clouds "hung in gloomy contrast, over the stainless field of white beneath." Emmons relieved him at four and he turned in, "dreading no Evil & confident that we would succeed in finding Land ere we were Many days older." The sun was bright, a light breeze blowing, the sea smooth and of a dark green cast still. The appearance of land remained strong and Captain Hudson, who was about during most of the night, remarked that he intended to run toward it as far as possible for the purpose of "getting hold of it." At five in the morning they hove to in a small bight and got a cast of the lead (in eight hundred fathoms this time) which again came up covered with mud. There was a light leading wind, the ice was still sufficiently open to work the ship, and Hudson left orders to stand in for the supposed land until their passage was obstructed.

Eld was at breakfast when, as he recalled, "I was almost thrown off my seat by a tremendous crash, that appeared as if the whole bow's Must be stove in." But a calmer man than this big Connecticut Yankee could hardly be found, unless in the cabin. Eld sat stolidly eating for a few moments so as not to alarm his messmates. Then he made for the hatchway. At the quarterdeck he learned that the rudder was knocked loose. The ship was surrounded by loose ice that parted here and there into channels and as often came together again. In tacking to avoid contact with a piece of ice ahead the *Peacock* had got sternway and struck a piece astern. The rudder had borne the shock in nearly a fore and aft position, and the cant this gave the ship, together with the grinding action of the ice, parted the starboard wheel rope and wrenched the rudder-head until it was useless—indeed worse than useless, slewed as it was from the vertical. The rudder crashed again and was nearly lost altogether. They were drifting further into the ice now and in the little space available attempted to steer by sail, but this only produced more collisions, often with pieces larger than the ship itself, and she continued to drift implacably toward an ice island some six miles square and upwards of a hundred feet high.

The carpenters reported from a staging got over the stern—and several times knocked down—that the rudder was beyond all help in the vessel's present position and would have to be unshipped. (A spare had been brought from the States, but it rested safely in the hold of the *Relief*.) How to stop the drift toward the ice island? "Scarcely a Moment passed," Eld noted, "without the Ice striking in some quarter, bow beam & counter, Every crash of which appeared as if it would annihilate her hull & Knock the Masts out of her." An officer was stationed at the pumps to sound the bilges and make frequent reports to Hudson and Emmons. If the ice island was to be avoided it would be necessary to get the ship onto the other tack, and to this end a boat was lowered to carry an ice anchor to a nearby floe. They planted it firmly enough, but before they could take a turn on the windlass, a piece of ice drifted past and swept the line from their grasp.

They were back where they started, with one ominous exception: the ice island was nearer now and they were bearing down upon it in a gradually freshening wind. Well might the men now remark of their plight, "It is all day with us." But not quite yet, not with William Hudson's ship. In brisk response to a rapid series of orders from the quarterdeck, a spare topsail yard was set up to brace the mainmast against the impending collision and, furling all but the fore and aft sails, attempts were again made to fetch her to the ice. The boats proved to be almost as unmanageable as the ship and the men did as much fending as rowing among the driving and grinding bergs. Yet they succeeded again in planting the anchor, got the hawser inboard, and the crew ran away with the slack until it was taut. Suddenly—"Great God the Anchor dragged," someone shouted—it went limp.

Minds dwell on curious things at such times. Henry Eld saw that there was now "no alternative but to await our fate; it was inevitable we Must fetch up against the immense Ice Island that was towering over our head's," and toward which they ponderously moved at a steady three knots. "We Many of us had wives, and children, and all had dear & near relatives, Mothers, Sisters, & brothers, & almost Certain death stared us in the face," instant death probably, but if not, the more terrible fate "of being saved to inhabit an Ice Berg" that might not exist a month hence. "I settled in my mind," Reynolds recalled, "that it would be best to go down with the Ship." It was "enough to appal the stoutest heart & spread Consternation," yet Eld found himself admiring the "grandeur & beauty" of "this stupendous Mountain of Ice." With few exceptions hearts remained stout. Everyone, he found, was as "Calm and collected as possible, orders were issued & carried into Effect the same as usual. No blustering or unnecessary Noise, but cooly awaited the Event & preparations Made for Making sail if she did not go down, & should cant the right way." The men were in the rigging and every officer at his station. As the *Peacock* drifted close in, the officer standing next to Eld called out, "*Look out for the Mizen Mast*, stand from under we shall have it on our heads!"

She struck with a tremendous crash at her weakest part—stern to. The recoil threw the officers to the deck.

Together with Hudson's foresight, it also saved them all. The concussion snapped the spanker boom "like a pipe stem," crushed the stern boat "into ten thousand atoms davits & all," drove forward the whole bulwarks from the taffrail to the gangway in a domino movement that was only arrested by the

"No alternative but to await our fate." The *Peacock* in
contact with the iceberg, by Alfred T. Agate.
(*Narrative*, 2: facing p. 318, Western Americana
Collection, Yale University Library.)

signal gun at the starboard gangway, and set the masts to quivering like "coach
whips." While spars and upper works crashed and splintered, all eyes were
upon the overhanging ledge of ice and snow that towered above the
mizzentopmast head. If it gave way, all would be up with them.

The elasticity of the ship gave impetus to her recoil, while the spanker
boom's initial contact gave the vessel just the right cant to clear her rigging. In
this moment, as the *Peacock* lay aslant a little away from the ice, pushing little
waves and pieces of ice before her as she slewed through the sea, Hudson
called out commands to the officers and men he had made certain were
standing by to receive them. The jib was run up, and as the ship began to
stand off, the fore, main, and mizzen topsails were set and the yards braced to
clear the towering wall of ice. Wonderfully, the wind began to take effect, the
Peacock gathered headway "& shot clear of this ugly customer," as Emmons
described it. Aft, a roar and crash followed by a great spout of water brought
news that a large piece of the overhanging shelf had fallen in their wake.

Ahead lay a clear but narrow channel, perhaps half a mile long, alongside the ice island and no more than a ship's length from it. Their task now was to navigate this channel without further collision and this they could accomplish only by manning all brails and halyards, then making sail at one end and taking it in at the other. The ship would surge ahead for half her length, stop against the ice, surge again, laboring all the while in an ominously rising swell. Eld was astounded that the old ship could bear the strain. "Every timber Must be Started," he thought, and every few moments some thing carried away—bobstays, bowsprit shrouds, the anchors bouncing ponderously and at last hanging only by their stoppers. But she cleared the point of the ice island, where they could see it trending off to the southwest.

To the amazement and admiration of all, dinner was piped at the usual hour. Hudson thought it would give the men something else to think about while the carpenters went to work on the rudder. The sky, which he had been closely observing the past few hours, clearly foretold a squall, and broken ice was already fast gathering about the ship. But with the aid of an ice anchor they succeeded in unshipping the rudder in the afternoon, or rather its two pieces and broken pintles. Until it was repaired the ship must be steered by her sails and brought to the opposite tack with ice anchors. Eld spent two hours in planting one of these. At these times the dark figures of men and boats in the ice stood in significant relief to the "dreary whiteness." Often they had to carry the anchors across planks laid from one piece of ice to the next, while others stood in the bow of the ship fending off the ice with spars. Where there was room enough to gather way, the alternative was to carom her against a floe, but this was risky, for the *Peacock* had commenced making water and the swell was increasing. Thus she moved in this congealing bay like some ponderous billiard ball, careening, halting, starting again, but reaching toward the open sea.

The ice was a frozen but turbulent desert with not a living thing to be seen, but in the afternoon a hugh sea lion stretched out upon a floe, lifting his head from time to time to stare, "wondering perhaps what Strange intruder had come to usurp his Element." For once the men took no notice. In the afternoon snow began to fall, the wind freshened and the hawser holding them to an ice island parted, and they made sail again, beating up for promising little passages that as often as not—and then the disappointment was audible—closed up again before their eyes. But by seven in the evening clear water could be seen from the masthead when the weather lifted.

But so could an ominous cloud in the west, which caused more dread than all the other dangers. For while the light breeze and swell had earlier driven them upon the ice, a squall would drive the ice upon them—a matter of an entirely different magnitude. Reynolds went aloft to see these shades approach and his hopes plummeted: "Here were two hundred of us, in the full vigour of health & strength: in a few Moments Not one would be left." They took in every rag of sail but for the rest could only stand helpless. "*Now,*" he observed, "you might See eye turned to Eye, seeking for Hope." Still there was no panic. The "funeral Cloud" drew nearer and nearer, then suddenly spread wide and dissolved into wreaths.

Once when the *Peacock* got a wrong cant, a puff of wind sent her flying back into the ice, but she was again got round with ice anchors and pointed toward the clear sea. The wind remained light but the rising sea tossed three of the chronometers out of their beds of sawdust, and crashed and ground the ship until Hudson was sure her bows would be driven in.

A hasty survey conducted in the early hours of January 25 revealed that the ice had torn away the special strengthening member at the waterline of the bow and was now grinding away at the bows. Ice lay in almost a solid bank across the mouth of the bay where they had entered; yet there was no alternative, so far as Hudson could see, but "to be ground to pieces by the Ice—and Sea—or drive her out." Drive he did. By four o'clock the weather was thick with snow but they were through the densest ice, standing out in a shattered ship from what the day before had been an open bay.

While coffee was served liberally through the night and never mind rationing by the pint, the carpenters worked without respite and finished knocking the rudder together during the forenoon. They hove to and by mid-afternoon had shipped this thing of bolts and splices and rigged a relieving tackle, and in a partially clear sea, "with our rudder hanging by the eyelids—the poor Peacocks feathers ruffled," as Hudson described their situation, they made all sail in snow and fog and cleared the outer barrier at two in the morning of January twenty-sixth.

Summoning the wardroom officers to his cabin, Hudson explained how matters stood. The damage was extensive. Repairs at Sydney, the only port in this part of the world with facilities for a ship of this size, would require at least a month, and during that time their services would be lost to the Expedition, which was scheduled to depart for the Fiji Islands on March 1. He called for a vote. Should they continue the southern cruise? Though George Emmons, who had ridden her down the ways a dozen years before, thought the good old *Peacock* might be patched up to continue along the barrier, most agreed with Hudson that they could best serve the Expedition by effecting the repairs without further delay.

They responded variously to the twenty rudderless hours in the ice. Eld was not one to multiply miracles but was convinced that "a Kind providence . . . must have stretched forth its hand," though he did not discount the ship's solid bottom that rendered her perhaps the strongest of her class in the Navy. Emmons gave no thought at all to the Hand but thanked a good ship that could bear such shocks, "the only one built expressly for exploring Service," and to every man's doing his duty. William Reynolds remarked of the beloved ship that had she gone to the bottom after the concussion, "I verily believe . . . she Would have gone down With three as hearty cheers, as Ever came from a hundred throats," though "god Knows What it is that should prompt a Man to send out his last breath in a hurrah!" But everyone agreed that major credit was due Captain Hudson. She was a stanch ship, declared Eld, but "above all Commanded by one who probably for Nautical Skill has not his superior in the service." As for Captain Hudson, that very model of an amiable Victorian gentleman thanked God, his officers and crew, and Mr. Jonas Dibble, chief carpenter.

"And so Ended our attempt South!" Reynolds lamented, "so vanished our bright hopes . . . true we had seen the land afar off, & had touched the bottom with lead but this was a lame tale to tell." The contrast between their present ignominious situation and that of three days before when there had been "every prospect of success" struck Emmons forcibly. "I almost think I will never be sanguine again," he reflected. As the *Peacock* limped along under easy sail to lessen the strain on her jury-rigged rudder, her men, greatly relieved, greatly chagrined, could only entrust the squadron's reputation to the *Vincennes* and the *Porpoise*.[1]

RUFFLED FEATHERS

10 A New World

Your Landfall, be it a peculiarly shaped mountain, a
rocky headland, or a stretch of sand-dunes, you meet at
first with a single glance. Further recognition will follow in
due course. . . .

Conrad, *The Mirror of the Sea*

Few expected Wilkes to succeed where Hudson had failed.
Shortly before leaving Sydney young James Blair of the *Peacock* had written
his influential father in Washington that this cruise south would be a more
formidable undertaking than that of the previous season, and not alone
because longer: the *Vincennes* would be along. "Some of us," he confided,
"have doubts as to the Vin ever returning if she should get into imminent
danger, for the First and Second in command of her are termed *no Sailors* by
the best Judges." He continued: "We, (of the Peacock) are blessed with a
Cap'n who is the best sailor in the Squadron and one of the best in the
Service."

This was not simply an expression of the lively esprit de corps of the
Peacock, for the best judges on the *Vincennes* concurred. Moreover, what
esprit survived in that ship was largely directed against the commander, whose
attempts at discipline only became more fitful and impetuous in the course of
the icy cruise.

Wilkes may not have been aware of this appraisal but the way in which he
managed the *Vincennes* during the first weeks off the barrier suggested that it
had some validity. The ship moved gingerly. On January 11 he ordered officers
of the watch to avoid entering brash ice and passing to windward of bergs. The
latter injunction was well taken, but in these waters no exploration was
possible without running in brash. To the exasperation of some of the officers

who heartily wished him more mettlesome, Wilkes ignored the mouth of the ice bay which the *Peacock* was entering at their last sight of her on the nineteenth and proceeded along the barrier to the west. It was foggy that morning and Lieutenant Alden, who had the watch, could hear the sea breaking on a berg close by and sent word to Wilkes. The fog had lifted a little when Wilkes came out, they stood looking for a moment, Wilkes muttered something about proper management of the ship, ordered Alden to stand away from the barrier, and was turning to go below again when Alden, pointing to the south, remarked, "There's something there that looks like land, Sir." Wilkes glanced up but made no reply and went on his way. As atmospheric conditions were unfavorable and Alden was not altogether confident he made no mention of the appearance in his log entry.

From the masthead on January 22, when their noon position was 66° 08' S., 149° 43' E., clear water could be seen between and beyond the bergs embedded in the barrier. Rather impertinently, Lieutenant Joseph Underwood of Rhode Island, an officer of education considerably above the average for the Navy and one whom Wilkes especially disliked, remarked in his journal, "I concluded that a vessel might go some 15 or 20 miles in that direction if it were thought to be an object." Indications of land were promising, he noted: the sea was of a "muddy greenish hue and some of the ice much discolored," and while bird droppings accounted for some of the latter, on one berg he spotted such a discoloration on the underside of a projection. Moreover, the seals and penguins hereabout seemed quite at home, appearing singly or in little groups; whereas, so far as was known, these species were to be seen at a distance from land only when migrating. Some on board thought they could actually see high land in the distance.

Unimpressed by these arguments, Wilkes instead fell to speculating on why icebergs tended to collect in this area. As they had seen no indications of land, he thought it "unwarrantable" to conclude that they were gathering around a terrestrial nucleus, and after mulling over the matter he decided that the phenomenon might be explained by their "attraction for each other which in large bodies and in so moveable an element may easily take place." The only force that could then separate them and account for the isolated floating bergs would be "very heavy gales of wind," which he thought rarely occurred in these latitudes.

Some thought appearances of land favorable on the twenty-third. Next day, while the *Peacock* was in trouble a few miles to the east, they were particularly strong, even to Wilkes, and the masthead reported that clear water was to be seen in the southwest, where bergs were few. Underwood so reported to

Wilkes but finding him unimpressed contented himself with recording on the log slate, "a ship could have looked in some miles further." Posted on the quarterdeck the observation was embarrassingly conspicuous and, upbraiding the lieutenant, Wilkes maintained that no opening had existed. When Underwood held his ground, insisting that a southing might have been made, Wilkes was much put out and, ordering the ship put about, declared that he would "search the same place again if it employed me a Month."

At eight next morning, January 25, the *Vincennes* was some distance southwest of the spot, and Underwood reported in his journal sarcastically, "it would have been imprudent to have gone in much further unless for a great object." Their noon position this day was 66° 39′ E. and the weather was perfectly clear. As they were watering ship from a small berg—lightly iced-over pools were often to be found on the upper surfaces of these—Lieutenant Augustus L. Case (whom Wilkes disliked only a little less than he did Alden and Underwood) reported from aloft that he saw "distant mountains at W.S.W. and some clear water in that direction." Underwood confirmed it from the masthead and several of the crew went aloft and agreed on the decided appearance of land.* But nothing was done, for "although the ice was loose," Underwood noted, "there was almost too much of it to run the ship through, as bad weather might come on."

Wilkes was furious, even before reading this latest installment in Underwood's journal. Denying that any real opening existed, this unusual explorer, seemingly more interested in discipline than discovery, ordered the ship put about again and cautioned Underwood that his conduct had "raised impressions in my mind that will not easily be effaced." Though when the commander promised him every opportunity to clear himself and Underwood came up with the testimony of thirteen persons and announced that the entire starboard watch would bear witness to his conduct on this occasion, Wilkes refused to hear them. The operations of the ship might be adversely affected, he said.

Standing along the barrier to the west once more, they spoke the *Porpoise* on the morning of the twenty-sixth. As this meeting was to assume significance in the future, it should be noted that a brisk breeze was blowing and as the vessels were within hail for less than a minute there was opportunity for only a passing remark or two. These were devoted mostly, perhaps wholly, to Wilkes' calling out the rate of the standard chronometer aboard the *Vincennes*. The

* Wilkes named this "Disappointment Bay." Exploration in 1958 by the Australian National Antarctic Research Expedition, supplemented by the aerial photography of the U.S. Navy Antarctic Developments Project of 1946–1947, shows it to be Cook Ice Shelf.

The *Vincennes* watering ship from iceberg in
"Disappointment Bay," 67° 04′ 30″ S., 147° 30′ E., from
sketch by Charles Wilkes. (*Narrative*, 2: facing p. 328,
Western Americana Collection, Yale University
Library.)

two vessels ran in company through the discouragingly large pieces of drift ice
until noon the following day, when the brig was lost to view.

On January 28 they were at 66° 35′ S., 140° 30′ E., and at ten in the
morning Lieutenant Alden, who was reefing topsails at the time, reported that
land was to be seen to the south. Wilkes gazed for some time and finally
announced, "There is no mistake about it." But before they could obtain a
better view, a heavy gale blew up with spits of snow and they had to wear ship
and stand off through fields of bergs whose outlines could be discerned only as
an "indescribable white glimmer along the upper edges," but which seemed to
overhang the decks as they swept past. The gale continued until the following
noon, when they made sail for the point from which land had been sighted.
And early on January 30 they ran into a deep bay "formed by solid ice and low
ledges of rocks," as Underwood described the scene, beyond which rose "long
high ranges of mountains, showing peak over peak covered with snow." *

* The *Vincennes* was in Piner Bay (which Wilkes named for his signal quartermaster, Thomas

A NEW WORLD

Underwood thought them five to six thousand feet high and perhaps twenty-five miles distant, but there were ledges of rock no more than three miles away. At 9:45 a cast of the lead touched bottom at thirty-five fathoms, and a rocky bottom at that, as shown by dents in the lead. But again the wind rose and an hour later they stood out of the bay in a light snowfall.

Regaining the barrier fifty miles farther west, they stood along it in thick weather and gales, with appearances of high land reported from day to day.* The ice here appeared more solid than any yet seen and some of it in the fantastic shapes of towers, forests, animals, wharves, and bridges—to list their favorite analogies—common the previous season. With land still in sight on February 12 when their longitude was 112° 16′ 12″ E., Wilkes felt certain that despite their inability to get further soundings† they had been coasting land for more than thirty degrees of longitude, or some eight hundred miles, and so

---

Piner) on the Adélie Coast, where outcrops of rock are occasionally visible. Land near the coast rises to over 3600 feet.

* On February 2, Alden, Wilkes, Green, Sanford, and Underwood noted sightings of land in their journals; on February 5 Alden; February 6 Underwood, Alden, Sanford; February 7 Alden, Wilkes; February 8 Wilkes; February 11 Alden; February 12 Alden, Green, Sanford, Underwood, Wilkes; February 13 Alden, Underwood, Sanford.

† Wilkes was probably aware that John Biscoe, three miles off Adelaide Island eight years earlier, had been unable to get soundings at 250 fathoms. Determination of when Wilkes was first persuaded of the proximity of land is complicated by his method of journal-keeping. As a rule he made entries on the right-hand page, reserving the left for emendations. He was afterwards to date his claim for the *Vincennes* from January 19, but in his regular (right-hand) entry for that day he makes no mention of the appearance of land, except in small, cramped script, obviously compressed so as not to extend beyond the margin: "with appearances of land to the S.S.E." On the left-hand page appears a revealing note, utterly uncharacteristic of a journal that is almost wholly factual and devoid of personal flavor. "I wish I could speak the Peacock to be confirmed in my opinion relative to the Land I feel confidence of existing to the S & E to S & W. There is no one on board My own Ship that I can communicate with. . . . It is provoking that we cant get through this interminable barrier and get with the Land that I am Confident exists now but I feel that every opportunity will be taken by me whatever may be the risk (if I know myself) to get to it. . . . No I must be patient, altho' I cannot help feeling how disgusting it is to be with such a set of officers (One or two I must except,) who are endeavouring to do all in their powers to make my exertions go for nothing—We shall however see how we will all come out of this scrape. I keep to my old motto *nil Desperandum*. . . ." It is my distinct impression that this heroic passage was written for other eyes and at a date considerably subsequent. Though on the left-hand page opposite his regular entry for January 15 (the day before Reynolds and Eld sighted land from the *Peacock*) Wilkes sketched a little bay in the barrier with a curved line over the horizon labeled "Supposed Land," otherwise January 20 is his first regular entry that mentions the appearance of land. Of the other journals kept aboard the *Vincennes* on this cruise and still extant, Ezra Green's and Midshipman Samuel B. Elliott's are the only ones that mention the appearance of land on January 19. The latter reads, "Discovered *Land* and field Ice from the lee ¼ to lee bow." But "Land" is written over the incomplete erasure of another word, evidently "iceberg." Underwood first notes appearance of land on January 22, Sanford on January 23. Elliott notes appearances on the twenty-third. On the twenty-eighth he is definite: "At 1.45 Discovered Land bearing South & SS.E.—" and on the thirtieth emphatic: "At 5 A.M.—*Discovered high Mountainous Land* to the South covered with snow." It will be recalled that it was on the afternoon of January 19 that Reynolds and Clark claimed to have seen land from the *Peacock*.

had "discovered the Antarctic Continent"—the name he chose to award it.[1]

To celebrate the national achievement with a "treat of Champagne," the commander unbent slightly and invited to the cabin all the officers except those who had been heard to agree that he was "too d----d lucky a fellow." The man had discovered in spite of himself.

Hoping to determine the continent's extent, they made land again the next day an estimated fifteen miles distant. The sea was green, but there were no soundings at three hundred fathoms and the weather being unsettled, they tacked and stood off. But the fourteenth was clear and the *Vincennes* stood through some miles of drift ice for the land that could be seen distinctly, again no more than fifteen miles away, rising to some three thousand feet and covered with snow. At eleven in the morning and in 65° 59′ 45″ S., 106° 18′ 42″ E., they were stopped by closely packed floe ice but with land so near that Underwood could make out "all the ravines and separate hills," which he thought not nearly so high as those seen on January 30.

On duty—and off, February 14, 1840, at 65° 59′ 45″ S.,
106° 18′ 42″ E., from sketch by Charles Wilkes.
(*Narrative*, 2: facing p. 344, Western Americana
Collection, Yale University Library.)

A NEW WORLD

Guarding the mysterious land beyond, the ramparts of ice held them forever at bay. It was the more frustrating now that land was so often in view, but in the afternoon the intruders discovered that not all of it lay within the barrier. From one iceberg more than usually discolored (and "three times larger than Boston Common," one Massachusetts man noted) the boat crews collected sand, pebbles, and stones. Quite on the top, some ninety feet above the sea, they found a stone weighing upwards of seventy pounds, which they duly lugged aboard, and, inaccessible beneath a ledge, they spotted a much larger one. The crews amused themselves by sliding down the iceberg's slopes and generally cavorting about while the officers conducted magnetic observations. After collecting some five hundred gallons of "very delicious water" from a pond in one of the berg's ravines and placing the *Vincennes'* Signal Number One atop it with orders to Hudson and Ringgold to continue the cruise westward until March 1, they gathered up their specimens of the new continent and at eight in the morning stood to the west in hopes of adding a few more degrees of longitude to their discovery.

By February 17, having passed more earth-stained bergs and explored a large bay, Wilkes was persuading himself that they had gone far enough. The hours of darkness were lengthening, the crew was weary, with the sick list approaching thirty, and he himself was feeling unwell. They had reached their westward goal of 105° E. some days earlier and confirmed the continental proportions of their discovery. And besides, he assured himself, Hudson and Ringgold would find their new orders and continue to the west.

Accordingly, on February 21 Wilkes mustered all hands (including three convict stowaways who had appeared at the morning muster on January 5 in borrowed uniforms and were entered on the ship's rolls with Wilkes' assurance that they would be turned over to the authorities at Sydney at the end of the cruise) and informed them that the ship was now bound north, thanked the men for their good behavior, and awarded an extra tot all round. And so the *Vincennes* "bid a hearty adieu," Ezra Green remarked, "to the *Barrier of ice* which so obstinately prevented our landing upon our newly discovered Continent." *

While the *Vincennes* was turning northward, the men of the *Porpoise* were celebrating Washington's Birthday some twenty-four degrees to the east. In honor of the day, fresh meat and vegetables were served out to the crew from

---

* Since leaving Piner Bay, the *Vincennes* had proceeded along the Claire, Bonzare, Sabrina, Budd, and Knox Coasts to what Wilkes labeled "Termination Land" on the edge of Queen Mary Coast.

the hospital stores, which had been of little use on this particularly healthy ship. Extra grog was allowed, and the day "passed off with great hilarity." Mustering all hands, Ringgold thanked them for their "uniform good conduct," expressed regret that their arduous efforts had not been crowned with the discoveries all had hoped for, and, unaware of his new orders floating somewhere in the west, announced his intention of returning north in a few days more. In the wardroom toasts were drunk and speeches made in the afternoon. Not surprisingly, the day's run was only eighteen miles.

The *Porpoise* had followed in the track of the *Vincennes* but had seen little of the continent her sister ship had coasted for thirty-six degrees. At its first appearance the barrier had damped the hopes of many, who concluded with Doctor Holmes that though in all probability the pieces composing it had been carried by the wind to the shores of "some great obstacle such as land" lying hidden at its center, the ice was "far too thick to discover land if it were under our noses. It would be no joke," he concluded doubtfully, "if our southern Cruise of exploration . . . should be 'knocked up' by this icy barrier." But though they sailed in the *Vincennes'* wake and explored several promising bays, the barrier did most decidedly knock up their cruise and cast a pall over the hopes of all. Holmes' journal is a catalogue of disappointments. In the middle of January, after having beat to the westward some five hundred miles, he noted that the barrier, a hundred feet high in places here, still preserved "its old station and I seriously fear will prove a complete obstacle to southern exploration," though he did note "marked appearances of land" in the evening. Two days later, still coasting the "intolerable ice float": "Fortium Aves not favor us, and we shall reap little glory from Southern exploration."

They sighted the *Peacock* for the last time on January 23, entering the ice bay where she was to find bottom at 320 fathoms and stones in the penguin's craw. The brig was leaving it, having found only that the barrier was impenetrable, "so that if we do not get far south, we have the best possible reason to give for our failure." On the morning of January 27 they saw the last of the *Vincennes* and a gale blew up that lasted three days, obliging them to haul off. On the afternoon of the thirtieth when they made the barrier again in the neighborhood of 64° 50′ S., 135° 27′ E., they made out two vessels under easy sail on a northerly course. Taking them for the *Vincennes* and *Peacock*, Ringgold determined to speak them. But on nearer approach they appeared to be strangers. After some speculation it was agreed that the English expedition under Ross had probably sailed from Cape Town and was now engaged on its first southern cruise. Ringgold hoisted colors and the men stood ready to cheer the discoverer of the north magnetic pole. But in answer the strangers ran up

A NEW WORLD

French colors and the larger the broad pennant of a commodore. It was Dumont d'Urville then. No matter. To cheer the prince of French explorers the *Porpoise* set a course that would carry her under the *Astrolabe*'s stern. It was the stuff of high drama, this unprecedented meeting of two national expeditions at the edge of the last continent, but misunderstanding instantly reduced it to farce. For when the brig was within short pistol shot the strangers suddenly made all sail. Astonished and a good deal miffed, Ringgold hauled down his colors, bore up on his course "without a moment's delay," and as Holmes remarked disgustedly, "left these ill-mannered Frenchmen." The doctor had never witnessed a "more selfish and ungentlemanly act," and the flames of indignation spreading to the imagination, he speculated on the results this "churlishness" might have had. "Suppose . . . we had been in danger of perishing from want of provisions? We might have perished within hail of the French flag." They had in fact mistaken the French intentions, for Dumont d'Urville, seeing the brig approaching at a fast clip and wishing to communicate, had made sail only that he might keep pace. And so, the one indignant, the other much puzzled, and both sensitive to national honor, the two explorers went their separate ways, each reflecting on the other's deplorable manners.*

On reaching longitude 133° E. and finding the barrier higher and firmer than ever, Holmes like Wilkes began to doubt the dictum that ice never forms in an open sea. Doubts remained firm until February 12, when they reached the western limit set by their instructions. Though having failed, understandably, to sight Wilkes' decorated iceberg, they came upon evidence during the morning that nonetheless impelled them a little farther—a piece of black ice, which, towed alongside, was found to be composed of alternate layers of ice and snow, the latter mixed with sand and containing pieces of rock the size of apples. They gathered more next day, a hundred miles farther on. But still the land itself eluded them, and Holmes himself concluded that these pieces had probably drifted from Kerguelen's Island to the northwest.

On February 14 they gave up westering, wore ship, and ran to the east, disappointed of course but well satisfied they had done their duty, as Holmes persuaded himself they had. "Nothing has been seen by us to warrant the belief that land exists anywhere in our vicinity. We have coasted along the field ice from 165° E. to 100° E. and have found *one solid, unbroken, impenetrable barrier of ice*" and "if anything *could have been done,* I have no hesitation in saying that *we should have done it.*" [2]

* Astonishingly, there was to be a similarly fruitless encounter with the French at the Auckland Islands in March.

Wilkes expected no more of the schooner than his officers did of *Vincennes.* She was small and fragile and if the masthead of the brig was not lofty enough to raise the continent, still less was to be seen from the *Flying Fish*'s. Perhaps she would have accomplished little even had Wilkes esteemed her and her commander and furnished men and provisions accordingly, but the cruise would have been considerably less miserable for all on board.

She had made the barrier at three in the morning of January 21, and with only four of the crew well enough to perform duty took up the long journey to the west. Once during his watch Sinclair brought her in close under the lee of a mile-long berg to have "a good look" at some discolorations. The ice stole their wind and they had to resort to the sweeps to keep her off—and none too soon, for a huge mass broke off above "with a noise like thunder and the snow flew into the air so as to look as tho it was smoking," and the resulting swell set the schooner to rolling seas aboard. "I was quite satisfied with my scientific experiment," Sinclair concluded ruefully. They saw many birds and seals, observed the greenish cast of the sea, and were sure this vast body of ice must be attached to land. But with not enough hands to haul the lead line they could not venture a deep cast. On January 22, within a few miles of the *Peacock*'s position when Reynolds and Eld first saw land in the distance, they made out with spyglasses "large masses of rock" embedded in the field ice about a mile from the barrier's edge. But there was no way to reach them even if there had been able men enough to make a boat's crew.

Fine weather and a sharp lookout won them that much before the snow squalls struck and fog. Then they could steer only by the sound of waves crashing against the barrier to port and the bergs to starboard, sometimes roaring into caverns to spout fifty or sixty feet into the air. Sinclair found it a "most Blood chilling sound, fully equal to the rattling of the Chain Cables at Noir Island." Often through the fog they could hear the cry of penguins, but far from taking heart at the voice of life in the otherwise forsaken world, they found it "a mournful sound amidst the howling of the Tempest."

Things grew worse. Another man fell sick, leaving but three able to take the helm, and the officer of the deck had to divide his watch between looking out for bergs as he stood lashed to the foremast and spelling the helmsman to warm himself at the cabin stove. The schooner labored mightily in the heavy seas, plunging under to the heel of her jib-boom, yet even with all hands they dared not attempt to reef the foresail for fear of losing the only sail they could lie-to under. When the incessant pounding opened her seams the crew had to man the pumps. Of this able-bodied trio one had "the Venereal" and another's feet were so swollen that he was standing the four-hour helm watch

A NEW WORLD

in stocking feet. They relieved the pitching somewhat by shifting their coal aft but still had to pump continuously. As the constant wetting rendered the berth deck uninhabitable and left only the cabin stove useable for cooking—and even it was forever being drowned by the sea washing over its pipes—the crew were taken into the cabin with the officers.

In the cabin of the *Flying Fish,* from sketch by Alfred T. Agate. (J. C. Palmer, *Thulia: A Tale of the Antarctic,* New York, 1843, p. 19.)

When the weather lifted a little on February 3 Pinkney thought he could make out land to the southward, but Sinclair disagreed. It was "too high for land" and probably only a cloud mass with clearly defined edges. But even he thought land near and was sure that, could they but make it, a cast of the lead would touch in a hundred fathoms.

By February 5, the gale still blowing and the sea running high, the crew had had enough. Confined as they now were, officers and crew constituted a miniature and, one would suppose, intimate community, yet the men addressed to Pinkney a formal and decorous letter representing that, whereas their clothes and bedding had been waterlogged for days and the ablebodied among them reduced to three, they could not much longer bear up under sufferings which "must soon terminate in DEATH." Himself down with a high fever, Pinkney called for the written opinions of his officers, who replied unanimously that neither vessel nor crew was fit for this cruise. The petitioners were so informed and shortly before noon, having worked westward to 143° 09′ E. (as best they could make out from sights taken from the tossing deck) they bore up for the north, a miserable lot of invalids, one slowly starving, one immobilized from the "Poo Poo & Pox," another covered with ulcers, the boatswain afflicted with *tic douleureux,* the cabin boy down with "rheumatism in the head."

But on reaching the fiftieth parallel the sick men came crawling out "like Galapagos Terrapins" into the sunshine and a week later were sufficiently recovered to get into a fight and one to receive a dozen of the cats. Sinclair could joke again. One day off the barrier he and Pinkney had seriously feared attack by a large whale cavorting near the little vessel. But now, in the cruising ground of whalers off the south coast of New Zealand, they laughed over the need to run with all caution, "lest we should find a harpoon driven into us." On March 9 Sinclair mustered the "Ghostly crew in their best bib & tucker," looked them over and remarked in his journal, "Such a set of human beings I never saw, Falstaffs troop would have been left in the back ground by comparison." Next day they anchored in the harbor, thanked God for preserving them from the ice and, finding themselves first in, from their commander's greetings.

They found the scientists waiting (all but Couthouy, who, the Sydney doctors despairing of his recovery, had taken ship for the Sandwich Islands, via Tahiti again, in search of a more salubrious climate) and waiting in no very good humor. They had been there a month and, without the means to pursue their investigations any distance into the interior, had therefore had to limit themselves to the neighborhood of Bay of Islands, where, Peale complained, they had "gathered all the plants, shot all the Birds, caught all the fish, and got heartily sick of the Natives, in spite of their tatooing and carving." They had fared better in Australia, where Dana had tramped over the mountains of the Illawarra district with William B. Clarke, whom, more interested in geology than theology, he found "a strange man for a clergyman," collecting fossil shells and noting evidences of stream erosion, and where in search of vocabularies Hale had traveled by steamer and stage to the frontiers of settlement.

On March 26, the *Porpoise* came in and four days later, the *Vincennes,* with news of the *Peacock*'s arrival at Sydney, where she was undergoing repairs after near disaster. "Thus we are all safe again from this most perilous cruise," rejoiced Sinclair, who likened the *Peacock*'s sailing while her spare rudder was in the storeship to a man traveling with his pistols in his trunk. The poor *Peacock* had anchored at Port Jackson on the night of February 21, truly without a pilot this time, after a nerve-wracking voyage during which, to spare the rudder, they had steered mostly by the sails. Hudson took his ship over to Mossman's Bay, a snug place on Port Jackson's North Shore which he found ideal, removed as it was from the "Rum Shops and the various arts" of Sydney's crimps. A man with a novel "diving machine"—an "India rubber suit with a metal helmet" fitted with "glass eyes," Emmons observed—inspected the bottom and reported that the damage was largely confined to the bow. To effect the repairs they ran her onto the beach at high tide. What her officers saw at ebb made them gasp. The gripe and cutwater were eaten away below the waterline, at several places to within an inch and a half of the butts of the planking. Emmons estimated that they would surely have gone down had they remained "sawing an hour longer," for once brought into contact with the ice the plank ends would have sprung wide and "no human force could have kept the ship afloat."

While workmen swarmed over the ship and riggers, sailmakers, carpenters, and armorers busied themselves ashore, Emmons visited the Sydney Library. Though unimpressed by the natural history museum housed in the building, he found something to think about in a newspaper account of the expedition that Britain was sending to circumnavigate the South Pole under the experienced Arctic explorers Captain James Clark Ross and Captain Francis R. M. Crozier. As their ships had been built expressly for service in the ice no doubt their explorations would be something to reckon with, though he could not foresee how bitter the reckoning would be, or how soon it would begin.

On March 11 the *Vincennes* arrived at Sydney, Wilkes having decided not to put in at Hobart in Van Diemen's land. At Fort Macquarie he turned the three stowaways over to the authorities, and the youngest, a Cockney who had become a great favorite with all on board, was claimed by the sergeant of the Fifty-Sixth Regiment as his drummer boy. (It was afterwards heard that he was sentenced to one hundred and ten lashes and actually given ninety-three, the final five posthumously.) The *Vincennes* carried by far the longest sick list in the squadron and probably the bitterest set of officers then afloat. Surgeon Gilchrist came ashore with his baggage, dismissed from the squadron, and Blunt, Underwood, and Case requested transfer to the popular *Peacock*, which Wilkes cursorily refused, though with Case he unbent enough to add that solely "as respects myself I should be most happy to exchange your Services . . . for those of any other officer in the Squadron." By the time the *Vincennes* reached New Zealand, so many requests for transfer reached her cabin that Wilkes was compelled to issue a general order to regulate the matter in the "interest of the service." Jim Blair was privately investigating all these difficulties and to set his father straight reported that despite Wilkes' attempt to delay the *Peacock*'s arrival at the south, Hudson's bold motions had placed the "good old Ship" so far in advance of the rest that Wilkes was badly stung with jealousy. Blair was sure that when the details were made public at home, Captain Hudson, "the best leg that the Expedition stands upon," would be acclaimed its hero.

Still, it was the *Vincennes* that had put the "great question" at rest and redeemed the Expedition, whose track would now "be conspicuous on all Charts, for ages to come." She had run "terrible risks," it was acknowledged with some surprise, and her accomplishment so impressed those aboard the *Peacock* that their own discovery dropped out of mind, though not of memory.

The secret was to be kept until Washington could be informed. Hudson prepared his report to the Secretary of Navy in a document dated March 3, in which he stated that the *Peacock* on January 19 made "what we believed to be Land" (failing to mention that he had not believed it to be such at the time), and again on January 23, when they had seen "high Land—at least so far as 'terra firma' can be distinguished—where every thing is covered with snow." But as there was no opportunity to send his dispatch Hudson submitted it to Wilkes on the latter's arrival.

On March 12, the day after the *Vincennes* arrived at Sydney with the glorious news, a vessel put in from Hobart with the report that the French explorers had arrived and were letting it be known that they had discovered land within the Antarctic Circle on the evening of January 19 at 66° S., 130° E. Alden was aboard the *Vincennes* when he first heard this news and greeted Wilkes at the gangway with the remark that the French had beaten them. No doubt having learned of the claim ashore, Wilkes rose to the occasion. "Oh, no," he replied, "don't you recollect reporting to me of land on the Morning of the 19th?" Alden did not, and even his examination of the log entry barely brought the incident back to his mind. Shortly afterward the United States consul came aboard to draw up a statement for the press. Alden happened to be in the cabin at the time, working on the charts of the southern cruise (Wilkes himself was to supply the topography) and with astonishment heard him read the announcement that was to appear in the *Sydney Herald* next day.

The newspaper had it "on the highest authority, that the researches of the exploring squadron after a southern continent have been completely successful. The land was first seen on the morning of the 19th of January, in latitude 66° 20′ south, longitude 154° 18′ east." The *Peacock*, by getting soundings in a high latitude, had established "beyond doubt the existence of land in that direction," and the *Vincennes*, by running down the coast some seventeen hundred miles, taking frequent soundings, and returning with specimens of rock and earth, "completed the discovery." Though questioning whether the researches would prove of "any essential benefit to commerce," the *Herald* was effusive in its congratulations and hopeful that "so noble a commencement in the cause of science and discovery" would induce the American government to regard it as precedent for future endeavor.

The praise was generous enough to please the most red-blooded of the explorers, but the same column of newsprint carried an article from the *Hobart Town Courier* reporting the French discovery. When news of the French expedition first reached the United States in 1837 it was widely (and correctly) assumed that the "strong representations and effective arguments" in Congress and about the country in favor of polar exploration had stimulated "our ancient ally to redouble vigor." There had been sentimental predictions about the "sons of those sires who stood shoulder to shoulder on the redoubts of Yorktown," praising with "equal cordiality" one another's daring "amid the storms of Antarctic seas." The American explorers had heard that Louis Philippe had promised his officers "any thing, should they get the farthest South," but this claim was almost the only news they had received of the French effort. Sailing a year before the Americans, the French had skirted the fringes of the Weddell Sea and stood off the coasts of the South Shetlands and the Palmer Peninsula during the season of 1837–1838. Some of their junior officers had spread a "Cock & bull Story about the discovery of a Continent," but investigation showed that the supposed discovery was only Palmer's Land, or Louis Philippe Land, as they termed it. They had spent the following season in the Pacific "& this year When we thought them all on their way home," Reynolds wrote his family, "lo & behold! they were close at us!"

When the Americans heard the astounding news that the French also claimed to have sighted land on January 19, memories were suddenly refreshed, recollections brightened, and asseverations and solemn depositions appeared on every hand. Reynolds lamented that Hudson had treated so lightly the report of land that he and Eld had made on January 16. So did Hudson, whom he now found "quite ready to believe, that Eld & I had not been deceived! but how to remedy it?" Jealousy for his own ship overwhelmed by a greater jealousy called national honor, Wilkes himself took eager note of Reynolds' and Eld's claim and at New Zealand lent a willing ear to Ringgold's recollection (not to be refreshed by reference to the *Porpoise*'s log, which made no mention of it) that on going aloft on the afternoon of January 16 he had seen beyond the ice "an object, large, dark, and rounding, resembling a mountain in the distance," which contrasted sharply with the "light and brilliant" icebergs. He had concluded that it was an "island surrounded by immense fields of ice" and now expressed surprise that Wilkes had failed to mention his own discovery when the *Vincennes* and brig hailed one another on January 26. Oh, had not Ringgold heard him ask if he (Ringgold) had seen the land? No, Ringgold had not, but then it was blowing fresh, and they were within hail only briefly.

Only the *Flying Fish* was now discoveryless—which fact doubtless served to lower her even further in Wilkes' esteem—and George Sinclair, who saw the ships come into Bay of Islands trailing laurels, thought it "somewhat strange that we did not hear that the Porpoise had seen land before the arrival of the Vins but now that the Vins had discovered a new World, it appears that the Porpoise saw it, before she did. . . . We are a great Nation!"

But whoever saw it first, it was the *Vincennes*' train of successive landfalls that won the prize by showing that a continent, "& Not so Many Islands," lay within the ice. As they saw it, the French, who might have accomplished as much, ran only a hundred and fifty miles along the ice before putting back, for "Frenchman like," observed Reynolds, "they must run away to tell of their Success, and that has ruined them!" Though the Americans remained unaware of the hardships the French had suffered, the charge was less than generous in view of the latter's having effected a landing.

Reynolds did not know that Wilkes also had an ambition to tell and that by doing so he almost ruined their own accomplishment. At New Zealand in early April, Wilkes addressed a long letter of advice to Captain Ross, together with a tracing of the chart he had made, and dispatched them to Hobart Town to wait the Englishman's arrival. Though a violation of Paulding's injunction to secrecy, it was an act natural enough for one who had just discovered the continent that the English expedition was to search for, and if it exuded too much of the bravado that Americans were noted for, that failing might have been discounted by its recipient. It was unfortunate that the Englishman would see impertinence and subterfuge in what was only self-congratulation, for while Dumont d'Urville merely contested priority of the discovery, Ross was to suggest rather forcefully that it had never been made.

But that controversy lay in the future, and when the *Vincennes, Porpoise,* and *Flying Fish* stood out from Bay of Islands on the morning of April 6, 1840 (the *Peacock* having already sailed on March 30) Wilkes had every reason to congratulate himself. Seeing good ground for a wider distribution of credit and assuming that "Capt. W . . . would not in his vanity, acknowledge it," Dana sent his and Captain Hudson's congratulations to J. N. Reynolds in New York, "that his expectations respecting the Southern Continent have been realized." [3]

11 *Among the Feejees*

The old Savage King became a most devout Christian, and
a statesman into the bargain . . . , he handed his Country
over to Queen Victoria. . . .

A Peripatetic Parson

For once even the midshipmen knew what the next port of call
would be. "We are bound for Tonga Taboo!" Reynolds recorded in delight.
The little that was known of the Tonga Islands was from accounts of the
wandering preachers of the London Missionary Society and the celebrated
book by William Mariner, who had lived there for some years after twenty-six
of his shipmates of the *Port-au-Prince* were massacred in 1806. Everyone knew
that Cook had named these the Friendly Islands out of total misapprehension
of the nature of their inhabitants.

The *Peacock* had sailed from Sydney on March 30 and, alternately buffeted
by contrary winds and left dead in the water by calms, did not sight the Tonga
Group until a month later. When they finally worked through the reef that
surrounded Tongatabu it was only to find the other vessels getting underway
and the *Vincennes* flying the signal, Join Company. They had to content
themselves with spyglass glimpses of the green island and the accounts of those
who had got ashore.

The *Flying Fish*, under George Sinclair's command now, the popular
Pinkney having been confined to the *Peacock* after another sharp exchange
with Wilkes, had made the group on April 21. She had anchored off
Nukualofa, a large and handsome village of some five hundred huts
surrounded by a closely woven fence of reeds and timber some ten feet high
and presenting an appearance of surpassing neatness. The chaplain was happy
to find it a community of Christians, "moral, industrious and clean" and

186

"almost white." (John W. W. Dyes was more skeptical, being "greatly surprised," he wrote home, "to hear from the first native that spoke English the question if I could give him a bottle of rum, and I asked if the missionaries had not learned him better, he shrugged up his shoulders in reply and said, 'I am missionary.' ") English Wesleyans had been here since 1826 and the *Flying Fish* was no sooner anchored than they were breathlessly recounting their tribulations to the explorers. One frankly told Sinclair that the only solution to the "difficulties of the Island" was to exterminate the heathen party. But their suggestions fell on deaf ears so long as they had to deal with the men of the *Flying Fish*, who found the heathens fully as engaging as the Christians and the women of both camps "enough with their little winning ways to trap an anchorite."

With the arrival of the *Vincennes* on April 24, however, the missionaries gained an ally of sorts, and the explorers had their first glimpse of large numbers of armed savages one day when they were treated to the novel sight of the missionaries' war party strung out across the harbor in canoes, Wilkes in his gig at their head, followed by George (Taufa'ahau), chief of nearby Ha'apai, and his warriors. As they approached the *Vincennes* with paddles flashing in the sun, the whole party broke into "Old Hundred." "The tenner tribbl & Base was well sung," Dyes noted appreciatively, "& I must confess I never heard any thing that sounded Better." Wilkes summoned a peace conference: but though the converts, headed by King Josiah (Aleamotu'a), were amenable, their "ghostly advisers," as Sinclair called the missionaries, held out for total surrender. Fearing Christian treachery, the heathens simply kept clear and the proceedings came to nought, to the great satisfaction of George Sinclair, who inclined to the view that "The most damnable and blood thirsty Tyranny that a nation can be subjected to, is that of a Bigoted religious sect."

Their faces swollen from mosquito bites and looking, Doctor Holmes observed, as though they had spent the night "fisticuffing one another," the explorers weighed anchor and stood away for the Fijis early on the morning of May 4. Wilkes had read a great deal about the group for which they were bound and with the smugness that never ceased to infuriate his officers, calmly observed to the English pilot taken aboard at Nukualofa, "You will find when we get to the islands, that I know as much about them as you do." The officers, who had more than once heard Kotzebue dismissed as a "liar" and King as "a drunken fellow," naturally wondered on hearing this announcement why Wilkes had bothered to engage a pilot at all and rejoiced to hear the latter reply, "You may know all about them on paper, but when you come to the goings in, and comings out, you will see who knows best, you or myself."

Actually the squadron needed all the assistance it could get. The Fiji Group, Reynolds noted as they stood to the northwest before a fair breeze, had "a hard name with Navigators." And deservedly so, for the three-hundred-odd islands were a wilderness where the elements met in enmity, the land a crazy patchwork, the water a bedlam of treacherous currents, with many places that could accurately be described as neither land nor water, where the bottom would lie at fifty fathoms one moment and three the next, with nothing for a man to fix his eye on. The labyrinths of reefs and shoals that wrenched the ocean currents into every point of the compass made navigation a problem primarily for the man at the masthead. The inhabitants had proved uncooperative in attempts at accurate charting, and a century after the squadron's appearance some of the islands were still not surveyed in detail or even named.*

The charts available to the Americans were of little use. One obtained from an English trading schooner at Tongatabu was both unreliable and a little intimidating. Presenting "a frightful display of rocks & reefs" ornamented with such ominous bits of intelligence as "Eliza lost," "American brig lost," and the like, it seemed little more than a collection of maritime epitaphs, and in an access of bravado Wilkes let it be known that he fully expected to lose at least two of his own ships here.

But these islands owed their hard name as much to their culture as to their configuration. These were the "Cannibal Isles." The Tongans had doubtless told the explorers something of their neighbors to the west, from whom they had learned how to strangle widows and eat human flesh, and among whom they found relief from the tiresome peace that obtained for long periods in their own country. On the brief passage in thick and rainy weather from

---

* Abel Tasman had first sighted a few of them in 1643 and had come near losing his two small ships in the process. William Bligh in 1789 had been the first to realize their extent when after the famous mutiny in Tongan waters he had sailed his six-oared open launch unarmed straight through them, with good fortune rare in that unhappy life emerging unscathed at the western end. Bligh managed to assemble the materials for a chart, and Captain James Wilson of the *Duff*, who made further discoveries in 1797, drew up another. Further clarification came early in the nineteenth century with development of the trade in sandalwood, a commodity in plentiful supply on the largest of the Fijis, Vanua Levu, whose Sandalwood Bay (Bua) became one of the busiest ports of the South Seas. By 1815 the groves were gone, but in Martin Arrowsmith's chart of 1814 the trade had produced the first approximately accurate representation of even a part of the group. In 1820 Bellingshausen had added a few more islands to the Low Archipelago, or Windward Group, to the east. Dumont d'Urville had come to the center of the group in 1827 seeking, unsuccessfully, to solve the mystery of La Pérouse and again in 1838 in the *Astrolabe* and *Zélée* to destroy the town responsible for killing the captain and many of the crew of *l'Amiable Josephine* four years earlier.

Tongatabu some of the officers busied themselves with drawing up their wills.

Though the explorers had no way of knowing, they came at a time of unrest and therefore danger. A violent storm early in the year was followed by an awesome flood at Rewa Roads, ominous portents to a superstitious people. The chiefs of the island of Bau, an emergent center of power, were raiding in every direction so that war was nearly constant. In short, the people were in an ugly temper and William Reynolds spoke better than he knew when after two weeks in the islands he remarked lightheartedly, "Well, we are among the Feejees, & I have not been Killed nor Eaten, nor wrecked yet."

The Expedition, now approaching the closing months of its second year, found itself entering a largely unexplored archipelago strung along nearly six degrees of latitude and five of longitude. A survey of a substantial portion of it might alone be deemed justification enough for the expedition, and to the approval of all Wilkes sensibly divided the task. The *Porpoise* dropped behind to survey the Low Archipelago, while the *Vincennes* and *Peacock* proceeded to Ovalau. The schooner tarried long enough to receive the traditional Fiji welcome by spending an alarming night atop a reef that removed some ten feet of her false keel.

The lofty ruin of a giant volcano lying just off the northwest coast of Viti Levu, Ovalau for some years past had been the chief center of European settlement in the group. Its port of Levuka, constricted to the beach by the massive heights beyond, was an assemblage of thickly thatched, high-gabled native houses that resembled haycocks and a scattering of houses of European style. Aloft on the *Peacock* as the ships approached, one homesick reefer gave a cry of joy at sighting a cow on the hillside, "whisking her tail among the bushes, & feeding just as quietly as our own Cows at Home." Working their way through the crowds of curious natives gathered on the beach they found the town oddly intersected by walls of stone and earth, erected, they correctly assumed, for defense.

The inhabitants were apparently constructed to the same end. Tall and vigorous, clad only in a bit of tapa at the loins, begrimed and bedaubed with red paint and soot, ears slit and hanging nearly to the shoulder with a bone or shell thrust through the hole, hair grotesquely frizzed out from the head, dyed various hues and teeming with life—they presented a "spectacle of mingled hideousness & ferocity" that struck the explorers as an apt expression of the character they bore, and the visitors were disconcerted to learn that these savage warriors performed all the culinary tasks and handled children "with all the tenderness imaginable." It seemed quite out of place for "Men of their Calibre."

White men had been living in the islands since the wreck of the *Argo* in the first decade of the century, rendering various services to the sandalwood and *bêche-de-mer* ships, trading and fighting. The company of ten or so now resident at Levuka were a remarkably industrious and law-abiding group in this notoriously lawless track. They were chiefly English and American, though one day a short, thickset old fellow, almost as dark as the natives but with bright blue eyes and a white beard that left off only where his *maro* (a loincloth made of tapa) began, came out to the ships. He was Patrick Connel of County Cavan, he announced in a rich brogue, eighty-five years old and in these islands for forty. Transported to Botany Bay after the Irish rebellion of 1798, he had escaped aboard a French privateer, then jumped ship in the Fijis. Welcomed by Tanoa, chief of the Bau district, he had become a power in the islands. But now reduced in circumstances he lived with his remaining three wives on nearby Batiki, wishing only, by adding two offspring, to round off his progeny at a hundred and fifty and, "plase Jasus," provide each son with a hatchet. The explorers concluded, however, that he was a white man yet, for seven years before he had warned the crew of the *Charles Daggett* of approaching attack and, when twelve men were lost despite his warning, had purchased their bodies from the natives. The officers and scientists spent hours listening to this Irish Sinbad's tales of the Fijis.

Connel was only the most spectacular of an odd lot. William Valentine came from a good New York family. Salem was represented by James Magoun, eight years in the Fijis, and Nantucket by Jacob Cunningham and David Whippey. A resident now for eleven years, Cunningham had been wrecked here with Captain Vanderford, now the *Vincennes'* interpreter and trading master, and had seen a fire blaze for his roasting before being rescued by some natives from Bau. The widely respected Whippey, who had run away from a *bêche-de-mer* ship in 1822, had built the first vessel ever constructed in the Fijis, taken several wives, and become a great favorite with the chiefs. Thirteen years before, he had rescued his fellow Nantucketer William Cary from captivity after the *Oeno* disaster and put him aboard Vanderford's *Clay*. In the 1820's, after the sandalwood groves were gone, Vanderford himself had founded the trade in *bêche-de-mer*, which quickly became an American monopoly dominated by Salem, and in a few years there were as many ships "fishing" for the sea slugs as formerly had come for sandalwood. His arch rival in the trade was Captain John Henry Eagleston, who sailed for Stephen C. Phillips of Salem, a vigorous supporter in Congress of the Exploring Expedition. The two captains had fallen out over jurisdiction of a *bêche-de-mer* reef many years since and cordially detested one another. Master now of the *Leonidas*, Eagleston was working the reefs around Vanua Levu (where the natives had recently killed one of his men) with the assistance of a small sloop built at Levuka and whimsically christened *Who Would Have Thought It*. This little fraternity* was to prove of great assistance to the explorers, who were delighted to converse again with white men who were not missionaries.[1]

At the time he was shipwrecked Vanderford had been rescued by the great chief Tanoa, called "Old Snuff" by the Levuka whites from the peculiar nasal whine of his speech that made him appear to be forever on the verge of a sneeze. Probably about seventy now, a spare and twisted mass of wrinkles with red-rimmed eyes and a long matted beard, this offensive old fellow was a daring navigator and one of the great chiefs of the islands. Those explorers who thought it good fun to entertain him on board with all the ceremony appropriate to a reigning monarch failed to reflect that his erratic tyranny made him precisely that.

As Dyes described the usual visits the Fijians would scramble aboard and immediately assume a squatting posture on the deck, "With hans under ther Hunches some times holding their Privates Whitch is tuck up in a Little pece of tapper." Not so Old Snuff, who, had he squatted, would not have deigned to employ his own hands. He stepped aboard in a white maro, long enough to form a train, his face blacked with charcoal and a slab of pearl shell hanging from the neck. The *Vincennes* was dressed in flags about the quarterdeck and the marines were turned out in full dress to parade with the little makeshift band that at the instigation of some wag struck up "The King of the Cannibal Islands." Escorted through the ship to see the arms supply, the operation of the lathe, and, most impressive of all, the armorer at work, the party wound up in the cabin, where out of deference to his rank, Tanoa was given whiskey, which Reynolds thought he downed "with the air & relish of an old toper," and one of Hall's Patent Rifles with brasses. Agate painted miniatures of some of the party and after a lecture on the proper care of white men, which Reynolds thought "as well received as lectures in general," Tanoa signed the usual commercial treaty, agreeing among other things to set aside a plot of ground for raising turnips, radishes, beans, and pumpkins.†

The old chief took a great liking to the *Peacock*, and to William Reynolds, whom he embraced and called son, much to the young man's discomfiture. It

---

* The Levuka whites were a puzzle to George Emmons. "The custom of Polygamy is the only indulgence that I am aware of," he mused, "that they would not enjoy under the Laws of our Land—to counterballance which, they are denied nearly all the natural rights belonging to Man."
[1]The treaty ceremony was repeated with the chiefs of Rewa, Bau, Cakandrove (the district above Savusavu Bay), and Macuata during May and June.

"Old Snuff." The Fijian chief Tanoa, by Alfred T.
Agate. (*Narrative*, 3: facing p. 58, Western Americana
Collection, Yale University Library.)

was said that Tanoa had eaten many men in his youth and indulged his palate in private still. Fred Stuart, captain's clerk of the *Peacock*, took one look at Fijian heads and concluded from the phrenological evidence that the cannibal propensity was marked.

Peale was early put on guard when he noted that one of Christ's emissaries kept a musket under the seat of his canoe and, phrenologists or not, most of the others were wary at first, though things went so smoothly for a time that caution wavered. Shortly after arrival, Wilkes determined to ascend the island's highest peak, Nadelaiovalu, which rose to some two thousand feet, and he took along several of the officers and scientists with natives to carry the instruments. The day was hot, the way steep, and about midway along Henry Eld, who although large was never very strong, gave up. The native with him betrayed great anxiety, sprinkling Eld's face and fanning him with leaves and finally running ahead to get help, which he succeeded in doing by announcing that a "big chief" had "laid down on the way—saying God dam!" Emmons helped his shipmate down to the boats, both wondering who was more afraid of whom.

While they were at Levuka, the *Vincennes* set up a scientific station that resembled a small village in itself. There were the "portable houses" for the pendulum and transit (the former some twenty feet square), the drying shed Brackenridge erected nearby for his seeds and plants, three tents and the huts assembled from bush, and the whole was surrounded by a bamboo fence. They also hired a few Fijians to carry wood and water and to do the cooking, for everyone agreed that there was not a cook in the squadron to equal them and that the breadfruit, yams, taro, pig, and chicken prepared in the Fiji manner were "most excellent." As the encampment lay on a thoroughfare leading from the mountains, the islanders trooped by daily to trade and see the ships. They would swap anything—spears, war clubs, bows and arrows, shells of all kinds, necklaces of human teeth (an item of which the explorers took careful note), and pubescent girls who went freehold for a musket and a whale's tooth. A present from a local chief, one of the girls climbed into Hudson's bed one night, putting the good captain to flight. He spent the night by the fire listening to Paddy Connel's tales.

That could only be taken as hospitality. But then Captain Eagleston, who ought to know, said "Never to trust a Fegee man," a maxim he observed to the full by keeping a hostage aboard, a sentry on watch, allowing only one canoe alongside and it only at the stern, and rarely going ashore himself. Wilkes took him at his word in drawing up regulations for the survey boats. So did Brackenridge, who on his excursions kept a brace of pistols at hand, explaining,

"I hold them all in the light of savage barbarians nevertheless the many flattering reports to the contrary that have been pawned upon us . . . by the various Missionary sects." But constant wariness was difficult. And perhaps it was uncalled for.

That was a point many times argued aboard the *Flying Fish*, Underwood taking the view that cautiousness only begot mistrust. Show confidence, he would say and laugh at Sinclair's caution in arming the boats. Once on the beach at Maola a large number of natives approached Underwood's boat with shouts and angry gestures. The white resident called out, "You had better stand by your arms, Gentlemen. They are after mischief." He hauled off promptly enough but remained unshaken. Sinclair later thought they had come close to bloodshed, but by then other events had colored his views.

Of the vessels only the *Flying Fish* was suitable for survey work and, taking aboard Tom Granby, an English resident of Levuka, as pilot, she covered an immense extent of coastline. On the first of these cruises she carried a Tongan chief whom the officers called "Tuvo," actually Tubou Totai, a prince of the blood and well known bon vivant who had once visited Sydney and learned some English and still delighted in displaying the invitations he had received. The other passenger was a Bau chief they called "Corydaudau." On arrival at Lakeba the officers were about half sorry to lose the company of the two, who had taught them much about the islands. For his part Corydaudau had adopted the knife and fork, still putting away an entire fowl at a sitting but in a less offensive way. Dressed only in one of Sinclair's monkey jackets, which stopped short of the big man's "stern post," he cut a singular figure but possessed a mind, Sinclair observed in surprise, "capable of comprehending almost any subject." By way of farewell, he presented Sinclair with the bone with which he dressed his hair—a mark of great esteem as it was the shin bone of the first man he had killed in battle and eaten.

The schooner's officers found Wilkes, who was also often aboard, a less agreeable passenger, with an annoying penchant for interfering in the management of the vessel—to no advantage whatever, as he had no experience with fore-and-aft rigs. Once they ran aground on Goat Island because he obstinately refused to heed Tom Granby's warning. On another occasion Sinclair awoke early to find the flying jib boom nearly over the beach and the vessel hard and fast. Wilkes had been at it again. Later in the day they came near homing in on the same strand because he refused to let the pilot come about. "I never, in my life, have seen a man handle a vessel as Capt Wilkes does," Sinclair remarked wonderingly.

At the conclusion of one cruise they found the British surveying schooner

Starling, consort to Captain Edward Belcher's ship *Sulphur,* at Ovalau. The *Sulphur* had lost her rudder and pintles on going aground at Rewa. (Indeed it was learned that she had grounded no less than fifty-two times in these islands and the *Starling* twenty-three.) While a boat was dispatched to the *Peacock* for a set of spare pintles Wilkes paid a courtesy call upon Belcher, who had been out five years, mostly in the Pacific, surveying the islands and the Northwest Coast of America. The visit lacked cordiality, for Wilkes found the stout, dark Englishman a secretive and prickly fellow who evaded his request for information on the Northwest Coast and comparison of magnetic data. Unknown to Wilkes, the Englishman was still smarting from an unfortunate episode at Rewa, where he had applied to the local chiefs for water and provisions, only to hear them gleefully demand payment, citing the new regulations Wilkes had provided which, contrary to custom, failed to exempt warships.

Belcher's officers were less reticent and gave the Americans "a terrible account of the difficulties & dangers" to be met at the mouth of the Columbia River, where both vessels had grounded, the *Starling* losing her rudder. But what at the moment was more alarming to the weary officers, the Englishmen said there was no use going on that coast between September and May and that it was "absolutely impossible" to remain after October. This seemed to mean that the squadron would not reach the Columbia before the following spring and so be home a year later than they had hoped. What Wilkes was planning of course no one knew for certain, but Henry Eld spoke for all when he remarked that a year added to "our now tedious cruise is considered too long."

That they should be weary was no wonder, for aside from the schooner only small boats could be used to survey these islands. Accordingly, Emmons was placed in charge of the *Peacock*'s launch and cutter and assigned the south coast, together with the reefs and nearby islands, of the largest of the archipelago, Viti Levu, as far to the west as the little island of Malolo. Wilkes allotted him the absurdly small space of twelve days in which to complete the task. If leisure remained he was to survey Malolo as well. Lieutenant Alden was given charge of the *Vincennes'* launch and cutter and was to survey the north coast, joining Emmons at Malolo. Other parties took up the survey of other islands and for the next three months the boats were constantly employed.

Most were whaleboats, some twenty-eight feet long and five in the beam and double-ended, which meant cramped quarters in bow and stern. Quarters were further cramped by mast, sail, oars, and ground tackle, howitzer, blunderbuss, rockets, muskets, pistols, and cutlasses, surveying gear, personal kits, and the provisions: a large bag of bread, food chest, and three large breakers, two of water, one of whiskey. That left space for five men to sit bolt upright. Sleeping was the chief problem, for they dared not sleep ashore. And they were often hungry. Except for taro and coconuts, provisions were in short supply almost everywhere, and they accounted themselves lucky when they could buy or catch a large fish to be eaten with a liberal sprinkling of antiscorbutic lemon juice. Indeed not only the boats but the squadron as a whole suffered from shortage of fresh provisions. In the middle of July, Wilkes ordered rations reduced, as those on board had to last for ninety days. They tightened their belts and thought fondly of the good ship *Relief* that perhaps in pique, and certainly in misjudgment, had been left behind.

The boat expeditions were poorly organized, too, especially on the *Peacock*, where the whole endeavor was left to the officers commanding the boats. "The Captain of this Ship," Reynolds remarked with equal parts vexation and affection, "the second in command, in the first great American Exploring & Surveying Expedition, is a perfect Seaman, & a very good Man . . . but he knows nothing of Surveying! And he is too old to learn!" They would leave in the early morning with nothing in the way of breakfast but cold wormy bread, pull five or six hours and scramble about a reef and heave the lead before taking a half hour for rest and grog. In the afternoon they broke off once more to dine on the bread left from breakfast, then toiled until dark, when they returned for a supper of leftovers while reminiscing of "the good things in Season, at Home: the Early vegetables of Spring—the fruits of summer: the cool room: the siesta after dinner; and the walk at Evening, with the girls."

And the heat. Sometimes the sextant became too hot to hold. They had longed for such days while among the ice but the hot and humid air was enervating and the surveyors labored against lethargy. The boats were equipped with awnings against the sun, and these were much prized, but since they spent almost as much time in the water as in the boats, soon everybody was peeling from sunburn and stinging from the salt. Sometimes a squall would suddenly descend to carry away the awning, and perhaps sails and mast as well. To cap it all, there were times when a day's labor would be wiped out because, attracted by the bright colors, natives would walk off with the station flags from which they took angles.

Moreover, Wilkes' penchant for assigning too much work and regulating everything by the clock made some of these cruises terribly long—so long that the officers took to sending letters to one another by passing boats, which were received almost as eagerly as if they had come from home. Blunt and Emmons were out for nearly two months one time, and many of the others for forty days. They would return with feet sore from coral cuts, some crippled with rheumatism, and all "very much pulled down" from the weeks on short rations.

Still, most were able to adjust. A man learned to travel light in this work. Drawers and stockings disappeared early from the kit, for they only served to keep you wet. Trousers, shirt, a jacket with plenty of pockets, heavy shoes, and a hat filled the bill well enough. And boat life had its exhilarating aspects. A lively officer preferred the command of his own boat to a subservient position aboard ship and if sensitive to such things could bear the hardships for the delight of occasionally walking on sand or among trees. William Reynolds felt the delight one day soon after their arrival as he took up the survey of the Rewa River. "The sun was just rising as we entered it," he recorded, "& the fresh air of morning, came most pleasantly to our senses, charged with the fragrance of flowers, & with the unusual odors of the land, that is always so perceptible & so grateful, to one, just from the Sea. I have known this feeling an hundred times, & if I could write poetry, I would certainly commemorate its delights in song." The trees were alive with birds—parrots of brilliant plumage—and the reefs "gorgeous beds of coral" embroidered with the graceful darting motions of brightly colored fish. Sometimes the beauty was breathtaking. Toward sundown one day, with a light breeze blowing, Reynolds' boat passed along the shores of Goloa, off the north coast of Vanua Levu, where he found the scene "lovely beyond all telling, and as the boat floated along, in the deep shadow caused by its shores, I forgot every thing in the world . . . and just gazed on, with my whole soul in my Eyes." He gazed until his companion, young Midshipman Hudson, unable to restrain himself, commenced "shouting his raptures aloud."

Although orders forbade their landing except for provisions or at uninhabited places, they did not observe them to the point of absurdity. In the mornings all looked forward to going ashore to stretch their sore and cramped limbs and, if no natives appeared, to bathe in fresh water and cook a breakfast of pork and yams seasoned with lemon juice and washed down with a cup of chocolate or a "drink of strong waters." The alternative was strong waters and raw pork in the boats, and sometimes strong waters alone.

And, orders or no orders, they necessarily saw a good deal of the natives, who often gathered to watch them take angles. They had no notion what the instrument of polished brass was doing to their sun and were utterly confounded on seeing one of the men "unship four of his teeth, toss them from hand to hand, & then replace them." They raised their usual cry of wonder: "Whoo! Whoo! Whoo!" It was a "strange feeling," one of the officers wrote, "& one which touches a Man's pride, to be so regarded, by beings upon whose admiration he has no claim, save that of superior knowledge . . . a claim that is not readily granted by man to man, among ourselves."

Fijians entertaining the explorers with a club dance, by Alfred T. Agate. (*Narrative*, 3: facing p. 198, Western Americana Collection, Yale University Library.)

On occasion a chief disposed to be friendly beyond the ordinary would stage a dance for their benefit and a bevy of naked girls would undulate with motions "slow & regular as machinery: gestures decent & very graceful" to the accompaniment of a horde of children beating a rhythm on the ground with sticks. Here only the women were tatooed and they only about the labia, from which carefully drawn arcs of blue tracing extended upward over the belly. Doctor Holmes found that they displayed these embellishments readily, although Sinclair discovered that a "small piece of Tobacco" was gratefully received.

The never-ending labor in the cramped quarters honed the feelings of the men to a nicety that astonished their officers. On one occasion, near

Monkey-Face Passage, one of the crew took offense at some remark, refused to mess with the rest, and held out for a week on raw pork, sitting by himself while the others enjoyed a well cooked meal. But for a wonder no one commented, and the officer left it to hunger to tame the sulker's pride, which it did, for one morning he simply joined the others without a word, was received "with Kindness & not a single joke was cracked at his Expence."

But Reynolds was inclined to think that "two Months passed in such a Manner, would shorten ones life a year or two at least." After only two or three weeks' absence it was as good to get back to the ship as it had been to leave it in the first place. On returning from one expedition Reynolds hurried into the cabin with the chronometer to find Captain Hudson just sitting down to dinner. There was no better ship to come home to, for he noted in his entry for that day that Hudson, "Welcomes me back & asks me to take my chance with him—I told him I was not in a very fit condition: but he said never mind— Sit down as I am. . . . Placed myself opposite the Captain's decanter—ready to do justice to Meat & drink; he helped me bountifully & for a time I was to busy to talk, so he very considerately kept up the conversation himself—he thinks Boat service is the very Devil; having had 3 days experience himself. . . . It may be noted as a remarkable fact, that there was not a drop in the decanter when we left the Cabin."

During June the survey work was somewhat complicated and the explorers rendered a little more wary by the first unquestionably hostile movement in the never-ending testing and probing. At Wilkes' orders Hudson was to capture the chief responsible for the attack on the *Charles Daggett* seven years before. Paddy Connel identified the culprit as Vendovi, brother of Tui Dreketi, King of Rewa, and one of the survivors, James Magoun of Levuka, bore him out.

Hudson carried out his mission with a treachery that was a match for anything the natives might have plotted. He entertained Vendovi's brother Phillips (Cocanauto) on board in company with one of the local missionaries, and a few days later received Tui Dreketi himself with presents and ceremony (though with only one and a half rolls of the drum, for the steward who flourished the sticks lost his way and the salute terminated in a few "abortive squeaks of the fife, breathed by the ship's cook"). When Tui Dreketi next came aboard the *Peacock*, he came in confidence, bringing his wives and household, two brothers, Phillips and Qaraniqio, and a retinue of over a hundred. The wary Vendovi was not among them, but no matter. In the midst of the festivities the drum beat to quarters and Hudson announced that all would be held on board until Vendovi was produced. Instantly Tui Dreketi's "blood *was up*," Reynolds observed, and he roundly denounced Hudson for treachery, but then he directed Qaraniqio to fetch their brother, alive if possible, and sat down to smoke Hudson's cigars and drink cava (the ceremonial beverage of this part of the Pacific, produced by community mastication of the root of an indigenous shrub) from his dish covers.

In the large powerful fellow brought in next morning some of the officers were astonished to see the guide they had employed a few days earlier. A trial of sorts was held in the cabin before King, ship's officers, and missionaries. His face painted black in Fijian fashion and wearing a woebegone expression, Vendovi denied nothing but only pleaded the excuse that had exasperated the missionaries ever since their coming and was to ring often in the ears of the explorers in the weeks ahead, "that he had only followed the Fegee custom & done what his people had often done before."

Hudson delivered the sentence. Instead of being killed, Vendovi would be taken to America to be made a better man of, and then returned to them imbued with the knowledge "that to kill a white person, was the very worst thing a Feegee could do." The brothers could not believe that the "big chief" in America would not kill Vendovi and went about the ring of officers asking each if this was indeed so. But they remained unconvinced and, one of the officers noted, "we actually beheld the singular spectacle of a group of Savages in Tears."

The affair left the officers a little uneasy, though not because of the devious role they had played. They generally agreed that however dastardly Vendovi's deed they could hardly string him up at the yardarm "in these times of refinement," but most doubted with William Reynolds that the "Leopard could change his spots." Their doubts grew when Qaraniqio, who had remained silent during the proceedings, was heard to remark disconcertingly "that he would like to go to America & he supposed all he would have to do, was to Kill a White Man."

The explorers had made the first move and now awaited the response. They doubled guard at the observatory and at Rewa the boats surveyed under the *Peacock*'s guns. Feeling did run high at Rewa, and when poor Belcher later arrived he was accorded so cool a reception that he abandoned his intention of surveying the group—or so he later claimed. But as there were no signs of retaliation the explorers resumed their probing of this curious culture.

The officers of the *Porpoise* remained in ignorance of the whole affair, for they were still surveying the Lau Group to the westward and forming favorable opinions of the natives. One gray-headed chief carried a letter of recommendation from a group of shipwrecked seamen he had rescued many years before.

Vendovi, "who only followed the Feegee custom," by
Alfred T. Agate. (*Narrative*, 3: facing p. 142, Western
Americana Collection, Yale University Library.)

Another chief recognized the likenesses of Napoleon and Washington in the
brig's library. Doctor Holmes was happy to observe the absence of idols. He
found only one, though it was disgusting enough, being the figure of a man,
"with large genitals; there was nothing like proportion about it." Wilkes, too,

AMONG THE FEEJEES

took an interest in exotic religious beliefs and, putting on a solemn expression, gravely asked one of the chiefs what his people believed happened to them at death. Henry Eld impassively recorded the reply: "That would be the end of them . . . some foolish persons thought they would live in some other world but they were very ignorant and there were but few of such."

After a few weeks among these seemingly benign people, even New Englander Holmes unbent to the extent of sampling cava. But they heard horrendous tales about the people in the main, or Leeward Group, who were said to strangle or bury alive the aged and infirm and who killed merely to gratify their depraved appetites.* The *Porpoise* moved westward with foreboding.

In the meantime the boat parties were substantiating these rumors one by one. Lieutenant Budd bought a club carved with forty notches. Sinclair, finding the island of Yadua inhabited solely by women, wretchedly poor and so abjectly afraid that they dared not make a fire, was told that they had been raided by the chief of another island when, owing to the hurricane earlier in the year, they had been unable to pay the customary tribute in yams. The raiders had eaten the men "instead of the Yams." The Levuka whites assured them that cannibalism was practiced throughout the archipelago, and that Phillips had been nurtured on human flesh until grown in order that he might become a great warrior. Still, even they had not actually witnessed the rite. As children of their century some of the officers were inclined to agree with philosophers who dismissed such accounts as merely "the bug bear stories of Voyagers." Others suspected that they were being subjected to a bit of leg-pulling, an art in which they themselves became adept as they sought to impress the natives with the prowess of their own tribe.

But evidence mounted. On the Fourth of July some of the officers paid a visit to the hot springs at Savusavu Bay, a particularly beautiful spot where the dense and dark green foliage rose high against the light blue sky and gave the whole a "somber & impressive appearance" that was enhanced by the wisps of rising steam. It was precisely the sort of scenery that most appealed to the connoisseur of romantic landscape. A group of natives invited them to share the meal just prepared in the boiling water and in the midst of it informed their guests that this was the site of their "cannibal feasts." In such a spot it was easy enough to believe.

---

* According to one contemporary, the killing of the incapacitated was regarded as virtually a religious duty, "and the giving of such assistance was a quite friendly and natural act . . . ; and the patient looked to receive such assistance with as little hesitation as the still active friends had in giving it."

What doubts remained were dispelled one day early in July when a native scrambled onto the *Vincennes'* quarterdeck munching on a human head from which he casually plucked an eye "and Eat it, smacking his lips at the same time, with the greatest possible relish." * There was a moment of shocked silence before the officers drove him away. Below in the canoe they could see the cooked legs lying with baked yams on a bed of plantain leaves, just as "a man would place his roast beef," Dyes noted in dismay. "The smell the smell. I never shall forget it. It inough to make a mans blood run cold to think of sutch." But dismayed or not, they recalled that this was a scientific expedition and purchased what was left for their collections.

Reynolds detected an air of delicacy at dinner: "A Sensitive man would have gone into hystericks." There were no hysterics; rather, a remarkable agreement that cannibalism, like the treachery and warfare that were universal here, was solely the concern of the natives, "the custom of the country." They were here as observers, not missionaries, and interference was no part of their job—so long as Fijians ate only Fijians.

But although they could not know it, the explorers faced a problem of definition. Their mere presence was interference. By simply beaching their boats they called into play the customs of the country—quite literally, for custom prescribed that all boats cast upon these shores, except those of the dreaded chiefs, were legitimate salvage. On July 11 the inevitable happened near Solevu, in Wainunu Bay on the southernmost headland of Vanua Levu, where the *Vincennes'* launch and first cutter were operating. Midshipman Samuel Knox missed stays and his boat drifted implacably onto the reef, where a crowd gathered. The natives were armed, as usual, and as they yelled and danced about, more appeared from behind the mangrove bushes on the beach. The boat touched and the chief stepped forward to take possession, explaining to the outraged Knox that it was the custom of the country and signaling the explorers to be off.

Knox looked to his arms only to find them soaked. The men gathered up most of the gear and went sloshing down the inner edge of the reef to board Alden's launch, which, loaded to the gunwales, succeeded in beating out next day. At last sight the natives had succeeded in floating the cutter and were dragging it up the beach near their village.

The resident whites were hard put to explain why the Fijians had spared the men's lives on such an occasion, for according to them it was the first time the

---

* Before the introduction of firearms, the Fijians' essentially vegetarian diet was varied only with the flesh of their enemies. Two English castaways resident here earlier in the century saw no evidence of any other form of cannibalism.

natives had resisted their "habits." But understanding of local superstition restored neither boat nor dignity, and with Wilkes and Hudson commanding, the *Flying Fish* and eleven boats set off for Solevu, all heavily armed and provisioned for two days.

After some argument Whippey persuaded the islanders to surrender the cutter. Only some trifles were missing, but Wilkes, unappeased, dispatched a landing party with orders to fire the village and shoot all who resisted. To the surprise and relief of everyone, the villagers took to the hills beyond, while the men, seizing brands from a cook fire near the beach, ran through the village setting alight each hut in turn. It was quick work. But having made the mistake of firing the town on its windward side, they found themselves facing a problem in terrestrial navigation. Hearing Lieutenant Alden call out, "Follow me!" they cut to their left. But Alden was soon "nearly up to his stern post" in the mud of a taro patch, and they made their way to the boats through swamp and thickets as best they could.

Participation in the attack by "the Great Commodore," as Reynolds derisively called Wilkes, was limited to firing a couple of rockets from his gig at the natives on the hillside. But these caused the greatest consternation. "They all disappeared in a moment," Emmons observed, and afterwards on other islands the explorers were to hear the most exaggerated accounts of these "flying devils." Doctor Holmes heard of the incident three days later on meeting the *Flying Fish* on the north side of Vanua Levu and jotted down a prediction and a prayer. "So ended the first aggressive act of the natives: God grant it may be the last. But," he added, "I doubt." [2]

12 *Affair at Malolo*

I asked a native who was in the room, to sing me a
certain hymn-tune. . . . He had a rich, full voice, and sang
correctly all except the semitone below the keynote at the
end; for is it not an interval unknown in barbarous music?

A Peripatetic Parson

Operations were deceptively routine for the next ten days. The
Peacock and *Vincennes* proceeded from Sandalwood Bay through Monkey-
Face Passage to Macuata ("Mudwater" to the Americans), off the north coast
of Vanua Levu, anchoring there on July 24. It was a pleasant place. They
rambled among the trees and bathed in a nearby stream, and Reynolds got
himself tatooed. All were in good spirits. Their stay in the Fijis was nearing an
end, for they had worked their way westward from the Lau Group, surveying
all in their path, while Emmons was finishing up the westernmost, the
Yasawas. But though Emmons was dependable in surveying as in all else,
Wilkes had boarded the schooner in order to give the Yasawas his personal
inspection. At the largest of the group, Naviti, he had dispatched Alden and
Underwood in boats to survey the small islands of the Mamanuca Group,*
lying a little to the south between Naviti and Malolo, with orders to
rendezvous with the *Porpoise* and *Flying Fish* at Malolo at sunset next day,
July 23.

Alden and Underwood anchored in the bay on Malolo's eastern shore in
the late afternoon. As they were low on provisions Underwood led a party,
well armed at Alden's insistence, to a high point on shore in hopes of sighting
the *Porpoise*. On the way up they met a boy with an armload of war clubs. He

* First discovered by Christopher Bentley of the Rhode Island vessel *Ann and Hope* in 1799.

dropped them and ran. But they caught him and forced him to return to the beach, where a crowd of natives had gathered and appeared to be much disconcerted at finding their arms-bearer in the custody of the strangers. There was no sign of the brig and even the trusting Underwood agreed that in the attempt to procure provisions here they must adopt "every precaution." The residents of Vanua Levu could have told them as much. Lying near the main trade routes between the two largest islands, the pirates of Malolo were the terror of the archipelago.

The men in the boats went supperless but hopes of getting a meal rose next morning when they sighted the *Flying Fish* at anchor some eight miles to the east. (As usual, Wilkes was being none too meticulous in observing his own orders and had spent so much time ashore taking angles at nearby Vomo that he had decided to postpone the rendezvous. And he spent much of the following day making observations from a low sand island some six miles east of Malolo, where Alden and Underwood observed the schooner at anchor.) At nine Emmons arrived from Vomo, equally hungry. When shortly afterward John Sac returned from the shore with the information that provisions could be had, Underwood, who never missed an opportunity to treat with the natives wherever the squadron called, cast off with nine men and a good stock of the usual stuff of trade—cotton cloth, scissors, jew's harps, and fishhooks. He was followed by Alden's promise to join him as soon as the tide permitted and some banter from his messmates about the dangers of the explorer's life. Emmons, as hungry as when he arrived, departed about the same time to make observations on Malololailai, a smaller island to the southeast, very nearly linked to a tongue of land that extended from the larger. Only a narrow passage lay between.

Underwood's launch, though of shallower draft than the cutter, ran aground in this passage and some fifteen or twenty natives came out to help drag it over, heaving in rhythm to a song they sang with the crew. It was hard going and they gave up a half mile from the beach, anchored the boat, and waded ashore. Alden kept an eye on the proceedings through his spyglass. Growing somewhat apprehensive as he saw more and more natives come down to the beach, he moved in to find that there was just enough water now for him to get alongside the launch, in which Underwood had left the customary hostage. He transferred the man to his own boat. A seaman came off to report on the negotiations and when he returned to the beach Midshipman Wilkes Henry waded in with him.

Then three natives came out and exchanged some words with the hostage, who became agitated and when the canoe pushed off attempted to follow. But

Alden restrained him and ordered the provisions brought off without delay. The tide had risen somewhat and the launch was making for the shore when the hostage suddenly leaped out and began scrambling through the shallows for the beach. Alden leveled on him, but as a dead hostage is no hostage, held his fire and was just calling to Emmons' boat to pull after him when his words were drowned by the sharp report of firearms from the beach, where, flinging round, he could see a wild struggle in progress.

The boats flew shoreward before a fresh breeze but soon met the launch pulling out and heard someone cry that Underwood was killed. Leaping out, they opened fire upon the Fijians, who were now hastily retreating with their dead and wounded.

Seaman J. G. Clark was staggering delirious in the shallows, his lip hanging by a thread. On the beach no man stood. Underwood's stripped body lay with its face to the sky and Henry's nearby.

Stunned, for the affray was over almost as soon as begun, Alden and his men tramped back along the beach. "With heavy hearts we bore our murdered comrades to the boat," Alden wrote that evening.

Patching up the survivors as best he could, Emmons learned that the natives had attacked when the hostage jumped. Underwood had immediately ordered his men back to the boat while he and Henry covered their retreat. The two fought desperately, Underwood killing one man, Henry two, before being overwhelmed. The last anyone remembered seeing of Underwood, he was hauling a spear out of his shoulder with both hands and urging the men to the boats.

The *Flying Fish* was still at anchor and Wilkes ashore collecting shells when the officers sighted the boats flying the ensign union down. They returned to the schooner just as the cutter came dashing alongside, Alden in the bow, his clothes smeared with blood, calling out, "Great God, Sir, Underwood and Henry are murdered!"

After posting three boats to row guard around Malolo, next morning a mournful little procession carried the bodies, sewn up in hammocks, to a common grave on one of the little cays a few miles northeast. Agate read the service and, Sinclair noted woefully, "Earth met Earth with a solemn heavy sound." They stood in silence for a moment, listening to the breeze in the leaves overhead, fired three volleys, then shrewdly eradicated all traces of their visit.

The shock of the loss was the greater because these two officers were who they were: the good-natured Rhode Islander Underwood had been one of the first to sign on the Expedition under Commodore Jones, originally as draughtsman to the scientific corps; and Henry, as the only son of Wilkes' widowed sister, had carried himself well and had been popular with his messmates in what Reynolds described as "circumstances of peculiar embarrassment & delicacy."

Anguish also surrounded the question of who was to blame for the loss. Alden, for letting the hostage escape? Underwood, for overconfidence? Wilkes, for failing to keep the rendezvous? Wilkes, for failing to provision the boats sufficiently to render them independent of the shore? Or, to cast further back, Wilkes, for having detached the supply ship? Wilkes blamed Alden, but everyone agreed with Doctor Holmes' outraged observation, "That two such men should be treacherously murdered on these distant islands, by a band of cowardly and cruel savages, is enough to rouse every spark of feeling in the breasts of all who knew them, and to mingle thoughts of terrible vengeance with our just plans of punishment"—a comparatively mild expression of the sentiment prevailing.

The afternoon and night after the burials were spent in filling cartridges, cleaning muskets and pistols, and organizing attack parties. Similar preparations were being made ashore. They could see the savages in the firelight, painted for war, some running along the shore to taunt the men in the boats.* "All of which," Emmons patiently observed, "we were of course obliged to submit to for the present."

In the morning Wilkes got the *Flying Fish* under way to lead the attack on the north side but to his mortification she immediately grounded on a shoal and lay helpless. The main party of some eighty men organized in three divisions landed unopposed on the south shore at ten o'clock. Ringgold, who had arrived in the *Porpoise* shortly after the burial, mustered them on the beach with a little speech on the necessity for what they would now do and the command to "destroy *every thing* save women & children," after which the divisions separated to cut their separate swaths of desolation and meet again before the village on the eastern shore. Destroying banana trees and patches of sugar cane, yams, and taro on the way up, without seeing a single native, Lieutenant Johnson's division paused briefly on the island's summit, where a "most beautiful and animated Scene" opened below. One party was already

---

* The historian of the group points out that these jibes were a part of the local military tradition. "From behind their shelters and stockades the rival parties would hurl brave words and stinging taunts, in which there was often something of good humored banter. This war of words was waged in the hope that warriors thirsting for renown would work themselves into a frenzy of reckless valour, and approach or sally forth. If a few dead bodies could be obtained in this way honour was generally satisfied, and the attackers would retire in triumph."

drawn up before the fortified town and the other was winding through the tall grass. They could hear the shouts of the warriors mingled with the cries of women and children and the squealing of pigs. Outside the stockade two of the chiefs in their long white maros were "whooping and calling out" and "flourishing their spears & clubs in the most threatening manner." The sight occasioned some surprise, for who would have supposed that these savages would offer fight to such a force? Spears and arrows came out in clouds. But when a rocket burst inside the stockade and was followed by a general volley of musketry, the taunting chiefs suddenly disappeared from view. Johnson's party remained on the hilltop only a few moments before descending to the fray.

They found the stockade surrounded by a dry moat, perhaps fifteen feet wide and six or seven deep. Hurrying across it on a narrow causeway, Sinclair discovered a man in the act of hurling a spear and gave him "15 buckshot, which sent him to Kingdom Come." Ringgold ordered him back, shouting that they had come "to punish the natives and not ourselves," but, unable to retreat without exposing himself, Sinclair was forced to remain where he was, a superb vantage for the scene within. The gate ahead was "like a kind of mouse trap, so that you could go in, but could not get back so easily," and just inside was another ditch, freshly dug, where the natives were lying "thick as pigs," safe until they raised their heads but also, because the bows could not be fully drawn in that position, harmless. Sinclair fired at one man, no more than four feet away, with a single ball which, he swore, the man "absolutely dodged, the ball passing over his right shoulder." Luckily, the captain of the *Porpoise's* maintop was at hand and shoved a bayonet into him. As Sinclair ducked at a warning yell from behind, a club flew up that staggered the gatepost. The savage who threw it was drawing another when Sinclair put a pistol ball through his head and he fell "like a bag of sand."

All the while, the men of the ships were coming up to the gate "two and two" and firing into the midst of the defenders no more than twenty feet away. Sinclair's own double-barrel became so hot that he had carefully to avoid its metal. The firing had lasted perhaps thirty minutes, the air was filled with the wails of women and the moans and shouts of men, when a rocket landed on the roof of a hut. To the astonishment and admiration of all, a native leaped on top and began hauling off the flaming thatch. Almost immediately a dozen guns were leveled at him and he came rolling down to thump on the packed dirt below.

Within, the spreading flames caused consternation. "I hope I am not a savage in disposition," Eld remarked later in reflecting on the day's events, "but . . . I felt a degree of savage like satisfaction every time I did or thought I had Killed one of those Miscreants." But it was not only Henry Eld, among the gentlest of men, who suffered a pang when in the midst of the din and scurrying a child appeared through the smoke to stand at the palisade crying bitterly.

The streamers shooting upward kindled the thick crowns of the coconut trees which flared for an instant like giant torches. The sharp reports from the exploding bamboo that framed the huts sounded for all the world like successive volleys of musketry. To Sinclair the spectacle was "grand, & beautiful and at the same time horrible." The explorers raised a cheer as the defenders began to flee. "There they go!" "Shoot that fellow!" It was difficult for the officers to prevent the crews from shooting the women, whom they had not expected to find in the town at all and who fought as tenaciously as their men. A few of the latter still stood their ground to die in defense of the village.

When a half hour later the Americans ventured gingerly onto the ground where the village had stood they found large hampers of yams, calabashes of water, pigs, and other supplies laid in for the anticipated siege. Near the ring of ashes that had been the palisade was the body of the crying child. To render the survivors utterly helpless the men made a great bonfire of the spears, bows, arrows, and clubs, and in derision of the custom of the country tossed on a body lying at hand and followed it with some yams. But Fiji had the last word when one of the natives who had been taken aboard the brig the day before and who had guided them to the village stepped up to Holmes and to the surgeon's infinite disgust, "with the air of an epicure told me how good it would be to eat!"

Reforming in divisions they resumed their course of destruction toward the other village five miles away, only to find on reaching it at sunset that Alden had anticipated them. Sinclair thought it must have been "a most beautiful place."

Back aboard they took stock. No one was wounded seriously, and they estimated that eighty-seven Fijians had been killed. "Never before, had there been such a day of slaughter in all Fegee," Reynolds rejoiced with pardonable exaggeration. The inhabitants of some of the less frequented islands had looked upon the explorers as white gods, or so it had seemed to many.* Though a little amused by it, they had rather admired the image and were happy now to see it established at Malolo.

* The affair at Malolo showed the natives to be hardly more credulous than the white gods, who pretty much agreed that the Fijians were so quick as to be able to dodge musket balls and that their heads were "so hard, that they turned the Edges of the cutlasses, and our men in some cases had to finish them off with their boat oars."

White god Wilkes announced that he intended to land in person next morning to direct the killing of "Every man on the island." But then a woman appeared on the beach to surrender Underwood's melted watch and the barrel and frame of Henry's bowie-knife pistol and beg for mercy for the island. Taking second thought, Wilkes ordered the survivors to assemble at noon on the shore. The appointed hour had passed when the explorers, occupying a small hill, first heard "a singular moaning sound" in the distance. After a time a party of some forty, nearly all of them women, emerged from the trees and falling on hands and knees began crawling slowly up the hill, heads drooping and keeping time with a guttural sound which terminated at intervals in a prolonged grunt, then commenced anew. This went on for two hours before they were seated and an old man rose to plead mercy. The officers, he confessed, had been killed without provocation but the perpetrators were all dead now, and many others beside.

In reply the great white chief "dwelt in proper terms" (the officers agreed) on the atrociousness of the crime, announced that the United States was "a great Nation, a powerful people," and signified his unalterable determination to destroy every man on Malolo—unless they now watered and provisioned the vessels with all the yams and coconuts on the island.

In the course of the ensuing operations the officers rejoiced to hear the natives, sleepless for two nights past, complain of fatigue, but some still thought Wilkes too lenient. Remarking that the cup of vengeance had been drained "almost to the dregs," Sinclair felt for a time that "we ought to take another sip," but he finally concluded that the decision to leave a few survivors was the wiser, for their reports of the "irresistable force of the arms of the white man" would surely deter all Fiji from future acts of aggression.

Such reports did precede them—everywhere. Yet on reaching Somosomo a few days later they nonetheless found the missionaries living in terror. Making a feast of two enemies near the missionaries' houses, the chief's son* had noted the missionaries' expressions of abhorrence and the weeping of their wives and, much offended, had threatened them all with "death and Mastication," as Sinclair put it. When Wilkes paid a call and referred pointedly to the effects of the rockets at Malolo, the old chief promised to protect the missionaries and offered anything on the island for just one Flying Devil to use against his enemies. Wilkes proposed a fireworks display instead.

In the evening hundreds of natives lined the beach. A blue light was burned

* Kilakila, who in 1854 was murdered in his sleep by his son, who was soon killed by his brother, who was murdered in turn in 1857—a not untypical conclusion to a Fijian family spat.

and a rocket fired to burst into splendid corruscation high overhead. The multitude on the strand responded with a swelling roar of shouts. A second elicited another roar. The third fired by the white gods was more spectacular still, for it hung in the musket barrel and its fire got under the apron of the adjoining twelve-pounder, which, primed and loaded with grapeshot, now blazed away at the same time that the rocket escaped the musket. The effect was grand and next day the missionaries reported that they were enjoying unwonted esteem. Somehow farce forever hovered near.

Off Macuata on August 9 the ships all joined company for the first time since entering the Fijis. Wilkes returned to the *Vincennes* and two days later the five white pilots of Levuka, who had proved good friends to the Expedition, as everyone but Wilkes heartily acknowledged, cast off from the *Flying Fish* and gave the little vessel three cheers as she filled away. The *Porpoise* was detached on a round of duties—making return visits to check on the treatment of missionaries, completing surveys in the Tuamotu Group that should have been finished the year before, inquiring at Turtle Island about the survivors of the *Shylock*, wrecked on the same reef that had claimed the *Oeno*, and calling again at Samoa before meeting the rest of the squadron at Oahu. Then Wilkes discovered that he had neglected to survey the great coral reef off the north coast of Vanua Levu, and recalling the *Flying Fish*, ordered her to take on additional men and provisions, and complete that task. Meanwhile the *Vincennes* and *Peacock* stood bravely on for the Sandwich Islands.

Three months among a treacherous people, three months' hard work on a steady diet of yams, taro, and everlasting pig, and even that in short supply, were unlikely to kindle fond memories of any place, but the Fijis had drawn blood. Holmes spoke for all in his fervent hope that their farewell was "for ever." As the vessels made their final departures at various times and places the explorers reflected on their accomplishment in these islands and some penned little essays in their journals on the strange people they had been among. Even the scientists generally agreed that the squadron's greatest achievement here would be found on the charts. Hudson estimated that the *Peacock*'s boats had sailed more than ten thousand miles. Recalling the words of the Nantucket memorial, "Many ships have gone into those seas, & not a soul has returned to tell their fate," Pickering found some satisfaction in reflecting that in the year 1840, instead of sending its fleet "a pond-sailing in the Mediterranean," the United States had conducted a "famous survey" of this graveyard of the Pacific. Sinclair cautiously concluded that the group had been surveyed in a manner reflecting great credit on the Expedition, "when all things are taken into consideration." The chart would not be flawless—it would be impossible for any force to survey accurately the whole of this vast area in so short a time—and he only hoped that Wilkes would not claim too much, since they had seen little of the interior of the larger islands. With two more months and provisions from "the good old ship Relief" they could have completed a nearly perfect survey.

Still, many doubtful positions were established beyond cavil, and many of the blanks on previous charts filled in with new names: Peacock Harbor ("in compliment," Emmons noted, "to my floating Home . . . for her Many good qualities & the Singular good fortune that in so many instances attended her"), Exploring Isles, Flying Fish Shoal, and Budd Reef, as well as Murderers' Bay and, the cay of burial, Henry's Island in Underwood Group. Taking the work all in all, it left the Fijis "as well surveyed as any Group in the Pacific, but none the less," Sinclair cautioned, "I would advise navigators to Keep their Eyes open when running in this group, even if they should have a cargo of charts aboard."

The scientists, too, had done good work here. They had experienced no difficulty in getting ashore when they wished and most found the Fijian sojourn all they had hoped for when with J. N. Reynolds they had first laid plans for the great national expedition. On looking over the botanical specimens on the day of departure, Brackenridge, recovered now from the fever that had laid him low for many weeks, was pleased to discover that six hundred species had been collected and preserved—including a new "Tomatoe, very fragrant and superior in taste"—though he suspected that another five hundred remained in the interior of the larger islands for the botanist who had the "temerity to go in quest." In the time left over from drawing the botanical specimens, Agate had managed to build up a fine set of portraits of the natives, and Drayton, though ailing (from too much medicine and too many cigars, some thought) had completed a large number of zoological drawings. Dana had gathered some hundred and thirty-five species of corals and been able to figure the animals of most of them, together with some four hundred species of crustacea, nearly all of which he was sure would prove to be new. The collection of coral animals was very nearly unprecedented, but Dana himself took greater satisfaction in having given two of the officers, one of them Captain Hudson's son, the final push "from death into life, the life of the Gospel."

They had picked up a few specimens of culture as well, sometimes to their horror. They had learned, for example, that the completion of a chief's canoe was celebrated by launching it over ways of live bodies, and that a man was planted along with the piling of a new spirit house as a sort of living cornerstone. And they took note, with what satisfaction there was in it, that they had finally given the lie to "many of the most eminent men in the world," who preached that cannibalism existed nowhere in the world of the nineteenth century. Some others had contended by way of extenuation that the Fijians ate only their enemies. It was an idle enough observation, Pickering remarked, "in a country where a man dare not go alone to a neighboring village. It is nearer the mark to say that they do not kill their next-door neighbours for the purpose." It was easy to observe, as did Silas Holmes on his departure from the group, that the Fijians were the ultimate in human degradation ("I am almost ready to blush that I am a man, when I remember that they too, bear the human form."), but some made an attempt to understand. Sinclair questioned his friend Corydaudau on the matter and received an answer that he was forced to admit made a perverse kind of sense. For, "in a most sincere manner," the chief expressed wonder at the palate that preferred swine fed on offal to men nourished on "the very best of food." But Sinclair still thought it "unnatural" and suggested that it probably originated "when the population was super abundant and animal food scarce." He thought that moral preachments could not now eliminate it without the introduction of more domestic animals. Chickens, then, might well accomplish more than mission-aries. The explorers had already seen enough of the Pacific to disenchant them with missionary efforts and were rather inclined to see commerce as the hope of the future. Already, they noted, some of the Fijians were curing their own *bêche-de-mer*.

The explorers talked less confidently now about "the spirit of the age" and reflected more on the nature of savagism and the meaning of nature itself. Charles Pickering's was a mind of subtle cast, and from long training and reflection he was able to grasp some of the complexities of nature, yet here he found that all was paradox. "What are we to call these People?" Pickering asked in exasperation. "They are not Savages, for they live in towns, some times of one or more thousand inhabitants—in all that relates to the cultivation of the soil, they are great adepts." They were superb cooks as well, and their *okalalos*, a pudding of bananas of different flavors and coconut, baked in the ground in a calabash lined with plantain leaves, was held in high esteem by the explorers. (Charlie Erskine, a great fancier of puddings, duffs, and cakes, thought *okalalos* "left them all far astern.") They had a theology, and in every village spirit houses that doubled as inns. They were excellent navigators and ingenious in various arts and manufactures. They had no written laws, to be sure, but their customs were so rigidly observed as to serve the same purpose. They were clearly intelligent. One of the missionaries testified that he had "never seen children at home, learn their lessons half so fast," and one chief (that would be Phillips) had taken the pains to learn English and French and other European languages and was always delighted to find someone who could speak a tongue unknown to him.

Were such a people savages? "Wearing a dress adapted to the climate, certainly does not make them savages! If they are cowardly & treacherous, they are not afraid of death." In loyalty to their chiefs, "they go beyond any thing recorded in the age of Chivalry." They had "their reasons for everything." A man may decide that his mother has lived long enough because, perhaps, "she is no longer able to bring down 200 *lbs* of yams on her back, from the mountains." He digs a hole at some little distance and tells her that he is going to kill her. The old woman replies, "Well my son, if I am no longer of any use, I had better be dead." She kneels at the hole and the son finishes her off with a club or a garotte of tapa. "The Son returns to the house, without any more apparent emotion than if he had been slaying a pig, & may be in a month, will hardly recollect it."

The only sign of affection Pickering ever observed was for children and chiefs. "The Tonga or Samoa native you can make your friend, and can trust him to the death," but not the man of Fiji. "He may seem pleased as a child, ready & eager to oblige, will undergo fatigue & danger for you, but beware how you give him the least advantage. Poor Henry was knocked in the head by the very Chief, who ten minutes before was patting him on the shoulder." Loyal yet treacherous, cowardly yet brave, an artistic and industrious people whose chief pastime was war, a reasonable people with a logic uniquely their own—what indeed could one make of them? Here was not savagism, he wrote his friend Morton in Philadelphia, but "rather a *new species* of civilization."

Reynolds was to remember how often in these islands it had seemed to him "strange & unnatural, that the Sun should shine as brightly, & the rain fall, the same as in other Lands." [1]

13 · Sandwich Islands

The light of science and the gospel of our Christian faith
have moved hand in hand together through the world . . .
overriding the barriers of custom.

Isaac Israel Hayes, *The Open Polar Sea*, 1867

The cruise to the Sandwich Islands was no pleasure. The usual
tedium rendered these long sea passages difficult enough, but Wilkes, finding
cabals in the camaraderie born of shared hardship, invariably made them more
so by shaking up assignments. He removed a number of officers from their
accustomed berths just before leaving Fiji and assigned them to different
vessels, where the process began anew.

This "reckless & pell mell system," as Reynolds termed it, was not rendered
any easier to bear by the prospect of *"two years more*, in this accursed
Expedition, the healthfullness of which is gone." Some predicted that it would
not hold together half that time. Three days out, Wilkes threw a tantrum
when he was unable to find the survey notes on the Samoan Islands and
accused Hudson of having had them last. Hudson denied it and blamed
Wilkes and to the delight of the officers the two carried on like schoolboys for
a time. But Wilkes had the last word when he announced that the notes on
the Fijis had not been written up in the prescribed form and sent them all
back to the *Peacock* to be recopied, several weeks' work. The Samoan data
never were found and the *Peacock* and schooner would have to do that work
over again, too.

Two days later the crews were mustered and read another pronunciamento:
All shells and other specimens collected belonged to the government and were
to be turned in. But shortly afterward Wilkes changed his mind and ordered
Peale to select those he thought the government collections required,

purchase them, and return the rest. It was precisely the plan Couthouy had proposed long since in the face of Wilkes' irate intransigence, as the officers were well aware.

On these long passages Wilkes saw to it that on the *Vincennes* at least the bonds of discipline remained taut. As they answered the beat to quarters, he would take trumpet in hand and sing out, "Silence fore and aft, wet and sand the decks, knock out your ports, take off your muzzel-bags, withdraw your tompions and cast loose your guns." Then the captain of the gun would take over to exercise his crew. "Chock your luff, stop, vent, and sponge your guns, cartridge," he monotonously called out, "wad and ram home, round shot, canister or stand of grape, wad ram home. . . ." And some of the men responded with the undertone litany, "A couple of round shot, canister, stand of grape, two midshipmen and a master's mate, wad and ram home. . . ."

As their track was an uncommon one, there was some expectation of making discoveries along the way, the prospect of which ordinarily decreed deployment. Instead they were frequently hove-to while boats scurried to and fro transferring officers and orders. It was exasperating but not wholly beyond control. By August 14 the *Peacock* had had enough. In the clear moonlight of the early watch they "unaccountably" lost sight of the *Vincennes* ahead. The officers of succeeding watches neglected to caution the lookout to keep awake and the helmsman to "steer steady." At daylight the *Vincennes* was nowhere to be seen. A grin went round the ship. Noting that Captain Hudson failed to inquire, they concluded that he was "as well pleased as the rest of us."

They had sailed on short rations, expecting, despite adverse northeasterly winds, to reach Oahu within forty days. Yet at the end of the thirty-seventh the *Peacock* was still a full two weeks away. According to J. N. Reynolds' list, several islands of doubtful position lay near their track, but they dared not risk the consequences of searching for them. The *Vincennes* did, and having made landings on three of them, Wilkes named the whole, the Phoenix Group, after an American vessel said to have made a discovery there. Meanwhile on board the *Peacock*, coffee, tea, sugar, and flour were exhausted, and other supplies were fast giving out. Soon the men's diet was reduced to the crumbling remains of the worm-infested bread, a daily pound of yams per man, and stinking beef that resembled mahogany and was hard enough to take a polish—all stuff that would have been jettisoned in better times. They attempted to get an easting so as to follow Cook's and Vancouver's sixty-year-old track but were cursed with bad weather, and bad sailing, too, for the exhaustion of stores and provisions had left the *Peacock* light in the water. On the forty-seventh day the yams ran out and the water turned putrid.

Cockroaches (which ladies at home, Reynolds noted, were now delicately calling simply "roaches") infested the ship in such numbers that the vessel stank of them and they had to be fished out of every dish served.

After parting company the *Flying Fish* had made for the great sea reef lying west of Marli and traced it all the way to Round Island. The task was finished by August 15 and Sinclair wore his vessel round on a course for Oahu. A few days out the mast began to work in its step again, and dangerously. There was no carpenter aboard, or even carpenter's tools, but some trade hatchets remained and with his accustomed ingenuity Sinclair inserted them as wedges. They performed well enough. He was more fortunate in his course than Hudson, making Honolulu in thirty-five days. Residents said it was the fastest such passage ever made. One of the merchants of Honolulu, who customarily took over when the harbor pilot was in his cups, which he customarily was, brought them through the reef into the inner harbor. He briefly grounded the schooner on a mudbank but native canoes soon had her off and Couthouy came aboard. The conchologist had been here five weeks adding to the collections.

But neither Sinclair's skill nor Couthouy's industry would weigh with Wilkes. On his arrival Sinclair collected letters for some of the officers of the *Vincennes*—they had agreed to look after one another in this way—and put out immediately on sighting her five days later. On learning that there were no letters for him, Wilkes flew into a rage, stamping about the gangway and shouting at Sinclair, finally ordering him to get the *Flying Fish* under weigh and stand off and on until further orders. These did not come until the following morning, when both vessels moved inside the reef and Sinclair delivered his chart of the Fiji reef. Sinclair reflected in his journal on the nature of an officer who comported himself so. "It seems that we have sailed, under the National flag and Pendant, beyond the influence of the law of the United States, but I do sincerely trust, that when we again get within the sphere of their action, conduct so unjust and unlawful, will not be allowed to go by unnoticed."

Many another fervently hoped the same, and when Robert Pinkney, who had written Wilkes a disrespectful letter, was allowed ashore for the first time since leaving Tongatabu six months before, he compiled the formal charges and specifications for a court martial. Because Wilkes had ordered that all communications to the Navy Department were to pass through his hands, Pinkney requested acknowledgement of receipt and their prompt dispatch to Washington. Wilkes' acknowledgement took the form of charges of disrespect against Pinkney, in addition to those he had already prepared, and an order for his arrest. All the officers could do now was wait.

Wilkes was under no such handicap. Immediately upon arrival, he took over a large stone house lent by Governor Kekuanaoa of Honolulu. The first floor became a chartroom, where six of the officers labored, and the second Wilkes' office and living quarters. From that eminence he lashed out at those who had crossed him in the months since leaving Sydney. He ordered all journals submitted during the first week of October and was unmoved by Doctor Guillou's objection that his contained personal matter. The Doctor offered to present it sealed and addressed to the Secretary of the Navy. No, Wilkes would send nothing to Washington without first examining it. When Guillou then removed the pages in question, Wilkes presented charges against him, some dated ten months previous, and ordered him suspended and placed under arrest. Popular with all but Wilkes, the peppery little surgeon, who spent his spare moments sitting cross-legged on the deck tailoring coats and trousers, and whose tender care of the sick everyone remarked on, was to spend the rest of the cruise in confinement.

Couthouy's separation was a foregone conclusion from the time Wilkes had unwillingly adopted his plan for the collections. Early in October Wilkes seized Couthouy's journals and specimens and dismissed the conchologist on charges of having attempted to "promote dissension, bring me into disrepute, and destroy the harmony and efficiency of the Squadron." For the rest of the scientific corps, loss of the indefatigable Bostonian meant that they would have to shoulder an additional burden of work. It also meant that in their commander's peculiar scheme of values, matters of petty discipline came before science.

Wilkes next turned to disciplinary problems of lesser moment. On October 11 and for eighteen days thereafter a gun was fired and the jack hoisted at the *Peacock*'s mizzen to announce that a court martial was in session. In reviewing the sentences Wilkes mitigated a number, including that of a marine whose fifteen lashes and dismissal he reduced to fifty lashes alone. Whether that won him gratitude among the crew is not recorded, but clearly Wilkes was thinking of problems other than discipline. The crews had signed on for only three years. Their term would expire November 1, and unless they could be induced to sign over, it would be necessary to resort to the embarrassing expedient of filling their place in the Great National Expedition with Kanakas. Accordingly, a little drama was enacted on each of the vessels in turn, and again on the *Porpoise* when she arrived the second week in October. It varied little from ship to ship. On the *Vincennes* Wilkes made a long speech about patriotism and duty—and bounties and liberty ashore. Those who would re-enlist for another year and a half would receive two months' pay and a week's liberty now. John Dyes noted that "this did not go very Well." What went even less well was Wilkes' announcement that those who insisted on leaving the squadron would be left to get home as best they could. He acknowledged that it was a hardship and certainly regrettable, especially to a commander who held the welfare of his men first among his obligations. But the number of explorers who faced up to the hardship was embarrassingly large.

Hudson tried his hand a week later. He, too, offered liberty with money to spend. Still, no one was obliged to sign over and any man not of a mind to could cross to the port side of the deck. Forty-four promptly stamped across—and this on Hudson's ship. Later in October Wilkes promised that the cruise would not extend beyond May 31, 1842, "unless prevented by an Act of God"—the first intimation the explorers had received of the new date of their return. Moreover, they would henceforth receive extra pay. Many continued to stand their ground, taking a chance on getting passage home aboard some ship or other, and as he watched the "old Explorers" take "their Hammacks and Bages" ashore, John Dyes found it "a sorrowful sight to see . . . , tha were some of the Best men in the Expedition." However, after a round of drinking and whoring in Honolulu, nearly all the *Peacock*'s reluctant ones returned to put their names or marks to the articles. Forty-eight of the *Vincennes*' did not. Wilkes simply ordered three of the *Vincennes*' marines to re-enlist and when they refused, ironed and lodged them in the fort ashore to reconsider. When the ship moved over to Hawaii early in December they were placed in double irons below and on the fourth and again on the seventh were taken up into the sunlight and flogged before all hands as Wilkes himself stood by to ask mildly at each blow if they would now do their duty. On the eighth they answered aye before the cats could fall again. That act of coercion was a mistake that in another time and place would cost Wilkes dearly.

It was not only those whose enlistments were up who wanted out. During the stay in the Sandwich Islands desertions were a nagging problem, though they dropped off somewhat as the men learned how difficult it was to hide from the servants of God, who displayed a special animus against sailors. Some escaped only by smuggling themselves aboard merchant vessels in the harbor.

Blessed with the longest liberty they had yet been offered, the explorers were doubtless the largest naval contingent ever to have been loosed on the town. When they went ashore to visit bethel or brothel as might be, they found themselves in a novel culture: a remarkable mixture of races and skins, of dissipation and piety, of Yankee hustle and island langour, all jostling and jarring under the baleful eyes of the last of the New England Calvinists. Honolulu had a population of only about nine thousand, four streets, two hotels, seven bowling alleys, and a good sprinkling of grog shops, but it was of considerable commercial importance, owing to its large secure harbor and its location on the track of vessels from North and South America bound for the East Indies. It was also the frequent resort of whaleships from the whaling grounds "on Japan." Charlie Erskine found the town to be full of "beer-drinking Germans, pipe-loving Dutchmen, French dandies, conceited Englishmen, Yankees, Hoosiers, California Indians, and almond-eyed, sallow-faced Chinamen." Everything was covered with dust, and some of the islanders with little else. Men were seen dressed in shirt, vest, and coat without trousers. One fellow sported an unlikely pair of white mittens, and the women wore that favorite item of missionary haute couture, the ugly and unlikely Mother Hubbard.

The long-awaited explorers were given a friendly welcome by respectable Honolulu. The local newspaper, *The Polynesian*, which the remarkable young New Englander James Jackson Jarves (1820–1888) had established a few months before, hailed the squadron's brilliant success in discovering "the great Antarctic Continent, which Cook sought for in vain," expressed the hope that the surveyors would clear up some points of geography in these islands, and wished all hands a visit of "unmingled satisfaction." King Kamehameha III, residing at Maui, where his chaplain and advisor, William Richards (1792–1847), endeavored to keep him safe from the sins of the flesh, came over to extend a formal welcome and within a few days the officers were joining him for some bowling, at which he was adept.

But bowling aside, the squadron had come at a bad time, for there had just been a religious revival touched off at Hilo in 1837 by the missionary Titus Coan. Early in the squadron's visit laws were decreed "for the protection of the Sabbath" which stopped Sunday riding, milk delivery, and work aboard ships in the harbor. What lay in store for seamen in future was suggested in a provision of the new constitution that decreed "That no law shall be enacted which is at variance with the word of the Lord Jehovah, or at variance with the general spirit of His word." The men on liberty found that they were everywhere followed by armed police, who were quick to seize a man for unseemly conduct and lodge him in the fort.[1]

Restriction was the harder to bear because of the elysian reputation these islands had enjoyed in the maritime world of the west before the *Thaddeus*

Street view at Honolulu, by Alfred T. Agate. (*Narrative*,
3: p. 415, Western Americana Collection, Yale
University Library.)

arrived one spring morning in 1820 bearing young zealots from the New
England hill country. Offended beyond endurance at the sight of half-naked
girls lounging on windlass and bowsprit and the sound of their lewd laughter
as, hanging on the arm of officer or seaman they sauntered out of wardroom or
forecastle, the missionaries had attempted to stop them from swimming out to
the ships. In retaliation one irate crew shelled Lahaina. The first American
naval vessel to visit the islands, the *Dolphin*, created a scandal when it called
during a period of moral retrenchment in 1826. On learning of the new
regulations, the popular, rough-mannered John Percival announced that
national honor had been impugned, expostulated with the chiefs, and offered
to shoot the provincial and bigoted but able Hiram Bingham, whom he rightly
held responsible. Percival had his way in the end and, emptying the two
mission schools, the girls poured out in a steady stream for the three months
the happy ship was in port. When reports of this affair, eagerly communicated
by missionary Richards, reached respectable ears at home there was a fearful
row and a court martial, from which Percival was rescued by Mahlon
Dickerson, of all people.

But all that was past. Honolulu now bore a good many resemblances to a
New England village. There were church spires and clapboard houses, some
even with cupolas, and a temperance society. Natives pledged themselves to
give up the "great evil" of smoking and Wilkes and Hudson found the

Sabbath observed with a "decorum and quietness that would satisfy the most scrupulous puritan." [2]

Wilkes gave a grand "pic nic party" under a "tent of the stars and stripes" a few miles out of town ("The collation was beautiful," the missionaries were to recall in wonderment) and visited missionary homes, where he found "cheerful, contented faces," simple furniture, and only a girl for servant, or "help," as she was called, and heard from the missionaries "none but the most charitable expressions toward their assailants." Accounts of the persecution of Catholics had been "much exaggerated," and, anyway, the priests had appeared here "in direct defiance of the law."

As the island culture was extinct, Wilkes had to content himself with hearsay evidence, but he found little reason for lament. By instituting marriage the missionaries had assured better maternal care for children, and it was not true that they had thereby instituted abortion and infanticide as well: the sharp decline in the native population was owing rather to "former licentiousness" and the desire to avoid the pains of childbirth, or childhood sex and masturbation, or emigration, or maybe the decline was only imaginary, the result of a faulty census. The schools were packed with devoted young scholars whom Wilkes found "staid and demure, having the quiet looks of old men." Inquiry revealed that "after mature deliberation and experience," the missionaries had found it best to deprive them of their "heathenish enjoyments." Still it was good to see the occasional lad engaged in the wholesome amusement of flying a kite.

Some of Wilkes' officers shared his approval of Protestant efforts in the Sandwich Islands. Hudson was always on the side of Christian Endeavor, and Dana, in his concern for the spiritual welfare of his shipmates, had been acting like a lay missionary ever since the ships sailed. But others dissented. Doctor Holmes' observations were confined to Honolulu and its environs, but in that restricted area he found that though the converts could read and write, attended church and preserved the Sabbath, the women among them were "totally destitute of modesty or virtue" and suspected that the missionaries had made their usual mistake, curtailing the "innocent enjoyments of the natives" in accordance with their own "unjust and illiberal" views. Then to protect their wives from "contamination," they established "distinctions of caste . . . as well marked as at home, with relation to color." Observing that the Catholic priests recently arrived at Honolulu recognized no such distinction, he predicted great success for them.

James Alden was even less impressed, noting that the missionaries were entitled to no credit for the destruction of idolatry and the tabu system, quite fortuitous events that, antedating their arrival, prepared the ground for "Christian seed & cultivation—Alas for the harvest": a people once celebrated for cleanliness and gaiety, "now dirty and miserable" and reduced by half, because "men ascetic, fanatical, sectarian and . . . ignorant" had come to save them with the "blue laws of Connecticut."

On the other hand, the packs of randy sailors were doubtless a sore trial to the missionaries. At first the men took their pleasures innocently enough and went marching about town on the heels of a makeshift band, belting out patriotic airs and waving the American flag. Emmons thought they were "behaving very well, every thing considered." But John Dyes had better opportunities to observe, and the days the crews of the *Vincennes* and *Peacock* went ashore he saw Honolulu "turned upsydes down the sailors Horse ridign . . . & Cruising throu the streets raised sutch a dust as to Nerly blind one," and later watched them straggle back to the ship "nerly use up . . . sick with pox & auther wise Hurt by Horse & mair Riding, Dancing & getting Drunk." One day he attempted to quell a waterfront row and had to record with wounded feelings, "the Natives throw me overbord of the Warfe." After divine service next day, another fight erupted, "in whitch the Natives pounded Severly a Number of ouer men." And there were several occasions like the one Dyes witnessed aboard the *Vincennes* at Hilo and dolefully chronicled: "Nerley all day the Ship Has Been filled with Yellow *Hores* of the worst description." After tracing the general itinerary of "these Loos Ladyes of Pleasure," he added that this took place in the "Captains Absence."

The *Vincennes* found herself at Hilo because, despite the fact that the Sandwich Islands were a good deal more familiar to the world than Samoa or the Fijis, Wilkes felt that the survey work had to be carried on. The scientists boarded the *Flying Fish*, commanded by Sam Knox since the day Wilkes had inspected Sinclair's journal, to examine Kauai at the northwest end of the chain, then Oahu and Hawaii. Wilkes himself chose to lead the most spectacular of the excursions—the ascent of Mauna Loa, at nearly fourteen thousand feet the largest of active volcanoes. It began inauspiciously. Refitted and repainted, the *Vincennes* was ready to sail from Honolulu early on the morning of December 2, but the pilot arrived both tardy and drunk, there were fiery words, and he stamped ashore, leaving Wilkes to find his own way by buoying out the narrow channel from the boats.

From Byron's Bay at Hilo the men of the *Vincennes* could see their objective clearly, a great stone dome sixty miles away. An observatory was set up near the beach so that meteorological observations could be made simultaneously with those at the summit, and two hundred bearers were rounded up. When every man and thing was assembled at daybreak on December 14, Henry Eld, whose task it was to impose some kind of order, was reminded of a caravan he had once seen fitting out for Mecca. The cargo collected was enormous—portable houses, tents, instruments (including the pendulum apparatus that required ten men to carry it), and provisions stowed in the giant island calabashes. The bearers were a clamorous, half-naked mob, bound for the snowy summit clad only in the maro with a piece of tapa thrown over the shoulders and sandals of ti leaves. Getting them under way with their loads of fifty pounds per man Eld found "a most serious job," and it was noon before the first party started. Wilkes and Peter A. Brinsmade, a Honolulu businessman, Bible teacher, and U.S. Consul who had come along "to share our troubles and fatigues," set out two hours later in sedan chairs, each carried by four natives. They tramped through canefields (including missionary Titus Coan's), woods, bogs, lava beds, and patches of pandamus and fern, the natives suffering all the way with shoulders so galled that Eld found it a painful task to drive the shirkers from the bushes along the way.

On the sixteenth they pitched camp under the rim of Kilauea's crater—a chasm a thousand feet deep and something over two miles long, with a cherry red lake at the bottom. (It had boiled over the previous May, leaving a flow that was still hot near the shore.) As darkness fell the scene became hellishly beautiful, with an illuminated cloud of silvery brightness suspended above, the condensed vapor from the boiling mass at their feet. The howling wind seemed to rush to the chasm to support the mighty fires within, where, caught by the wind, they danced across the surface, Eld imagined, like "some fiery monster skipping . . . for its prey."

Proceeding over beds of solid lava and eerie fields of scoria, the party reached the summit of Mauna Loa on Tuesday, December 22, and remained atop the Pacific world until the middle of January. The violent winds, which smashed several instruments despite the maze of stone walls they were continuously building, the cold, the clear moonlight with massive clouds undulating below the horizon brought back vivid memories of Antarctica. Though many were sick and everybody so sore and exhausted from the interminable wall-building and unnerved by the ever-howling gales, they succeeded in triangulating the summit, in determining the depth of the craters and direction of the lava flows, the speed of sound and the temperature at which water boiled in the rarefied atmosphere, the dew point, and one another's pulse rates. Seaman Clark, recovered from his Malolo wounds, cut a commemoration in the lava, "Pendulum Peak, January 1841," and when some

The camp on Pendulum Peak atop Mauna Loa, sketch
by Charles Wilkes. (*Narrative*, 4: facing p. 155, Western
Americana Collection, Yale University Library.)

of his shipmates protested that so anonymous a legend might be ascribed to a
gang of Her Britannic Majesty's blokes, he rose early next morning to cut
additional letters below: "U.S. Ex Ex." On January 15 Eld "Got that
intolerable bore the Clock off among the first things," and bade goodbye to
the peak with a passage in his journal that came as near being a complaint as
anything recorded there: "I never left a place with more pleasure." The last of
the summit party reached the ship forty-two days after setting out.

Titus Coan was waiting to show the commander around the Hilo mission,
where he set the pupils to reciting, and then presented Wilkes with a bill for
damage done to his sugar cane. Ten dollars. Wilkes regarded it as "a piece of
extortion" but paid up. Whether he ever knew that his ship had been full of
"yellow hores" during his absence there is no knowing. But as shortly before
departure he received from Coan a complimentary note on the "exemplary
conduct" of the crew during their stay at Hilo, he at least knew to leave well
enough alone.[3]

On March 23 the *Porpoise* returned from her second independent cruise.
She had arrived from the Fijis in early October after surveying Farewell Island

(Cikobia), Fawn Harbor, and Natuva Bay on Taveuni; beating up to Somosomo to check on the welfare of the missionaries, who had been obliged to witness another cannibal feast before their very doors (in evidence of which Holmes had a vertebral column he found awash in the nearby surf); then turning finally to Turtle Island, where they learned that the survivors of the *Shylock* had been rescued. In mid-November Wilkes had dispatched her again, with orders that sent her sailing all over the central Pacific. After failing to locate Manuel Rodriguez Shoal (Kingman Reef), which Edmund Fanning had reported some nine hundred miles south of Honolulu, they threaded their way in gusty, rainy weather through the reef-strewn waters of the Line Islands, surveyed several of the Tuamotus improperly laid down on Kruzenstern's chart, and made Carlshoff (Aratika) on December 15—a low and desolate reef where, to his disgust, Lieutenant Johnson was landed for a month with boring apparatus and twelve men, since Wilkes, finding it impossible to believe that the activities of tiny animals could produce entire islands, had discovered an interest in coral. Prospects for the landing party brightened only a little when Johnson spotted two or three "tolerably pretty" girls among the only inhabitants. The weather continued squally, pipes and augers broke, the coral kept caving in. Some days they were able to penetrate no more than a foot and at twenty-one they gave up. The single unattached girl proved to be impenetrable, too. Johnson fell sick and, to cap it all, when an English brig put in, most of the Kanakas of the *Porpoise*'s crew deserted.

Meanwhile the *Porpoise* proceeded to the southwest past "Vincennes" Island (Kauehi), Raraka, and Katiu, into the Daevski Group of atolls that Bellingshausen had discovered in 1820. Surveying the lot, Ringgold renamed them Sea Gull Group, consisting of Sea Gull, Bacon, and Reid (probably Tuavaka, Tepoto, and Hiti). The natives were helpful but the flies voracious, and Sinclair concluded that the "principal occupation & amusement" here was scratching.

Changing course to the northeast to seek out reported islands, they enjoyed "far from a Merry Christmas" in hot and squally weather but broke out a bottle of champagne in the wardroom and toasted distant friends, Sinclair vowing, "if Ever I am caught again an any thing but a man of war I'll be——." Farther on they found a place on the charts for Barclay de Tolly (Raroia) and Wolconsky (Takume).

The weather improved early in January and the brig sped to the southwest before a spanking breeze that carried her along at seven and a half knots. Working from an old manuscript chart on board, they searched for the islands that Quiros had sighted in 1606—Santelmo, San Pablo, Los Quatro Coronados—made Margaret's (Nukutipipi) and Anuanuranga (which they took to be Los Quatro Coronados) in what is now called the Duke of Gloucester Group, and a little to the west sailed over the position assigned on Kruzenstern's chart to Archangel, finally locating it so far from its designated position that credit for its discovery would go to Ringgold. Picking up the frustrated drillers ("However," Sinclair consoled them, "Science, Science—Squalls or no Squalls, War or Peace") they bore away for Tahiti and anchored in Papeete harbor on the twenty-second to take to the boats once more in order to connect surveys earlier made by the brig and *Peacock*.

Under way again a week later they surveyed Flint, a detached island to the northward whose exact position had never been determined, then fixed the position of Staver's (Vostok), reported by an American whaler only a few years before. For two days they searched the different positions assigned to Penrhyn's (Tongareva) by two whaling captains and were on the point of giving it up as another mirage when the lookout raised it to the northwest. It proved to be really a large lagoon, perhaps ten miles long and eight wide, almost completely surrounded by coral islets that rose no more than fifteen feet above the sea.

Early in the morning the islanders began coming out in their light canoes to congregate at the gangway and scramble up the side, shouting and gesticulating all the while in peculiarly harsh voices, accompanying their words with the most diabolical facial expressions, "Every muscle being brought into play and made to quiver apparently with rage & excitement." They were, at least in their present excited state, a strangely popeyed people, and in apparent ferocity they outclassed the Fijians and seemed to be the original Yahoos.

There was some uneasiness aboard. The islanders had lined the bottoms of the canoes with eight-foot spears and pieces of coral of handy throwing size. Still more were putting out from the beach and soon some three hundred were alongside. On gaining the deck they seized everything in sight. First went a peajacket, then the ropes from the gangway, and one was hauling away at the brass poop stanchions. They quickly darted their booty into the canoes and spun round for more, "clamorous as a parcel of Mag-pies" all the while in a language that neither the Kanakas nor the Tahitians aboard could understand. Ringgold broke out the arms chest, Johnson recovered the stanchions by making a pass with his cutlass, and Sinclair belted one man with the flat of his sword.

Undaunted, they took up trading with the same heedless vociferousness, accepted anything offered and, without pausing to appraise it, tossed it into the canoes. But curiously they always gave fair return in fishhooks and necklaces of their own manufacture.

They were an olive-skinned people, the men with mustaches and beards, and some of the women, making "gestures too significant" to mistake, handsome, with remarkably fine breast development—"immense," Doctor Holmes pronounced it. They seemed to recognize no rank but treated one another with as little ceremony as they did the visitors, knocking the women and old people about and battering the fingers of one gray-beard who, having fallen overboard, tried to haul himself into a canoe. The old fellow seemed to know where he was not wanted and swam off for his own canoe.

As their numbers continued to increase, Ringgold ordered the decks cleared and weighed anchor. This elicited a well-aimed hail of stones from the canoes, but no one was injured. Their most fearsome weapon proved to be their unremitting racket, which seemed to be the medium of their lives. Holmes watched one fellow deliver a harangue that lasted "at least ¾ of an hour, in a tone which it would have seemed impossible for any human being to have sustained . . . he hardly stopped to take breath and kept up a constant and most violent gesticulation. No body paid any attention to him, as each was nearly as busy with his own tongue." A collective sigh of relief passed through the vessel as the sails filled. But even then the canoes followed in a little cloud of sound and in the surveying operations they dared not use the taffrail log from the certainty it would be stolen.

Since by now there was neither sufficient time nor provisions to permit charting the Isles of Danger and Palmyra, as Wilkes had directed, they bore north for Honolulu. The *Porpoise* was sailing badly, for her copper was ragged, her sails so worn that they split time and again, and her hold almost empty. Rations were reduced three times, and a week after passing Washington Island, which Fanning had discovered in 1798 about half way between Penrhyn and Oahu, their all-important antiscorbutics, pickles and kraut, were gone. They were down to twenty days' provisions on reduced allowance, three hundred miles dead to leeward of their port, and working to windward, Sinclair observed, "like a crab." There was a good deal of grumbling and some pregnant speculation about "Bad management Somewhere," as one officer noted darkly, for they had begun this cruise at a port where there was a "superabundance of Every thing." When they finally anchored at Oahu on March 24 Sinclair discovered that "For the first time since the gale off Noir Island in the Relief, the clink of a Chain Cable did not make me feel nervous."

Boats came out with the latest news. Queen Victoria had a new daughter and the United States a new President, for as Purser Waldron liked to put it in his pompous way, much mimicked by the officers, the "great Moral and religious community" had elected Old Tippecanoe four months earlier and "retired Mr V Buren." Of more immediate interest to the officers, however, was the rumor that the sloop-of-war *St. Louis*, Commander French Forrest, was bound for Honolulu. If Forrest should indeed appear, Wilkes would find himself outranked at last, and all were curious to know what would then be the fate of the broad pennant that had waved so proudly from the *Vincennes'* main ever since their departure from the *Falmouth* at Callao.

Curiosity was to remain unquenched, however, for the task of overhauling the *Porpoise* began next day at a furious pace—whether owing to the rumor no one could say. She was stripped and hauled alongside the wharf, where for some reason, Wilkes himself insisted on superintending the operation of heaving-down, a procedure that involved exposing one half her bottom then the other, in order to re-copper. In the midst of "more noise & confusion than would be made in heaving down the whole navy at home," her sailing master found that everything went "head over heels." It was bad enough when in his obstinacy Wilkes insisted on demonstrating his command of seamanship where there were no witnesses except the explorers themselves. Here where the shore was lined with onlookers, sea dogs blushed.

At the first heave the lashings of the main purchase block parted. This was repaired amid "confusion & mismanagement" and noise reminiscent of the people of Penrhyn and late in the afternoon they got her down, but as Wilkes had made no provision to prevent her falling when below her heaving bearings, the topmasts crashed flat upon the wharf. Still, that saved her from capsizing. Carpenters went to work on the bottom, while the officers, ears burning, cast covert glances at the shore. "For myself," Sinclair confessed, "I could have crawled into the bunghole of the smallest sized water breaker." Work slacked off on Sunday out of deference to the customs of the country, though twenty-four men were kept constantly at the pumps. The effort to right her produced equal confusion, and entertainment: "Many smiled, some laughed outrite." Work continued into the next Sunday, when a message arrived from the fort announcing sternly that they were "violating the laws of the Country, by working on the Sabbath." Feeling a little more pious than usual, the weary officers thought it a nice irony that a people so recently rescued from barbarism should have to teach a civilized nation its Christian duty. But they did not like Wilkes' acquiescence either and thought the proper reply a curt "Necessity."

SANDWICH ISLANDS

On Monday, April 5, with a long sick list and every man jack on board exhausted, the *Porpoise* and *Vincennes* got under weigh for the Northwest Coast, where they expected to meet the *Peacock* and *Flying Fish* no later than the first of May.[4]

14 Secret Service

There exists somewhere—I have been informed—a society
for the extermination of native races. . . .

A Peripatetic Parson

An old merchant captain in Honolulu who came down one
bright day to have a look at the exploring vessels had pronounced the *Flying
Fish* a "half-tide rock." A head sea would keep her wet. And as a fresh breeze
bore her southward from Honolulu in mid-December she was indeed diving
under a good many waves. Still, she managed to keep company with Hudson's
ship, a feat rarely accomplished with Wilkes'. They were off on an island-hunt-
ing mission of their own, with orders to proceed westward along the Equator
to the Phoenix Group, then southward to the Tokelaus and Samoa again,
thence northwestward to the Ellice and Kingsmill (Gilbert) Groups, following
the trend of the island chains to a small group of doubtful position known as
the Pescadores, and stopping at Strong's (Kusaie in the Carolines) and
Ascension (Ponape). All along this tortuous route they were to search for
reported islands and arrive at the Columbia River in time to meet the
Porpoise and *Vincennes.* Again, there was too much to do in the time allotted.

After searching five different positions, on January 11 they finally sighted
the low coral island fringed with coconuts that Fanning had named
Washington, but the weather came on squally, and they gave up the search for
others reported in this sector of the Line Islands. Instead they crossed the
Equator, and on the twentieth made the bold and barren shores of Jarvis, or
Bunker's Shoal as it was called, which, lying almost exactly on the Equator and
the one hundred and sixtieth meridian, had been discovered twenty years
before. They surveyed it by a method that became almost automatic when an
island was sighted and allowed the two vessels to work in efficient harmony on

this part of the cruise. While the *Peacock* stood off and on, the schooner ran down the shore a few miles but remained well in sight. With one of her great guns the *Peacock* then fired base, and the interval between the flash and the report provided the distance between the vessels, the base line that was the foundation of their triangulation as they then moved around opposite sides of the island.

Proceeding southwestward, they celebrated Christmas on a course for the Phoenix Group. On the *Peacock* both Hudson and the "young gentlemen" joined the others for dinner in the wardroom, which they topped off with a large Christmas cake one of them had received from a lady friend at home. On the tossing schooner the celebration was of a different order. William Reynolds and his sole companion, "Old Sam Knox" (Knox was not quite thirty but he had spent most of those years on salt water and, bald now, his face lined and weathered, he looked old enough to be a grandfather) spent the day in the cramped little cabin in the stern, where the vessel was hardly more than six feet wide. Such conditions do not usually nourish friendship, but though no two officers in the Expedition were more unlike—the one romantic and ebullient, the other placid and rather old-fashioned in his ways—the two got on famously. Between islands, as Reynolds wrote in his secret journal this day, they had "nothing to do, from Morn till Night, but to Stare at Each other, & to talk about any and Every thing—but we get weary staring, & We cant talk for Ever—then we are puzzled." There were no books ("they are too stingy to lend us any from the Peacock, though I paid $3.00 in Oahu for a lot of New ones") and writing was difficult from the wet, for the hatch spewed water "like a Shower bath." They could not even stand erect in the cabin, yet fifty-five days were to pass before they stepped off the schooner.

And so on this day the two friends reflected on Yuletides at home. In place of turkey they dined on salt beef ("salt horse"), pickled pig, and bread ("*Monstrous dry* is the *best* of Sea biscuit"), sure from the texture of the beef, from which chips flew when cut, that the animal had been a contemporary of their childhood. At times like these the disgusted Reynolds would vow "to let the Sea alone in future, and secure fair treatment of my interior, by living on shore," but then would come the "glorious feasting days in port" with fresh fruits and vegetables and meats, and vows would be forgotten.

The area of the Pacific they were now bound for was little known to the charts, though a number of islands had been reported. On January 9, 1841, they made what they took to be Enderbury, reported by Captain James Coffin of Nantucket in 1823, and here for a few moments when the wind was just right, they caught the essence of these seas, the secret scent of earth and

In the forecastle of the *Flying Fish*, from sketch by
Alfred T. Agate. (J. C. Palmer, *Thulia: A Tale of the
Antarctic*, New York, 1843, p. 25.)

flowers, and many remarked the occasion in their journals. Ordered to proceed
with the survey while the *Peacock*'s officers made a landing, Knox and
Reynolds found it particularly tantalizing.

While nothing like so difficult as in the Fijis, navigation here was still a
delicate procedure. On a clear day these low islands—Birnie, for example,
which they surveyed two days later—could be seen from the masthead at a
distance of eight or nine miles, and at twelve to fifteen if there were trees, but
darkness and high seas made them difficult to detect. They rose so abruptly
from the ocean bottom that soundings and the color of the sea yielded no
clue.

After searching in vain for several of the islands listed in "Reynolds' Book,"
they found one on January 17, Sydney, which the *Vincennes* had sighted on
her passage from Fiji. The scientifics—Dana, Hale, Peale, Rich, and Agate

were aboard the *Peacock*—methodically set about adding to the government collections, followed closely now by the crew, who were acting "not Exactly per bono publico," Fred Stuart remarked in amusement, "but for the good of No. 1—leaving hardly a stone unturned in search of something new." But the yield was skimpy and the island showed no signs of habitation.

Standing to the south before a moderate northeast breeze, they made Duke of York (Atafu), the northernmost of the Tokelau Islands, on January 25. It proved to be inhabited, contrary to the evidence of the chart derived from the visit in 1791 of the *Pandora* in search of the *Bounty* mutineers. Three large double canoes put out, their occupants singing loudly and keeping time with the paddles, occasionally breaking off to gesticulate, "which was all admirably done to the same time," Emmons observed, adding approvingly that unlike most such exhibitions he had witnessed among the islands, their gestures were "divested of vulgarity." Some scrambled up the accommodation ladder to trade their mats, paddles, and fishing implements with great enthusiasm but still pausing from time to time to burst into song.

Others kept off—in fear, one explained, lest the ship rise into the sky. In this remark some of the officers saw themselves reflected, like the Conquistadors of old, as children of the sun, but Fred Stuart came to the less flattering conclusion that these people had dealt with white men before and knew "too well their true character." And indeed one of the officers later found in the village some suspiciously secular cooper's tools. All hope of enticing the wary ones aboard disappeared when the *Peacock* fired for base. Stuart happened at the time to be gazing idly at a chief standing in the middle of his canoe. The man "jumped at least 4 feet high—plunged into the sea and sank," remained a remarkable length of time underwater, and on finally reappearing, leaped "most dexterously into the canoe" and lost no time in shoving off.

The survey completed, boats went ashore. On this, his fifty-fifth day aboard the schooner, Reynolds complained so bitterly ("after having fretted ourselves to death in finding this Island, We Might as well be in the Kitchen chimney at Home") that Knox determined to send him ashore even at the risk of a dunking, for their only boat was stove in. But it stayed afloat as far as the reef and he swam the rest of the way. On the beach, as they took up the instruments for determining dip and intensity and position, it was flattering to be handed coconuts to drink—"which they gave us for nothing," one man noted in astonishment, "and only seemed to wonder how we could empty so many . . . us poor dogs, who had . . . nothing but brackish water for the last two months." But the affectionate rubbing of noses hampered observations, and the singing never ceased.

Women and children were huddled in canoes out of reach in the lagoon, but the men, tall and well built, resembled Samoans, though phrenologically superior in many points. However, their language was unique, and they had no acquaintance with tobacco. Stuart found that "On presenting one a Segar (thinking at the time I was doing him a great Kindness) he accepted it—put it to his nose then looked significantly in my face—and pitched it into the Sea." Not a weapon was to be found among them, and as a mark of esteem Hudson suggested that the officers' messes make them a present of a boarand two sows—which was done without any grumbling at all.

Calms prevented a complete survey of Duke of Clarence (Nukuonu), sighted the next day a few miles to the southeast; but moving eastward, they found themselves at daylight on January 28 close in with a fine green island. A fleet of canoes soon put out with what appeared to be a cluster of spears across the stern of each and began maneuvering in a suspiciously hostile manner. On the *Peacock* they brought up arms and made preparations to repel boarders, then felt a little foolish at discovering on nearer approach that the spears were fishing poles and the canoes maneuvering from shoal to shoal. The islanders showed no interest in mirrors, hatchets, gimlets, or nails but merely concentrated all the harder at fishing—until fishhooks were offered, when they eagerly held out fish and coconuts in return. Still the slightest thing alarmed them—the taking up of a spyglass, or the smoke of a cigar, would send the canoes scurrying away.

Next day they formed a procession and accorded the explorers a formal reception, leading them to their old chief, who rubbed noses and wept copiously over Hudson—much to the captain's discomfiture, his clerk noted. Crowded into canoes in the lagoon behind the village floated at least five hundred women and children. Only a few pretty girls remained—diversionary offerings to the celestial navigators. Into the. public and private collections went paddles, mats, shells, tools fashioned of wood, and neatly made buckets that resembled the common butter tubs at home, a great load of stuff that the islanders helped them stow aboard the vessels.

This was one of the few peoples they had visited who seemed to know no other land or people. So the island was a new discovery, the Expedition's own, and the scientists begged Hudson for another day or two on the ground that the "originality of the People" made the island of unusual importance to science. But they were low on water and no doubt Hudson had had enough of being wept over. He proudly named it Bowditch Island (Fakaofo is the native name) "after our worthy and indefatigable astronomer," and the group in which it lay with Duke of York and Duke of Clarence, "Union Group," and thus "dovetailed the name of our republican countryman" with "the royal pair." Privately he vowed to persuade the missionaries in Samoa to establish a station there.

Bearing southward, they raised the high coral island in the southern part of the Tokelau Group that Hudson had learned of at Tahiti from the Nantucket whaleman Captain Jonathan Swain II, who had sighted it in 1820. They surveyed it in a squall, and the high sea that made a boat landing too dangerous to attempt broke Master Baldwin's from its mooring and swept it with full crew onto the beach, where, undaunted, they proceeded with the usual scientific observations. Hudson named it Swain's.[1]

On February 5 they sighted the high land of Savai'i again, where instead of feasting, bathing in waterfalls, and rambling in cool groves, Reynolds and Knox found themselves redoing the survey of Upolu. They came this time in the wet and stormy season, and they paid the price. Alternating calms and squalls and never-ending rain made the work difficult, at times impossible. But three weeks saw it done and, rounding the eastern end of the island, they rejoined the *Peacock* and followed her into the harbor of Saluafata, where to their astonishment Hudson announced that they were to attack and burn the town next morning.

The trouble this time stemmed from the murder of an American seaman some months before. Hudson had demanded that the chief of the district either punish or deliver up the murderer in accordance with the treaty signed at Wilkes' insistence fifteen months before. But the chief could only reply that the culprit was protected by chiefs greater than he, who would fight rather than yield him up. So would the fugitive, who sent word that he chose to kill "a few more white men" before surrendering.

In the still air of morning the guns of the *Peacock*, loaded with round shot and grape, slowly and deliberately fired into Saluafata, only a stone's throw distant. Under cover of the guns the three ships' boats landed and, unopposed, fired the five villages comprising the town, and after returning aboard for a round of grog—hot work this—destroyed two more at the foot of the harbor. Watching from the deck, Fred Stuart found the scene "Most Beautiful and grand . . . the dense volumes of Smoke intermingled with Towering flames or sheets of fire rising far above the Cocoa Nut Trees." Emmons thought the villages "almost too pretty" to burn, but burn they must "as a just punishment—and the only one left to us for the Murdering of one of our countrymen." By good fortune no one was injured, native or crew, and they sailed away as the smoke rose against the green hills.

For a time there seemed the possibility of further action, and next day to his delight Reynolds was posted on "Secret Service" in an attempt to take a particularly savage chief named Opotuno, who was notorious for his depredations on visiting white men. Small, bespectacled against myopia, and boyish at twenty-five, as unsuspicious a character as could be found in the squadron, Reynolds was the ideal choice for the role. On Sunday morning, while the boats went through the innocent motions of surveying, he was landed on Manono, the thickly peopled islet inside the barrier reef on Upolu's western end, with orders to capture Pare, the old chief of the island and Opotuno's uncle. That accomplished, it was assumed that Pare's people would deliver up the nephew as ransom.

Everyone was in church, and he followed an empty path through the trees, enjoying the songs of the birds in the galleries above and the prodigal verdure on every hand until he met the congregation approaching. Wearing their outrageous Christian bonnets ("a sorry substitute," he thought, for "wild flowers in the raven hair! the Missionaries have no poetry in them") the women greeted him warmly. But the men were cool, and on learning that he had been at Saluafata, one announced, "You are no good," and walked on.

At the house of the resident missionary, Mr. Heath, he received a scarcely warmer welcome, and one of the English ladies looked at him in horror. Heath asked if it was true that the explorers had come to seize the island's beloved old chief. Shaken, for he himself had been told of the plan only twelve hours earlier and was under instructions to learn what he could from the missionary while revealing nothing, Reynolds found his maneuvering "knocked in the head; and diplomacy had to go on the other tack."

Here was a quandary. The capture of Pare would only raise a "tremendous outcry" through the islands and accomplish nothing, for while the old chief was without influence beyond Manono, Opotuno was everywhere dreaded. The whole enterprise suddenly seemed "so silly, and . . . fraught with Nothing but Evil" that his exciting mission became a loathsome thing. Huck Finn was to face a similar dilemma when tempted to help Jim escape the slave catchers. But Reynolds was more steadfast than Huck and explained to himself, "I was fully aware of the orders of my Superiors. My sense of duty would not allow me, to mar their plans by any scruples of My own." Perceiving that his only course was to deceive, he launched into "such a complicated mass of falsehoods, and discussed the pros & cons of the affair with so much coolness, treating it altogether as an improbability," that he was sure Heath believed it all. In a "Most Artful manner" he learned which of the huts was Pare's. But art nearly deserted when the missionary remarked offhandedly, "Well, I suppose I may as well tell Pare's friends, that they need not be alarmed any more, about him, that you have not come to do him harm. They are still waiting and are anxious to know." It was a bad moment, but Reynolds faced up to duty once more and walked away with cheeks burning.

At Pare's he was welcomed by two pretty, bright-eyed girls. While he was on the point of greeting them, a troop of natives suddenly rushed up the path armed with fish spears and clubs. Not wishing to be made a hostage himself, he gallantly removed his hat and began an animated conversation, and while the natives stood about disconcerted, he put on his hat again, bade the girls goodbye, and sauntered on his way. No one followed.

Replying with feigned astonishment to the many questions put to him along the way, he completed the five-mile circuit of the island. At the beach again he accepted a penitential cup of cava, his first, from a group of pretty girls busy spitting it into a bowl. "The fact is," he admonished himself, "custom has Every thing, to do, in these matters": a Samoan might be as repelled at sight of the sweaty arms of a farm wife kneading bread. And so, "Viewing the Affair in this Enlightened, philosophical & rational light, my delicacy & fastidiousness vanished, and I felt there was another degree added to my cosmopolitanism." And so vanished, too, William Reynolds' career as secret agent.

Next morning Emmons tried his hand at stealth. Everywhere he was greeted civilly. At the house of one of the minor chiefs he remarked politely on the beauty of the chief's daughter. The chief replied graciously that he was welcome to her but must take care not to let the missionaries hear of it. "I thanked him and gave him to understand that that was not my object in paying so just a compliment," Emmons recorded primly. At another, he was greeted by two pretty little girls, their hair dressed with flowers, who took him by the hand to meet their mother, gave him a coconut to drink and bade him goodbye with a kiss on the cheek. "Quite captivated," George Emmons wound his way along the leafy path to the boats, reflecting that "had I felt my existence as much of a blank as some Foreigners who have taken up their residence in these Islands, and forgotten my own Land of Liberty I am sure I should have turned 'Samoa' too." Which was a remarkable admission for the duty-bound Emmons to make.

When Lieutenant Walker, sent to capture another chief, also returned emptyhanded, the explorers gave up. That night they could see bonfires blazing in celebration of deliverance, and Reynolds, who lately had entertained such savage sentiments at Upolu, spoke the minds of all when he remarked in his journal that night, "I was not at all sorry, that the Expedition was now to be abandoned."

All hope of martial glory faded, the two vessels put to sea at sunset, March 7, and stood to the northwest. Eight days later they surveyed the circular reef dotted with islets called Ellice's Group (Funafuti, one of a larger number now known as the Ellice Islands) and at next daylight were in De Peyster's Group (Nukufetau). Swarms of canoes hampered the survey and Reynolds and Knox grew a little alarmed, for, with low freeboard and no bulwarks, the schooner would be helpless before a determined boarding force. Confidently announcing that the little vessel was taboo, Reynolds motioned them on toward the *Peacock*. They promptly pushed off, repeating the word to one another, and with gestures "not of the most decent nature," urged the visitors to call ashore. On the *Peacock*, where they swarmed up the rigging as high as the mizzen topmast head, Fred Stuart read treachery in their cranial conformation, and when Agate had finished sketching two albinos the decks were cleared and they hurried on. The wind lay dead in their teeth and time was precious now, so they did not linger at Tracy's (Vaitupu—though not on the charts, it appeared on Jeremiah Reynolds' list in very nearly its correct position) and Nui (though Wilkes would later name it Spieden, after the *Peacock*'s purser). On March 24 they surveyed an uninhabited island, tiny and lagoonless, which they took to be a new discovery, Nanumanga (Wilkes would name it Hudson).[2]

For navigating among the low coral islands of the next archipelago to the north—the Kingsmill Group they were then called, a term now applied only to the southern Gilberts—they had only a very incomplete, and as they were to learn, inaccurate chart based on Captain Louis I. Duperrey's exploration of the area in the *Coquille* in 1824. Had they been able to beat to windward with greater success, they would have sighted several of the group to the east and perhaps have made new discoveries. As matters stood, the first they reached was Drummond's (Tabituea), largest and most populous of the group. This was on April 3.

It was no accident that it was to Drummond's they had at length come, for at Oahu the explorers had fallen in with a survivor of the English whaleship *Corsair*, wrecked here in 1835. The captain, his wife and child, and a boat's crew had gained the shore—and never been heard from since. Four other boats, attacked by canoes, had fled with a handful of provisions and after a harrowing voyage reached the Ladrones. But quite apart from that, the explorers were curious about these islanders, who were known to be a "new people," distinct from those of the Ellice Group.

Some fifty canoes were soon about the ships, sailing craft ingeniously fashioned of small pieces of plank lashed together and handled with a skill that all admired. Hale set about adding a new language to his collection, and Agate sketched the curiously tattooed men in conical caps of straw. Calling first for "tobaga," then rum—clear evidence, Emmons wryly noted, of "two prominent steps toward civilization"—they brought forth fishnets and lines, baskets, fish, chickens, and coconuts. The men were light-skinned and bearded and well-formed—though one of the explorers pronounced them "the most depraved ill looking cut throat beings . . . with Villany stamp'd in their very Eyes." The shapely girls were something else again, and the same critic remarked that he "never was struck more forcibly with the beauty and form of any race of people than with the girls of Drummonds Island." The only flaw he could find "after a strict overhaul" was their bad teeth.

Lieutenant Emmons was the first to test the temper of these people. When his survey party stepped ashore to take compass bearings they were immediately surrounded by a crowd who made a great nuisance of themselves with demonstrations of affection. Some very pretty women sought to entice him to their village, but George Emmons was a man who knew his duty.

Next morning there were ninety-two canoes about the *Peacock*. In the boats Emmons took care to prevent any natives from boarding and one of the exasperated islanders began hurling stones. Emmons pointed a pistol, but to no effect, and he supposed that these people had no acquaintance with firearms. There was a bad moment later in the day when the boats were chased by canoes before escaping through a narrow passage in the reef. Angered but determined to prevent bloodshed, Emmons continued with the survey, finding to his satisfaction that Duperrey's chart was a poor piece of work. The Frenchman had somehow got the lagoon on the wrong side of the island.

On boarding the *Peacock* again on the seventh, Emmons found a pretty and very pleased girl seated in the cabin, turning this way and that as Agate painted her likeness. But the news was alarming. During his absence Hudson had gone ashore with some of the officers, taking no guard of marines because as he had remarked in his indulgent way to Purser Spieden, he believed there was "no harm in these people." The natives had met them in great numbers. With their tastefully tattooed navels, the women were decidedly pretty and their gestures alarmingly provocative as they sought to attach themselves to the explorers—quite literally, hanging about their necks and pulling them toward the village. (Strange company it was for Captain Hudson: good husband and father, did he pass it off as island foolishness?) One could hardly take offense at this sort of welcome, but the explorers soon discovered that while the women dallied, the men were efficiently picking their pockets. Others who had strayed alone had to force their way through importunate crowds. Becoming suspicious of these people among whom they were "so promiscuously huddled," to use Reynolds' graphic description, they straggled back to the boats—all except Seaman John Anderson of the *Peacock*'s first cutter. There had been some commotion in back of the village and some said they heard shrieks as from "some person in mortal fear & agony." Lieutenant Walker and Passed Midshipman Davis went off well armed in search, calling often and loudly, John Anderson! John! But no answer came, and as they returned to the boats through taunting crowds, some throwing stones and brandishing spears, they felt pretty certain that Anderson had followed one of those Eves to her garden of death and been taken by surprise. Still they held the boats offshore until sunset purely out of hope before returning to the ship vowing vengeance.

The village of Utiroa, Drummond's Island, by Alfred T. Agate. (*Narrative*, 5: facing p. 54, Western Americana Collection, Yale University Library.)

It augured ill for Anderson when next morning no canoes came off from Utiroa. From other villages they did, and their occupants gave the Utiroans a bad name. Even the tolerant Hudson grew alarmed and, concluding that Anderson was dead, made up his mind that duty and consideration for future navigators decreed punishment. As preparations for battle began once more,

Reynolds took thought. It seemed that his journal was chronicling one attack after another, "that our path through the Pacific is to be marked in blood. We commenced at the very first Island we made, and more than once since we have been obliged, unfortunately for ourselves & for the Natives, to go to the Extreme, and to take life, to pay for life." But there was no help for it. "If a person should be of such fine spun humanity, as to condemn our proceedings . . . I can only recommend to him a voyage to the Islands. A little Experience & a reasonable regard for his own Safety, & for that of others, Who might follow in his track would open his Eyes to the . . . *humanity* of the course we have pursued." No one disagreed with this reasoning. Reynolds was exceptional only in that he was at pains to explain the bloody wake.

"Villany stamp'd in their very Eyes." Drummond's
Island Warriors, woodcut. (*Narrative*, 5: p. 50, Western
Americana Collection, Yale University Library.)

Preparations were soon completed. From the canoes that swarmed about the schooner Reynolds managed to acquire, of all things, several suits of armor, which with weapons and women were offered in exchange for "a few plugs of tobacco." These suits of armor were made of stout rawhide set with sharp flints, with helmets of toadfish skin bristling with stiff barbs; they were perfect of their kind in workmanship. He also bought wooden swords studded with sharks' teeth and spears pointed with the tail of the stingray and was shown how properly to use them in removing heads and laying open bowels. Sending one suit to Peale for the public collections, he hung another at the squaresail yard and, standing well back, sent the balls of his double-barrel through it as he observed with satisfaction the astonishment and dismay on the faces of his audience in the canoes.

From the *Peacock*, lying in what is still called Peacock Anchorage, eighty-seven officers and men set out next day to carry "fire and the sword" to the village of Utiroa. Lieutenant Walker commanded. The boats drew up line abreast within pistol shot of the beach, where seven or eight hundred warriors crowded, some wading into the sea to lash the surface with their spears and all shouting defiance and ridicule.

It was hoped that bloodshed might yet be prevented if the islanders would surrender Anderson or even his remains, if it came to that. But attempts at parley came to nothing when, with deafening shouts, the warriors attacked the boats. Pulling back into line, Walker ordered Emmons to fire a rocket. But the fiery devils that had so terrified the Fijians created only a momentary diversion here. Sharpshooter Peale shot a warrior dead. But still they came. He dropped several more, but to no effect. A volley of musketry killed many others, but with a boldness that astonished all, most held their ground until the boats beached; then after another volley they fled into the trees and offered no further fight. Before applying the torch the landing party made a hasty survey of the town, which proved to be a mile long and thickly studded with houses and canoes drawn up in supposed safety. In one of the houses Emmons found a nine-pound iron ball, in another an iron chain plate and a strap to a deadeye.

Fred Stuart, now in the way of becoming an experienced military observer, watched it all from the *Peacock*'s deck. The canoes about the ship had beat to windward at the first sound of gunfire and their sails now stood snow white against the heavy column of dark smoke "intermingled with fire and Sinders" that soon covered the deck with ashes. Following the progress of the shore party as the fire spread first to the right, then to the left, he could "fancy them applying the lighted torch . . . to the Huts of what only an hour before had composed the neat and powerful Village of Utiroa." On the schooner, chafing to be at the "Hell Hounds" himself, Reynolds could feel the heat and, watching through his spyglass, saw a "tremendous glow" light up the sky.

Having taught the people of one more island (some twenty natives had been killed) what certain devastation "would be visited on their heads" at "the taking of a single White Man's life," the explorers went about their business before the smoke had ceased to rise, bidding "Adieu to Drummonds Island and our poor Ship Mate Anderson."

By the end of April they had completed surveys of nearby Sydenham (Nonouti), where they again showed the French to be in error, Henderville (Aranuka), Hall's (Maiana), Hopper (Abemama), and Woodle's (Kuria). Working northward under fresh breezes, they spent two days surveying Knox, a long harp-shaped scrap of land that Americans of a later century were to know as Tarawa, once again catching Duperrey out and resolving three of his islands into one. At nearby Charlotte (Abiang) the *Flying Fish* ran aground in dirty weather and then was chased by a fleet of canoes until they put a shot close by the ear of the leading steersman, who promptly jumped overboard, followed by all the others, while the schooner made blue water and safety.

In pleasant weather again they put Matthew's (Marakei) in its proper place, then Pitt's (Butaritari) and Makin (Little Makin). Now five months out of Oahu and short of supplies, Hudson announced that the Carolines, many of which hung in a latitudinal limbo, would have to go begging, and with them Ascension (Ponape), whose lofty péaks and fertile valleys had won it acclaim as the most beautiful of islands and whose mysterious prehistoric ruins had piqued the romantic curiosity of the age. Still, they sailed with the satisfaction that they had learned something of the language and customs of this race of men, had corrected the positions of ten islands on the charts—which had proved to be almost wholly unreliable—and had surveyed the area "with sufficient accuracy to answer all the purposes of Navigation."

Hudson chose a course through the Marshall Group, which by his reckoning would give them sufficient northing to pick up the trades that would carry them to Oahu. Forced by the shortage of provisions to run through a hazardous and little known sea, they sped past Arrowsmith's (Majuro) and the large atoll called Pedder's, or Daniel's (Arno), and on May 5 surveyed the Pescadores without seeing any signs of habitation. Leaving the schooner to search for survivors of a vessel lost there in 1834, the *Peacock* departed for Honolulu.

She was weary. Her boatswain, carpenter, gunner, and sailmaker were almost constantly employed at repairs. To conserve water, soup and tea were dropped from the menu, and on May 18 the last of the Samoan coconuts gave out and with them the last of the milk. They made a great loop to the north, proceeding to the thirty-fifth parallel before turning northeastward, and there was some fretting at the delay, for all were anxious now to reach the

Northwest Coast. If this gallant vessel's company could have known what lay in store for them upon that far shore, all aboard would have rejoiced at every day's delay.

The *Flying Fish*, as usual, was first in, although as badly in need of repairs as the *Peacock*. Her sails came down in rags in every blow, her decks leaked with every sea, and provisions were in even shorter supply. The water remained both plentiful and potable until May 24, when it was found that there were more dead mice in the casks than anyone had realized. The main fare consisted of vermin-infested bread and briny beef, which when the supply of wood ran out they were forced to eat uncooked. Once they harpooned a porpoise as a school crossed the bow. Economy being the order of the day, they strained out the oil and fried the brains and black steaks in one portion of it and used the rest to fuel the fire, over which they brewed a pot of tea as well. The flesh proved palatable enough to men who at one time or another on this cruise had dined on dog, kangaroo, and raw pork, as well as the omnipresent bad beef. But the cockroaches were a nuisance, and the rats became incredibly bold, carrying on their daily activities quite oblivious of the men—traveling in packs and fighting, screeching, biting at the woodwork until it was impossible to get a night's sleep. The men would throw shoes at them, bang on the bulkhead, or get up and light a candle to search their bunks.

Served by the wind only in puffs, they finally sighted the high land of Oahu on June 13, when as if in mockery a steady breeze blew up and carried them crowded with sail into the harbor.

The *Peacock* came in thirty hours later and the officers set off to enjoy the delights of the shore. William Reynolds, always slight, discovered in dismay that this latest cruise had cost him fourteen pounds.

To no one's surprise, three of the schooner's crew deserted. But they were soon replaced and on June 21, watering and provisioning completed and ships' companies refreshed, the two vessels hoisted the cornet to recall absentees, weighed anchor, and stood out of the harbor in company, bound before the trades for the Columbia River. They were, of course, almost two months behind Wilkes' original schedule.[3]

15 Oregon

The entrance to the Columbia is impracticable for
two-thirds of the year. . . .

Alexander G. Findlay, *A Directory for the Navigation of
the Pacific Ocean*, 1851

On July 4, on board the *Peacock* and *Flying Fish*, there was an
extra ration of grog all round to celebrate the day and warm the body. The
temperature had dropped to the low fifties, but the trades held fresh and both
ships sailed better now that they were properly laden.

The general good feeling had not been so widespread since they had sailed
with hopes bright as morning from the Virginia capes. They were homeward
bound—not their own homes of course, but what they called their "native
land," or "the sod of America," thereby anticipating greater skill from their
diplomats than they had any right to expect, for the Oregon territory was still
under joint occupation with Britain in accordance with the treaty of 1818,
though to be sure the spread-eagle element was growing more and more restive
under its restrictions. The Explorers' views of Oregon's great river were a little
more complicated; the Columbia loomed large in their thoughts because their
surveys there would mark not only "a great era in the history of the
Expedition," but also the Expedition's "grand finale." But they dreaded the
river, too. Later, Reynolds swore that he and other of the officers had shared a
presentiment that "disaster & distress or death" lay in ambush on that far
shore. If so, it would hardly have been surprising, for they knew that William
Gray, the Boston captain who discovered the river, had told of a current so
overwhelming that he had waited nine days for a gale of wind strong enough
to carry him through. (Gray was lucky, for a wait of a month or more was not
uncommon.) Many had read Irving's *Astoria* and the tales of voyagers to the

region, a good percentage of them melancholy enough, and the stories told by merchantmen they spoke fully bore out the river's reputation. The old preacher Samuel Parker, who had crossed the continent as advance agent for the American Board of Commissioners of Foreign Missions, had observed on leaving the river, "Perhaps there have been more lives lost here in proportion to the number of those who have entered this river, than in entering almost any other harbor in the world." (Owing to northwest gales and dense fog in summer, a mean tide range of seven and a half feet, and a five-knot current, at last published count 234 vessels have met with disaster at the river's mouth since the white man's appearance.)

Still, they had the chart Vancouver had made of the mouth in 1792. And better, because more recent, they had directions, including compass bearings on shore points, for crossing the bar, obtained at Honolulu from Captain Josiah Spalding of the *Lausanne*, who had recently deposited a group of missionaries on its banks.

At 9:40 on the morning of July 17, sailing on a southeast breeze through passing banks of fog and patches of kelp, the *Peacock* got first soundings: one hundred and ninety fathoms. Shortly afterward they made out the misty outlines of the low promontory on the south bank that Captain Gray had named Cape Adams (by this time it was called Point Adams) and got the anchors off the bows and bent the chains. At five they got soundings at forty-one fathoms and when the fog lifted discovered the bold promontory of Cape Disappointment on the south bank. One of the men hooked a shark. In recollection these hours were to stand out with uncommon clarity.

As the wind was light and the fog had become so thick that the vessels were invisible to one another, even though shouted orders and even the usual deck noises could be heard clearly across the water, Hudson prudently chose to stand off during the night and signaled the *Flying Fish* accordingly. The breeze freshened in the early morning, a Sunday. The lead showed fourteen fathoms, and in wearing ship some five miles out they began to feel the effects of the current on the helm. To enter the river it was necessary to run in on the flood, for at ebb the current may reach five knots. At eleven-thirty Hudson calmly ordered divine service, then called all hands to work ship into port.

On the *Flying Fish* Knox was discovering that the rats had made a sieve of his dress coats, and Reynolds rallied him a little by loudly congratulating himself on his foresight in leaving his own dress wardrobe in safety aboard the *Peacock*. There was a heavy swell running, and the weather continued thick, but it lifted from time to time and they could see high breakers inshore and the *Peacock* putting in for them.

The *Peacock* held her course, hugging the wind. Lookouts were perched at various points in the rigging—Perry at the foretopmast head, Midshipman Clark at the foretopsail yard. The leadsmen were in the chains—the sea was so charged with sediment here that color told nothing—and Hudson himself on the bow, glancing from the scribbled directions in his hand to the line of rollers and calling orders to the helmsman. On relieving Perry aloft Emmons could see a continuous line of breakers extending apparently the entire four miles from Point Adams to Cape Disappointment. As the depth gradually shoaled to five fathoms, the ship's head was put to the north along the line of foam, and at one point in the line Emmons observed that the sea was breaking only occasionally. Soon this opening could be seen even from the deck. But Hudson was not satisfied and repeatedly called to the lookouts for reports. They replied that this was without doubt the most favorable spot and as the bearings on shore agreed with his directions, Hudson ordered the yards braced and the ship's head put toward the spot. It was one o'clock.

Five minutes later she struck. Not hard at first, but it was impossible to reduce sail before a heavy swell slammed her violently against the hard sand bottom.

Hudson sought immediately to bring her by the wind to haul offshore, but caught between the surge of the Pacific and the driving current of the Columbia, the *Peacock* was unmanageable. The sails were furled and signals run up—"Aground I am!" While Emmons put out in a boat to sound about the ship, the guns were buoyed, the stream anchor and cable readied, and the first cutter lowered to carry them out—only to be instantly smashed. (What you do with a smashed boat is break it up for firewood, and so closely was routine followed in Hudson's ship that orders were given and the task carried out promptly.) By four o'clock the *Peacock* had dug her way into the hard sand until there were only ten and a half feet of water at her bow. In the early evening she began to strike heavily and the leadsman reported nine feet. To ease her, grape and round shot were heaved overboard, the topgallant masts and rigging sent down and a stream anchor got out by a tackle from the foreyard to bring her bows-on to the sea. This presented a problem, for when she swung, water poured in at the hawseholes and flooded the gun deck, but the problem was solved by the cable's breaking. She swung broadside once more and the pounding resumed. She was leaking now and though the pumps were kept going continually the water slowly gained in the hold, where it was joined from time to time by more cascading down the hatches from the gun and spar decks. More poured in when the iron tiller, lashed amidships, broke off at the rudderhead and the rudder lumbered to and fro until it finally stove in the stern, tore away the pintles, and sank, leaving a hole large enough for a man to crawl through.

At seven the men were mustered and divided into gangs to man the pumps through the night. Shortly after midnight the sea began breaking over bow and beam. As she was lurching heavily, the masts whipped dangerously. The time had come to cut them away, a critical operation from the danger to hull and crew, performed only in the last extremity. But that would not do here, for the masts were needed for lowering the boats, and the boats could not be lowered until the sea fell, as the experience with the first cutter had shown. And so at four in the morning young Davis closed his entry in the log with the observation, "Water above the chain lockers. . . . We have no hope, but of saving the crew." And even that hope was hardly justified by anything in their situation, for there seemed little likelihood of the old ship's holding together till daylight.

Hudson had been privately of the same mind for some time. When Emmons drew alongside soon after the ship struck to report the results of his soundings, Hudson beckoned him nearer and leaning on the rail directed him in a low voice to pull for Cape Disappointment to search for a landing and bring off anyone who claimed to know the channel. Pulling against the flood in a heavy sea—one man bailing continually—Emmons saw that the shores were too bold for landing. In putting about he was swamped, but the current carried the boat through the outer line of breakers, he bailed her out and was soon back aboard.

Still the *Peacock* held, even though at daylight a great quantity of sand was seen washing to and fro in the hold, grim evidence that her bottom was broken up. The terrible pounding continued and the sea remained rough but the tide was ebbing and as it did so the line of breakers followed, approached the ship, swept over in a mighty roar and crash, and marched beyond to take up a new stand to seaward. Everyone agreed that this was the last opportunity to attempt a landing and in the early light Emmons saw to lowering the six boats. The sick went first, followed by the scientifics, the charts, books, ship's papers, marines, then crew and officers, leaving some thirty persons still aboard. Emmons led them into Baker's Bay in the lee of Cape Disappointment. It was nearly noon now, the sea was getting up again and the line of breakers once more roiled inshore of the ship, and Lieutenant Walker, who had the watch, was sure she would go over on her beam. But then Hudson had dinner piped at the usual hour. For all the alarm he showed, they might have been in the placid waters of Matavai Bay. In the boats the men at the oars saw the masts cut away one by one, commencing with the fore, until only the stump of the mizzen remained, standing in undignified surrogate to a once graceful rigging and flying the signal of distress—the ensign, union down. The explorers had seen no sadder sight. But the hull lay more easy now.

As they pulled for the ship once more, the lead boats seemed to stand on end in the breakers. And for a moment Gunner Thomas Lewis' launch did just that, before capsizing end over end as a heavy roller caught it. De Haven picked up the crew and the swamped boat drifted away out of sight. Assuming that the signal at the mizzen meant that the ship was going to pieces, Emmons pressed on hurriedly until Hudson signaled him to turn back. He had no choice but to obey. To persevere would endanger lives already saved and jeopardize the sole means of deliverance of those still on board. Returning sadly to Baker's Bay, he posted a lookout on top of the Cape to report when conditions for rescue were favorable.

The *Peacock* tossed dying in her bed of sand. All the upper works on the port side were knocked away, her bottom stove in, and water up to the berth deck. But in the afternoon the line of breakers marched seaward again, Emmons brought out the boats, and the thirty-odd officers and men followed by Captain Hudson took their places and pulled for Baker's Bay. There the scientists, the sick, the marines and the sailors gathered on the shore and gave their captain three hearty cheers.

The *Flying Fish* had also had an anxious night. Because of the fog, the *Peacock* had been aground almost an hour before Knox and Reynolds saw her crew frantically furling the sails in a sea of wild foam. They saw a boat sounding about her, they saw the launch smashed and by and by the pieces floating past. Knox made for her until warned off by the signal "Danger," then "Stand to Sea." Sadly they obeyed, to spend a sleepless night of alarms, illuminated only by the *Peacock*'s distress rockets shooting up through the fog, and to vainly wonder whether they would ever see their friends again. The schooner darted here and there like a lost child in search of its parent. Because the fog was so thick that they had been unable to see the boats depart, they had a bad fright when at earliest light no trace of the *Peacock* was to be seen, except for pieces of the superstructure that floated past, until with the aid of spyglasses they picked up her bowsprit and a bit of the mizzen. The *Peacock* was gone and with her more than a hundred men! They were heading in for what they took to be the channel when a boat hove in sight and George Emmons was soon aboard with a one-eyed Indian named George, who claimed to be a pilot, and they learned that all were safe.

All hands were saved, but the cargo was another matter. Hudson had rescued his journal (as had Emmons and some others of the once reluctant

The wreck of the *Peacock*, by Alfred T. Agate.
(*Narrative*, 4: facing p. 524, Western Americana
Collection, Yale University Library.)

journalists) and the surveys, the master his chronometers, Agate some of his
sketches, and some of the men a few relics. But the collections and all else
were lost. Including William Reynolds' wardrobe. Jim Blair got ashore with
nothing more than the clothes on his back and a miniature likeness of General
Jackson his mother had given him the day the Squadron sailed.

And the *Peacock* herself was gone. It was as if she had bravely held her
decks above the sea until the last of her affectionate crew was safe. Then she
had drifted into deeper water and settled with a weary sigh. It remained for
him who had known her longest to pen her obituary. "Thus I have witnessed
the beginning and end of the Peacock," George Emmons wrote in his journal,
"having been launched in her at New York in 1828, and wrecked in her on the
Columbia Bar in 1841. She may be ranked among the first vessels in our service
for the good she has done the country. . . . And there is some consolation in
knowing that after the many narrow risks she has run this cruise—that her fate
has finally been prolonged until reaching her native shore."

Indian George brought the *Flying Fish* into the placid waters of the cove
called Baker's Bay, an almost shockingly idyllic spot after the horrors of the
turbulent seas no more than two miles distant. Some members of the

American Methodist Mission at Point Adams who had witnessed the disaster came over laden with tents, blankets, cooking utensils and provisions, and James Birnie, the agent of the Hudson's Bay Company at Astoria (or Fort George as it was now called) brought more. When Indians came to sell venison and fresh salmon, the explorers sat down among the flowers "and feasted away as if there had been never a shipwreck at all." And indeed the only indications that there had been were some of the *Peacock*'s spars and the "Pearl," the capsized launch, which was found high and dry on the beach.

The northern scene seemed strange to them and wild after so many months among the "Soft Isles of the South." Here the forests were truly primeval, the glades sylvan, and all seemed solemn and somehow "stricken" in the silence and solitude. Their only duty aboard the schooner was to familiarize themselves with the channel when weather and mood permitted. Taking up more permanent quarters near the site of John Jacob Astor's old fort, two miles from Fort Clatsop where Lewis and Clark had wintered in 1805–1806, the men of the *Peacock* erected huts of pine branches and wigwams of old planks, and Purser Spieden set up shop in Birnie's hen house. The novelty of life on this green shore caught their imagination and the paths soon sported street signs and one of the wigwams a barber's pole. They called it "Peacockville." Chenook and Clatsop Indians arrived daily to peddle fish and meat, then sat on the ground and gambled away the proceeds. Hudson saw one fellow walk away in nothing but a borrowed blanket.

But idleness palled, and there was some grumbling at the cause of it—Captain Hudson's ignorance of how to conduct surveys. The weather was favorable, boats were at hand, and experienced surveyors ready to work. But Hudson had learned nothing of the technique. Even the boyish midshipmen had many times been employed on duties he, like Ringgold, was incapable of performing. "The mysterious properties of a right angled triangle are utterly beyond their Comprehension," Reynolds observed in exasperation. Except for the forty men who went in gratitude to help the Hudson's Bay Company harvest its crops, most of the *Peacock*'s crew remained idle for nearly three weeks, while only two boats were employed in surveying and the schooner traced out the channel.[1]

Only a few miles to the north there were many who would have been happy to share some of their idleness. Those aboard the *Vincennes* and *Porpoise* had been very active indeed since the morning of April 28 when, at the end of a wet and sickly passage, they had first sighted Cape Disappointment. The turbulence at the bar quickly convinced Wilkes that it would be best to commence operations elsewhere, and so, signaling the brig to follow, he turned north toward Juan de Fuca Strait. The following morning they very nearly came to grief in the fog. Discolored water was reported where by Wilkes' calculations it should not be and where he was confident it was not. Shortly afterward came reports of breakers ahead. In a moment the ship was among them. She was hauled by the wind, bows diving under. Then a man aloft called out, "Land on the lee bow." As Wilkes' reckoning told him land was elsewhere, he refused to credit the report until he too saw it loom high through the mist and spray, with the sea breaking tremendously against it.

Booming along under full canvas they cleared the low outlying rocks by a third of a mile, but just as they were congratulating themselves, "Breakers ahead & to leeward" rang out again. A quick cast of the lead showed five and a half fathoms, breakers were washing over the bows, and a large rock was discovered about a pistol shot to leeward, though it passed almost as soon as seen. Astonishingly, "the old beer Keg," as the purser's steward called the *Vincennes*, ran clear and made an offing. She had made her own discovery of Grenville Rocks—fortunately not in the night, or she would have come off a good deal worse than even the *Peacock*. For the *Porpoise* it was, if possible, a nearer thing still, and she escaped, the sailing master admitted, more by "good luck than good management." A revealing episode, this, of the character of the "Grand Commodore," as Reynolds sarcastically called Wilkes. Wilkes' assurance was no affectation, whatever else about him might be. No fully witted navigator would have approached this fog shrouded coast on his reckoning alone, merely to keep up appearances. Wilkes' self-confidence might oftentimes have been misplaced, but it was genuine.

Entering the Strait of Juan de Fuca in a gray mist, they sailed through a forest of stupendous evergreens to anchor at Port Discovery forty-nine years to the day after Vancouver's arrival.

As they proceeded along the bold channel they relied on Vancouver's chart and narrative, both of which proved to be remarkably accurate. It was only the first of many debts the explorers were to owe their British predecessors. The Hudson's Bay Company dispatched the mate of its famous sidewheel steamer *Beaver* to pilot them to Fort Nisqually at the southern end of the sound, and they moored in "one of the most majestic sheets of Warter," John W. W. Dyes had ever seen, "the forrist trees of the largest size grow to the Very Warters Edge where you may cut a mast . . . for a Line of Battle Ship."

They were astonished at the cordiality of the Bay Company's reception. "Instead of throwing impediments in our way, as we thought they would," Sinclair remarked when the pilot saw them safely moored and then sent aboard a present of fresh beef for the crews, "they offer us every facility."

Captain William H. McNeill of the *Beaver* and young Alexander C. Anderson, agent in charge of the fort, came over for tea and were sufficiently emphatic in their determination to be of assistance to arouse Wilkes' suspicion. But not even his mistrustful nature could withstand the continuing onslaught of the Company's hospitality.

As his conviction grew that the *Peacock* and *Flying Fish*, overdue since the first of May, had met with shipwreck in the coral islands and perhaps massacre or famine as well, Wilkes directed the enterprises on land and sea with redoubled vigor. The observatory was set up near Fort Nisqually, and while Ringgold was dispatched in the *Porpoise* to survey Admiralty Inlet, easternmost of the great sound's arms, Lieutenant Case, with Totten, May, and Colvocoresses, went in four of the *Vincennes'* boats to survey Hood's Canal and the coast as far north as Fraser River, where the two surveys would join. For the first time in the course of the cruise, extensive overland exploration was possible, and Wilkes organized two parties. Lieutenant Johnson took command of one made up of Pickering, Brackenridge, T. W. Waldron (captain's clerk of the *Porpoise*), Sergeant Stearns of the marines, and two of the crew. They were to cross the Cascade Range north of Mount Rainier and proceed eastward to Fort Colville on the Columbia, near its junction with Clark's River in the Flathead country, then south to the Company's Fort Walla Walla, returning along the Yakima and back across the mountains.

The less ambitious of the expeditions Wilkes chose to lead himself. Taking most of the horses supplied by the Company—and leaving the disgusted Johnson to haggle with the Indians for more—he set off with Drayton, Purser Waldron, and a Canadian guide to take his measure of the more settled part of the country. At the Methodist mission at Fort Clatsop, operated by ex-shoemaker Joseph H. Frost, they were served dinner by Mrs. Frost on the china she had treasured round the Horn—"an attempt at showing off," Wilkes ungraciously described it, that "only proved how she had been brought up."

As they approached the great stockade of Fort Vancouver, Doctor John McLoughlin came galloping up in welcome. The establishment was impressive—warehouses, quarters for agents and their families, chapel, bakery, forges, carpenter's shop, trade store, hospital, magazine, and meteorological observatory, and upstream a saw mill from which Company vessels carried lumber to the Sandwich Islands. There were also two brass ship's cannon in carriages that had originally meant business but, the guests carefully observed, had long since become mere ornaments. The man responsible for it all was John McLoughlin, a tall commanding figure of an open, florid countenance that betrayed his Scottish descent, who as governor of all Company posts in the west ruled an empire a good deal larger than the thirteen states that had made up the original Republic.[2]

The Doctor furnished Wilkes and Drayton with a large bateau, lined with mats for comfort, nine men to row it, and a variety of camp equipment from the Company stores, and suggested the use of many articles that Wilkes in a fit of humility confessed he was ignorant of. Thus outfitted they set out to examine the Willamette and its settlements. Portaging around the falls, where salmon were leaping and lamprey eels worming their way up the rocks, they took shelter at the house of one William Johnson, who said he had fought aboard "Old Ironsides" during the War of 1812. He had married an Indian—his "woman," he called her—kept two Indian slaves, and seemed no longer to mind the flies and fleas. A half dozen of Johnson's neighbors called to see "the Commodore," one of whom, William Cannon, had come out with the overland Astorians. To his dismay, Wilkes found them "all agog about laws & legislatures, with governors, judges, & the minor offices all in embryo," and muttering about McLoughlin's overweening power.

He was in no mood to talk politics with these people, "an uncombed, unshaven, and a dirty clothed set," and set off for the mission across the plain, there to dine "a la Methodist" again at a crowded table to which the officers of God's outpost came "higgledy piggledy," addressing one another as "Brother" and "Sister." (Was it "Brother Wilkes," too?) Afterward a committee materialized seemingly out of nowhere, for with the appearance of the naval vessels bearing more armaments than most of them had ever seen before hopes ran high for relief from British tyranny. But the unsympathetic Wilkes put it to them straight—at least by his own account. As crime was non-existent, a code of laws would serve no purpose beyond antagonizing the Company and almost certainly the Catholic settlers. They should wait, he told them, "until the government of the United States should throw its mantle over them."

In the hope that the lost vessels would yet appear, Wilkes wrote out orders for the *Peacock* and the *Flying Fish*, dispatched them to Fort George, and set out for Nisqually on June 17. Discipline had slackened in his absence but he soon had things shipshape again by reprimanding several of the officers and, as purser's steward Robinson described it, kicking "up a terrible breeze all around the board, Keeping every body on the 'qui vive' and making every body uncomfortable, as he always does." But Wilkes prided himself on his knowledge of "Jack," and to return all hands to good temper, planned an elaborate Fourth of July. On the fifth—for the Fourth fell on Sunday—the gunner fired a sunrise salute on shore and at nine every man and officer of the *Vincennes* (the *Porpoise* was off sounding the Strait of Georgia), except Vanderford, who was sick, marched out in "span-clean" white frocks and trousers with drums beating and colors flying, Wilkes leading and Vendovi in his chief's dress bringing up the rear. In passing the fort they gave three mighty cheers, which the "redcoats" on the ramparts answered half-heartedly, and proceeded to a prairie bordering a lake, where an ox (courtesy of the Company) was roasting on a windlass, as the men called it. After dutifully planting five stands of colors, they took up the real business of the day, "some riding like wild men to & fro over the plain," some playing foot ball. (A good fellow, Wilkes threw in the ball, calling out heartily, "Sail in, my shipmates!") The more excitable fell to "dancing like mad" to the screech of a fiddle, which "very mutch astonished" the Indian onlookers, Dyes noted. The day was brought to a close with an extra ration of "old Rye." Perhaps no one enjoyed it more than the poor savage Vendovi, ashore for the first time since his capture.

Scientific exploration in the Oregon forest, by Joseph Drayton. (*Narrative*, 5: facing p. 122, Western Americana Collection, Yale University Library.)

For Bob Johnson's party, battling mosquitoes and rattlesnakes in the Yakima valley, the Fourth was less pleasant. The exploration had begun agreeably enough, through forests of spruce with trunks "so straight and clean," Brackenridge noted in admiration, "that it was seldom you Could find a branch closer than 150 feet to the ground." By May 29 they had reached the headwaters of the Spipen beyond the mountains, where, short of provisions—the Indian bearers more or less delicately refused the government salt pork—they purchased dried salmon from the Indians and some cakes these tribes made from the camas root dug up in the meadows. Finding the Yakima too deep to ford, they swam the horses and inflated their "gum elastic bolsters" to form a raft for the packs. On reaching the Columbia they followed its banks upstream through rolling prairies to Fort Okanogon, where the Company extended its accustomed welcome with lodging and remounts. On June 15, they had reached Fort Colville.

There was a bad moment on the return trek when they came upon several hundred Indians engaged on a "rooting excursion" and a "stout Savage looking fellow" seized one of their horses, announcing that it had been stolen from him, walked calmly up to his lodge, and was leveling his rifle when Brackenridge and Tom Waldron stepped up and cocking their own pieces let him know that if he presented at any one they would "instantly blow his brains out." That was good enough for the Indian. He had only intended to shoot the horse, he said. Glad to be "rid of such a band of Ruffians," the explorers passed on.

Indians engaged in spearing salmon ferried them across the Snake and they moved rapidly over the prairie, one day making forty miles, to Fort Walla Walla, where they met Doctor Marcus Whitman, who had ridden over from the mission on the Waiilatpu. On fresh Company horses they regained the Yakima, followed it through barren country dotted with wormwood bushes and tufts of grass, proceeded up the Spipen, and crossing the mountains again, reached Nisqually on July 15, sixty days after their departure.

Brackenridge drew two conclusions from the journey. A, on the leadership: "A Sailor on shore, is as a fish out of Water." B, on the nature of this country about which there had lately been so much ballyhoo at home: "It appears to me, that we certainly must have viewed it in a very different light from the Majority of Writers that have come out so boldly in its favour." Not two acres out of a hundred north of Walla Walla would pay the farmer for his trouble.

There was still no news of the missing ships and men, whose absence occasioned not only much doleful speculation but extra work as well, for exploration and surveying had to be completed before the weather turned dirty in September. Accordingly, the *Vincennes* was dispatched up the Sound, her boats triangulating all the way, en route to the Columbia's mouth. Four days after his return from the overland trip, while still busy with the specimens collected, Brackenridge received orders to join a party under Henry Eld to survey Gray's Harbor at the mouth of the Chehalis River a few miles overland to the southwest. The weather was foul with fog, rain, and gales of wind. The so-called harbor was largely mud flats, and provisions became so short that by the middle of August they were subsisting on berries, occasional clams, and the dead fish deposited by the surf. With the aid of some friendly Indians—directed, oddly enough, by a "Squaw Chief" whose husband appeared to Brackenridge to be "only a meere tool or pro forma in her presence"—they completed the survey in twenty-four days, knocked off, and, as Eld put it feelingly, took leave of "this miserable hole." The only moment of pleasure recorded in the journals came one day when De Haven and Baldwin appeared with a few provisions and the glorious news that their shipmates were safe, though the *Peacock* lost. The news was not a complete surprise, for some days before a Chehalis Indian had gravely informed Brackenridge that a large "Boston Ship" had "got broke" at the Columbia bar. Another portage brought them to Fort George and a joyful reunion with "old friends and shipmates."

Fearing to trust the *Vincennes* to the Columbia's mouth, Wilkes had sent her on to San Francisco Bay. He had also, after some negotiation, purchased the Baltimore brig *Thomas W. Perkins* as a replacement of sorts for the *Peacock*. He had been prepared to discharge the *Peacock*'s crew at Vancouver rather than pay the vessel's asking price—if any objected he could point out that, after all, their enlistments had expired some time since—but McLoughlin, not relishing the prospect of a batch of stranded sailors "getting into quarrels, with the natives, and bringing the whole country into trouble," offered to buy the cargo, chiefly whiskey, and the bargain was concluded. Wilkes rechristened the brig *Oregon*.[3]

Not wanting to miss any bets, Wilkes had also decided to send one party overland to San Francisco Bay. For this task, he selected Emmons, Eld, Colvocoresses, Brackenridge, Agate, Rich, Dana, and Peale, and the invaluable sergeant of marines, the black-eyed, bright-faced Albert Stearns, once a fancy dyer in Massachusetts, now a master of both keel and saddle. Even with the generous cooperation of the Hudson's Bay Company, it was the devil's own job to get the party organized, and the month of frantic inaction that ensued was a little reminiscent of the difficulties in getting off the First Great National Expedition itself. They consulted mountain man Tom McKay and heard him tell of having killed over a hundred Indians and discovering everything worth discovery between here and California—which latter was only a white lie at worst.* There was a poignant moment here when in buying horses the sailor Eld asked the trapper for gentle ones, confessing that he and Dana were poor riders. A little farther on, they had halted for dinner at the farm of an eighty-year-old Canadien who "hopped & skipped about like a youth of 16" as he prepared a meal of mutton steaks for the explorers. He had wintered with Lewis and Clark at Fort Mandan thirty-seven years before. Finally, at two in the afternoon of September 7 (the morning was spent rounding up strayed horses) they set off. With guides, hunters, trappers, woodsmen and their squaws, together with several families bound for California who joined for escort, they made up a party of thirty-nine. One of these families, Joel Walker's, had been, a year earlier, the first to cross the mountains for the purpose of making a home in Oregon and was now to be among the first of the many Oregonians moving to California, which Mrs. Walker would be the first white woman to reach overland. Walker planned to enter the employ of the Swiss impresario Captain John A. Sutter, who was setting up a large establishment on the banks of the Sacramento.

With eighty horses loaded with stores, powder, and ball, they made an impressive caravan. That an impression must be made everyone was certain. Toward the end of July a rumor reached Vancouver that a party led by Walker's brother Joe (who as lieutenant in Captain Bonneville's travels of 1832–1835 that Irving had written about had been the first to cross the Sierra Nevada mountains from east to west) had been wiped out somewhere east of Fort Hall on the upper Snake. And reports of the bad character of the Indians to the south reached the party almost daily. Large numbers were said to have fortified themselves at the more difficult passes, determined, Emmons heard, "to put to death all Whites who attempted to pass through the country." [4]

But the big problem for a week or more to come was not the Indians but the horses. They caused no end of trouble, and the whole of the second day was given over to rounding them up. Gradually the animals grew more accustomed to restraint, but some nights wolves ate the trail ropes and they tended to wander farther afield as grass became scarcer to the south. That

* In acquiring horses, guides, and information about the trail, the explorers met, besides McKay, at least two other of the great mountainmen, Robert (Doc) Newell and Joseph L. Meek, and several of their colleagues—Calvin Tibbets, George W. Ebberts, Bill Craig, Caleb Wilkins, John Turner. Emmons called them "hired men," and Eld put them down as "a parcel of scheming fellows" who anticipated "a money making & pleasure party to and from California" while drawing two dollars a day of the government's money. The mountainmen's opinion of the web-footed greenhorns one can only guess at. Nearly all withdrew from the venture, offering a variety of excuses, and having found no common language, they parted, never really having met.

bother aside, their trail southwestward across a hilly prairie, charred by a recent grass fire, across Tongue Creek and through the Calapuya Hills into the Elk Mountains and the Umpqua country was not too difficult. For the most part their troubles were of the nuisance variety—insects, fever, bears. Mrs. Walker fell sick and wasps got among the children "& created some music." One evening a group of Calapuyas, among them a very pretty squaw, wandered into camp; and Agate drew the likeness of the pitiable old chief who stood motionless in his deerskin mantle. Another day one of the Walker boys chased through the bush what he took to be a missing mule loping ahead, but it turned out to be a grizzly instead and he returned to camp in disgust. The explorers were coming to have a good opinion of these animals until one afternoon toward the end of the second week on the trail the lead party came upon one "of an enormous size" that advanced on them, rearing up in menace. Peale put a ball in his lungs and he bounded away, pursued by riders who shot him twice more but never did succeed in killing him. Emmons was disappointed. He had hoped to preserve the skin of the animal "for our National Museum—that I trust—*is to be*." And he recorded his impression of the species as a whole in words remarkably similar to those Meriwether Lewis had used nearly forty years earlier: "Among all the animals I have ever seen I do not think that I have witnessed so formidable an enemy."

On reaching the Umpqua, Emmons and Agate rode a few miles downstream to the Company's fort to get some first-hand information on the temper of the Indians. They found the fort in a state of alarm and very nearly got themselves shot for Indians by the defenders—five men, two women, and nine dogs—and while the explorers took "a bad cup of Tea sweetened with dirty sugar," the agent in charge kept repeating excitedly that the Indians hereabout were "terrible mauvais savage," angered just now by the reappearance of the white man's smallpox. He urged the greatest caution, "little suspecting," Emmons reflected complacently, "that I had had frequent intercourse with even worse people for the last three years."

At the camp Eld had kept the men busy running balls for cartridges. The air was thick with smoke and fog that made the sun a dark bloody color and no larger than a doubloon. Rounding up the horses they broke camp at ten o'clock in the morning of the eighteenth and proceeded over the prairie. A thin line of fire was crossing it, too, crawling slowly before the wind and ascending the distant hills. These fires were not dangerous in themselves, but they were a devilish bother, for not only did they deprive the party of game and the horses of feed, they also exposed small stones that lamed the horses. And as Oregon horses were rarely shod, it became necessary to halt from time to time while the mountain men, whose professional acquirements included smithing, nailed on shoes.

Proceeding up the south fork of the Umpqua they entered hilly country that seemed to be inhabited solely by grizzlies and Indians, though only the grizzlies were conspicuous. The banks were high here and as they wound their way along them in the morning silence broken only by the squeaking of saddles and harness and the rattle of gear, they could look down on the placid waters two hundred feet below. The Indians' handiwork was becoming commonplace, not just deliberately set brushfires but boughs artfully tied together from opposite sides of the trail to sweep the riders from their mounts. One dumped Emmons quite effectively and thereafter the advance party carried cutlasses to hack a way through.

On September 22 they reached the pass through the Umpquas. The woods were charred from a recent fire and the trail dust turned them all black. In the evening one of the horses arrived in camp with its pack burst. As the pack had held Peale's belongings, among them his Oregon journal, drawing instruments and sketchbook, this was a serious loss, and hoping to recover it, and also to rest both the horses and those delirious from fever, they laid over a day.

The search was unsuccessful and they got "under weigh" again on the twenty-fourth. (The landlocked mariners continue in their journals to use the language of the profession and "set course" on the trail, "steer E. by S.," "make two knots the hour," and the like, as well as appraising trees as potential timbers and spars.) Indian signs were numerous now, and once on investigating a rustling in the bushes, they found an ambush so hurriedly evacuated that it still contained some highly agitated squaws and dogs. They were among the Rogue or Rascally Indians, and they could see them on distant hilltops calling in seeming communication and lights in the woods at night flickering here and there.

With everyone "on the *qui vive* for trouble," they came down out of the hills and on September 25 crossed the clear and rapid waters of the Rogue. Just ahead, where the river narrowed and the trail clung to the edge of a mountain that jutted into it, was a notorious place of ambush which the explorers had taken to calling "Bloody Pass." On the opposite bank Indians ran "whooping & hallowing in advance" and others could be seen in partial concealment. How many were concealed on their own side of the river they could not know, but Emmons took care to lead an advance party into the defile, fully expecting to enter a crossfire.

But the Indians hurled nothing more deadly than taunts. The river turned east here and with a sigh of relief, the explorers parted company with it, "fully convinced of the propriety of its name," Emmons remarked.

Still, the "Shasty" Indians ahead had no better reputation, and the trail was beginning to take its toll. Many in the party were wracked with fever—some so completely out of their heads that it was necessary to disarm them—but as game was growing scarce and the horses had been slowly starving ever since crossing the Umpqua they had no choice but to cajole the sick into the saddle every morning. On September 29 they crossed the forty-second parallel and caught their first glimpse of the rugged snow-covered crest of Mt. Shasta, small vapor clouds forming under its lee, rising until they reached the easterly current that swept the summit, then gradually disappearing into the west. Ahead lay the Boundary Mountains, which divided the rivers in their courses and separated the Oregon territory from Mexico's Alta California.

The explorers could not know it and they kept on the alert, but as it happened their Indian troubles were over. One evening six members of the Shasta tribe came into camp, conducting themselves "with great propriety," Brackenridge noted approvingly, to sell fish and bows and arrows and quivers made of wildcat skins, and after some persuasion allowed Agate to sketch them. Afterwards, to test the Indians' skill the explorers hung a button on a tree some twenty yards away. They were astonished when the arrow hit it every time. Even Brackenridge, no friend of the red man, was moved to admiration. "For my own part," he observed, "I would as soon at one hundred Yards distance—have a musket discharged at me as an arrow from one of those Indian bows."

It was a strange country, full of curiosities and freaks of nature—immense pine trees and cones that measured sixteen inches; a soda spring, its waters loaded with iron; another of "Sulphurated hydrogen"; a tuber called the soap plant that, mashed a little, made a very serviceable substitute for the soap that was fast disappearing from their stores. Sometimes the hunters managed to bag one of the amazingly fleet antelopes, the first such animals these sailors had ever seen. But there was little feed for the horses, for whom the trail, turning now into round pebbles and steep ascents, was becoming all the more difficult. There was no relief from the "intermittents," which the awful heat seemed to bring on more frequently. And the smoke covered all.

On October 2 they reached the Destruction River in the shadow of Mt. Shasta and followed its rocky banks to the Sacramento. The soil here was poor stuff, parched and stony, but Brackenridge found it rich in plants unknown to botany, and the hunters' task was easy in a country abounding in bear, elk, antelope, deer, and wild cattle. Once they came into camp with six grizzlies, which the explorers found to be "very palitable" when served up in a stew.

Following the Sacramento, they reached the Feather River on October 18, at a dreary spot cluttered with hundreds of skeletons where the tertian fever had wiped out an entire Indian village. The horses were so starved and weary as to be very nearly useless—all but the fractious mare that, loaded with the cooking gear, they called "Frying Pan." Undaunted by starvation and exertion, she invariably kicked up in the mornings when the belly band was hauled taut. One morning toward the journey's end, as the little caravan was moving quietly along, she suddenly began kicking and running against the other animals with a clatter of pots and pans and kettles. Several men tried to lasso her but at sight of the rope she shot off across the prairie at the top of her speed, closely pursued, "but being accustomed to this game," Emmons observed, "she escaped by dodging & in her effort to do mischief bursted her bellyband, & having created another excitement, away she dashed again ahead of the Party, Pots & pans flying in all directions—& it was nearly half an hour before she was finally captured. Some of these scenes," he noted, "are gotten up without much previous notice, and are certainly entertaining, if they are sometimes troublesome & expensive." There were many scenes of this overland journey that would live on in memory after the misery and helplessness of the chills and fevers were forgotten—the trail, for one, as they got under way of a morning with bridles jingling and packstraps squeaking, the clank of iron on stone from the occasional horse that was shod, and dust settling over all. The campfire scenes, for another, the talk as outside the circle of light the watch rode herd on the horses, the explorers swapping the story of the wreck for some tale of a fight with Crows, with perhaps a few references to the willing women of Tahiti or the Nez Perce tribes thrown in, spinning yarns until the embers glowed only faintly through the ashes. It was a superb lenitive for the weariness of a hard day's travel.

At the American River on October 19 they met Captain John A. Sutter, a stout figure in undress uniform with sidearms buckled on, who welcomed them with a cordiality reminiscent of Doctor McLoughlin. Though Brackenridge thought he talked "a little largely" as he showed them about the station he called New Helvetia, he nevertheless ran seven thousand head of cattle, twelve hundred horses, a thousand sheep; his vineyard supported a winery and a distillery; and he had Russian, Indian, and American trappers under contract.

But there was little hereabouts to detain the scientists, although upstream, in the vicinity of Shasta Mountain, Dana told Sutter that he had seen "the strongest proof and signs of gold." On learning from Sutter, who had recently visited on board the *Vincennes* at San Francisco Bay, that Wilkes had not yet arrived with the *Porpoise* but that Ringgold had long since completed his boat survey of the Sacramento, Emmons took the sick aboard a boat Sutter provided for the hundred-and-fifteen-mile trip to the ships. They made the bay without incident on the twenty-third, breakfasting on a stew of wild goose, and pulled along the shore—firing into the air from time to time to get oar room among the ducks that obstructed their way—until a breeze sprang up. Then they made sail and reported aboard the *Vincennes* at Sausalito, or Whaler's Harbor, as it was generally called. Wilkes actually commended Emmons on his conduct of the expedition.

Coming overland five days later, Eld paid off the woodsmen and trappers and sold the horses, which, Emmons observed, wore "a look that plainly told of their sorrows." [5]

16 Homeward Bound

On dropping your anchor in New York Bay, you will pay to
each of your crew ten dollars. . . .

Charles Wilkes, Singapore Roads, to C. Ringgold,
February 26, 1842

San Francisco was a far smaller place than the number of ships
lying in the magnificent harbor led one to expect. Though John W. W. Dyes
observed gloomily that there was "plenty of Rum & desopation Here," the
place was no Babylon: a couple of stores, remarked the purser's steward, "a
kind of Hotel where they sell some wine & jawbreaking cigars & have a small
billiard table—a sailors grog shop or so . . . & the whole of St Francisco is
before you." Those not busy with the surveys on bay or river could find little
in the way of entertainment ashore.

Things were more lively aboard ship. The mess was as good as the explorers
had ever enjoyed, with fresh provisions four times a week, and the flow of
visitors nearly constant, among them some aristocratic ladies of scandalous
morality, and once a "baldheaded Padre" who got "rather fuddled aloft, &
. . . kicked up the deuce" before Ringgold put him ashore in disgust. Some
came to shake hands with the cannibal Vendovi, under marine guard in the
forecastle and much reduced from long confinement, others came to be
entertained at parties got up by the ship's officers, until it seemed to Emmons
that visiting the ships had become "quite the fashion in this country." On the
third anniversary of the squadron's sailing the Vincennes' officers, with
Captain William D. Phelps of the Alert, the popular captain of the port,
William Antonio Richardson, and some others "had quit a blow out," the
ship's moralist noted. "By Night tha Were drunk Enougth Singing Halloing &
making the most Hedious Noise." But the officers were only making up for

266

Wilkes' stiff-necked deportment. For the commander, although he entertained a few dignitaries, struck the Californians as "severe and forbidding,"
too busy to be sociable, and altogether a disappointing exception to the
distinguished captains who had visited this coast in the past. Governor
Rotchef of the Russian-American Fur Company preferred the junior officers,
to whose tales of the South Seas he listened by the hour, and once he sent
down a troop of his best horses to convey them the sixty miles to Fort Ross for
a visit.

But then the Golden Land itself left Wilkes unimpressed. From what he
saw of it—the road between San Francisco and Santa Cruz mission while on
an outing with Hudson—the commander concluded that "⅗ of California is a
barren waste incapable of yielding anything." That was an opinion few shared.
Most, comparing Oregon to California, were inclined to believe that the
United States was laying claim to the wrong place. However, that was for
history, or destiny, as some called it, to settle.

When Wilkes arrived the frolic ended, the surveys were hurried to
completion and preparations made for departure. (The *Flying Fish* had been
left to complete the Oregon surveys before making rendezvous at Honolulu.)
Alterations to the *Oregon* were completed on the last day of October.
Alterations were also made in the organization of the squadron. The
unpopular chaplain now sent in his resignation and was left to make his way
home as best he could—to the considerable satisfaction of the officers.
Horatio Hale, too, left the squadron. Fascinated by the languages of the
Oregon country, he had requested permission to stay a while longer and
pursue his own way home. Wilkes promptly agreed—and thereby changed the
course of future anthropology. Captain Hudson had declined command of
another vessel and traveled as supernumerary in the *Vincennes*. Carr was given
the *Oregon*.

In part the shake-ups were owing to necessity, for the *Oregon* had to be
officered and manned, but they owed more to the commander's latest fit of
pique, for Wilkes was wearing his crown of thorns again. He had had an
exasperating time of it in surveying both Puget Sound and the stretch of the
Columbia up to Fort Vancouver, especially the latter operation. Attempts at
survey before his arrival had been made "without the requisite knowledge &
comprehension" and had all to be done over.

The redoing had begun badly. Taking command of the *Porpoise*, he had
proceeded up the river with the *Flying Fish* in company and promptly
grounded off Astoria—to the delight of William Reynolds, who was piloting
the latter and thus had "the honor of anchoring the first public vessel of the

United States, in the waters of this famous place." Another day both the *Oregon* and the *Porpoise* were aground at the same time on sandbanks. A launch towed off the former, but the latter lay with her masts at a forty-five degree angle and had to be shored up with spare topmasts as the tide ebbed. In coming to her assistance next morning, the *Oregon* ran aground again on the opposite side of the channel. Holmes was amused to observe how the two vessels "formed excellent bouys, pointing out the dangers on either side." The humor of it escaped Wilkes, who, fretting over problems that ran the gamut from tobacco spittle on the deck to missing station flags, confided to his journal with a wearied air and spake thus: "Verily I have many things to contend with." He was persuaded that the cause of his difficulties lay chiefly with the officers of the late *Peacock*, who, despite three years on this service, were still "little influenced by the cords of discipline." And for that, he blamed Hudson.

Wilkes was also sorely tempted to blame Hudson for the loss of the *Peacock*. Although immediately on learning of the disaster he had summoned statements of the facts from all the ship's officers, and then issued a general order absolving Hudson of all blame; although he privately took note of Hudson's "good management" in saving lives and chronometers at the time of the wreck; although he suspected that local magnetic attraction aboard had affected the compass bearings—still, Wilkes was sure that Hudson had "not made himself fully master" of Captain Spalding's directions, and, anyway, he should have sent the *Flying Fish* ahead of his own deep-draft vessel. But most of all, Wilkes found fault with the *Peacock*'s delay in reaching the Northwest Coast, which he now called "the most important part" of the cruise.

Hudson's distinction, however, lay merely in his rank among the offenders, for the commander was "disgusted with ignorance, idleness, want of thought, & want of proper energy & exertion," and more or less privately looking forward to the "happy day when I get rid of them all." Week after week he reprimanded, suspended, arrested. Walker was suspended for requisitioning three bottles of brandy for his boat crews, who sweated and choked in the smoke that lay low on the river. Alden was suspended for reasons he never knew. Budd was suspended by error. Perry and Knox were denied permission to leave the squadron. Charlie Guillou remained under arrest and was shuttled from ship to ship (Wilkes seemed bent on leaving him in Oregon, but he had friends on the *Flying Fish* who took him aboard) and Johnson was placed under arrest in July after some hot words with Wilkes on the *Vincennes'* quarterback. The two prisoners showed little contrition and enjoyed an idyllic respite at Fort George, where Bob Johnson put up a shack for himself, held a well-attended housewarming, and found himself elected mayor and the town renamed Bobsville. Guillou became schoolmaster to the little Birnies, and Reynolds, paying a visit, was almost as amused as the children to see the two men playing "hunt the slipper." The men of the crews offended, too, but it was unnecessary to dignify their offenses with suspension and arrest. The cats would do the trick.

By the end of October all was in readiness and Wilkes asked port captain Richardson to pilot the vessels out of the bay on the thirty-first. Since the day arrived on the heels of a strong southeast gale, Richardson, observing the heavy sea breaking over the bar, urged him to wait. But wind and wave held no terrors for Charles Wilkes and at the appointed hour the vessels stood down the harbor. They sailed without Richardson (though they had Beechey's excellent chart, which they had used on entering) and without much wind. The *Oregon* and *Porpoise* were a little in the lead as they approached the bar that the boats had surveyed only a few days before, and on the *Porpoise* Sinclair noticed that the rollers came near breaking over it. Later he wondered how this had escaped the notice of the commander. As the light breeze showed no signs of increasing, the *Vincennes* let go her anchor and smartly furled sail. But as she swung to atop the bar itself, certain forces of nature began to act in dire conjunction: the wind failed completely, a heavy swell set in, and in the early evening the ebbing of the tide brought the ship broadside to. By eight o'clock a tremendous sea was running and she lay rolling helplessly in its troughs, channels under. The chain cable very nearly tore loose and seas breaking over the bows cascaded down the main hatch. Everything was suddenly afloat or awash—chests, boxes, bureaus, kettles on the berth deck, livestock, chain cables, vegetables on the gun deck. For hours she pitched bows under and there was no sleep for anyone. In the early hours of morning, James Allshouse, marine, was going up the forehatch to the spar deck when a heavy breaker struck abreast the larboard forerigging and swept the length of the ship, capsizing the two boats stowed amidships, carrying away the spare topmasts stowed on the booms, and crushing Allshouse, who died three hours later.

At eight-fifteen that morning a light breeze sprang up, the *Vincennes* fired a gun as signal to get under weigh (for the fog was thick) and set all sail. The brigs replied and, ringing their bells, worked along by soundings until signaled again to half-mast their colors and anchor for a burial service. The officers of the brigs, which had been lying only a short distance away "perfectly quiet & comfortable" in fifteen fathoms, were astonished to learn of the night of hardship and death and, when the fog lifted a little, to see the state of the

Vincennes, with portions of her bulwarks carried away and three boats stove in. They could only congratulate themselves on the distance they had been running ahead the previous afternoon. Some saw a guide here to the future conduct of their own vessels.[1]

So the body of James Allshouse was committed to the deep with the full honors of war, and his shipmates, with heavy hearts for him and curses for the Commodore, set sail once more. Yet for all their bitterness against Wilkes, officers and men sailed with light hearts. The important work was done and they would soon be homeward bound. At Monterey, the *Vincennes* and *Oregon* stood off and on while the *Porpoise* called for letters. When she did not return promptly, they set sail without her. Wilkes just might make good on his "Sacred pledge" to get them home by the end of May.

The ships took a more southerly course than usual for Oahu in order to search for more reported islands. But the voyage was uneventful save for splitting the occasional sail and—on the *Vincennes*—lashing the occasional back. Anchoring off Honolulu on November 17, they learned that the sloop-of-war *Yorktown,* Captain John Aulick, had departed a fortnight before. With a glance at the proudly flapping blue pennant, Sinclair was moved to bitter admiration at the man's luck: "Another narrow escape" for the "Commodore."

The *Flying Fish* arrived at three the same afternoon after a passage that had been eventful enough. Ordered to complete the survey of the Columbia River, then of the coast as far south as the Umpqua, Knox had telegraphed the *Vincennes* for permission to re-enter the river to refit, for the schooner's sails and rigging were rotten. But he had received the curt reply: "Refit at Sea." And that, piecemeal, he was to do, although the rejection and the thought that they were to be denied a glimpse of California put his men in no happy frame of mind. Trouble began the next day when a gale blew up and their only foresail (which had to double as stormsail) split at the clew. They took a reef and carried it until the wind moderated on October 15, when repair was possible. The sea remained high and it was not until the twentieth that it calmed enough for them to anchor off the bar and complete the survey by boats. After ten days' delay, eight hours' work saw the job done.

That, as it happened, was to be the last of their survey work, for as they made their way to the south the weather came on thick. It was exasperating. Time was running out, they could not work, and they were getting no nearer home. On the twenty-fifth it was again blowing a gale and parts of the standing rigging began to give way. They made repairs as best they could, working under water half the time from the force of the sea. Three days later, while

At the helm of the *Flying Fish*, from sketch by Alfred T.
Agate. (J. C. Palmer, *Thulia: A Tale of the Antarctic*,
New York, 1843, p. 31.)

being treated to a spectacular display of the elements—rain, hail, thunder and
lightning, even a whirlwind that luckily changed course just off the bow—they
were astonished to see land ahead and all along the lee, probably the mouth of
the Umpqua. Attempting desperately to tack away, they set the jib. It split.
Then the foresail split clean across and the vessel lay drifting under bare poles
in the dark. Luckily the wind was dying out but the sea still ran high, waves
coming aboard all round. Knox quietly set to work, as was his wont, at bending
the jib, while one of the crew stitched the foresail together as best he could in
the shafts of moonlight that filtered between massive clouds. In the total
absence of wind the enormous heaving of the sea seemed unnatural, as though
Nature had set aside her usual procedures for the sole purpose of bedeviling
the poor *Flying Fish*. All hands labored in a desperate silence broken only by

the shouts of the man stationed to warn of the approach of the really big waves, at whose cry all sprang into the rigging, except the helmsman, who clung to the tiller "like grim death." The last log entry for the day presented this estimate: "We are now Entirely at the Mercy of the Weather, having Neither sails, nor Standing rigging to trust to." But they finished bending the jib, the wind began to rise—mercifully from the northwest this time—they hoisted the main, and the *Flying Fish* walked rapidly away. At daylight land was no longer in sight. "Saved again!" Reynolds exclaimed in his journal. Then the mainsail tore out at the clew, gales alternated with calms, and on November 3 they abandoned all attempts at surveying and stood to the west. Although patching and splicing all the way, they made a speedy passage. When Knox went ashore to report, he bore "particular directions" from his messmates to bring back "all the Eatables the Hotel might afford in a state for instant mastication, and a dozen of fat ale."

The big news at Honolulu was from the Antarctic, where it was said the Expedition had been outdone—undone, some said. On his arrival from New Zealand a few weeks before, Captain John H. Aulick had announced that during the previous spring and summer Captain James Clark Ross had surpassed Weddell to establish a new "farthest south" at 78° 04′ and in doing so sailed his *Erebus* and *Terror* over areas that Wilkes had marked as continental on the chart he had provided the Englishman. George Emmons thought it might be true. Conditions might well have favored Ross as they assuredly had not the American squadron. "To those at all acquainted with Antarctic navigation," he calmly observed, "it is well Known that a large portion of the sea may be covered with impenetrable ice today—& a week hence be perfectly free & open." And there was always difficulty in distinguishing land from ice. What most worried Emmons was the prospect of unfavorable publicity prejudicing opinion at home against the Expedition. Henry Eld was equally certain the rumor could not be true and, if the response of the people of Honolulu offered any clue, could not harm the Expedition's reputation. He thought Aulick's mischief not only discourteous but unpatriotic.

The town's good feeling was a balm to the furious Wilkes, who ascribed the charge to Aulick's thwarted ambition to command the squadron and to Ross' envy. He was never to forgive either. But Aulick had also served notice that discoveries made at the world's end would have to be established at home.

With the vessels watered and provisioned and the rigging of the *Flying Fish* repaired, the squadron stood out of Honolulu harbor for the last time on November 28. After much signaling and maneuvering on a fresh breeze next day, the brigs stood to the northwest, the *Vincennes* and *Flying Fish* to the southwest, all under sealed orders. It was supposed the voyage would be a speedy one, but that was more wish than anything else, for this was an exploring expedition still. The brigs were to survey the islands and reefs of the northwestern area of the Sandwich Islands, from French Frigate Shoals to Pearl and Hermes Reef. But the weather was foul, as was to be expected in this season, and after beating about until December 11, Ringgold decided to bear away for the appointed rendezvous at Singapore, a course that carried them past Wake, past the high cone of Assumption (Asuncion) in the northern Marianas, past Monmouth (Bataan) in the northern Philippines and across the China Sea. On January 22 they entered the Straits of Singapore and anchored in the early evening in a harbor that many had become acquainted with in the pages of Reynolds' *Voyage of the Potomac.* At daylight they found themselves amidst a motley collection of shipping flying the flags of every nation and ranging from the swarms of yellow-striped half moons called junks, with their delicate stick masts and squaresails of bamboo matting, each sporting a great painted eye on either bow and a lurid dragon on the stern, through bumboats, sampans, proas, Dutch galiots built of teak, and Baltimore clippers, to the *Constellation* and *Boston* of the East India Squadron.

They remained in idleness for nearly a month before the *Vincennes* and *Flying Fish* arrived. While a gang of wiry Hindoo laborers caulked the decks, the explorers toured the city, for they were sightseers again as they had not been since leaving Peru. But the markets were for sightseeing only, for by someone's oversight, there was no money aboard.

The *Constellation* and *Boston* remained at anchor until February 5, when, the rest of the squadron not appearing, they sailed, and the broad blue pennant was saved again.

The *Vincennes* and schooner had parted company two days out of Honolulu, the little vessel unable to keep pace before the wind. After searching unsuccessfully for various islands and reefs reported by Arrowsmith, the *Vincennes* made Wake Island on the morning of December 20, finding it on the third attempt after searching at two other charted positions. The scientists spent a few hours among the rats and birds that seemed to be its sole inhabitants, while the boats took up the survey. They fixed its position—for the first time with anything like precision—and sailed away to the west before sunset.* They passed between Assumption and Maug on December 30, four

---

* The explorers left some names on Wake: Peacock Point, the apex of the larger (Wake) island, and Peale and Wilkes Islands, continuations of the north and south arms.

days ahead of the brigs, but beyond Bataan headed due south along the coast of Luzon and on January 12 put into Manila's crowded harbor for nine days. The *Flying Fish* arrived the same day. Sailing again on January 21, the schooner surveyed Apo Shoal, off Mindoro Island, while the *Vincennes* surveyed Mindoro Strait and the waters of the Sulu Archipelago, the notorious pirate hangout, where the scientists carried on their investigations under the watchful eye of the local sultan, who could promise them little protection from his cutthroat subjects. There was more boat work in Balabac Strait before favorable northeast winds brought them into Singapore on February 19.

Wilkes immediately suspended poor Knox, who was ashore sick, for he had missed a rendezvous in Balabac Strait. A court of inquiry, the usual fate of those who commanded the *Flying Fish*, sat for five days and listened to a parade of witnesses, then to Reynolds' delight "found not the shadow of a cause for Either Enquiry or censure."

As the Expedition was now finished with reefs and shoals and as it was feared that the *Flying Fish* might not survive the voyage round the Cape of Good Hope in the hurricane season now at hand, she was duly surveyed, condemned, and sold to an admiring English resident. Even Reynolds, when the order was given to haul down the ensign on February 24, felt regret, having "the same sort of regard for her that a man must Entertain for a gallant horse, that has carried him safely through the fight." George Emmons would have accorded her "a place in our National Museum—if we ever have one." At any rate she deserved a better fate than he believed would now befall her, for though the new owner waxed enthusiastic over his "beautiful Yacht," Emmons rightly suspected that he intended to make her "a smuggler of opium."

The "mortifying sight" of British colors flying from the schooner left a universal bad taste and, in a mood less elated than might have been expected of voyagers homeward bound, the "Miserable remnant of the Exploring Squadron" got under way on February 26. Sounding frequently, they sailed between the high shores of Sumatra and Java for the Cape of Good Hope and, it was supposed, home. The long voyage seemed in some poetic sense to have ended a few days earlier when the Down-Easter George Porter died of dysentery contracted at Singapore. For Porter was the seaman who on the passage to Madeira three and a half years before had narrowly escaped death by hanging when thrown from the main topgallant yard. Also, the promotions that Wilkes got around to recognizing on February 24 seemed to come as well-merited rewards for the years of arduous duty. The *Porpoise's* sailing master, George Sinclair, was bemused to contemplate that he had served in the Expedition at one time and another as midshipman, passed midshipman, master, lieutenant, and commander.

If the winds that were to waft them home should come on unfailingly fresh, it was still possible for all of them to be in New York by May 31—just barely. Wilkes made that impossible when on passing Java Head he announced that the *Vincennes* would proceed to New York by way of the Cape of Good Hope and St. Helena—as direct a course as could be shaped. The brigs were to make for Rio to purchase scientific specimens, after proceeding a few hundred miles off course to St. Helena in order that Wilkes, arriving later, might learn how they were coming on. The men of the brigs knew that most flags fly for the first in and Reynolds imagined the commander "chuckling, with a devils satisfaction, at having so deceived us." As though to make doubly certain that they should not outdistance him, Wilkes ordered the brigs to sail in company and twice daily heave to for soundings with the deep-sea thermometer. This arrangement caused widespread discontent among the crews, especially on the *Porpoise*, for the *Oregon* was a dull sailer on a wind, and in his private journal Reynolds would have consigned Wilkes to "hanging, only that he deserved impaling, long long ago."

There was heavy weather in the Indian Ocean and it was a month before the *Vincennes*, with a lead of a day or two, picked up the coast of Africa. The passage was a chastening one, for on March 20 the steady and popular old Captain Vanderford, unwell for some months, became deranged and the next day was "crazy as a bedlamite." His shocked messmates sat up with him all night and next afternoon the Fiji captain died quietly under opiate, age sixty-four. It was awful, observed the purser's steward, to watch the death of "one who has ate and drank with you, suffered with, and rejoiced with you, and with whom you have encountered dangers many and oft." It was most awful for Vendovi, who lost in Vanderford his last link with home. Free to wander about the ship now, playing his ever-present jew's harp, the big savage was popular with all hands and, though suffering for some time past from a cold, had remained in good spirits. But after Vanderford's death the surgeon noticed that his sickness was assuming a "dangerous character."

The *Vincennes* remained at the Cape only three days, watering and provisioning under Table Mountain, while the officers went ashore to visit the observatory where Sir John Herschel had recently spent four years mapping the southern heavens, and ladies and gentlemen from Cape Town came out to view the Feejee chief reclining on the berth deck.

Taking aboard six of the crew of the American brig *Uxor*, wrecked on

Prince Edward Island during a gale the previous October, the *Vincennes* got under way on April 17. She made St. Helena on May 1 after a passage notable chiefly for the suspension of George Emmons from. duty for two days—even the dutiful Emmons—because of some little distraction at the taffrail while dip observations were in progress in the cabin. But Wilkes could be deliberate, too. On April 19 he determined to take action on the letter sent almost exactly four years earlier by "All the Ships Company" of the *Macedonian* to the Secretary of the Navy protesting the appointment of a new commander when they had signed on in the expectation of serving under Commodore Jones. He now appointed Walker, Emmons, and Case to determine whether the letter had been instigated by officers now on board. The three gave the order less than twenty-four hours of "the most mature reflection," before returning it on the grounds that the signers had been "perfectly at liberty under the constitution."

As it was learned that the brigs had arrived at St. Helena a week before and sailed the same day, the *Vincennes* sailed again on April 2, "Homeward Bound" as all exclaimed in their journals. And as the ships made their separate ways (the brigs continued in company) their officers reflected on the meaning of the past four years. William Reynolds' messmates on board the *Porpoise* told him that with the benefit of better food and accommodations he looked ten years younger than when he first transferred from the *Flying Fish*. And, looking back, he could write in the private journal that he had no intention of surrendering to the government, "I look upon the hardships, dangers & servitude that we have undergone in this expedition, as parallel in their Extent, to the worst years of the 'Revolutionary War' & if its operations had been protracted for 48 months longer, Every one of us would have been *Expended*, from a *wearing out* of the system." He found his shipmates "all very much changed: all the boys have grown into men, and the Men have become wrinkled and gray," all a sad contrast to those earlier beings who sailed from Hampton Roads "full of glorious hopes & so abounding with confidence in our Commander."

Damn "this Everlasting Expedition," then, and its commander, who, they discovered on reaching Rio on May 12, had sent the brigs all this distance out of the track to pick up five small boxes of minerals, shells, plants, and birds, "light Enough to all be lifted, by one hand!"—at an expense to the government, Sinclair estimated, of ten thousand dollars and an untold amount of good faith. Five years had passed since some of the men had shipped for three. Oh, to be home once more, amid kind faces, "green fields & the sweet woods," there to forget "the rude people we have mingled with."

But homesickness would soon be cured, and if recollections of the "reckless tyrant" would rankle many down the years, few would fail to agree with yeoman Ezra Green, who wrote home to say, "I shall never regret this voyage." Even Reynolds, who had recorded enough of its "wondrous & lovely scenes" to assure that memories would not "become blunted, as years creep over my head," could in cooler moments reflect, "I hope they will last in all their freshness, as long as I have life."

And there was pride remaining for the "Everlasting Expedition," too, as Reynolds realized when he boarded the *Delaware* in Rio harbor and the officers "looked at me, as if I were a Natural Curiosity: they had not seen *an Explorer*, in full bloom." They felt it on June 22, when they left Rio on a fresh southwest breeze and were cheered by the *Concord* and *Potomac* and *John Adams* and the *Delaware*'s band struck up "Home Sweet Home" as they passed under her stern. Silas Holmes nearly wept as the "sweet sad Music . . . came breathing over the waters." Except perhaps for those who were to fight at Vicksburg or Port Royal, the Expedition, after all, would be the great event of their lives.

Everybody treasured a few mementos, and the order to surrender these, issued on all the ships during the Atlantic crossing, caused universal dismay. All journals, rough notes, memoranda, drawings, sketches, paintings, specimens of all kinds were to be turned over to the government, and this order was "to be construed in its *spirit* as well as *literal* construction." On the *Vincennes* Wilkes directed Hudson, Emmons, and Pickering to inquire of every man on board "if he has given up all & every thing connected with the Expedition or that may be important to it in the illustration of any part of it, or of facts relative to it," from whomever obtained, all to be reported to Wilkes in writing together with lists of everything received. It was a humiliating business. No one relished serving on this committee enjoined to extract every scrap and relic from men who had labored four long and arduous years, their few pitiful souvenirs now to be tossed into the government's great maw and regurgitated in New York or Washington for God knew what purpose. Emmons thought officers and men might at least be permitted to retain duplicates. He himself found it difficult to part with the souvenirs he had rescued from the *Peacock*, particularly a Fiji bow and arrows that Maury had presented to him after their boat fight off Malolo. "But here they go & if Government wants them I have not another word to say"—journal and sketchbooks and shells, a flattened Indian skull from the Northwest Coast, a Shasty arrow presented to him by Doctor McLoughlin, a shark's tooth sword from the Kingsmills, a manila mat and some copper coins. The most prized of the Expedition's relics, Vendovi, was still ailing.

And so the little hordes were relinquished—a piece of each man with them—and packed in boxes marked "U.S. Ex. Ex." With apologies for lack of elegance the officers closed their journals as self-consciously as they had begun them four years before—even those who had forgotten to be embarrassed by the act of journalizing.

The passage home was as speedy as ingenuity and generally favorable winds could make it. Aboard the *Porpoise* on the first day of June it was discovered that someone was trying to increase the day's run. The deep-sea thermometer, which in order to lower the necessary hundred fathoms, required that they stop dead in the water every day, was missing. "An eloquent Speech was delivered on the occasion by Capt. Ringgold," Sinclair noted with scarcely concealed delight, and a hundred dollar reward was offered for information. None was volunteered but next day Sinclair had to record in dismay, "A new Sounding apparatus made and the Experiments Continued."

The *Vincennes* was just then emerging from the calms of the Sargasso Sea into a fresh northeasterly breeze and a choppy head sea. In a great hurry now, Wilkes issued a standing order not to shorten sail without his consent. Emmons had the watch. The ship was straining and, fearful that spars or rigging might give way, he sent an officer to consult Wilkes. Back came an order to make more sail. When, accordingly, Emmons set the fore topgallant sail and jib, she made a few more plunges and her bobstay parted. To save her masts he immediately put the helm up and reduced sail aft. This brought the commander stamping angrily onto the deck, shouting contradictory orders in all directions, which Emmons had no choice but to repeat to the crew, "that he might not accuse me of disrespect" and at the same time be made to see "what a mess he had got every thing in." In a fury now, Wilkes ordered Emmons below and sent for the First Lieutenant, who saved the masts by reducing sail. Bobstay secured, the ship was brought again upon her course.

It was Wilkes' last character performance but one before the officers and men of the *Vincennes*. She struck soundings near Sandy Hook on June 10, one hundred and ten days out of Singapore, and next day a pilot came aboard and the steamer *Hercules* towed her in. The ship's company watched the proceedings now with great interest. Ever since Wilkes had first hoisted the stars of the broad blue pennant they had waited in suspense for the *Vincennes* to speak another navy vessel. There had been some narrow misses over the years, but by good luck and perhaps good management, confrontation had been avoided. Now they were sure they had their counterfeit captain boxed in.

"Curiosity was now on tip toe" as they entered the harbor bound for the Navy Yard. Would he dare to flaunt his usurped pennant before the lawful one flown by the commandant, or would he tamely haul it down to appear in his proper colors as lieutenant commanding? To the fury of some and the grudging admiration of others, he did neither, but coolly mustered the crew, delivered a short my-lads address thanking them for service to country and adding that he had a better opinion of them now than when four years before they had demurred at sailing with him, and had himself set ashore at the Battery. And never mind the prescribed courtesy call upon the commandant of the yard.

The promised date of arrival having expired ten days since without the hand of Providence being anywhere discernible, the crew stood on their rights—and on their commander's example, some remarked. They would go ashore and the ship could moor herself. But the officers kept them aboard until they had done their full duty by the government. Then with a curse for the Expedition they stamped ashore—John Brown, Bill Briscoe, George Butter, Jasper Cropsey, Charlie Erskine, Ezra Green, John Jones, Bob Pully, John Smith, Sam Stretch, and the rest, men who had not run at Callao, or Sydney, or Oahu (to name only the more popular ports of debarkation) but stayed on to survive dysentery, drowning, and flogging. Some had joined at Rio, or Honolulu, or Sydney, some—a little more than half—had "served the cruise." Now they were shipmates only for a last fling in the gin shops and porter houses of the "Hook" and "Five Points," where most would be scalped and skinned by waterfront "landsharks," though a few might put up in respectable houses bearing the imprimatur of the Seaman's Friend Society.

> Let the lower lights be burning!
> Send a gleam across the wave!
> Some poor fainting, struggling seaman
> You may rescue, you may save.

Some might again share a berth in the odd ship or whaler, or even a naval vessel chosen with care, and talk over the old days as South Sea Surveyors. But damned if they would ever sail again under old Wilkes. There they go, then, humping their seabags that contain all they possess (including perhaps the occasional arrowhead, Indian skull, or packet of seashells) to join the ranks of the anonymous ones who set the sails and lay the railroads of the world and rest forever in the gloom of history.*

---

* William Reynolds, who kept careful track of the disposition of the crews during the four-year voyage, rendered this final accounting: The Expedition sailed from the United States with 346

Vendovi's condition was so grave that afternoon that the surgeon, despairing, had him carried to the hospital ashore. The chief was heard to express wonder at the size of the building. Surely it was the white man's spirit house, and the Great Spirit awaited him within. A few hours later he died, quietly, as befitted a chief. The great adventure was ended.[2]

men. Desertions among these, 46. Discharged at Oahu, enlistments expired, 48. Died, lost, discharged (elsewhere than Oahu), sent home, 71. Returned with Squadron of the original number, 181. Whole number on the books during the four years (not including natives of Sandwich Islands), 524. Of these, 178 shipped abroad. Desertions among those shipped abroad, 80. Total number of desertions, 126.

17 Courts Martial

Farewell, dear Fitz-Roy, I often think of your many acts of
kindness to me. . . .

Charles Darwin

Vendovi's death was a blow to the Expedition. As the most
spectacular of the specimens collected, he might well have served as the
Symmes' Hole of the later years, calling the country's attention to the
Expedition's accomplishments and summoning public funds for study of
the collections and publication of the results, perhaps even dispatching new
expeditions. Already in the few short hours between mooring and Vendovi's
death, James Gordon Bennett's *New York Herald* had launched the ballyhoo
in the half column it allotted to the squadron's return by announcing
Vendovi's illness as a "consequence probably of having no human flesh to
eat." For a while afterward it looked as if the cadaver itself might serve
publicity purposes. There was talk of a renowned anatomist's delivering a
lecture over it. The *Herald* announced that the head had been pickled, adding
for the statistics-minded of its readers that the hair was "thirty inches long on
each side." A few months later the skull turned up as Ethnological Specimen
No. 30 in the Expedition's collections.

It was a pity the squadron had not returned a two-headed kangaroo, but
editor Bennett did what he could. When there was delay in paying off the
Vincennes' crew, a good many of them called at his office to be informed that
he would pay their expenses to Washington if they would promise to beat
their money out of the Congressmen. They were finally paid toward the end of
the month without having to resort to such drastic action, but in years to come
some of the explorers were to see merit in the proposal.

The *Oregon* arrived on the last day of June, the *Porpoise* on July 2. Two days later the explorers found the streets alive with processions and military parades, flags flying, "boys firing pistols, guns, & fireworks, in ones face, & under ones feet, terrible hubbub." But the natives were only observing the annual tribal rite. No flags flew to celebrate the return of the First Great National Exploring Expedition. Taken altogether it hardly added up to a hero's welcome for men who had been trailing clouds of glory round the world for the past four years. In fact, several newspapers remarked on the public apathy and, worse, the tendency to dismiss the Expedition as an "idle and useless" enterprise. As future undertakings might make some demands on "American genius and courage," one wished "to see every completed effort duly honored—at all events, until the habit of doing great things is well established." The *New York Tribune* blamed widespread ignorance of its purpose and accomplishments. As it had been primarily a scientific affair, its judges must be men of science, but the *Tribune* could report that the few sufficiently acquainted with its results to form an opinion were predicting that it would "worthily rank" with the great British and French expeditions. In his column of welcome in the Washington *Globe* Francis Preston Blair expressed confidence that forthcoming evidence would give the lie to Captain Ross, called upon the officers to "lay aside all feelings of discontent" (one wonders how son James responded) and upon the administration in Washington to do justice to the Expedition, and remarked on the "happy coincidence in the bequest of *Mr. Smithson*, the establishment of a National Institute for the Promotion of Science at Washington, and the great national exploring enterprise."

For a time in 1842 it was an open question whether indifference might not serve the Expedition better than attention, for in the House of Representatives its friends failed in an attempt to get up a resolution of commendation. In the Senate, a proposal to invite Wilkes and his officers to appear was voted down and a movement was afoot to deny Hudson's promotion on the ground of his having served under an officer below him on the list. Hudson won his promotion but the affair boded ill.

Yet if the results of the past four years were not to be lost, the greater part of the task lay ahead: the safekeeping of the collections, their description and classification by the country's best authorities, the engraving and publication of the results in a manner befitting a national showpiece, together with a narrative of the cruise.

Wilkes blamed the Whig administration for the general lack of attention to the Expedition, or as he put it, the opposition "to my receiving any honors or gratifications on my return." So far from being showered with honors, he found himself left off the promotion list for the year. That was injury. Insult came with the discovery that Doctor Guillou had been promoted in the normal course of events. Calling upon Secretary of the Navy Abel Upshur within three days of stepping ashore, he met with a "very cold" reception. The heated discussion that ensued destroyed all prospect of future favors from that quarter. At the White House he found President Tyler seated at the center of a semicircle around the fire, half a dozen "ruffian-looking fellows" on either side, "all squirting their tobacco Juice into the fire, and over the white Marble hearth." As it was apparent that the President did not know who he was, at the earliest opportunity he fled the "vulgarity and boorishness of this squad of politicians." His next call was on John Quincy Adams, who listened as the commander "complained bitterly" of the "cold and insulting silence." Adams could say little in reply. "I . . . must wait to hear the statements of the other side."

There were more sides to this enterprise than even Adams realized, and he had only to wait a few weeks before hearing some of them. Wilkes had filed charges against May, Johnson, Pinkney, and Guillou, and they against him. Wilkes had wanted the whole matter disposed of by a court of inquiry and had complained to Secretary Upshur that further delay would be "cruel and harassing to my feelings." But Upshur had coolly replied that he would have to take his chances with the rest before a court that was to sit for one hundred and five days and hear nineteen cases.

People were eager to hear of the adventures of the "celebrated exploring expedition," which ever since its sailing, one newspaper commented, had been "like a sealed book," and looked forward to something like a narrative of the cruise in the daily coverage of the trials by that paragon of democratic journalism, the *New York Herald*. The scene was impressive—"A galaxy of our naval pride," one reporter called them, never before having seen so many of "our veteran heroes" in a single group, in full regalia boarding their barges at the Battery at nine o'clock each morning to hold their great court aboard the *North Carolina*, Captain Francis H. Gregory. The explorers gathered for the last time, to attend the sessions daily from ten to three and spend their evenings talking over the day's proceedings.[1]

The trials of the junior officers revealed disappointingly little about the events of the cruise but told much about Wilkes as commander. That of Passed Midshipman William May, charged with disrespect, ran for four days. May had purchased a box of shells in the Fijis after Wilkes' agent had refused them. When the order was issued for the surrender of all specimens, he had "disrespectfully" marked the little box as private property. The trial hung suspended for a time on the question of whether May had placed the box on the deck with the marking up or the marking down. In the end, testimony disclosed that he had refused to obey an order. It disclosed a good deal more about Wilkes.

A procession of officers testified to their commander's style of command. Walker found him "violent, overbearing, insulting, taxing forebearance to the last degree." Knox: "incoherent & rude withall." Alden: "his manner is exceedingly overbearing and offensive to a gentleman." Couthouy, who testified without benefit of his notes and journals, Wilkes having lost them: "his language was . . . offensive in the highest degree." Was there a contrast then between Wilkes' manner and that of the other commanders? "I can't conceive of a stronger." North followed, then Reynolds, Maury, Emmons, Howison (Wilkes' own clerk), Perry, even Carr—all testified to the same effect. It was clear that when excited the man's rudeness was unparalleled; and all, even Hudson, testified that he was easily excited. The *New York Tribune*, grumbling that the charges were altogether too "petty" to occupy so much of the court's time, concluded that "The chief point of interest developed is the excitability of Lieutenant Wilkes."

In his defense, May put into words a conclusion the more reflective had long since reached: "He who would survey the world must first sound the depths & shallows of his own character." The court found May guilty of refusing to remove the offending label and sentenced him to public reprimand.

Wilkes positively savaged Pinkney with charges and specifications, but after hearing testimony for eight days, the court found only one specification of the six charges even partly proven and declared him guilty of writing disrespectful letters. He was sentenced to public reprimand and six months' suspension. Johnson, charged with disobedience and "wasting public property," examined witnesses himself and won acquittal in a trial that lasted only two days and was remarkably free of rancor.

Not so Guillou's. Clearly out to nail the peppery surgeon, Wilkes presented a battery of charges growing out of the affair of the pestle and mortar at Sydney, some missing journal pages, and a heated exchange or two. The Doctor's messmates testified as best they could in his behalf, and the sympathy for him among the spectators was almost palpable, but the court sentenced him to dismissal from the service—though after a prolonged bombardment of pleas from fellow officers and prominent medical men and politicians, President Tyler mitigated the sentence to a year's suspension.

Long before these trials were concluded, interest shifted from the trivialities on which they turned to the approaching trial of Wilkes. The explorers' quarry was come to bay. The court went into adjournment for a few days before it was to begin, and William Reynolds rushed home to Lancaster to "conclude" his marriage (cases of matrimony among the explorers approached epidemic proportions during the next twelve months). But he was back in New York in time for this event of real significance for him.[2]

The charges were brought by Guillou and Pinkney. The Doctor leveled seven—Oppression, Cruelty, Disobedience of Orders, Illegal Punishments, violation of terms of enlistment, Scandalous Conduct Tending to the Destruction of Good Morals, and the same Unbecoming an Officer—that filled twenty-six manuscript pages. Those most anxious to see Wilkes convicted deplored that they were "so wordy" and imprecise and pinned their hopes instead on the four similar charges, resting on different specifications, brought by Pinkney, for they dearly wanted Wilkes rebuked for the blue broad pennant and the captain's epaulettes.

Many of the charges came as no surprise to those who had heard the previous testimony or read the record of the earlier trials. No doubt Wilkes had delayed an unconscionable time in forwarding Guillou's and Pinkney's complaints to the Department, no doubt he had discriminated against the Doctor in the matters of promotion and pay; no doubt he had publicly harangued Guillou from a piazza in Honolulu, had goddamed Pinkney on the deck of the *Vincennes* and forced him to lay out five hundred dollars of his own money to repair the *Flying Fish* at Bay of Islands. And Guillou's charges of cruelty to natives probably counted for little with the public and met with no sympathy among the explorers. When Bob Johnson was asked by the court whether he considered the attack on Malolo necessary for self-defense, he replied candidly enough, "It was not in self-defense. I went on shore for the purpose of revenging my messmates." The remarkable number of floggings that ran from eighteen to forty-one lashes (Guillou cited twenty-five such instances) did attract attention, especially among those aware that for the past forty-two years the Rules and Regulations had permitted a captain to assign no more than a dozen.

But it was Guillou's sixth charge, the catch-all of conduct unbecoming, that caught the public eye and that was to bear most heavily on the Expedition's repute with future generations. For Guillou charged that in his report to the Secretary of March 11, 1840, Wilkes "did utter a deliberate and wilful falsehood in the following words, to wit, 'On the morning of the nineteenth of January we saw Land to the Southward and Eastward with many indications of being in its vicinity such as penguins, Seal and the discoloration of the water but the impenetrable barrier of ice prevented our nearer approach to it,' the said Lieutenant Charles Wilkes well Knowing that land to the Southward and Eastward was not seen on said Morning as asserted by him."

On Saturday, August 27, James Alden was called and sworn and as the procession that followed was heard the explorers found themselves once again among the ruined cities of Antarctica. Alden was asked what he knew in relation to the sixth charge. He had had the four-to-eight that morning aboard the *Vincennes*.

"I never heard of any discovery of land or any Claim set up for the discovery of land on that day," he testified, "until we arrived at Sydney," when Wilkes, having learned of the French claim, reminded him of the sighting on the morning of the nineteenth. But Alden had not entered the event in the log, and Wilkes himself had given the original report no credence, indeed had ordered Alden to haul the ship off. Further questioning brought out that by the chart they had made, the alleged discovery had been distant forty-eight miles and visibility that morning had been poor. But about later sightings from the *Vincennes*, Alden had no doubts—on January 28, when they were four hundred miles farther to the west, and again on February 13.

Perhaps Wilkes had not been much on deck during the southern cruise, perhaps he had not acquainted himself with the logbook? Here the testimony of all the witnesses in all the trials to Wilkes' untiring industry and perseverance was turned against him. De Haven, master of the *Vincennes* during the southern cruise, testified that Wilkes had been on deck most of every day—and every night as well. Nothing had escaped the man's attention. Moreover, a standing order required that the logbook be brought to him daily at two o'clock. Question: "Did he ever find any fault that land was not recorded as discovered on the 19th?" Answer: "Not to my recollection."

So much then for Wilkes' claim to have discovered the Antarctic Continent from the *Vincennes* on the morning of January 19. Had the *Peacock* done so? Lieutenant Davis, who was now called, stated that he had seen strong indications about five in the afternoon of that day and during the watch from eight to midnight made an entry in the rough log to that effect but was ordered by Captain Hudson to "erase that, & to state that it proved to be an Ice bergh." But he still believed it was land and read to the court two entries from the log that recorded appearances of land during the afternoon watches: by Emmons at 3:30 and Perry at 5:00.

Both Reynolds and Eld testified that they had seen land from the *Peacock* on the nineteenth, but late in the afternoon. Eld had spent between two and three hours at the masthead that day, and what he had seen was "much higher than any Ice bergh or Island I have ever seen, [and] I had been Cruizing two years south." There had been a good deal of excitement aboard in consequence. But without a substantiating entry in the *Peacock*'s log, and indeed testimony by Davis that he had been ordered to erase the claim made in the rough log in the evening, whence Wilkes' claim for discovery?

In a desperate attempt to regain lost ground, Wilkes dredged up a witness willing to testify that he had seen land from the *Vincennes* the morning of the nineteenth, between nine and ten o'clock. The gunner, John G. Williamson, recounted, "I was standing on the larboard Gangway, Capt Wilkes was on deck at the time, he came to me and asked what I thought of the appearance of the land, my answer was, if it was not land, I had never seen land." But it was a lost cause. No one came forward to corroborate the gunner's testimony.

At this point Wilkes' veracity would seem to have been pretty thoroughly compromised and through it the national honor. But this, two officers of the *Peacock* would not permit. A lot of water had passed under the keel since Henry Eld and William Reynolds had accorded high repute to the word of Charles Wilkes, but they knew what they had seen from the *Peacock*'s rigging on the southern cruise and now told of it, and in the telling they salvaged both the nation's honor and the *Peacock*'s. They had listened to a great deal of talk about the events of January 19, and in response to the judge advocate's question, "Did you see land on any day prior to the 19th & when?" both had something to say about the events of the sixteenth. Both testified, in words that carried conviction, that they had seen land that day. (And their journals, had they been placed in evidence, would have borne out their testimony, as Wilkes' journal would not have borne out his.) Eld put it very clearly.

"I saw it on the 16th between 10 and 11 A.M. I went to the Main topmast Crosstrees in company with Lt Reynolds as it was my custom to do every day while cruizing in those Seas. We both of us immediately exclaimed and I believe simultaneously—there is the land. There were three remarkable peaks, one of a Conicle—and two more of a dome like appearance. Much like mountains of volcanic formation. After looking at it for some time, we sent down for a spy glass, and examined it very closely. And I came to the conclusion that it Could be nothing else but terra firma. . . . It was a very clear and beautiful day."

Reynolds bore him out. Captain Hudson was then called. He had not believed at the time that he had seen land, but he did believe so now. A man could change his mind about these appearances—and all witnesses agreed on this—because "Those who had seen land down south before would recognize it after more readily."

Wilkes' defense proved to be just "such a production," Reynolds wrote home, "as was to be expected from him—Arrogant, careless, dictatorial in its tone to the Court & full of malicious abuse . . . taking a sly chance at us all." The truth was not in it. Wilkes read the first part himself until weariness and ill-health forced him to relinquish the task to counsel, who read on in "monotonous & hurried tones," stumbling so frequently that Reynolds wondered that he could be reading his own words. By turns impudent, petulant, and ingratiating, they bore the marks of Wilkes, not his counsel. Here stood a modest but enterprising officer, a man of science, to be sure, but one who had learned his science on the heaving deck and so none the worse for it, who to preserve the honor of the Service had accepted the command after his superiors had declined it and had carried it out with energy, sparing neither himself nor his officers and men—though, mind you, never pressing them "beyond the limit of proper exertion," as witness the loss of only eight men by disease. (No reference to the invalids shipped home, to the one hundred and twenty-four desertions that far outnumbered the rescued castaways.) And this in the face of many hardships, the most galling of them the "cabal" his officers formed "to thwart all the objects of the Expedition, which were not consistent with the ease of the gentlemen who composed it."

On the charge of excessive punishment, the only one of the lot, he asserted, which caused him any apprehension, he asked the court to judge leniently. It had all been unavoidable in view of the difficulty in finding the time and the officers to hold a court martial. (Captain Isaac McKeever of the *Falmouth* had appeared out of the past to pay his debt of gratitude by testifying that the squadron had been altogether too busy at Callao for a proper court.)

The Court delivered its verdict and sentence. Guilty in seventeen instances of illegal punishment. Sentenced to "a public reprimand by the Honorable the Secretary of the Navy." Many of Guillou's specifications and charges had been ruled out from defects in places and dates, and how was one to prove that Wilkes had not seen land on the morning of January 19, even if no one else on the *Vincennes* had?

The officers were disgusted with the lightness of the sentence. But Wilkes' reputation nonetheless suffered, and to the extent that he was the public personification of the Expedition on its new landlocked career, the Expedition's reputation suffered, too.

For the scientifics, some of whom were called to testify in the course of the trials, it was all a great tribulation that obliged them to remain idle, separated from notes and specimens while they ought to have been busy preparing for publication, "before many things fade from our memories," as Pickering complained.[3]

18 Friends of Science

The main army of science moves to the conquest of new
worlds slowly and surely. . . .

Thomas H. Huxley, "Advance of Science in the Last Half
Century," 1887

Charles Wilkes' first public act on the squadron's return was to
address Washington's National Institute, a newly formed national society of
scientists and friends of science. Referred to somewhat grandly as "Washington City," the capital was really a southern village struggling painfully to fulfill
its role. Its avenues were now paved, though poorly, its streets remained dust
and mud. Its only "creditable" buildings, noted one who had taken up
residence there three years before, were the Capitol itself, though its
unfinished dome resembled a large model of Symmes' Hole, the President's
house, and the government Departments. Washington was a "cheerless" place,
he added, "simply endurable by political and public receptions," the only
other diversions being the gambling houses and a poor theater. By 1842 he
might have added the National Institute.

For decades men of culture who found themselves in Washington for
whatever reason had complained of the lack of institutions of learning—no
college worthy of the name, let alone the national university that a succession
of Presidents had solemnly urged upon Congress. Down the decades public-
spirited men had founded a dreary train of institutions—the United States
Military Philosophical Society, the Metropolitan Society, the Columbian
Institute, the American Historical Society, to name only those of most
imposing mien—only to see them crumble through apathy and neglect. Two
events of the thirties, however, gave new impetus to attempts to upgrade the
reputation of the city and the nation, and brought them into confluence with

another train of endeavor in these years, the attempt to establish a national scientific community.

In 1835 the nephew of James Smithson died in England without heirs. Three years later the Exploring Expedition put to sea. The nephew left a fortune of a half-million dollars, which now by virtue of the uncle's will passed to the United States for the establishment at Washington of an institution, to be known as the Smithsonian Institution, for the "increase and diffusion of knowledge among men." There followed a decade of haggling in Congress over the bequest. Once it was determined that acceptance would not compromise national honor, the fund was promptly invested as internal improvement in speculative Arkansas bonds, while Congressmen debated a variety of proposals for increasing and diffusing knowledge: a national high school, an astronomical observatory, an institution for improving agriculture, a library, a university.

The debates in and out of Congress over disposal of the Expedition's materials were fully as long-winded. It is not clear that anyone in authority had any notion when the explorers sailed, of the extent of the collections they would bring back, or of what was to be done with them. The small natural history collections returned by earlier, overland expeditions had knocked about the country from one scientific society to another until they became scattered and finally lost, except for the occasional relic—a stuffed sable from the Lewis and Clark Expedition, two live grizzlies from Pike's—that wound up in the Philadelphia museum founded by Peale's father. Accordingly, Secretary of War Joel Poinsett had made arrangements with the present owners of this museum, now called the American Museum and managed by Titian Peale's brother, Franklin Peale, to care for the zoological specimens. The prominent Philadelphia florist and seedsman Robert Buist agreed to care for the live plants and the roots, bulbs, and seeds.

All parties to these casual agreements had second thoughts when the first shipment arrived—fifty thousand specimens collected, prepared, and packed by the scientific corps and shipped from Rio, when their labors were hardly begun. Over the next three years boxes both wood and tin, whiskey barrels and kegs, and canvas bags and baskets arrived by the hundreds. The total collections of all previous government expeditions amounted to no more than a fraction of this one. No museum, or greenhouse, or even scientific society had the resources for housing, caring for, and displaying it. Private enterprise, in short, proved as inadequate for this purpose as it had for conducting scientific exploration in the first place. Yet some provision must be made promptly if the materials were not to be lost—and some disenchanted naturalists were resigned to just that—for many of-the kegs and crates in which they were consigned to passing ships arrived in damaged condition and the contents required immediate care. Further inroads were made by Congressmen begging seeds and plants for influential friends and enterprising nurserymen among their constituents. An unprecedented and confused situation demanding prompt action, it called for administrative resources of the order that Joel Poinsett had demonstrated at an earlier and equally critical juncture in the history of the Expedition.[1]

In one of his last acts before leaving office in the spring of 1841 Poinsett persuaded Secretary of the Navy Paulding to order the collections sent down to Washington from Philadelphia. For their care he proposed to act on an old vision of his and at the age of sixty-two quit politics to launch in the years that remained to him a truly national scientific society. As early as December 1838 he discussed the disposition of the Smithson funds and the Expedition's collections with John Quincy Adams, chairman of the Smithsonian Bequest Committee of the House; and the following July he wrote to various scientific societies for advice on the establishment "in Washington City, in accordance with the Smithsonian bequest," of a "National Museum, with Professors who shall perform the double office of Curators & Lecturers." Pointedly ignoring the maelstrom of schemes and utopias that swirled about the Smithson money, he gathered a group of seventeen at his house on the evening of May 7, 1840, to confer then and in several meetings thereafter on the expediency of establishing "a Cabinet of Natural History." He chose the group with care. It included John Quincy Adams, Senator Thomas Hart Benton, and men who had spent enough of their years in the service of government that they had ceased to fear it—Col. Joseph G. Totten (1788–1864), chief of the Army Corps of Engineers, conchologist, and mineralogist; Col. John J. Abert (1788–1863), chief of the Corps of Topographical Engineers and a naturalist; Ferdinand Hassler of the Coast Survey; Francis Markoe, Jr., a clerk in the State Department, naturalist and amateur geologist; and Dr. Henry King of St. Louis, a geologist in the service of the Ordnance Bureau.

They agreed that an institution in Washington "intended to embrace the whole circle of Science" was of "great importance in a National as well as a Social and Scientific point of view." Of one obstacle that was to loom larger and larger in the years to come, they took only passing note, remarking merely that facilities in Washington were "equal if not superior" to those of any other city in the country for reasons "too evident and well known to need particular enumeration." The one facility they did trouble themselves to enumerate was the "important aid" the society would derive from "its connection—although indirect—with the Government." They further agreed to defer a request to Congress for a special act of incorporation for their "National Institution for the Promotion of Science" until the next session, when its "usefulness, if not its necessity" would be more apparent and all might "join heart and hand" in creating an institution that would confer upon the nation "as high a standing in the literary and scientific world as it already enjoys in the political society of Nations."

Short of revealing their designs on the Smithson funds, the founders made the connection with government as direct as possible by choosing as ex officio directors the Secretaries of Navy and War, and as "Counsellors" men of proven political acumen and influence—Adams, Abert, Totten, and Fourth Auditor A. O. Dayton—and by stipulating that all collections in the care of the institution should be the property of the government. A membership drive netted some ninety prominent Washingtonians, a good sprinkling of whom held membership in Congress as well, and an equal number of prominent citizens in the nation at large elected as corresponding members.[2]

In June 1840, the members of the moribund American Historical Society agreed to merge their organization with the Institute and become its Department of American History and Antiquities, and the Columbian Institute was proposing to do the same. The government collection of several thousand geological specimens housed in one of the rooms of the War Department was now in the Institute's charge, and it was confidently expected that other government collections would follow—David Dale Owen's rocks and minerals, the collections of the Indian Bureau, and those from the Exploring Expedition, which it was predicted, would be "rich & extensive." Although Congress had made no final decision about the disposition of the Smithson funds or the chartering of the National Institute, it had appropriated five thousand dollars for transporting the Expedition collections to Washington and for arranging and preserving them. A month later, in March 1841, the crates and barrels holding the Expedition's collections began to arrive from Philadelphia, as Paulding had arranged, and the Institute, with its newly acquired funds, appointed Dr. Henry King curator at a salary of five dollars a day. Shortly afterward, twenty tons more of material arrived at Boston and were brought down to Washington.

As the first few boxes were opened, the wisdom of the new arrangement for their custody became evident. About a quarter were marked as the private property of Titian R. Peale. In one crate all the choicest specimens were so marked. Some of the Institute's officers wondered which of the earlier shipments deposited in Philadelphia had been lost to the museum there, and on investigating those boxes found that some contained very few specimens but an abundance of wood shavings and doubted "if Shavings were an abundant article with the Squadron." Others were stuffed with another article of unlikely abundance, Philadelphia newspapers of recent date. Colonel Abert was inclined to find "some apology for Peale" so long as everyone had assumed that the government would display its traditional indifference toward its scientific collections, but with a sense of discrimination sharpened by long government service for what was and what was not government property, the Colonel remarked that as matters now stood, "it would be a Shocking outrage of propriety to countenance the idea that this expedition was got up, and these naturalists paid, by the U.S. for private benefit." It was indeed a precise and flagrant example of what good democrats most feared: private gain from public patronage. In preventing such depredations in the future, the Institute might perform a real service.[3]

The relationship now developing between government and science was not the result of far-seeing statesmanship in either camp, though far-seeing statesmen in both had been urging some kind of relationship for many years. The Secretary of the Navy wanted nothing more to do with the Expedition and informed the scientifics that so far as he was concerned the enterprise was "at an end upon the return of the ships." The matter was before Congress, he noted, "& doubtless some suitable provision will be made for securing the results of the Expedition." The Smithson bequest made decision the more urgent. Arrival of the collections made it imperative, indeed almost an act of self-defense. True, the debate over the Englishman's money had dragged on for years and was to drag on for a few more, but the prospect of putting it to the use of the Expedition made it possible for even the more rigorous upholders of laissez faire to envision a government scientific institution without blanching. The mysterious Englishman had simply rendered the objections of strict constructionists irrelevant. But even before the irrelevancy was generally recognized, the arrival of specimens had forced Congress to take the unprecedented step of appropriating money for the care of scientific collections. It soon became clear that those collections were going to require even more attention. While the shells and skulls and warclubs came out of their boxes under the supervision of the Institute's curator, a small corps of taxidermists was stuffing fifteen bird skins a day. As things were set up for display in the Patent Office Building that the Secretary of State had obligingly made available, the Commissioner of Patents began to wonder aloud why he had been chosen to plug the dike (he had a new building with a spacious and handsome hall, that was why); and he announced in his annual report that

FRIENDS OF SCIENCE

while it afforded him pleasure to promote the welfare of science, he wanted it on record that the accommodation could only be temporary. He was to put it on record annually for a good many years to come.

(The Commissioner could swim, if need be. The local museum-keeper, John Varden, could not. After some years of collecting "curiosities," Varden had set up a museum in 1829 close by the City Hall, advertising it as "a safe Depo" for "anything like birds or beasts that are a grate deal of trouble to take Care of." By 1841 he had added two Egyptian mummies and a few specimens sent by one of the Explorers and, as he later explained, was "in a fair way of making a living when the U.S. Ex. Exped. returned," and he was forced to close the doors of his Washington Museum, as visitors now "could see a much larger collection free gratis for nothing." The first American martyr to government enterprise in science, Varden took the path trodden by the Columbian Institute and the Historical Society and sold out to the National Institute, following his curiosities to the Patent Office, where he became assistant curator for the collections.)

Within a few months of the Institute's founding, its collections in natural history swelled enormously through purchases but mainly through donations from its members, who seem only to have been awaiting establishment of something akin to a national museum to dispose of their cabinets. The long rows of glass covered cases offered something to every taste, and the Hall of the Patent Office quickly became one of the city's great attractions. Aside from its natural history collections, the Institute displayed products of domestic industry—a case of buttons, samples of cloth, the best iron castings. For the history-minded there were one of the original drafts of the Declaration of Independence and a piece from the coffin of the Father of His Country, and for the merely curious, several Turkish sabers, horse covers once owned by the Sultan of Muscat, and a shawl presented by him to "Lt. Foot's Lady." For those of a more reflective cast there were the great collection of portraits of Indian chiefs that the Washington artist Charles Bird King had painted at the request of the War Department ("But for this gallery," a guidebook noted, "our posterity would ask in vain—'what sort of a looking being was the red man of this country?'") and James Smithson's fine cabinet of minerals that the Institute had rescued from the customs shed in New York. The Expedition collections were kept under lock and key until mounted for display, but everyone heard that they were monumental and the secrecy only whetted the appetites of visiting scientists.[4]

As more of the specimens were unpacked, however, uneasiness crept into the relationship between the Expedition and the Institute. Before the ships returned, Dr. Henry King, who was signing himself "Supt. Col. U.S. Ex. Ex.," and a group made up at one time and another of Couthouy (down from Boston), John Kirk Townsend, Professor Thomas Nuttall, the Harvard botanist, and various employees of the Institute were at work on the specimens. But by the end of 1841 they were at an impasse—out of space and out of money. The Expedition collections had filled up half the hall and were encroaching on the Institute's, and the work of unpacking, preparing, and displaying them was hardly begun. Of fifteen hundred bird skins in hand, some four hundred had been cleaned, stuffed and mounted. But they were as yet eyeless, and required labels and scientific arrangement. (One expert taxidermist could prepare six moderate sized birds a day if the skins were not too much twisted from the packing; a large bird might require two days.) Of one hundred and sixty quadruped skins, fifty had been stuffed and put in cases. Some two hundred glass jars, two barrels and ten kegs of mollusca, fishes, and reptiles remained to be prepared. Little as yet had been done with the approximately fifty thousand botanical specimens, beyond Professor Nuttall's appraising the collection as equal, perhaps superior, to any of its kind in the world. Of the three thousand specimens of insects, the greater part had been arranged, but only as to genus. Only a few of the several hundred thousand shells—thirty to forty bushels—had been cleaned, but conchologists had already pronounced it the finest collection in the country. Some seven thousand mineral specimens were now in display cases, but fifty boxes remained to be opened. Curator King remarked that it would require five years to arrange the specimens already in his possession. Small wonder the Institute men, as they informed the Secretary of the Navy in January 1842, were "now looking with some anxiety for additional shipments from the exploring squadron." And beyond those they foresaw the return of the ships themselves with specimens equal in number to all those yet received.

They continued to work without pay while the Directors of the Institute (whose object, they now announced, was "to 'increase and to diffuse knowledge among men' ") pleaded with the Secretary for more money and more space. But Congress declined to act until the ships returned and it was August before it did so by making available twenty thousand dollars from the Navy appropriation, "if so much be necessary," the members added with almost touching innocence. Delay on such grounds augured ill for the Institute, for if it was not to have charge of funds as well as collections, then the avalanche of crates would be a threat instead of a prize.

Charles Wilkes could not see why the Institute should have command of either. He insisted that the only institution that Congress had established (in the words of the enabling act) "to extend the bounds of science and promote the acquisition of Knowledge" was the Expedition itself. There was a curious, malign hostility toward it in Washington, he wrote Senator W. C. Preston, a cabal of silence that by denying any expression of thanks to the explorers on their return represented a departure from national custom and contrasted sharply with the practice of the French and English in honoring explorers who had accomplished a good deal less. Somehow it must be overcome, for "if what has been attempted and succeeded in is not now finished," the whole enterprise "shall become the laughing stock of Europe." In short, government must retain the exploring scientists, whom Wilkes judged to be more essential now than at "any other period of the cruise." The careless phrase is significant, for in Wilkes' plans the cruise was no more than begun. Preston thought he exaggerated the hostility to the Expedition—perhaps it was no more than indifference—but Wilkes saw the issue clearly enough. The Expedition must now address itself to research and publication and the government must pay the bill.

Charles Pickering sided with Wilkes. In his view, the collections should pass as soon as possible under the eyes of those best acquainted with them, to whom every facility should be accorded, including the Expedition's scientific library of several hundred volumes and, not least, adequate compensation. "We do not look to the dollars and cents," Pickering wrote, "but we would like to be placed on a respectable footing. We cannot but feel that the intellectual reputation of our country stands committed before the world in the late Expedition; that we have it in some degree in our keeping, to be vindicated through our means." He drew indelible lines between the aims of the Institute and those of the Expedition, between the museum-keeper and the scholar. The collections were not knowledge but only the means to knowledge, and the only way of proving the worth of the Expedition was "not by producing specimens to which an unfortunate importance has been so often attached but by the communication of facts."

It was a distinction that did not sit well with the Institute. Its little group of officers, acting without the aid of precedent but only their own considerable knowledge of the unique requirements of American science and the possibilities of politics to guide them, had sought to fill the vacuum that lay between government and science. They had designed their Institute to serve scientists as the Bank of the United States had served the commercial community: as a clearing house for natural history it would upgrade the coinage of American science. And they had acted in an atmosphere of suspicion as profound as that which had brought down that august establishment. Politicians suspected scientists of grabbing for privilege (and therefore denied the Institute banking privileges), and scientists had not forgotten the government's dismissal of their colleagues from the Expedition's corps four years earlier. Indeed, some of those scientists still had a memorial for relief before Congress.

The Institute hoped that Congress would make provision—and appropriation—for publication of the scientific results under the Institute's imprint. "This would give *eclat* to the Institute," Col. Abert remarked, "and take none from the Scientific Corps." And perhaps the Expedition and science would have been well served, for as Abert understood, the scientifics were "a Jealous class of men," who would not gladly bring forth their volumes under the superintendence of any man. But as Congress had yet made no appropriation for publication, that issue was a little academic in the early winter of 1842–1843.

The matter of preservation and arrangement of the specimens was not. Abert and others would have had the Institute made curator of the Expedition collections not by permission merely but by right, vested by law with their care and disposition and with management of the appropriations for the purpose. As the officers of the Institute were a majority of them officers of government as well, and by the Institute's charter always would be, they reasoned that there should be no fear in granting them the power. This "Board of Management," consisting of friends of science who had spent their careers in government, might be made the "vehicle of union & confidence between the two." [5]

What most got their wind up was Pickering's remark about the unfortunate importance attached to specimens. "One of the prominent objects of the present appropriation and of the Institute, undoubtedly is that of establishing a National Museum," they announced, and in a counterproposal urged that the Institute's "controlling power" over the collections and over all persons at work on them be reaffirmed. Otherwise there would be no end of "embarrassments and difficulties." But there were embarrassments and difficulties, largely set in motion by Wilkes and brought to fruition by a Congressional ally of his, Senator Benjamin Tappan (1773–1857) of Ohio. A humorous and urbane Democrat whose aristocratic bearing was lightly mocked by an eye that stolidly contemplated his nose, Tappan was chairman of the comparatively insignificant Joint Committee on the Library of Congress, and he was also—in his spare time—an eager conchologist. As an amateur scientist he had taken a great interest in the Expedition, the more perhaps as Secretary Paulding at dinner one evening in the spring of 1840 had promised him as many shells as he wanted from the Expedition's store. That promise, he noted at the time, "I

Senator Benjamin Tappan. (From *Appleton's*
Cyclopaedia of American Biography.)

shall not be likely to forget." Nor did he. He had supported the Institute's
plan for disposition of the Smithson legacy when the issue had first come to his
attention more than a year before the squadron's return, but then Wilkes had
come bearing grievances—and perhaps shells. Mutual friends performed the
introductions and Wilkes at once confided in detail his discovery of the
administration's determination to "ruin" him. Tappan responded by drawing
up a bill providing for publication of the Expedition's papers at government
expense. He also arranged for the Library Committee to become the
Congressional overseer of the enterprise, and he persuaded members of the
Committee from the House to put into the annual Navy appropriation bill,

twenty thousand dollars for the arrangement and classification of the natural history collections. As this left Secretary Upshur to determine how the sum should be expended, Tappan and Senator Preston called at the Navy Department—Preston to plead the cause of the National Institute, Tappan to urge that the enterprise be kept a purely government one. The scales ultimately tipped against the Institute, and Upshur agreed that Pickering, as the Committee's agent, should draw Navy pay for superintending publication of the scientific volumes and overseeing classification and arrangement by such persons as he deemed qualified.[6]

As a naturalist of recognized standing in the country at large, Pickering was quite acceptable to the Expedition's "Scientific Gentlemen" (with the exception of the exasperated Peale), who looked upon his appointment as assurance that the collections would not be taken from the hands that had gathered them and turned over to "closet naturalists" to be written up, as some had feared they would if the Institute continued in custody. After some suspenseful maneuvering, Wilkes was commissioned by the Committee to write the narrative of the Expedition, and he who on becoming its commander had been at such pains to make it a Navy enterprise now assented without murmur to its being a purely civil one.

As Congress thus removed control of the collections from the Navy Department, by whose act alone they had been committed to the care of the Institute, the latter found itself increasingly ignored, and it soon became apparent that the frail administrative structure its members had managed to erect was too weak to support their plans. Still hoping to recover official control of the collections and to effect a legal union with government, the Institute, a little superfluously, appointed Pickering curator of its own collections and talked of setting up a system of exchanges to greatly augment them. But when late in December 1842 Congress got around to making the recommended appropriation for publication, the Institute lost all hope of attaching its name to the volumes.

The new alliance between the Library Committee and the Expedition, between Tappan (who, as Abert ruefully noted, controlled the Committee though his remarkable "activity of management" and the lassitude of the other members when confronted with scientific matters) and Wilkes, rendered the ground beneath the Institute uncertain. But it was the collections, their popular appeal as "curiosities" as much as the sheer tonnage of them, that were to bring the Institute down.

New wonders came to light daily as the boxes and bags were opened, and all visitors pronounced them unprecedented. Positions on the scientific staff were in great demand, and there was some grumbling at the decision to employ the scientists of the Expedition to arrange the collections and to write up the results as well. But having gathered them, they knew the collections better than any others and with some exceptions were as well qualified as any in America for the task. They also realized how essential the spectacular "curiosities" would be to the prying loose of future appropriations from Congress, however useless to science Pickering might think them once they were classified and described, and so made every effort to set up exhibits as soon as possible in the Great Hall of the Patent Office.

The building itself was new. Its cornerstone had been laid in 1836 on F Street between Seventh and Ninth and the structure that materialized was a handsome one of doric columns (sixteen, each eighteen feet in circumference and modeled on the Parthenon's, visitors were informed) and spacious stairways, built of freestone on a granite base at a cost of over four hundred thousand dollars. Even Dickens, whose enthusiasm for things American was limited, had recently pronounced it an "elegant structure." It was in fact the American Spirit House. In its spacious columned halls dwelt the Spirit of the Age, whose icons were displayed on every hand, the products of American ingenuity and Know-How. The room on the upper floor, two hundred and sixty-five feet long and painted the stark white of the meeting-house, was now filled with natural history collections only because the Expedition returned before enough mousetraps were invented. Visitors increased as the collections were arranged in their glass cases and Pickering willy-nilly found himself superintending a museum.[7]

Swinging south on a lecture tour in January 1843, Emerson found the collections to be, after the Capitol, "the best sight in Washington." Lieutenant Walker came to gaze wistfully at the little cluster of shells he had purchased at Manila after losing all his other mementos in the *Peacock*, and William Reynolds, come to view his contributions, encountered Wilkes himself and, still feeling strongly, had "the supreme gratification of cutting him dead. God everlastingly damn him!" The crowds grew so large that Wilkes had signs posted for their guidance and, for the protection of the floor of tesselated stone from tobacco juice, directed a large number of spitoons to be placed well away from the columns. When these were found to be inadequate from indifference or ineptness, he directed an attendant armed with a pail of water and an enormous sponge to follow closely any visitor with a lump in his cheek. This worked better.

At the little greenhouse in the rear, Brackenridge had to contend with similar annoyances and an additional one that posed a greater threat than the odd plug of tobacco. It was no sooner known in the city that the government had a greenhouse than applications began to pour in for flowers and plants, and many of them from very important people indeed. These were a trial to Brackenridge, who took great pride in his plants, and with Wilkes' support he simply refused them all. President Tyler's wife called one day to collect some flowers only to be refused by a man working in shirtsleeves and she bustled off to complain to the Commissioner of Patents. The laborer turned out to be Brackenridge himself, and the Commissioner begged to inform the President's lady that the matter was entirely out of his hands. The rule held only until the plants were sufficiently well established, but even so enough politicians and their wives were offended that a serious attempt was made to cut off appropriations for the enterprise.

Another problem was more difficult of solution. Some plants never reached the greenhouse at all. A good many seedlings of the Norfolk pine, for example, had been sent in a passing Salem vessel from New Zealand. At Salem some were stolen. But as they were, so far as was known, the first of their species to be introduced into the country, they stood as accusing sentinels here and there at New England doorways.

As the Expedition exhibits grew they pressed upon the Institute's. Ostensibly, both were under the same curatorship, but the Expedition's were the center of scientific interest and were accorded the major share of curatorial attention. The officers of the Institute were resentful but helpless. Actually the hall had been inadequate from the beginning. The scientists admired its appointments but found it lacking in suitability as workroom and museum. Pickering was complaining of the lack of space as early as the fall of 1842, when many of the boxes were yet unopened. As great a source of friction between the two institutions was the explorers' dissatisfaction with the quality of care bestowed upon the collections before the squadron's return. They made no secret of it, and the Institute's depredations became legendary among the next generation of scientists in Washington. Wilkes complained that the collections had been ignored, the scientists that they had not. As Peale imagined the scene on the arrival of the first shipments, "the seals were broken and a general scramble for curiosities took place by irresponsible members of the Society, in which some 'Honorable' men thoughtlessly took part. Many valuable specimens were lost, particularly shells and skins of birds." Peale complained to George Ord that one hundred and eighty specimens of birds that he had collected were missing, including some new species. And Dana complained publicly of the treatment accorded the crustacea, many of which, removed from their bottles and dried and sometimes even transfixed with pins by those eager to mount them for display, were too much damaged for description.[8]

In the summer of 1843, anxious to pursue his own researches and persuaded that the task of arranging was largely completed, Pickering resigned the superintendency and set off for Egypt. When Tappan then persuaded the Library Committee to replace him with Wilkes—one of history's scrappier martyrs, Wilkes remarked that the task would be a thankless one, but he was willing to make the sacrifice "for the sake of the Expedition"—the battle of the collections was joined. On taking command, Wilkes gave the hall the kind of inspection he was accustomed to give the *Vincennes* or the *Flying Fish*—and with like results. He found "a want of order and neatness and I think some waste that will early claim my attention." The collections were so crowded that the Expedition specimens could not be viewed to best advantage, the Institute's china teapots really ought not to be displayed cheek by jowl with shells, corals, and birds, and the "good taste and propriety" of some of the Institute's exhibits were questionable—this perhaps in reference to a bit of half-naked nubility in one of the Indian portraits. And though Commissioner Ellsworth seemed an agreeable enough fellow, ought Patent Office models to take precedence over Expedition specimens? But what galled Wilkes most was the public's impression, which he was sure the Institute's officers were at pains to encourage, that this was the Hall of the National Institute.

Though Ellsworth was not to be moved, Wilkes soon had the hall shipshape and with Tappan's assent—their cooperation extended even to such trivia—placed a large sign above the entranceway at the top of the staircase that proclaimed in large gold letters that none might mistake, "Collections of the United States Exploring Expedition." To Abert, who, taken aback, wrote to inquire what plans he had for the Institute's collections, Wilkes replied with an asperity that suggested he had been crossed on the deck of his own ship. He belittled with blunderbuss sarcasm the Institute's exhibits ("a few specimens and articles were pointed out to me as belonging to the Nat. Inst.") and observed that the staff were paid by the government for government work and no other. No doubt it would become necessary to remove the Institute's collections some time in the future. Due notice would be given.

In a long and eloquent letter, reasonable in tone, Abert urged Wilkes to forego the quarterdeck manner, as he was now, for all administrative purposes, a civilian—the successor of King and Pickering. A little offended by the slur on the Institute's collections, he pointed out that they were by no means the paltry thing Wilkes made them out to be but large, valuable, and ever-growing—as indeed most contemporary assessments suggest they were. In his own office were twenty-four cases of specimens shipped from Asia and Mexico which had not been sent to the Hall, where another sixty boxes stood unopened, because he had been informed that they would not be received. A situation had arisen, he suggested, that "Science and national pride must bitterly regret," for all the labor, all the contributions, from whatever branch of service, civil, diplomatic, naval, military, "are for the scientific reputation of our common country."

Hopeful of government patronage but dependent upon membership dues and contributions, the Institute absolutely required facilities for displaying its own collections. When Wilkes refused these, it languished—creature and victim of the Expedition specimens. Donations continued to arrive, and in a little while there were more than a thousand boxes, barrels, and trunks scattered among private rooms, garrets, cellars, and government departments, the prey of insects and neglect. Yet in its meteoric career, the Institute had gone a long way toward fulfilling the explorers' dreams of a national museum that would display their contributions to American science and had set precedents that were to prove fruitful when out of the welter of schemes for utilizing the Smithson money there finally emerged a Smithsonian Institution, partly private and partly public, its administrative structure a complicated contraption of many parts, that nonetheless would prove to be a stable and truly national institution of science.[9]

19 The Muse

Man is said to be naturally a gregarious animal, that an
interchange of civilities and kindness is a natural
propensity of the creature; it may be true of the species at
large, but two very prominent exceptions are Englishmen
and Yankees. . . .

[Nathaniel Ames], *Nautical Reminiscences*, 1832

Of all the Expedition's exhibits the one most eagerly awaited by
the public was the story of the cruise itself. As government foresight played no
more decisive role here than in disposition of the natural history specimens,
there was a vacuum. Wilkes rushed in.

Ever wary, he had watched as the outlines of a new cabal took shape in the
weeks after his return. It was not Mister Knox and Mister Reynolds this time,
but the President of the United States, his hatchet-man the Secretary of the
Navy, and their flunkies. He watched with mounting ire as they subjected him
to court martial, embroiled him in red tape with the auditor over payment of
his salary, and kept him off the promotions list while finally promoting
Hudson as a matter of course.* When he discovered a move afoot to appoint a
favorite of the President's to write the narrative of the Expedition, a
"half-crazy" employee of the State Department, he watched no longer, he
acted.

By the orders he had issued at the beginning of the cruise, orders that
converted old salts into fancy journalists and enjoined all to secrecy, he had
tried to assure that he would not be scooped as Lewis and Clark had been.
And in the ensuing struggle he had one great advantage: the journals were in
his possession. When Upshur directed him, at his convenience, to deliver all

* Wilkes was finally promoted to the newly created rank of commander in the summer of 1843.

305

records and journals to the Department, Wilkes confided to friends that the Secretary was attempting to undermine his defense at the court martial and, calling upon Democratic Senator Silas Wright, told him that he would never find it convenient to surrender the materials. "I would rather have committed them to the flames," he wrote thirty years later, incensed again at the memory. Friends pushed a resolution through the House that left them in his custody until Congress should make provision for their disposal. (He lodged journals, charts, portraits, and some of the specimens as well in his home, where he put them to good use, one day enticing John Quincy Adams from his desk in Congress to come inspect them.)

It was to secure his claim as much as to call attention to the Expedition that Wilkes agreed to address the National Institute on June 13, 1842. As he saw it, his performance made it "fully clear" that the writing of the narrative was "justly due" him. When the Library Committee gained jurisdiction, it quietly assigned him the task; and, agreeing reluctantly since Wilkes was still under court-martial sentence, Upshur ordered him to the duty. Thus an assignment Nathaniel Hawthorne once sought and many another experienced writer would have welcomed—J. N. Reynolds, Robert Greenhow (the able historian in the State Department), or one of the Expedition's own officers or scientists, several of whom wrote to good effect in the plain-sailing, matter-of-fact style of Cook—went to Charles Wilkes. But confidence and industry, he was sure, would fill the void that art left, though "Old Mr. Adams" was at pains to admonish him that he had "a beautiful monument to build for the glory of the country" and would be held to account if there was "a stone omitted or a blemish found."

The writing of official voyages had reverted to an older tradition since Captain Cook's return in the *Endeavour*, when the First Lord of the Admiralty had let it be known that the papers were in his possession, in rough draft and unarranged, and he "should be much obliged to any one who could recommend a proper person to *write the Voyage*." He had handed them to a man of polite (and sententious) letters who knew nothing of islands, seas, or ships, and owing at least in part to that vacuum, Dr. John Hawkesworth's hastily written account had managed to offend everyone, captain, ship's company, and literary critics alike. After that disastrous innovation with the most spectacular of voyages, Cook had seen to his own books and re-established the tradition of Dampier. Thereafter, commanders, or at least participants, wrote their own narratives: Bougainville, Bligh, Beechey, Kotzebue, Fitzroy and Darwin, and of late Dumont d'Urville. Captain Belcher's account of his own voyage appeared in 1843. Other things being equal, there was obviously a good deal gained in a participant's writing up the voyage. The trouble was, other things were never equal.[1]

Thus what might have been haunts the modern reader of the *Narrative*, as it tantalized contemporary critics. Enthusiasm for books about the sea continued unabated, if one may judge from the flood of cheap romances that appeared in the forties. On a higher level, Richard H. Dana's *Two Years Before the Mast* (1840) reinvigorated an older tradition of realistic treatment of maritime life, and for twenty years thereafter an outpouring of recollections told of anywhere from five to forty years before the mast. And the islands of paradise that had captured the literary imagination before their geography was fully known were to do so again in this very decade. That Wilkes' effort was certain to disappoint this audience became clear with the appearance of the *Synopsis* of his address before the National Institute. When that pamphlet reached the editor of the Honolulu *Polynesian*, he was pleased to reprint Wilkes' remarks about Honolulu hospitality but he was shaken by the total lack of "perspicuity in writing." To be sure, the scenes and events of the voyage might reasonably be expected to survive any writer's handling, but the editor only wished that the task had fallen to one of the explorers "whose literary talent had already been tested"—to Dana, for example, who had published a brief account in *Silliman's* that showed a disciplined command of language.

For Wilkes it was simply another job of work. In the past four years, as he saw it, he had been the stern but just commander, the intrepid seaman, the unwearied observer for science. At present he was overseeing publication of the scientific results, lobbying before Congress for appropriations, conducting a series of pendulum experiments to test the accuracy of the Expedition instruments, and warding off the demands of some of the officers for the return of their journals—their only defense against the criticisms in his address before the Institute. To authorship he brought the same energy he devoted to these tasks. The nature of the job, as he conceived it, insured that the narrative would be the first volumes through the press. For as Pickering was classifying fishes, so he set himself chiefly to organizing the observations in the journals—discovering only then, to his anger and dismay, that several of the young gentlemen had kept only very cursory accounts, no more than defective copies of the ships' logs. That done, he sent the manuscript to his brother-in-law, James Renwick, for comment. Replying that the quality of the prose made him "tremble" for its author, Renwick offered some lengthy criticisms that represented a good deal of effort. Wilkes blithely rejected the lot. Having "no pride of authorship to maintain" and aspiring only to give the country "an intelligible account," he explained that he had no need of art. There would be criticism from "my enemies or those who feel disposed to rob me of the credit that my exertions ought to entitle me to," but posterity would accord him his "due." Driving on the artists, engravers, and proofreaders, he saw the five volumes and atlas through the press in the spring of 1845.

Gilt-edged, their dark green morocco bindings stamped with the eagle and Seal of the United States, the *Narrative of the United States Exploring Expedition* bore the imprimatur of Congress. Wilkes was immensely proud of the volumes, and justifiably so. No expense had been spared. "In style of execution, they have not been exceeded in this country," noted the *American Journal of Science.* They were lavishly illustrated with plates, vignettes, and wood engravings made from the paintings and sketches of the artists Agate and Drayton, the officers (Totten, Dale, Eld, and the lamented Underwood), Fred Stuart, Peale, Pickering, and Couthouy. A few were by the commander himself. Everything used in the preparation of the volumes, it was noted proudly, was "strictly American." They were indeed superb examples of the American bookmaker's art.[2]

As examples of American prose they were a national disaster. Reviewers had a field day. They also took occasion to comment on the phenomenon of the nation's sending out an expedition in the first place, on the manner in which it was conducted, and on its results. For the innovation and the mass of information collected, they had only unqualified praise. Author and commander came off less well. They deplored, as one put it delicately, the "taste for accumulation" that swelled the book to enormous size with "entirely irrelevant matter" ("The undersigned's" order banning mustachios), with facts long known ("wine is the staple commodity of Madeira"), and with long "politico-statistical chapters," as the London *Spectator*'s weary reviewer called them, that were no more than paraphrases of widely available histories. Most of what lay between the magnificent covers was scissors-and-paste.

Coming upon such occasional "gems" as the fine description of the Malolo burial, reviewers found it difficult to believe that the same hand had written other passages and correctly ascribed the "variety of styles" to "free use of the private journals." Transcending animosities, Wilkes had in fact transcribed long passages written even by men he had dismissed—by Couthouy, for example, whose acuteness of observation served him well—and did so nearly always without acknowledgment, as the journalists among the explorers promptly noted. Indeed Wilkes' name might better have appeared as compiler, a more modest office, but an honorable one if competently performed.

Repetitiousness and turgid syntax apart, what astonished reviewers most was the bitterness between commander and command that had apparently prevailed through four long years and was prolonged here in the petty recriminations directed at those from whose journals the book had been assembled. English reviewers found this sort of thing incomprehensible in a "national work." Wilkes blanked the crews with avuncular contempt. The seaman was always "Jack," by whom the commander invariably "could not but be amused." The officers, if possible, fared worse. Even Poinsett, Wilkes' most steadfast supporter, was dismayed. "We cannot but regret," he remarked anonymously in the *Southern Quarterly Review*, slipping into the contrived indirection of the sentences he had so long been reading, "that Captain Wilkes should have introduced his private grievances . . . in the body of this national work."

For all the critical dismay, the *Narrative* sold briskly at ten dollars the set when Wilkes brought out an unofficial edition. It also won Wilkes the Royal Geographical Society's Founders' Medal, an honor earlier accorded John Biscoe, Robert Fitzroy, and James Clark Ross. More surprising is the imprint the book left on the literary imagination. The *Edinburgh Review* applauded its realistic treatment of the Polynesian cultures, and credited it with knocking the props out from under the sentimentalists, like the popular French novelist Eugene Sue. More important, the *Narrative* reached beyond the critics to men who, if repelled by the quality of the prose, were excited by the exotic settings and the drama of the voyage itself. As Joseph Conrad would find raw material for fiction in Belcher's *Narrative*, so American writers would find abundant material in the account of this expedition's cruise. James Fenimore Cooper, a friend of Wilkes' banker uncle Charles Wilkes, had remained sympathetic toward the commander during the court-martial ordeal and had spent some time with him in the Philadelphia hotel the two shared while Wilkes was assemblying his big book. When Cooper sought material on the Pacific islands for his novel *The Crater* (1847) he drew as heavily from Wilkes as from Cook. For *The Sea Lions* two years later he drew incidents and details of the fur seal trade from Benjamin Morrell and Edmund Fanning but took his Cape Horn topography and the terrors of navigation among the ice from the compendious *Narrative*. The iceberg as ruined alabaster city he took as unblushingly from Wilkes as Wilkes had taken it from the officers' journals, although Cooper gave credit.[3]

Small wonder that when Herman Melville reviewed Cooper's book, the polar scenes reminded him of "the appalling adventures of the United States Exploring Ship in the same part of the world." Among his own first purchases from the royalties of *Typee* (1846) had been a set of the *Narrative*. Melville, who had few illusions about man's nature and fewer still about civilization, had called at Tahiti shortly after the explorers' return and when he wrote *Omoo* and *Mardi* supplemented his own observations with theirs and presented a view of missionary endeavor that accorded much more with the officers' opinions than with Wilkes' official endorsement. For the writing of *Moby Dick* (1851) the *Narrative* yielded a good deal of information on native life and customs, as well as incidents—the sale of shrunken heads at New Zealand by the steward of a missionary vessel—and the lineaments of character, most notably Queequeg's, modeled on the New Zealand chief Kotowatowa. With covert amusement, Melville found a factual basis in the *Narrative* for scenes painted by his most outrageous whimsy.

Those were unexpected influences and hidden ones. What the general public most eagerly sought was information on the Expedition's most spectacular achievement, the discovery of a continent. It was of course a considerable one for the nation's first overseas exploring expedition. When the news of Wilkes' discovery first arrived in the summer of 1840 it made a hero of him, "another Columbus" to a generation of boys, including ten-year-old Sam Clemens in Hannibal, Missouri, and there was crowing in the press at the United States' victory over the British. A glance at the latest Admiralty chart of the South Polar Sea, issued in June 1839, was convincing evidence of the American accomplishment, for there the entire sweep of land coasted by the Expedition appeared as a blank, except for "indications of land" noted by the English whaleman John Balleny in 117° E. "Such was the ignorance of the British Admiralty . . . of the existence of a Continent," commented the *New York Journal of Commerce*. The discovery was honorable to Wilkes and the Navy, "honorable to science and the American name." [4]

But that was the excited first response of 1840. Foreseeing no use to which the discovery could ever be put, sober second thought suggested that it was "barren glory." (Anticipating this grubby view, John Pickering observed impatiently that "*national honor* is of positive *utility*.") Then came news of the French claims and the British charges. By the time the ships returned indifference and skepticism had cooled the embers of excitement. Poinsett observed that the discovery was calling forth less attention "than any of the hundred tales of misery and crime" that daily filled the papers, and Dana estimated that "not one tenth of those who know any thing of the Expedition believe that they discovered land in the Antarctic regions." Dana exaggerated, but the indifference of the explorers' countrymen became a species of international scandal that even the haughty Ross was to deplore. French geographers, though they surrendered no part of Dumont d'Urville's claim, were far more generous in their esteem and frankly acknowledged that if the Americans' observations and surveys were as accurate as they were extensive, then their expedition was, "without doubt, one of the most important ever undertaken for the advancement of the sciences" and their young nation fairly launched in scientific exploration "in a manner calculated to excite the emulation of the great nations of the world." As the controversy with Ross' countrymen developed, the French urged the Americans to publish their Antarctic chart with precise indications of the landfalls of each vessel.[5]

Public indifference was owing in some measure to delay in publication. While a chart of the French discoveries of January 1840 appeared the following June, and Ross' of January 1841 appeared the following July, the American chart awaited publication of the *Narrative* in 1845. And although priority in geographical discovery is less dependent upon publication than is scientific discovery or invention, it is nevertheless first announcement that fires the popular imagination.

When Wilkes' account did appear, it left a good many people puzzled. To a matter demanding the greatest accuracy, he brought only ambiguity. The *Vincennes* had proceeded to the west from 158° E. to 94° E., sailing between the parallels 62° and 67°, a distance of over fifteen hundred miles. On the map accompanying the *Narrative,* land appeared at short intervals as seen on twelve occasions, and on the strength of these sightings Wilkes proclaimed it a continent, rather *pompeusement,* it was thought in France.* Further, the dates of discovery were not at all certain. What was clear to every careful reader of the *Narrative* was that discovery was not recorded in the logbooks until January 28, even though the date Wilkes claimed was January 16. Of course this was the whole point at issue with the French, who did not claim discovery of a continent, but only priority in discovery of land: they had gone ashore on January 21 and brought off rocks and earth. They (though not their dashing captain, who with his family had died in a railway holocaust in 1842) now argued with plausibility that had the Americans been driven from those seas before January 22, no certainty of the existence of land there would have resulted from their explorations.

The explanation Wilkes offered for what one reviewer called the "unusual omission of the most important fact of the cruise in *every* record of its incidents" was shockingly disingenuous: no one on board was anticipating

---

* In his *Synopsis* he had claimed that the land mass extended as far eastward as 160°, but the easternmost point appearing on his map, "Ringgold's Knoll," lay in 158° 30′ E., a difference of thirty to forty miles.

discovery. "Who was there, prior to 1840, either in this country or in Europe," he asked, "that had the least idea that any large body of land existed in the south of New Holland?" The obvious answer was, very many, including Charles Wilkes. The *terra australis incognita*, one of the oldest speculations of geographers, had disappeared from charts only with the voyages of Kerguelen and Cook and remained a literary convention for the allegorical voyage. Wilkes' explanation led the old French mathematician and natural philosopher Jean Baptiste Biot to marvel at the slow pace at which America absorbed European ideas. Wilkes knew of Palmer's Land, indeed had sighted it. He knew of the British captain John Biscoe's discovery, in the *Tula* and *Lively* in 1830–1832, of Enderby Land, just without the Antarctic Circle at about 51° E. He had ordered Pinkney on the *Flying Fish* "to note all appearances of land," and in the *Synopsis* had called attention to the "remarkable circumstance of two national expeditions meeting in this entirely unfrequented sea, with avowedly the same objects in view." Most assuredly those expeditions were expected to come upon something more substantial than wind and currents.*

Wilkes' account of the Antarctic cruise served to no better effect in the dispute with James Ross, which was all over the newspapers on the squadron's return. Ross had sailed in the *Erebus* and *Terror* at the end of September 1839. At Hobart Town in Van Diemen's Land he learned of the French and American discoveries and received Wilkes' long letter on how to explore Antarctic seas, together with a "Tracing of the Icy Barrier attached to the Antarctic Continent discovered by the United States Exploring Expedition." Already a good deal put out that Dumont d'Urville and Wilkes should presume to explore an area they very well knew he was preparing to investigate, he was in no mood to rejoice for them and said so. (His peer in generosity of spirit, Wilkes was to sharply admonish him for "bad taste and egotism.") And in consequence he placed a broad interpretation on his instructions and chose to explore to the eastward, where Balleny had reached 69° the year before.

In January 1841 the ships broke through the ice pack—an unprecedented achievement—into clear water at 69° 15′ S., 176° E., in what is now called the

* Wilkes had not then learned of Captain John Balleny's discovery, in *Eliza Scott* and *Sabrina* in 1839, of the Balleny Islands on the Antarctic Circle between 162° 15′ E. and 164° 45′ E., or of the appearance of land that Balleny had noted in March of that year in about 117° E., which is now considered to be part of the continent and named Sabrina Coast. Wilkes gave this area configuration on his map by virtue of its proximity to one of the landfalls, "Totten High Land."

Ross Sea, to search for the south magnetic pole. On the eleventh they sighted a range of mountains, which Ross named the Admiralty Range, and proceeded southward along it to discover two volcanoes, Mounts Erebus and Terror. Having reached 164° E., they had discovered, Ross proclaimed, Victoria Land, and by stretching to 78° 04′ S. had broken all records for farthest south. (The next year he established yet another *ne plus ultra*, 78° 10′, which was to stand for sixty years.) Returning home in September 1843, Ross was accorded a knighthood instead of a court martial.

On the tracing sent Ross, Wilkes had hatched the area about the position 65° 40′ S., 165° E., the marks indicating to Ross mountainous land trending southwest and northeast a distance of sixty miles. As his ships, dull sailers both, approached this berg-infested position in darkness and gale winds there was much anxiety until daylight showed that they were running over it with land nowhere in sight. And this on such a "perfect Mediterranean day" that land of any altitude would be seen at a distance of sixty or seventy miles. A search of several days went unrewarded.

In reply Wilkes admonished the provincial Englishman that science knows no nationality and chided him for failing to recognize that the hatched area represented, as he now stated, John Balleny's discovery of 1839. The positions were "almost identically the same." But as Ross had sailed over it, he added impudently, Balleny's must have been no discovery after all.

Ross' account of his voyage, published in 1847, took a very lofty view of the American claims and sparked the controversy anew. Debate would drag on into the new century as explorers claimed to have run over Ross' landfalls and Wilkes' and one another's as well. French observers were inclined to be a little amused by the *polémique fort vive* between the Anglo-Saxons and as the controversy only acted to deprive the Expedition of the public confidence it badly needed during its years of mendicancy before Congress and the nation, it was a pity that all parties could not have acquiesced in the judgment of the French observer who concluded that there was glory enough for all: Dumont d'Urville discovered the land, Wilkes explored it to the greatest extent, and Ross visited the portion nearest the pole.*

---

* Bringing out his book in 1847, Ross was in a position to collate the three rival voyages and provide on one chart the outlines of the supposed continent. He found room for Dumont d'Urville's Terre Adélie and supposed (for the Frenchman had seen it only as a sixty-mile-long wall of ice) Côte Clairée, for Graham Land, Enderby's Land, Balleny's Sabrina Land and Islands, and his own Victoria Land. The American landfalls were another matter. Wilkes had explained that his sketch displayed a more or less continuous coastline because he believed himself warranted in

Aside from this controversy, the *Narrative* gave offense to a good many persons. Missionaries, their appetite for praise unsated by Wilkes' almost invariably fulsome observations on the craft, seethed over his uncomplimentary remarks about their warmongering brethren in Tonga. Some of the Californios were offended by the author's belittling references to them, and the Oregon jingoes, metamorphosed into boosters now by the settlement with Great Britain, were incensed by his unfavorable report on the commercial prospects of their river*—but they did appoint a pilot for it.[6]

Then a congressional committee was at Wilkes for having copyrighted his book and brought out extra printings at his own expense very nearly simultaneously with the official edition. But he was firm with the senators and cleared that obstacle by pleading the persecutions he had already suffered at the hands of government. He maintained a list of persecutions that was quite up to date. High on this list were the efforts by twelve lieutenants and a passed midshipman memorializing Congress to hear their defense against the libels upon them and their distant shipmates.

Wilkes acted promptly in urging the Library Committee, to which the memorial was conveniently referred, not to allow "the Cabal" possession of the logs, which, bent on destroying the Expedition, they would not hesitate to alter. After some dithering, he finally decided that the Committee's best course lay in "putting down this memorial entirely" by printing his reply, announcing that further investigation would not be deemed necessary (thereby saving valuable time and showing "Charity" toward the memorialists) and issuing as its report the model he provided. All of which the Committee dutifully did.

---

laying down the land, "not only where we had actually determined it to exist, but in those places in which every appearance denoted its existence." Ross, professing to be taken aback by the practice, "entirely new amongst navigators," of laying down the land where it was not seen, concluded in the interest of accuracy to ignore the American landfalls, except insofar as they confirmed the discoveries of explorers who showed greater respect for geographical science.

* The Expedition's work in Oregon probably affected the final settlement by persuading Britain that the United States was not prepared to accept the Columbia as the boundary. In opposition to Senator Thomas Hart Benton and others who favored compromising at the forty-ninth parallel, Wilkes pointed out to Congress in 1846 that, as the Columbia's mouth would never provide a suitable harbor, the United States must hold out for the Straits of Juan de Fuca, Vancouver Island, and Queen Charlotte Sound. His testimony was promptly substantiated by the latest news from Oregon. Dispatched in the twelve-gun schooner *Shark* to establish the American presence there, Lieutenant Neil M. Howison had taken aboard a pilot, a black man who said he had been there six years (no doubt the *Peacock*'s erstwhile cook, James De Sauls, who had deserted after the wreck) and who took charge with a knowing air, but, Howison reported tersely, "In twenty minutes he ran us ashore on Chinook shoal." Though Howison succeeded in refloating her, the *Shark* was finally carried on the south spit and went down a total loss almost atop the *Peacock*. All hands escaped to set up camp at Astoria and build their first fire from what they took to be planks from the *Peacock* that littered the beach. Howison's report on the river's commercial possibilities was unenthusiastic.

It was as Henry Eld once remarked of this man in a moment of admiration: "like a cork he cannot be sunk." But victory had its price: the bickering and maneuvering would ultimately cost Wilkes and the Expedition a good deal of credit in Congress and the rest of the nation.[7]

20 Democratic Science

They live in the future, and make their country as they go
on.

Francis J. Grund, *Aristocracy in America*, 1839

Amos Binney, the Boston naturalist and authority on land
mollusks, was familiar with the results of the various French and English
expeditions; and when Pickering showed him through the Patent Office, he
saw at once that these "discoveries made by our friends" equaled and perhaps
surpassed in quantity and significance those of any previous expedition. "The
attention of the scientific world," another visitor announced, was now focused
on Washington, awaiting "with much anxiety" the government's response to
the claims of science.

In the years since the squadron had sailed, American scientists had hardly
been able to believe the good fortune to science and now they watched closely
to see what steps the government would take to make the results public. If
placed in the proper hands the enterprise promised to go a long way toward
advancing the sciences, not alone by making the results available to
investigators, but also by establishing a precedent for government patronage.
Beyond that, as Binney remarked, it promised to do "great honor to the
scientific character of the Country." Many another was inclined to wonder
whether the movers of events in Washington were fully aware what such an
accomplishment required of them. Binney only hinted at what was required
when he pointed out that the publications must fully illustrate every new
specimen, showing its anatomy in precise detail, for one of the great desiderata
of natural history at mid-century was "the execution of accurate figures which
may forever be referred to as authentic and correct." Only the government
could hope to undertake such a task successfully.

Moreover, publication must be prompt. The Boston conchologist A. A. Gould, admittedly eager to arrange the shells, called attention to the new species from the Ross and Dumont d'Urville expeditions that, already being described, were stealing glory from the American expedition.

Liberality and promptness, then, were required of Congress. At the very thought Audubon retreated into reverie, to muse on what he would make of the enterprise, "did I possess the wealth of the Emperor of Russia, or the King of the French." But James De Kay, who had been serving as geologist with the New York State Survey since declining J. N. Reynolds' invitation to join the explorers, now added his practical voice to the many pleading with Tappan to make certain that the publications were done in a creditable fashion. He had some experience in these matters, and estimated that the engraving and printing for the New York survey, although not yet completed, would certainly cost at least $150,000. As the explorers had surveyed not a state but a world, the expense would be correspondingly greater. That much understood, De Kay concluded, "the expense of the publication should not for a moment be considered."

But the matter of expense was one to which Tappan, Wilkes, and everyone involved had to give no end of consideration. Early in 1843, at the urging of Senator Tappan, who was anxious to get a further appropriation for publication, the scientists made an informed estimate of what they had in hand. Dana found that the geological report would require a volume of some four hundred pages, with forty-five quarto plates to illustrate the three hundred fossil species collected, many of which were new discoveries. Of the four hundred species of corals, some two hundred were either entirely new or their animals were (a hundred of the latter were already drawn and colored) and these would require some sixty folio plates and a volume of three hundred pages devoted to species descriptions and a long article on the structure and formation of coral reefs and islands. Of the thousand species of crustacea, Dana estimated that upwards of six hundred were new. Drawings were already made of five hundred species, fewer than fifty of which had been previously described. Another three-hundred-page volume and ninety folio plates would see this job properly done. He thought that all four volumes might possibly be completed in a year's time if an artist were engaged to complete the corals.

Peale, in his departments, found eleven new species of mammals in the fifty collected, and fifty new species of birds out of the one thousand specimens. Together, these would require some four hundred pages of description and at least fifty plates. The latter he could turn out at the rate of one a week if an adequate library were available—his own had gone down with the *Peacock* and the Library of Congress was wholly inadequate to the purpose—and if he were allowed to take specimens to his rooms, where the day might be "devoted to drawing, and the evening to the preparation of mss."

The sheer bulk of the botanical collections made estimates difficult, and the Oregon and California plants had not yet arrived by the summer of 1843.* Some cases were never to arrive. In the greenhouse, where Brackenridge was caring for the live plants, eleven hundred plants, representing two hundred and fifty-four species, were growing nicely in pots and others springing up from the seeds of an additional six hundred and eighty-four species. Most of these Brackenridge had collected himself. After a cursory inventory, the official head of the botanical department, the ineffectual Rich, estimated that one hundred folio plates and five hundred octavo pages of letterpress would suffice for the new genera and species. (In consequence of his inattentiveness Rich found himself dismissed from the corps until he had apologized and provided a more exact estimate.) If all went well the plants collected up to the squadron's arrival at the Sandwich Islands might be described and drawn by the next session of Congress.

Horatio Hale thought he could make do with two volumes for the philology and ethnography, one hundred plates for portraits and illustrations of crania and native artifacts, and some maps to illustrate the ethnological provinces.

Congress responded with a magnanimity that seemed breathtaking—at first glance—for the volumes of the *Narrative* were lavish and set a good precedent in the high quality of engraving and printing. But all the publications were to be limited to one hundred copies: after all, the reports were only to proclaim America's scientific accomplishment to an admiring world. To scientists both at home and abroad this restriction could only signify a contempt for science, particularly since the additional cost of printing a thousand copies, once the plates were made and the type set, would be negligible. As matters stood, almost none of the copies would be available to the scientists themselves, for by another resolution even the few to be printed were not to be sold but held for presentation to the several states, foreign governments, and the command-ers of the *Vincennes, Peacock,* and *Porpoise.* The only way an author could have a copy of his own work was to have the scribbled-over proof-sheets bound. As these limitations did not apply to the charts, the botanist or

* Tracing these required some detective work. Pickering discovered that the vessel on which they had been shipped from the Sandwich Islands at the end of 1840—direct for the United States, it was supposed—had touched at Valparaiso, then proceeded on a voyage to China, thence to Europe, where she was sold. The plants stayed in her and were unloaded at Havana on her next voyage, and Pickering was then endeavoring to get them passage to Washington.

geologist was left to conclude that only the "useful" sciences were to be honored with adequate printings.

However, further appropriations would in any case be necessary along the way, and it was felt that Congress could perhaps be brought to see its error. If not, there was always the path that Wilkes took with his *Narrative*, when he secured copyright and plates and printed as many copies as he pleased.

Publication of the reports was an enterprise of unprecedented magnitude. Scientists, artists, and engravers weary of giftbooks and banknotes—including J. F. Watson in Philadelphia, who had been Jeremiah Reynolds' companion in Chile—called attention to the contributions they could make. Down the crowded years they came to labor for a time among the collections and go away again for reasons as various as their natures. Some completed their tasks. Replacements had to be found for others. For Wilkes it became a way of life as he saw himself a scientist among his peers, yet a warrior still—the Cincinnatus of Science, one might say. Wilkes took command of his scientific crew with his customary addiction to discipline, his correspondence full of the military imperative. But as over the years he was forced more and more to rely on scientists who had not sailed in his command and were men of stature in the community of learning, he was compelled to relax his manner somewhat, on occasion to reason them out of some ill-found prejudice or other, humoring them as it were.

It was a lesson that did not come easily and as his "quarter deck insolence," as John Torrey irately called it, did not sit well with many, he was fortunate the while in having the services of Joseph Drayton and Hudson's erstwhile clerk Fred Stuart. Both developed a fine talent for getting things done. An engraver, draughtsman, and expert print colorist, Drayton had a wide acquaintance within these crafts that served him well as he dispensed contracts and developed a sharp eye for the frauds of the go-getting entrepreneur. He was adept, too, at the infinitely delicate enterprise of persuading authors to observe some reasonable approximation to deadlines. He bore them no reverence. "It has been a long settled fact, that these d——d proffessors have all kinds of sence, but common sence," he wrote Wilkes after one particularly trying exchange. No more in awe of politicians, he simply designated his congressional bosses "Boss A," "Boss B," and so on and, by a variety of devices—he once appealed to Gray to name a new species for a member of Congress friendly to the Expedition—managed to remain on good terms with all, even, indeed especially, with Wilkes, to whose children he was always Father Drayton.[1]

At the outset, the Expedition scientists were duly grateful to Tappan and

Wilkes for breaking with European precedent to decree that the explorers themselves should write up the reports. When amateur naturalists of means and political influence at the highest level sought to displace them, Dana spoke for all the corps in observing to Professor Silliman that though Tappan was a less genial master than one might wish, "his stubbornness" was needed in the face of attempts at "delivering over the departments to the lowest bidder."

But in the end the policy proved not to be feasible. The magnitude of the collections made the task an immense one for the individual scientist, who in some departments, most notably botany, had to work with many thousand specimens. And although it was soon decided that only new species should be described, one still had to determine which were new. Doing so involved examination by microscope, an instrument in such short supply in the country that as late as 1847 only one was available to the corps in Washington. And the latest journals published at home and abroad had to be consulted, as well as the standard authorities. This done, one might still remain uncertain of precisely what one's predecessor had described, necessitating a search of the predecessor's collection. Having determined that the Expedition's specimen did indeed represent a new discovery, one had then to communicate the information to fellow investigators by describing and drawing it. Of course the opportunity to examine, describe, and name new species and to do so not in the hours left from tending patients or parishioners, but as a full-time occupation for which one was paid a salary, was attractive indeed, and many naturalists in the country would have leaped to it—a fact of which the chosen were ever aware as they labored and grumbled in Washington.

Their grumbles were legitimate enough. First among them was the requirement that the work be done in Washington. Designed to prevent the loss of specimens and the disruption of their display, it seemed a reasonable enough rule to those not actually doing the work. And even to those who were, Washington was acceptable for the first few months after their return. Any city would have been, and Dana for one was agreeably surprised to discover "so much good preaching in this center of gayety and fashion." By the spring of 1843 the Patent Office was humming with activity and the enterprise moving along as nicely as one could wish. Dana was indefatigable in preparing his materials for publication, and there was no doubt in Pickering's mind that he would "get out something that will do honour to the Country." Peale, who was working mostly in his own rooms, hurried in from time to time to seek out some skin or carcass, and even Rich was observed to be "industriously engaged." But preaching aside, the city held few attractions for someone whose career was outside politics; and the lack of books—the Library of

Congress limped along on a small annual appropriation and was much behind in collecting the latest journals—and the absence of like-minded investigators, made it the last city where a scientist would have chosen to labor. Hale, who was not bound to the natural history collections, insisted on working in Philadelphia, and other members of the corps were forever hurrying off to Philadelphia or Boston to consult the standard works. Their absences gradually lengthened until they were journeying instead to Washington when absolutely necessary. For the rest, Drayton and often Wilkes himself were away, hurrying up and down the seaboard to consult with the Scientific Gentlemen. When in 1846 Tappan decided "to *drive* the team myself for a while" and ordered Dana to Washington, the geologist simply refused, willing if it came to that to give up the appointment. "It is perfectly absurd that I should be able to prepare my reports in a city where there are no books," he complained to Gray.

But the intellectually sterile atmosphere of the capital was not the sole reason for withdrawal. The miles the scientists were able to put between themselves and Wilkes and Tappn represented so many units of freedom from regulations they often thought preposterous and always found restrictive. There was something of an uproar in 1843—indeed it became a cause célèbre in the scientific community for a time—when Wilkes announced a policy based on "modest merit." Couthouy had reluctantly withdrawn from the corps, complaining that the National Institute men had so mistreated the specimens in his absence that he could no longer make heads nor tails of them—though the real reason was probably his realization of his inadequacy to what was essentially a task for the learned specialist, in critical ways a different one from the collector's. When Pickering, who it was assumed would succeed to the shells, set sail for the Red Sea instead, Augustus A. Gould applied for the appointment, promising to complete the report with dispatch. But Wilkes, who seemingly had learned nothing about the limits to what the untutored might attain in science by sheer industry, insisted that Joseph Drayton, who had already drawn many of the shells, could perform the task well enough. "There is one thing about the Expedition that I have always looked to with satisfaction hitherto," he wrote, "that it will show and does show already what can be done by unknown and . . . untried hands." True, a conchologist's descriptions might be "very different" and "more scientifically written," but with the advice of some "among the many friends of the Expedition" knowledgeable in shells and Latin, Drayton would provide accurate ones enough.

When Gould urged haste, for "every steamer brings intelligence of objects newly described abroad," Wilkes was unmoved. To his mind the collections represented a fund of opportunity for the worthy and industrious, access to which he was duty bound to keep open. Curiously in one ruthless enough in reaching for the goals of personal ambition, he took a generous (and quite false) view of rivalry in science. A few months delay would not matter: "Every one must be aware of the time when our collections were made."

Appalled at such innocence, Gould pointed out to Tappan what was surely obvious to one who had himself published scientific papers: "It is not the date of the *discovery* of an object which gives precedence to it among scientific men, but the date of *publication*." To him who first described went the prescriptive right to name the species. Claims of loyalty were irrelevant here, and Gould advised following the precedent of European explorers: simply procure "the best science & the greatest expedition," and ignore all other considerations. "It would be no credit to your Conchologist," he informed Tappan, "to be publishing a book of old stories, as something new."

Amos Binney backed him up and urged immediate publication of short technical descriptions of new species in the proceedings of some of the scientific societies. "In matters of Natural History," he bluntly informed Tappan, "Capt Wilkes has not sufficient information to enable him to judge, what the arrangements in those departments should be, what the present condition of the Science requires, or what is due to the scientific character of the country." Still conceiving it his duty "to protect modest merit all in my power," Wilkes professed in his inimitable way to be "not a little astonished to see these references to Europe," where opportunities were open only to the few—"thank God it is not the case on this side of the Atlantic & I trust it never will be in my day." Though William Reynolds would have explained Wilkes' tender concern for modest merit in science as much of a piece with his employment in marine surveying of the modest talents of Hudson and Ringgold, Wilkes was actually no less solicitous of the national character than were Binney and Gould. The difference was that to his way of thinking that character was to be read as much in the chances the country afforded a worthy man to get ahead as it was in scientific accomplishment. He clung to his doctrine of democracy in science with a tenacity that Tappan was able to overcome only after a year's delay that cost the Expedition more new species, and then only by suggesting that concern for Drayton was all very well, but the Expedition must come first.

How damaging such delay could be was well brought out in the fate of the entomological specimens. Prowling through the collections in the Patent Office early in 1845, Peale discovered a box of insects supposed to have been lost and saw that many represented new species. As most of the other insect specimens had gone down with the *Peacock*, these were few and the usable ones fewer still, owing to neglect and loss of the tags signifying locality.[2]

But the number of competent entomologists in the country was also small. Tappan approached Samuel S. Haldeman of Philadelphia, a well-known conchologist who was taking an interest in entomology. But Haldeman was reluctant, pointing out that neither collections nor the requisite books were to be found in the United States. Of course, should he be allowed to take the specimens to Paris, Berlin, or London, that would be a different matter. But though he promised to preserve them from the prying eyes of foreigners, he clearly had little hope for his proposal. Then it was discovered that the Expedition specimens had become mixed with those of the Institute. As only Pickering knew both collections well enough to separate them, all work in this department was at a standstill until his return. Two years later, and after some haggling over terms, Wilkes engaged John Lawrence Le Conte, twenty-two years old and fresh from medical school, to write up the report in six months for a hundred and fifty dollars. (Wilkes hoped he would do it gratuitously but in the end had to order some books for him as well, which he then hoped the Smithsonian would buy "& thus relieve our fund.") The manuscript was duly delivered, but publication was delayed. Within four years the species had all been described by others and Le Conte's work never saw print.

Clinging to his precepts of discipline, Wilkes also failed to see that his publication policies could not be made to apply with equal force to all the sciences. Dana, especially, chafed under the injunction that only new species be published, for in the corals he found material for "the most complete work on the subject ever published." The few studies in print were less than satisfactory, and even the best of them were without figures. Corals were so peculiar in their forms and so little known that description alone conveyed little idea of the species, and drawing one species in a genus was not sufficient as it was in conchology. Relaxation of the rule came to seem the more urgent as Dana worked through the collection. Having described one hundred and ninety new species by November 1844, and having found that the same name had been applied to many distinct corals and different names to others that were identical, he crisply informed Wilkes that adding new species was really of less importance than correcting existing errors.

But even here Wilkes knew best. He assured Tappan—not entirely in jest—that he and Drayton knew more about the coral collection than Dana, whose importunities need cause no concern. Wilkes was inclined to view any deviation from the rules and regulations as self-seeking and possibly mutinous, and when on receipt of the manuscript he discovered that Dana had interpreted the rule as he saw fit, even to including a notice on zoophytes in general, there was trouble. But Dana stood his ground and summoned all the support he could, overshooting a link or two in the chain of command to carry his appeal to Senator George Perkins Marsh, a known friend to science. Beyond that he laid plans for supplanting Wilkes with a committee of scientists who would oversee the publications. At this point Asa Gray, who in 1842 had taken over Harvard's Fisher Professorship of Natural History, hastened to his friend's aid. Having read the proof sheets of the book, he thought its plan quite proper. Dana's discoveries, he pointed out to Tappan, had been not alone of "new facts, but *new principles* also," and it was these which rendered Dana's "*the* standard work" on the subject and thereby connected "fully and forever" the "expedition with the systematic history of the Zoophytes." For what it was worth, Gray added that at the Royal Society in London he had heard "high eulogium" passed upon Dana's work and sarcastically advised that something might be safely left to the author's "discretion in minor matters, as to what it is necessary or proper to publish."

Beyond the jealousy with which Wilkes guarded his power, Gray perceived the issue with precision: there was no room in Wilkes' plan of publication for presentation of new principles. Gray made little attempt to conceal his astonishment that a naval officer and a Senator should presume to question the decision of a scientist in a scientific matter. Privately, he did not bother. "Wilkes demurs against the publication of extraneous matter," he scribbled on the back of an envelope, "A pretty fellow he who has fitted up his volumes not only with what he has *stolen* from his Corps—but with all sorts of stuff, borrowed."

Dana had his way in the end, in part because of the support of Gray and others, but also because he went at his work with a single-minded determination that left the rest of the corps somewhat shaken and convinced Wilkes of his indispensibility. Drayton put him down as one of "the Workies of the Ex. Ex." The young man's career was launched, as he himself was well aware. He read a string of papers before the Association of Geologists in 1843 and 1844 and fairly peppered *Silliman's* with contributions, which, being occasionally pompous and falsely modest, displayed something of the cannibal instinct not uncommon among emerging aspirants in the professions. In the spring of 1843 he turned on his friend Couthouy and publicly accused him of having committed plagiarism in a paper on corals that Couthouy had read before the Boston Society of Natural History in December 1841.* In making the "simple

* The quality of Couthouy's paper gave Dana sufficient grounds for alarm, for it was an astonishing performance. In opposition to Charles Lyell, he came out strong for the Darwinian

and courteous, but decided" charge, as he characterized it, Dana announced that he was impelled by no feelings of animosity but "solely a regard for right," solely "the interests of science." His notes and journals still missing, the flabbergasted Couthouy fortunately was able to produce letters written to friends at home which proved his ideas to be his own. Dana publicly withdrew the charge at the next meeting of the Association with expressions of "deep regret," but in no confusion. The retraction was as forthright as the accusation.[3]

Activae pustulata. (James D. Dana, *Zoophytes: Atlas,* Plate 1, No. 2, Western Americana Collection, Yale University Library.)

Ethnography and Philology was the first of the reports to appear. Hale had completed the manuscript while the *Narrative* was still in press, then, leaving the proofreading to his redoubtable mother, he had set off for Europe and the East in search of more vocabularies. The book came out in the spring of 1846. Dana was close behind. He completed the coral manuscript at the end of February 1845, but because the text contained references to the plates of the companion atlas, publication was delayed until the tedious task of engraving was well underway. *Zoophytes* thus appeared in the spring of 1846, some

---

view of the role that subsidence played in the formation of coral reefs, citing much specific evidence in substantiation, and he did it all from memory. In the midst of the dispute that followed, Couthouy's notes and journals, which, committed to Wilkes' custody, had been missing since the time of the courts martial, were triumphantly found and opened to Dana's inspection by Tappan and Wilkes.

copies with a preface, and some—by Wilkes' order—without. The Atlas, with all of its one thousand and eight drawings done by Dana himself, followed three years later. He submitted his geology report before the end of 1846 but with too many maps and drawings—nearly four hundred—for the budget to accommodate. At Wilkes' suggestion these were reduced to four maps and one hundred and sixty-one small figures in the text (all done by Dana), and that volume came off the press at the end of 1848. The geology Atlas appeared the following year, after which Dana settled down to work on the crustacea.

Wilkes was pleased with the books and with the enthusiastic reception accorded them by reviewers fortunate enough to see them either in manuscript or in the author's unofficial issue. Tappan was so pleased—his own gilded set made a handsome display on the shelves—that he concluded the Expedition could stand on its own feet. Full of years though still vigorous, he had given up his Senate seat in March 1845 but he had remained as the Committee's agent for the publications. He had also continued to work hard on plans for the Smithsonian Institution, so that it might serve to increase scientific knowledge and provide a museum to house the Expedition collections. Confident by the spring of 1846 that they would get "a good Smithsonian bill" passed, he turned in a full report on the progress made by the Expedition's scientists, and with it his resignation.

Wilkes bade goodbye to a warm and influential friend, but the transition was the easier as he was elevated to Tappan's place as agent of the Committee. More disruptive was the death in January 1846, to the grief of all, of the amiable and hardworking artist, Alfred Agate, at the age of thirty-three. As he left his natural history drawings only half completed, a replacement had to be found. The new chairman of the Library Committee seemed all that Wilkes could have wished for—the quiet, dignified, and utterly humorless Whig senator from Maryland's Eastern Shore, James Alfred Pearce. A Princeton man and professor of law, he was regarded as a scholar, at least by fellow senators, with whom he had a reputation for being the chief protector of science and scientists in government.

Wilkes took command briskly, ordering the scientists to report on their progress forthwith and every two months thereafter and announcing that no disbursements would be made without his signature. But his tribulations were multiplied, for he had to pass on every detail now, even the most trivial—the purchase of charcoal, lime, and plant tubs for the greenhouse, of water-closets for the Gallery (such was the volume of visitors), the lending of Expedition skulls to Seth Eastman for illustrating the great national work on the Indians, and of other natural history specimens to Professor Silliman for his course of lectures in Washington. Some troubles were simply beyond solution, as when Drayton called one morning at Adams' Express in Philadelphia to collect a bundle of Gould's manuscript and discovered that "Adams' dog, during the night of its arrival here, chewed it all to pieces."

Relations with Congress proved less difficult than might have been supposed. Each new Congress roiled the waters a bit but rarely threatened to sink the enterprise. Wilkes had a way with politicians that proved invaluable over the years, as congressional patience wore thin at the Expedition's ever-growing demands. By 1846 the estimate was eighteen volumes of text and eleven atlases, to be completed in two years at a cost of one hundred thousand dollars.[4]

Wilkes viewed the scientists as the most persistently aggravating of the problems he faced. The defections began with Couthouy. The shock of the knowledgeable Pickering's departure was cushioned by the understanding that he was taking leave only to further his researches and would return to write the reports. But Peale and Rich were another matter. Peale had returned from the cruise, his "exile," he called it, to find his children "running wild" and his own prospects bleak. After describing his sixty new species of mammals and birds, which would "form a very pretty volume, if completed," he would be out of employment and could only look forward to a reward of "poverty, and a broken constitution." He grumbled at the lack of books in Washington and at his salary, which was once, like that of the rest of the corps, three months in arrears while "our masters" were off electioneering and Wilkes was in Philadelphia, "looking after *his book* while we poor devils have to market on credit, whine to our landlords, and bully our shoemakers." What was worse, three of these terrible Washington years carried off as many members of his family—a baby, his wife, and his beloved daughter Florida, whom he had delighted with seashells and affectionate letters from the world's far places. And, considering himself an experienced museum man, he resented Pickering's appointment as curator—the more so as President Jackson (as Peale recalled) had told him before the cruise that he had it in mind to establish a national museum with Smithson's money and the explorers' specimens and that Peale, naturally, should be intimately associated with it.

Peale was indeed more of a museum man and painter than a systematic naturalist. He had learned his natural history in tramping the fields and brakes with his flamboyant father, friend of Presidents and Indian chiefs alike, in search of specimens for their famous museum. Then by wielding art and science on the Long Expedition, he had emerged as one of the rising lights of American natural history. Many established naturalists had thought him quite well qualified to advise the commander of the great expedition to the South Seas and fully approved his forthright recommendation to trim away the fripperies of specialism from the scientific corps. His father dead now, the venerable museum little more than a sideshow, Peale was puzzled and angry when he found his claim before Congress, for personal losses suffered in the sinking of the *Peacock*, opposed by his erstwhile commander on the ground that he had been "incompetent to his position" in the first place. That was not necessarily so. The world moves on and science with it, sometimes after the fashion of the great Fijian war canoes that Tanoa was said to have launched upon ways of human bodies. That Peale now found himself adrift was a measure of how far science had traveled during the century. The sound he heard was not so much (as he thought) the malicious muttering of Charles Wilkes as it was the bell of time tolling the passing of the old-fashioned naturalist and summoning to his stead the coolly proficient writer of technical monographs, who addressed himself not to Nature but to atoms and cells. Peale never fully grasped the implications of what had happened when art and science went their separate ways.

Peale was too proud to accept Pickering's aid, but when his Philadelphia friends discreetly confided to Wilkes that someone must be found to revise and correct the manuscript and Wilkes circumspectly made the necessary arrangements, it seemed for a time that the mammals and birds would be ready when called for. By the end of 1846, the manuscript was completed— even to the Latin descriptions, which had to be farmed out—and in the hands of the copyist. Then things began to go wrong. Already suspicious that Peale was plotting with the "cabal" of officers, Wilkes found that he had disobeyed orders by writing an introduction (which was also "very objectionable" in tone) and by neglecting to include a catalogue of all the species collected. Finally, he had given the book too general a title, "Zoology." Wilkes had the introduction deleted, a catalogue inserted, and, for the sake of economy, ordered the backgrounds of the plates sharply reduced. Peale was not flattered. Fed up with the Expedition, he descended the grand staircase beneath Wilkes' big signboard and took a job as Assistant Examiner of Patents. Wilkes angrily consoled himself that it was "happy riddance," the plates would be finished anyway. By whom, he failed to suggest.

Peale's book, mutilated and promising eighty-four plates that had never appeared, was in press near the end of 1848, but shortly afterward Wilkes held up distribution, possibly even the printing. The search for an artist dragged on for a year before Wilkes concluded that the drawings yet to be made might best be done under the close supervision of someone "better informed" than

Peale—someone who might also prepare a supplement to his faulty text. In June 1850, Drayton, who spent much of his time in Philadelphia overlooking the engraving, sat down to examine a copy of Peale's book with John Cassin, Corresponding Secretary of the Academy of Natural Sciences and owner and manager of Philadelphia's principal engraving firm. An expert at the technical monograph, Cassin was the very model of the new specialist in natural history. He was able to point out several species marked as new that were really "as old as the hills," as well as a number of errors in syntax and Latin and at Drayton's urging agreed to examine the collections in Washington and name a price for finishing the job. It was an awkward situation, one scientist's taking up the unfinished work of another, but to Drayton's surprise, Cassin "brightened up like a Drummond light" and announced "that as Mr. Peale has abandoned the work he dont know what he has got to do with Mr. P." He found Cassin to be the very "Pork & Beans." [5]

John Cassin well knew where the future of science lay—and his own as well, as Wilkes was to learn when Drayton's initially confident feelers dragged into two years of tedious negotiations. When once it was decided that the book must be rewritten and Wilkes proposed terms, Cassin only laughed and countered with terms of his own that staggered the commander. Cassin could "do the thing up brown," Drayton reported, for two thousand a year for five years. Wilkes had no choice, and in August 1852 Cassin was able to report to a friend that he had received "a very polite letter" from Wilkes—by his reckoning only the second such in all the welter of their correspondence—with the information that the "Hon. Comm." had accepted his terms.

Cassin met his deadline promptly and his *Mammalogy and Ornithology* with atlas appeared in 1858, a triumph of the new science. Some ten of the nineteen woodcuts in the text were Peale's, as were thirty-two of the fifty-three plates in the atlas, and though many of the classifications and descriptions were new, the text drew heavily from the field notes of Peale and Pickering. Cassin took meticulous care to give full credit to each.

It had been a bothersome business for Wilkes but no more than that. Developments in the department of botany were a good deal more threatening. Ever the amateur in science, Wilkes envisioned a single author for the botanical report, and an American one at that. Though this science had branched into separate studies of phanerogamia, cryptogamia, filices, lichens, musci, algae, fungi, and still another on the geographical distribution of all, there is no evidence that Wilkes was led to reflect on his own naïvete in once having flattered old Dickerson by agreeing that the scientific corps was too large. The process of specialization was now developing at such a pace that by

Procellaria nived. (John Cassin, *Mammalogy and Ornithology: Atlas*, plate 42, Western Americana Collection, Yale University Library.)

the time the last of the botanical reports was published, even J. N. Reynolds' views were long outdated. To meet this onslaught of proliferation all Wilkes had to offer was William Rich.

In the spring of 1846 the Ohio botanist William Starling Sullivant called at the Patent Office to view the collections. "Lots of new genera and species," he reported happily. But he found the official botanist "a used up case" with a "very scanty library & still scantier brains to use it." By this time it was clear even to Wilkes that the dilatory Rich was not to be entrusted with the writing of anything like the complete report, and he determined to restrict him to the flora of the Pacific islands, give the ferns to Brackenridge, and the rest to Pickering (who returned home that summer) and perhaps to non-exploring scientists as well. When a year later no manuscript or even parts of one had been submitted, Wilkes assured Rich, with unwonted tact, that the assistance of Pickering and Brackenridge would be available to him at all times and "most cheerfully rendered." With that assistance, presumably, and that of professors at Georgetown College in furnishing the Latin descriptions, Rich submitted his manuscript before the end of 1846. Then, to the astonishment of everyone, he suddenly saw his patriotic duty, joined the army and went off to California.*

Wilkes and everyone else who read the manuscript soon discovered the reason behind the fit of patriotism. It was so "good for nothing" that only the costly engravings would be salvageable, and perhaps not even those, for Rich had taken little care in dissection and had not even troubled to name the new genera and species. No other botanist who valued his reputation would touch it. Wilkes suddenly expressed mortification that a man "so incompetent" should have been employed by the Expedition and chose to blame Asa Gray, of all people, on the pretense that Gray had recommended him. Pickering and Brackenridge would have to do the descriptions anew. And Wilkes hoped to utilize John Torrey, Gray's mentor and peer, who, knowing that Rich had done "nothing but smoke cigars & tell Stories during the Expedn.," was privately eager to take it up himself "& so do good to the cause of Botany, while I draw a little pay from the Treasury!" but he had had a disappointing experience many years before with Stephen Long's government exploring expedition and was chary.

The great obstacle stemmed from Wilkes' ignorance of the strides botany had made during the century. To his mind a botanist was just that and equally at home with all species. Aside from setting Brackenridge to the ferns and young Edward Tuckerman of the talented Boston family to the Cryptogams, he clung to the notion of turning over the rest to one investigator. The sharply contrasting view of the professional botanist was well summed up by Asa Gray when he wrote to his English friend Joseph D. Hooker (to whom he wished the Antarctic plants might be assigned) that as matters stood he himself would not think of touching any but the Oregon and California plants, considering

---

* In 1846 the Expedition also lost the services of its cartographers, when Budd, Totten, and Eld went on active duty.

himself "totally incompetent to do such a work without making it a special study for some years, and going abroad to study the collections accumulated in Europe." Torrey told Wilkes the same thing to his face. "No one botanist could do justice to such an immense collection." He suggested that the proper mode of proceeding would be to give editorship to one man and farm out the principal families to monographers, including Europeans. "It will have to come to this, sooner or later, if the plants are to be published at all," he admonished.

Wilkes merely "pughed at the suggestion—& said the work must be done at home." When informed that he must secure a foreigner to describe the algae, he declared that he could not believe it and would be "mortified to think that in all our population of some 20,000,000 there cannot be found one who is willing to undertake to describe them." Wilkes and Torrey finally came to terms of a sort in April 1847 when Wilkes offered him fifteen hundred dollars for descriptions of the Oregon and California plants alone and sealed the agreement by sending off two boxes of specimens. But what of the thousands of other specimens? Mindful of the necessity to economize, Wilkes gave thought again to Rich's miserable manuscript. It had cost him four thousand dollars: surely it could not be totally useless. But to his annoyance Gray and Pickering agreed that it was beyond salvage and refused to complete the descriptions. What he called "The doggedness of the one and the obstinacy of the other" put the commander quite out of patience. He appointed a new committee of Torrey, Pickering, and, to embrace the "practical as well as the scientific branches," Brackenridge. To his dismay, they unanimously pronounced the manuscript worthless. "This is going a little too far," he complained to the chairman of the Library Committee. Confronted with another "clique," this one endeavoring "to produce the impression that there are but three or four botanists in the U.S. who are competent," he determined to deal with it as he had dealt with cabals on the cruise—by employing "some talented young botanist who has ambition and a desire for distinction." He turned to the Reverend Moses Ashley Curtis, reported to be a good botanist, a hard worker, and a poor man. The task would surely be "a great object to him in a pecuniary point of view." But although Curtis was approached with delicacy and some butter—it would be too much to say that the commander was mellowing, but he was gaining an unaccustomed grasp of the amenities—he nevertheless declined. Wilkes next turned to Dr. George Engelmann of St. Louis, a German immigrant and one of the rising lights of American botany. But there was no help there either.

As Torrey had frankly told Wilkes, Engelmann was his final resort before turning to Gray. And that was an awkward step to take, for Asa Gray, he felt, had abandoned the Expedition on the eve of sailing, acquiesced in the appointment of that presumptuous incompetent Rich, advised that plants be sent abroad, publicly ridiculed the "concentrated intelligence" of the Library Committee for the policy of limited printing, and now was refusing to help "poor Rich." Back he went to Torrey with a new proposal. Would he take over all the botany, employing whomever he chose to do the parts? The serpentine mind was seeking to take by subterfuge what it could otherwise capture only at too high a cost in pride. Wilkes was aware that Torrey and Gray were collaborating on a Flora Americana and had concluded that by enlisting Torrey, "We should have the talents of both." But Wilkes, never very adept with muffled oars, failed and was faced with disorder in the botanical department. He could not abide disorder, and Gray accepted his surrender gracefully. Not wanting to force the commander's hand on the matter of European specialists, Gray substituted a trip to Europe at government expense to do the work in "Hooker's or [George] Bentham's, or Garden of Plants herbarium" and otherwise set his own price—one hundred and twenty dollars a month for five years—a stiff one that Wilkes met without quibbling. Gray was even able to bring in his favorite draughtsman, Isaac Sprague, who had come to his trade via carriage painting in his youth.[6]

It was a victory not only for Asa Gray and for botany, over the provincial commander; not only for the scientific community over the "big folks" in Washington, as Brackenridge called his political masters in tolerant contempt; but also for the scientist over the naturalist and thus for the cause of American science. The best possible man had been secured, one who promised to bring forth the Botany "in the best & most creditable manner." Thus Gray rejoined the expedition for which J. N. Reynolds had selected him a dozen years earlier. Neither he nor Torrey could know that they were joining for life. When Gray journeyed with his bride to Washington in June and called at the greenhouse, Brackenridge told him that with Torrey's help the job "could be done" in three years but probably would take somewhat longer owing to the "few small stumbling blocks" that would occasionally appear in the way.

At long last it seemed that the botanical department would be able to stand unaided. Brackenridge's Ferns was proceeding apace under the fostering eye of Torrey, ever ready with words of encouragement ("You know far more of the subject than I") books, advice, and gossip foreign and domestic from the world of botany with which the unknown horticulturalist had little personal acquaintance. Just before graduating from Harvard in 1846, young Edward Tuckerman, another of Gray's circle, took charge of the lichens on the sole condition that he not be required to work in Washington. He completed his part of the job to everyone's satisfaction within the year. William Starling Sullivant, the Ohio surveyor turned botanist and soon to be acknowledged as the country's premier bryologist, took over the mosses. (Knowing Sullivant to be independently wealthy, Wilkes delicately suggested that money was not to be mentioned in connection with Science, offered none, paid none, and proudly reported his coup to the Library Committee, unaware that for his part Sullivant was anticipating "smart money.") The small collection of algae went to Jacob Whitman Bailey (1811–1857), professor of chemistry and geology at West Point and a pioneer American microscopist. Moses Ashley Curtis agreed to do up the few fungi (he found eight of the thirty-one species to be new) and was paid one hundred dollars to alleviate his poverty. John Torrey's prediction came true when two foreign botanists were called in, the Dublin professor William Henry Harvey (1811–1866) to work with Bailey and the Englishman Miles Joseph Berkeley (1803–1889) with Curtis.

A population of twenty millions and only half an algologist and half a mycologist in the lot! It seemed to Wilkes that there was a lamentable lack of patriotic ardor among American scientists of this new breed. With the attack on his policy of modest merit he had begun to suspect a lack of democratic sentiment as well. Though his own commitment to intellectual equality represented the "spirit of the age," it was bound to bring him into conflict with the highly self-conscious community in science that, paradoxically, was emerging with views that outraged that spirit. When they cropped up in the troublesome department of botany, his suspicions were confirmed and the stumbling blocks emerged.

In September 1849 the gardener Brackenridge asked the botanist Torrey to "overhaul" his manuscript on the ferns, a task which involved reading proof, adding references, and translating the English descriptions into botanical Latin, and Torrey generously consented. But when after several weeks' work Wilkes suddenly informed him "in true quarter-deck style," that the specific character must appear, word for word, in English as well, this to be followed by a detailed description containing all that had already been said twice (a quick calculation showed that this recipe would add five hundred superfluous pages to the volumes) Torrey bridled. Calling at New York to determine the nature of the explosion, Drayton had to report that the Professor would have nothing more to do "with people that orders things they know nothing about;" and when Wilkes appeared Torrey let him know that he was prepared to resign before submitting to so absurd a requirement. Poor Brackenridge, whose manuscript was the battleground, had none of Torrey's or Gray's prestige and, aware that Wilkes might declare him expendable, could take little part in the fight. But he knew that Torrey was doing much more for his manuscript than merely serving as translator and that its quality as a book would owe much to him and nothing to Wilkes. Moreover, he could read Latin if not write it and was well enough acquainted with the form of botanical monographs to recognize that the one Wilkes was prescribing would create "a regular piece of tautology from beginning to end."

The form a botanical monograph should take was a seemingly trivial enough issue over which to fight a skirmish; but the skirmish became a battle and then a transatlantic war that would drag on for almost two years and leave a heritage of mistrust, both in the scientific community and in Congress, from which the Expedition would never fully recover. And indeed, fed up with Wilkes' management, Sullivant advised printing "in *Chicasaw* or *Choctaw*" if the commander wanted it so. The battle assumed the proportions it did in the eyes of the antagonists because they were who they were. Jacksonian Democrats had launched a scientific expedition to assert the cultural equality of the Republic, but their relations with the scientists employed were marked with irritation and soreness on both sides. The first irritation and the first great crisis for the Expedition had appeared on the eve of sailing in the disagreeable affair over whether to employ naturalists or professional scientists. In the decade since then, the professionals had grown in reputation and strength in the country as a whole and lost none of their determination to press their campaign to victory—to make a place for science in American life, to upgrade the reputation of American science in world opinion, and through it all to accept the judgment of none but their peers. The great enterprise of publishing the reports had sent the naturalists hurrying down to less rarefied altitudes, leaving the professionals in sole possession, and the thought of now surrendering ground so hardly gained seems not to have occurred to any of them. With banners flying they entered the fray.

Did Gray, Torrey wanted to know, mean "to submit to these chaps"? Not noticeably. Writing in the office of Sir William Hooker, "who is at my side," at the Royal Botanic Gardens, Gray replied promptly and decisively in a letter that was to enjoy wide circulation among Expedition scientists. He had no particular objection to printing the descriptive matter in English, "tho' in a work only to be looked at by botanists, and of a strict Scientific Character— not at all *ad populum*," Latin would be more useful. "But surely I will not do so silly a thing as to write out English translations of the *Latin specific Characters*." It was, anyway, he added, a matter with which Wilkes had nothing to do.

To Wilkes' way of thinking the Expedition from beginning to end was *ad populum*, and here was only another expression of the detestable exclusiveness of a "clique" of willful men of science. He had been forced to make room for some of these superior people in the squadron, to employ them again in writing up the reports, but he would not permit them to conceal the fruits of the Expedition from the American people. And he would not have surbordinates calling his orders silly. Wilkes replied scornfully that he permitted Latin to appear in the publications at all only as a courtesy to foreign botanists. This was a book, he told Torrey, intended by Congress "for the people & not for any class of scientific Men & I am truly surprised that Dr. Gray should venture at this day to express such an obsolete notion." If Torrey and Gray insisted on acting on "Anti-American notions," he would cut off their pay.

Both botanists knew that even "at this day" the people would have little success in untangling the technical nomenclature of botany, whatever the language in which it appeared. (Since all assumed that Congress would authorize further printings, no one raised the point that few of the people would be affected.) But they responded with a vigor quite out of proportion to the questionable logic of Wilkes' position. They were ready, Torrey exclaimed, to "get up such a representation, by the *real naturalists of this country*, as well as many in Europe, as will compel the 'Committee' to yeald," or if it came to that, to themselves resign, confident that they would only be "solicited to take it on again by those who are competent judges." Perceiving the threat to science and so to the national reputation if their work was to be controlled by non-scientists, Torrey wrote to Brackenridge: "We shall see before a great while, whether the quarter deck is to be the rule for men of science."

Disdaining to address Wilkes, Gray took the matter up with Senator Pearce, who explained with disarming courtesy the purpose of the Committee's provision for English translation: it would be less likely to antagonize members of Congress who had opposed the enterprise from the first and would mollify those who, objecting to the "Strictly Scientific character of the works," desired to see them "popularized by such descriptions as might be more generally understood." Pearce invited further correspondence. There was no issue between Gray and Pearce, who agreed that there would be a brief Latin technical character, followed by a detailed description with locality, observations, and general remarks in English.

But Pearce was not Wilkes, and when a portion of Gray's own manuscript arrived from England in April 1852 Wilkes insisted that if the Committee desired his further services, the diagnosis in English must be a direct translation from the Latin and distinct from the general and detailed description.

"Has Wilkes stopped your 'pap'?" Torrey asked Gray. In fact, Wilkes did stop Gray's pap in the spring of 1852, an act of pettiness that was too much for Joseph Henry, who now undertook to advise his friend Pearce. The Latin descriptions were intended for botanists alone, Henry assured the Senator. In any event, "no translation can make them plain" to Wilkes, who it now appeared knew so little Latin that he had allowed Gould's manuscript to slip by without literal translations, and whose argument that everything in the reports ought to appear in "ordinary language" Henry found preposterous: "The results of science may sometimes be given in ordinary language but not the details or the processes." *

On taking up the role of mediator ("I will defend you peacefully if I can or forceably if I must," he wrote Gray) Henry found that Pearce wanted the matter settled without its coming before the Committee and quite possibly the whole Congress; and so did Wilkes, once his attention was rather pointedly directed to that eventuality. Not having yet declared himself publicly on the matter, the commander offered to abandon his position on the form the botanical report should take if Gray would consent to retrace one step. Though Wilkes professed not to have noticed so insignificant a matter, Henry, experienced in the ways of Washington's inner politics, was not surprised to discover that Gray had committed "the highest indignity which could be offered to a naval gentleman" by violating the chain of command. He had submitted his accounts to Pearce instead of Wilkes. If Gray, then, would only withdraw them and present them "officially and formally" to Wilkes, Henry was sure the matter would be at an end. "In Washington," advised this statesman of science, "there is considered a wide difference between a personal and an official intercourse."

And so it was done. Taking the whole of Henry's advice Gray wrote to Pearce pleading ignorance of protocol and formally presented his accounts, apologizing to Wilkes for the "inadvertance." As was to be expected, Wilkes had the last word by niggling over a detail in the accounts but gave his approval to the manuscript. The freedom of science was preserved, at least for the moment, Wilkes was mollified, and Gray learned a lesson in protocol that he would have learned many years before had he sailed with the Squadron— how to suffer fools, he plainly considered it.[7]

* Compare Hale on the intent of his own volume: "It is hardly necessary for me to say that the volume shows only results, and such as none but those versed in these matters can rightly appreciate."

21 Strange Notions

It is the business of these infants perdus of science to make
raids into the realm of ignorance wherever they see, or
think they see, a chance; and cheerfully to accept defeat, or
it may be annihilation. . . .

Thomas Henry Huxley, "Advance of Science in the Last
Half Century," 1887

The tempest over the botanical monographs put scientists on
their guard, and many had second thoughts about the millennium of
government patronage of science. Most were never aware of another, more
desperate struggle in Washington against a then more ominous threat to the
freedom of science. Determined, as he had put it in a letter to Tappan, to
produce "a work that every American will be proud of, and which will show
those across the Atlantic that we can compete with them in many more ways
than they have as yet given us credit for," Wilkes never gave thought to the
possibility that there might be scientific discoveries in which Americans would
not take pride. Even if he had, it would hardly have occurred to him that the
reticent Pickering would be responsible for them.

From the banks of the Potomac the whole enterprise assumed a very
different aspect from what it did in Boston or New Haven. Where the
scientists saw a Navy officer who, by some quirk of the republican system, was
administering a great scientific endeavor for a niggardly government, Wilkes
impatiently viewed the scientists as a set of cross-grained fellows whose
peccadilloes half amused him at times but for the rest left him furious at their
multitude of niggling complaints and their inability to grasp the unhappy fact
that he was no longer his own master but as much subject to political
pettifoggers as they—indeed a good deal more so.

They were not his kind of crew and, no fonder of Pickering than of Peale, he would gladly have jettisoned them together. Though Wilkes managed to forgive Pickering for surrendering superintendency of the collections and publications to him and quite approved his preference for American scientists over European ones in writing the reports, the little naturalist was annoying in a variety of ways. He had sided with Gray in refusing to see any saving grace in Rich's manuscript, he wrote only slowly, read proof reluctantly, and refused to waste his energies on merely descriptive botany. "As to getting the 'critter' to do any thing but just what he pleases," Drayton grumbled, "we might as well try to pump thunder into a feather bed." His worst offense was his indispensability. His voluminous field notes were the most extensive kept during the cruise, and his exhaustive knowledge of the collections as a whole made him indispensable not only to the work on birds ("Cassin can do nothing" without "old Pick," Drayton reported), but on the plants (including Brackenridge's ferns), the fish, shells, reptiles, and insects as well. His twenty months' absence had sorely tried the staff in Washington, and on his return in May 1845, Wilkes found himself journeying to New York and waiting all day for the ship to dock.

Pickering took up the writing of his report on the races of man with encyclopedic thoroughness, but the manuscript was nonetheless ready in 1845. The impossible situation that now arose grew out of his insistence on erecting a superstructure of theory upon the massed stones of Baconian fact. Peale had tried his hand at this in the introduction to his report that Wilkes had suppressed as irrelevant as well as offensive. There were two reasons why Wilkes wanted no "personal matter" in the scientific reports. First, he failed to grasp the fact that natural history was beginning to move beyond simple taxonomy and description (at the very time these were demanding increasing precision and giving rise to the "closet naturalist," developments that had a common root in recognition of the complexity of specific relationships and of geographical distribution as a species criterion); and second, he assumed that everything of a "personal" nature worth saying he himself had said in the *Narrative,* and he wanted the series to appear as shipshape, anonymous and uniform catalogues. The sole exception was to be the work of Pickering, tacitly recognized as the chief naturalist of the Expedition, "a man," Spencer Baird remarked, "who combines in himself the scientific accomplishments necessary to make a dozen eminent naturalists." Apart from reports on the reptiles and fish, it was understood that his volumes on the races of man and the geographical distribution of plants would naturally go beyond the type of descriptive catalogue.

Pickering had set forth in 1838 to examine Pacific peoples with the eye of an "experienced naturalist," which he thought might well detect physical aspects that would escape the philologist, the ethnographer, and even the anatomist, before those peoples were wholly corrupted by contact with civilization. Intrigued by the phenomena of species extinction, generally accepted as fact since the turn of the century, and of the origins of existing species, he suspected that both might turn on the fascinating correspondence of species to environment that everywhere obtained. And he thought the most promising field of investigation would be small islands far distant from the continents, which often displayed "peculiar animals and plants." It was a course of reasoning Charles Darwin was following about that time when he happened upon Malthus' essay on population, and it carried Pickering away from descriptive natural history and into the field of geographical distribution, which he was never thereafter to leave.

One additional piece of intellectual luggage with which he sailed was the belief that there were five races of men. This was standard doctrine, given currency by the German anatomist J. F. Blumenbach (1752–1840). But from the Fijis Pickering wrote, in strict confidence, to his Philadelphia friend, the geologist and anatomist Samuel George Morton, that he had already seen eight and expected to find others before the cruise was ended. Here the course of his reasoning took a turn away from the one Darwin was to follow.

Physiological evidence suggested that all the races of men had originated in the tropics. "If Europe were the Natural Home of the White Man, he would most assuredly be born with Clothes!—One therefore need be no Solomon to perceive, that time has been, when there was no member of the human family without the Tropicks." There was little novelty in this idea among students of the natural history of man, but there was in what followed. From his observations of the variety of peoples who had long retained their racial integrity in the face of the general uniformity of the tropical climate, Pickering was persuaded that these races had "different origins, or, were originally placed in different localities," and arrived at the axiomatic observation that "Among the millions of species of plants & animals, scattered over this immense Globe, we never find a being, modified or moulded by Climate,—but always *adapted by Nature* precisely to that climate in which it is naturally found." He would not say that these races were really species, for as the world seemed to prefer that there be only one human species, "I am content to let them have their way." But as Pickering found the races to be as separate and distinct as their origins had been, and concluded that "a *hybrid race* (or a new race) cannot now originate, or be continued," the concession to public opinion was only a semantic one. The notion was exciting, for it explained at one stroke a phenomenon which had long haunted naturalists of all stripes: the remarkable correspondence of a species to its environment, and the phenomenon of race as well.

Short of clinging to the ancient notion, still a certainty in the religious community but becoming more and more suspect in the scientific, that the species were immutable, the only other course that lay open was the one Samuel S. Haldeman had taken in his neglected paper on molluscs. He had suggested that some individuals of a species were better adapted to the environment and so reproduced their kind, while those less well adapted tended to succumb. But Haldeman offered this explanation only tentatively and only for the emergence of varieties within the species, not for the emergence of species themselves. Two years after the Expedition's return the English editor Robert Chambers addressed himself directly, though anonymously, to the problem of the origin of species in a book, *Vestiges of the Natural History of Creation*, which disturbed the tranquility of the scientific community almost as much as it did that of the religious, though not entirely for the same reasons.

What Benjamin Tappan thought of Haldeman's and Chambers' notions is not known, but it is clear that he promptly made up his own mind about Pickering and his ideas. The two had evidently disliked one another on first sight and it had been a relief to both when Pickering resigned his superintendency and set off to observe man in the Near East. Tappan's objection to Pickering's manuscript occasioned Wilkes much anxiety, for, as he told the Senator, many looked upon the report on the races of man as "the most interesting branch of science to be developed by our researches" and would not be satisfied by Hale's dry vocabularies and scholarly search for linguistic affinities. After consulting with Pickering's philologist uncle, whom Tappan held in high esteem, he was happy to report that Charles Pickering seemed to have given up many of the "strange notions" Tappan had complained of and was willing to delete the objectionable parts of the manuscript. Wilkes hoped that Tappan would now consent to its publication, since rejection would sorely offend its author, and "You are well aware how necessary Dr. P. is for many of the Departments, and how full his journals are of local and particular information."

The strange notions Tappan complained of were coming to be shared in these years by an increasing number of the scientific community under the intellectual leadership of Pickering's friend at the Academy of Natural Sciences, Dr. Samuel George Morton, who from his measurements of the unprecedented collection of skulls he had gathered—it was known as the "American Golgotha"—concluded in his *Crania Americana* in 1839 that the racial distinctions they manifested were owing not to climate, but more likely (though he was cautious here) to separate origins. With the appearance of *Crania Americana* the assault on the scientific basis of equalitarianism was launched and with it what, ironically, came to be known in the western world as the "American School" of anthropology. A few weeks before the Expedition's return, Morton informed the members of the Boston Society of Natural History that as his investigations showed the American Indian to be morphologically the same throughout the hemisphere, the theory could no longer be supported that the races of men represented the response of the organism to local climate and constituted only varieties within the species.

Morton's (and Pickering's) English friend George R. Gliddon (1809–1857), the rowdy publicist for Egyptology who was telling Americans in his popular lectures that Egypt was the cradle of civilization and her monuments a certain key to the earliest records of mankind, showed that the races were as distinct at the acme of Egyptian civilization as at the present. And it was doubtless at Gliddon's suggestion that Pickering had gone to the Near East to see for himself—calling at Malta and Cairo, then proceeding down the Red Sea to Mocha, Aden, and Zanzibar and across the Arabian Sea to Bombay, gathering antiquities for his own collection and papyri for his Uncle John, as well as voluminous observations on the races of men.[1]

When Dr. Morton, now the acknowledged leader of American anthropology, adopted the conclusion of Dr. Josiah Clark Nott (1804–1873) of Mobile that the races of men were not varieties that interbred freely to produce equally fertile offspring, but species whose intermixture produced degenerate and short-lived progeny, the materials were assembled for a scientific theory that was both profoundly anti-equalitarian and profoundly anti-scriptural. And when the great Swiss naturalist Louis Agassiz arrived in 1846 to examine Morton's crania and announced in his Lowell Institute Lectures at Boston that year his own conversion to the theory, it gained in both popular celebrity and scientific distinction.

Southerners, embattled by the abolitionist attack on their Peculiar Institution, were quick to perceive the social significance of a dispute that the scientists, increasingly exclusive and self-conscious now, sought to keep within the confines of the emerging fraternity of science. That endeavor was a lost cause from the beginning, if for no other reason than the anti-scriptural implications of the theory. Indeed the South Carolina cleric-botanist Moses Ashley Curtis was one of its earliest critics.

For his part, Pickering took his good time in submitting the manuscript, perhaps because in 1846 he was hoping to be appointed Secretary of the new Smithsonian Institution and wished to avoid giving unnecessary offense (the appointment went instead to Professor Joseph Henry in December) but certainly because he was reluctant to submit his work to a group of politicians unlikely to give dispassionate consideration to a subject on which "the Public mind is peculiarly sensitive." Attempting to evade their censorship, he sought some assurance from Wilkes that the manuscript would be published whether the Committee liked it or not. This the commander could not give and once he understood what Pickering was requesting, he attempted to explain the matter in an unvarnished letter to Dr. Morton, who had interested himself in his friend's cause.

Wilkes wrote that he did not believe anyone on the Committee had "any scruples whatever on the subject—whether we are derived from a single pair or fifty; few of them have ever troubled their minds about the subject. . . . But a Committee, however freely they may think themselves, on these subjects, may deem that it is extremely necessary to be cautious in publishing any new philosophical inquiries relative to the History of man, wishing to avoid though willing that the subject may be treated most fully, anything that might shock the public mind, and in this I cannot but see great propriety as well as consideration for the public feelings." Wilkes saw here an advantage to Pickering himself, who doubtless wished to "avoid any departure from highly moral & correct views in treating of his subject" but could not be "so good a judge as others might be." True, the members of the Committee might not understand the subject "at all scientifically," but they could "save him from expressions" that might shock the public mind "without at the same time interfering with the proper elucidation of his subject." Wilkes wished to make himself clear: "Be assured the Committee have no idea . . . of meddling with the treatment of his subject, but they may point out where alterations might be made advantageously." Anyway, the Captain observed in conclusion, Pickering had no choice but to surrender his manuscript. If the Committee did not approve of it, he would be free to publish it himself. But, Wilkes added, with an eye on the field notes, as an employee of the government, the naturalist must "deliver up" any documents belonging to the government.

Wilkes' double-talk aside, it is clear that what would have shocked the public mind—if not Benjamin Tappan's—and what prevented the theory's being highly moral & correct, was not its anti-equalitarian implications, for agreement on the unfortunate anthropological status of the Negro was general: it was, rather, its anti-scriptural quality, its flat contradiction of

Mosaic natural history, that offended pro-slavery Southerners and anti-slavery Northerners alike. When it ultimately met defeat in the marketplace of ideas, it fell before objections that were wholly extra-scientific and wholly religious.

In the scientific community as a whole, probably few were aware of Pickering's offense against propriety. But whether or not they would have subscribed to his theory, for all concerned with the Expedition his manuscript posed a crisis. If scientific reports must pass the scrutiny of a congressional committee standing guard over the public feelings, if scientific principles as well as language must be *ad populum*, then government sponsorship of science would bear thinking about anew.

At the end of 1846 Pickering reported his manuscript completed but did not submit it. Wilkes requested, Wilkes demanded, Wilkes cut off his salary—though allowing him to continue working in the Patent Office. The Committee, less persuaded than Wilkes of the naturalist's indispensability, resolved that he be given only one more chance. He would submit his work or be dismissed. Pearce requested, Pickering refused. But Wilkes, the more anxious now as it was becoming clear that Rich was not to be relied on, found that he still had room to maneuver, for although the scientists served under the Committee, their appointments as well as their pay were from the Navy Department. He took steps to assure that defeat would not be total. Having patched up a recent misunderstanding with Secretary of the Navy John Y. Mason, he urged the Secretary, if Pickering should be dismissed, to "claim the Public property"—manuscript journals, "remarks, writing, drawings, sketches and paintings, as well as Specimens of every kind collected and prepared during the voyage," for these were "*absolutely* necessary" to complete the reports. It was all a little out of the Secretary's line and he left the decision entirely to Wilkes, who then somehow persuaded Pickering to submit his manuscript and won Pearce's consent both to its publication and to Pickering's retention.

Wilkes informed the Chairman that the report presented "much curious information" and predicted that, taken together with Hale's book, it would provide "the best work on the races extant, and as to its having any bearing on Revelation, I consider it entirely devoid of objection, on that score." Still, he confessed himself "disappointed in it as a whole, perhaps I expected too much from him, it is difficult for him to let his information leak out unless he is well tapped." The remark was a piece of willful obtuseness, for how was information to leak when considerations for the public feelings stopped every vent? Dr. Oliver Wendell Holmes was not being obtuse but merely unaware of congressional censorship when he pronounced the book (it appeared in 1848 as

The Races of Man: and Their Geographical Distribution) "the oddest collection of fragments that was ever seen . . . amorphous as a fog, unstratified as a dumpling and heterogeneous as a low priced sausage." Another Bostonian who was unaware of events in Washington and who, like the author, had spent some time observing other cultures at first hand, took note of the publication. Francis Parkman had not yet read the book but heard that it was "obscure" in "method and Arrangement" and derived the races of men "from one source."

Significantly, it is only the chapter on "Zoological Deductions" that is obscure. For the rest, in a style characterized by an ease and grace that Wilkes might well have envied, Pickering follows the squadron among the races of men, noting the physical and cultural peculiarities, the footprints of language, the broken twigs of art and custom, the scent of introduced plants, in order to track mankind to its original center. By the time his search is ended he has added three more races to the eight he described to Morton from the Fijis. And he can find, he says, "no middle ground between the admission of eleven distinct species in the human family, and the reduction to one." Many of his readers, including some of the staunchest defenders of Christian orthodoxy, were to nod approvingly at this statement.* For it was surely absurd to speak of eleven species within the genus man. But Pickering found no evidence that the races were owing to the circumstances of different environments and so were merely varieties that changed or disappeared with their dispersion into new localities—as new varieties of plums, apples, and pears had sprung up in America since the introduction of the parent stocks from abroad. There was no evidence—even on the monuments of Egypt—that a new race of men had ever appeared. The objection that race characters were insufficiently pronounced to admit of their being considered specific distinctions was really no objection at all, for naturalists of all stripes knew that "slight external" differences sufficed to establish a species. "If we could suppose separate species," he reasoned, in the recurring conditional mood in which one can discern the hand of politics, the problem would be solved.

The track led Pickering in the end (his examination of Egyptian monuments only reinforced his already firm opinion) to regions just below the

* For the London edition of 1851 a Sheffield physician wrote a seventy-two-page "Analytical Synopsis" of the book to emphasize what he was sure was its theme: *"That the black man, red man, and white man, are links in one great chain of relationship, and alike children which have descended from one common parent."* And the South Carolina parson-naturalist, John Bachman, the ablest and most persistent critic of the American School, quoted this passage approvingly in his attack.

equator, where a being without natural covering might be expected to thrive, to the East Indies and Africa, where the migrations of men and plants by land and sea seemed to have begun and where the "general consonance" of the zoological productions seemed most to favor the appearance of man among the other spectacular creatures these regions boasted—the "showy birds of the Malay Peninsula . . . ; the long-nosed Ape of Borneo; the Sumatran Tapir and Rhinoceros," and the orangs of Borneo, Sumatra, and western Africa, "which of all animals, in physical conformation and even in moral tempera- ment, make the nearest approach to humanity."

The twentieth century is suspicious of speculation on race—it is, under- standably, one of our modern taboos—and is inclined to blame those of the past for the modern predicament. Very nearly as much foolishness, in consequence, has been written about writers on race as on race itself. It is an unwarranted act of egotism to view the past as no more than a preparation for the present, and it requires some measure of intellectual humility to reflect upon how far short one's own age falls of the expectations of an earlier. The superficial investigator who takes his bearings from the fads of his own day will relegate Pickering to the dustbin of dead anthropologies. That will be error compounded. For Pickering was a man of his own age and country, and he sought, with Morton and Agassiz and the others, to render anthropology truly scientific, so that he might with some hope of precision satisfy his curiosity about the origins of man. If others were to find objectionable extra-scientific implications in his endeavors, they were none of his doing. Beyond that, Pickering's remains a viable and intellectually respectable concept, in its main outlines finding authoritative expression today in the work of the dean of American anthropologists, Carleton S. Coon.

But judged even by the shallow standard of guilt for the twentieth century, Pickering comes off well. He exalted none of his eleven races, least of all his own. For sheer destructiveness, as he had written Morton from the Fijis, he found no equal to the "race of plunderers" he called txe White Race: "From the Soul-inspiring works of Greece to the Simple Grave of the American Indians, whatever monument has been erected, by the head or hands, has had to deal with some other enemy than Time." So prevalent was the proclivity that it might justly be said to serve as a species character.

If Pickering was a man of his age, within its confines he was his own man, distinctive among the students of prehistory from the professional "Cauca- sian," who glorified the mythical tribe that supposedly descended from the heights of "frosty Caucasus" to give itself to the world. Determining that

America was sufficiently accessible to Asians by way of the Aleutians and to Polynesians by reason of the prevailing winds, he found no ground for agreement with his friend Morton (to whom he promptly sent three copies of his reprinted edition, designating one for Gliddon), who was sure a race of men had been created in and for America. Nor could he agree with Morton's friend Ephraim G. Squier—whose own book on the Mound Builders of the Mississippi Valley the Smithsonian Institution published as the first of its volumes the same year, after similar objections were raised in Congress and met with like devices of circumlocution—who expressed agreement with Morton and questioned the accepted biblical chronology as well. And to what could only have been the dismay of his Egyptomaniac friend Gliddon, he concluded that the Ethiopian profile had "furnished the model for the Egyptian features of the earliest monuments," that the slaves of Ancient Egypt were usually white, Negroes serving principally as soldiers—and, he suspected, as a queen on one occasion at least. And neither Josiah Nott (to complete the American School) nor the bibliolators among the defenders of slavery could have been pleased with Pickering's conclusion that Negro slavery was "of modern origin."

With an equanimity that was not prescribed by Congress—for it character-ized his letters from the Pacific as well—he put the races (and the racists) in their place. Insofar as he possessed a philosophy of race, he set it forth in his chapter, "Relations between the Races." Men were, to be sure, essentially alike. Still, no one doubted the existence of character, "distinguishing not only individuals, but communities and nations," as well. He himself was persuaded that "there is, besides, a character of race. It would not be difficult to select epithets, such as 'amphibious, enduring, insititious'; or to point out, as accomplished by one race of men, that which seemed beyond the powers of another. Each race possessing its peculiar points of excellence, and at the same time counterbalancing defects, it may be, that union was required to attain the full measure of civilization.

"In the organic world, each new field requires a new creation; each change in circumstances going beyond the constitution of a plant or animal, is met by a new adaptation, until the universe is full; while among the immense variety of created beings, two kinds are hardly found fulfilling the same precise purpose. Some analogy may possibly exist in the human family; and it may even be questioned whether any one of txe races existing singly would, up to the present day, have extended itself over the whole surface of the globe." [2]

What the book would have been had the insititious members of the

Committee and their amphibious and enduring agent refrained from prescribing and proscribing, no man can say, but even after their depredations it remained, as Wilkes in some measure predicted, the most comprehensive survey of the races of men that, based on direct observation, had ever been published.

22   Interesting Flotsam

So he is a fool, and a d——d fool;
but he can take Rangoon.

Wellington

By the late 1840's, Wilkes was making every effort to complete the Expedition's volumes in the expectation that, once the job was done, Congress would order a new printing. Despairing of Pickering's ever bringing out the report on snakes and fishes, he took the naturalist's own suggestion and in 1850 persuaded the great Professor Agassiz to take on the fishes. The following year he induced Spencer F. Baird to supervise the herpetology report, on the understanding that the actual work would be done by his assistant Charles Girard. A decade earlier, Baird, then a young ornithologist, had journeyed to Washington to gaze longingly at the newly arrived collections; but he was now the Assistant Secretary of the Smithsonian and in charge of its natural history museum. Girard's report appeared in 1858, five years late for its deadline. Agassiz was less prompt.

Asa Gray returned from Europe in 1852 and after two years in press and proof, the first part (Phanerogamia) of his projected two-part report on botany was published in 1854 and its accompanying atlas two years later. In 1854, too, Brackenridge's report on the ferns was published. Though he was long since "heartily sick" of the "crooked affair," it was still a proud moment for the gardener. Indeed, written at a time when he carried the sole burden of running the greenhouse and was assisting the noted landscape architect Andrew Jackson Downing in improving the public grounds, the work was a remarkable accomplishment. With a loan from Asa Gray, he provided the paper for printing an extra one hundred copies. As booksellers could not be found who would take them all, they remained at Gaskill's Philadelphia bindery, where in

April 1856 fire destroyed twenty-four copies of the official edition and all of the extra printing except for the ten copies that had been sold, most of them abroad.

Gould's report on the shells was delayed by his discovery, in 1848, of a hundred and fifty additional species to be described and by the loss of one of the Expedition's best engravers, W. H. Dougal, who, to the infinite disgust of Wilkes, rushed off to dig gold in California. Dougal returned in 1851, somewhat the richer from successful operation of a livery stable in San Francisco, and the book appeared in 1852. But the volumes were not coming out steadily enough to suit Wilkes, who grew quite out of patience with the dilatory authors. He himself had no difficulty in bringing out books. In 1850 the first volume of his great folio atlas of fifty-five charts, designed to accompany his report on hydrography, was published, and the next year saw his eight-hundred-page volume of meteorological tables, based on the meteorological journal of the *Vincennes*. And this during a period of frequent illness and loneliness brought on by the death of his wife. He spent much of 1849 and 1850 in the North Carolina mountains, from whose heights he laid siege to another Navy Secretary. This one had disappointed him by ordering his midshipman son John to sea just when the boy was most needed to help prepare the meteorological tables. But he could battle secretaries with one hand now and, wearying of the enforced idleness and dismayed by the wild inaccuracy of the accounts of the West Coast that were appearing in the wake of the Gold Rush, with the other he assembled (from the *Narrative*) a book on *Western America* (1849) to set the public straight. He also began writing his report on physics. He could not understand men who devoted years to preparing a single book and could only conclude that the scientists preferred "*Uncle Sams pap* . . . to rank or reputation." The delay was no fault of his.[1]

It was none of Drayton's, either. The peppery old factotum busily prodded his "big bugs"—Curtis on the "toad stools," Cassin on the "Birds & Beasts," Bailey on the "sea weed," the independent Pickering on geographical distribution ("There is one thing I would remind you of, and that is, when his foot is down you might as well try to ram a 32 pounder down his throat as to make him do what he won't do"). Engravers gave him almost as much trouble as authors, for aside from the Coast Survey and the geological surveys of New York and Pennsylvania, which required the services of engravers for years on end, so many other scientific volumes were in press during the fifties—Henry Rowe Schoolcraft's six volumes of *Historical and Statistical Information* on the Indian tribes, with their lithographs and steel engravings, and Gould's and Binney's five volumes on *The Terrestrial Air-Breathing Mollusks of the*

INTERESTING FLOTSAM

United States—that good ones were hard to find. He was constantly on the move. When Samuel George Morton died in 1851, Drayton gathered up the Expedition skulls that Morton had been measuring for his study of the "Physical Type of the American Indians" and returned them to the collections at the Patent Office.

In the meantime the scientists did what they could to satisfy the universal curiosity of the learned community by issuing preliminary reports in the journals and proceedings of the scientific societies. Dana prepared a score of these, several appearing in the *American Journal of Science*, of which he became an editor in 1846, and Cassin, Gould, and others followed suit. But this practice, while it kept the members of these societies informed and established the explorers' claims to the discovery of new species, merely whetted appetites for the formal reports. "There is need of influence in behalf of the Exped. & Science," Dana wrote the Academy of Natural Sciences on one occasion, for "Congress, as you know, requires frequent efforts before even a good object can be secured." The scientists of the country knew only too well and responded to such appeals with a show of mass support. Time and again, often with Wilkes' active assistance, individual scientists and their societies petitioned Congress for a larger edition and for the donation of at least some copies to schools, colleges, and learned societies. From Harvard, Louis Agassiz wrote to offer his support for what it was worth—which was usually a great deal. Because the natural history reports *"surpass in scientific importance"* those of any similar European enterprise, "nothing," he announced, "could be more timely, more productive of immediate advantage to the cause of science than . . . a large edition of these works, especially if it can be made accessible to the universally limited means of scientific men."

True, the authors might use the type and plates of the official edition to bring out a printing of their own; and, aside from Wilkes (who retained one hundred and fifty copies of the original press run of the *Narrative* and brought out a number of cheaper editions), Dana, Pickering, Gould, and Gray did so. But a book on vocabularies or ferns held few attractions in the marketplace, as Brackenridge's experience showed. Consequently, no complete sets of the reports were obtainable except by the captains and the kings, and the very elements seemed to conspire against the few copies in print. They were dispatched from Washington like seeds from the Patent Office, with no thought given to whether they reached their destination. Those presented to the Czar were lost at sea and their replacement required special sanction from Congress. An American visiting Canton in 1858 came upon the Chinese Emperor's gift set in a market stall and, thinking his friend Dana might enjoy having a copy of his own book, purchased the *Geology* for him. (At home they were held in higher esteem. In 1861 Fred Stuart, who had been Hudson's clerk on the *Peacock* and who had somehow managed to assemble one of the few complete sets in private hands, was asking fifteen hundred dollars for it.) The Christmas Eve fire of 1851 that destroyed thirty-five thousand volumes in the Library of Congress consumed one hundred and eighty-four copies of the reports. On the night after Christmas, flames leaped at the Expedition again in the great Philadelphia fire that raged for five days, leveling hotels, shops, and Barnum's Museum. Drayton could only stand helplessly watching the "vast columns of smoke & steam" rise in the icy air, but this time the Expedition lost only a hundred-dollar shell plate.[2]

The petitions, the memorials, the criticisms of the learned community were not without effect. A representative body, Congress responded by mending its ways. To the consternation of the scientists, it appropriated three hundred and sixty thousand dollars for printing fifteen thousand copies of Commodore Matthew C. Perry's three-volume account of his expedition to Japan.* But it did nothing for the father of all American overseas expeditions.

To the explorers it looked very much as though their expedition were the victim of a congressional conspiracy more to be feared than fire, for soon the question was less whether Congress would authorize a second printing than whether it would complete the first. After an interview with Pearce and John S. Meehan, the long-time Librarian of Congress who served as secretary of the Library Committee, Drayton reported a lack of "that warmth and solicitude, as was always manifested before." That was no wonder, for Pearce was much out of patience with Wilkes over the botanical monographs flap, but the Senator's new attitude was the more ominous because he was also a member of the Finance Committee, several other members of which had proved unfriendly to the Expedition in the past. It was the first hint that time might be running out. The previous Congress (in 1849) had appropriated only fifteen thousand dollars for the Expedition, while awarding the princely sum of $184,000 to the Coast Survey, in spite of the fact that, as Wilkes complained, "our labours will do as much for the honour and welfare of the country." When a recent enlargement of the Patent Office had displaced the plants and necessitated erection of a new greenhouse on the vacant area just west of the Capitol grounds, there had been strenuous opposition to even that small

---

* Ten thousand copies were distributed free to members of Congress, two thousand to the Navy Department, one thousand to Perry. "As for the public," Perry's biographer comments, "it would get its return for its three hundred and sixty thousand dollars by repurchasing copies from the thrifty congressmen."

INTERESTING FLOTSAM

appropriation. (Brackenridge, finding that his men were more or less sick with chills and fever during much of the year, soon concluded that the new site was "one of the most unhealthy sinks" in the city.) But delay in the appropriation for 1850 was owing less to congressional opposition than to the great crises of that year—Senator Seward's proposal to abolish slavery in the District of Columbia and the debates over the Fugitive Slave Law, the Texas claims, Oregon, and the rest—which accumulated in such numbers that people in Washington seemed to consider the Expedition's needs "of little moment." Finally, at the end of September, Congress appropriated twenty-five thousand dollars and the work resumed.

The next year there were further rumblings, and relations with Pearce grew so strained that Drayton rejoiced to see in the newspapers that a lady in the Senate gallery had dropped her parasol on the head of the chairman of the Library Committee, drawing blood. "I wish the confounded woman had been on the top of Mauna Loa," he exclaimed. But the appropriation passed in August. However, in March 1853 the customary twenty-five thousand dollars was appropriated for "completion," rather than "continuance," of the publications.

Wilkes professed indifference. He had had enough of the author-scientists and happily anticipated an end, he wrote Tappan, to "My Wars with these troublesome people," who were forever attempting to "bolt" after drawing "a large amount from Uncle Sams coffers." The end was in sight anyway: the charts were completed, Gray's Botany was "well advanced," Agassiz's manuscript was said to be finished, and Sullivant, Bailey, and Pickering were in press. Audacious as always, Wilkes believed the time was ripe to press for a reprint of the whole, perhaps in a cheaper edition. He also chose this moment to demand that the government purchase his copyright on the Narrative.

Then fire struck again, more boldly this time, at Gaskill's Philadelphia bindery in December 1853. Drayton lost all his records and papers, even his clothing—all "licked up like a pinch of Cotton in a lighted candle," he reported. The plates in press were lost but the rest remained safe in the "fire proof" that Tappan had long ago insisted on as the depository. But this fire and that in the Library of Congress in 1851 had consumed a good many copies of the bound volumes, and as the Expedition now had powerful enemies in Congress, it was not at all certain that appropriations would be made for their replacement.

For a few days in March 1855 the future hung in doubt while Pearce fought for another sum and urged a new printing of a thousand copies of all the reports. Congress responded with money for replacing the volumes lost in both fires and put up $29,320 again for "completing" the publications, but refused to reprint. Wilkes was grateful to Pearce for his efforts, since the amount would keep the enterprise going for another two years, by the end of which time the publications would be near enough to completion that Congress would surely see fit to reprint. But gratitude soured into resentment when he learned that Pearce had won this appropriation only by promising never to ask for another and now insisted that all reports not completed within the year must be discarded.

Wilkes fought back, not for himself, he let it be known, whose only reward had been "many hard knocks . . . from the Executive, the Judiciary, and the public," including men of science, "many of whom have *cut* my acquaintance entirely," but for an enterprise that had "done much to elevate the character of the Country." The delay could not be helped. It was idle to speak of hastening the work of a man "standing at the head of Science as Profr. Agassiz does." Unless government wished to employ scientists on a full-time basis, which would cost five times what was now paid them, there was no way to hurry them: "it is in Science as in Law, you must expect to pay well for talent." Anyway, he expostulated, taking up another line of attack, the nation was pledged to complete the work in "its full proportions." Anything less would do "great injustice to the Science of the Country in the eyes of the World," for it could never be concealed that "for a few thousand dollars this Great Country" turned its back on Science at the behest of "a few ignorant and narrow minded men" incapable of grasping the simple truth that "a publication might cost a large sum and yet be very cheap for its value." Besides, reduction would mean the loss of forty-seven new genera—and several hundred species, of which Drayton had completed between six and seven hundred drawings—as well as the money paid Agassiz and Pickering.

But Pearce was adamant. Seven years had passed since Pickering had finished his book on the races and he had since completed only an introduction—albeit at one hundred and sixty-eight pages a small volume in itself, which he had published at his own expense in 1854. This amounted to "abandonment." Agassiz, who had not submitted a page of manuscript after six years and nearly four thousand dollars paid him, must also go. Funds would permit publication of four volumes only—Gray's, Cassin's, Wilkes' Hydrography, and the collection of botanical monographs. Moreover, the number of plates, which occasioned the greatest single expense in publication,* must be

* When Sullivant, anxious for the publication of his monograph and informed that economy was now the watchword, suggested that his own plates be lithographed, Wilkes politely declined

sharply reduced and lithographs perhaps substituted for copper engravings.[3]

Here for a time matters rested, Wilkes implacable, Pearce immovable, both bristling. To make matters worse, the indispensable Drayton severely injured himself when, rushing to view another fire that had broken out in a nearby building in Philadelphia, he fell on the ice and a hose carriage ran over him. While he was recuperating, no work was done on the coloring of Gray's plates or on the atlas of shells. Still confident that Congress would not scrap the great enterprise to save the estimated twelve thousand dollars that would bring it to completion, Wilkes spent the month fending off attacks by "designing fellows not to call them rogues" and, generally, as he wrote his daughter, "Watching over the old Expedition with which the name of Wilkes is more than ever allied."

The blow fell on April 7. The Committee determined to confine the publication within the present appropriation, with the understanding, however, that once the works were completed, they would recommend another for the printing of Agassiz's report. The irony must have struck Wilkes forcibly that the Expedition's very success in scientific discovery had brought it to this sorry pass; the collections that had once sunk the National Institute now threatened the Expedition itself.

A few days later, disaster struck again in the form of another fire. Drayton, who, although ill, had been in Washington adding his pleas to those of Wilkes, hurried off to Philadelphia to inspect the damage. Gaskill's bindery had burned to the ground on the night of April 11, reducing to ashes even the contents of the fireproof safes. Drayton discovered that of the unbound printed sheets thirty copies each of ten volumes were destroyed, together with all the first printing of Wilkes' Hydrography—over ten thousand dollars' worth.

Still, Wilkes did not give up. Pearce found it maddening, and finally sent for Drayton in hopes that he would be able to make clear to the Captain the simple fact that, except for the volumes in press, the Expedition was at an end. Wilkes himself would not consent to abridgement but he did turn over his duties to Drayton, who did consent and who was in every way competent if his health would permit. It would have been treachery in another, but Wilkes accepted it in good grace from his longtime obedient servant whom he had come to regard as friend. It was as well, for the cigar-chomping old artist, who had entertained the Explorers so many evenings under Pacific skies with his

with the reminder that this was "a govt work and on it the reputation of the Country at home and abroad is at stake."

violin, lay ill in Philadelphia in November and died early the next month, claimed by the Expedition as surely as the men of the *Sea Gull* had been. Senator Tappan was dismayed at the news of Drayton's death and would have written an obituary, he told Wilkes, were he not near the end himself. He died in April 1857.[4]

When Senator Pearce now came hat in hand, Wilkes "made him feel his situation" but, taking command once again, tried to gather up the loose ends. For Drayton's place he chose Fred Stuart, Captain's Clerk on the *Peacock*, who since his return from Cadwallader Ringgold's North Pacific Expedition had been assisting with the work in Washington. Wilkes set about recovering the shells sent to Tappan and the algae that Bailey had described, for the microscopist had died in February. He also sent another memorial to Congress for a new printing, announcing that the publication was now drawing to a close. But his plea went unheard, for with the return of Ringgold's expedition and Lieutenant Thomas J. Page's to the Rio La Plata, senators were confessing themselves weary of "very heavy works" on "bugology" and other "unimportant and useless branches of natural history" and were inclined to regret the precedent they had set with "Wilkes' Expedition."

Attempting to hurry the authors, Wilkes was a little too sharp on occasion. To his surprise, Sullivant refused to submit his drawings until the government promised to pay for them, and there was a brisk exchange conducted through Sullivant's friend Gray, who, accustomed now to the Captain's asperity, only begged him to "be so good as to avoid expressions . . . neither required nor warranted by the occasion."

"I have my public duties to perform," Wilkes replied with a flounce of the coattails. The drawings were sent, but too late to avoid delay in publication of the botanical volumes. There was unpleasantness with John Torrey, who Wilkes thought was overpaying his artist at twenty dollars per drawing, and when Wilkes called on him in New York, Torrey, by his own account, "treated him very roughly." This was followed by a warm exchange over the style of Baird's introduction to the volume on reptiles, in which Wilkes had made a few alterations, thinking them to be corrections until Baird objected that they were ungrammatical and did "most respectfully protest against the signing my name to what . . . will make me appear ridiculous."

Nonetheless, by 1858 there were new volumes to show for Wilkes' prodding—Cassin's *Mammalogy and Ornithology* and atlas, and Girard's *Herpetology* and atlas of handsome drawings, many of them by the accomplished J. H. Richard. Wilkes' *Hydrography* was finally printed, together with the second volume of his atlas and charts, although the former was not actually issued until much later. The moss plates were given over to the printer, an artist was making progress with Agassiz's fish, and Torrey was examining the plates for his volume. With the end in sight and certain that no Congress would dare put a stop to it now, Wilkes sent for Torrey's, Sullivant's, and Pickering's manuscripts. In 1859 Congress appropriated $8220 for completing the volumes "now nearly finished." Drawing and engraving continued until the meager sum was exhausted. Another $11,000 were made available in 1860 to pay arrears due authors and artists, but since there were no funds for printing, Wilkes sought to divert the sum to drawing, printing, and binding. He hoped to finish the work in hand before the next session of Congress, so that it might perhaps agree to pay for the Agassiz and Gray volumes, as well. But by that time Congress had other things to contend with.

The Expedition was becalmed while at home the nation went to war with itself and abroad Charles Darwin conducted a revolution in natural history no less far-reaching in its consequences. Neither science nor the nation was to be the same again. Meanwhile, Fred Stuart deposited the Expedition plates, a hundred thousand dollars' worth, in the Philadelphia Exchange, believed to be thoroughly fireproofed. The collections also found a haven, insofar as wartime Washington might be considered one, but only after causing a good deal of concern among those who cared about them most.

The act of 1846 that established the Smithsonian stipulated that it should take custody of the Expedition collections as soon as arrangements were made for their reception. None too pleased "that this National Collection should . . . be taken care of by the funds of a foreigner," who left them to the United States only as "a last resort," his "bastard heir having died," and persuaded that the people running the Smithsonian "have not the cause of science at heart," Wilkes was delighted to discover that the Smithsonian's Secretary was equally unenthusiastic and complaining that the collections would be his "elephant's foot." Secretary Joseph Henry was equally unenthusiastic about the Smithsonian's quarters—that great towered pile of brown sandstone, designed in the "Lombard" style by Professor Renwick's son James*—but he saw the eight years required for its erection as so many years of grace in which to escape the fate that had befallen the National Institute when, crushed beneath the collections, it was reduced to beseeching alms of Congress.[5]

---

* At least one member of the art community agreed with Henry. The sculptor Horatio Greenough recorded his own first impression of Renwick's masterpiece: "Suddenly, as I walked, the dark form of the Smithsonian palace rose between me and the white Capitol, and I stopped. Tower and battlement, and all that medieval confusion, stamped itself on the halls of Congress, as ink on paper! Dark on that whiteness—complication on that simplicity! It scared me. . . . Is no *coup d'etat* lurking there? . . . Perhaps they are an allopathic dose administered to that parsimony which so long denied to science where to lay her head."

With the Commissioner of Patents desperately seeking to rid himself of them and Henry as desperately trying to escape them, there was considerable speculation about the fate of the collections while the Smithsonian was building. The naturalist J. G. Anthony had betrayed the sentiments of some scientists by putting the question bluntly to Tappan: "By the way, will there be any chance of plunder among the Shells?" Wilkes suddenly began to interest himself in the affairs of the moribund National Institute (together with, of all people, Walter Johnson, a man of singularly forgiving nature), which was showing some signs of life again. Abert and Markoe had retired and Wilkes thought it might be rebuilt "on a new and better foundation."* Perhaps Congress would endow it with enough of the public lands to provide for the collections and permit a system of exchanges, as scientists about the country were urging. The Institute found strength to protest against the transfer to "a private establishment, founded by a benevolent man it is true, but a foreigner," of "this truly national collection" gathered by the nation's "first and greatest Expedition of purely a scientific character" and every year viewed by many thousands of plain citizens who regarded them as "trophies gathered in honor of their country." But it was only a last gasp, for the Institute was soon overwhelmed by the American Association for the Advancement of Science, which, newly emerged from the Association of Geologists and Naturalists, was absorbing the enthusiasm of those who had worked to found a national scientific society.

Henry wholeheartedly agreed with the Institute. "Smitten with a chronic monomania on a single subject," as one of his congressional critics put it with greater insight than economy, Henry felt that the Smithson money should be spent only on the "development and publication of new truths." In his 1849 annual report he asserted that the collections should indeed be "preserved as a memento of the science and energy of our Navy, and as a means of illustrating and verifying the magnificent volumes which comprise the history of that expedition," but preserved by the government, not the Smithsonian, where they would occupy space that might be put to better use than the display of curiosities "from which the harvest of discovery has already been gathered." While they remained in the Patent Office, to be viewed by ever larger crowds, Henry twisted and turned in anguished attempts to evade them. By 1854 time was running out. The great lower hall—fifty by two hundred feet—was ready and Assistant Secretary Baird was displaying the Smithsonian's own collection, which, devoted to the natural history of North America, was the best of its

* In the Institute's annual presidential election in 1849, Wilkes received one vote.

kind, and the miscellany of government collections that had come into the Institution's custody. The next year the ingenious Secretary conceived a way to turn his two liabilities to profit. If a museum was wanted so desperately, then let government purchase his great pink elephant of a building for the purpose. It was of no proper use to a research institution anyway. "Indeed," he added, "it would be a gain to science could the Institution give away the building for no other consideration than that of being relieved from the costly charge of the collections."

Congress was not eager to have the charge of Henry's Lombard incubus, and Henry and the Regents of the Smithsonian finally agreed in 1857 to relieve the Commissioner of Patents (still complaining annually) if Congress would pay for the transfer of the collections and the cases to house them and make an annual appropriation for their maintenance. Congress obliged, providing handsome display cases designed by the capital architect, and the stream of ogling sightseers—a hundred thousand a year now—shifted from the Patent Office to the far more spacious hall of the Smithsonian, where they could view the collections, enriched by some newly prepared specimens that for want of space had never before been exhibited, in the long series of alcoves arranged in two storeys. John Varden, who followed in their wake, was on hand to answer questions.

Meanwhile, someone had painted the legend "National Museum of the United States" above the door to the hall, and the often expressed wish of the Explorers as they collected warclubs and birds on atolls and reefs was granted. Their Great National Expedition had created a great national museum, whose "interesting flotsam and jetsam," as Major John Wesley Powell called it, would provide future generations of scientifics with materials for research and both enlighten and amuse the public, though not always in that order of priority.

The live plants had reached a secure haven in 1852 when they were placed in the National Botanic Garden. Through the efforts of John Torrey during the sixties, the dried plants, together with those of later expeditions, were mounted and classified, and arranged to serve as type specimens. As such, they constituted the United States National Herbarium, the largest and richest in the nation (they filled thirteen hundred shelves) and became the training ground for another generation of botanists. Alternately for some years in the keeping of the Department of Agriculture and the Smithsonian, they found a resting place in the Smithsonian in 1896.[6]

The war increased the stream of sightseers, many of them in uniform now, but it put a halt to the work of the scientists. Old John Torrey found himself inspecting ships' boilers and the Captain (he was promoted to the rank in 1855) broke off his meteorological experiments to go to sea in his country's defense. It was doubtless a great relief to him once again to be able to give an outright order in the full expectation of its being obeyed. He conducted his part of the war by his own lights and, as the old explorers might have predicted, his tour of duty, though hazardous to him, was a good deal more so to his country. He was briefly a public hero when, commanding the *San Jacinto*, he seized the British steamer *Trent* on the high seas in November of 1861. Bands played along the seaboard and even Congress, so niggard with praise in the past, enthusiastically tendered its thanks. But his action made a shambles of relations with Great Britain and President Lincoln had to pick up the pieces. Wilkes next turned to designing ironclad canoes modeled on some he had seen in the far Pacific. These menaced only their crews and, complaining that his specifications had been ignored, he set out to catch the Confederate raiders *Alabama* and *Florida*. In the course of the chase he seized the swifter vessel of a fellow officer specially dispatched on the same mission and commandeered two vessels of Admiral Farragut's Gulf Squadron. But in clearing the seas he seized the ships of other nations as well, calling up further international crises. And before being recalled in the summer of 1863 he had managed to offend not only Britain, but Spain, France, and Denmark as well.

He managed to offend Secretary of the Navy Gideon Welles, too; Welles brought against him court-martial charges of disobedience, insubordination, disrespect, and conduct unbecoming an officer. The President of the Court, Rear Admiral Francis H. Gregory, who had once commanded the Expedition for a few brief hours before Mrs. Gregory intervened, and then the *North Carolina* when it had been the scene of Wilkes' earlier trial, delivered sentence: another public reprimand and suspension from duty for three years. Wilkes was put to pasture as rear admiral (a rank created in 1862), a hero forgotten. His naval career had spanned half a century, but he had never in the course of it learned to be a subordinate.

The warrior laid down his weapons. (Except for the blunderbuss pen: he was still pursuing Gideon Welles with abiding hatred in 1869, when Fred Stuart pleaded with him to desist and "allow the Old Man to depart in peace.") That career at an end, Wilkes turned his thoughts to his great national monument, which still remained unfinished. In 1870 Commodore Augustus L. Case, once a passed midshipman in the Exploring Expedition, responded to the request of the Library Committee and again detailed Wilkes to the Expedition. Together, Wilkes and Stuart took stock of the work remaining. "Our unlucky rebellion," as Wilkes called the Civil War, had got terribly in the way of things. Torrey's manuscript on the plants of the Northwest Coast, completed in 1861, required considerable updating, since most of his work had by now been duplicated by others; although Professor Henry urged him to continue with "the great work that has been so much credit to the country," Torrey was old and weary and not at all enthusiastic.

Neither Gray nor Agassiz had done any further work since 1861, and the pay of both was in arrears. Still, Agassiz had reported that two thousand pages of manuscript and sixteen hundred and seventy drawings of fish were completed when the war began. As only some forty drawings remained to be done and the dean of American science was old and ill, Stuart urged that manuscript, drawings, and specimens be brought to Washington. If necessary, perhaps others could be found to complete the work. Pickering's manuscript, only one half of which had been printed, was in the hands of the Committee. Wilkes' hydrographical report was nearly all printed and his Physics volume almost ready for the press. Stuart estimated that $64,458 would see the whole job completed, not an exhorbitant sum if one bore in mind that $28,566 had already been spent on the volumes yet to be published.[7]

Two years later Congress responded somewhat less than half-heartedly by appropriating nine thousand dollars for publishing Wilkes' and Torrey's volumes. Torrey was seventy-six and, with no heart for the work, pleaded with both Henry and Gray to dissuade the Committee. "I am conscious of being old," he wrote Gray, and was much relieved when the younger man (Gray was sixty-three) offered to perform the task of revision. At the end of January 1873 the old botanist took to his bed, "greatly diminished, & my flesh has gone I don't know where," but he had strength enough to give warm approval to the plan for completion Gray sent him. One month later he was dead.

His volume appeared the next year, together with the monographs by Sullivant, Tuckerman, Bailey and Harvey, Curtis and Berkeley. All had been completed decades before, and indeed all the authors were dead now, except the English lichenologist Miles Joseph Berkeley and Edward Tuckerman, who had first addressed himself to the task when just out of college.

They were the last of the Expedition's publications. Wilkes' *Hydrography* was finally issued in June 1873, bearing the date 1861. The plates for Torrey's atlas, though they only required binding, never appeared in an official edition, for Wilkes was having trouble with the new chairman of the Library Committee, Timothy O. Howe of Wisconsin. Howe systematically harassed the enterprise from the day he became chairman in March 1873, and he finally discharged Stuart and refused to pay the thousand dollars owed him. With two of the three volumes on which completion hinged, in print, the third

(Physics) in press, and, for once, money in the account, the dismissal of Stuart, who had carried the main burden of resuming publication, brought all to a halt. Though seventy-seven now, Wilkes had lost none of his capacity for indignation. On learning that Sherman & Company of Philadelphia had stopped the printing of his Physics because Howe refused to make further payments, he urged Messrs. Sherman to pay no attention to a person "so entirely ignorant," so "malicious and wrong" as to attempt "to put a stop to the finishing of this Great National Work." A valid contract had been made and the proper course for Messrs. Sherman was to complete the printing and never mind Mr. Howe, who would have to approve the bills or resign as chairman. But Sherman would not take the risk, and so the great monument that Wilkes had been striving to raise remained truncated, while several large unhewn blocks lay at hand. Pickering's volume, the first part of which had gone to press back in 1853, remained unpublished, although in 1876 the old naturalist brought out a five-hundred-page volume on the geographical distribution of animals and plants in their wild state as a companion to the little book on domestic species. Even so, these two accounted for only about half of his manuscript report.

Agassiz's two volumes, intended to work a revolution in natural history, went unpublished when the great entrepreneur of American science died a few months after John Torrey, in December 1873. Although his careful descriptive work would have been an ornament to the publications, the revolution could have been no more than a skirmish at the rear. For the revolution was Darwin's, and Agassiz had been fighting for fourteen years to stay its spread. The seventeen hundred sheets of Asa Gray's work for the "everlasting" Expedition, together with the drawings for his atlas, also remained unpublished. At the dawn of his career Gray had let the Expedition down, badly. Now, when he stood very near the head of the world community of botanists, it repaid the blow.

Wilkes lived only to complete the Expedition and, failing in that, survived it but three years. If his monument was unfinished, he found solace in the reflection that the fault for that lay with others. He spent these last years filling ream after ream with his apologia. Age had not palsied the hand nor softened the heart. He wrote on and on with dour gusto, savoring anew the old animosities, reappraising his career and finding each step well taken, every decision judicious and timely. It was an exercise in introspective hagiolatry.

Yet this is not to say that the object of his devotions was undeserving. What indeed is one to make of this man who commanded an expedition of six ships and hundreds of men yet was neither seaman nor leader? Who seized command of all the sciences yet was in command of none? Dana thought he knew and perhaps his qualifications for judging were best, for he was devoted both to science and to the Expedition, and in the six years he had spent aboard ship he had come to know "well what Naval officers very generally are." In 1846, when there had been difficulties with Wilkes over the coral volume and his feelings were "hard as a brick bat," Dana had tried to convey his understanding to Gray. Wilkes was conceited and overbearing, stingy with praise, ready with blame, and often unjust. But Wilkes respected science, and in the Navy that rendered him unique. That being so, Dana much doubted that with any other commander "we should have fared better, or lived together more harmoniously." Gray was willing to take his friend's word for it, as he himself knew only the Captain of the Washington years. But during those years, especially, the Expedition could hardly have fared better under another. Puzzled politicians, "tired," as one exasperated Senator put it, "of all this thing called science here," but nonetheless obliged to deal with science now, were inclined to accept the word of one in whom they recognized the mark of their own practical kind and even, in the Captain who had entered Sydney harbor with such flair, of their own art. Without Wilkes' incredible energy and byzantine mind, the Expedition's achievements might have been no more lasting than the wake of its ships upon the waters of the world. Actually Wilkes' accomplishment was a different and more enduring one than he would have desired, for though neither would have wished to see their names paired in history, Wilkes had gone far toward carrying out Jeremiah Reynolds' design. By putting science into government and government into science he had made it possible for the American scientist to live by his profession—like other respectable people.

Long a familiar figure in Washington society, the Captain was remembered in the country at large, if at all, as "the hero of the *Trent* affair." When he died on February 8, 1877, many newspapers forgot to mention that he had commanded the First Great National Exploring Expedition.[8]

23 Splendid Contributions

. . . and knowledge shall be increased.

Daniel 12:4

Though Americans were not again to appear in Antarctica until Admiral Byrd explored it from the air in 1928–1929, the Expedition did establish a precedent for American polar exploration. There was a rumor in 1849 that Wilkes would lead a party in search of the distinguished Arctic explorer Sir John Franklin (who as Lieutenant-Governor of Van Diemen's Land had delivered Wilkes' instructions to Ross), from whom no word had been received since his departure in the *Erebus* and *Terror* in 1845 in quest of a northwest passage between Baffin Bay and Bering Strait. The search for Franklin, begun in 1847, had become an international cause célèbre. Though Wilkes was the logical man to lead the American party, he was ill during much of 1849 and 1850, suffering like so many of the explorers from ague and fever. When the New York merchant Henry Grinnell outfitted the brigs *Advance* and *Rescue* for an expedition that was to mark the beginning of American naval exploration in the Arctic, he gave command, together with the ensign saved from the *Peacock*, to Lieutenant De Haven, who had seen polar ice before. His surgeon and naturalist, Elisha Kent Kane, found De Haven "a capital officer, a daring sailor, with a dash of extra spirit for exigencies." Kane was the son of J. N. Reynolds' old tormentor in Philadelphia, but his enthusiasm for polar exploration had been fired by the exploits of the First Great National Exploring Expedition in his youth. Kane himself carried the *Peacock*'s ensign aboard the *Advance* on the second Grinnell expedition (1853–1855), and was rescued by the third American expedition to the Arctic, led by Commander Henry J. Hartstene, whom Wilkes had sent home in the *Relief*. Kane's surgeon and naturalist was Doctor Isaac Israel Hayes, who commanded his own Arctic expedition in 1860–1861, taking with him John Cleves Symmes' account of the holes in the poles as well as the now famous flag. (In 1871 Grinnell dispatched the flag a fourth time, entrusting it to the ill-fated Ohioan Charles Francis Hall.) But the tradition of overseas exploration that the great expedition established was not confined to the poles. It included the world between. In the single year 1853 no fewer than four Navy scientific expeditions were abroad; De Haven's had just returned from the Arctic, others from the Amazon and Chile.

Of the institutions of science that the Expedition produced, John Quincy Adams would have been proudest of its lighthouse of the skies—the Naval Observatory. On the squadron's departure, the Secretary of the Navy had authorized the purchase of all necessary equipment for observations in astronomy, magnetism, and meteorology and placed it all in the hands of Lieutenant James Melville Gilliss. Gilliss' attention to the work over the next four years was very nearly constant and wore down thirty-three assistants in succession. His was the government's first working observatory and he was the first American to give his full time to practical astronomical work. On the Expedition's return he succeeded in getting an appropriation for a permanent building, which he made into one of the world's first-rate observatories. (By way of welcome, startled astronomers at Berlin, Paris, Vienna, and Greenwich presented it with a library.) Gilliss published his four years' observations and later a star catalogue, both the first American works of their kind. Again the Expedition stood convicted of smuggling science over the border of free enterprise and minimal government.*

The Explorers' two-hundred-odd charts helped free American shipmasters from their dependence, so galling to cultural patriots, on foreign cartographers; the charts were everywhere acknowledged to be of the first quality. Some were still in use during World War II, for the engraved plates were transferred to the Hydrographic Office on its founding in 1866 and became the

---

* The Expedition had been a young men's adventure, but what it could mean to the older investigator and his science was well brought out in the career of William Cranch Bond, the Cambridge watchmaker and passionate astronomer. When in 1838 the Navy commissioned him (in addition to Gilliss) to conduct the observations that would serve as baselines (zeros of longitude) for the Expedition's survey of the universe, Bond was forty-nine and living in some poverty—owing in part to the expense of building and operating his own observatory—and what the Expedition conferred on him, as his equally distinguished son wrote in gratitude after the father's death, was "that *material* aid, in scientific pursuits, which is so necessary to success," and which, he might have added, was so rarely to be found in the United States. But the lasting benefit was to science, for, having been accorded this recognition by government, Bond was invited the next year to establish an observatory for Harvard, which in turn served as the model for Gilliss'. There Bond continued his observations for the Expedition and there with his son discovered the eighth satellite of Saturn and pioneered in star photography.

nucleus of its collection. The Explorers themselves were proudest of their chart of the Fijis, and not alone because it had cost them the most in lives and labor. It was the first reasonably complete chart of the group, as comparison with Dumont d'Urville's, made from the most recent prior survey, readily showed. Although their maps of the West Coast were accurate as far as they went, the rush of events in the late forties brought out the Coast Survey (much of whose work there, begun in 1850, was done under the direction of Lieutenant James Alden in the steamer *Active*), and because the Survey could spend years where the squadron had been allotted only weeks, its maps soon supplanted those made by the Expedition. Still the Explorers performed a real service, and their survey of the interior, much of it based on the explorations of Emmons and Eld, has been held to mark the beginning of accurate western cartography. When Fremont in the forties connected his explorations with the squadron's, the continent was joined with some precision for the first time.[1]

The scientific reports and their magnificent atlases were largely what they purported to be, descriptive catalogues of species collected. One searches in vain for some daring leap of imagination, for imagination was held in check and theorizing was taboo. Yet in the role assigned them, the reports won the general approval of the scientific community and most have stood the test of time. Gould's volume bore testimony not only to his own learning but to Couthouy's remarkable perception as well, for its particular value lay in its report on regions whose Mollusca were largely unknown—Tierra del Fuego, the Pacific islands, Puget Sound, and Oregon. In one genus (Succinea) Couthouy and Gould described as many new species as the total previously known. And the attention they accorded unshelled Mollusca and the living organism in all groups—the whole animal and not just the shell alone—was something of an innovation and marked a real advance. Even Peale's rejected volume has been accorded an honorable place, for the few zoologists who have had the opportunity to compare it to Cassin's find it little inferior.

Brackenridge, the gardener turned scientist by virtue, probably, of four years spent in the company of the learned Pickering, wrote a book—it was his only published contribution to science—that compared favorably with the work of contemporaries in the same field and the species he proposed have stood up well. "A most charming work," Sir William Hooker wrote him from Kew, "creditable to yourself & creditable to the U. States." In his *Herpetology* Girard changed too many established names, "through sheer whim," as one historian has put it, but even so he brought many new species to the attention of science. Among the smaller collections in botany, Tuckerman was able to describe about eight new species and varieties of Lichenes, Bailey and Harvey many new species of Algae, and Curtis and Berkeley some nine of Fungi. And among the flowering plants Gray's volume rose as a taxonomic monument.

Yet one who has followed in the Explorers' wake comes away from these reports with an almost overwhelming sense of waste. They had nursed the great pendulum around the world and meticulously observed the magnetic apparatus through how many nights and days for a volume that was never to see print. (Though it must be said that if the novel theories Wilkes launched in the *Narrative* and in papers read before the American Association provide any measure of his intentions for the projected reports on meteorology and physics, the loss was less than tragic.) They had seined the seas of the world for fishes that would never be drawn. As a consequence, their collection, the largest ever made by an exploring expedition before the British *Challenger* Expedition of 1873–1876 (and even that enterprise, the reports of which ran to forty-one volumes, failed to surpass the American expedition in numbers of new species) was still yielding new species as late as 1924.[2]

Several of the authors managed to evade the obscurity that Congress decreed for their reports by resorting to prepublication in the scientific journals. Lacking illustrations, these were no match for the official reports, but they did assure effective dissemination of knowledge and establish priority, which is what scientific reports are for. Gould published the new Mollusca as fast as he could describe them in the *Proceedings* of the Boston Society of Natural History from 1846 to 1850, and only a small portion of Girard's report was not published elsewhere. But restrictions on printing and distribution rendered many of the reports less accessible than the collections themselves. Curtis and Berkeley's monograph remained largely unknown even to specialists, and four decades after its publication only two algological papers could be found that made reference to Bailey and Harvey's. Brackenridge's volume, and particularly its atlas, enjoyed perhaps more repute as rare books than as a contribution to science. Delay in publication vitiated the effectiveness of Torrey's work.

Yet in terms of the contributions it made to science, the Expedition was greater than the sum of its parts. In some of the departments—geology, anthropology, philology—the purely systematic, descriptive approach was inadequate, even irrelevant, and the investigator was forced to address himself to theory. Among natural history men in the Western world in the first half of the nineteenth century, the paramount issue and the most promising area of investigation was the geographical distribution of species. In 1855 the French botanist Alphonse De Candolle published a great two-volume treatise, *Géographie botanique raisonée*, which put the problem squarely to the world scientific community, asked a great many pertinent questions and provided few answers. Peale had some glimmering of its significance in the determination of bird and mammal species; indeed, the modern concept of geographical species might justify reinstatement of some of his species that Cassin discarded. Before the squadron sailed, Pickering had pointed out that investigation of the phenomenon would be incumbent upon the naturalist, and he himself displayed astonishing insight into the core of the problem. (If after publication of the *Origin of Species* he ever re-read that passage in his own letter with its advice to concentrate on species divergence within clusters of distant island groups, he must have done so with mingled pride and rue.) When he came to report on the races of man he had settled upon the notion of separate creations to explain the remarkable suitability of the organism to its environment and hence the widespread dispersal of species that differed only in minute particulars. It was the majority view in science, except with regard to man himself. Pickering, who did not except man, rarely ventured into theory after that.

Asa Gray had been fascinated by geographical distribution for as long as Pickering and, like him, realized the futility of addressing it directly until the basic task of classification was well in hand. But if the bonds of taxonomy held him firmly for decade after decade, the eternal classifying and describing of exotic plants returned by the Expedition and by later surveys nevertheless conferred advantages of inestimable value to a mind venturesome enough to follow wherever the flowers might lead. Gray was America's leading botanist by the eighteen-fifties, and by virtue of the experience these collections (and particularly the one returned by Ringgold's expedition to the North Pacific) brought him, he was the first anywhere to acquire a comprehensive and accurate knowledge of the plant life of the whole Northern Hemisphere. Gray was thus in a position to view their relationships and to cut a path for empiricism in natural history in place of the aesthetically pleasing and theologically soothing design that naturalists, very much like the English artists of the eighteenth century who painted yew trees in Tahitian landscapes, had long been devoutly finding evidence to support. The breadth of Gray's knowledge enabled him to recognize the floristic affinities between eastern Asia and the northeastern United States and to explain the phenomenon without recourse to special creation theory; it made him the sole American scientist—after his receptivity had been politely but carefully tested—to whom Darwin would reveal his "notions," as he modestly put it to Gray two years before profoundly shocking the Western world with them. It made him Darwin's foremost American champion.

The presence of the same plant species in eastern North America and Japan was to be explained, Gray pointed out, not by separate creations in each but by the opportunity for migration offered by the contiguousness of land masses in the Arctic regions, as compared to their remoteness from one another in the tropics, where, as Pickering had suggested, terrestrial species were so numerous. Such contiguousness was not essential to the diffusion of marine plants, which explained why these were largely the same on both sides of the ocean. True, western North America was a kind of island of life in itself, with a generally distinctive flora, but surely that was because the path of dissemination lay along the isothermals, which swung far northward on the western coast of the continent, by-passing Oregon and California and leaving the region with a flora that was unique.

To explain the interchange of plant species between eastern America and Japan, Gray made use of the phenomenon of glaciation, which Agassiz had done so much to elucidate. Gray also sought the advice of his friend Dana, who assured him that in the period before glaciation the climate was warmer than at present. To Gray, this meant that plants might freely migrate across the Bering Strait. The coming of the glaciers had put an end to migration and separated the flora into two great colonies, which satisfactorily explained their identity at the present day. But the similarity did not end with identity of species: he found that the same pattern extended to genera as well, that in many instances Japanese and American plants differed only just enough to warrant their classification as separate species. If the individuals thus diffused shared a common ancestry, why might not the genera, whose differences were so small, also have a common ancestry? Gray's answer to the question launched him into transmutation and led him to take the first step along the path that Darwin had pointed out.

If the Expedition conferred benefits on Gray, it was the making of Dana. In response to Wilkes' cost-cutting foray of 1848 Dana protested—to good effect—that having devoted eleven years exclusively to the Expedition, he had never bothered to establish himself in a profession and if he must take the time to do so now, then Wilkes must wait for his reports. But in fact those very years had established him in a profession: geology. When the squadron had sailed, he called himself a mineralogist, having just published a textbook on the subject. He shipped as geologist, and when Couthouy was discarded, he became marine zoologist, as well. The cruise over, he retained his interest in the latter field because of its bearing on his chief interest, geology. The whole field of zoophytes, the plant-like animals that are now called coelenterates, and especially the corals, was a new one to science. Long the preserve of both poets and clergymen, it came burdened with many fancies and much moralizing. The coral structures actually afforded the most spectacular example of the role of the organism in modifying the earth's crust, but for some (including Charles Wilkes) it was beyond belief that these "animalcules," some of them microscopic, could build islands and reefs, which were ascribed instead to "the lightning of tropical regions, and the electric fluid engendered by sub-marine and other volcanoes which abound in the South Seas"—notions which Dana tartly labeled "the first and last appeal of ignorance." Others identified the masons as fishes that labored diligently with their teeth. Many who were willing to give credit to little animals, saw polyps as the patient builders, heaping up rock from the sea bed by their united labors to produce great structures that were both beautiful and useful. These "busy little builders of the deep" exemplified the virtues of selfless and patient industry, as well as the benevolence of the Creator in providing stone flowers for man's delight and sea walls for his protection. Occupying the border zone between the animal and vegetable kingdoms, they had been transferred by general consent to the animal kingdom only during the last century. (The place of a similarly confusing creature, the sponge, was still being debated.) Dana early perceived the task that lay before him: disabuse the poets, enlighten the clergymen, and put the subject on a scientific basis.

His observations on coral phenomena appeared both in his report on Zoophytes, where, to Wilkes' consternation, he devoted over seven hundred pages to recasting this entire branch of zoological science, and in his report on Geology, in which he dealt with the coral structures. The former was a monumental work that cost Dana a vast amount of labor, not only because the subject had been so little attended that 203 of the 261 Actinoid zoophytes and 229 of the 483 coral zoophytes he described were unknown to science (and even more were unknown in the living state), but also because coral animals and the Actiniae—organisms such as the sea-anemone which, though related to the coral zoophyte, make no coral—are among the most difficult groups of the animal kingdom to classify systematically. But if the work was onerous, it proved to be a milestone in science, for he not only classified the animalcules but also elucidated their physiology, both individual and communal, and ecology. As Asa Gray predicted in his review, the report long remained the standard authority on the subject and retains its validity after the passage of a century, for the large divisions he defined and a majority even of his species are still accepted. With its publication Dana became the source for all that was known of coral zoophytes and the Actiniae. He exploded a good many popular myths by showing that the polyp was among the simplest of animals, having only a mouth and a stomach, was fleshy and not jelly-like, as was commonly believed, was not invisible, for the most part, but commonly half an inch in width and two or three in length in some species; and that its calcareous exudation was an internal secretion more analogous to the skeleton of a vertebrate than to the shell of a mollusk or the hive of a bee.

The abundant opportunities that the Expedition afforded Dana to study the three great types of coral islands—atolls, barrier reefs, and fringing reefs—enabled him independently to confirm Darwin's theory, which Dana first learned of at Sydney in 1839, of the evolution of the structure through the agency of subsidence, the slow sinking of the ocean floor. On reading the American's book, Darwin, whose chances for observation had been fewer, was *"astonished at my own accuracy!!"* The limits that volcanic activity set to coral growth attracted Dana to volcanism, and the contributions he was able to make to this subject—the influence of stream erosion in shaping the cone, elucidation of the steps in the eruptive process, the geographical distribution of volcanic activity and its role in shaping the earth's crust—again reflected the unexampled opportunities for study that the Expedition had accorded him.

The popularity of some of these relatively specialized studies was remarkable. When Dana's observations on coral phenomena, originally embodied in the two reports, were printed as a separate book, *Coral and Coral Islands*, it passed through three editions during the author's lifetime. Of course the subject possessed an inherent appeal, but it is also true that Dana wrote extraordinarily well and, like the preachers and poets, perceived a design in nature that was pleasing and flattering to man. "The Madrepores," he wrote in a passage that Gray quoted approvingly in his review of the *Zoophytes*, "are crowded around in turfy clumps and miniature trees in bloom, or imitate spreading leaves and graceful vases filled with flowers; while Astraeas build up among the shrubbery large domes, embellished with green and purple blossoms, studding the surface like gems." *

The opportunities that the nation opened to Dana through his fifteen years' service with the Expedition he amply repaid in gratitude and in the honors that accrued to it through him. In Berlin in 1856, Samuel F. B. Morse heard the great Humboldt exclaim at how "much admiration in Europe"

---

* Gray's conceits tended to be more mundane, if no less apt. He noted that the polyps generally "are firmly attached to the rocks, or some other convenient support, to which they cling with the tenacity of an office-holder, while they gorge themselves with such pickings as fall within their reach. Some polyps, such as the Hydra, it is well known, may be turned inside out, like the fingers of a glove—or as the pliant office-holder turns his coat when the *ins* and the *outs* change places—and still feed and digest unconcernedly, and thrive and batten in all respects just as well as before."

American science was commanding, and go on to praise the work of Dana as "the most splendid contribution to science of the present day." Dana retired from Yale in 1890 at the age of seventy-seven, even though his health had been poor for some thirty years. Thereafter, the flow of books and papers slackened somewhat; and he died in 1895, having given generations of Yale men and of Americans an opportunity to join him on the great adventure of his youth. "If this work gives pleasure to any," he remarked toward the close of his life in the third edition of his book on coral, "it will but prolong in the world the enjoyments of the 'Exploring Expedition.' " [3]

It is no wonder that American science owed much to the dedicated life of Dana. But it is a little surprising that its debt should also be large to a man who gave it only the years of his youth and old age. The first third of Horatio Hale's report was devoted to the ethnography of the Pacific and the remainder to its philology. Reviewers noted that Hale gave "a very extensive meaning to the word ethnography," for instead of confining himself to the practice of late years, of giving an account of "the filiation of different races," he dealt with cultures—the native religion, mythology, cosmogeny, civil organization, customs and manners, manufactures, migrations. Much of this information was of course not new. What was new, Asa Gray noted in his review, was the facility with which he combined these materials to present "a gallery of ethnographical pictures, of the highest importance" that displayed a "remarkable acuteness and tact in discerning the characteristic peculiarities" of the peoples studied.

Each people was distinctive and something more than the sum of its parts. Yet Hale was persuaded that, taken together, they formed "a single nation." Addressing himself to the problem of the geographical distribution of language and scrutinizing languages and all that was directly related to language, including prosody and music, he sought to determine the original point at which separation had taken place and the paths each had pursued to its present abode. Comparing Polynesian vocabularies and grammars, he found forms in the western islands that were absent in the eastern and other forms complete in the western but defective or perverted in the eastern tongues. He concluded that the principal tribes of Polynesia could be traced back to Samoa and Tonga and, he was inclined to believe, to the island of Bouro, in the East Indian archipelago. In any event, the course of migration was from west to east, a discovery that tended to bear out the theory, widely accepted, that the interior of Asia was the locus of mankind's dispersion.

The collections Hale worked with were vocabularies and grammars, and as he gathered them at the last minute before the Progress of the Age overwhelmed the cultures they represented, they were never to be superceded. The philological portion of his book emerged as a monument in classical philology, the philology of John Pickering and Albert Gallatin, but it also, especially in his grammars, marked a sharp departure, for he presented an analysis of the language, as one scholar has noted, "unmarred by any preconceptions, based upon European philology, of what such a language ought to be like, but isn't." Hale was an investigator after Asa Gray's own heart, and Gray, no mean stylist himself, had only praise for the "elegant, terse, compact" quality of Hale's prose that made it "a transparent medium of expression for a richly informed, clear-thinking, straight-forward mind."

Since Hale brought out an unofficial issue of one hundred and fifty copies and since old Albert Gallatin, that last of the Jeffersonians, edited his materials on the languages of the Northwest Coast, the work escaped obscurity, and throughout the century the leading philologists and anthropologists of Europe continued to accord it respect, one proclaiming it "the greatest mass of Philological data ever accumulated by a single inquirer." To have reached beyond the acknowledged advantages that his own continent offered for philological investigation and by focusing on exotic peoples, to have placed himself in successful competition with the leading scholars of Europe was an astonishing achievement for a young man who had joined the Expedition while an undergraduate.

In the decades that followed, however, Hale disappeared from the world of scholarship. On returning from his travels he studied law, married a Canadian woman, and in 1856 moved to Clinton, Ontario, where for the next thirty-five years he practiced law and devoted himself to various enterprises of public utility—promoting a railroad and the education and co-education of women, delivering a eulogy at the re-interment of Red Jacket—but contributed nothing to science. He thought of the separation as only temporary. He still kept his library in Philadelphia, where he became a member of the Philosophical Society in 1872, and he continued to correspond with the Oregon missionary Myron Eells on matters of linguistics. But in 1869 he confessed to being "somewhat rusted in philological studies."

In some ways he was rusted. His book had been an answering shot fired at the American School of anthropology, which, taking the biological approach, had condemned philology as "a broken reed" and concluded that the races of men were separately created and therefore were separate species. Hale, by contrast, perceived beyond the differences a unity, and his years with the Expedition had provided an intensive and constant exposure to Polynesian cultures far beyond anything available to those contemporaries of his youth.

By 1869 that struggle was long past, for Darwin had shown how it was that varieties and even species, though differing as sharply from one another as the races of men, had descended from common progenitors. Ethnologists had thereafter become anthropologists, addressing their investigations to the species Man, instead of merely to the varieties of men.

The leading American investigator in the field that Darwinism had rendered so promising was Lewis Henry Morgan, a railroad attorney from Rochester, who had developed an interest in Iroquois culture and had set forth his findings in *The League of the Iroquois* (1815), which was hailed as "the first scientific account of an Indian tribe." For Morgan, the Indian was not just a savage, but a savage with prospects, to wit, a "primitive" whose culture evolved through laws of progress that operated as surely upon the Kingsmill Islander as upon the Iroquois. Tracking progress in the arts of subsistence, of government, in the development of the monogamous family from the primitive state of sexual promiscuity, and in the gradual emergence of the idea of private property, Morgan formulated these laws in his *Ancient Society* (1877). A revolutionary view of man's past, his study might have been taken as fulfillment of the Jeffersonian dream of placing the doctrine of equality on a scientific basis. It was hailed by many of the leading figures of American anthropology. But not by Horatio Hale.

Sniffing the sulphur of the old battle of his youth, the re-emergence of the qualitative distinctions of the American School, Hale set about collecting Iroquois materials in the same way and to the same end that he had gathered Polynesian materials thirty years before. He responded with a thumping commitment to the unity of man and once more dragged the caissons of language to the fray. It is remarkable that his argument should have been as relevant—indeed, as advanced—when he addressed Morgan in 1877 as it had been three decades before. Morgan had seen the Hawaiian kinship system as a relic of a promiscuous and barbarous past. "Why promiscuous and barbarous?" Hale wanted to know. Reminding Morgan that he had spent some time among the Sandwich Islanders (as Morgan had not) and "studied the language carefully in preparing my Comparative Grammar and Lexicon of the Polynesian dialects," he tried to point out that "brother" and "sister" and "cousin" had not meant in those islands precisely what they meant in Rochester. "I am, we will suppose, a married Hawaiian, living in a large house along with my married brothers and perhaps my married sisters and cousins. The little children who play about me when I am at work in my field or who go out fishing with me in my canoe are all alike dear to me. When I speak of or to them, I don't use the words son or daughter, niece or nephew. I classify

SPLENDID CONTRIBUTIONS

them. They are all 'little ones'; and, if necessary I may add the words *male* or *female* for further distinction. In like manner I am not in their speech a father or uncle. I am 'old one' or 'senior'; and, if necessary, they may distinguish the sex in like manner. Among themselves the children have no word exactly equivalent to *brother* or *sister* or *cousin*. They have expressions which mean 'mate' or 'comrade,' and they may further distinguish by adding words or using forms to indicate whether the mate is male or female, and whether older or younger than the speaker. All this is classificatory, and it is pure Hawaiian. *Keiki* is not *child* but 'little one.' . . . *Makua* means mature. It is applied to trees and fruit as much as to human beings. . . ."

"The lists of relationships which you have collected with so much industry and care seem to me to prove—not that men and women ever lived in promiscuous intercourse, nor yet that brothers and sisters had their wives and husbands in common—but simply and solely that in the early society of most races it has been customary for nearly related families to live together in large households, for mutual support and protection."

In viewing the kaleidoscope of the human condition, Morgan had not erred in recognizing "the common principles of the human character and intellect" (the phrase is pure Hale), for he had glimpsed the principle of the relativity of cultures, and that was so much gained. But he had not applied the principle rigorously enough and so had failed to perceive that the universal laws of progression he discovered were really only his projections into space and time of the values of his own culture.

When, in the 1880's, anthropology's Ichabod once more addressed himself to the community of scholars in a spate of books, articles, and papers, many in his audience, much influenced by social Darwinism, must have thought his ideas antique. They could not perceive that, instead, they were witnessing the first shot in a long war against theories of social evolution. Hale had a profound mistrust of all theories that made biological characters the determinants of human behavior or that ranked races and cultures in some hypothetical scale of social evolution.

Although the last survivor from the age of classical philology, Hale was nonetheless ahead of his time in his conception of the role linguistics should play in anthropology. Language, he insisted in a paper he read before the American Association for the Advancement of Science in 1887, was anthropology's only sure tool. From the influence of climate, to which physical traits were notoriously subject, language was immune, as could be seen in the Aryan languages that extended from Hindustan to Iceland and were radically the same, while the physical differences of the people who spoke them were very great. True, a man might adopt another language, but only when residing among those who spoke it. A community, he remarked in a nod to Darwin, "never adopts a new language except under the direct pressure of a stronger population, with which it ultimately becomes united in one people of mixed blood. If in this mingled race, one element is much stronger than the other, the weaker element is finally absorbed, leaving perhaps little or no apparent trace, either in the language or the aspect of the population. If both elements are strong, the aspect of the people and the form of the language alike show evidence of the mixture. The fact, therefore, remains that language is the indication, and the only sure indication, of the origin of a community." With a distinctive language emerged "a peculiar mental and moral character," a religion, "peculiar social organization, suited to the character and circumstances of the people," and peculiar arts and folklore. Folklore, containing specimens of language and thought and "the best of information as to native religion, law, and custom," was itself an avenue to the past and its study a valuable "sister science of comparative philology."

Finally, Hale's experience with the Expedition led him to insist that field work alone could yield the intimate familiarity—with language and all the other elements of a culture—that was needed to uncover the empirical data essential to any truly scientific view of man's past.

In the last decade of his life, Hale had the opportunity to turn his science into the channels these advanced views prescribed. In 1884 the British Association for the Advancement of Science chose Montreal as the site of its first overseas meeting, organized a separate section for anthropology, and, in view of the impending extinction of Indian cultures, appointed a committee of seven to investigate and publish reports on the tribes of northwestern Canada. Of the seven, it was Hale who interpreted the mandate and saw to its execution. Though evidently intending to take to the field himself in the 1885 season, he was sixty-eight and physically not up to the task. Two seasons passed before he acknowledged that the work must be done by another. In 1887 he met Franz Boas, a thirty-year-old German anthropologist who had been studying the tribes of British Columbia. Impressed with Boas' grasp of the science, especially with his insistence on field work as the only valid approach, Hale offered him the position, sending along a copy of his paper on "Race and Language": "From what I have seen of your writings, I entertain the hope that your views will accord with those which are suggested in this paper. There can be no better opportunity of testing them than in the mission now proposed." On receipt of Boas' acceptance, he made certain that they would be tested by laying out a comprehensive program in a succession of letters sufficiently detailed to rankle the younger man, and ventured to refer him to "my account of the Oregon tribes, written more than forty years ago. . . . You will find many deficiencies, as I had but about three months for a large territory of whose ethnology hardly anything was known. I had to travel hundreds of miles through a wild country, with no companions but Indians and half-breeds, and often very few interpreters. I gave my attention chiefly to the languages and less to customs, traditions, arts, and physical traits than I should now. My impression is that I rated the character of those Indians too low. I was then a young man of twenty-four, fresh from College, and technological science was far behind the present stage. . . . It seems desirable that your report and map should connect with mine."

Boas complained to his wife of the old man's nagging, "saucy" letters, which showed "clearly that he knows nothing about general ethnology." They were nagging and detailed not only because Hale was guardian of the interests of the British Association and supervisor of research that was urgent and must be complete: he saw himself as preparing Boas for a future which would be his own only insofar as it was the younger man's. When Boas' results exceeded the old man's expectations, he set him free. "I will not hamper you with specific instructions," Hale wrote in relation to the 1890 season in the field. "You will consider yourself entirely at liberty to act on your own judgment."

Long after Hale was gone, the use of native texts continued to be a characteristic of Boasnian anthropology. By teaching him how to use the data of language, "the true basis of ethnology," to solve the problems of ethnology, Hale made it inevitable that in the future American anthropology would be peculiarly sensitive to its significance, and his unyielding insistence (in the face of exasperated protest) that Boas address himself to the groups of the entire geographical region, taking careful note of their differences and affinities, assured that it would be directed less to social analysis than to reconstruction of cultural history. When death ended the life-long "love affair with language" on December 29, 1896, Boas wrote the obituary. "Ethnology has lost a man who contributed more to our knowledge of the human race than perhaps any other single student." [4]

Coda

Of the Explorers few outlived Hale. The amiable, prosaic Hudson, promoted captain on the same day as Wilkes in 1855 and esteemed as one of the Navy's premier seamen, commanded the steamer *Niagara* in laying the first Atlantic cable in 1857–1858. His ship's surgeon was James Palmer of the *Peacock*, celebrant of the *Flying Fish* and a man of surprising ingenuity, who devised a method for splicing the cable in mid-ocean. Hudson died quietly at his home in Brooklyn, October 15, 1862, aged sixty-eight.

Cadwallader Ringgold led the North Pacific Exploring Expedition of 1853–1856, sailing from Norfolk again in the *Vincennes* and *Porpoise*. Fred Stuart went as his clerk, draughtsman, and assistant astronomer, and Lieutenant Alonzo B. Davis, once of the *Vincennes*, as commander of the storeship. Ringgold became ill—some said insane—from the old Expedition complaint, intermittent fever, and returned home. In the Civil War he commanded one of the vessels in the attack on Port Royal that Wilkes was too busy to participate in, retired as Rear Admiral in 1866 at the age of sixty-four, and died the next year in New York, a few months before the *Relief*'s commander, Andrew K. Long, who had retired as captain in 1864.

Many another died young. The Rhode Islander Silas Holmes drowned at Mobile in 1849; Henry Eld, the big, beloved New Englander who first sighted the new continent, succumbed to yellow fever at Rio at the end of another three-and-a-half-year Pacific cruise. De Haven, his health broken by his cruise in north polar seas, retired as lieutenant in 1862 and died in Philadelphia three years later at forty-nine. Jim Blair's career was shorter still. He went to California again in 1849 to assist in the new survey of the coast being conducted by James Alden. Finding San Francisco almost deserted, except for incoming passengers who promptly rushed up the river in search of gold—frequently on the heels of the ships' crews—and possessing a considerable knowledge of the harbor, he set up as pilot, charging a thousand dollars a vessel. With these profits he bought a steamboat, the first on the Sacramento, and soon owned a small fleet. Then he bought lands along the bay that became the business district of the city. Homesick, he kept trying to leave "this country of avericious strife," but the money poured in too fast to permit. In 1854, only thirty-three and still professing a determination to return home, he died, leaving a fortune to his family.

Some who had joined up for the cruise alone resigned from the Navy to take up various careers ashore. But the salt had entered the veins of others, and something else as well—perhaps the craving for adventure that had called them to the Expedition in the first place. Ringgold, Stuart, Davis, and De Haven could not leave exploration alone, nor could Overton Carr, who surveyed the Rio La Plata in the steam frigate *San Jacinto* in 1854–1855. The peppery Couthouy could no more find repose in the countinghouse than among the specimens of the Patent Office, and he returned to the soft isles to complete his observations. In 1854 he set forth in command of a vessel in search of sunken treasure supposed to have gone down with the Spanish man-of-war *San Pedro* half a century before in Venezuela's Bay of Cumaná. Returning from a three years' fruitless search, he lost his ship in a violent snowstorm on Cape Cod. When the Civil War came, he commanded four small vessels in succession, then the gunboat *Chillicothe* on the Red River in Louisiana. On April 2, 1864, while on deck directing the fire, he was shot down by a sniper and died the next day. "As brave and gallant a soul as ever trod a deck, and a lively and always interesting companion," remarked a friend, echoing the sentiments of the Explorers, scientists and officers alike.

Shortly after the Expedition's return the Down-Easter James Alden made a voyage round the world again, in the old *Constitution*, then participated in the capture of Tuxpan, Tabasco, and Vera Cruz. With the Coast Survey in the interwar years he made a reconnaissance of the Pacific coast aboard the little wooden paddle-steamer *Active*, fighting Indians at Puget Sound and very nearly British naval forces as well. His Civil War career was almost covered with glory, for in command of various vessels he saw action at Fort Pickens, Galveston, Fort Jackson, New Orleans, Vicksburg (where he twice ran his ship past the savagely belching batteries), and Fort Fisher. It was marred by only one small blot. Commanding the *Brooklyn* at the van of the column of wooden ships at Mobile Bay, Alden was momentarily appalled at the sudden sinking of the monitor *Tecumseh*, and when torpedoes were reported ahead, he backed water, evoking Admiral Farragut's exasperated imprecation on the torpedoes. Promoted commodore at the war's end and rear admiral in 1871, he commanded the European Squadron, became Chief of the Bureau of Navigation, and retired in 1873. He died in San Francisco two days before his old commander on February 6, 1877, but, as he would perhaps have wished, a continent away.[1]

Both Thomas Craven, Wilkes' first lieutenant left ashore at Valparaiso to await the vanished *Sea Gull*, and Samuel P. Lee, among the first to be shipped home, served with distinction in the Civil War and became rear admirals. The judicious George Emmons and the New Yorker Augustus L. Case came to their admiralties in 1872. Emmons led expeditions in California during the Mexican War, saw service in the Civil War from Charleston to New Orleans and Pass Christian and, commanding the steam sloop *Ossipee* in 1866–1868, carried the United States commissioners to Alaska and hoisted the flag over the new territory. Between wars he wrote a history of the Navy and its ships. He retired with twenty-three years' sea service to spend his days in Princeton, where he died in 1884. William Reynolds, the private chronicler and arch cabalist, was plagued by ill health and retired in 1855. But he went again to Honolulu in 1857 to serve as Navy storekeeper for four years, then commanded a vessel at Port Royal. He rose rapidly after the war, became rear admiral in 1873, and assumed command of the Asiatic Squadron. In 1877 he retired for good and died in Washington two years later.

Only a few of the Southerners went South when the crisis came. Perhaps men who had committed their careers and lives to an enterprise designed to upgrade the nation's reputation were not men to attack the nation itself on whatever provocation. But William Reynolds, recording the fate of his old shipmates in the endpapers of his journals, had to write "Rebel" by the names of some. Of these, Commander Henry Hartstene was highest in rank and reputation. He was present at the evacuation of Fort Sumpter and commanded a gunboat that guarded Charleston Harbor. However, he went insane in the summer of 1862. The volatile George Harrison and William L. Maury became commanders in the Confederate Navy, and Bob Pinkney, James H. North, and the Virginian George Sinclair were captains, Sinclair commanding two vessels during the war.[2]

Charles Pickering stood aside from the tumultuous new age and spent the last sixteen years of his life assembling his twelve-hundred-page *Chronological History of Plants*. A work of immense labor and learning, it was not only a record of the migration of plants from Egypt, "the country that contains the earliest records of the human family," but a chronology of botanical investigation that touched in passing on the other sciences and a great miscellany of subjects as well, but never on theory. He died on March 17, 1878, having seen only half the book through the press. Although recognized by his contemporaries as the Nestor of natural history, Pickering was a man of modesty and tranquility who to some extent foresaw his own fate: years before, in a quandary as to whether to accept a post in Reynolds' expedition, he had written John Torrey, "I do hope . . . that my whole life may not be made up of neglected opportunities."

Titian Peale's position at the Patent Office gave him security and a modest salary until his retirement in 1873, when he went home to Philadelphia to live in genteel poverty. He painted, took an enthusiastic interest in photography, wrote a few scientific articles, and worked among the ethnological collections from Polynesia that he had deposited with the Academy of Natural Sciences. By then they were the best of the kind to be found anywhere, as the official collection in Washington had somehow been misplaced. (In 1896 it was discovered in the Smithsonian cellar under several tons of coal.) He grumbled a good deal about the way the Expedition had been mismanaged, but on looking back at the age of eighty-one he was nonetheless very proud of his part in an enterprise that had produced so many scientific institutions and served "to elevate our country in the rank of Civilized nations," besides "exploring . . . a west coast for our people who followed there, and now count by millions." Living alternately in boarding houses and with his grandson, he remained alert and healthy until felled by a single day's illness on March 13, 1885.

Brackenridge had never really developed a taste for life on the fringes of the world, and in 1855 he bought an orchard near Baltimore, where he set up as nurseryman and landscape gardener and edited the horticultural department of the *American Farmer.* Quite "contented in mind and still vigorous in body," as he reported to Wilkes, he lived a quiet life among his flowers until in his eighty-third year death overtook him suddenly, on February 3, 1893.

The *Vincennes* went on her fourth Pacific cruise in 1846, conveying Commodore Biddle on his unsuccessful attempt to "open" Japan, and in five hundred and eighty-six days at sea she "behaved well under all circumstances," her commander reported. At San Francisco in 1850, she welcomed the newest state into the Union, though losing many of her crew to the gold fields in the process. When she sailed with the North Pacific Expedition she had been twenty-seven years in service, half of them in the Pacific. In 1867 she was sold, a thing of beauty still, but no match in speed and firepower for the contraptions the late war had spawned. The *Vincennes* had returned from the North Pacific without the *Porpoise,* for the brig had gone the way of the *Sea Gull.* Last seen on September 21, 1854, in Taiwan Strait, she was presumed lost in a typhoon with all her eighty hands. The *Relief* served as storeship during the Mexican War and, though never a speedy sailer, she bequeathed her unique rig to the faster sloops and corvettes that followed.

The man who helped start it all, Jeremiah Reynolds, became, of all things, a

Texas banker. Musing in his later years—he died in 1859—on Time's "patient noiseless tread," he concluded that growing old was just as well. Living a million years would not be worth "an hour of what may be ours—this is a pretty fair sort of world [and] if we dont expect too much we may find a great many good fellows in it." Fortunate beyond most, he had found his hour and his good fellows.[3]

And the United States, the intellectual outcast of the Western world, had succeeded in returning light—even if, as Joseph Henry grumbled, more energy was being expended in its diffusion than increase—and won for herself a new respect. Contrary to all precedent at home and prediction abroad, that was an accomplishment envisioned only by the informed and discerning. Many who viewed the democratic japes of the Expedition's beginnings could only observe the workings of a law of cultural impoverishment in a land where all was submitted to the judgment of the many. Few but Peale's dedicated father, who, working to disprove that law, had shrewdly displayed in his scholarly museum a five-legged, six-footed, two-tailed cow giving milk to a two-headed calf, would have perceived (had he lived on) the seriousness that Jeremiah Reynolds knew to lie at the heart of the endeavor and have dared to suggest with a wry smile that by making a place for men who sought neither wealth nor public acclaim but only the opportunity to live by their calling, the efforts of republican dreamers, village cranks, practical merchants, jealous navy officers, and single-minded scientists might help to render the life of the mind acceptable in and to American society.

That was indeed a gain to science and a notable achievement for a people who saw the embodiment of science in the Patent Office models. Yet, as that experienced navigator on the Seas of Credulity, Jeremiah Reynolds, understood, it was that quality of innocence that made it all possible. From Captain Symmes' fervent foolishness to the final subterfuge of the Smithsonian, none of it would have surprised Tocqueville—or Barnum. So the legacy was not alone, nor even chiefly, to science: by undercutting the endemic contempt for intellect and—through the institutions it fathered—rendering the japes and subterfuges less essential if not superfluous in the future, the Exploring Expedition helped to bear the equalitarian society through its cruelest test, the survival of intellect, and in so doing placed liberty in debt to science.

Notes

ABBREVIATIONS USED IN NOTES

ANSP   Academy of Natural Sciences of Philadelphia

APS   American Philosophical Society

DAB   *Dictionary of American Biography*, ed. Allen Johnson and Dumas Malone, 20 vols. (New York, 1928–1936)

HLF   Historic Letter File, Library of the Gray Herbarium, Harvard University Herbarium

LC   Library of Congress

LRWEE   Letters Relating to the Wilkes Exploring Expedition, Rolls 1–7 of the National Archives microfilm publication, Records Relating to the United States Exploring Expedition Under the Command of Lt. Charles Wilkes, 1836–1842 (Microcopy 75)

Citations consisting only of name signify the manuscript journals listed in the Bibliographical Note.

NOTES TO CHAPTER 1

1. R. T. Gould, "The First Sighting of the Antarctic Continent," *Geographical Journal*, 65 (1925), 220–225; Edouard Stackpole, *The Voyage of the "Huron" and the "Huntress": The American Sealers and the Discovery of the Continent of Antarctica* (Hartford, Conn., 1955), pp. 16–17, 22–23, 51–52; E. W. Hunter Christie, *The Antarctic Problem: An Historical and Political Study* (London, 1951), pp. 82, 84, 85, 91; Benjamin Morrell, Jr., *A Narrative of Four Voyages, to the South Sea, North and South Pacific Ocean, Chinese Sea, Ethiopic and Southern Atlantic Ocean, Indian and Antarctic Ocean, from the Year 1822 to 1831* . . . (New York, 1841; first published 1832), p. 68; Kenneth J. Bertrand, *Americans in Antarctica, 1775–1948*, American Geographical Society Special Publication No. 39 (New York, 1971), p. 97.
2. Andrew Sharp, *The Discovery of the Pacific Islands* (Oxford, 1960), pp. 166–167;

Edouard Stackpole, *The Sea-Hunters, The New England Whalemen During Two Centuries* (Philadelphia, 1953), p. 274; Abby Jane Morrell, *Narrative of a Voyage to the Ethiopic and South Atlantic Ocean, Indian Ocean, Chinese Sea, North and South Pacific Ocean, in the Years 1829, 1830, 1831* (New York, 1833), pp. 113–114, 161–164.

3. Samuel Eliot Morison, *The Maritime History of Massachusetts, 1783–1860* (Boston, 1921), 113–117; Alfred Stanford, "Blunt's Coast Pilot . . . ," *Colophon*, Part 14 (June 1933), no pagination; Abby Jane Morrell, *Narrative of a Voyage*, p. 185.

4. James D. Richardson, *Compilation of the Messages and Papers of the Presidents, 1789–1897*, 11 vols. (Washington, 1897), 2:865–883; *Richmond Enquirer*, December 10, 1825; A. Hunter Dupree, *Science in the Federal Government* (Boston, 1957), pp. 7, 9–11, 14, 27; Review of APS *Transactions*, n.s. 2 (1825), in *North American Review*, 20 (1826), 1–13; Florian Cajori, *The Chequered Career of Ferdinand Rudolph Hassler* (Boston, 1929), pp. 90, 91, 92, 110; Nauticus, "On a First Meridian," *National Intelligencer*, February 2, 1819.

NOTES TO CHAPTER 2

1. James McBride, *Pioneer Biography: Sketches of the Lives of some of the Early Settlers of Butler County, Ohio*, 2 vols. (Cincinnati, 1859–1861), 2: 225–252; Cincinnati *Western Spy*, April 24, 1819; Elmore Symmes, "John Cleves Symmes, the Theorist," *Southern Bivouac: A Monthly Literary and Historical Magazine*, n.s. 2 (1887), 555–566, 621–631, 682–693; *Western Spy* Supplement, November 6, 1818; *National Intelligencer*, December 17, 1819; September 15, 1820.

2. *National Intelligencer*, September 29, 1818, September 18 and December 28, 1819; *Cincinnati Advertiser*, November 19, 1822; April 10, 1824; *Western Spy*, August 21, September 11, October 23, and November 13, 1819; T[homas] J. Matthews, *A Lecture on Symmes' Theory of Concentric Spheres, Read at the Western Museum* (Cincinnati, 1824).

3. *Senate Journal*, 17 Cong., 1 sess., 171; *Annals of Congress*, 17 Cong., 1 sess., 278; 17 Cong., 2 sess., 191, 699, 792, 928.

4. *History of Clinton County, Ohio, Containing a History of the County; Its Townships, Cities, Towns, Schools, Churches* (Chicago, 1882), 580–585. Reynolds is largely forgotten and biographical sources are few, but see Henry Howe, *Historical Collections of Ohio*, 3 vols. (Columbus, 1891), 1:430–432; and two complementary attempts at rediscovery—Robert F. Almy, "J. N. Reynolds: A Brief Biography with Particular Reference to Poe and Symmes," *Colophon*, 2 (1937), 227–245; and Aubrey Starke, "Poe's Friend Reynolds," *American Literature*, 11 (1939), 152–159.

5. Symmes, "John Cleves Symmes, the Theorist"; *Philadelphia Gazette and Daily Advertiser*, January 7, February 2 and 8, March 8 and 11, 1826; *United States Gazette*, March 10, April 3, 1826; *Freeman's Journal and Philadelphia Daily Mercantile Advertiser*, March 25 and April 3, 1826; *New York Statesman*, April 8 and May 5, 1826; *Niles' Weekly Register*, 29:427–428 (February 25, 1826), and 33:80 (September 29, 1827); Boston *American Traveler*, May 22, 1826.

6. J. N. Reynolds, *Remarks on a Review of Symmes' Theory, which Appeared in the American Quarterly Review, by a "Citizen of the United States"* (Washington,

1827); Reynolds to Southard, June 27, November 6, 1827; July 1, 1828; Southard to Reynolds, July 6, 1827 (draft) in Southard Papers, Princeton. An excellent brief biography of the open polar sea fancy as it applied to the Arctic is Edward L. Towle, "The Myth of the Open Polar Sea," *Proceedings of the Tenth International Congress of the History of Science*, 2 vols. (Paris, 1965), 1:1037–1041.

7. *House Doc. 88*, 20 Cong., 1 sess.; *House Journal*, 20 cong., 1 sess., 197, 308, 417; *House Report 209*, 20 Cong., 1 sess.; *Register of Debates in Congress*, 20 Cong., 1 sess., vol. 4, Part 2, 1746, 2731.

8. John Quincy Adams, *Memoirs of John Quincy Adams, Comprising Portions of His Diary from 1795 to 1848*, ed. Charles Francis Adams, 12 vols. (Philadelphia, 1874–1877), 7:446; 8:37, 45, 57–58; Reynolds to Southard [1828]; July 13, 1828, in Southard Papers; Reynolds to Southard, June 27, August 12, 1828; Southard to Reynolds, June 30, 1828, Miscellaneous Letters for 1828, Navy Branch, National Archives.

9. J. N. Reynolds, "A Report of J. N. Reynolds, in relation to islands, reefs, and shoals in the Pacific Ocean, &c.," *House Exec. Doc. 105*, 22 Cong., 2 sess.; Reynolds to Southard, July 30, 1828, in Misc. Letters for 1828, Navy Branch, National Archives; Edmund Fanning, *Voyages Round the World, with Selected Sketches of Voyages to the South Seas, North and South Pacific Oceans, China, etc . . .* (New York, 1833), 151–282; Robert Greenhalgh Albion, "Edmund Fanning," DAB.

10. Reynolds to Southard, July 4, 13, 15, October 28, November 10, 11, 1828; De Kay to A[sbury] Dickens, October 5, 1828, in Southard Papers; Joseph Delafield to Southard, June 28, July 14, 1828; Southard to Delafield, July 3, 1828, in Misc. Letters for 1828, Navy Branch, National Archives. On Renwick, see James P. C. Southall, "James Renwick," DAB.

11. *New-York Mirror*, 6:103 (October 4, 1828), 111 (October 11, 1828); Reynolds to Southard, July 4, 10, November 2, 1828; [Southard] to Jones, n.d.; orders to members of the scientific corps, [n.d.]; Wilkes to Southard, October 5, 1828; in Southard Papers; Southard to Reynolds, November 4, 1818; Southard to Benjamin Pendleton, November 6, 1828; Pendleton to Southard, November 12, 1828; in Misc. Letters for 1828, Navy Branch, National Archives.

12. *House Exec. Doc. 2*, 20 Cong., 2 sess.; Reynolds to Southard, October 10, December 8, 10 [?], 1828, Southard Papers; *House Journal*, 20 Cong., 2 sess., 66, 134; *Niles' Weekly Register*, 35:357 (January 24, 1829); *Congressional Debates*, 20 Cong., 2 sess., 5:214.

13. Reynolds to Southard, December 3, 22, 1828; De Kay to Southard, December 11, 1828; De Kay to Reynolds, December 18, 1828; Wilkes to Southard, December 5, 1828, and January 1, 14, and February 14, 1829, in Southard Papers; W[ilkes] to Jones, January 6, 1829, draft in Ms. Journal of Midshipman Charles Wilkes, Jr., Commanding S. S. O'Cain, March 26–October 15, 1823 (Appendix D-39), Naval Records Collection of the Office of Naval Records and Library, Record Group 45, National Archives (hereafter referred to as O'Cain Journal; I am indebted to Nathan Reingold for bringing this revealing document to my attention).

14. *Congressional Debates*, 20 Cong., 2 sess., 5:50–52, and Appendix, 27–30; [Wilkes] to Jones, January 6, 1829; [February, 1829?]; March 29, 1829; to "Mr. Editor," [1829?]: drafts in O'Cain Journal; *Sen. Doc. 94*, 20 Cong., 2 sess.; *Senate Journal*, 20

Cong., 2 sess., 139, 176–177; *Army and Navy Chronicle*, 3:390–391 (November 10, 1836); John Quincy Adams to Rev. Charles W. Upham, February 2, 1837, in Adrienne Koch and William Peden, eds., *The Selected Writings of John and John Quincy Adams* (New York, 1946), Item 176.

15. Reynolds to Adams, September 3, 1829, Papers of John Quincy Adams (Letters Received and other Loose Papers), Adams Manuscript Trust, Massachusetts Historical Society; Reynolds to Southard, September 28 and October 11, 1829, Southard Papers; Eaton to Southard, October 18, 1828, Misc. Letters for 1828, Navy Branch, National Archives; New York Lyceum of Natural History Minutes, August 31, September 7, October 12, 19, 1829, New York Academy of Sciences. These minutes were brought to my attention by Richard O. Cummings, "The Organization of the American Antarctic Expedition of 1830," *Proceedings of the Tenth International Congress of the History of Science*, 2:1031–1035. Eights is a shadowy figure, but see Joel W. Hedgpeth, "James Eights of the Antarctic (1798–1882)," in Louis O. Quam, ed., *Research in the Antarctic; A Symposium Presented at the Dallas Meeting of the American Association for the Advancement of Science, December, 1968*, (Washington, 1971), pp. 3–45. For the little that is known of Watson, see Nicholas B. Wainwright, *Philadelphia in Romantic Age of Lithography* (Philadelphia, 1958), pp. 22, 85.

16. "Expedition to the South Seas," *New-York Mirror*, 7:95 (September 26, 1829); "Southern Polar Expedition," *ibid.*, 126 (October 24, 1829); Reynolds to Southard, October 25, 1830, Southard Papers; Memorial of Edmund Fanning and Benjamin Pendleton, *House Exec. Doc. 61*, 22 Cong., 1 sess.; A. A. Gould, "Notice of the origin, progress, and present condition of the Boston Society of Natural History, Boston, Feb. 1842," *American Quarterly Register*, 14 (1842), 236–241; James Eights, "Description of a new Crustaceous Animal found on the shores of the South Shetland Islands, with Remarks on their Natural History," *Transactions of the Albany Institute*, 2 (1833), 53–69; "Description of a New Animal Belonging to the Arachnides of Latreille: Discovered in the Sea along the Shores of the New South Shetland Islands," *Journal of the Boston Society of Natural History*, 1 (1835), 203–206; "On the ice-bergs of the Ant-arctic Sea," *American Quarterly Journal of Agriculture & Science*, 4 (1846), 20–14; Charles Darwin, "Note on a Rock seen in an Iceberg in 61° South Latitude," Royal Geographical Society of London *Journal*, 9 (1839), 517–528; C. L. Shear and Neil E. Stevens, eds., "The Correspondence of Schweinitz and Torrey," *Memoirs of the Torrey Botanical Club*, 16 (1915–1921), 119–300; "Memorial of Edmund Fanning," *Sen. Doc.* 10, 23 Cong., 2 sess.; Alexander S. Palmer, ms. draft of affidavit, County of New London, Connecticut, n.d., in Palmer-Loper Papers, LC. For Eights' bibliography see Hedgpeth, "James Eights of the Antarctic."

Listed in the presumed order of his experiences, Reynolds' articles are: "Leaves from an Unpublished Journal," *New-York Mirror*, 15:340–341 (April 21, 1838); "Mocha Dick: or the White Whale of the Pacific: A Leaf from a Manuscript Journal," *Knickerbocker*, 13 (1839), 377–392; "Rough Notes on Rough Adventures," *Southern Literary Messenger*, 9 (1843), 705–715. On Melville and "Mocha Dick" see R. S. Garnett, "Moby-Dick and Mocha-Dick: A Literary Find," *Blackwood's Magazine*, 226 (1929), 841–858; Charles Roberts Anderson, *Melville in the South Seas* (New York, 1966; first published 1939), p. 14.

17. Reynolds to Southard, May 6, 1830, Southard Papers; Florian Cajori, *The*

Chequered Career of Ferdinand Rudolph Hassler (Boston, 1924), pp. 153, 161; *Cong. Debates*, 24 Cong., 1 sess., vol. 12, Part 4, Appendix, 16–19; *Sen. Doc.* 262, 24 Cong., 1 sess.; Edouard Stackpole, *The Sea-Hunters: The New England Whalemen during Two Centuries, 1635–1835* (Philadelphia, 1953), pp. 290–298; Ralph D. Paine, *The Ships and Sailors of Old Salem: The Record of a Brilliant Era of American Achievement* (New York, 1909), pp. 538–560; William Endicott, *Wrecked Among Cannibals in the Fijis*, ed. L. W. Jenkins (Salem, 1923); W. G. Dix and James Oliver, *Wreck of the Glide, with Recollections of Fiji and Wallis Island* (New York, 1848).

18. [A. A. Gould?], Draft of memorial from the Boston Society of Natural History, n.p., n.d., Museum of Science, Boston; J. N. Reynolds, *Address on the Subject of a Surveying and Exploring Expedition to the Pacific Ocean and South Seas, Delivered in the Hall of the House of Representatives on the Evening of April 2, 1836, with Correspondence and Documents* (New York, 1836), pp. 13–15, 22–24, 70–73, 100, 272–273, 278; *Cong. Debates*, 24 Cong., 1 sess., vol. 12, Part 2, 1298–1299; Part 3, 3467–3478; *Cong. Globe*, 24 Cong., 1 sess., 3:396–397, 408, 410.

19. Charles R. Erdman, "Mahlon Dickerson," DAB; Martin Van Buren, *Autobiography*, ed. J. C. Fitzpatrick, American Historical Association *Report*, 3 (1918), 183; Mahlon Dickerson, Ms. Diary, Mahlon Dickerson Papers, New Jersey Historical Society; *Army and Navy Chronicle*, 3:290–291 (November 10, 1836); J. N. Reynolds, *Pacific and Indian Oceans: or, The South Sea Surveying and Exploring Expedition . . .* (New York, 1841), pp. 489–490.

20. Charles Lee Lewis, "Thomas Ap Catesby Jones," DAB; Fletcher Pratt, *Preble's Boys: Commodore Preble and the Birth of American Sea Power* (New York, 1950), pp. 385–386; *House Exec. Doc.* 147, 25 Cong., 2 sess. (hereafter cited as *Doc. 147*), 6, 7, 8–10, 13–16; Reynolds, *Pacific and Indian Oceans*, p. 488.

21. *Doc. 147*, 2–3, 16, 22–23, 24, 26, 28–29, 37, 52, 55–56, 73–76, 86–87, 181–185; Edmund Fanning, *Voyages Round the World*, p. 170.

22. *Doc. 147*, 8–9, 13, 14, 16–17, 23–24, 43, 77–78, 103–105, 111–113, 118; Benjamin Jones et al., "To his Excellency the President of the United States," July 2, 1836, ms. copy in LRWEE, roll 2; *Niles' Weekly Register*, 53:32 (September 9, 1837). On Melville's references to Armstrong, see Charles Lee Lewis, *Books of the Sea: An Introduction to Nautical Literature* (Annapolis, 1943), p. 31.

23. *Doc. 147*, 2–3, 22, 27, 28, 39, 49–50, 52–53, 72, 77, 79–80, 97, 124, 153, 154, 155, 156; *Army and Navy Chronicle*, 5:90–91 (August 10, 1837); Howard I. Chapelle, *The History of the American Sailing Navy, the Ships and Their Development* (New York, 1949), pp. 385–389, 390.

24. *Doc. 147*, 96, 147, 173, 223, 230, 242–243, 247–249, 251, 291, 304–312, 312–349, 404; Ezra Green to brother, January 12, 1838, Ezra Green Papers; Daniel Ammen, *The Old Navy and the New* (Philadelphia, 1891), p. 28.

NOTES TO CHAPTER 3

1. Metrique, "South Sea Expedition—Survey of the coast—Weights and Measures," *Army and Navy Chronicle*, 4:74 (February 2, 1837); [Review of Reynolds' Address], *North American Review*, 45 (1837), 361–390. Daniel C. Haskell, *The United*

States Exploring Expedition, 1838–1842, and Its Publications (New York, 1952), item 149, ascribes this review to Horatio Hale.

2. [J. N. Reynolds and Mahlon Dickerson], *Exploring Expedition, Correspondence Between J. N. Reynolds and the Hon. Mahlon Dickerson* . . . (n.p., n.d.), p. 28; *House Exec. Doc. 147*, 25 Cong., 2 sess. (hereafter cited as *Doc. 147*), 38–39, 117–118; Gray to John Torrey, [July] 1836, Simon Gratz Collection, Historical Society of Pennsylvania; Gray, *Elements of Botany* (New York, 1836); Torrey to Dickerson, September 29, 1836, LRWEE, roll 1; J. D. Dana, *A System of Mineralogy* . . . (New Haven, 1837). For the applications, see *Doc. 147* and LRWEE, rolls 1, 2, 3. On Gray's relation to the expedition, see A. Hunter Dupree's fine biography, *Asa Gray, 1810–1888* (Cambridge, Mass., 1959), Ch. 3; and on Dana's part, Daniel C. Gilman, *The Life of James Dwight Dana* (New York, 1899), Chs. 5–8 and *passim*.

3. Gilman, *Dana*, 53; John Pickering to General Andrew Jackson, September 23, 1836, LRWEE, roll 1; Asa Gray to Moses Gray, October 8, 1836, in Asa Gray, *Letters of Asa Gray*, ed. Jane Loring Gray, 2 vols. (Boston, 1894), 1:61–62; *Doc. 147*, 102. On Pickering, see Asa Gray, "Charles Pickering," in Charles S. Sargent, ed., *The Scientific Papers of Asa Gray*, 2 vols. (Boston, 1889), 2:406–410; W[illiam] S. W. Ruschenberger, "Charles Pickering," Academy of Natural Sciences *Proceedings*, 30 (1878), 166–171.

4. *Doc. 147*, 108–109, 512–553; Sir James E. Smith, *A Specimen of the Botany of New Holland* (London, 1817), p. 9, quoted in Bernard Smith, *European Vision and the South Pacific, 1768–1850*, a pioneering work to which I am much indebted.

5. Dana to Father, July 27, 1835, in Gilman, *Dana*, pp. 31–32; [Augustus A. Gould?], Draft of a memorial for the Boston Society of Natural History, n.p., n.d., Museum of Science, Boston; *Doc. 147*, 110, 113–114; Charles Pickering to John Torrey, March 30, 1836, John Torrey Papers, New York Botanical Garden; *New-York Times*, October 24, 1836.

6. *Doc. 147*, 113–115, 164; Dickerson to Gray, October 8, 1836; Dana to Gray, December, 1836; Harlan to Torrey, October 8, 1836; William Darlington to Gray, October 10, 1836, in HLF; Darlington to Torrey, October 11, 1836, Simon Gratz Collection, Historical Society of Pennsylvania; *Army and Navy Chronicle*, 3:346 (December 1, 1836); Gray to W[illiam] J. Hooker, October 10, 1836, in Gray, *Letters*, 1:59–61. Presumably Rich was one of the founders in 1825 of the Botanical Club of Washington and, with John Andrew Brereton, editor of the *American Botanical Register*, published in Washington in three issues between 1825 and 1830. See Max Meisel, *Bibliography of American Natural History*, 3 vols. (Brooklyn, 1924–1929), 2:443, 525.

7. *Doc. 147*, 10–13, 169–172, 604; Gray to Dickerson, January 16, 1837; Dana to Dickerson, January 7, 1837; Agate to Dickerson, January 7, 1837; Drayton to Dickerson, January 7, 1837, in LRWEE, roll 2; William Dunlap et al. to Dickerson, LRWEE, roll 1. Other letters of acceptance may be found in *Doc. 147*. On Agate, brother of the better known Frederick S. Agate, see William Dunlap, *Diary* . . . , *1766–1839*, 3 vols. (New York, 1930), 3:758, 785, 794–795; and Mantle Fielding, *Dictionary of American Painters, Sculptors and Engravers* (Philadelphia, 1926), which has a note on Drayton as well.

8. *Army and Navy Chronicle*, 5:146–147 (September 7, 1837), from Boston *Journal* of unspecified date; *Doc. 147*, 105, 271–274, 281–282, 365–366, 545; William Ford to Dickerson, January 18, 1837, LRWEE, roll 1.

9. *Doc. 147*, 135–138, 162–163, 233, 258–259, 260–261, 265–266; *Army and Navy Chronicle*, 4:92 (February 9, 1837); *House Doc. 138*, 24 Cong., 2 sess.; Couthouy to Gray, March 17, 1837, HLF.

10. Gray to Moses Gray, January 4, February 10, 1837, typescript copies at Harvard University Herbarium (brought to my attention by Dupree, *Asa Gray*); Reynolds to Southard, February 5, 1837, Southard Papers; *Army and Navy Chronicle*, 4:302 (May 11, 1837), 396–397 (June 22, 1837); 5:46 (July 20, 1837); *Doc. 147*, 317–320. On the British response, see the generous remarks of Captain Basil Hall before the Royal Geographical Society: "New Expedition to the Pacific and Antarctic Oceans," Royal Geographical Society *Journal*, 6 (1836), 440.

11. [Reynolds and Dickerson], *Exploring Expedition*, 5, 8, 21, 25, 27, 28; *Army and Navy Chronicle*, 6:145 (March 8, 1838); *Doc. 147*, 327–331, 333–334, 336–355, 357, 359, 363, 366–368, 379–380, 474–477, 491; Jones to Dickerson, February 12, 1838, LRWEE, roll 4; Dana to John W. Dana, June 11, 1837; and to Harriette Dana, July 3, 1837, Historic Mss., Yale.

12. [Reynolds and Dickerson], *Exploring Expedition*, 91, 128–129; Dickerson, Ms. Diary, July 18, 1837, Dickerson Papers, New Jersey Historical Society; *Army and Navy Chronicle*, 5:57–58 (July 27, 1837), 90–91 (August 10, 1837), 204 (September 28, 1837), 271 (October 26, 1837), 276–277 (November 2, 1837); Dana to Edward C. Herrick, August [21?], 24, 1837, Dana-Herrick Correspondence; *Doc. 147*, 470–471; *Niles' Weekly Register*, 53:383 (February 10, 1838); Daniel Ammen, *The Old Navy and the New* (Philadelphia, 1891), pp. 31–32.

13. James Glynn to [George F. Emmons], October 21, 1837; John B. Dale to Emmons, April 17, 1838, Emmons Papers, Western Americana Collection, Yale; Dana to E. C. Herrick, November 10 and [December 10?], 1837, Dana-Herrick Correspondence; *Army and Navy Chronicle*, 5:310, 315 (November 16, 1837); 6:145 (March 8, 1838); *Doc. 147*, 28–29, 34–36, 238–239, 283–284, 364–365, 366–368, 389, 417–418, 458–459, 460–461, 470–471, 503–504, 507–553, 562–564, 565, 572–573, 574–575, 596–597, 599–600, 601–603.

14. Edmund Fanning, *Voyages Round the World* . . . (New York, 1838), pp. 261–263; Percival to Dickerson, December 12, 1837; John H. Aulick to Dickerson, December 15, 1837; Hull *et al.* to Dickerson, December 25, 1837; Charles G. Ridgely to Dickerson, December 20, 1837, LRWEE, roll 4; *Cong. Globe*, 25 Cong., 2 sess., 14, 16, 168, 189, 192, 210, 245, 248, 273–274, 280, 292; *House Exec. Doc. 255*, 25 Cong., 2 sess.; *House Journal*, 25 Cong., 2 sess., 473; Dickerson to Isaac Hull, December 20, 1837, Western Americana Collection, Yale; [Reynolds and Dickerson], *Exploring Expedition*, pp. 121–131.

15. Andrew Denny Rodgers III, *John Torrey, A Story of North American Botany* (Princeton, 1942), p. 89; Pickering to the President and members of the American Philosophical Society, September 12, 1837, APS Archives; Kane to Dickerson, September 29, 30, 1836, LRWEE, roll 1; Elsie G. Allen, "The History of American Ornithology Before Audubon," APS *Transactions*, n.s. 41 (1951), pp. 387–591; Ord to Charles Waterton, March 27, 1838, Ord-Waterton Letters, APS; to Dickerson, January 5, 1838, "Private and Confidential," LRWEE, roll 4.

16. Dana to E. C. Herrick, December 8, [1837]; January 8, 1838, Dana-Herrick Correspondence; *Doc. 147*, 603; Reynolds to Southard, June 5, 1838, Southard Papers;

Army and Navy Chronicle, 6:9 (January 4, 1838), 72, 76, 80 (February 1, 1838); J. N. Reynolds, *Pacific and Indian Oceans: or, The South Sea Surveying and Exploring Expedition* . . . (New York, 1841), pp. 457–460; Perry to Dickerson, January 23, 1838; Poinsett to Walter R. Johnson, February 14, 1838; Beverley Kennon to Dickerson, [April 13, 1838?]: LRWEE, roll 4; Fanning, *Voyages Round the World* (1838), pp. 307–316; Gregory to Poinsett, February 13, 22, 26, 1838; Poinsett to Gregory, February 19 and n.d., 1838; Poinsett to Smith, March 22, 1838; Smith to Poinsett, March 1, 1838: Poinsett Papers, Historical Society of Pennsylvania; Smith to Wilkes, April 21, June 4, 22, 1838: Wilkes Papers, Kansas State Historical Society.

17. Renwick to Poinsett, March 18, 1828 [i.e., 1838], Poinsett Papers, Historical Society of Pennsylvania; Poinsett to Dickerson, April 19, 1838; C[ornelius] K. Stribling, "To the President," April 3, 1838, in LRWEE, roll 4; Smith to Wilkes, June 4, 1838; Jane Wilkes to Wilkes, March 25, 1838; Thomas T. Craven to Wilkes, April 1, 1838, in Wilkes Papers, Kansas State Historical Society. Poinsett's public though anonymous explanation of the appointment was to appear in two articles of his: "Synopsis of the Cruise of the United States Exploring Expedition . . . by . . . Charles Wilkes . . . ," *North American Review*, 56 (1843), 257–270; and "The First three volumes of a narrative of the United States Exploring Expedition . . . by Charles Wilkes . . . ," *Southern Quarterly Review*, 8 (1845), 1–69.

18. Percival to Wilkes, March 29, 1838, Wilkes Papers, Kansas State Historical Society; *Army and Navy Chronicle*, 6:72 (February 1, 1838), 416 (June 28, 1838); *Cong. Globe*, 25 Cong., 2 sess., 296–297, 409–410, 411; Fanning, *Voyages Round the World* (1838), pp. 307–316; John Quincy Adams, *Memoirs of John Quincy Adams* . . . *1795 to 1848*, ed. Charles Francis Adams, 12 vols. (Philadelphia, 1874–1877), 9:491; Wilkes to Dickerson, May 19, 1838, LRWEE, roll 4; Dana to E. C. Herrick, July 22, 1838, Dana-Herrick Correspondence; [Wilkes], ms. "Memorandum," n.d., LRWEE, roll 5.

19. [Reynolds and Dickerson], *Exploring Expedition*, 42; Wilkes to Poinsett, May 1, 1838, Poinsett Papers, Historical Society of Pennsylvania. Poinsett's approval of Wilkes' recommendations appears on the reverse of Wilkes' "Memorandum" cited above.

20. Thomas W. [?] Boyd to Wilkes, April 19, 1838; Peale to Wilkes, May 5, 1838, Wilkes Papers, Kansas State Historical Society; Wilkes to Poinsett, May 1, 1838; Dickerson to Poinsett, June 21, 1842, Poinsett Papers, Historical Society of Pennsylvania; Gray to J. F. Trowbridge, July 18, 1838, Gray, *Letters*, 1:65–66; Dana to E. C. Herrick, July 21, 1838, Dana-Herrick Correspondence; Pickering to Gray, April 21, HLF; Wilkes to Aaron Johnson and others, August 18, 1838, *Niles' Weekly Register*, 55:11 (September 1, 1838). For Wilkes' own boast of having reduced the expedition, see Wilkes to W. C. Preston, July 16, 1842, in George B. Goode, "The Genesis of the National Museum," U.S. National Museum *Report, House Misc. Doc. 334*, Part 2, 52 Cong., 1 sess., 173–380.

21. Gibbs to Poinsett, May 25, 1838; John Pickering to [Poinsett], June 1, 1838; Poinsett to James Kirke Paulding, July 29, 1838, LRWEE, roll 4; Sarah J. Hale to Levi Woodbury, June 17, 1838, Wilkes Papers, Kansas State Historical Society. On Hale's Harvard triumph (*Remarks on the Language of the St. John's or Wlastukweek Indians, with a Penobscot Vocabulary* [Boston, 1834]) see "Sketch of Horatio Hale," *Popular Science Monthly*, 51 (1897), 401–410, and for further biographical information,

Horatio Hale, *The Iroquois Book of Rites*, ed. William N. Fenton (Toronto, 1963), pp. vi-xxvii; and Jacob W. Gruber, "Horatio Hale and the Development of American Anthropology," APS *Proceedings*, 111 (1967), 5–37.

22. W[illiam] B. McMurtrie to Poinsett, August 1, 1838; Gray to Rich, July 27, 1838, Wilkes Papers, Kansas State Historical Society; Jones to Johnson, August 21, 1837, Dreer Mss., Historical Society of Pennsylvania; Johnson to Dickerson, February 27, 1838; Johnson to Paulding, August 2, 1838; Gray to Paulding, July 10, 1838; Reynolds to Paulding, June 30, 1838, LRWEE, roll 4; Reynolds to Southard, June 9, 1838, Southard Papers; Pat Neill to [Whom it may concern], February 28, 1834; [Frederick] Otto, for Mr. William Brackenridge, April 1, 1827: Brackenridge Papers, Smithsonian Institution Library; "Editorial Notes," *The Gardeners' Monthly and Horticulturist*, 26 (1884), 375–376; O. B. Spurlin, "Our First Official Horticulturist," *Washington Historical Quarterly*, 21 (1931), 218–229, 298–305; 22 (1931), 42–58, 129–145, 216–227. On Gray's separation from the corps, see Dupree, *Asa Gray*, pp. 67–69.

23. *Southern Literary Messenger*, 5 (1839), 313–314, 414–415; *Cong. Globe*, 25 Cong., 2 sess., 295–297, 301, 313, 314, 409–410; *Senate Journal*, 25 Cong., 2 sess., 449, 500, 520; Reynolds to Paulding, August 17, 1838, LRWEE, roll 5; Reynolds to Southard, June 5, 1838, Southard Papers; John B. Dale to Wilkes, March 31, 1838; George F. Emmons to Wilkes, April 23, 1838; [John] Percival to Wilkes, March 29, April 10, 1838; Isaac Percival to Wilkes, September 21, 1838; S[tephen] C. Phillips to Wilkes, July 19, 1838 (endorsement by Wilkes on reverse), Wilkes Papers, Kansas State Historical Society.

24. Ezra [Green] to brother, January 12, 1838, Ezra Green Papers; All the Ships Company to Dickerson, March 7, 1838, LRWEE, roll 4; Craven to Wilkes, May 29, August 4, 1838, Wilkes Papers, Kansas State Historical Society.

25. Wilkes to [Paulding], July 10, August 12, 1838; Gilliss to Paulding, August 14, 1838; Nathan Dunn and Franklin Peale to Poinsett, July 21, 1838; Kane to Poinsett, July 10, 1838, LRWEE, roll 4; N. L. Rogers and Brothers to J. H. Williams, April 11, 1838; R. R. Pinkham to John Reed, June 22, 1838; Craven to Wilkes, June 10, 1838, Wilkes Papers, Kansas State Historical Society; James B. Longacre to Poinsett, July 10, 1838, Poinsett Papers, Historical Society of Pennsylvania; *Army and Navy Chronicle*, 7:26 (July 12, 1838), 63 (July 26, 1838), 72 (August 2, 1838), and 93 (August 9, 1838, from Norfolk *Beacon* of unspecified date); J[ohn] F[itzgerald] Lee to S[amuel] P[hillips] Lee, August 1, 1838, Blair-Lee Papers, Princeton; R. M. Patterson, John Vaughn, and J. K. Kane to Wilkes, July 31, 1838, Wilkes Papers, LC.

26. *Army and Navy Chronicle*, 7:103 (August 16, 1838), 111 (August 15, 1838); Whittle; "Sailing of the Exploring Expedition," *Sailor's Magazine*, 11 (1838), 67–68; *Niles' Weekly Register*, 54:385 (August 18, 1838, from Norfolk *Herald* of August 15), 403 (August 25, 1838); Henry Eld, Jr., to [Henry Eld, Sr.], August 17 [1838], Henry Eld Papers, LC.

NOTES TO CHAPTER 4

1. J. L. Elliott; W. L. Hudson; Emmons; Johnson; Patricia Jahns, *Matthew Fontaine Maury & Joseph Henry, Scientists of the Civil War* (New York, 1961), p. 46;

Robert V. Hine, *Edward Kern and American Expansion* (New Haven, 1962), pp. 99–100; Howard I. Chapelle, *The History of the American Sailing Navy* (New York, 1949), 356–359, 365; "Sailing of the Exploring Expedition," *Sailor's Magazine*, 11 (1838), 17–68; *Army and Navy Chronicle*, 5:90–91 (August 10, 1837); Hartstene; Wilkes, *Narrative*, 1:xvi; George F. Emmons, *The Navy of the United States . . . with a Brief History of Each Vessel's Service and Fate as it Appears upon Record* (Washington, 1850), pp. 16–17, 26–27, and *passim.*; Allan B. Cole, ed., *Yankee Surveyors in the Shogun's Seas, Records of the United States Surveying Expedition to the North Pacific Ocean, 1853–1856* (Princeton, 1947), p. 5, notes 1 and 4; *Niles' Weekly Register*, 50:44 (March 19, 1836).

2. Sickels; Emmons; Reynolds to [Lydia M. Reynolds], August 30, September 3, 1838, Reynolds Papers; J. L. Elliott; Reynolds, Private Journal; Johnson; Briscoe; Dyes; Holmes; Peale to Florida and Sybilla Peale, August 13, 1838, Peale-Sellers Papers, APS; Long; Peale; Emmons; W. L. Hudson; Wilkes, Autobiography, pp. 859, 860, 971, 993–994; Poinsett to Hudson, June 5, 1838; Hudson to Poinsett, June 16, 1838 (copies in Hudson, vol. 1); Ridgely to [Poinsett], July 7, 1842, Poinsett Papers, Historical Society of Pennsylvania; Daniel C. Gilman, *The Life of James Dwight Dana* (New York, 1899), p. 58; Wilkes, *Narrative*, 1:Appendixes 11, 13. For biographies of Hudson and Knox, see *Appleton's Cyclopaedia of American Biography*. On Ringgold and Reynolds, see *ibid.* and articles by, respectively, Allan Westcott and Louis Bolander in DAB.

3. Reynolds, Private Journal; to [Lydia M. Reynolds], August 30, November 21–25, and December 4, 1838; Ms. criticism of Wilkes' *Narrative*, in Reynolds Papers; Erskine; Sickels; W. L. Hudson; Wilkes, *Narrative*, 1:31, 34, 35, 40–41, 43, 67, 69–74, Appendix 15; Autobiography, pp. 873–887, 974–979, 997, 1001–1008, 1016, 1024–1025; "Notice to Mariners. The Exploring Expedition," *Sailor's Magazine*, 11 (1839), 137; Johnson; Peale; Gilchrist; Emmons; Holmes; Long; Briscoe; J. L. Elliott; Anonymous journal kept aboard *Vincennes*; Hartstene; Couthouy; Dana to [E. C. Herrick], January 2, 1839, Dana-Herrick Correspondence; Wilkes to Nicholson, December 3, 5, 29, 31, January 3, 1839; Nicholson, endorsement of Waters [?] Smith, Surgeon of the Fleet, to Nicholson, December 5, 1838; to Wilkes, December 3 and 30, 1838, and January 2, 1839; to Paulding, January 8, 1839 (copies in LRWEE, roll 1).

NOTES TO CHAPTER 5

1. Wilkes, *Narrative*, 1:xxv–xxxi, 106–107, 120–121, 133; Emmons; Holmes; Peale; Claiborne; Wilkes, Autobiography, pp. 1027–1029, 1032–1038; Long; Ezra Green to brother, April 15, 1839, Ezra Green Papers; Sinclair; Reynolds, Private Journal; Couthouy; Johnson.

2. Reynolds, Private Journal; Johnson; Wilkes, *Narrative*, 1:136–142, 145, 149–153, 155–157, 160, 184, 205, 231 and Appendixes 30, 31, 37, 38; J. C. Beaglehole, ed., *The Journals of Captain James Cook on His Voyages of Discovery*, 3 vols. (Cambridge, 1955–1967), 1:46; Emmons; J[ames] C. Palmer, *Thulia: A Tale of the Antarctic* (New York, 1843), pp. 35, 37, 66, 67, 68, 72; U.S. Board on Geographic Names, Gazetteer No.

14, *Geographic Names of Antarctica* (Washington, 1956); Peale; Holmes; W. L. Hudson; Long; Sanford; Claiborne; Anonymous Journal kept aboard *Vincennes.*

3. Dana to mother, March 29, 1839; to [Asa] Gray, May 6, 1839: Historical Mss., Yale; Ezra Green to brother, April 15, 1839; Sinclair; Wilkes, Autobiography, pp. 1043–1047, 1053, 1062, 1063–1064, 1070; Wilkes to Long, May 25, 1839; Long to Wilkes, June 21, 1839, LRWEE, roll 5; Wilkes to Long, June 22, 1839, LRWEE, roll 4; Emmons; Reynolds, Private Journal; Gilchrist; Dale to Emmons, April 17, 1838; Hartstene, Emmons, Reid to James Glynn, January 28, 1838, in Emmons Papers; Johnson; Hartstene to Wilkes, May 23, 1839, Simon Gratz Collection, Historical Society of Pennsylvania; Hartstene; Jay Leyda, *The Melville Log, A Documentary Life of Herman Melville, 1819–1891,* 2 vols., pagination continuous (New York, 1951), p. 109; J. L. Blair to father, June 28, 1839, Blair-Lee Papers, Princeton.

4. Sinclair; Wilkes, Autobiography, pp. 1048–1049, 1051, 1076–1077; Sickels; Holmes; Long; Claiborne; Johnson; Emmons; Erskine; John W. W. Dyes, "Intemperance in the Isles of the Pacific," *Sailor's Magazine,* 13 (1841), 328–334; [Reynolds] to Lydia [M. Reynolds], June 2, 30–July 6, 1839, Reynolds Papers; [Pickering] to Mary [O. Pickering], July 12, 1839, Charles Pickering Papers, Massachusetts Historical Society; Eld to parents, July 12 [?], 1839, Henry Eld Papers, LC; Wilkes, *Narrative,* 1:232; Reynolds, Private Journal; Stuart. On De Haven, see Charles O. Paullin, "Edwin Jessie De Haven," DAB, and *Appleton's Cyclopaedia of American Biography.*

NOTES TO CHAPTER 6

1. Emmons; Holmes; W. L. Hudson; Johnson; [Wilkes] to Martin Van Buren, August 16, 1838, Charles Wilkes Papers, LC; Reynolds, Private Journal; Andrew Sharp, *The Discovery of the Pacific Islands* (London, 1960), pp. 73–74, 102–103, 185–186, 201–202, 220; Wilkes, *Narrative,* 1:309, 325, 337; Peale; Couthouy; Reynolds, Ms. criticism of Wilkes' *Narrative,* Reynolds Papers; Eld; Green; Brackenridge; Alexander G. Findlay, *A Directory for the Navigation of the Pacific Ocean . . . ,* 2 vols., pagination continuous (London, 1851), pp. 864, 870; George Robertson, *The Discovery of Tahiti, A Journal of the Second Voyage of H.M.S. "Dolphin" Round the World Under the Command of Captain Wallis, R.N., in the Years 1766, 1767, and 1768 . . . ,* ed. Hugh Carrington (London, 1948), pp. xxii, 209; J. C. Beaglehole, ed., *The Journals of Captain James Cook on His Voyages of Discovery,* 3 vols. (Cambridge, 1955–1967), 1:98, 121; Bernard Smith, *European Vision and the South Pacific, 1768–1850* (Oxford, 1960), *passim.*; John Davies, *The History of the Tahitian Mission, 1799–1830,* ed. C. W. Newbury (Cambridge, 1961), p. xliv.

2. Charles S. Stewart, *Private Journal of a Voyage to the Pacific Ocean, and Residence in the Sandwich Islands, in the Years 1822, 1823, 1824 and 1825* (New Haven, 1828); *A Visit to the South Seas, in the U.S. Ship Vincennes during the Years 1829 and 1830,* 2 vols. (New York, 1831); Otto von Kotzebue, *A New Voyage round the World . . . , 1823–1826,* 2 vols. (London, 1830), 1:102–104; F. W. Beechey, *Narrative of a Voyage to the Pacific and Beering's Strait,* 2 vols. (London, 1831); Reynolds to [Lydia M. Reynolds], September 12, 1829, Reynolds Papers.

3. Wilkes, *Narrative,* 2:3; Emmons; Couthouy; Johnson; Ezra [Green] to brother,

September 22, 1839, Ezra Green Papers; Holmes; Reynolds, Private Journal; Davis, *History of the Tahitian Mission*, pp. xxxiii, xlvi, 292–293; Eld; Erskine; Robertson, *Discovery of Tahiti*, p. 167; Cook, *Journals*, 1:clxxxviii, n. 2, 119; Gilchrist; Briscoe; Wilkes, *Narrative*, 2:41, 58, 328–334; John W. W. Dyes, "Intemperance in the Isles of the Pacific," *Sailor's Magazine*, 13 (1841), 328–334; Dana to mother, May 17, 1838; Dana to Gray, May 6, 1839; Dana to John [W. Dana], September 6, 1839, Historical Mss., Yale; W. L. Hudson; Wilkes, Autobiography, 1092–1094; Erskine; Wilkes to Queen of the Society Islands, September 18, 1839, LRWEE; Charles R. Anderson, *Melville in the South Seas* (New York, 1966; first published 1939), p. 213.

NOTES TO CHAPTER 7

1. Couthouy; Johnson; Holmes; Wilkes, *Narrative*, 2:80, 81, 95–97, 108–111, 121, 140–141; Reynolds, Private Journal; to [Lydia M. Reynolds], December 1–22, 1839, Reynolds Papers; Peale; Reynolds, Public Journal; Emmons; Louis B. Wright and Mary I. Fry, *Puritans in the South Seas* (New York, 1936), pp. 108–171; W. L. Hudson; Dana to Gray, May 6, 1839; to Benjamin Silliman, September 12, 1839, Historical Mss., Yale; to Redfield, August 14, 1838, June 24, 1839, and May 29, 1843, in Letters to W. C. Redfield, Rare Book Room, Yale; Reynolds, Ms. criticism of Wilkes' *Narrative*, Reynolds Papers; Court-Martial Records, vol. 44, no. 827, proceedings, 114, and Pinkney's charges against Wilkes, no pagination.

2. Wilkes, *Narrative*, 1:Appendix 5; 2:159; Wilkes to Ringgold, November 11, 1839, in Order Book; Court-Martial Records, vol. 44, no. 827, proceedings, 240; Reynolds, Ms. criticism of Wilkes' *Narrative*; Reynolds, Private Journal; to Lydia [M. Reynolds], December 1–22, 1839, Reynolds Papers; Holmes; Emmons; Alexander G. Findlay, *A Directory for the Navigation of the Pacific Ocean* . . . , 2 vols., pagination continuous (London, 1851), 821–822; Robert Coffin, *The Last of the Logan: The True Adventures of Robert Coffin Mariner in the Years 1854 to 1859* . . . , ed. Harold W. Thompson (Ithaca, New York, 1941), p. 125.

NOTES TO CHAPTER 8

1. Reynolds, Private Journal; Emmons; Dana to E. C. Herrick, January 28, 1840, Dana-Herrick Correspondence; Holmes; Peale to J. K. Kane, April 5, 1840, Misc. Mss. Collection, APS; Wilkes, *Narrative*, 2:208–209, 213–214; Autobiography, pp. 1130–1134, 1139–1140, 1148–1151; Order Book, September 24, December 6, 7, 11, 22, 1839.

2. Erskine; Emmons; Ann Mozley, "James Dwight Dana in New South Wales, 1839–1840," Royal Society of New South Wales *Journal and Proceedings*, 97 (1964), 185–191; Brackenridge; Wilkes, *Narrative*, 2:133, 184–198, 221, 175, 434–435, 449; Dana to [Asa] Gray, June 15, 1840, Historical Mss., Yale; Order Book, December 19, 1839; Reynolds, Ms. criticism of Wilkes' *Narrative*, Reynolds Papers; J. Biscoe, *Journal of a Voyage towards the South Pole, 1830 to 1832* (Edinburgh and London, 1834); "Nouveau continent découvert par le Capt. Anglais Biscoe commandant le brick 'Tula'," Société de Géographie *Bulletin*, 19 (1833), 165–167; Charles Enderby,

"Discoveries in the Antarctic Ocean, in February, 1839. Extracted from the Journal of the schooner Eliza Scott, commanded by Mr. John Balleny," Royal Geographical Society *Journal*, 9 (1839), 517–528.

NOTES TO CHAPTER 9

1. Wilkes, *Narrative*, 2:283, Appendix 25; Emmons; Sinclair; W. L. Hudson; Andrew Sharp, *The Discovery of the Pacific Islands* (Oxford, 1960), 191–192; Eld; Holmes; Underwood; Reynolds, Private Journal; Johnson; William H. Hobbs, "Wilkes Land Rediscovered," *Geographical Review*, 22 (1932), 632–655; Wilkes, Autobiography, pp. 1158–1159; Reynolds, Public Journal; Stuart; Court-Martial Records, vol. 44, no. 827, proceedings, 176, 183, 187, 192–193, 197, 200; *Sailing Directions for Antarctica*, Hydrographic Office Publication No. 27, 2d ed. (1960), Sections 6-1, 6-2; Reynolds to mother, March 4, 1840, Reynolds Papers. For the latest and most ambitious attempts to identify the Expedition's Antarctic landfalls, see Kenneth J. Bertrand, *Americans in Antarctica, 1775–1948*, American Geographical Society Special Publication No. 39 (New York, 1971), Ch. 10.

NOTES TO CHAPTER 10

1. James [L. Blair] to father, December 15, [1839], Blair-Lee Papers, Princeton; Order Book, 111, 112–116, 121; Sanford; Court-Martial Records, vol. 44, no. 827, proceedings, 153–154, 156, 157, 163, 164–165; Wilkes; Daniel Ammen, *The Old Navy and the New* (Philadelphia, 1891), p. 29; Underwood; Wilkes, Autobiography, p. 1142; Alden; "Recent Discoveries in the Antarctic Ocean. From the Log-book of the Brig Tula, commanded by Mr. John Biscoe, R.N. Communicated by Messrs. Enderby. Read 11th February, 1833," Royal Geographical Society *Journal*, 3 (1833), 105–112; Captain George E. Belknap, U.S.N., "Deep-Sea Sounding," *Naval Encyclopedia; Comprising a Dictionary of Nautical Words and Phrases, Biographical Notices, and Records of Naval Officers* . . . (Philadelphia, 1881), pp. 198–212; Kenneth J. Bertrand, *Americans in Antarctica, 1775–1948*, American Geographical Society Special Publication No. 39 (New York, 1971), p. 177.

2. Wilkes, Autobiography, p. 1141; Wilkes; Underwood; Erskine; Alden; Green; Holmes; Court-Martial Records, vol. 44, no. 827, "N"; Peale to J. K. Kane, April 5, 1840, Misc. Mss. Collection, APS; Wilkes, *Narrative*, 2:343–344; Jacques S. C. Dumont d'Urville, *Voyages au Pôle Sud et dans l'Océanie sur les corvettes l'Astrolabe et la Zélée Executés par ordre du Roi pendant 1837, 1838, 1839, et 1840*, 23 vols. (Paris, 1841–1845), 8:171–173; 9:97, 99–100.

3. Sinclair; Dana to [Asa] Gray, June 15, 1840, Historical Mss., Yale; Peale to Franklin [Peale], April 5, 1840, APS; Ann Mozley, "James Dwight Dana in New South Wales, 1839–1840," Royal Society of New South Wales *Journal and Proceedings*, 97 (1964), 185–191; Wilkes, *Narrative*, 2:245–268, 292–293, Appendix 24; Emmons; W. L. Hudson; Reynolds, Public Journal; Order Book, March 1, 12, 13, and April 15, 1840; James [L. Blair] to father, March 23, 1840, Blair-Lee Papers, Princeton; Reynolds, Private Journal; to mother, March 4–20, 1840, Reynolds Papers; Court-Martial

Records, vol. 44, no. 827, proceedings, 153–155, 159–160, 164–168; *Sydney Herald*, March 13, 1840; *Army and Navy Chronicle*, 4:302 (May 11, 1847); Dumont d'Urville, *Voyages au Pôle Sud*, 8:179–180, 187–188; 9:166.

NOTES TO CHAPTER 11

1. Reynolds, Private Journal; Emmons; Holmes; J. L. Elliott; John W. W. Dyes, "Intemperance in the Isles of the Pacific," *Sailor's Magazine*, 13 (1841), 328–334; Sinclair; Dyes; Ronald A. Derrick, *The Fiji Islands, A Geographical Handbook* (Suva, 1951), pp. 3, 275–280; Reynolds to father and mother, September 26, 1840, Reynolds Papers; Ronald A. Derrick, *A History of Fiji*, 3d ed. (Suva, 1957; first published, 1946), pp. 11–23, 39–47, 64, 65, 75–79, 94, 122–125; W. L. Hudson; Ernest S. Dodge, *New England and the South Seas* (Cambridge, Mass., 1965), 86–99, 102; Eld; R. Gerard Ward, ed., *American Activities in the Central Pacific, 1790–1870*, 8 vols. (Ridgewood, N.J., 1966–1969), 2:392.

2. Reynolds, Private Journal; W. L. Hudson; Derrick, *A History of Fiji*, pp. 19 and n. 60, pp. 58–62; Sinclair; Dyes; Peale; Brackenridge; Stuart; Eld; Emmons; Erskine; Wilkes, *Narrative*, 3:120; 4:117; Holmes; Wilkes, Autobiography, pp. 1201–1203, 1362; Edward Belcher, *Narrative of a Voyage Round the World*, 2 vols. (London, 1843), 1:288; 2:38–39; Reynolds to father and mother, September 26, 1840; William Heath Davis, *Sixty Years in California* (San Francisco, 1889), p. 131; William Lockerby, *The Journal of William Lockerby, Sandalwood Trader in the Fiji Islands during the Years 1808–1809*, ed. Evard Im Thurn (London, 1925), pp. cvi–cx.

NOTES TO CHAPTER 12

1. Reynolds, Private Journal; Sinclair; Alden; Clark; Emmons; Eld; Underwood to Dickerson, December 12, 1837, LRWEE, roll 4; Wilkes, Autobiography, pp. 1221–1226; Wilkes; Holmes; Ronald A. Derrick, *A History of Fiji* (Suva, 1946), p. 26; Green; W. L. Hudson; Pickering to Mary O. Pickering, August 8, 1840, Massachusetts Historical Society; to Samuel G. Morton, August 7, 1840, S. G. Morton Papers, APS; Brackenridge; Dana to [Asa] Gray, June 15, 1840, Historical Mss., Yale; Erskine.

NOTES TO CHAPTER 13

1. Reynolds, Private Journal; Emmons; Erskine; Reynolds, Public Journal; Brackenridge; Sinclair; Court-Martial Records, vol. 44, no. 826, proceedings, 60–61, 74–75, 93; no. 827, proceedings, 143; Wilkes, *Narrative*, 4:3–4, Appendix 4; Dyes; W. L. Hudson; Reynolds, Ms. criticism of Wilkes' *Synopsis*, Reynolds Papers; Sanford; Stuart; *The Polynesian*, October 3, 1840; Ralph S. Kuykendall, *The Hawaiian Kingdom, 1778–1854* (Honolulu, 1947), pp. 114–116, 230; Holmes.

2. Bradford Smith, *Yankees in Paradise, The New England Impact on Hawaii* (Philadelphia, 1956), pp. 130–133, 147–148, 199; Harold W. Bradley, *The American Frontier in Hawaii, The Pioneers, 1789–1843* (Stanford University Press, 1942), pp.

104, 156, 176–180, 188–189; Samuel Williston, *William Richards* (Cambridge, Mass., 1938), p. 38; Charles O. Paullin, *Diplomatic Negotiations of American Naval Officers, 1778–1883* (Baltimore, 1912), pp. 337–339; Hiram Bingham, *A Residence of Twenty-One Years in the Sandwich Islands* . . . (New York, 1947), pp. 383–389; Wilkes, *Narrative*, 4:52–54.

3. A. J. Allen, comp., *Ten Years in Oregon, Travels and Adventures of Doctor E[lijah] White and Lady* (Ithaca, New York, 1850), p. 135; Wilkes, *Narrative*, 4:5, 8, 11, 12, 46–47, 52–54, 58–74, 77–78, 90–103, 111, 112–117, 119, 136, 209–212, 231, 252, 259; Holmes; Dyes; Alden; Emmons; Eld; James D. Dana, "Historical Account of the Eruptions on Hawaii," *American Journal of Science*, 2d ser. 9 (1850), 347–364; 10 (1850), 235–244.

4. Wilkes, *Narrative*, 4:260, 263–264, 265–266, 267–271, 277–280, 281, Appendix 7; Holmes; Sinclair; [Robert E. Johnson], "Exploring Expedition, Letter from an Officer at the Figi Islands, January, 1841," *Sailor's Magazine*, 14:66–68 (November, 1841), from the *Raleigh Register* of unspecified date; Andrew Sharp, *The Discovery of the Pacific Islands* (Oxford, 1960), p. 185; Johnson; British Naval Intelligence Division, *Pacific Islands*, Geographical Handbook Series, 4 vols. (London, 1943–1945), 2:551–553.

NOTES TO CHAPTER 14

1. Emmons; Wilkes, *Narrative*, 4:102–104, Appendix 4; Reynolds, Private Journal; Stuart; Reynolds, Public Journal; W. L. Hudson. Fakaofo is still sometimes called Bowditch and the Tokelaus the Union Group, but there is uncertainty about the discoverer. See Alexander G. Findlay, *Directory for . . . the Pacific Ocean* (London, 1851), p. 995; Andrew Sharp, *The Discovery of the Pacific Islands* (Oxford, 1960), p. 220; Edouard Stackpole, *The Sea-Hunters; The New England Whalemen during Two Centuries, 1635–1835* (Philadelphia, 1953), p. 282; R. Gerard Ward, ed., *American Activities in the Central Pacific, 1790–1870*, 8 vols. (Ridgewood, N.J., 1967–1969), 2:304–318.

2. Reynolds, Private Journal, and Public Journal; Emmons; Stuart; W. L. Hudson; Wilkes, *Narrative*, 5:44. There is disagreement on the identity and discoverers of Nukufetau and Nuitao. See Stackpole, *Sea-Hunters*, pp. 279–280; Findlay, *Directory*, pp. 997–998; Sharp, *Discovery of the Pacific Islands*, p. 195; Ward, *American Activities*, 2:564–566.

3. Wilkes, *Narrative*, 4:Appendix 8; W. L. Hudson; Emmons; Reynolds, Private Journal; Stuart; Reynolds, Public Journal.

NOTES TO CHAPTER 15

1. Emmons; Reynolds, Private Journal; Samuel Parker, *Journal of an Exploring Tour beyond the Rocky Mountains* (Auburn, N.Y., 1842; first published 1838), pp. 310–311; James A. Gibbs, *Pacific Graveyard; A Narrative of Shipwrecks where the Columbia River Meets the Pacific Ocean* (Portland, Ore., 1964), p. 289 and endpapers;

Wilkes, *Narrative*, 4:489; Peale; De Haven; F. P. Blair to Andrew Jackson, June 17, 1842, Blair Family Papers, LC; W. L. Hudson.

2. Robinson; Sinclair; Wilkes; Brackenridge; Holmes; Dyes; Wilkes, *Narrative*, 4: 305–306, 309–310, 522–524, 528–530; Edmond S. Meany, "Last Survivor of the Oregon Mission of 1840," *Washington Historical Quarterly*, 2 (1907), pp. 12–23; Emmons. For a published version of Wilkes' Oregon journal, see Edmond S. Meany, ed., "Diary of Wilkes in the Northwest," *Washington Historical Quarterly*, 16 (1925), 49–61, 137–145, 207–223, 291–301; 17 (1926), 43–65, 129–144; 223–229.

3. Wilkes; Wilkes, *Narrative*, 4:353, 359; Robinson; Erskine; Dyes; Hubert Howe Bancroft, *History of Oregon*, 2 vols. (San Francisco, 1888), 1:189; Brackenridge; Eld; Wilkes to Samuel Varney, August 9, 1841, copy in Charles Wilkes Papers, LC; E. E. Rich, ed., *The Letters of John McLoughlin from Fort Vancouver to the Governor and Committee*, 2 vols. (Toronto, 1943), 2 ser., 95–105. Brackenridge's Oregon journal is printed in O. B. Spurlin, ed., "Our First Official Horticulturist," *Washington Historical Quarterly*, 21 (1920), 218–229, 298–305; 22 (1921), 42–58, 129–145, 216–227.

4. Eld; Albert Stearns, certificate of enlistment in Court-Martial Records, vol. 44, no. 827; Emmons; Charles Henry Carey, *History of Oregon* (Chicago and Portland, 1922), p. 420; Hubert Howe Bancroft, *Register of Pioneer Inhabitants of California, 1542 to 1848* (Los Angeles, 1964), p. 765; Bancroft, *History of Oregon*, 2 vols. (San Francisco, 1888), 1:73n.; Donald Jackson, ed., *Letters of the Lewis and Clark Expedition with Related Documents, 1793–1854* (Urbana, Ill., 1962), p. 429, n. 9; Washington Irving, *The Adventures of Captain Bonneville U.S.A. in the Rocky Mountains and the Far West*, ed., Edgeley W. Todd (Norman, Okla., 1961), pp. 16–17, n. 4 and *passim*.

5. Emmons; Eld; Brackenridge; Peale; Rodman W. Paul, *The California Gold Discovery: Sources, Documents, Accounts and Memoirs Relative to the Discovery of Gold at Sutter's Mill* (Georgetown, California, 1966), pp. 125–133; James D. Dana, "Notes on Upper California . . . ," *American Journal of Science*, 2d ser. 7 (1849), 147–164.

NOTES TO CHAPTER 16

1. Dyes; Robinson; Emmons; William Heath Davis, *Sixty Years in California* (San Francisco, 1889), pp. 121–125, 131–134; Wilkes; W[ilkes] to Hale, August 17, 31, 1841, Letterbook, Charles Wilkes Papers, LC; Holmes; Reynolds, Private Journal; Wilkes, Autobiography, pp. 1321–1323; Wilkes, Letterbook, entry for October 26, 1841; W[ilkes] to Knox, October 28, 1841, *ibid.*; Alden; W. L. Hudson; Sinclair; Eld.

2. Emmons; Sinclair; Reynolds, Private Journal, and Public Journal; Eld; Wilkes, Autobiography, pp. 1235–1237, 1338–1344, 1369–1370; Robinson; Erskine; Holmes; Henderson D. Norman, "The Log of the Flying Fish," United States Naval Institute *Proceedings*, 65 (1939), 363–366; *New York Herald*, June 26, 1842; Wilkes to Walker, Case, and Emmons, April 19, 1842; Walker, Case, and Emmons to Wilkes, April 20, 1842, copies in Emmons at entry for February 19, 1842; Ezra [Green] to brother, November 1, 1841, Ezra Green Papers; P. P. Bliss, "Brightly beams our Father's mercy," 1877; Reynolds, Ms. criticism of Wilkes' *Synopsis*.

1. *New York Herald*, June 11, 17, 19, July 26, 28, 1842; Erskine; Ms. list of "Ethnological Collections of the U.S. South Sea Exploring Expedition," in U.S. Exploring Expedition Mss., Smithsonian Institution Library; Reynolds, Private Journal; *Niles' National Register*, 64:190–191 (May 20, 1843), reprinted from the *New York Tribune*; Washington *Globe*, June 16, July 5, 22, 1842; John Quincy Adams, *Memoirs of John Quincy Adams, Comprising Portions of His Diary from 1795 to 1848*, ed. Charles Francis Adams, 12 vols. (Philadelphia, 1874–1877), 11:177 (June 15, 1842), 192 (June 30, 1842); J. R. Poinsett to Commodore [Charles G.] Ridgely, July 4, 1842, Poinsett Papers, Historical Society of Pennsylvania; Wilkes, Autobiography, pp. 1373–1388; Court-Martial Records, vol. 44, no. 827.

2. Court-Martial Records, vol. 43, nos. 823–826; Joseph P. Couthouy, "Reply of J. P. Couthouy, to the accusations of J. D. Dana, Geologist to the Exploring Expedition, contained on pp. 130 and 134 of this volume," *American Journal of Science*, 45 (1843), 378–389; *New York Tribune*, July 30, 1842; Reynolds to father, August 7 [August 14?], 1842, Reynolds Papers.

3. Court-Martial Records, vol. 44, no. 827; Reynolds to father, [August] 21, September 10, 1842, Reynolds Papers; *New York Herald*, August 10, 14, 1842; Wilkes, Autobiography, pp. 1382–1387; Reynolds, Ms. criticism of Wilkes' *Synopsis*, Reynolds Papers; Charles Wilkes, "Defence: The following Defence of Lieut. Charles Wilkes to the charges on which he has been tried is respectfully submitted to the court" [Washington, 1842]; Pickering to Mary O. Pickering, August 1, 1842, Massachusetts Historical Society.

NOTES TO CHAPTER 18

1. Charles Wilkes, *Synopsis of the Cruise of the U.S. Exploring Expedition . . .* (Washington, 1842); John W. Forney, *Anecdotes of Public Men* (New York, 1873), p. 231; George B. Goode, "The Genesis of the National Museum," U.S. National Museum *Annual Report* for 1891, pp. 273–380 (vide 302–307); Jessie Poesch, *Titian Ramsey Peale, 1799–1885, and His Journals of the Wilkes Expedition*, APS Memoirs, 52 (Philadelphia, 1961), 95; Wilkes to Paulding, to Buist, to Franklin Peale, all dated December 25, 1838, LRWEE; "Original Invoices" in Smithsonian Institution Library; J. J. Abert to Poinsett, May 6, 1841, Poinsett Papers, Historical Society of Pennsylvania. On the inroads of politicians, see the many requests in the National Institute Papers, Henry E. Huntington Library.

2. John Quincy Adams, *Memoirs of John Quincy Adams . . .* , ed. Charles Francis Adams, 12 vols. (Philadelphia, 1876), 10:57 (December 8, 1838); Samuel George Morton to John K. Kane, July 23, 1839; Morton, "Extract from the Minutes of the Academy of Natural Sciences at Philadelphia, July 23, 1839," both in Misc. Mss. Collections, APS; Minutes of May 7, 8, 10, 14, 15, and June 20, 1840, in National Institute, Misc. Mss. 129, Smithsonian Institution Archives; Goode, "Genesis," p. 285. For a list of the Institute members in May 1840, see [National Institution], *Constitution and By-Laws of the National Institution for the Promotion of Science, Established at Washington, May 1840* (Washington, 1840).

3. Ms. Resolution of the American Historical Society, June 18, 1840, in National Institute Papers, Smithsonian Institution Archives; Richard Rathbun, "The Columbian Institute for the Promotion of Arts and Sciences: a Washington Society for 1816–1838, which established a museum and botanic garden under government patronage," in U.S. National Museum *Bulletin* 101 (1917); Francis Markoe to [Peter S. Du Ponceau?], September 8, 1840, Rathbun Mss.; Goode, "Genesis," pp. 185–186, 304; William J. Rhees, comp. and ed., *The Smithsonian Institution; Documents Relative to Its Origin and History, 1835–1899*, 2 vols. paged continuously, in Smithsonian Miscellaneous Collections, 42, 43 (Washington, 1901), 215–220; "A Citizen" [George Watterston], [Letter on the Smithsonian Legacy], Washington, January 2, 1844 [Washington, 1844?]; Abert to Poinsett, May 6, 1841, Poinsett Papers, Historical Society of Pennsylvania. Peale may be caught red-handed in Titian R. Peale to Franklin [Peale], April 5, 1840, APS.

4. Upshur to Brackenridge, July 13, 1842, Brackenridge Papers, Smithsonian Institution Library; Adams, *Memoirs*, 11:459 (December 23, 1843); Goode, "Genesis," p. 307; *House Doc. 74*, 17 Cong., 2 sess.; Varden to President & Members of the Columbian Institution in Washington City, June 24, 1836, copy in Rathbun Mss.; Washington *Globe*, July 9, 1840; Varden to John Cassin, May 16, 1854, typescript in Rathbun Mss.; William Healey Dall, *Spencer Fullerton Baird* (Philadelphia, 1915), pp. 73–76; Francis Markoe, Jr. to [Poinsett], June 20, 1841, Poinsett Papers, Historical Society of Pennsylvania; typescript "List of certain historical and industrial objects in Museum of National Institute," Rathbun Mss.; Jonathan Elliot, *Historical Sketches of the Ten Mile Square forming the District of Columbia* (Washington, 1830), pp. 165–168; Abert, Memorandum for the Committee of the National Institute, June 16, 1841, and Memorandum of May 21, 1841, National Institute Papers, Smithsonian Institution Archives.

5. Goode, "Genesis," pp. 308–309, 346–350; Rhees, *Smithsonian Institution; Documents* (1901), p. 239; Pickering to Upshur, August 18, 1842, in typescript copy of National Institute Minutes for September 12, 1842, Rathbun Mss.; *Sen. Doc. 229*, 16 Cong., 1 sess.; *House Report 832*, 27 Cong., 2 sess.; *Sen. Doc. 67*, 27 Cong., 2 sess.; Washington *Globe*, August 26, 1842; Abert to Poinsett, November 9, 1842, Poinsett Papers, Historical Society of Pennsylvania.

6. Markoe, Abert, Dayton to [Upshur], August 24, 1842, in typescript copy of National Institute Minutes for September 12, 1842, Rathbun Mss.; Benjamin Tappan, Ms. Senate Journal, March 5, 1840, February 15, 1841, December 23, 1842, and November 23, 1843; to brother [Lewis Tappan?], June 1, 1840: Benjamin Tappan Papers, Ohio Historical Society; Rhees, *Smithsonian Institution; Documents* (1901), pp. 166–168, 176–180; John S. Meehan, copy of resolution of the Committee on the Library, August 26, 1842, Benjamin Tappan Papers, LC.

7. Wilkes to Tappan, August 28, 1842, Benjamin Tappan Papers, LC; T. R. Peale, "The South Sea Surveying and Exploring Expedition," *American Historical Record*, 3 (1874), 244–307; Abert to Poinsett, February 6, 23, 1843, July 3, 1844, Poinsett Papers, Historical Society of Pennsylvania; to Charles Pickering, September 16, 1842, National Institute Minute Book, Misc. Collection 110, Smithsonian Institution Archives; Dall, *Baird*, pp. 76–77, 81; Pickering to Upshur, December 26, 1842 (copy); Upshur to Pickering, December 29, 1842, Benjamin Tappan Papers, LC; Charles Dickens,

American Notes (London, 1874; first published, 1842), p. 142; E. S. Streeter, *The Stranger's Guide or the Daguerreotype of Washington, D.C.* (Washington, 1850), pp. 23–25; George Watterston, *A New Guide to Washington* (Washington, 1842), pp. 114–119; "Place and Arrangement of the Hall when Cap'n C. Wilkes took Charge August 7, 1843," Rathbun Mss.; *National Intelligencer*, November 20, 1843.

8. Ralph L. Rusk, ed., *The Letters of Ralph Waldo Emerson*, 6 vols. (New York, 1839), 3:222–224; W. M. Walker to Tappan, March 20, 1843, Benjamin Tappan Papers, LC; Reynolds to Henry Eld, January 22, 1843, Eld Papers, Western Americana Collection, Yale; Wilkes, Autobiography, pp. 1394, 1396–1401; Abert to Charles Pickering, September 16, 1842, National Institute Minute Book; Goode, "Genesis," pp. 350–353, 354–358; Peale, "South Sea Surveying and Exploring Expedition"; Peale to Ord, March 14, 1843, Misc. Mss. Collection, APS; William H. Dall, "Some American Conchologists," *Proceedings of the Biological Society of Washington*, 4 (1888), 95–124; Baird, pp. 79–80.

9. W[ilkes] to Tappan, August 11, 1843, Letterbook, Charles Wilkes Papers, LC; Goode, "Genesis," pp. 313–315, 316–318; "Notice to Members of the National Institute," at beginning of *Bulletin of the Proceedings of the National Institute*, No. 4 (1845–1846); John Carroll Brent, *Letters on the National Institute, Smithsonian Legacy, the Fine Arts, and Other Matters Connected with the Interests of the District of Columbia* (Washington, 1844); John G. Morris to Markoe, February 19, 1844, typescript copy in Rathbun Mss.

NOTES TO CHAPTER 19

1. Wilkes, Autobiography, pp. 1373–1374, 1379–1382, 1391–1392, 1403; Wilkes to [wife], August 19, 1842, Letterbook, Charles Wilkes Papers, LC; John Quincy Adams, *Memoirs of John Quincy Adams . . . ,* ed. Charles Francis Adams, 12 vols. (Philadelphia, 1874–1877), 11:202 (July 9, 1842); Upshur to Wilkes, September 22, 1842, copy in Benjamin Tappan Papers, LC; Wilkes to [John Wilkes], April 22, 1855, Charles Wilkes Papers, LC; Horatio Bridge, *Personal Recollections of Nathaniel Hawthorne* (New York, 1893), pp. 82–83; Annie R. Ellis, ed., *The Early Diary of Frances Burney*, 2 vols. (London, 1907), 1:139, quoted in J. C. Beaglehole, ed., *The Journals of Captain James Cook on His Voyages of Discovery*, 3 vols. (Cambridge, 1955–1967), 1:ccxliii–ccliii.

2. Honolulu *Polynesian*, September 21, 28, 1844; [James D. Dana], "United States Exploring Expedition," *American Journal of Science*, 44 (1843), 393–408 (reprinted as *A Brief Account of the Discoveries and Results of the United States Exploring Expedition*, New Haven, 1843); Wilkes to Upshur, February 16, 1843; Wilkes to Renwick, February 26, 1845, in Letterbook, Charles Wilkes Papers, LC; Wilkes to Pickering, n.d., National Institute Papers, Huntington Library; "Narrative of the United States Exploring Expedition . . . ," *American Journal of Science*, 49 (1845), 149–166; *Morning Courier and New-York Enquirer*, June 3, 9, 13, 14, 18, 30, 1845. Wilkes' volumes bore the title *Narrative of the United States Exploring Expedition. During the Years 1838, 1839, 1840, 1841, 1842. By Charles Wilkes, U.S.N., Commander of the Expedition, Member of the American Philosophical Society, Etc. In Five Volumes, and An Atlas*, and were printed by C. Sherman, Philadelphia. On the

various other printings of these and all other Expedition publications, see Haskell, *United States Exploring Expedition.*

3. [Charles Henry Davis], "The United States Exploring Expedition," *North American Review,* 61 (1845), 54–107; "United States Exploring Expedition," *Southern Literary Messenger,* 11 (1845), 305–322; "The United States Exploring Expedition," *The Spectator,* 18 (1845), 85–86, 160–161, 447–448, 613–614; ["E."], "Narrative of the United States Exploring Expedition," *Westminster Review,* 44 (1845), 469–496; [Joel R. Poinsett], "The last two volumes of a Narrative of the United States Exploring Expedition . . . ," *Southern Quarterly Review,* 8 (1845), 265–298; *National Intelligencer,* June 12, 1848; *Edinburgh Review,* 83 (1846), 431–452; Norman Sherry, *Conrad's Eastern World* (Cambridge, 1966), pp. 141, 154–155; James F. Beard, ed., *The Letters and Journals of James Fenimore Cooper,* 6 vols. (Cambridge, Mass., 1960–1968), 4:430, 470–477; James Fenimore Cooper, *Early Critical Essays,* ed. James F. Beard (Gainesville, Fla., 1955), p. 43; W. B. Gates, "Cooper's *The Sea Lions* and Wilkes' Narrative," *Publications of the Modern Language Association,* 65 (1950), 1069–1075; "Cooper's *The Crater* and Two Explorers," *American Literature,* 23 (1951), 243–246; Thomas Philbrick, *James Fenimore Cooper and the Development of American Sea Fiction* (Cambridge, Mass., 1961), pp. 217–221.

4. [Herman Melville], "Cooper's New Novel," *The Literary World,* 4:370 (April 28, 1849); Jay Leyda, *The Melville Log: A Documentary Life of Herman Melville, 1819–1891,* 2 vols. paged continuously (New York, 1951), p. 241; Charles Roberts Anderson, *Melville in the South Seas* (New York, 1939), *passim.*; David Jaffe, "Some Origins of Moby Dick: New Finds in an Old Source," *American Literature,* 29 (1947), 263–277; Samuel L. Clemens, *Mark Twain's Autobiography,* 2 vols. (New York, 1924), 2:120–121; clipping from *New York Journal of Commerce* of undetermined date, in Emmons' journal at entry for June 20, 1841.

5. "Exploring Expedition," *Niles' National Register,* 62 (1842), 150; Pickering to Poinsett, July 10, 1840, Poinsett Papers, Historical Society of Pennsylvania; [J. R. Poinsett], "The Exploring Expedition," *North American Review,* 56 (1843), 257–270; Dana to Benjamin Silliman, February 13, 1843, Historical Mss., Yale; James Clark Ross, *A Voyage of Discovery and Research in the Southern and Antarctic Regions, During the Years 1839–43,* 2 vols. (London, 1847), 1:116; P[ierre] Daussy, "Exposé des travaux de l'expedition americaine pendant les années 1838, 39, 40, 41 et 42, lu a l'Institut national de Washington par son commandant Charles Wilkes, Esq . . . ," Societé de geographie *Bulletin* (Paris), serie 2, tome 19 (1843), 37–79; Auguste Laugel, "Le Pôle Austral et les Expéditions Antarctiques," *Revue des Deux Mondes,* XXVIᵉ Année, Seconde Période, Tome I (1856), 802–820; Jean Baptiste Biot, "Narrative of the United States Exploring Expedition," *Journal des Savants* (Paris, 1848), 672–687, 709–728; (1849), 65–83; [Joel R. Poinsett], "The first three volumes of a Narrative of the United States Exploring Expedition . . . ," *Southern Quarterly Review,* 8 (1845), 1–69.

6. Laugel, "Le Pôle Austral"; [Davis], "The United States Exploring Expedition"; Wilkes, *Narrative,* 2:282, 335; Philbrick, *James Fenimore Cooper,* pp. 229–230; Biot, "Narrative of the United States Exploring Expedition"; Wilkes, *Synopsis of the Cruise of the U.S. Exploring Expedition . . .* (Washington, 1842), pp. 20, 27; Ross, *Voyage of Discovery,* 1:116–117, 272–276, 269–299; Charles Wilkes, *Antarctic Discovery. Letter*

from Captain Wilkes to the Editor of the Union. Washington City, August 12, 1847 (Washington, 1847); The Spectator (Washington), November 19, 1842; Basil Thomson, Diversions of a Prime Minister (London, 1894), 199; Charles L. Camp, ed., George C. Yount and His Chronicles of the West: Comprising Extracts from His "Memoirs" and from the Orange Clark "Narrative" (Denver, 1966), pp. 211–213; Hubert Howe Bancroft, History of Oregon, 2 vols. (San Francisco, 1888), 1:584–589; John E. Wickman, "Political Aspects of Charles Wilkes' Work and Testimony, 1842–1849," Ph.D. dissertation, University of Indiana, 1964; House Misc. Doc. 29, 30 Cong., 1 sess.; George H. Himes, "Letter by Burr Osborn, Survivor of the Howison Expedition to Oregon, 1846," Oregon Historical Quarterly, 14 (1918), 355–365. On the great extent to which recent exploration has confirmed the Expedition's Antarctic landfalls, see Kenneth J. Bertrand, Americans in Antarctica, 1775–1948, American Geographical Society Special Publication No. 39 (New York, 1971), Ch. 10.

7. Wilkes to John W. Davis, January 28, 1845, Benjamin Tappan Papers, LC; Autobiography, pp. 1449–1452; to George Bancroft, April 30, 1845; to [John Wilkes], January 2, 1848, March 3, 1855, December 15, 1856, Letterbook, Charles Wilkes Papers, LC; J[oseph] Drayton to Tappan, May 4, 1845, Benjamin Tappan Papers; [Henry Eld] to father, March 27, 1844, April 25, 1845, Eld Papers, LC; House Doc. 32, 29 Cong., 2 sess.; Wilkes to James A. Pearce, January 7, 15, 23, 25, 1847, Letterbook, Charles Wilkes Papers, LC.

NOTES TO CHAPTER 20

1. Binney to Tappan, October 13, 1843; J. E. De Kay to Tappan, December 30, 1842, Benjamin Tappan Papers, LC; [Gould] to [Tappan], n.d., penciled draft in Science Museum, Boston; Audubon to Baird, July 30, 1842, in William H. Dall, Spencer Fullerton Baird (Philadelphia, 1915), pp. 78–79; De Kay to Tappan, December 30, 1842; Tappan to Pickering, February 13, 1843 (draft); Dana to [Tappan?], January 14, February 22, 1843; Peale to Tappan, February 22, 1843, Benjamin Tappan Papers, LC; Pickering to [Asa Gray], July 5, 1843, HLF; G[eorge] Brown Goode, "The Genesis of the National Museum," U.S. National Museum Annual Report for 1891, pp. 273–380; Rich to Tappan, February 14, 1843; Rich to Pickering, February 24, March 2, 1843; Hale to [Tappan?], February 14, 1843, Benjamin Tappan Papers, LC; 28 Cong., 2 sess., Joint resolution 5, United States Statutes at Large, 5:797 (February 20, 1845); J. B. Sutherland to David Henshaw, August 12, 1843, Letterbook, Charles Wilkes Papers, LC; Torrey to Asa Gray, March 18, 1851, HLF, quoted in Haskell, The United States Exploring Expedition, p. 22, n. 60; David M. Stauffer, American Engravers upon Copper and Steel, 2 vols. (New York, 1907), 1:69; Drayton to Tappan, April 24, 1843; Wilkes to Tappan, June 4, 1843, Benjamin Tappan Papers, LC; Drayton to Wilkes, August 6, April 27, 1850, Charles Wilkes Papers, LC; Drayton to [Asa Gray], May 22, 1851, HLF.

2. Dana to Silliman, February 13, 1843; Dana to mother, January 2, 1843, Historical Mss., Yale; Wilkes to Dana, March 17, 1847, Letterbook, Charles Wilkes Papers, LC; A. Hunter Dupree, Asa Gray, 1810–1888 (Cambridge, Mass., 1959), p. 24; Hale to Wilkes, October 3, 1843; Pickering to Tappan, April 24, 1843, Benjamin Tappan

Papers, LC; Tappan to son, March 15, 1846, Benjamin Tappan Papers, Ohio Historical Society; Dana to Gray, March 16, 1846, HLF, quoted in Haskell, *United States Exploring Expedition*, p. 11; Gould to Tappan, September 18, October 17, December 17, 1843, December 6, 1844, January 3, 1845; Gould to Wilkes, October 7, 1843; Wilkes to Tappan, September 16, October 9, 18, Friday evening [December 8?], n.d. (between letters dated November 17, 1843, and January 31, 1844), 1843; Wilkes to Gould, October 14, 1843; Binney to Tappan, December 2, 1843, Benjamin Tappan Papers, LC; Peale to Wilkes, February 21, 1845, Wilkes Papers, Kansas State Historical Society.

3. Haldeman to Tappan, March 1, 1845, Benjamin Tappan Papers, LC; Tappan to Wilkes, March 26, 1845, Ohio Mss. Collection, Ohio Historical Society; Wilkes to Le Conte, March 4, 1847; Wilkes to James A. Pearce, April 5, 1847; Drayton to Wilkes, November 11, 1851, Letterbook, Charles Wilkes Papers, LC; Dana to Tappan, September 18, 1843, November 4, 1844, Benjamin Tappan Papers, LC; Dana to Wilkes, February 2, 1845, Western Americana Collection, Yale; Wilkes to Tappan, n.d., vol. 19, no. 3071, Benjamin Tappan Papers, LC; Marsh to [Dana], February 4, 1846, Western Americana Collection, Yale; Dana, "Private," to Gray, March 7, 1846, HLF; Gray to Tappan, March 11, 1846, Benjamin Tappan Papers, LC; [Gray], undated notation on envelope postmarked March 6, [1846?], HLF; Drayton to Wilkes, July 25, 1851, Charles Wilkes Papers, LC; James D. Dana, "On the Temperature limiting the distribution of Corals," *American Journal of Science*, 45 (1843), 130–131 (read before the Association of American Geologists and Naturalists, April 29, 1843); "Reply to Mr. Couthouy's Vindication against the charge of plagiarism," *ibid.*, 46 (1843), 129–136; Joseph P. Couthouy, "Remarks upon Coral Formations in the Pacific; with Suggestions as to the Causes of Their Absence in the Same Parallels of Latitude on the Coast of South America," *Boston Journal of Natural History*, 4 (1841), 66–105, 137–162, read December 15, 1841; "Reply of J. P. Couthouy, to the accusations of J. D. Dana . . . ," *American Journal of Science*, 45 (1843), 378–389; J. D. Dana and J. P. Couthouy, [Acknowledgements of J. D. Dana and J. P. Couthouy, relative to a charge of plagiarism], *ibid.*, 47 (1844), 94–134. For a review of the controversy see *ibid.*, 46 (1844), Appendix.

4. [Asa Gray], "Scientific Results of the Exploring Expedition," *North American Review*, 63 (1846), 211–236; Tappan "To the Honl. James A. Pearce, Chairman of the Joint Committee on the Library" [March 1846]; to Benjamin Tappan [Jr.], April 13, 1846, Benjamin Tappan Papers, LC; to brother [Lewis Tappan?], November 6, 1844; to Eli Tappan, March 20–April 2, April 7, 1846, Tappan Papers, Ohio Historical Society; Joint Library Committee of Congress, Receipt of Tappan resignation as agent of the Committee, May 20, 1846, Benjamin Tappan Papers, LC; Bernard C. Steiner, "James Alfred Pearce," *Maryland Historical Magazine*, 16 (1921), 319–339; 17 (1922), 33–47, 177–190, 269–283, 348–363; 18 (1923), 38–52, 134–150, 257–273, 341–357; 19 (1924), 13–29, 162–179; Brackenridge to Wilkes, November 1, 1848; Wilkes to [John] Varden, November 13, 1850, February 3, 1852, National Institute Papers, Huntington Library; Drayton to Wilkes, April 27, 1850, Charles Wilkes Papers, LC; *Sen. Doc. 405, 29 Cong.,* 1 sess., 8.

5. Peale to G[eorge] Ord, March 14, 1843, November 26, 1844, Misc. Mss. Collection, APS; Jessie Poesch, *Titian Ramsay Peale, 1799–1885, and His Journals of*

the Wilkes Expedition, APS Memoirs, vol. 52 (Philadelphia, 1961), 95, 98; T. R. Peale, "The South Sea Surveying and Exploring Expedition," *American Historical Record* . . . , 3 (1874), 244–251, 305–311; Spencer F. Baird to John Cassin, March 1, 1851, Baird copy-press letterbooks, Smithsonian Institution Archives; Wilkes to Tappan, May 28, June 22, 1845; Wilkes to Pearce, December 27, 1846, January 23, 25, April 5, May 18, December 30, 1857, Letterbook, Charles Wilkes Papers, LC; Haskell, *United States Exploring Expedition*, p. 55; Drayton to Wilkes, June 17, 18, 1850, Letterbook, Charles Wilkes Papers, LC. On Cassin, see T. M. Brewer, [Obituary Notice of John Cassin], Boston Society of Natural History *Proceedings*, 12 (1869), 244–248.

6. Drayton to Wilkes, November 29, 1850, Charles Wilkes Papers, LC; Dall, *Baird*, p. 280; Andrew D. Rodgers III, *"Noble Fellow" William Starling Sullivant* (New York, 1940), p. 174; Wilkes to Tappan, June 22, 1845; to Rich, June 24, 1845; to Pearce, December 27, 1846, April 5, May 18, June 7, July 13, August 1, December 30, 1847; to Torrey, April 10, [21], 1847; to Curtis, June 23, 1847, Letterbook, Charles Wilkes Papers, LC; to Torrey, April 15, 1847, Boston Public Library; to Gray, June 24, 1848, HLF; Andrew D. Rodgers III, *John Torrey, A Story of North American Botany* (Princeton, 1942), pp. 47, 182; Gray to J. D. Hooker, December 31, 1845, *The Letters of Asa Gray*, ed. Jane Loring Gray, 2 vols. (Boston, 1893), 1:337–338; Torrey to Gray, May 30, 1848, HLF; [Gray], "Scientific Results of the Exploring Expedition"; Dupree, *Asa Gray*, p. 187; Edward Harris, *Up the Missouri with Audubon: The Journal of Edward Harris*, ed. John F. McDermott (Norman, Okla., 1951), pp. 8, n. 18. On Curtis, see C. L. Shear and Neil E. Stevens, "The Mycological Work of Moses Ashley Curtis," *Mycologia*, 11 (1919), 181–201; Thomas F. Wood, *Sketch of the Botanical Work of the Rev. Moses A. Curtis* (Raleigh, 1885).

7. Brackenridge to Torrey, June 26, 1848, September 14, 1849, January 9, October 17, 1850, January 18, 1851, Torrey Papers, New York Botanical Garden; Torrey to Brackenridge, September 11, 1847, December 16, 1850, June 12, 1851, Brackenridge Papers, Smithsonian Institution Library; Torrey to [Gray], January 8, March 18, June 29, 1851; Torrey to Mrs. Gray, March 28, 1851, HLF; Wilkes to Tuckerman, March 5 [?], 10, 1846, Letterbook, Charles Wilkes Papers, LC; to Sullivant, June 2, 1847; to Pearce, June 2, 1847, April 13, 23 (copy), 1852; to Torrey, March 16, 1851 (copy); to Gray, n.d. [July 1852?], HLF; Tuckerman to Wilkes, March 21, 1846, Benjamin Tappan Papers, LC; Rodgers, *"Noble Fellow"*, pp. 174–175; Drayton to Wilkes, October 26, 1850, Charles Wilkes Papers, LC; Sullivant to Gray, July 8, 1852 (quoted in Dupree, *Asa Gray*, p. 194); Gray to Torrey, January 31, 1851, copy in Brackenridge Papers, Smithsonian Institution Library; Gray to [Pearce], April 2, 1851, June 18, 1852 (copy); to Wilkes, June 17, 18, 1852 (copy); Pearce to Gray, April 30, 1851; Henry to Gray, [May] 27, June 16, 1852, HLF.

NOTES TO CHAPTER 21

1. Wilkes to Tappan, June 22, 1845, November 30, 1848, Benjamin Tappan Papers, LC; to Tappan, May 28, 1845 (Letterbook); to Pearce, August 1, December 30, 1847 (Letterbook); Drayton to [Wilkes], fragment in "Personal Correspondence Undated"; and June 18, 1840, Charles Wilkes Papers, LC; William H. Dall, *Spencer Fullerton*

Baird (Philadelphia, 1915), p. 163; J. N. Reynolds, *Address on the Subject of a Surveying and Exploring Expedition* . . . (New York, 1836), pp. 153–155; Pickering to Morton, August 8, 1840, Samuel George Morton Papers, APS; S. S. Haldeman, "Enumeration of the recent fresh water Mollusca which are common to North America and Europe; with observations on species and their distribution," *Boston Society of Natural History Journal*, 4 (1844), 368–384; [Robert Chambers], *Vestiges of the Natural History of Creation* (Edinburgh, 1844; New York, 1845); Samuel George Morton, *An Inquiry into the Distinctive Characteristics of the Aboriginal Race of America* (Philadelphia, 1842); Pickering to Mary O. Pickering, November 2, 1843, April 18, August 28, 1844, Massachusetts Historical Society. On the "American School," see William Stanton, *The Leopard's Spots: Scientific Attitudes toward Race in America, 1815–1859* (Chicago, 1960).

2. J. C. Nott, "The Mulatto a Hybrid—Probable Extermination of the Two Races If the Whites and Blacks are Allowed to Intermarry," *American Journal of the Medical Sciences*, 6 (1843), 252–256; *Two Lectures on the Natural History of the Caucasian and Negro Races* (Mobile, 1844); L[ouis A[gassiz], "Geographical Distribution of Animals," *Christian Examiner*, 48 (1850), 181–204; "The Diversity of Origin of Human Races," *ibid.*, 49 (1850), 110–145; "Contemplations of God in the Kosmos," *ibid.*, 50 (1851), 1–17; [Moses Ashley] C[urtis], "Unity of the Races," *Southern Quarterly Review*, 7 (1845), 372–488; Pickering to Morton, September 7, 1846, Morton Papers, Library Company of Philadelphia; to Morton, June 12, 1848, letter mounted in endpapers of the ANSP copy of Pickering's book; Wilkes to Morton, November 6, 1846, Morton Papers, Library Company of Philadelphia; Wilkes to Pickering, February 8, March 4, 1847; to Mason, March 6, 1847; to Pearce, March 19, April 5, May 18, 1847, Letterbook, Charles Wilkes Papers, LC; Holmes to Morton, November 27, 1849, Morton Papers, Library Company of Philadelphia; *Letters from Francis Parkman to E. G. Squier*, ed. Don C. Seitz (Cedar Rapids, Iowa, 1911), pp. 18–30; John Bachman, *The Doctrine of the Unity of the Human Race Examined on the Principles of Science* (Charleston, S.C., 1850), p. 303; Pickering, *Races of Man* (London, 1851, the most widely available edition), pp. 191, 214, 289, 296–297; E. G. Squier and E. H. Davis, *Ancient Monuments of the Mississippi Valley; comprising the Results of Extensive Original Surveys and Explorations* (Washington, 1848). Quotations from Pickering's book are from the chapter "Zoological Deductions" unless otherwise noted.

NOTES TO CHAPTER 22

1. Wilkes to John Wilkes, March 10, 1855, John Wilkes Papers, LC; to [John Wilkes], February 2, 1854; to Agassiz, May 9, 1850 (Letterbook), Charles Wilkes Papers, LC; to Tappan, November 30, 1848, December 20, 1850, April 14, 1851, Benjamin Tappan Papers, LC; to Walter R. Johnson, February 26, 1849, National Institute Papers, Huntington Library; William H. Dall, *Spencer Fullerton Baird* (Philadelphia, 1915), pp. 255–258; Brackenridge to Torrey, December 20, 1850, April 18, January 18, 1851, John Torrey Papers, New York Botanical Garden; Haskell, *United States Exploring Expedition*, p. 89; Gray to W. J. Hooker, June 20, 1856, *Letters of Asa Gray*, ed. Jane Loring Gray, 2 vols. (Boston, 1893), 2:422–423; John S.

Meehan to Pearce, July 7, 1849, Letterbook of txe Librarian of Congress, LC. On Girard, see George Brown Goode, *The Published Writings of Dr. Charles Girard*, U.S. National Museum Bulletin 41 (Washington, 1891). Wilkes' report on meteorology was evidently not distributed until 1854; see Haskell, *United States Exploring Expedition*, p. 71.

2. Drayton to Wilkes, January 14, July 22, December 27, 28, 30, 1851, Charles Wilkes Papers, LC; Dana to Morton, January 26, 1849, ANSP; Agassiz to Wilkes, October 22, 1854; Wilkes to Drayton, March 13, 1849, Charles Wilkes Papers, LC; Wilkes to Tappan, December [?] 27, 1853, Benjamin Tappan Papers, LC; *Ballou's Pictorial Drawing-Room Companion*, 14 (1858), 399; Gilman, *James Dwight Dana*, p. 143; Torrey to Gray, March 9, 1861, HLF; John S. Meehan to Pearce, December 24, 25, 1851, Letterbook of the Librarian of Congress, LC. Morton's article appeared in Henry Rowe Schoolcraft, *Information Respecting the History, Condition and Prospects of the Indian Tribes of the United States* . . . , 6 vols. (Philadelphia, 1851–1857), Part 2:315–331. I am indebted to Miss Josephine Cobb of the National Archives for unearthing *Ballou's* report on the set in Canton. I assume that the visiting American and Dana's friend, the missionary-Sinologist-diplomat Samuel Wells Williams, were the same.

3. *Narrative of the Expedition of An American Squadron to the China Seas and Japan* . . . , 3 vols. (Washington, 1851); Edward M. Barrows, *The Great Commodore: The Exploits of Matthew Calbraith Perry* (Indianapolis, 1935), p. 348; Drayton to Wilkes, September 1, 4, 11, 14, 1850, December 14, 1852, Charles Wilkes Papers, LC; Wilkes to Tappan, November 25, 1850, December [?] 27, 1853, nos. 3076, 3490, Benjamin Tappan Papers, LC; to John Wilkes, March 4, 5, 10, April 22, 1855, John Wilkes Papers, LC; to Pearce, March 6, 13, April 10, 1855; Pearce to Gray, November 28, 1856, HLF; Pearce to Wilkes, March 24, 1855, Charles Wilkes Papers, LC; William J. Rhees, comp. and ed., *The Smithsonian Institution: Documents Relative to Its Origin and History, 1835–1899*, Smithsonian Miscellaneous Collections, vols. 42, 43 (Washington, 1901), paged continuously, 429–434, 487, 511; Richard Rathbun, *The Columbian Institute for the Promotion of Arts and Sciences: a Washington Society for 1816–1838, which established a museum and botanic garden under government patronage*, U.S. National Museum Bulletin 101 (Washington, 1917); Pickering, *The Geographical Distribution of Animals and Plants* (Boston, 1854).

4. Drayton to Tappan, March 10, 1856, Benjamin Tappan Papers, LC; [Drayton], "Losses by fire of the works of the Ex. Ex. . . . on the 11th of April 1856"; to Wilkes, September 9, October 22, 1856, Charles Wilkes Papers, LC; to Gray, March 10, 1856, HLF; Wilkes to Eliza [Wilkes], March 20, April 13, 1856; [Wilkes], "Copy of remarks of Mr. Drayton from Mr. Pearce, Washington July 5th 1856"; Wilkes to Pearce, September 1856; Pearce to Wilkes, April 7, 1856, Charles Wilkes Papers, LC; John S. Meehan to Pearce, November 12, 25, 1856, Letterbook of the Librarian of Congress, LC; George E. Lewis to Gray, November 25, 1856, HLF; T[appan] to Wilkes, January 12, 1857 (copy), Benjamin Tappan Papers, LC.

5. Wilkes to [John Wilkes], December 15, 1856; to Pearce, May 21, 1857, January 3, 1859, February 18, [1861]; to William W [?] Bailey, June 3, 1857; to Torrey, November 3, 1858; to Sullivant, November 3, 1858; to Pickering, May 22, 1858 (all in Letterbook); "To the Honorable the Senate and House of Representatives of the United States of

America in Congress Assembled," February 19, 1857; Pickering to Wilkes, January 1, 1858; Stuart to Wilkes, September 17, 1858, Charles Wilkes Papers, LC; Rhees, *Smithsonian Institution: Documents* (1901), pp. 429–434, 608, 627; Wilkes to Tappan, November 30, 1848, Benjamin Tappan Papers, LC; Horatio Greenough, *Form and Function: Remarks on Art, Design, and Architecture*, ed. Harold A. Small (Berkeley, 1966; first published as *Memorial of Horatio Greenough*, New York, 1853), pp. 36–38. *Hydrography* bears the date 1861 but was not distributed until 1873.

6. Anthony to Tappan, May 7, 1850, Benjamin Tappan Papers, LC; Wilkes to Johnson, February 6, 26, 1849, National Institute Papers, Huntington Library; to Tappan, November 25, 1850, Benjamin Tappan Papers, LC; National Institute Minute Book, 1842–1849, pp. 367–374, Smithsonian Institution Archives; Rhees, *Smithsonian Institution: Documents* (1901), 601, 1716, 1732–1733; George B. Goode, "The Genesis of the National Museum," U.S. National Museum Annual *Report* (1891), pp. 273–380; Smithsonian Institution *Report for 1858* (Washington, 1859); Rathbun, *Columbian Institute*; J. W. Powell, "National Agencies for Scientific Research," *The Chautauquan*, 14 (1890–1891), 37–42, 160–165, 291–297, 422–425, 545–549, 668–673; Andrew D. Rodgers III, *John Torrey, A Story of North American Botany* (Princeton, 1942), pp. 265–271, 332.

7. Smithsonian Institution *Report for 1861* (Washington, 1862); *New York Times*, November 19, 1861; *Cong. Globe*, 37 Cong., 2 sess., Part I, 5; James A. Rawley, *Turning Points of the Civil War* (Lincoln, Nebraska, 1966), pp. 71–95; Robert E. Johnson, *Rear Admiral John Rodgers* (Annapolis, 1967), p. 213; Clarence E. MacCartney, *Mr. Lincoln's Admirals* (New York, 1956), pp. 10–11; *House Docs. 102, 103*, 38 Cong., 1 sess.; Stuart to Wilkes, March 19, 1869, in "Receipts & Bills & Business Correspondence, 1853–1869," Charles Wilkes Papers, LC; Stuart to Gray, February 25, 1870, HLF; to A. R. Spofford, March 12, 1870, Charles Wilkes Papers, LC; Case to Wilkes, June 27, 1870, Charles Wilkes Papers, Historical Society of Wisconsin; Wilkes to Gray, March 30, 1873, HLF; Torrey to Stuart, March 9, 11, 1860, Misc. Mss., Personal Papers, LC.

8. Rhees, *Smithsonian Institution: Documents* (1901), pp. 611–627, 692; A. R. Spofford to Wilkes, February 7, 1873, Charles Wilkes Papers, LC; Stuart to Torrey, February 6, 1873; Torrey to [Gray], December 19, 1872, January 14, 21, February 10, 1873, HLF; [Wilkes], draft of memorandum, n.d. [1875?], beginning "By act of Congress July 1842 . . ."; Wilkes to Howe, January 20, 1875; to Messrs. Sherman & Co., April 6, 1875 (Letterbook), Charles Wilkes Papers, LC; Charles Pickering, *The Geographical Distribution of Animals and Plants, Part II. Plants in their Wild State* (Salem, Mass., 1876), p. iv; Haskell, *United States Exploring Expedition*, p. 99; Gray to Charles Wright, August 1, 1862, *Letters of Asa Gray*, 2:483–484; Dana to Gray, February 12, 1846, HLF.

NOTES TO CHAPTER 23

1. John McCline [?] to John Wilkes, June 12, 1849, John Wilkes Papers, LC; William Elder, *Biography of Elisha Kent Kane* (Philadelphia, 1857), p. 149; Jeanette Mirsky, *Elisha Kent Kane and the Seafaring Frontier* (Boston, 1954), p. 22; J. W. Buel,

World's Wonders, as Seen by the Great Tropical and Polar Explorers . . . (St. Louis, 1884), p. 576; E. K. Kane, *Arctic Explorations in the Years 1853, '54, '55*, 2 vols. (Philadelphia, 1856), 1:298; Laurence P. Kirwan, *A History of Polar Exploration* (New York, 1960), pp. 181, 183; "Notes by the Editor on the Progress of Science in 1852," *Annual of Scientific Discovery*, 4 (1853), pp. 5–29; *Sen. Docs.* 161, 172, 28 Cong., 2 sess.; *House Doc.* 219, 54 Cong., 1 sess.; Nathan Reingold, *Science in Nineteenth-Century America. A Documentary History* (New York, 1964), pp. 134–145; G[eorge] P. Bond to Wilkes, March 28, 1859, Charles Wilkes Papers, LC; William J. Youmans, *Pioneers of Science in America* (New York, 1956), pp. 223–233; Joseph Lovering, "Boston and Science," in Justin Winsor, ed., *Memorial History of Boston: 1630–1881*, 4 vols. (Boston, 1880–1881), 4:489–526; Wilkes to Tappan, December 30, 1850, Benjamin Tappan Papers, LC; Gustavus A. Weber, *The Hydrographic Office, Its History, Activities, and Organization* (Baltimore, 1926), p. 29; Ronald A. Derrick, *A History of Fiji* (Suva, 1946), p. 92 and n. 3; Carl I. Wheat, *Mapping of the Transmississippi West*, 5 vols. (San Francisco, 1957–1963), 2:177–179.

2. Harley Harris Bartlett, "The reports of the Wilkes Expedition, and the Work of the Specialists in Science," APS *Proceedings*, 82 (1940), 691–705; Hooker to Brackenridge, February 9 [?], 1856, Brackenridge Papers, Smithsonian Institution Library; Henry W. Fowler and Barton A. Bean, "Descriptions of eighteen new species of fish from the Wilkes Exploring Expedition, preserved in the United States National Museum," U.S. National Museum *Proceedings*, 63 (1924), Art. 19; and Henry W. Fowler, "The Fishes Obtained by the Wilkes Expedition, 1838–1842," APS *Proceedings*, 82 (1940), 733–800; Charles Wilkes, *Theory of the Winds* (Philadelphia, 1856); *Theory of the Zodiacal Light* (Philadelphia, 1857); *On the Circulation of the Oceans* (Philadelphia, 1859). One geophysicist, working with the surviving manuscript observations, was able in 1910 to work out the position of the south magnetic pole of 1840; see G. W. Littlehales, "The South Magnetic Pole. The Magnetic Inclination in the Approaches to It, as Deduced from Observations Made in 1840 by the United States Expedition Commanded by Lieut. Charles Wilkes, U.S.N.," American Geographical Society *Bulletin*, 42 (1910), 1–8.

3. William W. Diehl, "The Fungi of the Wilkes Expedition," *Mycologia*, 13 (1921), 38–41; Frank S. Collins, "The Botanical and Other Papers of the Wilkes Exploring Expedition," *Rhodora*, 14 (1912), 57–68; Bartlett, "The reports of the Wilkes Expedition"; Pickering to Reynolds, August 15, 1836, in J. N. Reynolds, *Address on the Subject of a Surveying and Exploring Expedition* . . . (New York, 1836), pp. 153–155; A. Hunter Dupree, *Asa Gray, 1810–1888* (Cambridge, Mass., 1959), pp. 69, 95, 214–215; American Academy of Arts and Sciences *Proceedings*, 4 (1857–1860), 192–196; Dana to Wilkes, November 4, 1848, Boston Public Library; Wilkes, *Narrative*, 4:168–169; Henry T. Cheever, *Life in the Sandwich Islands: or, The Heart of the Pacific, As It Was and Is* (New York, 1856), pp. 178, 179–196, 350; James D. Dana, "On Zoophytes," *American Journal of Science*, 2d ser. 2 (1846), 64–69, 187–202; 3 (1847), 1–24, 160–163, 337–347; [Asa Gray], "Report on Zoophytes; by James D. Dana," *ibid.*, 9 (1850), 294–295; J. Edward Hoffmeister, "James Dwight Dana's Studies of Volcanoes and of Coral Islands," APS *Proceedings*, 82 (1940), 721–732; Dana, *Coral and Coral Islands* (New York, 1890; first published 1872), preface, p. 7; *The Life and Letters of Charles Darwin*, ed. Francis Darwin, 2 vols. (New

York, 1897), 1:342; [Asa Gray], "The Scientific Results of the Exploring Expedition," *North American Review*, 63 (1846), 211–236; Gilman, *Life of James Dwight Dana*, 355–356.

4. [Gray], "The Scientific Results of the Exploring Expedition"; Bartlett, "The Reports of the Wilkes Expedition"; Jacob W. Gruber, "Horatio Hale and the Development of American Anthropology," APS *Proceedings*, 111 (1967), 5–37; Albert Gallatin, "Hale's 'Indians of North-West America, and Vocabularies of North America,' with an introduction by Albert Gallatin," American Ethnological Society *Transactions*, 2 (1848), Art. 1, preface, pp. 23–188; R. G. Latham, *The Natural History of the Varieties of Man* (London, 1850), preface; "Sketch of Horatio Hale," *Popular Science Monthly*, 51 (1897), 401–410; *Appleton's Cyclopaedia of American Biography*; Ruth Finley, *The Lady of Godey's, Sarah Josepha Hale* (Philadelphia, 1931), pp. 212–214; Horatio Hale, *An International Idiom: Manual of the Oregon Trade Language, or "Chinook Jargon"* (London, 1890), pp. 26–27; Samuel George Morton to John R. Bartlett, January 28, 1847, John R. Bartlett Papers, John Carter Brown Library, Brown University; John Wesley Powell, "Sketch of Lewis Henry Morgan," *Popular Science Monthly*, 18 (1880), 114; Hale, "Race and Language," *ibid.*, 32 (1888), 340–351. Gruber's excellent study represents the rediscovery of Hale; my discussion is greatly indebted to it.

NOTES TO CODA

1. "James Croxall Palmer," *Appleton's Cyclopaedia of American Biography*; James W. Gould, *Americans in Sumatra* (The Hague, 1961), pp. 137–138; Blair to Mary [Jesup Blair], March 31, 1850, Blair Family Papers, LC; William E. Smith, *The Francis Preston Blair Family in Politics*, 2 vols. (New York, 1933), 1:208–210; William H. Dall, "Some American Conchologists," Biological Society of Washington *Proceedings*, 4 (1888), 95–134; Thomas T. Bouvé, "Historical Sketch of the Boston Society of Natural History . . . ," *Anniversary Memoirs of the Boston Society of Natural History* (Boston, 1880), pp. 1–250; Arthur MacC. Shepard, "James Alden," DAB.

2. Charles O. Paullin, "Thomas Tingey Craven," "George Foster Emmons," DAB; Walter B. Morris, "Samuel Phillips Lee," DAB; on Case, see *Appleton's Cyclopaedia of American Biography* and George F. Emmons, *The Navy of the United States . . .* (Washington, 1850), pp. 116, 693; on Hartstene, see John Howard Brown, *The Biographical Dictionary of America . . .* , 10 vols. (Boston, 1906); on Harrison and Maury, see Henry A. Du Pont, *Rear Admiral Samuel Francis Du Pont, United States Navy* (New York, 1926), pp. 47, 72, n. 4; on Sinclair, see J[ohn] Thomas Scharf, *History of the Confederate States Navy . . .* (New York, 1887), pp. 819–820; *Naval Encyclopedia . . .* (Philadelphia, 1881), p. 404; Du Pont, *Rear Admiral Francis Du Pont*, p. 187; Rebecca Paulding Meade, *Life of Hiram Paulding, Rear-Admiral, U.S.N.* (New York, 1910), p. 191.

3. Charles Pickering, *Chronological History of Plants: Man's Record of His Own Existence Illustrated through Their Names, Uses, and Companionship* (Boston, 1879), p. 1; Pickering to Torrey, March 30, 1836, Torrey Papers, New York Botanical Garden; William Churchill, "The Earliest Samoan Prints," ANSP *Proceedings*, 67 (1916),

199–202; Jessie Poesch, *Titian Ramsay Peale* . . . , 105, 112–113, 116–117; Brackenridge to Torrey, March 12, 1855, Torrey Papers, New York Botanical Garden; to Wilkes, April 6, 1875 (draft), Brackenridge Papers, Smithsonian Institution Library; "Editorial Notes," *The Gardeners' Monthly and Horticulturalist*, 26 (1884), 375–376; J. F. O[tis], "Currente Calamosities, No. IV," *Southern Literary Messenger*, 5 (1839), 254–256; Reynolds to Thomas Corwin, July 30, 1850, February 13, 1853, Thomas Corwin Papers, LC; on the vessels, see Robert V. Hine, *Edward Kern and American Expansion* (New Haven, 1962), pp. 99–100, 112; Howard I. Chapelle, *The History of the American Sailing Navy* (New York, 1949), pp. 349, 358, 385–389; Emmons, *Navy of the United States*, pp. 104–105; Harold and Margaret Sprout, *The Rise of American Naval Power, 1776–1918* (Princeton, 1939), pp. 112–114; Allan B. Cole, ed., *Yankee Surveyors in the Shogun's Seas, Records of the United States Surveying Expedition to the North Pacific Ocean, 1853–56* (Princeton, 1947), p. 11; Emmons, *Navy of the United States*, pp. 16–17, 120–121; *Naval Encyclopedia*, p. 405.

Bibliographical Note

    With the exception of the large body of materials in the
National Archives, the manuscript sources are widely scattered. In the search
for these I was saved many months and much effort by the late Daniel C.
Haskell's accurate and very nearly exhaustive bibliography, *The United States
Exploring Expedition, 1838–1842, and Its Publications, 1844–1874* (New
York, 1942), a far more comprehensive volume than its title suggests. Of the
few additions I have been able to make to it, the chief have been the letters of
J. N. Reynolds, William Reynolds' journals and correspondence, James
Alden's journal, and the first volume of William L. Hudson's journal.

    The only document that covers the whole period of the Expedition's career
is Wilkes' autobiography in the Charles Wilkes Papers, Library of Congress.
Written with an uncritical enthusiasm for its subject that is evident on every
one of its nearly three thousand pages, its reliability as a factual account is
negligible, but if read chiefly for what it tells of the writer, it is an immensely
revealing document.

    The chief sources on J. N. Reynolds and his promotion of the enterprise are
the Samuel L. Southard Papers and the Blair-Lee Papers, Princeton; and
Miscellaneous Letters for 1828, Navy Branch, National Archives; and on the
organization of the enterprise, the half-organized mass of documents in *House
Exec. Doc.* 147, 25 Cong., 2 sess.; and the first seven rolls (Letters Relating to
the Wilkes Exploring Expedition) of the National Archives' microfilm
publication, Records Relating to the United States Exploring Expedition
Under the Command of Lt. Charles Wilkes, 1836–1842 (Microcopy 75).

    Useful on the cruise itself are the letters home to be found in various
collections: Reynolds' in the William Reynolds Papers, Franklin and Marshall
College; Peale's in the Miscellaneous Manuscripts Collection, American
Philosophical Society; Pickering's in the Massachusetts Historical Society, and
the Samuel George Morton Papers, American Philosophical Society; Samuel
R. Knox's, George Foster Emmons' and Henry Eld's in the Western
Americana Collection, Yale; Ezra Green's at the United States Naval
Academy; and James Dwight Dana's in three collections at Yale—Historic
Manuscripts, Dana-Herrick Correspondence, and Letters to W. C. Redfield.
Wilkes' Order Book is in the Wilkes Papers, Kansas State Historical Society.
Of the logbooks I was able to locate only that of the *Flying Fish*, and it proved

to be virtually illegible from water damage. No doubt others will one day be found in one or more of the Washington repositories, but the present lack is the less to be lamented as the journals are so abundant.

It is the journals that tell the story of the cruise. Probably all fifty-four of the officers, as well as the scientists and many of the crews, obeyed Wilkes' order and at least began to keep journals. Nearly all the remainder (Pinkney defiantly destroyed his, Reynolds smuggled home his private journal) were surrendered on the return voyage, but after Wilkes published his *Narrative of the United States Exploring Expedition, during the Years 1838, 1839, 1840, 1841, and 1842* (Philadelphia, 1845), many of the journalists collected their volumes from the Navy Department. Of these, some found their way into libraries, others have disappeared. Of those that remained in the keeping of the Navy Department, the National Archives has published on microfilm the twenty-three now extant: Records Relating to the United States Exploring Expedition Under the Command of Lt. Charles Wilkes, 1836–1842 (Microcopy 75), Rolls 7–25, which is cited below simply as National Archives. The incompleteness of the series of the scientists' journals is particularly unfortunate. Dana's volumes at Yale and Pickering's at the Academy of Natural Sciences in Philadelphia and at the Massachusetts Historical Society consist of little more than field notes and were perhaps rough notes for journals now lost. Worse, I have been unable to find Hale's, which, to judge by an excerpt copied into Hudson's (2: 253–287) was both comprehensive and perceptive.

The journals are as various as the men who wrote them. After a commendable start some neglected their daily entries, with Lieutenant Robert Johnson "voting a diary to be a d——d bore," until Wilkes reminded them of their duty. Others merely copied entries from shipmates; some prudent souls recorded only the bare essentials on the weather, ship's position, day's run, and the like. Of the nearly two score journals extant I found that the following would best tell the story:

James Alden	Mariners Museum, Newport News, Va.
Anonymous journalist aboard *Vincennes*	National Archives, Roll 10
William D. Brackenridge	Maryland Historical Society
William Briscoe	National Archives, Roll 13
Micajah G. L. Claiborne	National Archives, Roll 12
George W. Clark	National Archives, Roll 25
Joseph G. Clark	*Lights and Shadows of Sailor Life, As Exemplified in Fifteen Years' Experience, including the More Thrilling Events of the U.S. Exploring Expedition . . .* Boston, 1848
George M. Colvocoresses	*Four Years in a Government Expedition . . .* New York, 1852. Both the original journal and the book

	manuscript are in the Western Americana Collection, Yale.
Joseph P. Couthouy	Museum of Science, Boston
Edwin J. De Haven	National Archives, Roll 24
John W. W. Dyes	National Archives, Roll 11
Henry Eld	New Haven Colony Historical Society; Western Americana Collection, Yale
Jared Leigh Elliott	Library of Congress
Samuel B. Elliott	National Archives, Roll 17
Charles Erskine	*Twenty Years Before the Mast* . . . Philadelphia, 1896
George Foster Emmons	Western Americana Collection, Yale
Edward Gilchrist	National Archives, Roll 14
Ezra Green	U.S. Naval Academy
Henry J. Hartstene	National Archives, Roll 12
Silas Holmes	Western Americana Collection, Yale
William L. Hudson	American Museum of Natural History (vol. 1); Southern Historical Collection, University of North Carolina (vol. 2)
Robert E. Johnson	National Archives, Roll 15
Andrew K. Long	National Archives, Roll 18
Titian R. Peale	Jessie Poesch, *Titian Ramsay Peale, 1799–1885, and His Journals of the Wilkes Expedition,* American Philosophical Society Memoirs, vol. 52 (Philadelphia, 1961), 124–203. Original journals in Library of Congress.
William Reynolds	Franklin and Marshall College: "Journal on board the Vincennes" (cited in the Notes as Public Journal); "Journal 1840, 1841, 1842. Peacock, Flying Fish & Porpoise . . . From the Fiji Islands to St. Helena"; "Journal U.S. Ship Vincennes & Peacock 1838, 1839, 1840 . . . From the United States to the Fiji Islands"; "Private Notes from St. Helena to the U. States . . ." cited in the Notes as Private Journal, vols. 1, 2, and 3 respectively).
R. P. Robinson	National Archives, Roll 22
Joseph Perry Sanford	National Archives, Roll 19
J. Frederick Sickels	National Archives, Roll 16
George T. Sinclair	National Archives, Roll 21
Frederick D. Stuart	National Archives, Roll 20
Joseph A. Underwood	Western Americana Collection, Yale
John S. Whittle	Alderman Library, University of Virginia
Charles Wilkes	National Archives, Rolls 7–9

As the journals were not kept in a uniform way (pages are unnumbered in some, chronology is awry in others), I have cited only the journalist's name.

The courts-martial records, poorly arranged, are to be found in the National Archives microcopy publication cited above, Rolls 26 and 27.

The most fruitful sources on the National Institute are in the Archives of the Smithsonian Institution, particularly the material gathered by Richard Rathbun; the Henry D. Gilpin Collection and the Poinsett Papers, Historical Society of Pennsylvania; the National Institute Papers, Henry E. Huntington Library; and the Charles Wilkes Papers, Library of Congress.

Abundant material on the collections and their installation in the Patent Office is to be found in the Charles Wilkes Papers, Kansas State Historical Society; Charles Wilkes Papers and Benjamin Tappan Papers, Library of Congress; and, especially for invoices, U.S. Exploring Expedition Papers, Smithsonian Institution Library.

Manuscript sources relating to the publication effort are voluminous. The largest are the Charles Wilkes Papers and the Benjamin Tappan Papers, Library of Congress. Much correspondence among Wilkes, Drayton, Stuart, and the scientists is to be found in the Historic Letter File, Gray Herbarium, Harvard; Western Americana Collection, Yale; John Torrey Papers, New York Botanical Garden; Charles Wilkes Papers, Kansas State Historical Society; Boston Public Library; Simon Gratz Collection, Historical Society of Pennsylvania; Benjamin Tappan Papers and the Ohio Manuscripts Collection, Ohio Historical Society; the Letterbooks of the Librarian of Congress and the John Wilkes Papers, Library of Congress. In appraising the Expedition's scientific achievement, I was greatly aided by the articles in the American Philosophical Society's *Proceedings*, vol. 80 (1940).

Of the many books which have contributed to the making of this one, my greatest debt is to two special bibliographies: Daniel C. Haskell's *United States Exploring Expedition*, cited above, and Max Meisel, *A Bibliography of American Natural History: The Pioneer Century, 1769–1865* (Brooklyn, 1924–1929). With few exceptions, the history of American science in this period is to be found in biographies. The chief exceptions for my purposes have been A. Hunter Dupree, *Science in the Federal Government* (Boston, 1956); George H. Daniels, *American Science in the Age of Jackson* (New York, 1968); and William M. Smallwood, *Natural History and the American Mind* (New York, 1941). Dupree's incomparable *Asa Gray, 1810–1888* (Cambridge, Mass., 1959) and Edward Lurie's *Louis Agassiz, A Life in Science* (Chicago, 1960) have taught me much about American science and scientists of the period; and I have profited as well from Daniel C. Gilman, *The Life of James Dwight Dana, Scientific Explorer, Mineralogist, Geologist, Zoologist, Professor in Yale University* (New York, 1899) and William H. Dall, *Spencer Fullerton Baird* (Philadelphia, 1915), two studies of the nineteenth-century type that plug the gaps with useful bundles of correspondence; Andrew D. Rodgers III, *John Torrey, A Story of North American Botany* (Princeton,

1942); and Ferdinand Cajori's appropriately eccentric *The Chequered Career of Ferdinand Rudolph Hassler* (Boston, 1924). Early in this study Thomas Philbrick's *James Fenimore Cooper and the Development of American Sea Fiction* (Cambridge, Mass., 1961) opened the way to a large body of maritime literature, made me aware of its popularity during the first half of the nineteenth century, and impressed upon me that through most of that period the primary American frontier was the sea.

BIBLIOGRAPHICAL NOTE

Index

Abemama, 245

Abert, John J., 292, 293, 294, 298, 300, 303–304, 358

Abiang, 245

Academy of Natural Sciences of Philadelphia, 43, 329, 341, 351, 381

Active, 366, 379

Adams, John Quincy, 23, 28, 50; views of, on role of government, 4–5, 30; interest of, in expedition, 17, 62, 365; and Wilkes, 283, 306; and National Institute, 292–293

Adelaide Island, 147, 173 n

Adelie Coast, 173 n

Admiralty Inlet, 255

Admiralty Range, 313

Advance, 364

Agassiz, Louis: and glaciation, 27 n, 369; anthropological views of, 342, 346; and ichthyological report, 349, 353, 355, 357, 361, 362; urges larger printings, 351; Wilkes' reluctance to hurry, 354

Agate, Alfred T., 48, 83, 89, 207, 234, 252, 259; sketches natives, 191, 213, 240, 241, 261, 263; illustrations by, in Narrative, 308; death of, 326

Alabama, 360

Alaska, 380

Alden, James, 80, 118; and Wilkes, 139, 171, 208, 268, 284; reports appearance of Antarctic land, 170, 172, 173 n, 286; hears announcement of Antarctic discovery, 181–182; surveys in Fiji, 195, 203, 205, 206; battles Fijians, 204, 207, 210; on missionaries, 223–224; surveys West Coast, 366, 378; later career of, 379

Aleamotu'a. *See* Josiah, King

Alert, 266

Alexander I Island, 147

Algae, 334, 367

Allshouse, James, 269, 270

American Association for the Advancement of Science, 358, 367, 375

American Board of Commissioners of Foreign Missions, 248

American Coast Pilot, 4

American Historical Society, 290, 293, 295

American Journal of Science, 42, 307, 308, 351. *See also* Stillman's

American Philosophical Society, 6, 43, 46, 52, 54, 58, 59, 87, 373

American River, 264

l'Amiable Josephine, 188 n

Anderson, Alexander C., 255

Anderson, John, 242, 244, 245

Ann and Hope, 205 n

Annawan. *See* *Seraph* and *Annawan* Expedition

Antarctic Continent, 27 and n, 147; existence of, speculated, 16, 19, 27, proclaimed, 173–174; discovery of, claimed, 182–185, acclaimed, 310; disputed, 272, 285–287, 311–313. *See also* Antarctic Peninsula; Graham Land; Palmer Land

Antarctic Peninsula, 99. *See also* Palmer Land, Graham Land

Antarctica, 2, 26 n, 364

Anthony, J. G., 358

Anthropology, 267, 375, 376, 377; "American School" of, 342, 345 n, 347, 373–374. *See also* Ethnography; Ethnology

Antiscorbutics, 92

Anuanuranga Island, 228

Apia, 136, 137

Apolima, 141

Apo Shoal, 274

Aranuka, 245

Aratika, 122, 227

Archangel Island, 228

Arctic, exploration of, 364–365

Argo, 190

Arioi, The, 127

Armstrong, James, 38

Army and Navy Chronicle, 47

Arno, 245

Arrowsmith, Martin, 188 n, 273

Artists, 48, 319. *See also* Agate, Alfred T.; Drayton, Joseph

Arutua, 122

Ascension Island. *See* Ponape

Committee of, on the Library of Congress, 298, 299, 300, 306, 314, 326, 332, 333, 334, 336–337, 343, 344, 352, 353, 355, 360, 361. *See also* Howe, Timothy O.; Pearce, James Alfred; Tappan, Benjamin; Wilkes, Charles

Connel, Patrick, 190, 193, 199

Conrad, Joseph, 309

Consort, 39, 40, 52, 53, 69, 111

Constellation, 273

Constitution, 70, 379

Consul, 30

Cook, James, 101, 132, 186, 217; inaugurates scientific exploration, 41; Wilkes compared to, 62, 139; Antarctic exploration of, 102, 154, 221, 312; at Tahiti, 123, 125, 126, 135; tradition of, in writing voyages, 306

Cook Ice Shelf, 171 n

Coon, Carleton, S., 346

Cooper, James Fenimore, 37, 309

Coquille, 240

Coral. *See* Zoophytes

Corsair, 240

Corydaudau, 194, 214

Côte Clairée, 313 n

Couthouy, Joseph Pitty, 48, 50, 52, 64, 83, 123, 124, 126–127, 130, 296, 308; collects shells at Rio, 89, 91; treats with Fuegians, 105, with natives of Clermont, 116, of Disappointment Islands, 120; and Wilkes, 118, 119, 120, 121–122, 137, 217, 218, 219, 308; admires Tetiaroa, 123, Matavai Bay, 124, Tahitians, 126–127, 130; doubts missionary success in Tahiti, 127–129; explores Samoa, 132–133; given sick leave, 147, 180; dismissed, 219; at court martial, 284; resigns from scientific corps, 321, 327; accused of plagiarism, 324–325; paper of, on coral reefs, 324 and n; achievement of, 366; later career of, 379

Craig, Bill, 260 n

Crater, The, 309

Craven, Thomas T., 69, 83, 93, 109, 380

Crews, disposition of squadron's, during cruise, 279–280 n

Cropsey, Jasper, 279

Crozier, Francis R. M., 181

Crustacea, report on, 317, 326. *See also* Dana, James Dwight; Natural history collections of Expedition of crustacea

Cumaná, Bay of, 379

Cunningham, Jacob, 190

Currents, ocean, method of determining, 86

Curtis, Moses Ashley, 332, 334, 342, 350, 361, 367

Cuvier, Georges, Baron, 46

Daevski Group. *See* Sea Gull Group

Dale, John B., 80, 110–111, 308

Dampier, William, 306

Dana, James Dwight, 53, 58, 64, 81, 83, 93, 133, 234, 259, 260, 264, 320; early career of, 42–43, 45; and J. N. Reynolds, 44–45, 185; and Dickerson, 46, 47; and Wilkes, 88, 121, 137–138, 323–324, 363, 369; and Couthouy, 324–325 and n; on delays in departure, 42, 52, 59, 65; on Tappan, 320–321; interest of, in meteorology, 87–88; religiosity of, 129–130, 144, 223, 320; field work of, in Australia, 145, 180, in Fiji, 213; on care of collections, 302–303; report of on geology, 317, 326, 351–352, 370–371, on crustacea, 317; on corals, 317, 325–326, 369–371; benefits to, from Expedition experience, 369–372

Dangerous Archipelago. *See* Tuamotu Group

Daniel's Island. *See* Arno

Darwin, Charles, 44, 46, 306, 368, 376; on transit of Antarctic boulder, 27 n; theory of, on subsidence, 324 n, 371; reasoning of, on origin of species, 340, 374; works revolutionary change in natural history, 357, 362

Darwinism, 374, 375

Davis, Alonzo B., 159, 242, 250, 286, 287, 378, 379

Davis, Charles H., 90

Davis, John, 1

Dayton, A. O., 293

De Haven, Edwin J., 113, 114, 251, 259, 286, 364, 365, 378, 379

De Kay, James Ellsworth, 21, 23, 42, 44, 46, 317

De Peyster's Group. *See* Nukufetau

De Sauls, James, 314 n

Deakin Bay, 161 n

Dean, James, 48

Dean's Island. *See* Manihi

Decatur, Stephen, 35

Deception Island, 101

Delaware, 42, 277

Depot of Charts and Instruments, 29. *See also* Naval Observatory

Derrick, Ronald A., 208 n

Desertions, 54, 69, 113, 114, 130, 131, 136, 148, 227; total of, 279–280 n, 288

Destruction River, 263

Dibble, Jonas, 148

Dickens, Charles, 301

Dickerson, Mahlon, 6, 29, 45, 53, 54, 57, 58, 61, 65, 68, 222, 329; background and character of, 28, 33–35; opposes Expedition and urges reduction, 35, 37–38, 51, 57, 62; quarrels with Jones, 36–37, with Reynolds, 37–38, 56; and scientific corps, 40, 42, 47–48, 50, 52–53, 55,

Fanning, Edmund: career of, 18–19; interest of, in polar exploration, 19 and n, 26, 28; views of, on exploring vessels, 38–39, 56, 57; island discoveries of, 18, 227, 229, 232; and J. F. Cooper, 309
Farewell Island. *See* Cikobia
Farragut, David, 360, 379
Faun, 30
Fawn Harbor, 227
Feather River, 264
Fiji, 30, 30 n, 57, 167, 187–215, 226, 234, 340, 345, 366; domestic relation in, 211; military tactics of, 208
Fishes. *See* Ichthyology
Fitzroy, Robert, 121, 122, 306, 309
Flint Island, 228
Florida, 360
Fly, H.M.S., 109
Flying Fish: joins squadron, 71; described, 76; command of, coveted, 95–97; first Antarctic cruise of, 101–103; repaired, 130, 143, 285; second Antarctic cruise of, 148–149, 151–153, 155 n, 178–180, 184, 312; attacks Solevu, 204; at Malolo, 205, 206, 207, 208; at sinking of *Peacock*, 248, 251; surveys Columbia River, 253, 267–268, 270, Oregon coast, 270–272; sold, 274; passim
Flying Fish Shoal, 213
Forrest, French, 230
Fort Clatsop, 253, 255
Fort Colville, 255, 258
Fort Fisher, Battle of, 379
Fort George, 253, 256, 259, 268
Fort Hall, 260
Fort Jackson, Battle of, 379
Fort Macquarie, 143, 181
Fort Mandan, 260
Fort Nisqually, 255, 256, 258
Fort Okanogon, 258
Fort Pickens, Battle of, 379
Fort Ross, 267
Fort Sumpter, 380
Fort Vancouver, 255, 257, 259, 260, 267
Fort Walla Walla, 255, 258
Foster, Henry, 17, 101
Fox, J. L., 93–94, 139
France, 51. *See also* Dumont d'Urville, J.S.C.
Franklin, Sir John, 364
Fraser River, 255
Frémont, John Charles, 366
French Frigate Shoal, 273
Friendly Islands. *See* Tonga Islands
Frost, Joseph H., 255
Frost, Mrs. Joseph H., 255
Fugitive Slave Law, 353

Funafuti. *See* Ellice Group
Fungi, 334, 367

Gallatin, Albert, 6, 373
Galveston, Battle of, 379
Gansevoort, Hunn, 80, 111, 113, 114
Geographical distribution, 339, 340, 350, 367–368, 369; report on, 339, 340, 350, 361, 362, 367–368, 369. *See also* Agassiz, Louis; Gray, Asa; Hale, Horatio; Peale, Titian Ramsey; Pickering, Charles; Scientic reports, appraisal of
Geology, 42, 43, 63; report on, 317, 326, 370. *See also* Dana, James Dwight
George, 187
George, Indian, 251, 252
George V Coast, 157 n
Georgetown College, 331
Gibbs, Josiah, 48, 65
Gilbert Islands. *See* Kingsmill Islands
Gilchrist, Edward, 111, 137, 141, 144, 181
Gilliss, James Melville, 70, 365, 365 n
Girard, Charles, 349, 356, 366
Glaciation, 27 n, 369
Gliddon, George R., 342, 347
Glide, 30, 30 n
Glynn, James, 39
Goat Island, 194
Goloa, 197
Good Success Bay, 101
Gould, Augustus A., 317, 321–322, 327, 337, 350–351, 366, 367
Graham Land, 147, 313 n. *See also* Palmer's Land
Granby, Tom, 194
Gray, Asa, 44, 45, 46, 64, 137, 319, 321, 363, 371 n; and Reynolds, 42, 43, 47, 71; recommendations of, to scientific corps, 42–43, 48; and Dana, 42, 43, 370, 371; and Dickerson, 50, 58; resigns from scientific corps, 67–68; and botanical reports, 331–333, 334–337, 339, 349, 351, 353, 354, 355, 357, 361, 362; benefits to, of Expedition collections, 368–369; on Hale, 372, 373; on Wilkes, 49, 324, 356
Gray, William, 247, 248
Gray's Harbor, 259
Great Western, 70
Green, Ezra, 118, 173 n, 175, 277, 279
Greenhow, Robert, 306
Greenough, Horatio, 357 n
Gregory, Francis H., 60, 283, 360
Gregory, Mrs. Francis H., 60, 360
Grenville Rocks, 254
Grinnell, Henry, 364, 365
Grizzly bears, 262, 264

Guillou, Charles F. B., 111, 132, 144, 219, 268, 269, 283–285, 288

Ha'apai, 187
Haldeman, Samuel S., 323, 341
Hale, Horatio, 48, 52, 64, 83, 87, 88, 89, 121, 180, 234–235, 267, 341, 378; early career of, 65–66; and philological report, 318, 321, 325, 337 n, 372–373; and L. H. Morgan, 374–375; and Franz Boas, 376–377; contributions of, to anthropology, 373–377
Hale, Sarah Josepha, 65
Hall's Island. *See* Maiana
Hall, Charles Francis, 365
Hamer, Thomas L., 33
Harlan, Richard, 47
Harrison, George, 380
Harrison, John, 3
Hartstene, Henry, J., 89, 111, 364, 380
Harvard University, 365 n
Harvey, William Henry, 334, 361, 366
Hassler, Ferdinand Rudolph, 6, 19, 29, 45, 292
Hawaii, 220–224, 226. *See also* Sandwich Islands
Hawes, Albert Gallatin, 33
Hawkesworth, John, 306
Hawthorne, Nathaniel, 306
Hayes, Isaac Israel, 364
Hayne, Robert Y., 24–25, 28
Heath, Mr., 238
Henderville Island. *See* Aranuka
Henry, Joseph, 337, 343, 357, 358, 359, 361, 382
Henry, Wilkes, 206, 207, 208, 211, 215
Henry Lee, 110
Henry's Island, 213
Hercules, 278
Hermite Island, 98–99
Herpetology, report on, 349, 356, 366. *See also* Baird, Spencer F.; Girard, Charles; Natural history collections of Expedition, of reptiles
Herschel, John, 275
Hersilia, 1
Hilo, 221, 224, 226
Hiti. *See* Reid Island
Hobart, 147, 312
Hobart Town Courier, 183
Holmes, Oliver Wendell, 344
Holmes, Silas, 81 n, 87, 93–94, 187, 227, 268, 277, 378; on restrictions on scientific corps, 118; on Pacific missionaries, 123; on Tahitians, 131, 133; on trial of Samoan, 135; on Sydney, 144; on second Antarctic cruise, 155, 176; on meeting with Dumont d'Urville, 177; on Fiji, 198, 201–202, 204, 208, 212, 214

Honden Island, 119, 132
Honolulu, 218, 221–224, 232, 245, 248, 267, 270, 272, 279, 307
Hood's Canal, 255
Hooker, Joseph Dalton, 44, 331, 333
Hooker, William, 335, 366
Hope, 2, 19 n
Hopper's Island. *See* Abemama
Horne Islands, 141
Hoste Island, 94
Howe, Timothy O., 361
Howison, James R., 284
Howison, Neil M., 314 n
Hoyle, Raphael, 48
Huahine, 132
Hudson, William H., 197, 213
Hudson, William Leverreth, 77, 90, 137, 161, 175, 212, 218, 241, 245, 277; sermons of, 78; reputation of, 79; considerateness of, 94, 104, 150, 152, 199, 233; popularity of, 115, 232; seamanship of, acclaimed, 168, 169, 182; on condition of *Peacock*, 85–86, 148, 167; abandons first Antarctic cruise, 103–104; on Pacific missionaries, 130, 222, 223; as prosecutor at Samoa, 135; and Wilkes, 79, 141, 217, 268; ignores rendezvous, 153; response of, to reports of Antarctic landfalls, 157, 159, 184, 287; certain of proximity of Antarctic land, 162; determined to discover land, 163; extricates *Peacock* from ice, 164–167; and J. N. Reynolds, 185; ignorance of, of surveying, 196, 253, 322; trickery of, in Fiji, 199–200; attacks Solevu, 204; and expired enlistments, 220; discomfort of, at Fakaofo, 236; attacks Saluafata, 237, Utiroa, 242; and loss of *Peacock*, 248–251; joins *Vincennes*, 267; promoted, 282, 305; at court martials, 284–286; later career of, 378
Hudson Island. *See* Nanumanga
Hudson's Bay Company, 253, 254, 255–256, 257, 258, 259, 261
Hughes Bay, 2
Humboldt, Alexander von, 15, 371–372
Huron, 1
Huxley, Thomas Henry, 44
Hydrographic Office, U.S., 365–366
Hydrography, 59, 63; report on, 350, 354, 355, 356, 357, 361. *See also* Wilkes, Charles

Ichthyology: report on, 349, 357, 361, 367. *See also* Agassiz, Louis; Natural history collections of Expedition, of fishes; Pickering, Charles
Independence, 88, 90
Ingraham, Joseph, 2
Inman, Henry, 48

Magoun, James, 190, 199
Maiana, 245
Majuro, 245
Makatea, 122
Makemo, 122
Makin, 245
Malolo, 195, 205–211, 277, 285, 308
Malololailai, 206
Malthus, Thomas, 127, 340
Mammalia, report on, 317, 328, 329, 356. *See also* Cassin, John; Natural history collections of Expedition, of quadrupeds; Peale, Titian Ramsay; Scientific reports, appraisal of
Manihi, 122
Manila, 274, 301
Manono, 141, 238
Manua Islands, 132–133
Manuel Rodriguez Shoal. *See* Kingman Reef
Maola, 194
Marakei, 245
Mardi, 310
Margaret's Island. *See* Nukutipipi
Marianas Islands, 273
Mariner, William, 186
Marines, 53, 219, 220
Markoe, Francis, Jr., 292, 358
Marli, 118
Marquesas Islands, 2, 18
Marsh, George Perkins, 324
Marshall Islands, 245
Mason, John Y., 344
Massacre Bay, 134
Matavai Bay, 123–124, 131, 250
Matthew's Island. *See* Marakei
Matthew's Rock, 142
Matthews, Thomas Johnston, 11
Maug, 273
Maui, 221
Mauna Loa, 224–226
Maupiti, 132
Maury, William L., 139, 144, 277, 284, 380
Mawson Peninsula, 159 n
May, William, 81, 139, 255, 283–284
Meehan, John S., 352
Meek, Joseph L., 260 n
Melville, Herman, 27, 111, 127, 130, 309–310
Meteorology, 42, 63, 87–88, 137–138; report on, 350, 367
Metropolitan Society, 290
Midshipmen, defined, 69 n
Mindoro Island, 274
Mineralogy, 42, 63
Missionaries: in Fiji, 193, 200, 211, 227; in Oregon, 252–253, 255; in Samoa, 135, 136–137, 238; in Sandwich Islands, 221–224, 225, 226; in Tahiti, 123–125 and n, 126, 127,

130; in Tau, 133; in Tonga, 187; explorers' opinions of endeavor of, 124, 127–130, 135, 136–137, 194, 214, 223–224
Mobile Bay, Battle of, 379
Moby Dick, 310
Mocha, 107
Mollusca, report on, 321–322, 350, 366, 367. *See also* Couthouy, Joseph Pitty; Gould, Augustus A.; Shells
Monkey-Face Passage, 199, 205
Monmouth Island, 273, 274
Monroe, James, 19 n
Monterey, 270
Moorea. *See* Eimeo
Morgan, Lewis Henry, 374, 375
Morrell, Abby Jane, 3, 4
Morrell, Benjamin, 2, 309
Morse, Samuel F. B., 48, 371
Morton, Samuel George, 53, 215, 340, 341–342, 343, 345, 346, 347, 351. *See also* Anthropology, "American School" of
Mount Erebus, 313
Mount Rainier, 255
Mount Terror, 313
Mountainmen, 259–260 and n
Murderer's Bay, 213

Nadelaiovalu, 193
Nanumanga, 240
Napuka. *See* Disappointment Islands
National Botanic Garden, 359
National Institute for the Promotion of Science, 282, 355, 357; founding of, 292–293; as depository for Expedition collections, 293–294, 295–296, 300, 302, 323; collections of, 295, 303–304, 323; care accorded Expedition collections by, 296, 302–303; and Wilkes, 290, 296–297, 298, 303–304, 306, 307, 358 and n; and scientific community, 297; and politicians, 297–298; and Tappan, 298–300; and scientific corps, 300
Natural history collections of Expedition, 58, 112, 281, 282; ownership of, disputed, 122, 137, 217–218, 283–284; proposed deposition of, 292–293; surrender of private collections to, 219, 277–278; volume of, 291, 296, 300, 316, 320, 330; hazards to, 252, 291–292, 293–294, 302–303, 318 n, 352–353, 381; arrival of, at Washington, 293–294; arrangements for deposition and preservation of, 293–301, 357–359; display of, 301–303; popularity of, 301–302, 326, 359; of birds, 296, 302, 317; of corals, 121, 317, 323; of crustacea, 302, 317; of ethnography, 318, 381; of fishes, 367; of geology, 317; of insects, 296, 322–323; of minerals, 296; of

plants, 296, 318, 326, 359, 366–367, 368; of quadrupeds, 296, 317; of reptiles, 296; of shells, 296, 358. *See also* National Institute for the Promotion of Science; Washington Museum

Natural History Survey of New York, 317, 350

Naturalist, supplanting of by specialist, 58–59, 327–328, 329, 333, 335. *See also* Peale, Titian Ramsay

Natuva Bay, 227

Naval Lyceum, U.S., 45

Naval Observatory, U.S., 365. *See Also* Depot of Charts and Instruments

Navigation, 3–5, 93

Navigator Group. *See* Samoan Islands

Naviti, 205

Navy, U.S.: scientific backwardness of, 19, 21, 42, 63, 73 n, 77; relations of, with Coast Survey, 6, 19; jealousy of civilians in, 19, 23–25, 37, 38, 39, 48; interest of officers of, in Expedition, 20, 23, 61–62, 68; Wilkes' criteria for exploring officers from, 21–22; scientific expeditions of, in 1853, 365; *passim. See also* Dickerson, Mahlon; Jones, Thomas ap Catesby; Mason, John Y.; Paulding, James Kirke; Secretary of Navy; Southard, Samuel; Upshur, Abel P.; Naval Observatory

Navy Commissioners, Board of, 35, 36, 86–87

Negroes, 347

New Hebrides, 143

New Orleans, Battle of, 379, 380

New York, 279–280, 350

New York Herald, 281, 283

New York Journal of Commerce, 310

New York Lyceum of Natural History, 19, 26, 42, 45

New York Mirror, 20, 26

New York Natural History Survey, 350

New York Tribune, 282, 284

New Zealand, 180, 184

Newell, Robert, 260 n

Nez Percé Indians, 264

Niagara, 30, 30 n, 378

Nicholson, John B., 88, 90–91

Nicollet, Joseph Nicholas, 49

Noir Island, 108, 229

Nonouti, 245

North American Review, 41

North, James H., 139, 284, 380

North Carolina, 283, 360

Northern Cook Group, 132

Northwest Coast, 195, 231, 246; languages of, 373

Nott, Josiah Clark, 342, 347

Nui, 240, 397 n

Nukualofa, 186–187

Nukufetau, 240, 397 n

Nukuonu, 236

Nukutipipi, 228

Nuttall, Thomas, 296

Oahu, 212, 224, 229, 240, 245, 246, 270, 279. *See also* Sandwich Islands

Oeno, 30, 190, 212

Oeno Island, 30 n

Olmsted, Denison, 48

Omoo, 310

Orange Harbor, 91, 94, 104

Ord, George, 58, 59, 302

Oregon, 247–263, 267–269, 314 and n, 377

Oregon, 267, 269, 270, 273, 275, 281

Orsmond, John Muggridge, 127

Ossipee, 380

Ovalau, 30 n, 189, 195

Owen, David Dale, 293

Pacific Ocean: extent of American commerce in, 16, 19, 23, 29; as field for natural history, 44–45; marine disasters in, 30 and n

Page, Thomas J., 356

Pago Pago, 133, 140

Paine, Robert Treat, 21, 48, 49

Pallas, 30

Palmer, Alexander, 26 n

Palmer, James, 378

Palmer, Nathaniel B., 26 n

Palmer's Land, 27, 99, 147, 154, 183, 312. *See also* Graham Land; Antarctica Peninsula

Palmer Peninsula. *See* Palmer's Land

Palmyra Island, 229

Pandora, H.B.M., 235

Paparno, 126

Papeete, 228

Papenoo River, 126

Paramatta, 144

Pare, 238–239

Parker, Samuel, 248

Parkman, Francis, 345

Parry, Edward, 62

Pass Christian, Battle of, 380

Passed midshipmen, defined, 69 n

Patagonia, 27

Patent Office, U.S., 351, 381, 382; building described, 301; as depository for Expedition collections, 294–295, 316, 320, 322, 326, 344, 352, 358, 359, 379. *See also* Commissioner of Patents; Ellsworth, Henry L.

Paulding, James Kirke, 37, 66, 67, 68, 71, 79, 184, 292, 293, 298

Peacock: launching and outfitting of, 20, 22; early career and description of, 29, 75–76;

condition of, on passage to Rio, 85–86, 88, to Sydney, 148, to Oregon, 246; collision of, with *Vincennes*, 109, with ice, 163–167; affection of ship's company for, 115, 168, 252; repairs to, at Rio, 88, at Sydney, 181; grounding and wreck of, 249–252; passim

Peacock Anchorage, 245

"Peacock Bay." *See* Deakin Bay

Peacock Harbor, 213

Peacock Point, 273 n

Peale, Charles Willson, 46, 291, 327, 328, 382

Peale, Florida, 327

Peale, Franklin, 291

Peale, Titian Ramsay, 21, 47, 78, 86, 87, 89, 104, 119, 134, 180, 216, 244, 291, 308; background of, 46, 63, 327–328; connections of, with American Philosophical Society, 46, 58, 59, 71; advises reduction of scientific corps, 63–64; relations of, with Pickering, 300, 328, with Ringgold, 93–94, with Wilkes, 63–64, 94, 120, 138, 327, 328, 339, with scientific corps, 83; on restrictions on scientific corps, 116, 118, 120–121; with overland party to San Francisco, 259, 262; and Expedition collections, 293–294, 302, 317, 320, 322–323; scientific inadequacy of, 327–328; zoological report of, 328; resignation of, 328; scientific contribution of, 329, 366, 368; later career of, 381

Peale Island, 273 n

Peale's Museum, 58, 291, 328

Pearce, James Alfred, 326, 336, 337, 344, 352–356

Pearl and Hermes Reef, 273

Pendleton, Benjamin, 26 n, 28

Penguin, 26 and n, 27

Pennsylvania Geolgocial Survey, 350

Penrhyn's Island, 228–229, 230

Percival, Isaac, 69, 111

Percival, John, 57, 62, 69, 222

Perry, Matthew Calbraith, 60, 352, 352 n

Perry, Oliver Hazard, 78, 80, 249, 268, 284

Peru, 30, 30 n

Pescadores Islands, 232, 245

Peter I Island, 147

Phelps, William D., 266

Philadelphia, 52, 53, 55, 58; fire in, of 1851, 352, of 1853, 353, of 1856, 355

Philadelphia Museum, 70

Phillips, 199, 202, 215

Phillips, Stephen C., 190–191

Philology, 65–66; report on, 318, 372–373. *See also* Hale, Horatio

Phoenix Group, 217, 232, 233

Physics, 48, 63; report on, 350, 361–362, 367

Pickering, Charles, 83, 89, 109, 116, 127, 132, 133, 139, 255, 354, 366; early career of, 43–44; and American Philosophical Society, 58; and Brackenridge, 366; and Dana, 320; and Dickerson, 47, 50; and S. G. Morton, 215, 340, 341–342, 345, 346; and Peale, 328; and J. N. Reynolds, 43–44, 46; and Ringgold, 93–94; and Tappan, 341, 343; and Wilkes, 49, 64, 65, 113, 118, 339, 343, 344, 357; on Fijian culture, 214–215, 340, survey, 212; opposition of, to National Institute, 297, 298; and Expedition collections, 277, 301, 302, 303, 397, 316, 318 n, 323, 329, 339; resigns superintendency of collections, 303, 321, 327; and publication effort, 289, 300, 308, 331, 332, 339, 353; anthropological report of, 338–348, misinterpreted, 345 n, assessed, 346–348, separately printed, 351; and American School of anthropology, 342–347; report of, on geographical distribution, 339, 350, 353, 361, 362, separately printed, 362, 380; views of, on geographical distribution, 368, 369; later career of, 380

Pickering, John, 43, 65, 310, 341, 342, 373

Pickering, Timothy, 43

Pike, Zebulon M., 291

Pilot, 39, 40, 52

Pinchgut Island, 149

Piner, Thomas, 172–173 n

Piner Bay, 172–173, 175 n

Pinkney, Robert F., 80, 312; berated, 138–139; refused request for detachment, 144–145; preparations of, for second Antarctic cruise, 148; on second Antarctic cruise, 179–180; relieved of command, 186; charged and arrested, 218–219; court-martial charges against, 283, 284; files court-martial charges against Wilkes, 285; later career of, 380

Pioneer, 39–40, 52, 53

Pitcairn Island, 30

Pitts Island. *See* Butaritari

Poinsett, Joel Roberts: assumes administration of Expedition, 60; appoints Wilkes commander, 61; divests Expedition of military character, 62, 96; agrees to reduce scientific corps, 63–67; arranges for deposit of Expedition collections, 68, 70, 291; visits squadron, 71; persuades Hudson to join, 79; founds National Institute, 292–293; reviews *Narrative*, 309

Point Adams, 248, 249, 253

Point Venus, 123, 125

Polar regions, speculation on, 8–9, 13, 15, 16, 19, 312. *See also* Antarctic Continent; Reynolds, Jeremiah N.; Symmes, John Cleves, Jr.

200; on response to cannibalism, 203; on vengeance at Malolo, 210; on life on board *Flying Fish*, 233, 246, 276; pursuit of, of Samoan, 238–239; observations of, on Expedition's hostilities, 243–244; presentiment of, on Columbia River, 247; witnesses wreck of *Peacock*, 251; grounding of *Flying Fish*, 267–268; observations of, on return, 276, 277; accounting of, of crews, 279 n; at courts martial, 284, 285, 286, 287, 288; at Patent Office, 301; later career of, 380

Reynold's Peak, 157 n

Rich, William, 83, 344; scientific background of, 47, 388 n; field work of, 134, 234; with overland party, 259; botanical report of, 318, 320, 332; defects, 327, 330–331; Gray blamed for appointment of, 333

Richard, J. H., 356

Richards, William, 221, 222

Richardson, William Antonio, 266, 269

Richmond Enquirer, 5

Ridgely, Charles G., 79

Ridley's Island, 99

Ringgold, Cadwallader, 96, 155, 227, 229, 266, 273, 278, 368; background of, 79; disagreements of, with Peale, 93–94, with Hartstene, 111, with Johnson, 144; on second Antarctic cruise, 175, 176, 177; claims Antarctic landfall, 184; leads attack on Malolo, 208–209; credited with discovery of Archangel Island, 228; ignorance of, of surveying techniques, 253, 322; surveys Admiralty Inlet, 255, Sacramento River, 265; later career of, 378, 379

"Ringgold's Knoll," 313 n

Río Negro, 92–94, 111

Rio de Janeiro, 75, 88–91, 275, 276, 277, 279, 291

Roberts, Edmund, 75

Roggeveen, Jacob, 132

Rogue Indians, 262

Rogue River, 262

Rose Island, 130, 132

Ross, James Clark, 234, 309, 317, 364; preparations for expedition of, 147, 181; French mistaken for expedition of, 176–177 and n; Wilkes addresses advice to, 184–185; Aulick reports on expedition of, 272; Wilkes urged to refute claims of, 282; deplores American indifference, 310; priority of publication of chart of, 311; accomplishment of, 312–313; and French and American claims, 312, 313 and n

Rotchef, Governor, 267

Round Island, 218

Royal Botanic Gardens, 335

Royal Geographical Society, 309

Royal Society of London, 15, 44, 324

Rurik. *See* Arutua

Russian-American Fur Company, 267

Sabrina, 27 n, 312 n

Sabrina Coast, 312 n. *See also* Sabrina Land

Sabrina Islands, 313 n

Sabrina Land, 175 n, 313 n

Sac, John, 117, 206

Sacramento River, 260, 264, 265, 378

Saint Helena, 275, 276

St. Louis, 230

Saluafata, 237

Samoa, 132–141, 212, 232, 237–240, 372

San Francisco, 265, 266, 378, 381

San Francisco Bay, 259

San Jacinto, 360, 379

San Pablo Island, 227

San Pedro, 379

Sandalwood Bay, 188 n, 205

Sandalwood trade, 16, 188 n, 190

Sandwich Islands, 16, 212, 218, 255, 273, 318, 318 n

Sanford, Joseph Perry, 173 n

Santa Anna, Antonio Lopez de, 39

Santelmo Island, 227

Sargasso Sea, 278

Sausalito, 265

Savai'i, 133, 141, 144, 237

Savusavu, 191 n, 202

Say, Thomas, 21

Schoolcraft, Henry Rowe, 350

Science, relations of, with government, 4–7, 11–14, 20, 29–30, 48–49, 363, advocated, 19, 31–32, rejected by astronomers, 48–49; projected role of, on Expedition, 41. *See also* Coast Survey, U.S.; Congress; Navy, U.S.; Reynolds, Jeremiah N.; Smithsonian Institution

Scientific corps, 40, 50, 54, 76, 77, 81, 98; advocated, 31–32, 41; selected, 21, 42–43, 47–48; projected role of, 57–58; meets with Dickerson, 52–53; disposition of, in ships, 83; relations of, with officers, 83, 93–94; Wilkes' restrictions on, on voyage, 116, 119, 120–121; 137–138. *See also* Natural history collections of Expedition; Scientific reports; Scientists *and* names of individual scientists

Scientific reports: selection of authors for, 300, 301, 319–320, 321–322, 323, 329, 331, 333–334, 349; provision for publication of, 298, 299, 300, 316, 318, 327, 352–355, 357, 361; speedy publication of, urged, 316, 317, 321; number of, estimated, 317–318, 327;

limitation on printing and distribution of, 318–319, 351–352; prepublication of, 351, 367; hazards to, 349–350, 351–352, 353, 356; publication of, terminated, 361–362; appraisal of, 366–368. *See also* Drayton Joseph; Pickering, Charles; Stuart, Frederick D.; Tappan, Benjamin; Wilkes, Charles; *and* individual sciences and authors

Scientists: role of, in American society, 45–46, 335, 351, 363, 382; interest of, in Expedition, 20–21, 31, 42; esteem of, for Reynolds, 44–45, 46; opposition of, to those selected, 58–59, 63; suspicions of, of government patronage, 47, 48–49, 298, 344. *See also* Natural history collections of Expedition; Scientific corps; Scientific reports

Sea Gull, 71, 73, 76, 79, 94, 95–97, 109, 110, 111, 356, 380, 381

Sea Gull Group, 227

Sea Gull Island, 227

Sea Lions, The, 309

Sealers, 1–2, 17–18. See also *Seraph* and *Annawan* Expedition

Sealing industry, 16

Seaman's Friend Society, 279

Secretary of the Navy, 91, 97, 285, 288, 293, 294, 296, 305, 306, 350, 360, 365

Sedgwick, Adam, 145

Seraph and *Annawan* Expedition, 26–28 and n. *See also* Reynolds, Jeremiah N.

Serle's Island, 118

Seward, William H., 353

Shark, 314

Shasta, Mount, 263, 264

Shasta Indians, 263

Sheffield, James, 1

Shells, 296, 298, 299, 358. *See also* Mollusca

Sherman & Company, 362

Shylock, 212, 227

Sierra Nevada Mountains, 260

Silliman, Benjamin, 42, 43, 45, 320, 326–327

Silliman's, 307, 324. See also *American Journal of Science*

Sinclair, George T., 108, 186, 227, 229, 254, 269, 278; and Wilkes, 139, 151, 202, 218, 224, 230, 270, 276; preparations of, for second Antarctic cruise, 148–149; comments of, on second Antarctic cruise, 178–181; on claims for Antarctic discovery, 184; disapproves of missionaries in Tonga, 187; on hostilities at Malolo, 207, 209, 210, 211; on accomplishment in Fiji, 212–213; reflections of, on Fijians, 202, 214; on science, 228, on Expedition experience, 275; later career of, 380

Singapore, 273, 274

Singapore Straits, 273

Sir Charles Saunders' Island, 132

Sirius, 70

Slavery, Negro, 342, 344, 347, 353

Slidell, Alexander, 36, 47

Smith, John, 279

Smith, William, 1

Smithson, James: bequest of, and Expedition, 282, 294, and National Institute, 282, 358, and Poinsett, 292, and Congress, 291, 293, and a national museum, 327, and Wilkes, 357, and Smithsonian Institution, 304, and Henry, 358; mineral collection of, 295. *See also* Adams, John Quincy; National Institute for the Promotion of Science; Poinsett, Joel R.

Smithsonian Institution, 291, 304, 323, 343, 347; and Tappan, 326; and Wilkes, 357; and Joseph Henry, 357, 359, 382; and Horatio Greenough, 357 n; natural history collections of, 358–359; Expedition collection deposited in, 359, discovered in, 381. *See also* Smithson, James

Snake River, 258, 260

Society Islands, 132

Solevu, 203

Somosomo, 211, 227

Sounding, method of, 161 n

South Sandwich Islands, 147

South Shetland Islands, 1, 2, 27, 101, 183

Southard, Samuel, 69; attempts as Secretary of Navy to organize Expedition, 17, 20, 21–22; as Senator, 28, 33, 50; on lack of science in Navy, 19, 24; Wilkes on, 25; and Dickerson, 35, 66; visits squadron, 53–54

Southern Quarterly Review, 309

Spalding, Josiah, 248, 268

Spectator, The (London), 308

Spieden, William, 125

Spieden Island. *See* Nui

Spipen River, 258

Sprague, Isaac, 333

Spy, 30

Squier, Ephraim G., 347

Starling, 195

Staten Island, 27

Staver's Island, 228

Stearns, Albert S., 255, 259

Stewart, Charles S., 37, 124, 129

Storer, Bellamy, 33

Strait of Georgia, 257

Strait of Le Maire, 94, 101

Straits of Magellan, 98

Stretch, Sam, 279

Strong's Island. *See* Kusaie

Stuart, Frederick D., 161, 235, 236, 252, 360;

industry of, testimony to, 139, 286; indecisiveness of, 140–141; grants leave to Couthouy, 147; cursed, 151, 301; ignores rendezvous, 153; Antarctic landfalls named by, 159 n, 161 n, 171 n, 172 n, 175 n; response of, to report of Antarctic landfalls, 171, 172, 186, 187; persuaded of existence of Antarctic Continent, 173–174; sightings of Antarctic landfalls by, 173 n, 187; system of journal-keeping of, 173 n; scientific speculations of, 150, 177, 227, 367, 370; refuses transfers to officers, 181–182; response of, to *Peacock*'s discovery, 182, to news of French discovery, 182–185; advises Ross, 184–185; ascends Nadelaiovalu, 193; meets Belcher, 195; orders capture of Vendovi, 196; investigates Fiji religion, 201–202; attacks Solevu, 204; inspects Yasawas, 205–206, 207; attacks Malolo, 208; claims reparations, 211; returns *Flying Fish* to Fiji, 212; compiles court-martial charges, 218; attempts to extend enlistments, 219–220; ascends Mauna Loa, 225–226; dispatches *Porpoise* to Isles of Danger, 229; directs heaving-down, 230; names Spieden and Hudson Islands, 240; arrival of, at Northwest Coast, 253–254; visits Fort Vancouver, 255–256, Methodists, 256; stages Fourth of July celebration, 256–257; dispatches overland party, 259; commends Emmons, 265; surveys Columbia River, 267; blames Hudson, 267; anchors on San Francisco bar, 269; response of, to Ross' exploration, 272; sells *Flying Fish*, 274; delays return of brigs, 275; return of, 278–279; welcome accorded, 282–283, 310; court-martial charges filed by, 283–284, filed against, 285–286; court-martial of, first, 286–288, second, 360; and National Institute, 290, 296–297, 298–299, 300, 302, 303–304, 358 and n; chosen to write narrative, 300, 305–306; oversees display of collections, 301, 313, 326–327; method of authorship of, 307–308; critical response to *Narrative* of, 308–310, claims of, to Antarctic discovery, 310–312 and n; brings out separate edition of *Narrative*, 314, 319, 351; advises on Oregon settlement, 314 n; elicits scientists' estimates, 317–318; takes

command of publication program, 319; restrictions of, on authors, 320–321, 323, 324, 326, 334–337, 352; seeks Drayton as author, 321–322; supports Dana against Couthouy, 324 n; assumes agency of Library Committee, 326–327; as lobbyist, 327, 363; rejects Peale's book, 328; ignorance of, of botany, 329–330, 331; seeks author for botanical report, 330–333; and Pickering's *Races of Man*, 338, 339–341, 343, 344, 348; employs Agassiz and Baird, 349; publishes *Western America*, 350; seeks larger printings, 352–353, larger appropriation, 354–355; surrenders superintendency, 355, resumes, 356; opposes Smithsonian custody, 357; Civil War career of, 360, 378; resumes superintendency, 360–362; appraisal of, 362–363, 382; death of, 363; and search for Franklin, 364

Wilkes, Charles (banker), 309
Wilkes, Jane Renwick, 61, 350
Wilkes, John, 350
Wilkes Island, 273
Wilkins, Caleb, 260 n
Willamette River, 256
Williams, John, 136, 143
Williams, 1
Williamson, John G., 287
Wilson, Charles, 125, 127
Wilson, James, 188 n
Wise, Henry A., 62
Wolconsky Island. *See* Takume
Wolf, George, 22, 23
Wollaston Island, 98–99, 101
Woodle's Island. *See* Kuria
Wright, Silas, 306

Yadua, 202
Yakima River, 255, 258
Yasawa Group, 205
Yorktown, 270

Zélée. See Astrolabe; Dumont d'Urville, J. S. C.
Zoology, 42, 47, 63, 328. *See also* Mammalia
Zoophytes, 369–371; report on, 323–324, 325–326, 371. *See also* Dana, James Dwight; Natural History collections of Expedition, of corals

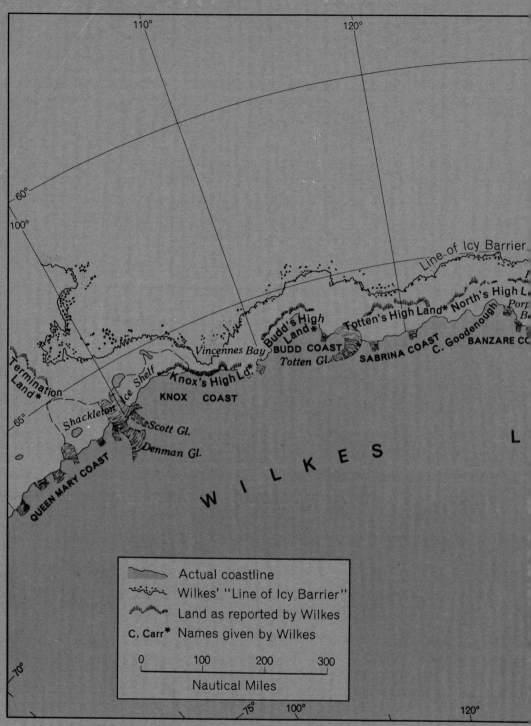

Antarctica's Wilkes Land, with Features Mapped by Wilkes. (Reproduced from Kenneth J. Bertran
Courtesy of the author and t